BOTTOM LINE'S

Balanced Healing

YOUR STEP-BY-STEP GUIDE

TO RAPID, REMARKABLE HEALING

TOP TREATMENT OPTIONS

FROM THE WORLDS OF CONVENTIONAL

AND ALTERNATIVE MEDICINE

LARRY ALTSHULER, MD

www.BottomLineSecrets.com

Bottom Line's BALANCED HEALING
Your Step-by-Step Guide to Rapid, Remarkable Healing
Top Treatment Options from the Worlds of Conventional and Alternative Medicine

Published by arrangement with Harbor Press, Inc.

IMPORTANT NOTICE

The ideas, positions, and statements in this book may in some cases conflict with orthodox, mainstream medical opinion, and are not suitable for everyone. Do not attempt self-diagnosis, and do not embark upon self-treatment of any kind without qualified medical supervision. Nothing in this book or on its cover should be construed as a promise of benefits or of results to be achieved, or a guarantee by the author or publisher of the safety or efficacy of its contents. The author, the publisher, its editors, and its employees disclaim any liability, loss, or risk incurred directly or indirectly as a result of the use or application of any of the contents of this book. If you are not willing to be bound by this disclaimer, please return your copy of the book to the publisher for a full refund.

Bottom Line® Books publishes the opinions of expert authorities in many fields. The use of a book is not a substitute for legal, accounting, health or other professional services. Consult competent professionals for answers to your specific questions.

Addresses, telephone numbers and Web sites listed in this book are accurate at the time of publication, but they are subject to frequent change.

ISBN 0-88723-409-7

10   9   8   7   6   5   4   3   2

Bottom Line® Books is a registered trademark of Boardroom® Inc.
281 Tresser Boulevard, Stamford, CT 06901

Printed in the United States of America

*To my loving wife Claudia, whose love, support,
and long-enduring patience have allowed and encouraged me
to help others achieve better and healthier lives.*

Visit Dr. Altshuler on the Internet at
www.balancedhealing.com

Contents

PART ONE

Balancing Conventional and Alternative Medicine: GETTING THE BEST OF BOTH WORLDS

PART TWO

BALANCED HEALING IN ACTION

Foreword

If you have ever watched an Italian waiter hold a tray of drinks high in the air as he moves between tables and throngs of people in an outdoor café, you will understand that finding balance is much more than a matter of Newtonian physics. He swivels the tray under his fingers, testing the very edge of equilibrium and teasing us with split second tilts in and out of a seemingly dangerous lack of equilibrium where all might crash. He makes it appear as if his attention is on those who require his service and that the silver tray stacked with drinks and biscotti might as well be weightless. In his accomplished poise, impeccable timing, and skillful attention to other's needs, the waiter reminds us that balance is both an art and a science.

This book is about both the art and science of finding balance in one of the most precious arenas of your life, your health. Because good health is so important, when something goes wrong, we tend to accelerate in one direction or another to find a solution, either focusing on alternative approaches to medicine or conventional (allopathic) approaches, instead of seeking a balance that combines the best of both worlds. The search for the remedy, and in some cases the cure, can lead us into a seeming labyrinth of options that run the gamut from medical systems that sometimes offer more technologies than treatment, to alternative approaches that may not distinguish hype from healing. Dr. Altshuler offers thoughtful and practical direction on finding this balance for yourself, and, in the process, achieving optimum health and well being.

When you are not well and you feel most vulnerable, you are often more susceptible to making rash choices. In addition to finding the right balance between alternative and conventional approaches, this book encourages you to research, research, research before making decisions regarding treatment. Once you commit yourself to such a quest, you may be shocked to discover that there is often more research available on complementary and alternative approaches than on areas of standard conventional medicine. But be forewarned: Research can be contradictory and confusing on both sides. And, yes, as Dr. Altshuler points out, isolated studies with dramatic findings may turn out to be corporate advertising in disguise, so ask lots of questions and do your best to separate fact from fiction.

You can be thrown way off balance when you're not well, and you can be deeply and dramatically tested. Sometimes a change of health is sudden, catastrophic and the result of injury or exposure to exotic disease. On the other hand, you might suffer from chronic health problems that affect you gradually, over many years. Whatever the cause of ill health, *Balanced Healing* will help show you that the most potent place of renewal emerges out of your own psychological and spiritual strength. When you combine your own energy with the knowledge, skill, and loving support of others, the potential exists for remarkable healing. In struggling to heal, you can, paradoxically, experience a greater level of wholeness by discovering your own incredible inner resources.

Your mental strength and the power of your mind to affect your body is so remarkable that it can dissolve the harshest experiences of victimization and, in some cases, even check or reverse the path of virulent disease. In fact, the history of your life, literally how you have lived and what you have been exposed to, is evidenced in your body. As the Taoist Master Mantak Chia suggests, you should practice smiling into your heart, lungs, liver and kidneys every day; they are the intimate recorders of love and compassion, as well as of torment and self-neglect. We are still learning much about the nature of healing, but this we can say with safety: Extraordinary healing powers can be activated from within. As we gain more evidence concerning the nature of the healing process, including exceptional human capacities, the power of prayer, and subtle energy, your conscious participation in the healing process remains a critical dimension of true healing. You cannot leave to others what can only be generated from within.

An inner confidence, openness, trust, and even peaceful acceptance are crucial for true healing to occur, and these qualities can be cultivated. Indeed, it seems if we really learn to reach in, we can also learn to reach out more effectively and experience the nature of human interdependence. The prayerful and caring support of others can play a significant role in accelerating the healing process and the vital knowledge and skill of professionals is often absolutely critical.

I am reminded of a conversation I had with the director of the Menzhekang hospital in Lhasa, Tibet, a few years ago. Menzhekang is the premier institution for traditional medicine in Tibet. We were discussing plans to assist the hospital in developing a modern surgical center for cataract surgery:

"I am interested that you are open to integrating some aspects of Western allopathic medicine into your traditional practice," I commented.

For a moment he looked puzzled, and then he smiled. "Like Western medicine, traditional Tibetan medicine is based on a great body of knowledge and on a science developed over hundreds of years. We have always been open to the discovery of the most appropriate and skillful means in furthering our work. In the case of cataract blindness it is quite clear that Western ophthalmic practice has developed the most skillful means to restoring sight to those blinded in this way. Scientists must always remain open."

I was executive director of the Seva Foundation at the time of this conversation and on a subsequent visit to the region, met with Nepali health workers who were working with traditional healers, found in almost every village of this captivating Himalayan kingdom. In this case, the healers had been trained to recognize cataracts and give advice on where to send patients, rather than attempting to use thorns or other homespun practices to remove them. The healers continue to work with emotional and spiritual issues and leave the surgery to others. They have found balance.

Dr. Larry Altshuler's book is offered in this same spirit and with the same wisdom.

You are like the waiter with his tray trying to move with poise through a complex dance of daily life, with things to carry and people to serve. Sometimes you are as fluid and graceful as a whirling dervish, and sometimes things fall and even crash. To regain your balance, you must turn inward to touch the deep wellsprings of compassion and energy that source your being, and then reach out with discernment and knowledge until you find wisdom. *Balanced Healing* will help show you the way.

— James O'Dea
President, The Institute of Noetic Sciences

Acknowledgments

This book is the culmination of decades of learning—about life, about people, about the intricate inner workings of the human body, and about the mystery of human emotions and the human spirit. Along the way, I have had numerous teachers and mentors, most of whom probably do not realize the impact they have had on my thoughts, my motivation, and my accomplishments.

First, I wish to thank my family: my wife Claudia and children Lindsey, Genevieve, Ben, and Vanessa, without whose support and time sacrifices I never would have wanted or been able to write this book. I would also like to thank good friends Bill Comstock, Renee Knox, and Leslie Dlugokinski, and family members Paula and Clarence Fickel, Andrea Gorman, and Karla Beaman, who helped keep my wife and me sane during the many hours, months, and years I isolated myself to complete this book. I would also like to thank my father, Jerome Altshuler, whose own journey and experience with mind-body methods opened my world to new ideas and possibilities when I was just a young boy.

I would also like to express appreciation to many of my teachers. In the conventional medicine world, these include Don Baxter; George Padilla, PhD; Lazar Greenfield, MD; and my many professors at the University of Oklahoma School of Medicine and Department of Internal Medicine. In the alternative world, I gratefully acknowledge Dean Sclecht, MDiv; Brugh Joy, MD; Carolyn Conger, PhD; Beverly Rapp, MEd; Andrew Gaeddert, herbalist; and Tsun-Nin Lee, MD.

I would further like to thank those who were instrumental in the development of this book: Debby Young, my editor, who expertly shaped my ideas and knowledge; Harry Lynn, my publisher; and Earlene Posselt, MD and Jim Maher, DC, OMD, colleagues who contributed their wisdom and knowledge while reviewing the book.

Finally, I would like to acknowledge those who taught me more about medicine than any book or lecture ever could—my patients.

Introduction

Just think of all the improvements and inventions of the past 100 years that have enriched our lives—cars, airplanes, air conditioning, elevators, subways, computers, nuclear power, satellites, space travel, and much more. They're incredible advancements that have changed everything about our lives. But to me the most dramatic changes of all have been in medical science and health care. In only a century, we've taken giant leaps toward knowledge and understanding. Vaccines and drugs have vanquished many diseases. Technology reveals the intimate workings—and malfunctions—of our body's structures and systems. Surgeons routinely replace damaged body parts with donor organs or mechanical devices. In just 100 years, life expectancy has nearly doubled.

Yes, we've achieved a great deal and made tremendous improvements in treating the ills and injuries that ail us. But our remarkable scientific progress has not come without cost or risk. For one thing, many of modern medicine's remedies often give us as many problems as benefits. Also, there's not enough of a focus on preventing disease, and in figuring out how to truly heal us once disease has caused damage. And despite the advances and advantages of technology, many of us, doctors and patients alike, are dissatisfied with the ways of modern health care. It's become fragmented, with multiple doctors independently examining and treating totally separate areas of our bodies as if they are separate. But they are not. The body functions as a whole. All of its myriad parts contribute to one's health and life. Caring for our health means caring for our whole bodies.

FROM ART TO SCIENCE: THE EVOLUTION OF HEALTH CARE

Humankind has always revered the healer. From ancient cultures to modern medicine, healers have blended art and science, gift and skill, compassion and knowledge, all for the betterment of human existence. The word heal comes from the Old English word hal, meaning "whole." And until the advent of medicine as a scientific discipline, the role of the healer was to restore wholeness, to make us whole again. But then, as early scientists began to study the human body and the mechanics of its function, their knowledge and understanding grew, and a new breed of healer emerged: the doctor. Doctor comes from the Latin word docere, meaning "to teach." Early in the modern medical era, the healer really was a teacher, sharing the information that helped people restore and maintain health and wholeness. For centuries, healing and teaching formed the foundation of health care.

The explosive growth of technology in the twentieth century changed everything. Discovery after discovery enhanced our knowledge of how the human body functions. And the discoveries came faster and faster. It took nearly four hundred years to chart the structures and network of the human body's nervous system, but only two decades for scientists to map the very essence of our existence, the human genome. The result is that we—both doctors and patients—have come to believe that "modern" means "more": more machines, more tests, more information. And, unfortunately, most doctors today are no longer teachers and healers, but specialists or subspecialists who interpret tests and recommend treatments based on technological solutions.

Your body, however, is more than the sum of its parts, and maintaining its health is more than treating its ailments. Your body requires an intricate balance that strives for wholeness. But technology, despite its many and amazing benefits, distances us from the concept of wholeness that is the essence of healing. Technology offers none of the characteristics of healing. It is not compassionate or understanding. It doesn't feel or care. We might have expected that as technology came to the forefront of the practice of medicine, health care would have combined technological advances with the art of healing to give us the best of both worlds. That is not what happened. Instead, we moved from one end of the spectrum to the other. But healing is balance, and balance lives in the center of this spectrum. True healing balances the advances of science with the insights of mind and spirit.

HOW CAN WE GET THE BEST OF BOTH WORLDS?

Ancient healers delivered effective therapy by using what the environment provided. Modern medicine need not be so different. Of course, ours is a much-expanded environment, with more extensive offerings. But what hasn't changed is our desire for personal care and natural, non-invasive treatment options that emphasize wholeness. What we want, and what we can have, is balance between technology and touch, between physical mechanics and the unlimited potential of the mind, between conventional medicine and alternative medicine.

More people than ever are growing disenchanted with modern medicine's overwhelming reliance on technological solutions, and they're exploring other options in search of balance and healing. A recent study published in *The New England Journal of Medicine* showed that nearly half of Americans, 42 percent, combine conventional and alternative therapies. But, too often, we don't have the information and knowledge to do so effectively and safely. Many people are reluctant to talk with their medical doctors about alternative medicine, and many medical doctors don't know enough about alternative therapies to answer questions from their patients.

So instead of finding balance, you might well find yourself caught in the middle. You may not like the impersonal, technological approach of conventional medicine and its technology, but you're unwilling to give up the proven benefits. On the other hand, you like the human touch and the promise of alternative medicine, but you have no idea whether the methods are safe—or even whether they really work. And when the practitioners from each side tell you that only their particular expertise is what you need, you experience even more doubt. Balance, especially about something as important as your health, should not be so confusing and distressing!

FINDING A BALANCED APPROACH TO HEALING

To find a practitioner who is knowledgeable in both conventional and alternative medicine would be ideal. Unfortunately, this is not so easy. Many doctors say they practice "integrative" or "complementary" medicine, but such labels turn out to be buzzwords without substance. These doctors may say they use both systems, but they actually use one system preferentially while using token treatments from the other. And many alternative practitioners say they practice integrative medicine when in fact they perform only one or two alternative methods (such as acupuncture or massage) and are not even trained in conventional medicine. The bottom line is that most people (including most doctors) are not aware of what works and what doesn't, or of what's really beneficial and what may be harmful. And even fewer people understand how to combine the two systems most effectively.

As a physician who was using both conventional and alternative medical practices long before it was popular to do so, I understand how to combine the best of both methods while avoiding the pitfalls of each. I also understand that disease and health depend not just on how your body works, but also on how your mind interacts with your body. And most importantly, I understand that each person is different and therefore requires a unique combination of methods to achieve true healing. I call my approach *Balanced Healing*. Balanced Healing does not favor one system over another, and it does not compete against either system. It simply enables you to choose and use the methods that are best suited to your particular needs so that you can achieve a true balance in your life . . . and in your health.

In this book, I'll show you how you can attain this unique balance for your health and wellness, based on your individual needs. I'll examine and compare the benefits and pitfalls of both conventional and alternative medicine, and I'll give you a basic knowledge of these two approaches to health care. I'll explain how they work and what you can expect from them. Then I'll tell you how to get the most from medical practitioners and how to choose those who are best suited for your needs. I'll also give you guidance about what you can do to ensure the best healing possible. Finally, I'll map out step-by-step strategies that use a balance of conventional and alternative methods to give you the capability and flexibility to make your own choices and take control of your own health and well-being.

Both conventional medicine and alternative medicine have a great deal to offer. I hope that this book will give you the knowledge and understanding you need to combine them and thus take advantage of the best of both worlds. Only by achieving this balance can you make the wisest possible choices for your optimal wellness.

PART ONE

Balancing Conventional and Alternative Medicine

GETTING THE BEST OF BOTH WORLDS

CHAPTER 1

Conventional Medicine
WHAT YOU NEED TO KNOW

Until quite recently, physicians and scientists knew very little about the human body. In fact, until the twentieth century, myth, superstition, and magic were the most important factors in diagnosing and treating health conditions. People lived much shorter lives, typically filled with illness and debilitation. But in the 1900s, new tools and new discoveries spurred an unprecedented medical revolution that enabled us to truly understand the human body and the diseases that ravage it. With this new and vast knowledge came the capability to diagnose and treat on the basis of fact rather than fiction. Today, for most of us, life is a lot healthier—and longer—than it was for our grandparents.

But technology has also created a lot of challenges and problems that make us question many of the practices of conventional medicine. One of these practices is the "fragmentation" of medical treatment. The technology that enables us to focus on a specific disease or body part also causes us to lose sight of the "wholeness" of health and wellness. You visit one doctor for this, a different doctor for that. Rather than looking at your health as a whole, modern medicine views your body as a collection of parts. And this view creates a distance between you and your doctor because tests and machines often take precedence over the human touch. Another problem is that technology has not only changed the way in which medicine is practiced, it has also added considerable expense to medical care. Medical costs are higher now than ever before.

On balance, however, the benefits of medical technology and modern medical care far outweigh the shortcomings if you understand both. In this chapter, I'll discuss the good and the bad of conventional medicine, and I'll give you the knowledge you need to keep the balance tipped in your favor.

THE BENEFITS OF CONVENTIONAL MEDICINE

Most Americans turn to modern conventional medicine as their first choice for taking care of the vast majority of their health problems. Among conventional medicine's numerous benefits are the following:

- **Life-saving emergency care.** When you're in a desperate situation, conventional medicine can mean the difference between life and death.

- **Timely medical care for nonemergency needs.** Conventional medicine offers a vast array of medical specialists practicing in a wide variety of clinical settings.
- **High-tech diagnostic technologies.** Conventional medicine has tests and devices that evaluate every part and function of your body.
- **Powerful and effective medications.** Conventional medicine uses drugs that are scientifically formulated and rigorously tested.
- **Surgery to remove or repair damage to specific organs or body parts.** Modern surgical techniques are highly sophisticated and effective.
- **Vaccines and other measures to prevent disease.** Conventional medicine has dramatically reduced or even eliminated diseases that used to ravage and kill whole populations.
- **Extensive training and certification processes for physicians.** Your doctor has had many years of classroom and clinical training and has been rigorously tested before being allowed to practice medicine.
- **Ongoing research to increase knowledge and create newer, more effective treatments.** Each year, billions of dollars fund research in universities, medical schools, and other institutions—research that will result in tomorrow's treatments and cures.

When There's an Emergency

Nothing beats conventional medicine when it comes to emergencies. If you suddenly develop crushing chest pains and shortness of breath, if you fly through the windshield in an automobile accident, or if you fall off a ladder while cleaning your gutters, the emergency department of a hospital is your best choice. You'll find the latest high-tech equipment and highly trained staff to detect or prevent potential life-threatening conditions, bring your heart back to life, stitch your wounds back together, and set your broken bones so they heal straight and true. More than 100 million Americans seek emergency medical care every year, and thousands of them would have died or suffered permanent debilitation without it.

Medical Doctors Are There For You

Even if your situation turns out to be more about discomfort or worry than life or death, odds are that there's a health clinic or doctor's office nearby to find out what's wrong and provide treatment that can help you recover and feel better. From doctors in individual or small group practice, to large clinics, to 24-hour, walk-in urgent care centers, modern medicine puts doctors and other health care professionals within easy reach. Americans log nearly 900 million doctor visits a year; that's an average of three visits per person. Whether it's an attack of gout, a sore throat, a bladder infection, or any number of other health problems, qualified health care providers and appropriate treatments are always available to help you—as Glenda and Ron, a young Southern California couple, were relieved to discover.

On a trip to visit relatives in Kansas, Glenda and Ron had just fallen asleep when they were awakened by the cries of their two-year-old son Ryan. The boy was hot, flushed, and pulling at his ears—all clear signs of an ear infection. Even though it was one o'clock in the morning, and they were in a motel 800 miles from home, Glenda and Ron remained calm. While Ron made Ryan a bottle of juice and changed his diaper, Glenda used the phone book to locate a 24-hour urgent care clinic just a few miles from the motel. The clinic was ready for them when they arrived. The doctor confirmed that Ryan did indeed have an ear infection, gave him an antibiotic and medication to relieve the pain and fever, and phoned a prescription for the full course of antibiotic treatment to a nearby chain drugstore that was also open 24 hours. Just two hours after Ryan woke up feverish and in pain, the family was back at the motel, and he was ready to go back to sleep.

Finding Out What's Wrong

When you're not feeling well, the first goal for you and for your doctor is to find out what's wrong. One of conventional medicine's greatest strengths is the capability it offers doctors to take whatever symptoms you have and diagnose their causes. There are thousands of symptoms, from simple ones that could be signs of serious disease, to complex ones that are more annoying than threatening. Now that medical advancements have removed much of the mystery from the inner workings of the human body, doctors can more easily discover what's causing these symptoms.

To find out what's wrong, doctors typically follow these steps:

1. Obtain a medical history from the patient
2. Perform a physical examination
3. Order diagnostic tests

A medical history is your description of your health history: your past health problems, concerns, and treatments, as well as what's bothering you today and why you are seeing your doctor now. Your medical history gives your doctor more clues to help identify the cause of your problems and point the way to potential treatments. When 45-year-old Frank, a software engineer, came to see me, he had an itchy rash on several areas of his body. The rash would suddenly appear and then just as suddenly go away. He had tried all sorts of lotions and creams and stopped eating certain foods and using new soaps and detergents, all to no avail. I asked Frank about his job and his family. As it turned out, he was working a lot of overtime. His company was struggling to overcome the loss of a major account, and many of Frank's work friends had already lost their jobs. The stress was almost unbearable. Those who were still working wondered how long they would have jobs. I asked Frank if he could connect the appearance of the rash with other stressful times in his life. After thinking about it for a moment, he realized that, indeed, whenever his life became stressful, he started to itch. This information clinched the diagnosis: neurodermatitis, or stress-related skin irritation. I prescribed Benadryl, an antihistamine, to ease the itching and discomfort of the rash, and I recommended some stress reduction methods that could help Frank head off stress before it gave him a rash. I saw him a few months later and asked him how things were going. He looked wonderfully relaxed, and he smiled when he told me that since he'd gotten a new job at a different company, he hadn't had a single episode of his skin problem.

After taking your history, the doctor will perform a physical examination, which may provide more clues about what could be wrong. This is the next step on the diagnostic ladder. A physical examination can find an abnormality that escapes detection during a medical history or other testing. Finding something suspicious during your physical examination can help your doctor rule out other possibilities and focus on the most likely underlying cause of your symptoms.

The Veteran's Administration hospital in which I was a resident had a regular patient named Charlie, a hotel desk clerk. This 55-year-old gentleman was well known to the staff because for four years he had been coming in every three or four months with various complaints, primarily stomach problems. None of the doctors ever found anything out of the ordinary, and the staff at the hospital soon came to view Charlie as a hypochondriac. In fact, most of the doctors stopped examining him and would just give him medications to pacify him. One afternoon he came in on my shift with his usual complaints of intestinal discomforts. After listening to his heart and lungs with a stethoscope, I had him lie flat on his back on the exam table. Knowing Charlie's history, I didn't expect to find anything, and we started talking about the baseball World Series game scheduled for later in the evening. Charlie had come in early so he would be home in time to watch the game. As we discussed batting averages, I carefully felt Charlie's abdomen. Much to my surprise, I found a small, painless lump low in his belly. I sent Charlie for further evaluation, and the lump turned out to be a small colon cancer, which fortunately had been caught early enough for a cure.

If a medical history and physical examination don't give your doctor the answers he needs, diagnostic tests can help narrow down the list of possible causes of your symptoms. These tests can be done from the outside or inside of the body; from the outside, doctors can examine samples of your fluids and tissues, or they can use machines to detect abnormalities on the inside. Here are just a few examples of these tests:

- **Blood and urine tests.** By taking just a few tubes of blood and a few drops of urine, your doctor can see how every bodily system is functioning. Blood and urine tests can measure enzyme and hormone levels, detect infection, discover some cancers, and more. These tests can also help your doctor decide what other tests, if any, are needed.

- **Diagnostic imaging.** CT (computerized tomography) scanning, MRI (magnetic resonance imaging), and other sophisticated high-tech imaging tests show your doctor the inside of your body in ways that would be impossible even if he opened you up! With computers, your doctor can construct 3-D images of specific organs or body parts. Diagnostic imaging can reveal problems in the way those organs or parts function, and it can help doctors find the most effective solutions to these problems.

- **Fiber-optic techniques.** With fiber-optic devices, your doctor can directly view tissues inside your body and take tissue samples for laboratory analysis. Such diagnostic procedures are especially good for examining the inside of the gastrointestinal tract, lungs, and even joints.

- **New techniques.** We're developing new diagnostic techniques all the time. One recent development is the "wireless endoscopy capsule," a grape-sized capsule that contains a microscopic camera. You swallow the camera, which then sends high-quality images of the intestines to a video monitor in the doctor's office. This technique could eventually replace numerous other gastrointestinal tests.

With blood tests, imaging machines, fiber-optic techniques, and other technological advances, plus a good history and physical examination, your doctor can detect the cause of almost any disease. The diagnostic methods and techniques of conventional medicine are powerful weapons in the effort to keep you as healthy as possible.

Strong, Effective Medications Help You Get Well

The technology of conventional medicine also enables doctors to effectively treat the diseases they have diagnosed. Medications are usually the first line of defense. Nature has created many of the medications we now use in conventional medicine, but it is technology that has enabled scientists to analyze, investigate, extract, and isolate the active ingredients—and to produce these medications for widespread use. But more and more of today's medications are not from natural substances. They've been designed and created by scientists who have learned to manipulate molecules to act upon particular cells to make them react in certain ways. Conventional medicine can provide very effective and potentially life-saving medications for almost every disease.

With the wonderful medications available today, you can live a normal and healthy life even if you have health conditions such as diabetes, hypertension (high blood pressure), heart failure, seizures, and bacterial infections—all of which would have been fatal only a generation ago. Sam, a 48-year-old high school teacher, is an example of what modern medicine can do. When he first came to see me, he was taking garlic, flaxseed oil, and niacin to reduce his cholesterol level, which initially was more than 300 (significantly above the normal range). After six months of this regimen, his cholesterol level was 258—a nice drop, but still too high. I prescribed what is called a statin medication, which lowered Sam's cholesterol to a normal level of 178 within one week and significantly reduced his risk of heart disease and death.

We now have drugs that, when given within three hours of a stroke, may prevent permanent brain damage. Other drugs can unclog arteries, minimizing or avoiding damage from a heart attack or stroke. Even commonplace drugs that you can buy without a prescription can deliver significant benefits. Researchers believe that ibuprofen, the pain reliever found in Motrin, Advil, Anacin II, and many other drugs may help prevent Alzheimer's disease, as well as colon cancer.

Then there are antibiotics. If you were born after World War II, you are too young to remember the devastating dread of infections such as pneumonia, which killed thousands of people every year until the discovery of the first antibiotics, sulfa and penicillin. People still die of pneumonia today, but in far smaller numbers than in the days before antibiotics. The same is true for infections such as meningitis, endocarditis (infection of the heart), osteomyelitis (infection of the bone), as well as infections of the kidneys, eyes, and skin. Antibiotics have saved countless lives in the past five or six decades.

Alysha, a quiet, intelligent sixth-grader, would have suffered long-term problems or even death had it not been for antibiotics. She came down with a rash, fever, and chills. Her mom was concerned and took her to the doctor. As the doctor examined Alysha, she asked the girl how she'd been spending her summer. Alysha started talking about the family's camping trip a week earlier. Right away the doctor shifted her examination from Alysha's throat and chest to the child's arms and legs, and within minutes found what she was looking for: a tick. Although Alysha's symptoms at first looked like a viral infection, Alysha had a far more serious condition, Rocky Mountain spotted fever, which is passed to humans through the bites of ticks. Left untreated, this condition could cause permanent kidney damage or even death. The doctor prescribed the antibiotic tetracycline, and Alysha made a full recovery.

The benefits of medication apply not only to acute conditions that erupt with sudden and severe symptoms, but also to chronic diseases—health problems that have been and will be present for long periods of time. As more and more of us become older, there will be many more cases of chronic diseases such as arthritis, congestive heart failure, diabetes, and emphysema.

Two of my patients, 78-year-old Ruth and 80-year-old Margaret, are examples of how today's medications can relieve many of the symptoms of these chronic conditions and allow people to continue enjoying life. The degeneration of Ruth's knee joints (osteoarthritis) was making it harder and harder to walk. I recommended a common anti-inflammatory medication, available without a prescription, to reduce the inflammation and pain. After two weeks, Ruth was almost pain free, and was able to return to activities her aching knees had kept her from enjoying for several years. Margaret had trouble walking, too, but for a very different reason: congestive heart failure, which made it hard for her heart to pump enough blood to meet her body's oxygen needs. After walking only a short distance, Margaret could barely catch her breath. I prescribed a diuretic (water pill) and an ACE inhibitor, which strengthens the pumping force of the heart. In just a few days, Margaret was back on her feet, once again taking delight in walking through her lovely garden and going down to the corner market in her neighborhood.

The medications that doctors prescribe today are well researched and well tested. Before you swallow a pill, it has been tested on thousands of people, it has gone through a rigorous approval process, and its benefits and risks have been carefully documented. Such scrutiny is not found in any other country in the world or with any other healthcare products (see page 11 for more information about research procedures).

Sophisticated Surgery for Every Part of Your Body

Medications can control many medical conditions, but they cannot always cure them. Fortunately, other effective conventional treatments can, in fact, help heal or cure a great many health conditions. In no other area of medicine is the impact of technology more profound than in surgery. Incredible technological developments enable surgeons to perform operations once thought impossible. Just a few of these remarkable advances include the following:

- Intricate eye surgeries that can reattach your retinas, replace the lenses of your eyes, and even correct your nearsightedness. Even more amazing is the recent development of an artificial eye that can be surgically implanted to allow some blind people to see well enough to walk and eat without assistance.
- Brain surgeries that can remove dangerous aneurysms (burst blood vessels), destroy areas of tissue that are causing seizures, relieve pressure from fluid buildup, and even control pain.
- Organ transplants that can save you from certain death and allow you to live a normal life again.
- Heart surgeries such as angioplasty and stenting that can relieve angina and prevent heart attacks without major chest surgery.
- Joint repairs done with arthroscopes, which require only a very small incision and allow you to start using the joint within a day.
- Joint replacements that give you an artificial shoulder, hip, or knee to replace a natural joint that has worn out.

Among the most miraculous surgeries are those that involve replacing limbs that have been severed. Special microscopes and instruments allow surgeons to reconnect almost every kind of tissue: blood vessels, ligaments, muscles, and even tiny nerves. These techniques can restore nearly full function to the limb after healing is complete. Equally incredible is a device that makes it possible for someone who is completely paralyzed to have the use of a hand. Implanted into the chest, the device uses a sensor that translates small shoulder movements into control signals to the arm and hand, so that patients can write, use a phone, groom, and eat and drink without equipment to assist them.

The fiber-optic technology so helpful in diagnosis also leads the way to many new techniques in surgery. Using flexible, lighted scopes, surgeons can make much smaller incisions that are far less traumatic to the body. Such procedures—arthroscopic, laparoscopic, or endoscopic—make healing and recovery much faster. Fifty years ago, for example, a surgeon who wanted to remove your gall bladder had to make an incision from your breastbone to your belly button. Now the tiny cut is about an inch long and barely visible. Even more advanced are "needlescopic" surgeries, which use instruments smaller than three millimeters in diameter to take out gall bladders, spleens, adrenal glands, and other organs—even portions of the colon! Thanks to modern surgery, Lance, a 20-year-old college student, was able to keep playing football. An aggressive and talented running back, Lance had injured his knee more times than he could remember. The knee was stiff and sore every morning when he woke up, and it would swell and hurt for days after a game. After the season, he had arthroscopic surgery to repair torn cartilage in the knee joint. By the end of the next season, he was his team's leading scorer, and all those morning aches were nothing more than distant memories.

Laser Technology: Better Surgery—and More Ways to Heal You

Surgeries are invasive: They require the surgeon to cut your body open or to enter it in some manner. But developments in the field of laser technology have made surgeries more efficient, faster, and less risky by using high-energy, "hot" lasers to make incisions and stop bleeding. The high-energy laser gives the surgeon greater precision and control than is possible with a conventional scalpel, and it causes much less tissue damage. Lasers can even help control or cure various conditions without invading the body. Low-level energy, "cold" lasers can help wounds heal faster and reduce swelling and inflammation. Lasers can heal nerve, joint, and spinal disc problems and even reduce arthritis symptoms for long periods of time (sometimes permanently), with no side effects, and without cutting into the body.

Cold-laser technology helped Vicki, a 40-year-old department store manager, avoid surgery on her spine. She'd been in a car accident when she was a teenager, and she suffered from chronic and unrelenting neck pain. After 25 years of various treatments—medication and physical therapy, and alternative methods such as chiropractic—Vicki's pain continued to rule her life. Surgery, the treatment of last resort, looked like her only option. She came to see me for a second opinion, and I recommended that she try low-energy laser treatment. She agreed that after 25 years of pain, delaying surgery for a few more weeks wasn't going to make a difference. After eight treatments with the low-energy laser, however, surgery was the last thing on Vicki's mind. Instead, she was planning a vacation cruise with her husband and shopping for a bicycle to go riding with her daughter. Pain free, for the first time in more than two decades!

My father, who loves to play golf, found relief from arthritis in his hands with low-energy laser treatment, and he now can play a full 18 holes of his favorite passion without any pain.

Prevention Is Really the Best "Cure"

Despite the high profile of medical technology to *treat* diseases, prevention is really the mainstay of modern medical care. Doctors have many ways to keep you from getting sick in the first place and to screen for diseases while they are still in their early stages and curable. The PAP smear alone has saved literally millions of women from dying of cervical cancer. Mammograms have done the same for breast cancer. Colonoscopy can effectively detect colon cancer in its earliest stages, when it can be successfully treated and fully cured. Other tests can often reveal genetic defects while babies are still in the womb, so that doctors and parents can plan for their treatment, or sometimes even treat them before they're born. Vaccines are among the most powerful preventive weapons we have. They have totally eliminated many lethal diseases—smallpox, polio, and certain types of hepatitis, just to name a few. Vaccines have also been developed for influenza and certain types of pneumonia, and they may eventually play a part in preventing AIDS and other viral infections, and even certain types of cancer.

Your Physician Is Extensively Trained and Highly Qualified

Medical doctors (MDs) in the United States spend a minimum of nine years in formal school and training. They then must pass a series of comprehensive written and practical examinations to become licensed to practice medicine. These requirements are unparalleled elsewhere in the world and are more rigorous than in any other profession. And, to keep their licenses, American physicians must complete specific continuing medical education courses throughout their careers. In Chapter 3, "Getting the Most from Your Practitioner: An Insider's View," you'll find more information about physician education and training.

Medical Treatments Are Based on Comprehensive and Well-Designed Research

Research helps unlock and solve the mysteries of the human body. By investigating and describing the incredibly complex functioning of our bodily systems, scientists can develop methods to prevent or stop the breakdown of these systems. Medical research deserves credit for curing numerous diseases, prolonging lives, and providing you with a healthier quality of life. Because of research findings, you can receive treatments proven to be beneficial, and you can be protected against those that don't work or are dangerous.

In the U.S., the federal government's Food and Drug Administration (FDA) approves all prescription drugs and medical treatments. Various medical organizations also issue guidelines for doctors to follow for using drugs and other treatments. Before any treatment or medication receives approval, researchers conduct extensive laboratory and field tests. Then other researchers at different medical centers or research facilities attempt to repeat the tests again and again to make sure the results are always the same. Billions of dollars are spent in the U.S. every year on medical and scientific research to give you the best diagnostic tests and treatments in the world.

Today's most advanced research, called gene therapy, involves influencing genes to control or cure disease. Genes provide the "blueprints" for cells to grow and produce the substances that run our bodies. Scientists are now using viruses and various substances (called vectors) to alter genes that have degenerated or gone bad and are causing disease. Medical scientists have already used gene therapy to prevent or alter several diseases or acquired abnormalities such as immunodeficiency disease and some cancers. Someday (and probably in the not-too-distant future), scientists, on the very day you are born, will be able to detect the diseases you are likely to develop during your lifetime. You can then take precautions if a disease develops, or even totally eliminate it before it occurs!

THE PROBLEMS WITH CONVENTIONAL MEDICINE

The medical achievements of the twentieth century have saved countless lives and helped millions of people. But the very same technology that makes medical miracles possible also opens the door for problems. And trying to correct these problems can cause even more difficulties that otherwise might not have occurred. While its benefits far outweigh its shortcomings, conventional medicine has its flaws, and no discussion can be complete without addressing them. If you know where errors in medical care are likely to occur, you can recognize and avoid, or at least minimize, the dangers. The hazards of modern medicine include these:

- **Relying on technology that is not foolproof.** Tests can indicate disease where there is none, and vice-versa. And over-reliance on technology can mislead doctors.
- **Impersonal doctor-patient relationships.** The extreme specialization of modern medicine means that a doctor seldom gets to know and understand the whole patient.
- **Side effects of medication.** Modern medications, powerful as they are, can have strong and dangerous side effects.
- **The risks inherent in every treatment and procedure.** Surgery and other medical procedures can cause unintended harm and even death (and a great many surgeries are unnecessary).
- **Human error in making diagnoses and providing treatment.** In hospitals alone, human error may cause as many as 250,000 deaths each year.
- **High costs.** Conventional medical treatments and drugs can cost hundreds or thousands of dollars.
- **Unreliable research.** Medical research is all too often poorly designed or otherwise flawed, which can lead to the wrong conclusions. The researchers may be biased in favor of a particular conclusion. Or the research might be too limited to be really useful.

Technology Is Not Foolproof

Today, all your doctor has to do is suspect a medical problem and then turn the investigation over to technology. Physicians have come to count on and trust in the technological marvels of modern medicine. Well, if these tests are so good, isn't that an advantage? Yes, and no. For all the advances and advantages we can attribute to technology, it has one major flaw: Technology is not foolproof. No diagnostic tool comes close to being perfect. As wonderful as all the machines and tests are, if a doctor places too much dependence on technology, errors and harm can result.

That's what happened with a 34-year-old tennis pro named Eileen. She went to her doctor because she was having abdominal pain. Her doctor ordered a scan of her liver and spleen, and the test revealed numerous spots on her liver. These spots had the appearance of cancer, and Eileen's doctor told her that she needed immediate surgery, followed by chemotherapy and radiation. When Eileen questioned this assessment, her doctor became stern and told her that even with these treatments, she had only a year to live. Eileen wisely sought a second opinion, as should anyone who receives such devastating news.

She came to me for the second opinion. As I examined her, I asked her to tell me about her symptoms and overall health. The pain seemed to come and go, she said, and had started several years earlier but seemed to be getting worse, which was why she went to the doctor. She had not lost any weight, she had no trouble falling and staying asleep at night or staying awake and alert during the day, and she went for a gynecological exam every year because she was taking birth-control pills. She might as well have waved a huge red flag! I knew that birth-control pills could cause small but harmless masses to develop on the liver, and that these masses could cause abdominal discomfort.

I requested that a second radiologist review Eileen's scan, and sure enough, this was the case. The spots were completely harmless. The only treatment Eileen needed was to stop taking birth-control pills, which she was more than willing to do when she learned they were the cause of her symptoms. Fortunately, this story had a happy ending. But can you imagine how different the outcome would have been had Eileen actually gone for surgery? Although the laboratory analysis of the masses would have revealed them to be benign (we would hope), Eileen would have undergone the pain and disruption of surgery needlessly. As it was, she went through an unnecessary and emotionally painful ordeal simply because doctors put so much faith in technology that they neglected the basics of good medicine: They failed to consider Eileen's medical history. Even worse, they saw her only as a liver and a spleen rather than a whole person. Those oversights could have had dire consequences for Eileen.

Another patient, a 23-year-old graduate student named Al, was not as fortunate as Eileen. He had a cough that just wouldn't go away, so he went to the doctor. Other than the cough, Al was in excellent physical condition. He was bringing up quite a lot of phlegm, so his doctor sent a sample of it to the lab. Much to everyone's surprise, the lab reported the sample positive for tuberculosis. Al's doctor prescribed the standard six-month regimen of two powerful medications to treat the tuberculosis, and he warned Al that a known risk of these medications was permanent liver damage. Within two months, Al did indeed have liver damage, so the doctors had to reconsider his treatment. Guess what they discovered. Al didn't have tuberculosis after all! An investigation showed that a lab technician did not follow proper procedures and contaminated Al's phlegm sample with phlegm from a person who *did* have tuberculosis. In retrospect, it was obvious that Al's doctor could have averted the entire problem by repeating the lab test. Al not only didn't have tuberculosis (nor was his lifestyle such that he had any exposure to this serious disease), he didn't have any symptoms other than a cough. The misdiagnosis, completely preventable, changed Al's life forever.

If you need more proof of the risks of relying totally on technology, here's one more example. When magnetic resonance imaging (MRI) became widely available in the mid-1980s, doctors rushed to use it to diagnose a wide range of previously puzzling conditions. One that garnered much attention was back pain, which can be difficult to diagnose and treat successfully. MRI findings became a key factor in determining whether a person with back pain should have surgery; if the MRI revealed an abnormality in one of the disks of the spinal column, it was off to the surgeon for that patient. Then a 1990s study in *The New England Journal of Medicine* disclosed that 74 percent of the people tested who did not have back pain had disk abnormalities on MRI. How surprising is it, then, that a large number of people who have positive MRIs continue to have back pain after disk surgery? These abnormalities are not the cause of their pain in the first place! Yet thousands of people have back surgery on the basis of MRI findings, whether or not they actually need it.

The Doctor-Patient Relationship Can Be Impersonal and Distant

Once upon a time (TV time, that is), there was a character named Marcus Welby, MD. This fictitious healer was both wise and compassionate. He knew his TV patients as friends, not diseases. He always had time for everyone, and most of his patients got better seemingly just because he listened to and talked with them. Marcus Welby might have been make-believe, but the character was drawn from a reality that has since gone the way of black-and-white television. It was a time when doctors made house calls and even stayed for dinner once in a while. Your family doctor knew not only that you'd had a heart murmur since your childhood bout of rheumatic fever, but also that you liked daisies better than roses (and he brought a bunch when he came to your house).

Today's doctors see patients in clinics and offices. Often, several to dozens of doctors share the same facility and staff. If you're an infrequent patient, you might not see the same doctor twice. And even if you have to wait for the doctor, your time with him or her is limited by the nature of the problem you said you were having when you called to schedule your appointment. Are you thinking a house call really would be nice? You have a better chance of winning the lottery than seeing your doctor on your doorstep.

Most doctors don't want their visits with patients to be so impersonal, but the changing medical climate has had a great impact on the doctor-patient relationship. Several factors have undermined this relationship (see Chapter 3), but technology has been the most powerful. If I were to rely primarily on technology and testing for diagnosis and treatment, there would be little need for me to get to know my patients beyond a very superficial level, and there would be a void in the doctor-patient relationship. This gap is unfortunate, because it limits the doctor's ability to get a truly accurate picture of your state of health and the factors that influence it.

As you can see, tests seldom tell the entire story. They can tell what has gone wrong inside your body, but they rarely tell you what caused your body to malfunction. Unless the underlying factors can be discovered through good doctor-patient interaction, the problem may continue, recur, or grow to include additional problems. Relying on technology creates distance between you and your physician, and this loss of contact can have serious repercussions for your health.

That's what happened with Dara, another patient of mine. An amateur rock-climber, Dara had always been very healthy. But a most unwelcome "present" when she turned 44 was the start of a two-year cycle of breathing problems and severe sinus allergies. The technology-driven approach her doctors chose to follow was extensive allergy and lung-function tests, which suggested nonspecific allergies. So Dara's doctors gave her antihistamine medications, allergy injections, and steroid medications when her symptoms were really bad. These treatments helped control her symptoms, but only temporarily and to a minimal degree. Unfortunately, they also caused her to be drowsy, gain weight (almost 40 pounds), and develop osteoporosis—all well known and fairly common side effects.

When Dara came to see me, I asked her to tell me about her life: her job and her family, her pets and her hobbies, her house and her neighborhood. Dara began telling me, with great enthusiasm, about the new house she and her husband had moved into two years earlier. Built in 1898, the house was on a lovely piece of property near a small lake. It had been remodeled a number of times through the years, most recently by a retired couple who did most of the work themselves. As we talked, Dara realized that her symptoms had gone away completely during a three-week vacation to Hawaii, but they had returned a week after they were home. Her symptoms went away again when she was away on business for ten days, and again returned a week or so after she got home. Whenever she was gone from the house she felt better, even just during the day when she went to her office.

I suggested that Dara have the state health department check her house for environmental pathogens or allergens—substances in the house that could be causing her symptoms. Sure enough, inside the walls, the health inspectors found significant mold growth, which sometimes occurs in older houses that have not been well maintained or properly cleaned before remodeling. Dara and her husband moved into an apartment while the house was completely gutted and renovated. Dara's allergy symptoms disappeared, but some of the side effects of treating them did not, and Dara had to begin treatment for osteoporosis. If only Dara's first set of doctors had obtained a good medical history! They could have put the pieces together and saved Dara the anguish of unnecessary, and, in the end, harmful treatment. Instead, they trusted the tests, which really didn't reveal anything, anyway, and Dara paid the price.

Sadly, such experiences are common today. Doctors and patients both feel rushed during appointments. Patients wait for questions doctors never ask, and doctors presume that tests will tell them what patients don't. How did your last doctor's visit go? If typical, a nurse or medical technician sat down with you and asked, "What brings you here today?" and wrote brief notes in your chart. The doctor came in, looked at what the nurse wrote, and examined whatever part of your body seemed to be the focus of your symptoms. Your doctor likely then ended the visit by referring you for tests or writing a prescription. If your symptoms went away, great. Problem solved. If not, more tests.

Technology further widens the distance between patient and doctor when the doctor is a specialist. With all of the technological advances and information, no physician can know it all, so the practice of medicine has become divided and subdivided into many separate fields. Nowadays, we have specialists and sub-specialists, and even sub-sub-specialists, for each system of the body and even for many diseases, with each physician concentrating only on one aspect of the total person. Yet how can doctors who examine and treat only one area of the body even begin to observe and understand the whole person? You know the answer: They can't. This fragmented approach causes other problems. The treatment that one specialist provides might interfere or negate the treatments of other specialists. Even worse, each specialist feels responsible for only one part of you, and often your medical care is not integrated or cohesive; it's inconsistent and confused.

Sixty-five-year-old Thomas, a retired public relations counselor, is an example of what can happen. This poor man felt as if he were 85. He had a long list of health problems, and an equally long list of specialists who were treating those problems. He had a rheumatologist for his arthritis, a gastroenterologist for his stomach reflux, a pulmonologist for his asthma, and a nephrologist for a recent problem with his kidneys. He had also seen an orthopedist to consider knee-joint replacement and a general surgeon for his ulcer. Each doctor prescribed various medications, and each medication ended up affecting other organ systems. The arthritis medications caused more stomach and reflux problems, the stomach medicine caused more kidney problems, and the asthma drugs caused more joint erosion and swelling. Yet each doctor kept focusing on only one organ system and just increased the dosages or added more drugs.

I treated Thomas' arthritis with a low-energy laser, which reduced his symptoms by 95 percent and allowed him to stop taking the arthritis medications. After another week, he noticed his stomach and reflux problems had improved significantly. Two months later, he was able to stop taking these medications as well, which ultimately resulted in his kidney problem clearing up. To our surprise, his asthma symptoms went away, and we realized that the asthma had been caused by the reflux. Today, Thomas feels like 45!

But it's not just physical causes that remain uncovered. Numerous studies have revealed that psychological and mental factors affect or cause almost 85 percent of all medical conditions, yet few physicians even broach the subject. For example, depression is a major cause of many physical ailments, especially in the elderly. Studies show that 25 percent of all elderly patients may suffer from significant mental disorders, yet 30 percent to 50 percent of the time, these disorders are not diagnosed and treated. And these percentages do not include those patients with mild to moderate psychological problems, which are much more common. Doctors often overlook these psychological factors because they simply rely on technology and do not look for depression as the cause of physical problems.

Rachel, 76, a retired kindergarten teacher, is a case in point. She had moved in with her sister Sue, a delightful grandmotherly woman who had been a patient of mine for years. Rachel's husband had died after a three-year struggle to recover from a major stroke. Sue became worried because Rachel seemed to sleep all the time and complained that her joints hurt. Rachel went to a doctor who ordered comprehensive blood tests, a chest x-ray, arthritis tests, and even a brain scan and MRI, all of which uncovered absolutely nothing. The doctor prescribed anti-inflammatory and sleep medications, but Sue didn't think her sister was getting any better and convinced her to come see me for a second opinion.

As I talked with Rachel, she burst into tears when telling me about her husband. She also told me that several of her friends also had died during the past two years. It was clear to me that Rachel was very depressed. I prescribed an antidepressant and gave her information about a local support group for older people who had lost their spouses. Within six weeks, Rachel was like a new person, back to being herself, Sue reported with great relief and joy. Rachel's energy was back, she slept well at night, and she was taking dance lessons with a gentleman she met at the support group. After six months, I was able to gradually reduce her medication until she wasn't taking it anymore.

Medication Can Be Dangerous

By far, the most common type of treatment in conventional medicine is medication. *The Physician's Desk Reference* (PDR), the "bible" of drugs, lists tens of thousands of medications and their uses. There is no way that a physician can become familiar with all of these drugs, their uses, and their adverse effects and still have the time to practice medicine!

All medications have side effects. Most of these side effects, such as rashes or intestinal upset, are immediately apparent, and you can stop taking the medication if they appear. Occasionally, however, you might experience a side effect that is uncommon, severe, or subtle. That's what happened to my patient Bob, a 35-year-old accountant. Bob started taking a prescription medication to control an irregular heartbeat. When I saw him on a follow-up visit two weeks after he'd started taking the medication, his heart rhythm was normal and he said he felt fine. A month later, however, he was back in my office. Some of his clients complained to him that there were numerous mistakes on their tax returns. At first, Bob thought he was just working too fast because he had so much work to do at tax time, but then his wife told him it seemed that he wasn't himself. He was forgetful and often confused, and at times it seemed that he didn't even recognize his wife. These very symptoms were an uncommon side effect of the medication I had prescribed for Bob. I switched him to a different drug that didn't have the potential for such problems, and in a week he was back to being both the astute professional his clients had come to know and trust and a dependable, loving husband.

Although Bob's experience, with its happy ending, became a great story for family gatherings, the side effects of medications can often have tragic consequences. Consider that, each year,

- More than 32,000 people suffer from hip fractures because of drug-induced falls.
- More than 160,000 people suffer from drug-induced memory loss or impaired thinking.
- More than 230,000 people are hospitalized because of prescription drug problems such as side effects and incorrectly prescribed medications (wrong drug, wrong dose, and so on).
- An estimated 160,000 deaths occur in hospitals from the adverse effects of properly prescribed medications.

Drugs can interact with each other and with other substances. The more medications you take, the greater the chance of untoward reactions and interactions. Unfortunately, additional medications might also be required simply to counteract all the side effects and interactions of your primary drugs. I commonly evaluate patients who bring in bags full of medications, many of which interact adversely with each other, cancel out each other's effects, or cause even more side effects. These problems occur especially with, and are especially harmful to, the elderly. As you get older, your body loses the ability to process many drugs efficiently, so those drugs can build up and cause more problems. But some of these medications might be unnecessary, and others can be replaced with a simpler combination that is just as effective. Statistics show that the use of prescription medications is increasing 20 percent each year, so we can expect that these drug interaction problems will only increase.

Sometimes problems arise not from the drugs themselves but from the ways they're used. The most worrisome example is antibiotics. Over the years, millions of people with colds have flocked to see their doctors and walked out of the office with . . . you guessed it . . . antibiotics. Many people expect a prescription, and many doctors are willing to give it. But if you take antibiotics too often when you don't need them, bacteria adapt to resist those antibiotics. These bacteria can later cause life-threatening illnesses that those antibiotics, once effective against them, can no longer control. A recent study done on streptococcus pneumonia, a bacterium that commonly causes pneumonia, found that resistance to the six major types of antibiotics had doubled in just three years!

Overuse of antibiotics created a serious problem for a young patient of mine named Ellen. At 18, Ellen was a promising track star, attending college on a full scholarship. One day at practice, she suffered a twisting foot injury that fractured and displaced a bone. Ellen had to have surgery. As is typical in such situations, the surgeon put Ellen on antibiotics after surgery to prevent infection. Several days later, she started having redness and swelling, classic symptoms of infection. Lab tests showed a staphylococcus infection, and Ellen's surgeon gave her additional antibiotics. Her condition worsened. A specialized test called a *culture and sensitivity* revealed the reason: The strain of staph causing Ellen's infection was resistant to the usual antibiotics used to combat it because Ellen had taken antibiotics so often in the past for a variety of health problems. Staph is normally present on the skin, and these bacteria invariably get into the surgical wound; that's why surgeons prescribe antibiotics after surgery. I had to give Ellen a high-powered antibiotic intravenously. This treatment eventually cleared up the infection, but not before the infection did permanent damage to her foot. Ellen could no longer run, and she had to quit track.

Doctors overprescribe or incorrectly prescribe not only antibiotics. Many commonly prescribed drugs—antihistamines, antidepressants, pain relievers, medications to reduce stomach acid—might not be the best treatment for a particular condition, although doctors routinely prescribe them for those conditions. Pharmaceutical companies eager to promote newly developed drugs ply doctors with samples and offer discounts for patients, sometimes encouraging doctors to choose drugs that might not be the best option for the condition.

Buying drugs on the Internet can make you even more susceptible to their dangers. Because drugs are often so expensive, people looking for the best deals have turned in droves to the Internet. Certain drugs can now be purchased on line from doctors who, for a fee, will prescribe a drug for you without examining you. But these "savings" could end up costing you your health or even your life. Many of the conditions for which these drugs are used can be discovered only by a proper examination, and self-diagnosis and self-medication can be very harmful to your health. You could easily end up taking the wrong drug or too high a dose of a drug.

When 67-year-old Stephen, a retired Marine colonel, began having impotence problems, his urologist wanted him to get a thorough physical exam from his regular doctor, primarily to check for any signs of heart disease, before he would prescribe the popular anti-impotence drug Viagra. In people with heart problems, Viagra can cause heart attacks, and because of his age, Stephen had a higher risk for heart disease. Looking for a shortcut, Stephen found a doctor on the Internet who prescribed the drug for him without an exam. Sadly, with the first dose, Stephen became a statistic; he suffered a heart attack and died. Although the Internet doctor had asked Stephen whether he had any heart disease, he said he had never had any heart symptoms, so he assumed he didn't have heart problems. Stephen's regular doctor would have checked his heart health with lab tests and a treadmill evaluation, which would have revealed that he did, in fact, have heart disease.

Prescription medications are not all that can cause harm if you use them inappropriately. Acetaminophen has been linked to liver poisoning in people who take too much for too long, who mix it with alcohol, or who take it in several different remedies together (such as cold/flu, headache, or sleep formulas). A recent study shows that acetaminophen overdoses might be a bigger cause of liver failure than the diabetes drug Rezulin, which was taken off the market because of this harmful effect.

Conventional Procedures Can Be Harmful

Although modern medicine is safer than ever, no treatments are without risk. Numerous procedures, particularly surgery and other invasive procedures, carry the risk of unintended harm and even death. This is true whether the procedures are done in the hospital, in an outpatient surgery center, or at the doctor's office. Certainly, surgery is often the best treatment option for some conditions. But at other times, it is done simply as a quick fix. In fact, a very common motto in surgery residencies is "When in doubt, cut it out." Mary, a financial planner who is now a patient of mine, was seeing a gynecologist who took this motto to heart when she complained of recurrent cramping in her pelvic region and intermittent menstrual problems. Testing showed several fibroids, so at age 37, Mary underwent a hysterectomy. But the cramping continued after the surgery. Further testing revealed a bladder problem, which was healed with medications. Mary's hysterectomy was totally unnecessary!

Such surgeries are often done because it is much easier to simply take out an organ than to try to find underlying factors that might heal the problem medically over several months. Or surgery becomes a last resort, even though the chances of success are doubtful, because conventional medicine simply has nothing else to offer. And statistics demonstrate this to be true:

- 770,000 hysterectomies are performed every year in the United States, nearly four times that of any other country, yet almost 50 percent of these surgeries might not be needed.
- Coronary bypass surgery, which has been the primary treatment for clogged heart arteries, is often unnecessary. Numerous studies show that in more than half of these patients, nonsurgical medical treatment is as effective and life-prolonging as the highly invasive surgery.

■ Well more than half the back surgeries performed in this country are unnecessary. Worse, many are done because a previous back surgery didn't help, even though the likelihood of additional back surgeries helping these patients is actually much lower with each successive surgery. Studies have corroborated that in a high percentage of cases, proper nonsurgical medical treatment can often reduce back pain more effectively and for a longer period of time than back surgery.

Every surgery and invasive procedure has a risk of harm or death. In addition, many of these procedures are ineffective, and some can make you worse, requiring even more procedures and additional treatment. Considering all treatment options before you decide on surgery—and to try conservative approaches first whenever appropriate—are clearly in the best interest of your health.

Human Error in Medicine Can Be Deadly

Inherent risks are always associated with medications and medical procedures, but when we add human error to the mix, we could be talking about the difference between life and death. Deaths or harm due to doctor or staff error are called iatrogenic and occur much more commonly than you might suspect. In hospitals, human error causes nearly a quarter of a million deaths each year, making hospital errors the third leading cause of death in the United States, after only heart disease and cancer. Here are some recent estimates:

■ Eighty thousand deaths each year from nosocomial infections (infections picked up in hospitals by patients who didn't have them when they were admitted).
■ Twenty thousand deaths each year from non-medication errors, such as those that occur during diagnostic procedures (biopsies, endoscopies, dye tests, etc.) or routine surgeries.
■ Seven thousand deaths each year from medication errors. A recent study showed that medication errors (both fatal and non-fatal) occur in nearly 20 percent of patients. In a 300-bed hospital, that's more than 40 potential adverse drug events each day.
■ Twelve thousand deaths each year from unnecessary surgery.

This data does not include adverse effects associated with disability or discomfort. *Each year more than one million people are injured while in the hospital.*

We have all this information because hospitals are required by law to report the data. Unfortunately, however, we don't know how many errors occur outside of the hospital setting, although we can safely assume that the numbers are significant. We do know that an average of 10 percent of all hospital admissions is made necessary by treatment that has been given to patients in doctors' offices. The most common errors that occur outside the hospital involve treatment with medications. Many patients get the wrong drugs as a result of incorrect diagnosis, a common consequence of placing too much faith in technology alone.

Sometimes the doctor makes a mistake and prescribes the wrong medication. Or the nurse or pharmacist might fill the prescription incorrectly. Sometimes the doctor's handwriting is difficult to read. That doctors have illegible handwriting is a classic joke, but it's not so funny when the consequence could be fatal. Tragically, 42-year-old Robert, the chief financial officer of a large corporation, paid with his life for one of these mistakes. When Robert developed heart pain, his cardiologist wrote a prescription for Isordil, a medication to increase blood flow to the blood vessels of the heart. The pharmacist misread the handwriting and instead dispensed Plendil, a blood-pressure medication, at a dosage eight times the maximum dose. A few days later, Robert suffered a heart attack and died.

The bottom line is that human error, inside or outside the hospital, does occur, and it can be harmful and dangerous.

The High Cost of Medical Care

Technology doesn't come cheap, and in a healthcare environment in which technology rules, the costs of medical care will continue to climb. If you have health insurance, you might spend from $300 to $1,000 a month for premiums and still have to pay deductibles and co-pays. If you don't have health insurance, you're probably praying that you don't need medical care. With doctor's visits averaging $125, routine blood tests ranging from $100 to $300, pacemakers costing $5,000 to $8,000, and coronary bypass surgery exceeding $25,000, the expenses can add up quickly, no matter what condition you have. That diagnostic MRI could set you back as much as $1,200. A fiber-optic scope exam could cost you $900 just for the doctor's services, with $500 to $1,700 more for the facility, lab, and anesthesia charges. Drugs are also very expensive. Common prescription anti-inflammatory drugs can cost $80 to $140 a month or more. New drugs to treat high blood pressure can ring up at over $200 a month, and if you have common heart problems, you may have to pay as much as $600 a month for the medications you need to keep you healthy.

An unfortunate fact is that most doctors prescribe the newer, more expensive drugs that become available, primarily because of intense marketing by drug companies to both doctors and the public. In addition, in the past year alone, doctors prescribed 34 percent more medications than in the previous year. It's no wonder that the huge increase in health care costs is partially due to the growing expense and use of prescription drugs.

Unreliable and Questionable Research

The research that I referred to earlier has allowed medical science to progress with a great deal of accuracy, safety, and confidence. Modern medical care relies heavily on research, so the quality of scientific investigations is extremely important. But there are several serious problems related to medical research.

Bad research. To begin with, not all conventional research is good. In fact, some of it is downright mediocre. A scientist or doctor receives a grant to conduct research, but that doesn't necessarily mean that the research is well designed, that it's conducted rigorously, or that it comes to the correct conclusions. A recent report published in a major medical journal pointed out that in many studies, the researchers' conclusions were not supported by their own data! Even worse, many researchers talk in terms of relative benefits rather than absolute benefits. For example, a study will claim that drug X is 50 percent more effective in reducing disease risk than drug Y. Only in the fine print, however, do you find that drug X really cut the risk only from 4 percent to 2 percent. This misleads you by making an effect look stronger than it is: The 50 percent seems impressive, but the real reduction is quite small. An analysis in a recent issue of the *Journal of the American Medical Association* (JAMA) found that studies in the best medical journals (including JAMA) overwhelmingly focus on the relative rather than absolute benefits.

Research may also be bad when it is incomplete, not done thoroughly, or not backed up by additional studies. These situations are actually quite common. Often, a study (or a number of studies) may show some possible benefit, and, despite the lack of corroborating or more comprehensive studies, doctors go ahead and use the findings to offer new treatments. An excellent example is hormone replacement therapy (HRT) using the synthetic hormones estrogen and progesterone. These hormones have been prescribed to post-menopausal women for decades, on the basis of initial studies that showed them to be beneficial in preventing heart disease and osteoporosis and many other studies since then showing these and additional benefits. Only recently (40 years later!) was a more comprehensive study done that showed that HRT could actually be more harmful than helpful to your health—and this study recommended that it not be used long-term. The U.S. Office of Technology Assessment has stated that only 20 percent of treatments in clinical practice has actually been proven effective through good, comprehensive research. Certainly, most conventional treatments have proven successful even without the proper studies, but how many treatments are we subjected to that do not help at all, or are unnecessary, or, most importantly, may be harmful?

The consequences of incomplete or flawed research are serious indeed. You might remember several high-profile examples. Rezulin (for diabetes), Seldane (for allergies), Pondimin (for weight control), Redux (for weight control), and Duract (an anti-inflammatory used for pain) were all released with great fanfare and then pulled from the market when it became clear that they had serious side effects that weren't detected during testing.

Conflicting results. Because different research projects vary in quality and design, many studies arrive at conflicting and opposing conclusions. For example, in 1992 a class action lawsuit was filed on behalf of thousands of women who had undergone silicone breast implants. This suit was based on a few studies that indicated that silicone in breast implants caused a variety of adverse bodily reactions. I examined more than 450 of these women, and I found that most of their symptoms could be attributed to other causes. My findings were backed up by more recent studies that demonstrated no adverse effects from these implants, except in a small number of patients. Another example is the weight-loss product referred to as Fen-Phen. After this drug combination (Fenfluramine and phentermine) had been used for more than a year, the Mayo Clinic reported that it caused heart valve defects in numerous patients. The drugs were taken off the market, and the drug company was sued—and it settled for billions. However, later studies reported that the incidence of these defects was much lower than originally thought. Many doctors now think that because Fen-Phen helped so many patients, the benefits outweigh the risks, and the medication could be used again, with specific guidelines and precautions.

Bias. Many researchers have preconceived expectations about how their research will turn out. This bias can definitely affect the way they conduct the research and the conclusions they reach. In some cases, many of the subjects are eliminated from statistical evaluation when they don't react as expected. In others, the research is done specifically to try to prove something and is designed to do just that. A good example is a recent study done by an HMO in the state of Washington that compared the results of various treatments on back pain. The authors concluded that just reading a booklet on back pain was as good as chiropractic treatment or physical therapy. Analysis showed that numerous errors were made in the study, and worse, that the conclusions did not agree with the data! Apparently the HMO wanted to prove that the booklets were just as valuable so that it wouldn't have to pay for the other treatments.

Sponsor influence. Much current research relies on funding from pharmaceutical companies that are trying to prove their drugs are effective and should be used in place of others. A recent study published in the medical journal *Lancet* found that of the studies financed by pharmaceutical companies, 94 percent had positive findings; in other words, in 94 percent of the studies, the researchers ended up endorsing the use of whatever it was they were studying! Furthermore, some of these companies either suppress unfavorable studies or insist that the researchers "spin" positive results from their work.

Limited findings. Certainly, a great deal of research is being conducted, but for what purpose? Many studies do not apply to the general population because the study participants are carefully selected and have medical conditions that are uncommon or occur in only a small subset of patients with the disease. In addition, literally hundreds of articles and research papers are published every month that simply repeat what has already been done and offer no new or important information. Many of these studies are conducted simply to obtain research money. Other studies concentrate on new drugs or surgical techniques that may be used on only a few patients. At a cancer research meeting I attended recently, a presentation reviewed 268 thousand research trials from 1940 to 1990 and concluded that in more than 90 percent of them, trials were designed to meet the needs of researchers and regulators, not patients.

BALANCED HEALING GUIDELINES
FOR USING CONVENTIONAL MEDICINE

As you can see, conventional medicine has some significant advantages and some equally significant drawbacks. The goal is to take advantage of the benefits and avoid the problems as much as possible. When you consider that, every year, millions of people take medications and undergo treatments and surgeries, it's clear that, overall, conventional medicine is fairly safe and effective. So just be more aware of what is happening and use the knowledge you gain from this book to make wise and appropriate choices. These Balanced Healing Guidelines can help you benefit from the best that conventional medicine has to offer:

1. **Do what you can to prevent illness and injury.**
   - Discontinue or cut back on unhealthy habits such as smoking and excessive drinking.
   - Eat nutritiously.
   - Get some sort of physical activity every day.
   - See your doctor regularly for check-ups and screenings.
2. **In case of an emergency, go to the hospital emergency department, urgent care facility, or your regular doctor. Take advantage of the excellent emergency care offered by conventional medicine.**
3. **Communicate with your doctor.**
   - Make sure your doctor understands your concerns and your reasons for seeking care.
   - If you're seeing a new physician or specialist, get copies of all your pertinent blood tests, x-rays, scans, and even medical records, and take them to your first appointment.
   - If your doctor does not ask about stress, emotions, or other psycho-social aspects of your life, you bring them up.
   - If you have a complicated condition that requires treatment from several physicians, make sure that you have one primary physician who can coordinate all the specialists and answer all your questions.
   - Don't be afraid to keep asking questions until you fully understand your condition and what needs to be done.
   - If your doctor is not willing to discuss your medical problems and listen to you, consider finding another doctor.
4. **Make sure you understand why your doctor has recommended a particular test and what you will be experiencing during the test.**
   - Ask if the diagnostic tests are really necessary, and what your doctor expects to learn from them.
   - Ask for a step-by-step description of the procedure to be sure you're prepared for it.
   - Ask what a diagnostic test or procedure will cost before you have it done. If it's too expensive, find out if there are other less costly testing options.
5. **After diagnostic tests are completed, confirm with your doctor that the results make sense and correlate with your symptoms.**
   - Be careful not to automatically assume that just because something is found, it is the cause of your condition. Your doctor could find something that is not related to your symptoms and that could be completely harmless.

- Be careful not to assume automatically that, just because something is not found, nothing is wrong. Sometimes further testing is needed to determine the cause of your symptoms.
- Remember that no test is 100 percent reliable. Every test has both false positives and false negatives.

6. **Explore all your treatment options carefully, and, if you have choices, take the option you are most comfortable with.**
    - Find out all you can about your treatment, including possible side effects, dangers, and expected results; ask how long it will take to work—and, if it doesn't, what the next step(s) will be.
    - Unless immediate treatment is necessary, go slowly and begin with the most conservative, non-invasive treatments.
    - Ask your doctor how often the treatment works and how you can tell whether it is truly effective. If the chances are no better than 50/50, think carefully before you proceed.
    - If your doctor or a specialist recommends a new procedure, ask to make sure he or she has been well trained in the method and has performed it many times before. Find out whether there is a clear advantage to using it—and clear scientific evidence that it works. If you're ever in doubt, get a second opinion, especially if the treatment involves surgery.

7. **Check your medications.**
    - Ask your doctor what benefits a particular drug might provide, and what risks there are in taking it (including side effects and interactions with other drugs or foods).
    - Ask your doctor how long the drug will take to have an effect.
    - If your doctor prescribes a drug you haven't taken before, ask for samples so you can make sure it works better than other medications and without side effects, before you pay for a full prescription.
    - If your medication is expensive, ask your doctor if there are other drugs that are equally as effective and cost less. Find out if there are generic alternatives, which will be much less expensive. When you hear commercials about new medications, realize that there are probably other medications that work just as well and are much less expensive.
    - If possible, avoid using new medications until they have been on the market for several years.
    - Make sure that all of your prescriptions are filled correctly. Ask your doctor to write the name of the drug (legibly, printed if necessary, so that you can read it), and compare it with the label. If you have questions, ask the pharmacist.

Your health is your concern . . . and your responsibility. While conventional medicine offers great benefits, it also has shortcomings you must be aware of to use this approach to your best advantage. Before you make decisions, learn as much as you can about the diagnostic tests and procedures, treatment options, and possible complications. Of course, it's important to trust the doctors who are treating you, but it's equally important to remember that for most health problems, there are several possible solutions. And you might discover that nonconventional treatments are just as effective, with fewer side effects and at less expense. Read on for more about alternatives to conventional medicine.

CHAPTER 2

Alternative Medicine
WHAT YOU NEED TO KNOW

Alternatives to conventional medicine encompass a staggering array of methods and products. Even the most conservative estimates indicate more than 340 alternative methods, 26 categories of practice, and almost 10,000 ways of using alternative approaches. Many alternative methods have been used since ancient times, while others evolved at the same time that technology was creating modern conventional medicine. Some methods are entirely new, and some have adapted modern technology to ancient techniques. Ancient physicians used acupuncture as far back as 3,000 years ago, for example, but only in the last hundred years did modern acupuncturists discover they could increase the stimulation of acupuncture sites by applying a mild electrical current to the needles.

As conventional medicine began to come of age in the twentieth century, its practitioners started referring to older healing methods as *alternative*. This term stuck through much of the century as conventional (also called *allopathic*) medicine became the standard of care. But in the early 1970s, patients and physicians alike began to recognize that technology could not address all health issues and concerns. A resurgence of interest in the traditional healing arts began. A key event was the experience of journalist James Reston. While traveling in China, Reston had emergency surgery to remove his appendix. His only anesthesia was acupuncture, and it proved to be very effective. His experience was well publicized, and it opened the eyes of many, including those in the medical community, to the benefits of alternative therapies. Today, an estimated 42 percent of Americans uses some form of alternative, or "natural," care.

Most people use natural healing methods in conjunction with, or to complement, conventional medical care, which is why you often hear alternative therapies referred to as *complementary medicine*.

One reason these therapies are so appealing today is that they address the body as a holistic entity that encompasses the physical, mental, emotional, and spiritual dimensions of an individual's life. Many people feel that this approach complements the often narrow focus of conventional medicine, which tends to treat a particular disease or organ rather than the person as a whole. In addition, many people use alternative treatments because they prefer natural treatments, both because of the potential dangers of drugs and/or surgery and because they've found that many conventional treatments just don't work.

As is the case with conventional medicine, there are benefits and shortcomings to alternative therapies. On the positive side, many alternative methods are simply more effective than conventional treatments for certain conditions; and many natural treatments have fewer side effects and potential dangers. On the negative side, some alternative therapies can turn out to be a waste of time and money, and they can even cause harm. As with conventional medicine, alternative medicine's benefits outweigh its shortcomings; but again, you must understand both the pros and the cons to obtain the best results.

In this chapter, I'll discuss the good and bad of alternative medicine. I'll help you decide when and how to use it, either exclusively for a particular condition, or in conjunction with conventional methods.

THE BENEFITS OF ALTERNATIVE MEDICINE

There are many alternative methods you can use in place of or in conjunction with conventional approaches. In fact, for some health conditions, alternative treatments can be even more effective than conventional methods. The benefits of using alternative therapies include the following:

- **Alternative methods and products can be very beneficial.** Many have withstood the test of time—in some cases, thousands of years. Modern research has confirmed that alternative therapies really can help you get better.
- **Treatments are more natural** (involving no drugs or surgery). Nature's pharmacy is stocked with thousands of remedies that can be obtained from plants, animals, fungi, and bacteria.
- **The approach to health and healing is holistic, integrating the body, mind, and spirit.** With alternative medicine, you understand and feel connected to the entire healing process, your treatments are tailored to you as an individual, you can be an active participant in your healing, and you can draw on the power of your mind to help you heal.
- **Alternative approaches give you additional options if conventional medicine isn't working.** Alternative practitioners use therapies that medical doctors often deny or ignore.
- **Alternative medicine can be more affordable.** Care, services, and products are generally less costly than comparable conventional treatments.

Alternative Therapies Are Time-Tested Methods That Work

Archeological findings reveal that humans have used natural medicine for tens of thousands of years. Ice-covered bodies of ancient humans have been discovered with pouches containing herbs and salves—ingredients we recognize today as substances used for healing. Acupuncture and mind-body healing have been used for many millennia. For centuries, grandparents and parents have passed down home remedies to younger generations, thus continuing ancient healing traditions. Why are these alternative methods and products still being used after thousands of years? It's simple: They work. They have benefited mankind for centuries, and now, through scientific research, modern medicine is beginning to provide proof of their effectiveness.

For example, acupuncture relieves a wide range of discomforts and health problems, even though modern medicine cannot yet fully explain how and why it works. Today, the National Institutes of Health (NIH) has concluded that acupuncture is clearly effective for nausea and vomiting caused by pregnancy, chemotherapy, or radiation, and for post-dental pain. The NIH also suggests that physicians consider acupuncture as complementary to conventional treatment methods for menstrual cramps, tennis elbow, fibromyalgia, stroke rehabilitation, addictions, asthma, headache, myofascial pain, osteoarthritis, low back pain, and carpal tunnel syndrome.

Conventional medical research has shown other alternative methods to be beneficial for a wide variety of conditions. Here are just a few examples:

MEDITATION	
Anxiety	Stress reactions
Depression	Psoriasis
Hypertension	Panic disorders
Insomnia	Infertility
Chronic pain	Immune system dysfunction or weakness
HYPNOSIS	
Overeating	Stress
Pain	Addiction (smoking, alcohol, drugs)
Psychological conditions such as anxiety, phobias, and depression	Side effects of surgery
Boosting the effects of painkillers	
MANUAL THERAPY (CHIROPRACTIC, OSTEOPATHIC)	
Neck and back pain	Cervicogenic headaches (from neck trauma)
MASSAGE	
Pain	Asthma
Diabetes	Arthritis
AIDS	Fibromyalgia
Chronic Fatigue Syndrome	Autism in children
Low birth weight in premature babies	Anxiety

In addition to these treatments, benefits have been documented for many other alternative methods, including yoga, Ayurvedic medicine, guided imagery and visualization, and homeopathy, to name just a few.

As these alternative therapies have gained popularity, mainstream medicine has begun to admit that there just might be something to them. In fact, a recent survey revealed that

60 percent of the time, physicians are willing to recommend or actually have recommended alternative methods. Many health plans now pay for certain complementary methods such as acupuncture and chiropractic. And 64 medical schools offer their students courses or lectures in alternative medicine. This acceptance by mainstream medicine, which for many years simply dismissed alternative methods, is proof that they're beneficial.

Alternative Treatments Come from Nature

Common bread mold produced the first antibiotic, penicillin. Native Americans chewed the bark of a willow tree to relieve pain, and we now call the bark's active ingredient

HERB	USES
Bilberry	Eye diseases, age-related changes in brain
Black Cohosh	Hot flashes
Cranberry	Urinary tract infections
Gingko	Brain deterioration or aging, dizziness
Echinacea	Colds, wound healing
Feverfew	Migraine headaches
Flaxseed Oil	High cholesterol, cancer prevention
Garlic	High cholesterol, cancer prevention
Ginger	Motion sickness, nausea, indigestion
Ginseng	Energy, stress, diabetes, hypertension
Green Tea	Cancer
Hawthorne Leaf	Heart failure, coronary artery disease
Horse Chestnut	Chronic vein problems, varicose veins, leg swelling
Kava Kava	Anxiety, stress, restlessness
Milk Thistle	Toxic liver damage, chronic hepatitis, cirrhosis
Saw Palmetto	Benign prostatic hypertrophy
St. John's Wort	Depression
Valerian Root	Insomnia
SUPPLEMENT	USES
Beta-Carotene	Sunscreen, exercise-induced asthma
Coenzyme Q_{10}	Heart failure, angina, diabetes, multiple sclerosis
DHEA	Lupus, osteoporosis, depression, AIDS
Folate, B_{12}, B_6	Heart disease, pregnancy
Glucosamine	Arthritis
Melatonin	Jet lag, insomnia, advanced cancers
Niacin (B_3)	Cholesterol and triglyceride level reduction
Riboflavin (B_2)	Migraine headaches
Selenium	Cancer prevention
Vitamin C	Iron absorption, hypertension, osteoarthritis
Vitamin E	Immune function, dementia, breast pain

aspirin. Before twentieth-century medical technology, doctors knew that the environment produced what was needed to heal their patients.

The NIH studied the 150 pharmaceuticals most frequently prescribed in the United States and found that of the best-selling drugs, 57 percent contained at least one major active compound either originally or still obtained from natural sources. Of these, about 20 percent was derived from plants, 20 percent from animals, 11 percent from fungi, and a small percent from bacteria. One drug was even derived from seawater.

With so many of today's treatments coming from natural sources, you would think that natural substances and healing methods would never have been abandoned. But conventional medicine did abandon these centuries' old cures in favor of the newer, high-tech substances and methods of the 1900s. Doctors became enthralled by technological advancements to achieve new treatments and cures because they and many researchers felt that these advances held out the greatest promise for the future of medicine.

But the past is becoming the future. For example, one of the new promising treatments for ovarian, breast, and lung cancers, a drug called Taxol, comes from the bark of the Pacific Yew tree. In fact, natural substances have once again become so important to medicine that the world's major pharmaceutical companies have teams hard at work analyzing every form of plant and animal on the earth and in the sea to discover new drugs.

In addition, conventional researchers are now studying the natural products that have been used effectively for centuries. So far, they've scientifically proven the effectiveness of numerous herbs and supplements. Here are some of the natural remedies that have been found useful for certain conditions (see Appendix B for a more in-depth discussion):

Alternative Therapies Integrate Body, Mind, and Spirit

Rather than focusing on and treating a malfunctioning body part, as conventional medicine often does, most alternative approaches explore your whole being. Conventional medicine dwells primarily on the physical, deals with the mind only as a separate specialty, and usually ignores the spiritual aspect altogether. But the mind, spirit, and body are all integrally related, each contributing to your health and well-being. Holistic practitioners address all these aspects, and this approach has a number of advantages:

- Holistic medicine allows you to feel connected with—and to better understand— the entire healing process. It's been estimated that more than 85 percent of all diseases are caused or influenced by negative emotions, stress, and other non-physical factors. If you focus only on a disease or a diseased body part, you ignore these other factors that could be significantly affecting your health. Ignoring non-physical factors also causes you to feel detached from the healing process. But if you understand your emotions and know how your mind affects your body, you can heal faster and more completely.
- Holistic medicine allows you to be an active participant in your healing and your health. It focuses on the mind-body connection as a critical factor in many of the health problems you may experience. Because only you can make significant

changes in your emotional state and mental outlook, almost all alternative methods require you to play an important role in the healing process. In fact, your active participation is often absolutely essential for true healing to occur.

■ Holistic medicine allows individualized treatment. Because you are a unique mind, body, and spirit, you respond to treatments in your own unique way. A holistic approach targets the specific underlying cause(s) of your health problem, yet gives you the therapy or combination of therapies that work for you as a whole person.

■ Holistic medicine draws upon the mysterious yet powerful functions of the mind. The mind can cause disease, and it can heal it, as well. Just having a positive attitude can make a huge difference in the speed and quality of your healing. Mind-body approaches such as meditation, yoga, hypnosis, and guided imagery use the mind to influence the body—and they do so with such success that many of today's major surgery centers offer these alternatives to help people prepare for surgery and heal more quickly afterward.

Alternative Therapies Give You More Options for Healing

Alternative medicine considers the causes of and treatments for many diseases that conventional medicine has either denied or ignored—or for which it has no answers. So you have additional options for healing, even when you think there is nothing more that can be done to help you. In the past, contemporary doctors often scoffed at new ideas and treatments. It's been barely 100 years since doctors refused to believe in germs because they could not see them. At the time, surgery under sterile conditions was unknown, and for a surgeon to eat lunch while he was operating—and then wipe his hands on his jacket and move directly to the next patient—was not unusual. The conventions of medicine can be quite rigid, and for physicians to change their minds and admit that new ideas or methods are valid often takes years.

While these conventional doctors of the time were busy denying new possibilities, alternative healers often considered them legitimate. In the late 1800s, the preferred treatment for heart failure was to apply leeches to reduce blood volume, a treatment that, although it succeeded in reducing the heart's workload, left patients so weak that they often died. Yet at the same time, folk healers were using a plant to treat the same problem, and with considerably more success. The plant? Foxglove, which contains an ingredient that has become digitalis, the most important heart failure medicine yet discovered.

Even in our time, conventional medicine has scoffed at medical conditions that research subsequently proved were, in fact, clinical diseases. Post-polio syndrome, chronic fatigue syndrome, fibromyalgia, and PMS (premenstrual syndrome) are all examples of medical problems that conventional medicine disregarded for years while alternative practitioners treated them. Without the influence of alternative medicine, who knows how many of these conditions would still be unrecognized!

Rather than being locked into the rigid treatment protocols of conventional medicine, alternative healers are generally more open to trying whatever might help the patient. This approach offers the flexibility to handle anything that might develop or manifest in the healing process. Linda, a computer game designer and a young patient of mine, got tremendous benefits from the options alternative medicine offered her. Now 32 years old, Linda had suffered from irritable bowel syndrome for 20 years. During that time, the only conventional treatments recommended were numerous medications, none of which controlled her symptoms adequately. I prescribed Chinese herbs, an alternative treatment dismissed by most conventional doctors, and they eliminated most of her symptoms. Linda was pleased, but she wanted to cure the problem more quickly than the several months it would take to finish the Chinese herbal treatment, so she underwent two acupuncture treatments, which allowed her to reduce the herbs she was taking but still didn't completely eliminate her problems. I added interactive imagery to her treatment. After four sessions, the rest of Linda's symptoms were gone. Without alternative medicine and the flexibility it provides, Linda would have continued to struggle with her disease for the rest of her life.

Alternative Care, Services, and Products Are Affordable

Alternative approaches are often less expensive than comparable conventional approaches. And not only do they cost less, but you get more for your money. Consider 37-year-old Mike, the owner of an auto-supply business. Mike had had allergies all his life. He had been on allergy shots for 12 years and still required inhaled steroids and antihistamines, yet he continued to have symptoms of nasal stuffiness, drainage, and sinus headaches. After three weeks on Chinese herbs and four acupuncture treatments, he was symptom free for the first time, at a cost far less than his conventional treatment. In fact, after just one treatment, he told me he could smell roses for the first time in 20 years!

Another example is Betty, a 46-year-old secretary with carpal tunnel syndrome. She had constant pain and numbness in her hands. The discomfort was so bad that it woke her up at night. Her hand specialist recommended splints and anti-inflammatory medications. Surgery was also a possibility, but Betty had heard from many others that it helped only a minority of patients, and the symptoms would often return a year or two later. So she decided to try acupuncture. After eight treatments, Betty's symptoms were gone.

I could give you many other examples of alternative procedures that can achieve healing without the high cost of conventional medicine. Reflexology or massage can correct many chronic problems such as headaches, muscle tension, and anxiety, and at a fraction of the cost of conventional methods. Acupuncture for pain relief is cheaper, safer, and quicker than narcotic medications, surgery, epidural steroid injections, and many other types of traditional pain treatment. Meditation is less costly than conventional methods for reducing stress, lowering high blood pressure, and improving immune dysfunction—and it's just as effective, if not more so.

THE SHORTCOMINGS OF ALTERNATIVE MEDICINE

Alternative medicine has many benefits and advantages, which is why many alternative therapies are quickly gaining recognition and becoming part of mainstream medical practice. But just like conventional medicine, alternative medicine has its drawbacks. Here are the most important ones:

- **Many claims of effectiveness have not been proven through research and scientific studies.** Despite the enormous amount of attention they've been given, some natural methods and products have not been proven effective and may be worthless. Even the most popular alternative products and treatments may not, in fact, deliver all they promise.
- **There are few standards for formulations and ingredients, and few standardized guidelines for taking or using alternative products effectively.** The label may not accurately tell you what you're getting. Minimal research has been done to establish effective and safe dosages, and no blood tests exist to determine whether you're taking the correct amount.
- **The marketing of alternative medicine can lead you astray.** Be wary of hype! Because herbs and supplements are not subject to the same regulation as drugs, their manufacturers can claim all sorts of benefits without having to back up their claims. If it sounds too good to be true, it probably is.
- **Alternative medicine does not always save you money.** Because there's so little reliable information and research, you can end up wasting a great deal of money trying to find what works and what doesn't, or buying the most expensive brand, which is not necessarily the most effective. And you may be wasting money by taking a lot of supplements, some of which may counteract the effects of others.
- **Alternative approaches can have side effects and hidden dangers.** Many popular supplements and herbs, as well as treatment procedures, can be just as dangerous as conventional medicine. It's not necessarily true that "natural" equals "safe." Many alternative products can cause allergic reactions, side effects, and even damage to your body.
- **Ineffective alternative treatments can be harmful.** It can be dangerous when you self-diagnose and self-medicate for a condition that requires a conventional treatment.
- **Education, training, and qualifications for alternative practitioners are often inconsistent or lacking** (see Chapter 3, "Getting the Most from Your Practitioner: An Insider's View").
- **Research on alternative methods is inadequate.** Compared with conventional medicine, there is little research on alternative approaches, and much of the research that does exist is fraught with problems.

Claims About Alternative Therapies May Be Unproven

Because so many people are interested in or have already sought out alternative approaches, we now have an abundance of information on alternative medicine. Hundreds, maybe thousands, of articles and books describe alternative methods and products, and many of these publications have soared to bestseller lists. Unfortunately, the abundance of information is itself a problem: Many people seek the "alternative of the week" without knowing whom to go to, what to do, or what they're really getting into.

Yes, scientific research supports the benefits of some alternative approaches, but many natural methods and products have not been proven effective and may be worthless. Even the most popular alternative products and treatments may not in fact deliver all they promise.

Part of the problem is that the federal Dietary Supplement Health and Education Act of 1994 defines alternative products as *dietary* supplements (in other words, food) rather than medical substances, so they don't have to undergo the strict testing and be governed by the effectiveness regulations that drugs and medical products do. Although manufacturers cannot make specific medical claims on the label, they can get around this restriction by alluding to possible benefits, with descriptions such as "for prostate health" or with labels such as "Heart Tonic." Unfortunately, these products may not deliver the described benefit. Here are some examples:

- **Chromium picolinate.** Studies have not borne out the claims that this mineral increases muscle mass, lowers cholesterol, supplies energy, and aids weight loss. Many of the studies that supposedly proved that chromium picolinate did all this were promoted and paid for by the companies that sell it. Independent studies have shown negative results.
- **Shark cartilage.** This treatment has been touted as effective for osteoarthritis, cancer, and AIDS, but studies so far have shown no such effects.
- **Vitamin C.** This vitamin has been marketed to treat cancer, but studies have not supported these claims. In fact, recent studies have demonstrated that vitamin C may cause as much harm as good when used in high doses for cancer.
- **DHEA, human growth hormone (HGH), and melatonin.** These three hormones have all been touted as anti-aging "miracles." Although they may be beneficial for some conditions, there has been no proof that they prolong life. In fact, most of the research studies on these hormones were done on animals. Although these substances can help prevent diabetes, clogged arteries, and cancer in rats, the human body processes these hormones differently, and short-term studies have so far failed to show any consistent benefits for health or longevity. Larger studies have been done on melatonin and aging, with very conflicting results. Initial studies on HGH have shown some short-term benefits, but they also have demonstrated potential long-term problems and many unanswered questions. Furthermore, the notion that aging is partly the result of hormone deficiencies is questionable. The people who recommend DHEA, HGH, and melatonin theorize that because hormone levels drop with age, if you get the levels back up, you'll become young again. We know that natural melatonin and DHEA do indeed decline between the ages of 20 and 60, but that could be because our bodies use these hormones to make organs develop properly, not to regenerate or maintain them.

Most alternative products have not yet been subjected to well-controlled studies to assess how they work for specific medical conditions—the kinds of studies that conventional medicine's substances must undergo. Until such studies take place, we have no idea whether many of them really work. Even those that work in the short term might have little or no effect in the long run, or they could cause additional yet undiscovered problems.

Alternative treatments might involve the same problems as alternative products. Even though many such treatments have received glowing testimonials from people who have used them (the scientific community calls this anecdotal support), they have not been subjected to rigid research—or, if they have, the research has shown negative or ambiguous results.

A patient named James, an investment banker, is just one case in point. At age 56, he had heart disease. An alternative practitioner told him that he could be cured by chelation therapy, in which a chemical called EDTA is injected into the bloodstream and purportedly binds calcium and toxic metals such as lead and mercury to prevent them from doing damage to the blood vessels—a claim that is not supported by research. After 30 treatments, James was no better, and his heart disease was worse. He wasted precious time that could have been used for conventional treatments that actually work.

The Mystery of Alternative Therapies: You Often Don't Know What You're Getting

You might find this surprising, but manufacturers of natural products do not have to prove the actual content or quality of the products they sell. Unlike conventional medications, which are highly regulated and subject to extensive quality-control measures, alternative products aren't controlled, and there are no quality standards to which manufacturers must adhere. Although you always know exactly what's in an aspirin tablet, you often don't know what's in an herbal remedy or supplement. Purity and potency can vary not only from product to product, but they also can vary even from pill to pill within the same bottle!

What's Behind a Label?

If the label says a particular ingredient is in a product, is it in there? You would think so. But when a consumer laboratory tested 54 ginseng products, it discovered that 25 percent of them actually lacked the main ingredient, ginseng. Alternatively, the product might contain ingredients that aren't listed on the label. Another study evaluated 12 Chinese herbal topical lotions used for skin problems. All of them contained steroids, yet not one listed steroids among the lotion's ingredients. If you don't get what you think you are getting, the product obviously will be of no benefit. And if you get something that you don't realize you're getting, you may suffer unexpected side effects or other harmful results.

How Much Is Really in There?

Even if a listed ingredient is in the product, there's no way to know whether the ingredient is concentrated enough to work. For example, feverfew, used for migraine headaches, requires 0.02 percent of parthenolide, its active ingredient, for the product to have an effect. But out of 32 feverfew products examined in a recent study, only one had enough parthenolide to have a beneficial effect. Melatonin products need 0.3 milligrams of the active ingredient to raise blood melatonin levels to where they should be during sleep. Many of the products contain only one-tenth of this amount. Concentration varies among products, too. The concentration of progesterone cream, sold over the counter and promoted to relieve hot flashes, prevent bone loss, and protect against heart disease, might not even appear on the label. The concentration ranges from 3,000 milligrams per ounce to less than 2 milligrams per ounce.

Is It Strong Enough to Produce the Claimed or Desired Effect?

Even if each pill contains the correct amount of herbs according to the label, the herbs themselves may or may not have the potency or effects they are supposed to have. Potency depends on when the herbs are harvested and on what part of the plant is harvested. For example, there are actually three different species of the echinacea plant, and in each one, a different part of the plant has medicinal applications. The potency of the herbs you buy can also be affected by soil chemistry, genetic line, and growing conditions (such as availability of water and sun). In addition, each part of the plant is more potent at certain times of the year. Yet some manufacturers simply harvest and package the entire plant all year round, without regard for which species they have, which part is most potent, and in which season it is most potent.

You might not even be buying the same herbs that the manufacturer shipped. The longer some products sit on the shelf, the less potent they can become. Heat and sun can also decrease potency. Flaxseed oil, which seems to have important effects that reduce cholesterol and prevent cancer, deteriorates very rapidly and should be used within three months of manufacture. Unfortunately, it may take weeks or months to be shipped and then may sit on store shelves even longer.

How Do You Know How Much to Take?

Even if you do know that you've bought a good-quality product that works, how do you know how much to take? Or, if you do know, how can you be sure that this amount is effective? How much should you take of any vitamin? Of any herb? Of any antioxidant? If you take too small a dose, you might experience no beneficial effect. If you take too large a dose, you can have adverse reactions. Unfortunately, no matter what book or article you read, the recommended dosages might not be suitable for your particular medical situation, so you can't be sure which information is right for you. Once again, the basic fact is that very little research has been done to resolve these issues, so your guess is often as good as anyone else's.

Some guidelines have been established, especially in Germany, for how often we should take specific natural substances. The major problem is that we all differ in our susceptibility to a particular product and the rate at which we metabolize it. So the amount that's effective for one person may be quite different from what someone else might need. With conventional medications, extensive research establishes effective and safe dosages, and there are blood tests to measure whether you are taking the correct amount. With alternative products, however, research has been minimal, and there are no tests for determining herbal blood levels. So you really cannot know for sure whether you are taking the right amount.

In my practice, I recommend alternative products in dosages based on the particular illness, as well as on other factors that might complicate the picture—your age, other medications you may be taking, and other medical problems you may have. Then I work with you to find a dose that achieves the desired result. Sometimes this process takes time and effort. That was the case with 65-year-old-Julia, a home health care worker. She had chronic venous insufficiency, a condition in which her leg veins did not function properly, causing her legs to swell. The herb horse chestnut has been shown to be effective for this condition, but the herbal texts recommend doses ranging from 125 milligrams to 900 milligrams per day. I simply had to start Julia on a low dose and then adjust it until I found the dose that relieved her leg swelling without causing side effects.

Besides knowing whether you are receiving an appropriate amount, how do you know how long to take a particular product? You should take some herbs only for a specified period of time—prolonged use may cause harmful effects—and others you must take for an extended period before you see results. Here are a few common examples of both situations:

- Many people take the immune stimulant **echinacea** every day to prevent colds, yet it is recommended for no longer than eight weeks.
- **Kava kava**, for anxiety, should not be taken longer than three months.
- When taking **ginseng** as an energy tonic, you should be re-evaluated after three months, and you should generally take it only five out of every seven days.
- You must take **gingko** for at least eight weeks before you know whether it will help memory or concentration problems.
- **Evening primrose oil** takes six months to have a beneficial effect on arthritis.
- **Glucosamine** takes two to four weeks, and **chondroitin** takes two to four months to be beneficial for arthritis.
- **Garlic** may take up to six months to lower cholesterol.
  (See Appendix B for more information on herbs.)

Is Brand A the Same as Brand M?

Different companies prepare products of the same name differently, resulting in widely variable potencies and concentrations. Consider echinacea again. There are several ways of preparing this herb, including a pressed-juice preparation, several types of extracts, and a root tincture. Do you know which preparation is in the bottle on your grocer's shelf? Do you know whether, or why, it matters? It does. Because of different processing procedures, the echinacea that you might take in the United States for your cold is not the same as the echinacea researched and approved in Germany for the same purpose, and the two forms work much differently.

You'll find these same kinds of discrepancies on every shelf in your health-food store. Certain manufacturers produce consistently reliable products, while others don't. When 43-year-old Jill, a high school history teacher, suffered from mild depression, she wanted to use natural products. She had already tried St. John's wort, but she told me it had not helped her at all. Because she had used a brand with which I was not familiar, I tried her on another brand that I knew to be of high quality. Within two weeks, her depression was under control.

What Are Functional and Fortified Foods?

Manufacturers recognize that we might not be inclined to take supplements and herbs, even if we think they may be good for us, so they have added them to everyday foods and drinks. The result is functional foods—products that claim to affect the function or structure of the body as an added health benefit. Food companies have added herbs such as echinacea, gingko, kava kava, ginseng, and St. John's wort to fruit drinks and snack foods. How about some echinacea chips, or ginseng candy? The main problem with these functional foods is that most contain negligible amounts of the active ingredient. In addition, people consume foods and beverages in varying amounts and at irregular intervals, so it's not likely that your body will use the beneficial substances effectively.

There's also a problem with fortified foods. Because of the popularity of supplements, many manufacturers are fortifying our regular foods, such as cereals, orange juice, and even burritos, with vitamins and minerals. The problem is that many people take both the fortified foods and supplements, risking a harmful overdose of nutrients. Examples include iron and niacin, which can harm the liver, and vitamin C, which can cause stomach irritation. Look at what happened to Ralph, a radio announcer, who at age 36 was worried about his family's history of cancer. He had read that selenium could help prevent cancer, so he started eating more selenium-rich foods and also started taking selenium supplements. After two months, he began feeling irritable and fatigued, he developed stomach pains, and he started losing his hair—all side effects of selenium toxicity. I told him to stop taking the supplements, and in three weeks his symptoms were gone (although it did take a month or so for his hair to return to normal). Ralph had overdosed on a supplement without realizing it was possible to do so or that he was doing it. Recent studies have shown that some fortified foods, especially orange juice, can interfere with the absorption of conventional medications such as antibiotics.

Watch for the Pitch, the Hype, the Outrageous Claims

There are no magic pills and no definitive answers to many of our health problems, but that does not stop companies or practitioners from making such claims. They know that marketing is the primary way of selling their goods, whether or not these products work. As a result, you may think a product is the answer to your problems when the claims actually are all hype. When the FDA changed the status of natural products from medical drugs to dietary supplements, it opened the floodgates for manufacturers to make whatever marketing claims they wished. The manufacturer doesn't have to prove that a product is beneficial or of high quality, as do manufacturers of conventional drugs and products. The only way an alternative product can be removed from the market is for the FDA to deem it unsafe.

Literally hundreds of products are promoted as beneficial or even life-saving, yet there is no proof whatsoever to support such claims. Consider these examples:

- A colon-cleansing product advertises that it will "burn disease out of your body."
- A self-promoting newsletter recommends a product with which "arthritis sufferers will grow new knees in as little as 90 days." The newsletter also promises that taking a new type of brain "lubricant" will eliminate Alzheimer's disease, and it promotes a product that is "successful in treating cancer, infection, leukemia, AIDS, and even autism."
- A supplement marketed as "natural DHEA"—and promoted as boosting energy and improving well-being—is derived from a wild Mexican yam. But some companies do not process it completely, which results in a form that cannot be utilized by the human body.
- "Vitamin O," which is 3 percent dissolved, stabilized oxygen, is touted as helping to eliminate everything from breathing problems and lack of energy to cancer and heart disease. It was even advertised in USA Today as a panacea that ". . . purifies your bloodstream, maximizes nutrients, eliminates poisons and toxins." A government lab analysis revealed that it was nothing more than distilled salt water.

The bottom line is that you have no way of knowing which marketing claims are true and which are hype. Manufacturers do not have to offer proof, so it's easy for them to lead you astray.

Buyer Beware: Alternative Medicine Can Cost You a Bundle!

For the most part, alternative products and methods are less expensive than comparable conventional medications and practices. But because there's so little reliable information and research, you can end up wasting a lot of money trying to find what works and what doesn't. And as if that's not challenging enough, many different companies market similar products; so even if you find something that works, what brand should you get? The most expensive brand is not always the most effective. Here are some areas to watch out for:

- **Avoid MLMs—don't pay for the middlemen.** Probably the most expensive way to buy alternative products is through multilevel marketing companies, or MLMs. In these pyramid set-ups, the profits from sales of herbals and supplements are divided among multiple levels of salespeople. Although many of these formulations are high quality and work well, you're still paying for all those salespeople. More often than not, you can buy the same combinations from a store for at least one-third less than the comparable MLM product.

- **Some alternative products are not worth the cost.** Many people take alternative products over comparable conventional medications believing that they will save money, but the savings are often elusive. Glucosamine, an anti-arthritic supplement, can relieve symptoms in many patients, but it costs as much as prescription anti-inflammatory drugs and much more than over-the-counter drugs such as Motrin, Aleve, and Advil, even though research shows these drugs to be equivalent in effectiveness. Some manufacturers combine additional products, such as chondroitin, with glucosamine for more potent effects, but this can double or triple the cost. SAMe, a supplement from Germany promoted and sold widely as another pain and arthritis reliever, may cost hundreds of dollars per month if you buy the top-quality product. Even the poorer quality SAMe products cost more than comparable conventional medications, which studies have shown to be just as effective as SAMe, if not more so.
- **Taking lots of products adds up quickly.** Your costs quickly mount if you think that you need lots of different alternative products to be healthy or prevent disease. In addition, when you take many alternative products at the same time, they may negate the effects of each other, meaning you're wasting even more money. For example, various manufacturers combine evening primrose oil (omega-6 fatty acids) and fish oil (omega-3 fatty acids) into one product to lower the risk of heart disease. Although each ingredient might have such a beneficial effect, the different fatty acids, when taken in combination, can compete against each other in the body and thus can cancel out each other's benefits.
- **You can't get reimbursed.** Even if the alternative method you want to use is effective and worthwhile, it still may be too expensive for another reason: insurance reimbursement—or, more accurately, lack of it. Most conventional methods and drugs require you to share the cost by paying a deductible or co-pay. But many alternative methods are not covered at all. If you want it, you pay for it. But a comparable conventional method could end up costing you far less.

Alternative Medicine May Have Side Effects and Hidden Dangers

Many people believe alternative products are safe because they're "natural." This is not true. Many alternative products can cause allergic reactions, side effects, and even damage to your body. High doses of gingko, ginger, garlic, and vitamin E can all prolong bleeding—a potentially serious problem if you're taking aspirin, which does the same, or blood thinners. Guarana, an herb included in many energy boosters, is more potent than caffeine and can cause a rebound effect of depression and extreme fatigue after it wears off. Even aromatherapy, believed by many people to be totally benign, can have unexpected effects. Many of its essential oils can be toxic, especially if used in too high a dose. Various oils can interact adversely with other oils, as well as with foods, perfumes, shampoos, soaps, and other products.

Thirty-two-year-old Cynthia, a newspaper reporter, is well acquainted with the dangers of alternative therapies. She came to me because she wanted a holistic approach to the allergy problems that were plaguing her. Cynthia had always been an anxious person. She read a story in a woman's magazine that aromatherapy could help reduce anxiety, so she decided to give it a try. She used several different fragrances in her bath and also burned aromatic candles by her bedside. Although she became more relaxed, she started having sinus and nasal congestion. Thinking she was having allergy problems from various pollens, she started taking antihistamines. But her symptoms got worse and the antihistamines didn't help anymore. So Cynthia went to her doctor, who put her on powerful steroids. The steroids not only failed to help Cynthia's symptoms, they made her tired and caused her to gain weight (both are common side effects of steroid therapy). When I asked Cynthia what treatments she was using for her symptoms, she listed everything except the aromatherapy. That came up only when I asked her what she was doing for her anxiety. Suspecting that the flower essences in the aromatherapy could be causing Cynthia's allergic response, I suggested she stop the aromatherapy. Within a week, her sinuses were clear.

St. John's wort is another natural product that could be harmful if used incorrectly. This herb can interfere with a specific liver function that is responsible for the breakdown of more than half the synthetically made conventional drugs. So far, this herb has been shown to interfere with the absorption of digoxin, a common heart-failure medication, and protease inhibitors, used for AIDS patients. Several more medications, including commonly prescribed antidepressants, are suspected to have similar interactions with St. John's wort.

Echinacea, which is related to ragweed, can cause allergic reactions in susceptible people. And recent studies showed that high doses of vitamin C, if given to cancer patients, may interfere with the beneficial effects of chemotherapy.

It gets worse: Many alternative products can cause more serious harm and even death. The herbal supplement ephedra (ma huang) contains ephedrine, a stimulant, and is touted as a weight-loss agent, muscle enhancer, and energy booster. It is even promoted as giving an "herbal high" and marketed to teens as "herbal ecstasy." When properly used, ephedra can be an effective decongestant and weight-loss supplement. Yet this herb has been associated with deaths as well as adverse effects, including heart attacks, stroke, angina, irregular heartbeat, and high blood pressure.

Another dangerous herb is pennyroyal oil. This herb is widely available at health food stores, and one cup of its tea can help menstrual cramps and regulate menses. Yet when used improperly, it can cause liver and kidney shutdown, profuse bleeding, and miscarriages.

Yohimbe, used for the same purpose as Viagra, has caused heart attacks (just like Viagra). A class of Asian herbs containing aristocholic acid has been linked to kidney failure and cancer. Blood root, deadly nightshade (belladonna), foxglove (digitalis), hemlock, jimson weed ("loco weed"), and sassafras are all herbs that can be quite toxic and must be taken with great caution, if at all. And even products that normally have few side effects may pose harm simply because they contain impurities or ingredients that are mistakenly included in the product.

As for alternative treatments, most are considered safe, although sometimes they can have unintended and even harmful consequences. People have suffered ruptured discs and even paralysis after receiving chiropractic treatment. Improperly performed acupuncture of the chest can cause a pneumothorax, a condition in which air outside the lung cavity compresses the lung and prevents free breathing. Chelation, a process designed to remove harmful chemicals from the bloodstream, can also remove important nutrients.

Unnecessary Alternative Treatments Can Be Harmful to Your Health and Your Pocketbook

Because some alternative products and methods have not been proven effective and may, in fact, be ineffective, you might certainly be wasting your time using them. But you might be losing much more than time.

Some alternative practitioners heavily promote treatment methods that are totally useless and thus totally wasteful of your hard-earned money. Alternative practitioners may call for all sorts of unusual lab tests that might cost hundreds or even thousands of dollars, yet that are inconsistent and have never been proven to give accurate results. Many alternative procedures and protocols that may cost in the tens of thousands of dollars have never been shown to be of any benefit at all. Even if you take a product or undergo a treatment that is relatively inexpensive, if it hasn't been proven effective and so doesn't work, you've just lost your money.

Ineffective treatments can also be dangerous, especially if you are receiving alternative care for diseases such as cancer and you don't seek needed conventional treatment. When 53-year-old Samantha, an accountant, was diagnosed with breast cancer, she declined conventional chemotherapy in favor of alternative methods and natural products she believed would cure her. Sadly, her cancer spread throughout her body within just two years. She received chemotherapy and radiation at that point, but it was too late, and she died.

Wes, a retired Army officer, was just as unfortunate. At age 67, he began having problems with urination. A search on the Internet led him to believe that he had benign prostatic hypertrophy (BPH), a swelling of the prostate gland. The same sources recommended the herb saw palmetto, so he started taking it without going to see his doctor. For several months, his symptoms improved, but then they worsened. Still Wes continued to treat himself by taking the saw palmetto, convinced that he just needed to find the right dose. One night about a year after he started taking the saw palmetto, he got up to urinate but couldn't. He had to go to the emergency room, where the doctor on duty catheterized him to drain the urine from his bladder and then referred Wes for an emergency consultation with a urologist. In less than 24 hours, the urologist diagnosed prostate cancer, which had already spread to Wes's bones. The treatments that could have helped a year earlier were now useless, and a few months later, Wes died. Could those treatments have cured the cancer and saved Wes's life? Of course, no one knows. But we do know that with early, appropriate treatment, prostate cancer is one of the most curable cancers.

Alternative Therapies Are Rarely Backed by Scientific Research

Until recently, much of the "research" done on alternative therapies in the United States has been done by practitioners touting their own methods and products. (Many studies have been done in other countries, but the results are published in foreign journals and not often recognized by the American medical establishment.) Unfortunately, many of the studies conducted by such practitioners have had poor methodology, poor design, and bias. Not surprisingly, many of these studies have also produced contradictory findings. Very few have been reviewed by experts or peers. Today, conventional doctors have begun to conduct research that can provide legitimacy and support for alternative methods, but there are still many problems.

Money Is Scarce

Several government agencies, including the NIH, branches of the armed forces, and the National Center for Complementary and Alternative Medicine, are providing funds for alternative medical research. However, the amount is minuscule compared to the overall resources of these agencies. The same is true for funds derived from private sources. There are so many alternative methods and uses, and there is so little money for research, that it will take a great deal of work just to figure out what needs to be done to pursue scientific study of these approaches.

Researchers May Lack Knowledge

The best research is done by practitioners who actively practice and understand the methods that they are studying. Although the truth of this statement seems obvious, the fact is that many studies of natural methods are done by conventional researchers who may not really understand what they are studying because they don't practice those natural methods themselves. You won't find a gynecologist conducting research on drugs to treat heart disease, but you might find a general research botanist (a plant specialist) conducting research on soy's effects on menopause symptoms! As a result, the studies may demonstrate negative results only because of the study design. This has been especially true in research on herbs or vitamins. Many studies have used amounts and dosages that are too small to have an effect in the first place, so it's no wonder the results are negative.

Alternative Medical Research Can Be More Difficult Than Conventional Medical Research

The standard for researching conventional medical methods is referred to as the RCT, or *randomized controlled trial*. This type of study is designed to compare a real medication or real method to a "dummy" pill or method (the *placebo*), without the patients knowing which they are receiving. But RCT assesses only one method or product at a time, while many alternative approaches require a combination of methods to have the necessary effect. For example, Chinese herbs are used together with acupuncture to provide the maximum benefits. If a single method does not help to a significant degree, it may be considered not useful, when in reality it might be effective in combination with other methods or products. *Traditional Chinese medicine* (TCM) uses the herb don quai for menopausal discomfort, but only in combination with other Chinese herbs. A recent study concluded that don quai had no effect on hot flashes and other menopause symptoms, but researchers studied only the herb by itself, although TCM practitioners never use it that way.

In addition, most conventional research uses standardized therapies—treatments that are the same for every patient. Yet many alternative methods are individualized for each patient, so standardizing these therapies for research may end up producing meaningless results. Some alternative methods, such as acupuncture, cannot be studied using a placebo (the "dummy method"); how do you fake inserting needles into someone? And studying herbs and other natural compounds is difficult because there are so many unknown factors that influence whether they work. For example, *phytochemicals*—substances that occur in vegetables and fruits and are thought to protect against cancer and other diseases—are widely advertised and sold as extracts (called *neutraceuticals*). However, research has so far failed to consistently document such protection because each researcher might use a different preparation. The same is true in studying alternative methods, because a particular method—acupuncture or homeopathy, for example—might have many different forms and schools of thought, some that work better than others in some people. So it's not surprising that contradictory findings are commonly the result of research on alternative methods and products.

Bias

As in conventional research, there is a great deal of bias in the research on alternative methods and products. Certainly, the companies that manufacture these products want to prove that their products are beneficial, just as the pharmaceutical companies want to prove that their drugs work, so bias is inevitable. But there are deeper sorts of bias where natural approaches are concerned. First, many conventional researchers do not believe in alternative methods and set out to disprove their benefits. Just as positive bias exists when a researcher sets out to prove something works, negative bias is present when a researcher wants to prove that something does not work.

Also, conventional doctors and researchers still have a strong bias against alternative medicine, as is evident from the fact that only a handful of alternative medical studies are ever published in the major medical journals, and most of those are the negative ones. There have actually been thousands of good studies published on alternative methods and products, but most of these are in foreign journals or sub-specialty journals that are infrequently read by most American doctors.

BALANCED HEALING GUIDELINES FOR ALTERNATIVE MEDICINE

As you can see, there are both positive and negative aspects of alternative medicine. In addition to the benefits, there are many serious pitfalls that you must consider. Natural alternatives can improve your health, but only if you understand how they work and if you use them appropriately. Here are my basic recommendations to help you use alternative treatments and methods to your greatest advantage:

1. **Before using an alternative product or treatment, evaluate it thoroughly, and learn how to use it effectively.**
   - There are unbiased sources of information on natural products and treatments,

and those sources are where you need to get your information. In addition, several labs in the United States perform regular analyses of plant-based supplements, allowing manufacturers that meet the standards to use their seal of approval. See Appendix C for more information.

- Find a doctor or alternative practitioner who's knowledgeable in alternative products and treatments and can guide you (more on this topic in Chapter 3).
- Don't just take a bunch of products hoping that one might work. Take only those products that are known to work and are specific for your condition.
- Don't believe a claim if it sounds too good to be true. Ninety-nine percent of the time, a product that sounds like a miracle cure does not work.
- Avoid products that do not list the amounts or concentrations of their ingredients, especially products that use combinations of different ingredients.
- Use products that state on the bottle that they are standardized. This means that the product is processed under industry standards and has to meet specific requirements.
- Use the alternative methods that are most common, have been researched, and are known to have benefited patients with your medical condition.
- Stop using alternative treatments if they're not helping you within a reasonable amount of time. Beware of any alternative treatments that are supposed to take an unreasonably long time to deliver benefits.
- Ask your conventional doctor to discuss your treatment with the alternative practitioner you're seeing, and then to monitor your progress.

2. **Spend less money on complementary medicine by using products appropriately.**
- Comparison shop; prices vary greatly. The most expensive products are not necessarily the best ones.
- In general, avoid products sold by MLMs (multi-level marketing companies) unless no comparable products are available from other sources.
- If you have insurance, check your policy to see whether it covers alternative methods. If not, consider changing to one that does.

3. **Use your knowledge and common sense to avoid the dangers.**
- Always remember that "natural" does not necessarily mean "safe."
- In general, avoid herbal weight-loss and energy-boosting products.
- Avoid high doses of any product. More is not necessarily better.
- Avoid taking numerous products at the same time.
- Because many alternative products may interfere with conventional treatment, always let your doctor know what you're taking.
- In general, do not take alternative products if you are pregnant or breastfeeding, unless they are recommended by a knowledgeable doctor.
- Look for substantiation beyond marketing claims.
- Do not self-treat. Always have your symptoms diagnosed by a doctor to rule out more serious causes.

Knowledge is one of the most important aspects of integrating conventional and alternative healthcare methods. It is essential for you to be an informed consumer, and to investigate both your doctor's recommendations and the claims of alternative products and methods. Only then can you make the decisions and choices that are right for your health and well-being. And one of the most effective ways to gain information is to seek care and guidance from qualified practitioners, both conventional and alternative. In the next chapter, I'll show you how to choose knowledgeable, competent providers to help you best meet your healthcare needs.

CHAPTER 3

Getting the Most from Your Practitioner
AN INSIDER'S VIEW

Both conventional and alternative medicine have great benefits and can offer you numerous ways to heal. But even with all the technological marvels of conventional medicine and the rediscovered uses of natural products and techniques, your health depends significantly on how these methods are actually applied to your specific condition, and on whether you have a practitioner who can guide you in using them as effectively as possible. For the best results, you and your practitioner need to work together as partners to do what's right for you. Yet, as in any relationship, many factors can define what's right. In this chapter, I'll offer guidelines on what to look for and how to choose practitioners who would be good partners for you.

First, let's get acquainted with the different types of practitioners by looking at the training that each receives.

ALL ABOUT TRAINING

Even the most ancient civilizations had healers, individuals who were noted for their medical skills and knowledge. Although these people no doubt had a natural inclination toward healing, they nonetheless developed their capabilities by learning from someone else who already possessed medical knowledge and skill. Until relatively modern times, most of this learning took place through informal and formal apprenticeships. Today, most people in the healing arts—both conventional and alternative—receive training that is a combination of classroom education (textbooks, classes, labs) and practical experience.

Training Medical Doctors: The Basics

Educating a doctor today is no easy task. It requires not only basic education, but also post-graduate training, training in one or more medical specialties, and continuing education. In the United States, a medical doctor's education starts with four years of college. Most doctors focus on science in their undergraduate studies, although most medical schools are now placing a little more emphasis on students being well-rounded.

After college comes medical school, four years of general medical training that lays the foundation of medical knowledge and skill. After medical school, a new doctor must complete an internship (an experience-based learning program similar to an apprenticeship) and then pass a series of tests to become licensed. Each state has different tests and licensing requirements.

Most doctors also complete a residency program, which generally consists of three to seven additional years of training. The more sophisticated the specialty, the longer the residency program.

The Spread of Specialists

As medical science has grown and expanded, so too has its knowledge base. Because modern medical technology requires additional understanding that goes well beyond standard knowledge of the human body, it's impossible for a doctor to know all there is to know about every area of medicine. So doctors specialize in areas of medicine that interest them, such as obstetrics, surgery, family practice, or dermatology.

Most Americans see a family practitioner or an internist for routine health care needs, as well as to determine whether a referral to a specialist is appropriate for specific problems, such as a broken leg or a hernia. There are sub-specialists as well, such as orthopedic surgeons, who only operate on damaged bones or joints, or internists (called nephrologists) who focus only on kidney disease. Generalists, specialists, and sub-specialists must take and pass extensive and often grueling exams, called *boards*, to become board-certified in their specialties.

Many specialties overlap; that is, more than one specialist can treat the same condition. For example, orthopedic surgeons, neurosurgeons, anesthesiologists, physiatrists (physical medicine/rehabilitation experts), and neurologists all treat patients who have back pain. But the care you receive may differ substantially depending on which specialist treats you.

Noel, a 58-year-old auto worker, longed for relief from the back pain that had bothered him for years. He went to several different specialists for treatment recommendations. His family doctor recommended medications and physical therapy, an anesthesiologist wanted to give him epidural steroid injections, and a neurosurgeon told him he needed surgery. Noel was unsure of what to do and came to me to help him decide. I recommended he start with physical therapy, the least invasive of all his treatment options, and consider the other options only if necessary. He improved with the physical therapy and didn't need the other treatments. Had he chosen one of the other treatments, however, the results might have been considerably different.

Training Alternative Providers

Training for most alternative practitioners can be quite different. *Alternative medicine* is simply a label that encompasses a diverse variety of methods, each one independent of the others. So, unlike conventional medicine, which is based on the same fundamental principles no matter what the specialty, alternative methods are based on widely differing premises. The training of alternative practitioners, then, is usually not standardized or regulated from one method to another. Whether or not you benefit from a particular method or treatment can depend on where, how, and how long your practitioner was trained. Sometimes it's not that the alternative method itself doesn't work; the problem is that it's not done properly.

Osteopathic medicine is the only alternative method that requires the level of training that conventional doctors receive. In most states, osteopathic physicians (DOs) are subject to the same licensing and practice standards as are medical doctors (MDs). *Chiropractors* (Doctors of Chiropractic, or DCs) and *naturopaths* (Naturopathic Doctors, or NDs) require four years of specialized training; chiropractors must also pass board exams before they can be licensed. To become a *Doctor of Oriental Medicine* (OMD) also requires a lengthy training period—at least four years. To become a licensed acupuncturist, you would need three to four years of training in the U.S., although doctors and chiropractors can practice acupuncture with only 100 hours to 300 hours of training. Licensing requirements for OMDs or acupuncturists vary greatly from state to state. *Homeopathy* typically requires one year of training and is a licensed practice in only a handful of states. *Naturopathy* is licensed in only nine states. *Massage therapy* programs in most states last 12 months, and graduates take an examination that includes both written and practical components. Passing the exam makes the practitioner a licensed massage therapist (LMT) or certified massage therapist (CMT), but only 31 states require licensing. Other alternative methods require training for periods ranging from a weekend to a few months. *Therapeutic touch*, for example, practiced by thousands of nurses, can be learned in a weekend (although there are longer courses), and there is no objective testing of the practitioner's abilities and no licensing requirements. (See Appendix A for further discussion and explanation of these and other alternative medicine practices.)

Except for chiropractic and osteopathic schools, most alternative methods are not taught consistently from school to school. This inconsistency often creates confusion for people seeking alternative care, because the practitioner's method or orientation isn't always clear. Consider the case of Robert, a 54-year-old carpenter who had tried three different acupuncturists to cure his low back pain. The first acupuncturist surrounded the area of pain with needles each time Robert came in, and the second acupuncturist taped seeds in Robert's ear acupuncture points for several weeks at a time. Both were valid approaches, but not what Robert expected or was seeking. Finally, the third acupuncturist used traditional body acupuncture (inserting needles in specific back and leg points), and Robert's back pain improved significantly.

Training the Doctors Who Practice Complementary Medicine

What about training for those doctors who practice both conventional and alternative medicine—that is, true complementary medicine? Because medical schools do not teach alternative approaches, those who wish to provide such methods must take additional courses or train themselves. Some experts in alternative therapies—especially acupuncture, herbal medicine, and mind-body techniques—teach their methods to doctors. Many of these courses are given by highly regarded conventional institutions such as the University of California-Los Angeles, Stanford University, Columbia University, and the University of Arizona, and these courses are recognized by the American Medical Association with valid credits in a doctor's continuing medical education.

Alternatively, many other alternative methods have no accreditation, and training is minimal at best, especially in fields that are not commonly recognized, or with treatments such as energy techniques and chelation that are not widely used. In addition, many conventional doctors who say they provide alternative medicine may simply sell herbs and supplements, or audio tapes/video tapes on such methods as guided imagery and Qigong. So it's really important to find out what training and certification (or licensure) a doctor has in a particular alternative method.

Staying on Top of the Latest Developments

For most health practitioners, the learning doesn't end with a diploma. New discoveries are being made every day. In fact, much of what medical students are taught every year eventually may be proven wrong or modified substantially. For example, doctors had been taught for more than a century that heart cells die from heart attacks and do not recover. In June 2001, a study revealed for the first time that heart cells can regenerate and repair the damage after a heart attack. Doctors used to be taught that brain cells die as we age, but another recent study demonstrated that even elderly people can make new brain cells.

Because almost every day brings news of new medical advances, it's essential that doctors keep up with the latest findings. Unfortunately, not all of them do. There are thousands of *continuing medical education* (CME) meetings that they can attend, but most of the meetings are held in beautiful vacation spots, and it's all too easy for the doctors to skip the meetings and do something else. New information is also available in hundreds of medical journals and books, and continuing medical education is now possible over the Internet; but many doctors don't have, or take, the time.

Unfortunately, a doctor's primary source of new information about medications today is the pharmaceutical company's representative. In fact, a survey by Harvard Medical School revealed that physicians learn 90 percent of their prescribing habits from these salespeople. The problem is that a drug company's motive is to sell its products, not to educate doctors, so the information that its salespeople provide is not always completely accurate. Studies show that physicians tend to prescribe drugs that pharmaceutical salespeople promote, even when these drugs may have little or no advantage over existing medications. Instead, by attending conferences and reading the latest findings in the medical literature, doctors need to do their own unbiased research on the most effective medications.

Continuing education in alternative medicine is both similar to and different from conventional medicine. In the states in which licensing is required, *continuing education credits* (CEUs) are mandatory for many alternative methods, including chiropractic, acupuncture, and massage. This system allows such practitioners to improve their techniques and to learn new techniques from other schools of thought. But, as with conventional medical meetings, local attractions may be the primary reason to attend such sessions, and practitioners might still just hold to their tried and true practice. Furthermore, because medical insurance covers relatively few alternative therapies, practitioners often devote time and energy to generating business for themselves because many people won't see practitioners who are not covered by insurance, so it can be difficult to build a practice. In fact, this becomes a major topic of interest at seminars and workshops.

But alternative practitioners, like medical doctors, must stay on top of new discoveries, for two reasons: First, new research studies are constantly evaluating the effectiveness of alternative methods; and, second, more and more practitioners are using these therapies together with conventional treatments. So doing something just because it's always been done that way is no longer good enough. Alternative practitioners also need to read the medical literature, attend conferences, and even learn about other alternative methods as well as conventional approaches.

ABILITY AND EXPERIENCE

Many well-trained doctors and practitioners are excellent caregivers, yet many others are not as good, even though their training is exactly the same. Why? The answer is that many factors influence practitioners' abilities, no matter what their training. Some people simply have more innate ability than others. Some people absorb and retain knowledge that they seem able to access faster than a computer draws from a hard drive. Unfortunately, there is no easy way for you to know which doctor has the most ability or which one has the characteristics that may influence your particular treatment, either positively or negatively. But you can evaluate experience. The more you do something, the better you become at it, whether you're bowling or performing brain surgery. Experience matters. Studies demonstrate that those physicians and hospitals that perform more operations and treat particular conditions the most have the best outcomes and the least side effects.

The capabilities of alternative practitioners vary even more than in conventional medicine, largely because there are fewer standards and requirements within alternative disciplines. Although a few alternative methods have requirements that practitioners must fulfill before they can begin training, many have none, and almost anyone can learn and practice the techniques. So it's important to consider not only experience but also *expertise*—the practitioner's level of knowledge. A practitioner who simply has used the same methods for years certainly acquires experience but might have limited expertise. A practitioner who studies new developments and tries new variations, however, gains both experience and expertise. The bottom line is that training alone, whether conventional or alternative, does not guarantee that the treatment will be successful. In general, the more experience and the more expertise the practitioner has, the greater the chance of success.

THE ART OF MEDICINE

As we discussed in Chapter 1, the ancient Greek physician Hippocrates observed many centuries ago, "What sort of person has a disease is more important than what sort of disease a person has." Certainly, many conditions can be handled with standard diagnosis and treatment, but when non-physical factors such as emotions, motivations, social interactions, and beliefs affect health (as they often do), they must be taken into account or the patient won't improve. The "art of practicing medicine" means uncovering *all* the factors that are causing the disease and using that knowledge to heal. To be effective in this art, the practitioner must reach beyond training and ability.

It's not entirely true, despite what most people think, that alternative practitioners are the ones who most often practice this art, while most doctors don't. In fact, many medical doctors still try to practice the art of medicine, while many alternative practitioners do not. Allan, a freelance writer, is grateful that he found a doctor who did. At 38, Allan had numerous medical problems. He was overweight, with hypertension, diabetes, and reflux. His doctor had treated each of these problems with medications, but Allan continued to have flare-ups and breakthrough symptoms. Allan was a hard-driving salesman, the top producer in his company. He traveled a great deal, so he ate fast food, didn't have regular meals, didn't exercise consistently, and never found much time for relaxation. In fact, he missed many of his kids' activities and had marital problems because he was never home, and when he was, he was too tired to do anything. His doctor had known Allan for a long time and had repeatedly encouraged him to change his lifestyle, but Allan insisted he couldn't. Until his heart attack, that is. His doctor told him that the next one would probably kill him, and that it was time for him to make changes if he didn't want his wife and kids to lose him. With the doctor's help, Allan changed to a job that involved less travel. He was able to exercise more regularly, eat healthy home-cooked meals, and enjoy his family. Within six months, he'd lost 40 pounds, he felt great, and he was able to reduce or stop taking his medications.

Your Practitioner's Attitude Can Be Bad (or Good) for Your Health

Your practitioner's attitudes toward you and your medical care are of the utmost importance to your health. If a practitioner is optimistic and caring, your health benefits can begin immediately. If a practitioner has a negative attitude, the chances that you will improve are reduced before you even start treatment. You want a practitioner who is open, caring, and has your best interests in mind.

This is not always what you get. Sometimes practitioners get pretty full of themselves and let arrogance and ego run amok. This attitude is not good for either of you. It can intimidate you into making decisions you don't want to make or failing to ask questions that concern you. And it can lead the practitioner to make mistakes that could have been avoided.

That's exactly what happened to 25-year-old Norma, a graduate student in art history. When Norma developed low back pain, her family physician referred her to a neurosurgeon, who recommended surgery. Norma asked him if she should first undergo other more conservative treatments, such as physical therapy or injections, but the surgeon replied that he knew what was best for her. Her family doctor advised her to go ahead with the surgery because this neurosurgeon was well recognized and experienced, and so she did. Unfortunately, the surgery was not helpful and, in fact, caused a nerve injury that left her unable to raise her foot (a condition known as *foot drop*). When she questioned the neurosurgeon about this problem, he simply replied, "Bad things happen. Life is not a bed of roses," and walked out of the room.

Arrogance can be found on the alternative side, as well. After 36-year-old Jody, an executive assistant in a large corporation, hurt her neck in a car accident, a friend recommended a chiropractor. Jody had never undergone manipulation, and she asked the chiropractor several times not to pop her neck because it was very stiff and she was afraid of hurting it more. He simply nodded, said, "I know what I'm doing," and proceeded to pop her neck. Jody developed excruciating pain, which later was diagnosed as a ruptured disc. It was months until conventional treatment with medications and physical therapy brought Jody's pain under control.

Not only might doctors or alternative practitioners be arrogant toward *you*, they can also be arrogant toward each other. If you have a condition that can be better treated by conventional methods, yet treatment is delayed because the alternative practitioner convinces you that conventional medicine won't help or is dangerous, your health can definitely suffer. Consider the story of Jean, a 46-year-old bank loan officer with asthma. She was tired of taking conventional medications and went to an herbalist/homeopathic physician, who told her the medications were harmful to her, and she needed to get off them and take herbs instead. Jean gradually stopped all her medications and began taking herbs and homeopathic remedies. After a week, she started having difficulty breathing and thought she should go back on the medications, but the herbalist told her to give the herbs more time. Unfortunately, Jean had a sudden asthma attack that required emergency treatment and hospitalization to save her life. After she recovered, she decided the medications weren't that bothersome after all.

Similarly, if a conventional doctor ignores or maligns an alternative method or practitioner, the patient may not receive treatment that is actually better and less costly. Such was the case with Rachel, a 65-year-old retired bus driver with back pain. Rachel came to see me for acupuncture and low-level laser treatment. A day later, she saw a neurologist, who told her that my treatments would not work and that he had her best interests in mind. He convinced her to undergo surgery, which she did, and it actually made her worse. She eventually came back to me to resume the acupuncture and laser treatments, which significantly reduced her pain.

Beatrice, a young investment banker, suffered a similar fate. When she was 32, she reached over to pick up a puppy and felt a snap around her shoulder. By the next day, she could not lift or move her arm very well. Over the next six years, the pain worsened, and Beatrice saw various doctors who did numerous tests, including an expensive, high-tech *magnetic resonance imaging* (MRI) test that showed a benign tumor in the neck. The doctors decided that the tumor was probably causing the pain, and that Beatrice would just have to live with it. Not satisfied, she went to an orthopedic surgeon who was convinced that she had a rotator cuff tear; he performed exploratory surgery of the shoulder, yet found nothing abnormal. Beatrice ended up with a pain management specialist who treated her with drugs and physical therapy. Mary, a patient of mine who frequently shopped at the store where Beatrice worked, told Beatrice about some of the alternative methods I was using, and Beatrice asked her doctor about them. He told her that alternative methods were a waste of her time and money, and that she should continue physical therapy, even though it hadn't helped. But after six more months of pain, Beatrice came to see me anyway. She had an obvious misalignment problem with her shoulder blade and ribs, which three treatments by osteopathic manipulation set right again.

You and Your Practitioner as Partners

I hope it's clear from what I've been saying that your relationship with your practitioner (conventional or alternative) must be a partnership in which you feel welcome to participate. This partnership requires an attitude of cooperation, understanding, and openness from both of you. Many doctors have poor bedside manner—they basically ignore you and don't answer your questions. They just want to direct your care totally by themselves, and they don't want you to take part in your treatment. This attitude leads to worry and doubt, which certainly do not help you heal.

Consider, for example, the case of Joe, a 64-year-old dentist and a patient of mine. Joe's cardiologist definitely did not approach his relationship with Joe as a partnership. This doctor had prescribed three different medications to control Joe's high blood pressure and, unfortunately, he had side effects—drowsiness and difficulty thinking—and so he asked the cardiologist whether he could change medications or do something else that would help reduce his blood pressure. The cardiologist told him that this was the treatment he needed and that it was too confusing to explain why. Joe wouldn't understand, the cardiologist said, and he should just take his medications. I urged Joe to start an exercise program, practice Qigong/Tai Chi, and lose some weight. Once he did this, his blood pressure dropped enough that I could simplify his medications. Your doctor should do what I did with Joe: treat you neither as a child nor as a medical school graduate, but as an intelligent person interested in his or her own health.

In general, alternative practitioners are more open and willing to interact with you and allow you to take an active role in your treatment. But this isn't always the case. Marilyn, a 52-year-old real estate agent, went to a chiropractor for her chronic headaches and neck pain. After three months of treatment, she had not improved, but the chiropractor insisted on continuing treatment. He wouldn't explain why it was taking so long, why she wasn't getting any better, or why more treatment was necessary. He simply told her that to resolve these problems sometimes took years of treatment. Marilyn eventually went to an osteopath, who instructed her to do specific stretching and strengthening exercises along with his manipulations. In a month, she was pain free.

The best practitioner, alternative or conventional, is one who wants you to do something to help yourself, thus enabling you to be a partner in the healing process.

Communication: The Key to Success

Communication between you and your health care provider is critical. Without it, your practitioner can't understand your symptoms and concerns, and you can't understand his or her recommendations. A study published in *The New England Journal of Medicine* revealed that of more than 3,000 patient-physician encounters reviewed, only 9 percent met the established criteria for good communication. Patients were informed about basic lab tests in only 17.2 percent of cases, and none were completely informed about decisions such as whether to use new medications. If you don't understand what your practitioner is doing or why, your health can suffer.

Communication is critical, whether you see an alternative or a conventional practitioner. One of each had correctly diagnosed depression in 37-year-old Carmen, a social worker, and both had recommended St. John's wort. But neither one told Carmen that this herb can interfere with the breakdown of digitalis, which she had been taking for mild heart failure. As a result, she became toxic from the medication—in fact, she almost died!

Communication means more than the practitioner or doctor telling you about treatments. It is also about *you* informing the practitioner about your symptoms, needs, concerns, and other relevant information. Communication is a two-way street, and your health depends on it. Will, the CEO of a family-owned business, is a 65-year-old patient of mine who came in because of pain in his pelvis. He had already been to a surgeon who had previously operated on his back and who thought the pain was referred from his back. X-rays of Will's back showed changes that usually occur with arthritis. Physical therapy and epidural steroid injections had been prescribed but had not helped at all. In fact, the pain worsened. I reviewed the records of the other doctors and took a complete history, but there was nothing there that pointed to the cause. The pain did not follow a typical pattern for disc problems, so I ordered an MRI and bone scan of the pelvis, which showed metastatic cancer of the pelvic bone. It was only then that Will told me he had been treated for prostate cancer a few years earlier. Instead of back treatment, he needed radiation, which was delayed months because he hadn't told any of his doctors his full medical history.

Taking the Time You Need

It doesn't necessarily take hours to diagnose most conditions; often it takes only a matter of minutes. What is crucial is that the practitioner spend the time necessary to correctly assess you and your condition, or else you can be led in the wrong direction.

Two of my middle-aged patients, Pam, a 42-year-old nurse, and Marilyn, a 48-year-old financial planner, came in with the same symptom—constant, burning pain in the feet. Pam had diabetes, so it didn't take very long to diagnose her pain as diabetic neuropathy, which was caused by a deterioration of the nerves in her feet, and begin a treatment plan. But there was no obvious explanation for Marilyn's pain, and her diagnosis took much more time. She had undergone three surgeries on her foot by a podiatrist and orthopedic surgeon, all without benefit. While reviewing a more extensive medical history with her, I noticed that she'd had a back injury some years before. Even though she wasn't having any significant back pain, I ordered further testing. The results showed an abnormality in one of her spinal nerves, and when that was treated, her foot pain disappeared.

Taking time for an accurate diagnosis is important for alternative providers, as well. Jane, a 43-year-old public relations counselor and a patient of mine, complained of chronic fatigue. She went to an alternative practitioner, who spent just 10 minutes with her and told her that she had obvious thyroid dysfunction. After a month of treatment with natural thyroid, she didn't feel any better. After a 5-minute recheck, he told her that the problem was not thyroid, but that her blood needed to be built up (although her blood tests were normal), and he simply gave her some supplements. When those didn't work, he took another 5 minutes to tell her the problem must be yeast overgrowth and that he wanted her to start on several supplements. Instead, she finally went to a traditional Chinese medicine (TCM) practitioner, who took an hour to explore her history and examine her, finally discovering the underlying problem, a syndrome that in Chinese medicine is called *qi* deficiency. She responded to acupuncture and a Chinese herbal formula that was made specifically for that problem, and her symptoms disappeared within two months.

MEDICINE AS BIG BUSINESS

Nothing interferes with a relationship like money. And when it comes to your health care, money is a big issue. Because we have so many new drugs and high-tech tests and therapies, medicine has become very expensive. As a result, medical cost control has become a major issue that has affected every aspect of medicine. Costs have to be contained somewhere, but it's not only the technology, medications, hospitalization, and treatments that are expensive. How doctors practice medicine can also determine how much it will cost you. Doctors and practitioners direct what is done, and often they can either save you money or cost you a lot more.

Unnecessary Tests and Procedures

In Chapter 1, I mentioned that numerous surgeries and other invasive procedures are done that should not be done or are not helpful. Why, then, are they done? One reason is money: A doctor makes more money performing high-tech procedures than treating a patient conservatively. Epidural steroid injection is an excellent example. The original purpose for injecting steroids into the space around the spinal cord was to decrease inflammation in the first month after an injury, so that the patient could start exercises that could heal the injury. But today steroid injections are done routinely for almost *anyone* who has neck or back pain, despite the fact that the injections work in only a small minority of these patients; and even if they work, the benefits usually are only temporary at best. But doctors charge up to $2,400 for the procedure—not bad for only 15 to 20 minutes' work!

Even when a procedure is necessary, you might get more expensive treatments when less expensive methods are available. Hillary, a stay-at-home mother of two, found this out when she started having abdominal cramps and menstrual bleeding. Her gynecologist diagnosed fibroids and recommended a hysterectomy. But Hillary was just 31 years old and wanted more children, so she went to two other gynecologists for their opinions, which were the same. Undaunted, she searched the Internet and discovered that an outpatient procedure called fibroid embolization (done by specialized radiologists), which could shrink the tumors in a large percentage of women, had been available for three years. However, few gynecologists let women know about this procedure because performing hysterectomies is a big part of their income. But Hillary asked her gynecologist to refer her for the procedure, and she was glad that she did. Her pain and bleeding ended, and she returned to her normal activities within a week.

Some doctors order tests or treatments simply because they are available. Consider Tony, a 36-year-old mechanic, who had a shoulder injury, diagnosed as a tear of the rotator cuff muscle. The routine tests showed that Tony also had carpal tunnel syndrome of the wrist, even though he had no pain or other symptoms. Nevertheless, the orthopedist suggested surgery on the wrist at the same time as the shoulder. His rationale was that "You'll be under anesthesia anyway, and it's easy to do." Unfortunately, as a result of the surgery, Tony started having pain, numbness, and tingling for the first time. In fact, the symptoms worsened and became so bad that the surgeon had to operate again—and that surgery made the symptoms even worse. But the surgeon made a lot of money from both surgeries, which, unfortunately, was his true motivation for recommending them.

Taking the Fast and Easy Way

Sometimes doctors find it easier to simply order a drug to treat symptoms than to address the underlying cause of an illness. That's what happened with 69-year-old Geneva, a college professor. Geneva had gas and bloating, which had started a few months before she came to see me. Her primary doctor told her she had acid reflux disease and gave her Prilosec, but it didn't help. He then gave her Prevacid and Nexium, both of which helped only a little. These medications had cost her more than $300, which Medicare did not cover. When I talked with Geneva about her health history, I noticed that she also had recurrent urinary tract infections, which doctors had treated with various high-powered antibiotics; she'd finished these medications just before the stomach problem began. I thought that the antibiotics had killed her normal stomach and intestinal bacteria that help digest food, and that she probably had an overgrowth of yeast. I gave her probiotics (bacteria to replace the ones that had been killed off) and digestive enzymes, which put her digestive system back on track in three weeks, and at much less cost. If her doctor had looked for the underlying cause of Geneva's problem, instead of going for the quick fix and treating her symptoms, her problem would have been solved much faster, without the high drug costs. Unfortunately, this approach is quite common, so pay attention and ask questions. If your doctor seems rushed or not interested in digging a little bit to solve your health problem, it's best to go to another doctor.

More Patients Equal More Money

Many doctors also try to maximize their income by seeing more patients in less time. I have already discussed the importance of time and communication in the healing arts, but the simple economic truth is that the more time doctors spend with you, the less money they make. Doctors also have been deluged by more and more paperwork, which not only limits their time even more, but also requires paying for additional staff. Many doctors try to make up for these increased costs by seeing even more patients. It's no wonder that you may have to wait hours just to see a doctor for a few minutes—and it's still expensive! Some doctors have simply opted to leave the medical profession altogether rather than work long hours for low pay and compromise their patients' health. These are usually good doctors, the ones you'd want to see, so losing them is unfortunate.

Doctors Who Invest in Themselves

Another reason for higher costs is that many doctors send patients to medical facilities—outpatient surgical hospitals, MRI centers, and physical therapy centers—in which they have a financial interest. Numerous studies have reported that physicians who have a financial stake in such facilities refer twice as many patients to them as doctors who don't. Unfortunately, these physicians don't have to tell you about their investments, so they rarely do.

Alternative Rip-Offs

Although alternative approaches are comparably less expensive than conventional ones, some alternative practices can end up costing you more. Greed is not limited to conventional doctors. Numerous alternative practitioners bombard you with all sorts of unnecessary treatment protocols, costing you thousands of dollars. Some will sell you ineffective or inessential herbs, supplements, and other products that serve only to make them more money. Others will convince you to undergo unusual testing that has never been proven accurate and is often much more expensive than conventional tests. Still other practitioners simply keep you coming back for endless treatments, just to "maintain" your health. And like some doctors, some alternative providers try to see as many patients as possible, maximizing their income while compromising your health. Remember to take an active role in your own health care, and follow the guidelines in Chapter 2 to avoid getting ripped off.

Problems with Insurance Companies

Doctors and practitioners can certainly be responsible for higher costs, but they are not the only ones. The greatest responsibility is on those who pay the bills, the insurance companies and the government. They decide how much to pay for the doctor and the treatments he orders, and their decisions directly determine how much it will all cost you.

There are several reasons why insurance companies increase health care costs. First, they are businesses, and profit, not ensuring your health, is their bottom line. In recent years, insurance rates have skyrocketed, not only because all the new technology is so expensive, but also because the companies' investments suffered huge losses in a weak economy. Second, to increase profitability, insurance companies often restrict services, limit reimbursement, or delay payments. Many insurance companies will pay for certain procedures but not others, even if the non-approved treatment is better, or they will pay for some medications, but not others. Although their ostensible purpose is to keep costs down, it is *their* costs they are keeping down, not yours.

Ironically, when they do pay, insurance companies reward technology and expensive procedures rather than less costly conservative care. Consider Leroy, a 38-year-old postal supervisor with back pain. He had been injured in a car accident, and his doctor ordered an MRI, which showed a few bulging discs. He had undergone physical therapy, but his insurance company would pay for only six sessions, which wasn't enough to help him. He told me that certain positions would alleviate the pain and others would make it worse, and so I thought his pain was due to sacro-iliac joint dysfunction and misalignment of the lower spine. Osteopathic techniques could have helped Leroy, but the insurance company wouldn't pay for them. Instead, he was sent to a surgeon, who recommended surgery, which the insurance company did pay for. As I could have predicted, it didn't help. Six months later, Leroy himself paid for the osteopathic treatment, which ended his pain in six treatments. You would think that insurance companies would consider more cost-effective, conservative treatments, but that just isn't what happens in many cases; they often restrict the less costly treatments and pay for the more expensive procedures. That's why surgeons and other specialists who provide high-tech diagnostics or treatments have a much higher income than primary-care physicians.

Similarly, most insurance companies don't pay for alternative methods, or they limit the number of alternative treatments you can receive, even if these treatments are more effective at less cost. Phyllis, a 42-year-old accountant, could teach her insurance company a thing or two about economics. For 20 years, Phyllis had taken numerous medications for her migraine headaches, at a cost of more than $300 per month that her insurance company covered. When she came to me, I recommended acupuncture, which has convincingly demonstrated its effectiveness in relieving migraines. The insurance company refused to pay for the acupuncture treatments, but Phyllis went ahead anyway, picking up the cost herself. After three acupuncture treatments, Phyllis said good-bye to her migraines. The cost to her: $255. What a bargain that could have been for her insurance company! Yet the insurance company opted to pay tens of thousands of dollars for years of drugs.

One of the largest insurers is the government, primarily Medicare. Although Medicare is not designed to make a profit, it must restrict services and reimbursements so as not to lose money. Yet, as with private insurance companies, Medicare primarily rewards technology and procedures, rather than less expensive options, including alternative methods. Of all the insurance payers, Medicare reimburses the least; in fact, many doctors lose money on Medicare patients. As a result, finding doctors who will accept patients who are insured by Medicare is becoming more and more difficult.

Because of the steady rise of medical costs, businesses that provide insurance to their employees have demanded lower-cost medical care. One result of this has been the creation of the *health maintenance organization* (HMO), designed to reduce costs by eliminating testing and treatments considered to be excessive. There is no question that this approach has decreased costs, but what has it done for medical care? Some HMOs provide excellent care, but others simply restrict services and consider many treatments to be excessive when they are really necessary. Anyone who has been in an HMO knows how difficult it is to get specialized care or even some necessary services that aren't provided by the HMO. The bottom line is that HMOs are businesses, with executives and investors whose main goal is to make money for themselves, rather than to improve your health. Very often, this approach means poor medical care for you.

Medical Marketing: The Promise of Health

Medical care now shares another characteristic of big business: self-promotion. You would like to think that the best way for a medical practitioner to attract more business is to build a reputation of integrity and providing excellent care. But that's not always enough in today's world of medical competition. To entice patients to their doors, many health care providers advertise and market promises of better health. Most hospitals, for example, spend millions of dollars annually to attract patients, rather than using the money to improve health care.

Unfortunately, many of the promises made in the spirit of marketing are exaggerated and difficult to fulfill. According to the medical establishment and the news media, conventional medicine provides and delivers medical miracles. These certainly do occur, such as when new procedures become available to treat chronic conditions, but these procedures usually help only a small percentage of patients. For most people with chronic diseases, there are no such miracles. This was the case with Elizabeth, a retail store owner, who at age 62 was diagnosed with colon cancer that had already spread to her liver. She had heard about a surgeon who could prolong survival by removing metastatic lesions from the liver, but when she underwent surgery, she was found to have so many lesions that the surgery could not help her. Elizabeth was devastated, and that could have been avoided if she had been presented with a more realistic prognosis.

It's not just doctors and the news media that are focused on marketing. Pharmaceutical companies are boldly making promises, directly advertising their drugs to you on national television, to the tune of several billion dollars a year. In these commercials, everything is beautiful and everyone is cured of whatever the health condition might be. These drugs may be beneficial for some people, but they are expensive, and the beautiful ads can create false hopes and unrealistic expectations.

Such promises are even more common and potentially harmful when it comes to alternative therapies. Because so many chronic diseases are not curable and cause much suffering, many people want to believe that alternative methods can help them. In some cases, they can, but in many others, they are just empty promises. Unfortunately, you can waste a lot of time and money on such promises. This was the tragic story of Bonnie, a 56-year-old graphic designer who had been diagnosed with breast cancer several years earlier. She had undergone appropriate conventional treatment, which put the tumor in remission. Unfortunately, the cancer recurred, but instead of receiving more conventional treatment, she went to a practitioner who advertised an "anti-cancer cream" purporting to contain a special clay that would suck out cancerous toxins. Of course, this is not possible; all that the cream sucked out, in the end, was Bonnie's money. Bonnie continued to worsen and eventually died. The cream was later analyzed by the government to be no more than a moisturizer, yet Bonnie spent almost $10,000 on this broken dream.

It doesn't matter whether it is alternative or conventional medicine, or whether the promises come from doctors, alternative providers, the media, or the drug companies. Promises can easily be made when the goal is money, and they can even more easily be broken. Make sure your expectations are realistic when you seek treatment, and that you don't automatically believe promises that seem too good to be true.

BALANCED HEALING GUIDELINES FOR CHOOSING THE RIGHT PRACTITIONER

Each person has different needs and desires. Whether you want a practitioner who just tells you what needs to be done and does it, or one with whom you can talk and who can help guide your decision-making process, the choice is yours. You must consider what *you* need, what *you* want, and accept nothing less.

Make a checklist of what you want in a practitioner, and, as you do, decide what's most important for you and your health. Here are some questions to consider:

- How, where, and when was the practitioner trained and educated?
- What specialty does the doctor practice, and which types of treatment does he or she typically recommend? Any time you see a specialist, be sure he or she has board certification. Those who do are always glad to show you evidence if you want it, and most include the information on their business cards.
- What experience has your practitioner had in his or her area of practice? How much experience has he or she had with your particular problem, and what treatments have produced the most successful results? Why have these treatments worked, and what other variables seem to influence the outcome?
- What reputation does the practitioner have with other patients, nurses, and other practitioners, both conventional and alternative?
- How do you feel after meeting the practitioner? Satisfied? Energized? Distrustful? Frustrated? It is your emotional reaction to the practitioner that will tell you whether you can achieve a healthy relationship with him or her.
- Does the practitioner give you the time that you feel is necessary to evaluate and discuss your condition, and does he or she give you information and recommendations that are understandable and complete? Is he or she willing to answer your questions?
- Does the practitioner appear to provide care that is as effective for your checkbook as for your health? Be sure the practitioner is willing to develop a treatment plan so that you know what to expect in terms of cost.

Two more pieces of advice: First, compare, compare, compare! Evaluate all your treatment options, both alternative and conventional, and get more than one opinion if you have doubts. Finally, refer to Appendix A when seeking an alternative practitioner. With each alternative method, there are specific ways to tell whether the practitioner is experienced, has the necessary abilities, and will give you ethical and effective treatment.

Finding the right practitioner isn't easy, but it's critical to both your health and your pocketbook. Yes, it can be challenging to ferret out all the information you need, especially when you're not feeling well in the first place. In this chapter, I've tried to show you some of the factors that get in the way of good care, whether conventional or alternative. If you're aware of them, it'll be a lot easier to find the practitioner who's right for you—and who can help you get better as quickly and economically as possible. Finding the right health care provider is a critical step to ensuring your optimum health and well-being. In the next chapter, we'll focus on other crucial steps necessary for you to take control of your own health and make the best health care decisions for your particular situation.

CHAPTER 4

8 Steps to Taking Control of Your Health

The best way to begin to take control of your own health care is to understand the bene-fits and shortcomings of the different approaches to healing. That's what I've tried to give you in Chapters 1, 2, and 3. Next, you need to know how to put that knowledge into prac-tice, with a balanced approach to health and healing. This chapter will help you do that by showing you how to choose the therapy that's best for your individual needs, whether it's primarily conventional, primarily alternative, or a complementary blend of the two.

In this chapter, I'll give you eight steps that can guide you to balanced healing, and I'll discuss each of these steps in detail:

1. Take an active role in discovering the cause of your condition and the best meth-ods to deal with your particular health problems and circumstances.
2. Rely on yourself to establish a healthy lifestyle to improve your health and prevent future health problems.
3. Examine your reasons for choosing particular treatments for your medical condi-tion. Make sure that you truly want to heal, rather than simply mask symptoms.
4. Ask every question you need to ask to fully understand both your condition and the treatment that's required to heal you.
5. Research your condition on your own, so that you can get the impartial informa-tion and knowledge that will help restore your health.
6. Consider all your health care options carefully. Make sure you understand every-thing that's available to you before you make a decision.
7. Trust that whatever method you have chosen will help you achieve wellness. If you don't believe that the treatment will work, it probably won't.
8. Complete the treatment regimens that you have chosen, and follow through with any lifestyle changes you need to make to achieve and maintain good health.

STEP 1: TAKE AN ACTIVE ROLE

You know from your experience with conventional medicine that the doctor typically does the talking and the patient unquestioningly follows the doctor's advice. But you must break with that tradition and become a full and active participant in your own health care. It's *your* body, after all, and you are ultimately responsible for your health and well-being. And no one knows your body better than you.

There are three big reasons why you should take an active role in your own health care. First, even the best practitioners may not know—or even be able to discover—all the possibilities for your healing. Often, you are the one who makes a discovery or finds a method that may work better. Marla is a case in point. This 55-year-old woman was diagnosed with breast cancer. She underwent a standard mastectomy and was to begin chemotherapy. Her oncologist informed her that she could expect side effects including hair loss, nausea, and fatigue, and that these were unavoidable. Marla came to see me, asking if there were any alternative approaches that could help her reduce or prevent these side effects. I recommended two Chinese herbal formulas and a specific Qigong exercise. Marla's doctor was quite surprised when she did not experience nausea or fatigue and lost only a small amount of hair. Marla took control of her situation and came to see me for help. She was able to minimize the side effects of chemotherapy by seeking answers on her own.

Another reason to take an active role in your health care is to avoid harm. Consider the case of 61-year-old Ethel, owner of a small chain of restaurants. Ethel went to her doctor, a colleague of mine, because she'd noticed that, over the past few months, every little bump seemed to turn into a bruise. Her doctor ran several blood tests: all normal. Because Ethel had no other signs of any diseases that would cause bruising, her doctor told her it was probably just part of aging and not to worry about it. A week later, Ethel was reading an article that mentioned that a few herbs, some of which she'd started taking a few months before, could increase bleeding tendencies and possibly cause a brain hemorrhage. Ethel stopped taking the herbs, and her bruises vanished.

The third reason for taking an active role is that much of the healing process depends on what *you* do. A practitioner cannot heal you with no effort on your part. I commonly see patients who simply expect me to give them something to cure their illnesses. They don't want to participate in their care by following up on treatment and learning how to keep from getting sick in the first place. They just want me to "fix" them.

The truth is—and I can't emphasize this enough—that your health begins and ends with you. So you must be actively involved in decisions about your health care, decisions that could make the difference between a long and healthy life and a life filled with illness, pain, and deterioration. The next seven principles will show you how to take this active role.

STEP 2: RELY ON YOURSELF

You don't necessarily have to consult either a physician or an alternative provider if you want to become or stay healthy. The simplest ways to achieve and maintain good health are available to anyone, anywhere: exercise, eat right, relax, and eliminate those bad habits.

Exercise for Optimal Health

Study after study has demonstrated that even moderate or light exercise helps to get rid of numerous medical conditions, and it helps to prevent even more. In fact, research has demonstrated that every organ system of the body, whether diseased or not, benefits from exercise. You don't have to join a gym or go to an aerobics class every day to get the benefits of exercise. Even housework, grocery shopping, and other daily chores can be beneficial.

And you don't have to exercise for a specified length of time; recent studies have shown that exercising three times for 10 minutes each can do you as much good as exercising 30 minutes at one time. Studies also show that you can get as much exercise at home as at a gym. To get the most benefit, use a combination of aerobic (for example, walking, swimming, tennis), resistance (weight-lifting), and stretching exercises. But don't stop at the minimum. Studies definitely show that the more you exercise, the better your health. Keep in mind, though, that any amount of exercise is better than none. (See "Simple Healing Steps for All Health Conditions" on page 79 for more specific recommendations.)

Proper Nutrition

Despite all the popular diets, nutrition books, and weight-loss programs, the number of overweight Americans is higher than ever—and the number continues to grow. Many studies show that if you are overweight, your risk for developing more medical problems and dying at an earlier age increases substantially. Why? You are what you eat, and the typical American eats too much of the wrong foods.

The average American diet, which contains too many processed and preserved foods that are high in fats, carbohydrates, and sugar, causes or contributes to numerous medical conditions, including what has become a national epidemic of obesity. Such was the case for 44-year-old Quinn, a newspaper reporter who was 50 pounds overweight. Her obesity led to arthritis of her knees, back pain, high cholesterol, and diabetes. She might have avoided all of these problems if she'd followed a nutritious diet and exercised regularly. Quinn's health problems improved significantly when she decided to eat more sensibly; and, so far, she has lost 35 of those extra pounds!

Even if your weight is normal, a poor diet can predispose you to many diseases. That was the case with 32-year-old Mark. His weight was fine, but his job as a truck driver meant that he ate most of his meals on the road. His steady diet of fast food provided very few vegetables or dairy products, and his meals were high in fat. So it was no surprise that he developed high blood pressure, heart disease, and gout (a form of arthritis). Mark was lucky. After he changed his eating habits to provide more balanced nutrition, all of these conditions were improved or reversed. You can achieve similar results by following these suggestions:

- Eat a balanced diet that includes foods from all five food groups. Don't eat just one or two types of food all the time.
- Eat at least three meals a day.
- Cut down on snacks, or replace high-calorie snacks with healthy substitutes such as fruit or low-fat yogurt.
- If you have a tendency to eat because of emotional factors such as loneliness, anger, or depression, replace the food with an activity you enjoy.

- If you are overweight, see the section on obesity on page 315 for more extensive recommendations.

Relaxation

Stress causes or worsens more than 85 percent of all medical conditions. So anything that can reduce the adverse effects of stress will improve your health. Of course, you can't always reduce the sources of stress in your life, so you must take action to counteract its effects on your body. An excellent antidote is relaxation. There are many forms of relaxation, and most of them are actually fun. Sports, walking, fishing, watching a movie, shopping, playing with your children, reading a good book, or just talking with friends can all be relaxing and can significantly reduce your stress.

My patient Norton is a good example of someone whose life stress had a great impact on his health and well-being. At age 43, Norton, a computer systems salesman, worked hard at his job, sometimes 16 hours a day and on weekends, to provide a good lifestyle for his wife and three children. But the costs were high indeed. Norton had all sorts of medical problems, including stomach pain, diarrhea, back pain, high blood pressure, and skin rashes. He told me that he worried that he would die before he could enjoy the fruits of his labors. His wife told me that there were problems in their marriage, and that Norton lost his temper easily with her and the kids. After several counseling sessions, Norton decided to cut back his hours at work and spend more time with his family, going on more outings, participating in his children's sports, and even watching TV with them at night. As Norton's stress eased, so did his medical problems. Now that he has a good balance between work and recreation, he is feeling good and everyone is happier.

If you don't have much opportunity for relaxation, try meditation. There are numerous audio tapes and teachers available (see Appendix A for examples and more information, and Appendix C for reference sources). Just 5 minutes to 15 minutes of meditation a day can really help you. The first time I witnessed the benefits of meditation, I was a small child. My father was going through a midlife crisis, and he worried constantly about everything, from the family to his job to national security. He developed an ulcer and heart pain. At that time, transcendental meditation was popular, and he learned and practiced it daily. After three months, he no longer worried, and his symptoms went away. After that, he practiced meditation whenever he became anxious or stressed. Dad is now 80 years old, stress-free, and in excellent health.

Whatever method you choose, just be sure that it is truly relaxing. If you enjoy sports but are very tense or get upset about the outcome, you'll just create additional stress. Some people travel to relax, but others find travel a major hassle. Do you feel the need for a vacation after you've been on one? You're not really relaxing! Try these suggestions:

- Make a list of what you enjoy, or would enjoy, doing, and then do something from your list.
- Examine your leisure activities and make sure they aren't producing more stress rather than less.

- Take at least 15 minutes every day and do absolutely nothing.
- Focus on the positive aspects of your life, and make a point to enjoy them.

Exchange Bad Habits for Good Ones

Being human means that we all have some bad habits, and we all do things that are potentially harmful. Some bad habits, such as not washing our hands enough, might seem insignificant, but they can be truly harmful. Hand washing is, in fact, the cheapest, easiest, most underrated, and most effective way to slow the spread of infection. A recent report revealed that, although 9 out of 10 people say they wash their hands after using a public restroom, only 2 out of 3 actually do. Even worse, those who don't wash can spread germs to faucets and door handles, which then spread infection to those who *have* washed their hands.

Other bad habits are even more dangerous. Drinking too much alcohol has many serious consequences, and I'm not just talking about the obvious problems associated with getting drunk (drunk drivers are responsible for thousands of deaths and injuries each year) or the alcohol poisoning that can result from binge drinking. Alcohol can adversely affect every organ of your body, including the liver, kidneys, pancreas, heart, brain, nerves, and muscles. But perhaps the most destructive habit is smoking, which significantly increases your risk for a wide variety of diseases. Smoking also can determine whether or not many medical treatments will work. For the body to heal properly, it must have good blood and oxygen flow to diseased areas. Smoking inhibits this process. Smoking is especially serious if you have surgery, because your body needs all of its resources to recover and heal. Surgeons recognize that smokers heal slower, have more complications, and have less successful surgeries. In fact, many surgeons will not operate on you unless you stop smoking.

STEP 3: KNOW YOUR MOTIVES

If someone asks you why you are seeking the services of a practitioner, you probably reply that you have a medical problem that you want treated or cured. On the surface, that seems obvious, but many patients have underlying, more subtle reasons for seeking medical care. And those reasons can significantly affect their present, as well as their future, health.

People go to see their doctors for many reasons. Some are looking for a real cure, but many others are looking for a quick fix. I see many patients with chronic pain, and they tell me that they want to find a permanent solution to their problem. But what they really want is a prescription for drugs to take away the pain, which is a short-term solution, at best.

If you don't address the underlying cause of the pain, it will come back before long. If you have tension headaches, are you going to the doctor to find out how to deal with the stress that is probably causing the headaches, or are you going just so that you can get medication? If you're really trying to get at the underlying cause, your headaches will probably be significantly reduced, and you will have less chance of developing other illnesses. But if you're just looking for a quick fix, you'll need to continue taking medication to be pain free—and that's not a real solution to the problem. To make matters worse, you'll probably develop other problems as your stress starts affecting other organs.

Some people want to prove to their spouses that they really can or cannot do a particular activity. This was the case with Trudy, a 67-year-old government agency worker who recently retired. She came to see me for treatment for her arthritis, and despite everything we tried—various medications, physical therapy, natural products, laser therapy, and acupuncture—her symptoms didn't get better. Then one day I received an irate call from her husband, who was upset that I couldn't cure her. During his ranting, he revealed that he was the one who had sent her in, wanting her arthritis to be cured so that Trudy could cook and clean house for him again. Later, Trudy admitted that she didn't want to cook and clean anymore, and her arthritis allowed her to have her wish. In a flash, I realized why none of the treatments had helped her.

Ignoring deeper issues is one of the main reasons people undergo so many unneeded surgeries every year. One of those surgeries was performed on Tammy, a 32-year-old personal trainer. Her husband wanted to start a family, but Tammy began having terrible cramping pain and excessive bleeding during her periods. She did not respond to medications and hormones, and so she opted to have a hysterectomy, despite the objections of her husband, who wanted her to try other methods.

The surgery stopped Tammy's symptoms, but Tammy and her husband started having marital problems. They went for some counseling, and it turned out that Tammy had been afraid to get pregnant because a relative of hers had been born with genetic defects. She was afraid that the same thing would happen to her children. Her pain was a defense mechanism, which could have been cured without surgery, and without leaving her unable to have children.

Why do people seek alternative treatments? Is it because they are less costly, have fewer potential side effects, are less invasive, are more holistic, or may work better than conventional methods? These are reasonable motives. But I've seen other motives that might be highly counterproductive. Some people might be desperate for a cure or looking for that magic pill. They might be frustrated with or distrustful of conventional methods. At best, such motives can waste money and time. At worst, they can lead to disaster if people delay proper medical treatment or get alternative therapies that are potentially harmful.

As you can see, your motives for seeking medical care can affect your health either positively or negatively. You won't know which result to expect until you understand why you are seeking a particular approach. I commonly ask my patients, "What do you want from me?" and they often look at me dumbfounded. Not many doctors ask such a question, and the answer seems simple. But when they start thinking about it, they are often surprised by their answers.

To give yourself the best chance for success, be sure you know why you're going to the doctor or practitioner, what your goals are, and what your motives are for choosing a particular treatment.

STEP 4: ASK QUESTIONS

Medical care can be complicated. Even doctors don't know or understand everything, and we commonly ask other doctors for help, or we review medicals books or the latest research. You might not fully understand your own health problems and their implications. You might have difficulty understanding why and how to use all the various products and treatments, conventional or alternative. So ask questions, and lots of them. Keep asking until the answers satisfy you. Here are some of the most common questions you should routinely ask:

- What is the diagnosis and what is causing the problem?
- Why is this procedure or drug or approach necessary, and how does it work?
- Is there some other method that can be used?
- Are there side effects, and, if so, what are they?
- How long and how much has this treatment been used, and for which conditions?
- Has it been effective with other patients? Does it work for some but not others?
- How long does it take to work?
- Does scientific research support this method, or is it based on unsubstantiated testimonials?

One area you need to ask questions about is prescription medications. Unfortunately, conventional doctors all too often make mistakes in prescribing medications. Along with their side effects, drugs can interact adversely with other drugs or with food. They can also build up and become toxic if you are elderly or have poor kidney or liver function. The good news is that many drug-induced disorders are predictable, and avoidable. If you ask pertinent questions about any drugs prescribed to you, you really can avoid potential disasters.

Here are the questions you should ask:

- What is the name of this drug? Write down what the doctor tells you, and compare that to the label on the bottle.
- What is the purpose of this drug?
- How should it be taken? With or without food? Again, compare your doctor's directions to the label on the bottle.
- How long will it take to have an effect?
- What are the major side effects? How soon might they occur?
- Will it interfere with my other medications?

What if you need a procedure, such as surgery, performed? Doctors are required to inform you of possible complications, but you can certainly ask more specific questions, such as the following:

- How many of these procedures have you done and what have your results been?
- How often do complications occur? How often have your patients experienced complications?
- What are the chances of infection?

- What is the hospital's infection rate? (Such figures are available every month, and your doctor receives a copy.)
- What are the expected results of the surgery or procedure?

When Jeri, a 25-year-old tennis pro, had arthroscopy of her knee, she asked her surgeon all of these questions. She went home from the hospital understanding what to expect and what problems to watch for. After a few days, Jeri was not able to walk, the swelling had not gone down, and the knee started turning red. She knew these were warning signs and immediately contacted her surgeon, as instructed. Jeri had developed an infection that could have rapidly destroyed her knee and even killed her. Fortunately, timely treatment with antibiotics cured the infection, and the surgery fixed her knee problems.

Everything I've said also applies to alternative therapies. If herbs or supplements are recommended, ask about their side effects or interactions. Herbs can cause allergic reactions, and they can interfere with the actions of conventional drugs. It's especially important to question alternative methods because they may not be backed by adequate research, and the practitioners using them are often not licensed. The more uncommon procedures are the most worrisome. Never blindly trust them or the practitioners who perform them. Ask every question you can, and don't hesitate to ask for proof that the treatment actually works, or to find out whether there's any potential harm from it.

It's important to ask questions not only to protect yourself, but also to give yourself peace of mind. If you're satisfied with the answers and feel that you've made the right choices, that alone can help you heal!

STEP 5: RESEARCH THE RESEARCH

Asking pertinent questions is one way to get information, but sometimes that's not enough. You might want to verify the answers you receive, or you might not know enough to ask the right questions in the first place. The answer is to do research and gather information on your own.

If you want to know about a conventional medication, review the *Physicians Desk Reference* (*PDR*) or write to the pharmaceutical company that makes the particular drug you're researching. The addresses are listed in the *PDR*, and companies will send literature if you request it. Most libraries carry copies of the *PDR*, or you can buy a copy at a bookstore. If your doctor gives you a sample of a drug, ask for the package insert, which gives you the same information that appears in the *PDR*. You might be able to get the information at the drug store; more and more pharmacies are now providing patients with written information about their prescribed medications. You can also ask your doctor whether there are other drugs that are equivalent, and then call local pharmacies to find out whether those drugs are more or less costly than what was prescribed.

If you want to know more about a conventional procedure or a particular disease, a trip to the library or bookstore is in order. You can find lots of books there that give good explanations of various conditions and the recommended treatments, and in laymen's terms. If you have a computer and an Internet connection, you have a vast wealth of information at your fingertips. Forty-three percent of the time, adults surfing the Internet are looking for health information from the more than 15,000 health-related sites on the Web, where you can find literature on almost every disease known to humankind. (See Appendix C for a list of recommended books and Web sites.)

If you want information about an alternative product, you can consult any of the hundreds of reference books available on everything from homeopathy to herbs to aromatherapy. In addition, you can obtain information from non-profit organizations such as the American Botanical Council (ABC), which has collected more than 120,000 studies and abstracts on at least 1,000 herbs. The ABC translated and published the German *Commission E* monograph, considered the world's most thorough research and recommendations on herbs. The Internet is also a huge source of information for alternative medicine products and treatments. You'll find Web sites developed by alternative practitioners and manufacturers, as well as many others managed by conventional medical institutions and companies. And the National Institutes of Health's National Center for Complementary and Alternative Medicine (NCCAM) provides information about research on complementary therapies.

A note of caution about researching: Obtaining your own information is very important, but you still have to be critical and skeptical about what you find. See whether you can find the same information in separate, independent sources. Research has its flaws and problems, as discussed in Chapters 1 and 2. A study may seem to prove something, or a book or article may come to a particular conclusion, but that doesn't necessarily mean the information is accurate. Try to determine who conducted—and who funded—the research. And be wary of the Internet, which is both an excellent source of diverse and detailed information *and* a huge grab-bag of material that's inaccurate. A recent study of Internet sites for conventional medicine showed that more sites contained incorrect than correct information! The problem is even worse with alternative medicine sites, many of which make claims that are misleading, inaccurate, or totally false in an effort to sell products. So when surfing the Net for medical information, look at several Web sites and compare. You can then discuss the information with your practitioner and get his or her feedback.

STEP 6: CONSIDER ALL YOUR OPTIONS CAREFULLY

It's important that you not lock yourself into—or out of—certain methods or treatments just because they are conventional or alternative. The path to balanced care requires an open mind and a willingness to consider various options, either separately or in combination.

My patient Sadie, a 16-year-old high school senior, is a prime example. Two years before she came to see me, she'd been involved in a car accident. She was thrown forward and hit her face on the dashboard. Several months later, she developed pain in her jaw. The diagnosis was temporomandibular joint (TMJ) syndrome, which affects the joint that moves your jaw for speaking and eating. She had been treated with a splint and anti-inflammatory medications, but they didn't help. Surgery was recommended, but the surgeon could not promise her a successful result. She wanted to check other options and came to me. I thought that her facial bones had been knocked out of alignment in the car wreck, and I recommended an osteopathic technique called cranial-sacral manipulation. She'd never heard of that treatment, but after I explained it to her and she researched it further herself, she wanted to try it. After three treatments, her pain was gone.

If you limit your options, you may limit your chances of healing. Whether alternative or conventional, consider all the treatment options, and you'll make the best choices possible.

STEP 7: TRUST IN YOUR CHOICES

The mind is powerful; belief is a potent healer. So rather than dismissing the power of the mind, all of us, practitioners and patients alike, should try to employ it. Whatever approach you eventually choose, if you believe that it will work or even believe that it has a good chance of working, this belief alone will have a positive influence on your health. This does not mean, of course, that all you have to do is believe in a method and it will cure you; that's just wishful thinking. You must also have knowledge to back up your belief and strengthen your convictions. Still, belief is an important factor in healing. If you tell me that no treatment has ever worked for you, and you doubt that I can help you, it is unlikely that you will improve. On the other hand, if you have confidence that I can help, you're much more likely to realize your goal.

If you want an example of the power of belief, consider the case of Carl, an 83-year-old retired railroad engineer and a patient of mine when I was a resident on the cancer ward of a large hospital. He had lymphoma, which caused his lymph glands to swell all over his body. During his hospitalization, we obtained a new experimental drug that had shown great promise in reversing this cancer. We informed Carl, and he wanted the drug as soon as possible. One day after the injection, all the swellings in his lymph nodes disappeared. Three days later, however, the company informed us that they had found that the drug was effective for no more than six months. We were obligated to inform Carl, and he became depressed. By the next day, his lymph nodes were swollen again. We realized how strong Carl's belief was, so a few days later we told him of another new drug that did show long-term results. After we gave it to him, the lymph nodes once again disappeared. He was discharged from the hospital, and the cancer never returned. The drug? Salt water.

Here's another story, but this time about the negative power of belief. At age 43, Evelyn, a school guidance counselor, came to the hospital because she was coughing up blood. An x-ray had shown a spot on her lung, and we removed a small section of tissue to examine under a microscope. Lab tests showed the lung tissue was cancerous. I gave Evelyn the bad news, but told her that with this form of cancer, she could live three to five years with proper treatment. She became very depressed and told me that she simply didn't want to go through the treatment, and she just wanted to die. Despite being very healthy at the time (other than the cancer), she died within two weeks.

It's clear that your trust in your choices can be a powerful healing force, and disbe-lieving can be disastrous. But please note: I'm not recommending blind faith. A healthy dose of skepticism is appropriate, which is why you need to ask questions, do your own research, consider your options, and follow the other steps in this chapter. Then, once you make a treatment choice, put your belief and your mind behind it, and you'll have the best chance of success.

STEP 8: FOLLOW THROUGH WITH TREATMENT

Once you have followed these first seven steps, it's critical that you listen, without preconceived ideas, to your practitioner, and then follow the treatment approaches that the two of you agree are most likely to result in success. If you don't follow through with prescribed treatments, you may never achieve your goal of healing.

The case of Harriet, a 24-year-old stockbroker, illustrates the importance of follow-through. Harriet came to me with a stomach condition called acid reflux (also known as gastroesophageal reflux disorder, or GERD). Other doctors had prescribed the standard conventional medications, which had helped control her symptoms. But for various reasons, including minor side effects and cost, she stopped taking them; so I started her on Chinese herbs. I told her to take three capsules three times a day for three weeks. When she returned in three weeks, she told me the herbs had worked at first, but then they stopped working. When I questioned her further, she admitted that she kept forgetting to take the herbs, so over the three weeks she had taken them much less often than prescribed. Harriet asked me to do acupuncture instead so that she didn't have to take anything. I scheduled her twice a week and she came to the first session but missed the next two, and she still wondered why she wasn't getting better. Several months later, she returned, and I convinced her to commit to the treatment plan. This time she followed through, and her symptoms went away.

I make a point of this because, unfortunately, failure to follow through with proper treatment is quite common, and it has predictable negative consequences. According to the American Heart Association, 79 percent of the time, people with high blood pressure are either not on therapy or are being inadequately treated, in many cases because they simply don't follow the doctor's recommendations. One study showed that people with high cholesterol did not fill their prescriptions 40 percent of the time, even though it's well known that these drugs will significantly reduce the chances of heart attack, stroke, and death. And health-monitoring statistics show that more than half the people who are diagnosed with diabetes fail to follow treatment recommendations, thus putting themselves at risk for heart, kidney, nerve, and eye problems.

You might have good reasons why you do not want to continue a certain method or medication. Maybe there are intolerable side effects, or it costs too much, or it doesn't seem to be effective. That's fine. But discuss your concerns and dissatisfactions with your practitioner; don't just stop treatments or medications on your own. Together, you and your practitioner should be able to find a satisfactory treatment approach.

THE BALANCED HEALING APPROACH TO HEALTH AND WELL-BEING

Whatever your medical condition, there are treatments, both conventional and alternative, that can help you. Even if your condition is not curable, treatments are available to help reduce your symptoms and provide you with a better quality of life. Use the knowledge provided in these chapters, and find the treatment or combination of treatments that's best for you.

Many factors work together to cause an illness. You are not just a physical being; you are also a mental, emotional, and spiritual being. If you don't understand and examine all of these aspects of yourself, you may never find the underlying causes and, therefore, the cure, for your health problems.

Whether you seek the help of a conventional doctor or an alternative practitioner, a *holistic* approach—one that looks at the whole person—is the best way to find and treat the cause of the problem. If neither conventional nor alternative methods alone can achieve this goal, then both are necessary. This is the essence of Balanced Healing—taking advantage of the best treatment or treatments for your particular health problem.

As I said earlier, the combination of alternative and conventional medicine is sometimes called *integrative*, but these two approaches are rarely fully integrated in the true sense—that is, used by practitioners who have expertise in and believe in both, and who use each one when it's appropriate. But in 96 percent of the cases, people who use alternative methods also continue to see their conventional physicians. Clearly, people seek what both approaches offer: true balanced healing.

In this chapter, I've given you the basic tools you need to take control of your own health care. Of course, you might need doctors and other practitioners to guide you and provide appropriate treatments. But don't just let them treat you without taking an active role. It's your body and *your* health, and whether you treat yourself and/or have someone else treat you, always be an active participant and understand exactly what's taking place. Part One of this book will help you do just that.

In Part Two, I'll give you step-by-step guidelines for preventing and treating specific medical conditions. These sections are intended only as a general guide. You may have your own individual response to one treatment or another, so it's important to consult with your doctor or practitioner and use the information contained in Part One before you pursue my recommendations. And remember: To achieve the best health possible, always take a balanced approach to healing, and involve your body, mind, and spirit.

PART TWO

BALANCED HEALING IN ACTION

Getting Started
HOW TO USE THE TREATMENT GUIDES

As you can see, both conventional and alternative medical treatments have benefits and shortcomings. For optimal health, you should use the methods that will work for your particular medical condition—whether you use just conventional, just alternative, or a blend of both. There is much that you can do on your own to improve many health conditions. However, in most situations, you should begin with an evaluation from an appropriate practitioner who can give you an accurate diagnosis and offer treatment recommendations. After you have an accurate diagnosis, the Balanced Healing Treatment Guide offers a step-by-step approach to help you apply the most effective treatments for common health problems—what methods you can use, when to use them, what results to expect, and when to seek additional professional help.

Your health is unique to *you*. Although the treatments I suggest in this section work for many people, they don't work for everyone. You sometimes need to evaluate various methods and combinations to find the treatment that provides the results you are seeking. The recommendations I make in this section are based on the current medical literature and my experience. There is no way that I can know everything about you. I don't know the results of your diagnostic tests or your physical examination. Therefore, my recommendations should serve only as a basic roadmap to assist you and your practitioner in determining your best course of treatment.

I have selected the common health problems that I and other practitioners treat frequently and that are most likely to respond to a balanced treatment approach. For each health condition, I include several kinds of information:

- **Common Symptoms** are the typical ones for each health condition. This information is for general reference only; please don't use this information to try to diagnose your health problem.
- **What You Need to Know** presents significant facts about the condition or its treatment.
- **General Recommendations** are general health tips for improving the condition.
- **Your Balanced Healing Action Plan** provides more specific recommendations for a particular health condition. Whenever possible, these are treatments that can

resolve the condition and that are directed at its cause rather than just its symptoms. Sometimes, however, all you can do is treat the symptoms. In general, you should use the steps in order, although some steps can be combined for better results. The key is to find what works for you.

QUALIFIED PRACTITIONERS

Although you can use many alternative methods on your own, I recommend that you at least begin by seeing a qualified practitioner of that method. This is especially important for traditional Chinese medicine (TCM) recommendations such as acupuncture and Chinese herbs, because these treatments will vary depending on your particular imbalances and syndromes, which the TCM practitioner must first determine by a proper tongue and pulse diagnosis. Because alternative practices and practitioners can vary in quality, you should review the summary of the recommended alternative methods in Appendix A.

It is important that you consult a physician to determine the conventional treatment that is best for your individual needs. Many conventional treatments require a doctor's prescription or authorization. Conventional physicians (MDs and DOs) should be board-certified in the specialties in which they practice; certification is your guarantee that they've met the knowledge and expertise requirements determined to be necessary for their specialty. Most doctors post their certification documents in their offices; if in doubt, ask.

APPROPRIATE TREATMENTS

In many conditions, conventional and alternative treatments may be equally effective. When this is the case, I recommend first trying those treatments that have the fewest side effects. Also, I often recommend treatments that avoid invasive methods or surgery, which often should be the last resort. When I recommend alternative products, I'll give you the dosages and uses most commonly suggested by research findings and alternative practitioners. Because these products may have side effects or interfere with other products and medications, you need to read Appendix B for a summary of the particular product you're using, in addition to consulting with your doctor and your other health-care practitioners. Also, dosages have not been firmly established for many products, so you need to look at Appendix B and talk to your health-care provider for more detailed information.

For conventional treatments, there may be several different drugs or procedures that are helpful. I discuss the most common one(s), but—depending on other diseases you have, medications you take, and other factors—some treatments may be more effective than others, and dosages may vary. So again, consult with your doctor first.

TO YOUR OPTIMAL HEALTH!

Whatever your health condition and treatment options, I hope that this guide will help you find and use the most beneficial balance of alternative and conventional methods for your personal and particular needs and conditions—and achieve true balanced healing. It is important to realize, however, that new medical findings are discovered all the time, and, because of this, the guidelines I provide now may have to be altered over time.

Simple Healing Steps
for All Health Conditions

Health and healing are matters of balance. Whether you want to maintain balance to help prevent health problems or to restore balance because you already have some health problems, I believe these four basics are the cornerstones for health and healing:

- Eat an appropriate diet.
- Get regular exercise.
- Meditate.
- Practice Qigong.

Certain conditions and diseases require specific variations of, or additions to, these methods, and I'll tell you about these modifications in the sections on the various conditions. But whether you already have a medical condition or you are completely healthy and wish to prevent disease, nearly everyone will benefit from following these first steps to balanced health.

It takes more than wishful thinking to restore and maintain balanced health. If you really want to be healthier, you must commit yourself to replacing any less-than-healthy habits with ones that support your good health. Change requires effort; the habits that define your daily life make life easier for you, and it can be hard to give up the comfort of letting them carry you through each day. But, believe me, change is worth the effort when it means improved health! Before long, and with consistent practice, your new, health-positive habits will become the patterns of daily living for you.

EAT A HEALTHY DIET

Improper eating is one of the primary causes of disease throughout the world. In fact, 5 of the top 10 causes of death—cancer, stroke, heart disease, diabetes, and chronic alcoholic liver disease—are directly linked to what we eat or drink. Numerous studies demonstrate that some groups of people have much lower risk for certain diseases, while others have a much higher risk, and the difference is entirely due to their diets.

When you think of "diet," what comes to mind? Losing weight? Yes, it's true that being overweight or obese is an increasingly significant problem around the world, but many people of healthy weight are also at greater risk for various diseases because what they eat and drink fails to support good health. You may not be overweight, but you are not home free when it comes to your diet. Diet is about healthy eating habits, not weight.

Countless diets have been promoted for both overweight and nonoverweight people. There are standard medical diets, such as those recommended by the American Heart Association, the DASH (Dietary Approaches to Stop Hypertension), and the Mediterranean. In addition, there are many diets developed and promoted by various individuals, including the very low-fat (such as the Dean Ornish program), Sugar Busters, the Zone Diet, the McDougall plan, and the high fat/high protein/low carbohydrate—or Atkins—diet.

Each of these diets has fans and critics, and each has advantages and disadvantages. For example, some low-fat diets can increase triglycerides, cause good cholesterol to be converted to bad, and lead to vitamin deficiencies—and they're very difficult to follow for long periods of time. Yet these diets are popular because people assume that low fat is healthier. But not necessarily. The high-protein, low-carbohydrate diet may cause side effects as a result of *ketosis*, a toxic by-product of protein and fat metabolism; it may also result in vitamin deficiencies or cause kidney stones. It addition, we don't know yet if it causes any harmful long-term effects. The Zone and Sugar Buster diets are semi-starvation approaches that can leave people hungry, and they're very complex to follow. (See the section on obesity for further recommendations on eating to lose weight the healthy way.)

If you are normal weight and want to maintain healthy eating habits, I recommend both the DASH and the Mediterranean approaches. For more information on the DASH diet, go to www.nhlbi.nih.gov/health/public/heart/hbp/dash/. If you'd like to try the Mediterranean diet, go to your local bookstore, where you'll find numerous cookbooks that will help you follow the guidelines.

Balanced Healing Eating Guidelines

Healthy nutrition is not complicated or difficult. The Balanced Healing Eating Guidelines are relatively simple and straightforward. Just about everyone can follow them—and enjoy eating, too! They're good, basic guidelines that will help prevent and reverse major diseases, and help you feel and be healthier, no matter what your current health status.

Step 1: Eat a Variety—and Balanced Proportions—of Foods

If you eat the same foods, or the same combinations of foods, every day, you won't get a healthy variety of nutrients. If you consistently eat too large a proportion of foods from any one food group, you increase your risk of developing problems such as those that are common in many fad diets. The bottom line is BALANCE! Eat a variety of foods from all the food groups to give your body the nutrients it needs to maintain your good health and to heal when you have health problems.

To learn about the different food groups and how much you should be eating from each group, I recommend using the Healthy Eating Pyramid, a guide to balancing your meals developed by Dr. Walter Willett at the Harvard School of Public Health. When you follow a food pyramid as a guide to eating, you eat more foods from the bottom of the pyramid and less as you go up to the top. In the Healthy Eating Pyramid, equal weight is given at the bottom level to whole grain foods and plant oils (including olive, canola, soy, corn, sunflower, peanut, and other vegetable oils), which you can eat at almost every meal. The next level of the pyramid includes vegetables and fruits, which can be eaten 2 to 3 times a day. Above that level are nuts and legumes, which can be eaten 1 to 3 times a day, followed by fish, poultry, and eggs, which can be eaten no more than 2 times a day. The next level of the pyramid includes dairy products, which can be eaten 1 to 2 times a day. At the top of the pyramid, you'll find red meat, butter, white rice, white bread, potatoes, pasta, and sweets—which should all be eaten sparingly. For more information about the Healthy Eating Pyramid, read Dr. Willett's book, *Eat, Drink, and Be Healthy*. (I don't recommend using the USDA food pyramid, probably the most well-known food guide, because it is outdated according to the most recent scientific research.)

Step 2: Eat At Least Three Meals a Day

Smaller and more frequent meals are key to keeping your body satisfied and your appetite at bay. Do you have coffee for breakfast and eat little or nothing all day until your evening meal? Do you eat only a big lunch? If you eat just one large meal per day, your body responds by absorbing more calories than if you ate the same amount of food divided into three meals. Your body needs refueling consistently, not off and on, to absorb the necessary nutrients and use them most efficiently.

Step 3: Balance Your Intake of Fats, Proteins, and Carbohydrates

Eat the foods within each food group that are the healthiest and that deliver the highest proportion of nutrients. For example, eat more unsaturated fats than saturated, eat more plant protein than meat protein, and eat more carbohydrates from whole grains and fresh fruits and vegetables.

Step 4: Eat a More Plant-Based Diet

I recommend that you eat three to five servings of vegetables and fruits every day to supply your body with valuable vitamins, minerals, and antioxidants. You don't have to be a vegetarian to be healthy. Meat has nutrients that are necessary for health and that vegetables often don't supply. What you need to do is limit your intake of animal meats. Rather than eating 12 or 16 ounces of meat at one meal, eat 4 to 6 ounces. You'll get the nutrients you need from meat, but you'll minimize the amount of fat—and especially saturated fat—that you eat. I typically order a 10- to 12-ounce steak, eat half, and keep the rest for another meal.

Step 5: Eat Raw Foods When Possible

Unfortunately, cooking can deplete your food of necessary nutrients, including enzymes, vitamins, minerals, and antioxidants. When possible, eat food raw. Eat lots of fresh vegetables and fruits every day.

Step 6: Make Olive Oil Your Fat of Choice

While you want to limit the amount of fat you eat, your cells do need a certain amount of dietary fat to carry out their functions. Because olive oil is monounsaturated, it does not contribute to elevated blood cholesterol levels. I recommend it as your first choice.

Canola and peanut oil are also monounsaturated. Polyunsaturated oils, including safflower and soy, are the next tier. Completely avoid saturated oils that are solid at room temperature—oils such as lard, butter, and margarine. If you feel you must have a saturated oil, butter is a better choice than margarine.

Step 7: Use Natural Herbs and Spices

Garlic, peppers, onions, and curcumin are among the best seasonings for the foods you cook. Not only do they add flavor to your food, but they also contain substances that have known health benefits. For example, grilling meats produce *carcinogens* (cancer-causing chemicals). But if you cook and eat meats with garlic, onions, or peppers, they can negate the harmful effects of the carcinogens by helping the liver get rid of these chemicals. Oregano, ginger, sesame, and rosemary also have antioxidant properties, so they can negate the harmful effects of eating fried and processed foods.

Step 8: Increase Your Consumption of Beneficial Foods

Foods with health benefits include whole grains, beans, and fatty fish (such as mackerel, trout, salmon, herring, tuna, halibut, cod liver, flounder, or sardines). If you snack, munch on foods such as nuts, which contain vitamin E, or fresh fruits and vegetables.

Step 9: Moderate Your Consumption of Sugars, Salt, and Alcohol

A little bit goes a long way with these substances. Using them to extremes can make it more likely that you will develop certain diseases, and excessive use can worsen whatever disease you have. Refined flours and grains are harmful, so eat whole wheat. On the average, we Americans eat 16 times the amount of salt that we need, so use it sparingly. Alcohol can be beneficial if you drink it moderately (about one glass or cocktail daily), but overdoing it is harmful.

Step 10: Avoid Processed and Fast Foods

Processed and fast foods are notorious for the high amounts of preservatives, salt, fat, and calories that they contain. They also contain minimal nutrients. Even worse, they are made with what are called *trans fats* (or trans fatty acids), which are produced by heating regular vegetable oil in the presence of metal and hydrogen (called *hydrogenation*). This process restructures the oil's carbon molecules into new chains, creating a product that stays solid at room temperature, is more stable for deep frying, and stays fresh longer. Of course, that's all great for food manufacturers. Unfortunately, trans fats raise your LDL (the bad cholesterol) and lower your HDL (the good cholesterol), contributing significantly to heart disease.

Processed and fast foods are certainly easier and less time consuming to eat, but they definitely take years off your life.

Step 11: Special Needs

You might need additional nutritional supplementation depending on your particular needs or desires. For example:

Vegetarian: If you don't eat any animal products, including dairy, you should supplement with vitamin B_{12}, and you may need extra vitamin D, iron, and calcium. These minerals and vitamins come mainly from meat and dairy products.

Organic Foods: Many people prefer organic foods because they are grown without insecticides, pesticides, and other chemicals. Federal law now requires organic certification. For organic produce, look for a notebook or display that contains certification papers. If the food is packaged, the label should reflect certification. In some products, however, only a certain percentage of the ingredients may be certified, usually because the cost of the nonorganic ingredients would be prohibitive if they were grown organically. (The labels will show the percentage.)

Low Dairy Consumption: If you do not like or cannot tolerate dairy products, you should take supplemental calcium at 1,000mg to 1,500mg daily. (See Appendix B, under "Calcium," for the best forms to take.)

Elderly: If you do not consume several servings of fortified milk on a daily basis and spend at least some time in the sun, you should be checked for vitamin D deficiency and take a supplement if your levels are low. If your diet is low in calcium, you're likely to be low in vitamin D and vitamin A as well. One in four older Americans gets insufficient vitamin B_{12}. Your doctor can check your blood levels and, if necessary, prescribe B_{12} supplementation through injections.

Smokers: Smokers are usually deficient in vitamin C. You should increase your vitamin C intake by eating more citrus fruits and fortified juices and/or taking supplements.

Low Calorie Diet: If you are on a restricted diet (less than 1,500 calories to 1,800 calories per day), I recommend taking a good multivitamin. (See Appendix B for recommendations and further guidance in choosing a good multivitamin.)

GET REGULAR EXERCISE

If someone told you there is a method that would take just two to three hours a week to prevent disease or improve your health, wouldn't it make sense to do it, and avoid all the trials, tribulations, and expenses of being ill? There is such a method: exercise. A number of studies have conclusively proven that improving or maintaining adequate physical fitness significantly decreases your risk of dying from all causes. It's easy to find excuses for not exercising, but when it comes right down to it, there are no valid reasons not to exercise. Even if you are in pain, have a disability, or are older, there are types of exercise that you can do and from which you can benefit.

- **Aerobic exercise** is any activity that increases the heart rate. Aerobic means "oxygen-producing." Every cell in your body needs oxygen to function properly. Aerobic exercise stimulates cells—and your body—to function more efficiently. Such activities as walking, bicycling, running, swimming, hiking, playing sports, walking up stairs, or even moving around your house are aerobic exercises.
- **Stretching** allows your muscles, joints, ligaments and tendons to become more

flexible. Greater flexibility decreases strain on your body and enables you to retain your energy and do a lot more with less risk of injury.

- **Strengthening (resistance)** activities build muscle mass by putting resistance against your muscles. Resistance exercise allows you to engage in more strenuous activities and helps protect you from injury. Isometric exercises, which use light weights and involve tightening and releasing major muscle groups, can be just as effective as structured, large-weight training programs.

Balanced Healing Exercise Guidelines

Whether you want to prevent disease from occurring or you presently have a health condition, exercise is an important element in maintaining and restoring better health.

Step 1: Get a Check-Up First

Before beginning an exercise program, get a thorough checkup from a doctor. This is especially necessary if you have heart problems, injuries, or other health conditions. But it's also important, if you haven't exercised in a long time, to check for potential health problems of which you are unaware. Knowing your challenges or limitations helps you to plan exercises and activities that will support and improve your health.

Step 2: Make Time to Exercise

You make time to eat, work, sleep, and watch TV. So make time to exercise! Once exercise becomes part of your daily routine, it becomes like brushing your teeth—just something that you do. It is important to know that you don't have to exercise 30 to 60 minutes at one time to receive benefit. Studies have demonstrated that exercising for 10 minutes three times a day is equivalent to exercising 30 minutes at a time. So fit it into your schedule, even if you have to break it into segments.

Step 3: Exercise Regularly

Your body gets the most benefit from consistent, regular exercise. Sporadic workouts have been shown to increase the risk of heart-attack deaths, while consistent, regular exercise reduces the risk for many health problems, including heart disease.

Step 4: Warm Up

Just a few minutes of moving your arms and legs to stretch and limber your muscles can help prevent injuries. I recommend doing it for at least 5 to 10 minutes. And don't forget to "warm down" after exercise, to help your muscles transition back to regular activity. You can do this simply by walking around, or again, by moving your arms and legs around. Do it for at least 5 minutes.

Step 5: Start Slowly and Build Up Gradually

The benefits of exercise begin immediately, whether you've been exercising regularly or you've been sedentary. So take your time, and don't do more than you can handle. There's no contest to see who can do the most. You'll be surprised to find out how quickly you're able to do more.

Step 6: Balance Your Activities

Use a balance of all three kinds of exercise. All can help you, but you'll get the maximum benefit if you do all three. Here are some guidelines:

- **Start with stretching.** Stretch slowly and stretch all your muscle groups for at least five minutes. I recommend daily stretching, because of its many benefits, even if you're not doing any other exercise that day.
- **Do strengthening exercises** at least three times a week (and daily if you are older). You can use weight cuffs that wrap around your ankles and/or wrists, or you can use a pair of dumbbells, from 1 pound to 10 pounds, depending on your current strength and goals. Lift the weights slowly and gently. Do two sets of 8 to 12 repetitions, resting between sets. As you are able to do more repetitions comfortably, you can increase your weights.
- **Do aerobic exercises** for 30 minutes three times a week. If time is a problem, you can do a 10-minute segment nine times a week. Doing more segments will give you greater benefits. The goal is to increase your heart rate to a specific level for the duration of the exercise time period (see Chart "Determining Your Heart Rates for Exercise" to determine your minimum and maximum heart rates for the most benefit). Start slowly, using the minimum training heart rate, and gradually increase to the maximum rate over several weeks to months. If you feel too tired or ill, you're doing too much. Walking, bicycling, swimming, and running are common activities that can provide aerobic exercise.

DETERMINING YOUR HEART RATES FOR EXERCISE	
Maximum training heart rate (MTHR)	185 minus your age = MTHR
Minimum training heart rate (MNTHR)	MTHR minus 20 = MNTHR

Step 7: Keep Your Body in Motion

Every chance you have, move! No matter what you do, it can become exercise, and every bit helps. You can

- Do shoulder rolls or stretches in the bathroom.
- Do mini-squats or marching in place at your desk or when you are on the phone.
- Do tummy tucks or reverse sit-ups while working at the computer.
- Walk up a few flights of stairs instead of taking an elevator.
- Park at the end of a mall and walk to the store you want to go to.

- Walk in place when you are in front of the television.
- Do isometric exercises at your desk or whenever you are sitting.

MEDITATE

Just as with exercise, I recommend meditation for everyone, whether you have a medical condition or are healthy. Even if you can meditate only five minutes a day, you'll get the benefits. Of course, the more you meditate, the better.

Balanced Healing Meditation Guidelines

There are many meditations you can do, and many audio tapes you can buy that will guide you. (See Appendix C for reference information.) You can also create your own meditation, tape it, and play it back to yourself. Whichever meditation you choose, do it as often as you can, whether during the day or as you fall asleep at night. The beneficial results will soon be evident. Here are two meditations to get you started.

Step 1: The Five-Minute Meditation

You can do the five-minute meditation just about any time and practically anywhere—while you are at work, watching TV, even sitting in traffic. It will energize and refresh you. Put your hands in your lap, laying one hand on top of the other, palms facing up, and close your eyes.

1. Take a deep breath, and hold it until the count of four. Then release your breath, and, as you do so, feel all the tension in your body drain away.
2. Take another deep breath, and hold it until the count of eight. Again, release the breath, and, this time, feel as if your entire body goes totally limp, as if gravity is pulling it down. Take a third deep breath, and this time hold it as long as you can. When you release it, again, feel your whole body relax, all the tenseness draining out.
3. Now take a few moments to concentrate on your breath. In your mind, see the air going into your mouth, filling and expanding your lungs. Then see your lungs squeezing the air out and the air flowing out of your mouth.
4. Do this several times, focusing on your breath going in and out. Then, as you inhale, imagine fresh energy flowing into your lungs, going into your blood vessels, and carrying the refreshing energy to all parts of your body. As you exhale, see all the tensions in your body being released back into your lungs and flowing out of your body.
5. Repeat this whenever you can.

Step 2: The Long Meditation

The long meditation allows your body and mind to fully relax and become free from tension and stress. There is no specific length of time for the long meditation; it is simply longer than the five-minute meditation. Most people do a long meditation at night before going to bed, or at a time when they know they won't be interrupted.

1. Get into a comfortable position. Begin the steps of the five-minute meditation.
2. After exhaling the third (longest-held) breath, focus on the toes of both feet, and relax them. When they feel relaxed, then concentrate on your feet, and allow them to relax.
3. Every time one body area is relaxed, proceed up the body, repeating the same process. Go to the lower legs, then the knees, the upper legs, the pelvic area, and the abdominal area. You can even relax the organs inside the abdomen by imagining the blood flow slowing down and the muscles of the organs (yes, they all have muscles, too) relaxing.
4. Move on to the chest, relaxing the ribs, heart, and lungs, again slowing them down. Feel a wave of relaxation every time you exhale and the chest wall falls. Then relax the back muscles, proceed up to the neck, and allow the shoulders to fall as they relax. Relax your fingers, hands, forearms, elbows, and upper arms.
5. Concentrate on relaxing your jaw, the muscles around your mouth, around your nose, and around your eyes. Relax the muscles of your forehead and temples, and finally relax the muscles in your scalp, underneath your hair, to your ears and the back of your head.
6. After completing this process, take a few minutes to scan your body from toes to head. If there are any areas that still feel tense, relax those areas again.
7. At this point, you can stop and just enjoy the relaxed feeling, or you can go on to achieve even deeper relaxation. One way to do this is to picture yourself at the top of a stairwell, with ten steps going down. See yourself walking down those steps, counting from 10 to 1 very slowly. Or picture yourself in your favorite place, such as lying on a beach or floating in a swimming pool. Or simply allow thoughts, feelings, and emotions to pop into your consciousness, observe them, and allow them to disappear (this is called mindfulness meditation).

For more information on meditation, see Appendix A, under "Mind-Body Techniques," and Appendix C, under "Meditation."

PRACTICE QIGONG (CHI KUNG)

By using a combination of movement, meditation, and breathing, Qigong (pronounced "chee gong") stimulates energy flow through the body and improves immune function, thus balancing or rebalancing all bodily functions. You must make time to do the Qigong exercises, and you should do them every day for the best results. You can get the immediate benefits of relaxation, but the significant benefits for reversing disease usually take several months. Tai Chi is a martial arts form that is an expansion of Qigong, and performing Tai Chi exercises is also very beneficial for your health.

Balanced Healing Qigong Guidelines

Qigong can range from very simple movements, similar to calisthenics, to very complex exercises in which brain-wave frequency, heart rate, and other bodily functions are altered intentionally. Although most people should initially be taught Qigong by experienced instructors, once you know the concepts of Qigong, you can develop your own exercises. Anyone can—and everyone should—practice Qigong.

According to the traditional Chinese medicine (TCM) foundation from which Qigong arises, there are five forces, all linked to specific "elements" or "energy phases":

1. Wood element, the tendency to expand out in all directions
2. Fire element, the tendency to rise
3. Water element, the tendency to sink
4. Metal element, the tendency to contract
5. Earth, which contains and holds the others together

To get you started, here are two simple Qigong exercises. The first is called La Chi, which you can do any time you have a few minutes, even when watching TV or sitting in your car at a stoplight. The second is called Five Forces Qigong, which gives expression to all these parts of your being, and it can be done in five minutes.

La Chi

Put your hands close to each other so that your fingers almost touch each other. Relax your shoulders and hands. Slowly open your hands to both sides, but don't pass the ribcage. Then close your hands, again very slowly, until the fingers almost touch. Repeat these opening and closing movements over and over again. Very soon, you will feel some sensation develop between your hands. These are Qi (pronounced "chee") (energy) sensations. When you feel this sensation, you can deliver this healing Qi wherever it is needed in your body by bringing your hands next to your body and imagining the energy flowing into the body and to whatever organ or tissue needs healing.

Five Forces Qigong

Start in the basic Qigong posture: Your feet are shoulder width apart, your tailbone is slightly lowered (a slight squat, with knees bent), and your tongue touches the roof of your mouth. Relax and breathe deeply.

Fire element phase: Make your left hand into a "beak," all four fingers converging on your thumb, and place your hand at the base of your spine, pointing up. Place your right hand palm up just above your head. Inhale as your left hand rises up the back. Then exhale as your right hand rises upward, then curves down to become the "beak" in the back, while at the same time, the left hand curves in front and up to the top of the head. Repeat nine times, alternating hands.

Wood element phase: Spread your feet wide and fling your arms up and out as far as you can. Look up and inhale as you expand out, then exhale as you lower your arms. Repeat nine times.

Water element phase: Bend your left leg slightly and place your weight on it, while you touch your right toe to the ground (heel up). Brush the back of your right hand across your right kidney area (just below the ribs in the back), then across the left kidney area, and then down the outside of your left hip and leg. Imagine your kidney energy going down and out your left leg. Meanwhile, pass the back of your left hand in front of your face from right to left, then heading toward your left kidney; repeat on the opposite side. Exhale when you brush down your leg, and inhale before brushing down your other leg. Repeat nine times.

Metal element phase: Stand in the basic posture, with your feet shoulder-width apart, but now slightly slump over with your shoulders pointed inward and your toes pointed in, and your palms facing each other in front of your navel. Imagine a ball of energy in between your hands. As you exhale, imagine squeezing a small ball of energy, then inhale and make the ball larger. Repeat nine times.

Earth element phase: Stand in the basic posture, but slightly hunched over, the backs of your hands facing each other in front of your navel. As you exhale, squat down until your fingers touch the ground between your feet. Bend your head to look at your fingers. Then inhale as you stand up straight and throw your head back and look up as your arms fly out and up, your palms facing up. Then start exhaling as you slump down again and the backs of your hands meet near your navel. Repeat nine times.

Stand quietly for a few moments as you imagine the energy flowing up your spine and down your front. Then rub your palms around your navel clockwise nine times to store the energy.

For further information on Qigong, see Appendix A, under "Qigong," and Appendix C.

IN SUMMARY

If you add these four Simple Healing Steps to your daily life, you'll not only help prevent many major health problems—you'll also help start healing any conditions that you already have. These methods do not interfere with any other treatments, can be done by anyone, are completely safe, are inexpensive, and are the most powerful tools for healing that mankind has discovered. But don't let the term "simple" fool you. Consider the four steps to be the foundation of a balanced, healthy lifestyle. Yes, they're easy, and anyone can use them. But they require both time and motivation. Even if you can do only one or two of them, the benefits will be significant. If you can accomplish all four, the results will be even better.

You might have to make changes in your lifestyle to incorporate these practices into your everyday routine. But making minor changes in your lifestyle is not as difficult as you may think. For example, if you smoke cigarettes, instead of smoking one, do the five-minute meditation or La Chi. You are doing two things that will benefit you: one that adds to your health, and one that takes away an action that is detrimental to your health. By examining your particular daily routine, you will find numerous periods in which you can apply the four steps, or use them in place of other nonbeneficial or harmful activities. Once you make them part of your daily routine, they'll become much easier. To help you be consistent, I suggest that you use the four steps with friends or family on a routine basis, so that you support each other.

But don't overdo it. It is possible to get too much of a good thing, and then you won't want to do it anymore. Even though these four methods are beneficial, other parts of your life, such as relationships and work, can suffer when you spend too much time exercising or meditating. The key is, as always, BALANCE.

Balanced Healing Treatment Guide for Common Health Conditions

ACNE

Acne is the most common skin disease and is a dysfunction of the skin pores. Hair follicles become plugged with sebum, a mixture of oils and waxes that lubricate the skin, and *keratin*, a protein that comprises the outermost layer of skin. When these substances build up, acne is the result. Acne can occur on the face, neck, chest, shoulders, or back. Myths abound regarding the causes of acne, from diet to uncontrolled sex drives, but heredity and hormones are the primary causes. The mild forms of acne will eventually go away on their own. But the more severe forms can cause permanent scarring of the skin if left untreated.

Common Symptoms

Lesions that may have one or a combination of

- Blackheads (dark spots with open pores).
- Whiteheads (bulging under the skin without openings).
- Pustules, nodules, and cysts, all of which are fluid-filled lumps.

What You Need to Know

The best approach to treating acne is to do what you can to prevent flare-ups. Try to avoid medications that can cause acne-like lesions, including steroids, drugs that contain bromides or iodides, Dilantin (for seizures), and lithium carbonate (for bipolar disorders). If you are taking any of these medications, **do not discontinue them without your doctor's advice!** Some forms of oral contraceptives worsen acne, while others improve it (check with your gynecologist for guidance). Avoid or minimize exposure to pollutants that cause acne—machine oils, coal tar derivatives, and chlorinated hydrocarbons. Cosmetics, overwashing, or rubbing your face can cause flare-ups.

General Recommendations

It is a common myth that eating greasy, high-fat foods causes acne. It is generally accepted that foods do not cause acne, and they probably don't aggravate it either. However, your diet can affect the health of your skin, which in turns allows acne treatments to work more quickly and effectively. For the healthiest skin, I recommend that you limit refined and simple sugars as well as high-fat foods in your diet. Avoid fried oils and processed foods with trans fats; these are the most unhealthy for your skin and your health overall.

Your Balanced Healing Action Plan for Acne

- For mild acne, start with Step 1.
- For moderate acne, begin with Step 6, and then return to Step 1.
- For severe acne, start with Steps 6 and 7, then return to Step 1.

Step 1: Use Acupuncture First

I recommend starting with acupuncture, which can be very effective in controlling acne for long periods. Principal points are found on the arms, legs, and feet. Ear acupuncture is also very effective, either alone or with body points. Principal points usually include lung, endocrine, testis, skin, and cheek. Always seek evaluation and treatment from a practitioner certified in acupuncture. (See Appendix A, under "Acupuncture," for guidance on finding a qualified acupuncturist and for explanations of different acupuncture techniques.) With acupuncture, you should notice improvement within six treatments.

Step 2: Use Topical Tea Tree Oil, Azelaic Acid, or Benzoyl-Peroxide Solution

Topical tea tree oil is the best *topical solution* (that is, a solution that you put on your skin) to use for acne because it kills skin bacteria and has the fewest side effects. Start with the 5 percent solution if you have mild acne. If you have moderate or severe acne, start with the 15 percent solution along with Step 6.

If you don't see the results you want after one to two months, it's time for a change. Switch to a solution containing 20 percent azelaic acid, another topical antiseptic. Apply this twice a day for at least a month, and then go to once a day for six months.

And if neither of these topicals is effective, then change to benzoyl-peroxide solution (5 to 10 percent concentration) or gel (12 percent). If you find that each of these topicals has some partial benefit, you can use them together, but apply them at different times. These products can dry the skin, so it is better if you use only one or two of them.

> When 15-year-old Tiffany came to me with moderate acne, she already had tried over-the-counter benzoyl peroxide in combination with antibiotics, but she continued to break out. I recommended tea tree oil along with a good multivitamin containing the supplements in Step 3, and I started her on Chinese herbs and acupuncture. After one month, her acne began subsiding, and after two months her skin was clear. She stopped the antibiotics, Chinese herbs, and acupuncture, and she was able to maintain clear skin using tea tree oil, benzoyl peroxide, and vitamins.

Step 3: Take Chromium, Selenium, Vitamin E, Zinc, Pantothenic Acid, and/or Chasteberry

If you find that Step 1 is only partially effective, take these supplements all together, once daily:

- Chromium (200mg to 400mg/day)—Helps break down sugars.
- Selenium (200mcg/day)—Helps inhibit acne inflammation.
- Vitamin E (400 IU/day)—Helps inhibit acne inflammation.
- Zinc (45mg to 60mg/day)—Improves skin health; use the effervescent sulfate or gluconate forms (identified on the package label).

If these four nutrients do not help completely, add 2.5mg of pantothenic acid four times a day. This compound reduces the production of sebum, the substance that plugs the skin pores. You should see improvement within one to three months. Another helpful herb is chasteberry, (solid extract, standardized to 0.5 percent agnuside, 175mg to 225mg daily), which has antibacterial properties and can help reduce acne in 70 percent of patients (but it may take six months to do so).

Vitamin A has been found to be effective in reducing sebum production as well, but only in high doses that can be dangerous, so a physician should monitor its use. **Do not use vitamin A unless your physician recommends it and provides regular follow-up care and monitoring.**

Step 4: Take Appropriate Chinese Herbal Remedies

There are several Chinese herbal formulas, usually containing cnidium seed and honeysuckle, that are effective for acne. I recommend *Cai Feng Zhen Zhu An Chuang Wan* or *Wu Wei Xiao Du Yin*. Consult a practitioner qualified in Chinese herbal medicine to determine which herbal formulas are the best for your particular syndromes (See Appendix A, under "Chinese Herbs.")

Step 5: Take Appropriate Homeopathic Remedies

If your acne continues, *Corynebacterium acnei* is one of the homeopathic remedies that may be beneficial, and you can use it with the previous steps. Consult a qualified homeopathist for guidance on which remedies and dosages will be most beneficial. You should see benefits within one to two weeks. (See Appendix A, under "Homeopathy," for more information.)

Step 6: Take a Prescription Antibiotic

If your acne persists, or is moderate to severe initially, your doctor can prescribe oral antibiotics such as tetracycline, erythromycin, or a cephalosporin (such as Ceclor). You can usually take these antibiotics for extended periods of time. Clindamycin, erythromycin, and metronidazole are antibiotics that come in topical solutions or gels, if you prefer to apply the medication to your skin rather than take a pill.

All these antibiotics are effective; your physician needs to determine which one and what dosage is best for you. But taking antibiotics for several weeks can cause vaginal yeast infections in some women. Antibiotics can also cause stomach problems because the antibiotic kills beneficial digestive bacteria as well. You can avoid both of these problems by taking probiotics. (See Appendix B, under "Supplements," for more information on probiotics.) It usually takes up to three months for antibiotics to deliver maximum benefit.

Step 7: Use Prescription Topicals

If Steps 1 through 6 fail to relieve your acne, or if your acne is severe, your physician might prescribe 0.025 percent to 0.1 percent Tretinoin (retinoic acid), a vitamin A derivative. Benzoyl peroxide (Step 2) may inhibit the healing effects of Tretinoin, however, so you must use them at different times if you are using both.

Step 8: Take Other Prescription Medications

For severe cases and cystic acne, isotretinoin used to be the treatment of choice. It may be taken off the market, however, because in some people, it may trigger depression and suicide, so many doctors have stopped prescribing it. If you are taking it or would like to explore the possibility of taking it, talk to your doctor and make sure you are closely monitored.

> Lara, a marine biologist, never had acne until she was 40 years old. She broke out on her face as well as her hands and upper torso. Over the next three years, she saw at least six dermatologists and tried every antibiotic and medication (including isotretinoin) used for acne. Some of these cleared her arm and torso acne, but not her face. Lara was so embarrassed that she didn't want to go out and be seen, so she virtually became a shut-in. I placed her on two Chinese herbal formulas and performed just one acupuncture treatment, which cleared her face completely.

If You Have Acne Scars

A dermatologist or plastic surgeon might be able to remove scars using one of two cosmetic surgical methods: *dermabrasion* or *chemical peeling*. Both are effective.

AIDS (Acquired Immune Deficiency Syndrome)

AIDS is a severe, and ultimately fatal, condition caused by the human immunodeficiency virus (HIV), which attacks the immune system. The damaged immune system makes people with AIDS susceptible to a large group of diseases and infections. With proper detection and treatment, people with HIV infection and AIDS can live much longer, avoid many of the complications, and have a good quality of life.

Common Symptoms

HIV infection may show no symptoms until the immune system is compromised. Then symptoms can appear either suddenly or more gradually.

Sudden Onset Symptoms

- Fever
- Sweating
- Malaise
- Fatigue
- Joint and muscle pain
- Sore throat
- Diarrhea
- Headaches
- Lymph gland enlargement
- Rashes
- Infection of the lung or mouth (yeast)

Subtle Onset Symptoms

- Progressively worsening fatigue
- Weight loss
- Fever
- Diarrhea
- Lymph node enlargement

What You Need to Know

Prevention is the best means of protection from this disease, yet despite widespread information on AIDS, many people (especially those at high risk) do not take precautions to protect themselves from this fatal infection. As many as 30 percent of people who have HIV don't know it, so they're putting themselves and others at risk. That's why you must protect yourself! A blood test can detect the presence of HIV, which is transferred from person to person via body fluids, particularly through any type of sexual contact (oral, genital, or anal). The use of a condom during sex is the best prevention, although it does not give 100 percent protection. Infected blood and infected needles (especially in drug abusers) can also transmit HIV.

Treatment with conventional drugs can put AIDS in remission for 10 to 15 years or longer. By adding alternative methods, you may be able to extend your survival, reduce your symptoms, and improve your quality of life.

General Recommendations

Diet: There is a strong association between nutritional status and immune function. Proper nutrition can slow the development and progress of AIDS. In addition to following the Balanced Healing Eating Guidelines on page 80 (see "Simple Healing Steps for All Health Conditions," page 79, under "Diet"), avoid sugar and smoking, both of which depress the immune system, and avoid alcohol, which depletes the body of vitamins and minerals. Taking a protein supplement is often helpful; I recommend soy protein as the best source. (See Appendix B, under "Herbs," for further guidance on soy products.)

Meditation and Qigong: Because the immune system is the primary target of the virus, any method that improves and strengthens the immune response is beneficial. Both meditation and Qigong are very helpful in enhancing the immune system. (See "Simple Healing Steps for All Health Conditions" on page 79, and Appendix A, under "Mind-Body Techniques," for further information and examples.)

Your Balanced Healing Action Plan for AIDS/HIV

Step 1: Take Prescribed Conventional Medications Such As AZT, Didanosine, Dideoxycytidine, and/or Protease Inhibitors

If you have HIV or AIDS, your doctor may prescribe *nucleoside* analogue medications such as AZT, didanosine, and/or dideoxycytidine, which help prevent the spread of the virus within your body. If your doctor prescribes AZT for you, also take L-carnitine (300mg to 500mg three times a day). This can prevent toxicity from AZT.

Many HIV/AIDS treatment regimens also include protease inhibitors, which help prevent the virus from reproducing itself within the body's cells. All these drugs do have various side effects, however, and the HIV virus can become resistant to them. If you are taking a protease inhibitor, do not take the antidepressant herb St. John's wort, which interferes with the metabolism of protease inhibitors, making them less effective. Garlic supplements have also been reported to decrease the blood levels of protease inhibitors (particularly saquinavir), so avoid them as well.

There is some controversy as to when to start the various types of drugs and which ones to use, so make sure you are always under the care of a physician who is an expert in the treatment of AIDS. Decisions about how to treat are based primarily on your CD4+T-lymphocyte count and your HIV RNA count (that is, the amount of virus particles). Each of us makes white blood cells that fight against viruses, called *T-lymphocytes*. In AIDS, T-lymphocytes that contain the so-called CD4 receptor fight the HIV virus, but they become depleted as the condition worsens. As a result, the RNA increases at the same time. If the CD4 count decreases and HIV RNA increases, then you have a greater chance of complications. If your CD4 count is less than 350 and HIV RNA is greater than 55,000, that's a very worrisome situation, and most doctors will start you on medication. When these levels return to normal, or near normal, you'll know that the treatment is working.

Step 2: Use Interactive Imagery

I highly recommend that everyone with AIDS use interactive imagery, which can reduce symptoms and improve the quality of life—and may help prolong life. This is a mind-body method in which you mentally interact with images that represent your emotions. It is a powerful method to uncover and deal with subconscious psychological issues of which you may not be aware. (See Appendix A, under "Mind-Body Techniques," for more information.) If you have AIDS, interactive imagery helps you deal with the basic fears, anxiety, and anger that commonly occur with this condition. It also helps with stress reduction, which in turn can reduce various symptoms and complications. Use interactive imagery with all the other steps.

Step 3: Take Vitamin E, Vitamin C, Alpha-Lipoic Acid, Selenium, Vitamin B_6, Vitamin B_{12}, Beta-Carotene, Curcumin, Licorice, Bromelain, CoQ10, and L-Carnitine

Many vitamins and minerals are depleted in people with AIDS. These and other supplements can help fight the virus. I recommend taking all of these supplements because AIDS is a lethal disease, and these vitamins and supplements may help prolong life and decrease complications through their nutritional and antioxidant effects. However, **do not take zinc, which can actually decrease your chances of survival.** Here are the dosages you should take as you follow Steps 1 and 2:

- Vitamin E, 800mg daily
- Vitamin C, 1,000mg daily
- Alpha-lipoic acid, 150mg three times a day
- Selenium, 200mcg daily
- Vitamin B_6, 100mg daily
- Vitamin B_{12} (active methycobalamin), 2mg daily
- Beta-carotene, 50,000 IU daily
- Curcumin, 2,000mg daily
- Licorice, in the deglycyrrhizinated (DGL) form, one or two 380mg chewable tablets before meals
- Bromelain, 1,200mcu to 1,800mcu daily
- CoQ10, 200mg daily
- L-carnitine, 6g daily

Step 4: Take Chinese Herbal Formulas for Complications of AIDS

If you still have symptoms of AIDS, such as *neuropathy* (nerve deterioration causing severe pain in the legs), night sweats, fatigue, and diarrhea, I recommend taking Chinese herbs and in particular a formula called Enhance. It has been used very successfully in the Quan Yin Herbal Program, a major treatment program for HIV patients in San Francisco. (See Appendix C, under "Chinese Herbs," for referral information, or contact Quan Yin Healing Arts at 415-861-4964 or by e-mail at qyhacinfo@aol.com.) Other Chinese herbal formulas may be useful for particular symptoms or complications. Consult a practitioner qualified in Chinese herbal medicine to determine which herbal formulas are the best for your particular syndromes, (See Appendix A, under "Chinese Herbs," for further guidance.)

Step 5: Undergo Acupuncture for Symptoms and Complications

Acupuncture can reduce many of the symptoms and other complications of AIDS, especially neuropathy, fatigue, and pain. Acupuncture is often used along with the Chinese herbs in Step 4. A qualified acupuncturist will use traditional Chinese medicine diagnostic techniques to determine the appropriate acupuncture points.

Always seek evaluation and treatment from a practitioner certified in acupuncture. (See Appendix A, under "Acupuncture," for guidance on finding a qualified acupuncturist.) You should notice improvement within six treatments, although more treatments may be necessary for maximum benefit. You might need maintenance treatments every few months.

> Tim, an electrician who's now 43 years old, has had AIDS for 10 years. Although his CD4 and viral-load counts have been stable, he came to see me because he was experiencing loss of appetite, fatigue, and burning pain in his lower legs (neuropathy). I started him on supplements and vitamins and Chinese herbs, which resolved his fatigue and increased his appetite. I also gave him acupuncture treatments, and, after just eight sessions, his leg pain was completely gone.

ALCOHOLISM

The World Health Organization (WHO) defines *alcoholism* as the consumption of alcohol that's beyond the limits accepted by your particular culture or that damages your health or social relationships. Alcoholism can cause numerous medical conditions, including heart disease (angina, heart failure), brain degeneration, decreased testosterone levels, esophagitis, gastritis, ulcers, high blood pressure, hypoglycemia, cancers of the upper GI (gastrointestinal) and respiratory tracts, cirrhosis and liver failure, muscle wasting, osteoporosis, pancreatitis, psoriasis, and psychiatric conditions. Alcoholism increases your risk of death, doubling the death rate in men and tripling the death rate in women. Overall, alcoholism lowers life expectancy by 10 years and increases the suicide rate sixfold.

Common Symptoms

Acute Alcohol Addiction
- Temporary blackouts
- Memory loss
- Excessive aggression
- Use of alcohol to relax, sleep, be happy, or deal with problems

Chronic Alcohol Addiction
- Husky voice
- Broken veins and capillaries on the face
- Tremors
- Chronic diarrhea

- Withdrawal symptoms, including anxiety, insomnia, headache, nausea, or *delirium tremens* (DTs, a type of hallucination)
- Malnutrition

What You Need to Know

The causes of alcoholism are a complex combination of hereditary predisposition and a variety of social, environmental, physical, and psychological factors. The condition is thus very difficult to treat. One type of treatment alone may not be effective because of the many factors involved, so treatments should be used in combination.

The goal of most treatments is to stop your drinking completely, but this may be nearly impossible for extremely heavy drinkers. However, a recent study has shown that in these cases, just reduction of drinking was very beneficial to overall health when abstinence could not be achieved.

General Recommendations

Diet: Most alcoholics suffer from nutritional deficiencies and have problems processing sugar and carbohydrates. Not only that, they actually crave these substances. Consequently, other problems may develop, especially in the liver, heart, and brain. To prevent these problems, you should eat three meals a day, avoid sugars, limit other carbohydrates (especially processed foods), and eat more protein. I recommend soy protein as the best source. (See Appendix B, under "Herbs," for further information on soy products.)

Meditation: Anxiety and insomnia are common symptoms in alcoholics, but they can be significantly improved with meditation. (See "Simple Healing Steps for All Health Conditions" on page 79, under "Meditation" for specific meditations and further information.)

Your Balanced Healing Action Plan for Alcoholism

Step 1: Seek Professional Help Through an Organized Program Such as Alcoholics Anonymous

The best action you can take for alcoholism is to get professional help. However, just seeing a doctor or psychotherapist may not be enough. Start with an organized program such as Alcoholics Anonymous to help you withdraw and end addiction. If that doesn't help, there are inpatient and outpatient programs, often affiliated with major hospitals and medical centers, available throughout the U.S. for those who need more extensive treatment. You can usually find an alcohol program in your area by looking in the yellow pages, but your doctor can also advise or refer you.

These programs are essential because the risk of relapse is high unless the underlying causes are corrected and you have full support from family and friends. In fact, most of these programs recommend that your friends and family get involved because their interaction with you may be key to preventing you from drinking again. The following steps will also help you reduce the cravings and symptoms of alcoholism and make it easier for you to stop drinking—permanently.

Step 2: Take Milk Thistle to Protect Your Liver

Take the herb milk thistle (200mg to 400mg per day using a standardized extract containing 70 percent silymarin) if you are still drinking alcohol, and for at least four months after you have stopped drinking. This herb helps protect your liver from alcohol damage, and it helps your liver regenerate new cells. Milk thistle can reduce many of the complications of alcoholism, including toxic hepatitis, cirrhosis, and liver or pancreatic cancer.

Step 3: Take a Multivitamin with Extra Thiamine and Magnesium to Replace Deficiencies and Reduce Cravings

Take a multivitamin with extra thiamine (30mg to 100mg daily) and magnesium (200mg to 300mg three times daily). These two nutrients are usually deficient in alcoholics. I also recommend taking glutamine (1g per day), which has been shown to reduce your cravings for alcohol. Once you have stopped drinking for several months and start eating more balanced meals, you can stop taking these supplements.

Step 4: Take Appropriate Chinese Herbal Remedies to Prevent Withdrawal Symptoms

I next recommend the Chinese herbal formula, *Chai Hu Gui Zhi Tang*, which is effective in reducing the symptoms as well as alcohol cravings during withdrawal. Take three tablets three times daily between meals for at least one month after you have stopped drinking. Your cravings and other symptoms should ease within a few days, but you may need to take the formula longer, depending on your symptoms. (See Appendix A, under "Chinese Herbs," for further information.)

Step 5: Use Ear Acupuncture

Acupuncture can also reduce alcohol cravings, and for my patients I prescribe it along with the Chinese herbs in Step 4. Ear acupuncture, usually the most effective and easiest form, uses press tacks—small needles embedded in an adhesive bandage and pressed on specific points in the ear. The points generally used are liver, lung, kidney, zero point, a point called Shenmen, and a point called sympathetic. You massage these points several times during the day to stimulate them. These needles remain in the ear for as long as possible (on the average, one week) and are replaced when they fall out, or until you no longer crave alcohol.

Step 6: Use Interactive Imagery

Relapses are common in alcoholism, in part because of underlying psychological and family issues. Sometimes these issues can be difficult to understand. Sometimes they're not fully resolved in an alcohol program. Interactive imagery can help you understand and deal with them. In this mind-body method, you mentally interact with images that represent your emotions. (See Appendix A, under "Mind-Body Techniques," for a more detailed discussion.) It's a powerful way to uncover and deal with subconscious psychological issues of which you may not be aware.

When Sam, a 40-year-old manufacturing executive, first came to see me, he had been an alcoholic for 10 years. He had completed several alcohol programs and had joined Alcoholics Anonymous, but he continued to have relapses, especially when he became stressed. I recommended that he again attend an outpatient program, but that this time he add acupuncture press tacks and Chinese herbs to help prevent withdrawal symptoms. After Sam completed the outpatient program, he used interactive imagery to help him better understand his reasons and triggers for drinking. He has now been sober for three years.

Step 7: Take Ativan, Buspirone, Propranolol or Clonidine to Reduce Withdrawal Symptoms

If you have withdrawal symptoms as you stop drinking, there are several medications that can help. Ativan or buspirone is beneficial for tremors, sweating, and anxiety. Propranolol or clonidine can help reduce elevated heart rate or blood pressure, tremors, and elevated body temperature. If you have seizures or hallucinations, your doctor may prescribe anticonvulsant or antipsychotic drugs. If you experience depression, an antidepressant may be helpful. Bupropion is the recommended one because it will also help you stop the urge to drink.

Step 8: Take Prescription Naltrexone, Disulfiram, or Ondansetron to Prevent Relapse

If you still cannot stop drinking after trying Steps 1 through 7, it may be time to start taking a prescription medication. Naltrexone is another drug that has been used successfully to block withdrawal symptoms and make it easier for you to stop drinking. Disulfiram (Antabuse) is designed to cause adverse symptoms (such as nausea and vomiting) whenever you drink alcohol, to reduce your desire to drink. Take these medications only if you are under a doctor's care and are being monitored carefully.

Another medication, ondansetron (Zofran) has been found to be very beneficial in reducing drinking if you have early onset alcoholism (before age 25) and a history of antisocial behavior.

Step 9: Use Liver- and Blood-Cleansing Herbs to Clean Out Toxins

The liver is the organ responsible for preventing toxins from accumulating in the body and for cleaning impurities out of the blood. Alcohol not only harms the liver itself, it also interferes with the liver's cleansing functions. This damage allows toxins and impurities to build up in the liver and blood. After you stop drinking alcohol, I recommend that you undergo an herbal liver and blood cleansing.

- A good liver-cleansing formula should include some or all of the following: dandelion root, milk thistle, Picrorhiza Kurroa (a perennial herb sometimes called Kutkin), and artichoke or beet leaf.

- A good blood cleansing formula should include some or all of the following: red clover, burdock root, chaparral, periwinkle, and goldenseal.
  The cleansing process takes two to four weeks to complete.

Step 10: Take SAMe If You Have Cirrhosis

If you have alcoholic liver disease (cirrhosis) as a result of alcoholism, your body abnormally produces liver-damaging chemicals that make your condition even worse. When this is the case, I recommend taking the supplement SAMe (1,200mg to 1,600mg daily) to inhibit these chemicals.

ALLERGIC RHINITIS (Hay Fever)

An allergy is an abnormal reaction by the immune system to a substance that is usually not harmful. *Rhinitis* means that allergy symptoms affect your nose. They can vary from mild to life-threatening. You can be allergic to a host of different things, including drugs and insect stings, but the most common ailments are upper respiratory allergies caused by substances in the environment and involving the nose (rhinitis) and sinuses (sinusitis).

Common Symptoms

- Sneezing
- Wheezing
- Nasal congestion
- Coughing
- Itchy eyes or throat

Severe Symptoms

- Throat swelling
- Irregular heart rhythm
- Shock
- Difficulty breathing

What You Need to Know

Testing from an allergy specialist can determine what substances are causing your allergic responses. Make every effort to eliminate from your environment the substances that may be causing your allergies, or reduce contact with them. The most common include pollen, dander, dust mites, tobacco smoke, perfumes, and pets. Try air purifiers, electrostatic filters, and/or hypoallergenic bedding. Use a dust mask when working outside or mowing the lawn.

The best treatments for allergies are usually the alternative ones. Conventional treatments (Steps 5 and 6) can at best control allergy symptoms, and you must continuously take the treatments. However, alternative methods such as acupuncture can reduce your symptoms quickly and provide long-lasting relief.

Your Balanced Healing Action Plan for Allergic Rhinitis

Step 1: Undergo Acupuncture

Acupuncture is the fastest and most effective way that I have found to reduce or eliminate respiratory allergies. The principal points are usually found on the hands and alongside the nose. There are also supplemental points on the forehead and two allergy points in the ear. Press tacks can be placed in the ear points and left for prolonged periods of time. These are small needles that are embedded in an adhesive bandage and then pressed into specific points in the ear. The needles remain in the ear for as long as possible (a week, on average) and are replaced when they fall out. You massage these points several times during the day to stimulate them.

You should notice improvement in your symptoms within four to six acupuncture treatments, but you might need additional sessions for maximum benefits. Some people need yearly maintenance sessions to keep their allergies at bay. Always seek evaluation and treatment from a practitioner certified in acupuncture. (See Appendix A, under "Acupuncture," for guidance on finding a qualified acupuncturist and for a discussion of different acupuncture techniques.)

Step 2: Take Appropriate Chinese Herbal Remedies

I recommend using Chinese herbals in combination with acupuncture for better results. There are several different formulas that are effective for allergies, depending on whether you have asthma, a stuffy or runny nose, sinus congestion, colored sputum, or other symptoms. Common formulas are *Cang Er Zi San, Qing Bi Tang, Xiao Qing Long Tang*, and *Yu Ping Feng San*. Consult a practitioner qualified in Chinese herbal medicine to determine which Chinese herbal formulas are the best for your particular syndromes (See Appendix A, under "Chinese Herbs," for further guidance.) You should see benefits within one to three weeks, but you may get results even sooner.

Caution: Ephedra is a Chinese herb often used for allergies, but it can be dangerous. You should not take it over extended periods or in high doses.

Step 3: Take Homeopathic Remedies

If the previous steps fail to help your allergic symptoms, homeopathy may be of benefit. *Arsenicum album* (6c) can be used for runny nose, itchy throat, and sneezing; *Pulsatilla* (6c) can be used for chronic, thick mucous; and *Allium cepa* (6c) can be used for runny nose and itchy eyes. Your symptoms should be better within a few hours to a few days. Consult a qualified homeopathist for guidance on which remedies will be most beneficial and for proper dosages. (See Appendix A, under "Homeopathy," for further information.)

Step 4: Take Stinging Nettle or Butterbur

If the previous steps are not effective or give you only partial relief, the Western herb stinging nettle can be very effective for respiratory allergies. You should use freeze-dried (cryogenic) preparations one to three times daily; take 300mg to 600mg a day. An herb from Europe, butterbur (8mg total petasine taken four times daily), has recently been shown to be as effective as conventional antihistamines but without drowsiness.

Step 5: Take Conventional Antiallergy Medications

If nothing else has worked for you, then it's time to try conventional medications. There are two types for allergic rhinitis, antihistamines and nasal steroid sprays. Although most people with allergic rhinitis use antihistamines, prescription nasal steroid sprays are actually better for "as needed" allergic symptoms during allergy season because they provide longer lasting relief and work better and faster when you find yourself repeatedly exposed to the substances causing your allergic response. Prescription steroid nasal sprays such as Vancenase, Beconase, or Flonase also have minimal side effects, and Flonase is less likely to sting your nose. However, these sprays may cause cataracts with long term use, so be sure to use them only when necessary (usually during the allergy season), and have your eyes checked regularly if you must use them long term.

If nasal sprays are not effective or give you only partial relief, try over-the-counter antihistamines such as Benadryl, Tavist, Drixoral, and Dimetapp. These drugs can be as effective at reducing symptoms as prescription antihistamines, but they often cause drowsiness, can interfere with learning and decrease work productivity, and may cause prostate enlargement or recurrent bladder infections. The prescription antihistamines, such as Allegra and Claritin, cause less drowsiness, but they are much more expensive. Try the over-the-counter antihistamines first, and use a prescription medication only if these drugs cause bothersome side effects.

Step 6: Try Immunotherapy (Allergy Shots)

Immunotherapy, or allergy shots, should be considered as your last resort. This method works by injecting increasingly larger amounts of allergens into your body so that your system becomes desensitized to them and no longer overreacts in response to them. However, it may take two to five years for these shots to be effective, and the effect can wear off. Some people fail to respond to immunotherapy, but you won't know if you are among them until you take the injections for years.

> Allan, 37 years old and a semi-pro golfer, was among the unfortunate allergy sufferers who didn't respond to conventional allergy treatments. He actually had to quit playing golf because he couldn't find a way to control his severe grass allergies. He had tried almost every antihistamine and steroid spray known, as well as allergy shots, all without success. After eight acupuncture treatments, which I gave him in combination with two Chinese herbal formulas, Allan's symptoms completely disappeared. Now he takes three to five acupuncture treatments at the start of each allergy season and enjoys spending his summers on the greens—symptom free!

ALZHEIMER'S DISEASE AND DEMENTIA

Alzheimer's disease is a form of dementia, a progressive degeneration of nerve tissue in the brain. It is thought to be caused by the buildup of plaque-like material and by nerve fibers that become tangled. These tangles and plaques are basically scars, composed of various unusable proteins and cell debris that end up choking and killing large areas of brain cells. Although there is no cure, there are many treatments that can slow the disease down.

Common Symptoms

- Mood changes
- Loss of memory and cognitive functions
- Depression
- Paranoia
- Agitation
- Anxiety
- Childish behavior
- Confusion
- Disorientation
- Inattention
- Dizziness

What You Need to Know

Estrogen has been shown to possibly help prevent dementia, so, if you are a woman, you should consider bioidentical estrogen replacement after menopause (see the section on "Menopause" on page 279 for specific recommendations on natural hormone replacement). If you have high cholesterol, the use of statin medications (such as Lipitor, Mevacor, and Pravachol) dramatically reduces the risk of dementia, whereas other cholesterol-lowering drugs do not (see the section on high cholesterol on page 168 for information on treatment using statins). High blood pressure (especially the systolic, or top number, reading) also increases the risk of Alzheimer's, so blood pressure control will help prevent dementia (for treatment recommendations, see the section on high blood pressure on page 244).

Keeping your brain active and engaged as you age has also been found to prevent dementia and Alzheimer's. Information-processing activities seem the most helpful; these include watching television; listening to the radio; reading newspapers, magazines, or books; playing games or solving puzzles; and visiting museums. The more of these activities you do, the less chance you have of developing dementia.

General Recommendations

Diet: Most biological processes in the brain require oxidation, which can produce byproducts called *free radicals*. These free radicals can harm brain cells and contribute to the scarring we see in Alzheimer's. Antioxidants, found in certain foods, especially fruits and vegetables, can neutralize free radicals. These foods can slow and sometimes help reverse the memory loss caused by the free-radical damage in Alzheimer's. Foods containing vitamin E and vitamin C have been shown to reduce the risk of dementia. B vitamins and folate are also important, so green leafy vegetables are especially good, as well as eggs, low-fat dairy, and low-fat meats. Omega-3 fatty acids from cold-water fish (such as mackerel, tuna, halibut, cod, trout, and salmon) may help fight inflammation in the brain caused by the clumps of protein.

In addition, I recommend light-to-moderate intake of alcohol. A recent study showed that alcohol can lower the risk of dementia. Any type of alcohol (not only red wine) has this effect. It is not known whether alcohol will improve your symptoms once you have dementia, but it may slow down the progress of the disease. However, high alcohol intake causes more harm than good, so you should limit your intake to not more than two drinks per night.

Your Balanced Healing Action Plan for Alzheimer's Disease

For moderately advanced Alzheimer's, begin with Step 2, and then return to Step 1.

Step 1: Take Nutritional Supplements and Herbs in Early Alzheimer's

Nutritional supplements and herbs can improve mental function. I recommend taking the following:

- Vitamin B_{12}, 1,000mcg twice daily (if blood tests show that you have a vitamin B_{12} deficiency)
- Vitamin E, 800 IU once daily
- Vitamin C, 1,000mg to 2,000mg once daily
- L-carnitine, 500mg three times daily
- Gingko biloba, 240mg daily (make sure the product you take contains at least 24 percent flavonglycosides, which is necessary for it to be effective).
- Huperzine A, an ingredient derived from Chinese club moss, 50mcg to 200mcg twice daily. Take all these vitamins/supplements/herbs together. Allow up to eight weeks to see improvement, although you may see results sooner.

Step 2: Take the Prescription Drugs Donepezil, Rivastigmine, Metrifonate, Phosphatidylserine, or Galantamine

If symptoms progress, your doctor can prescribe donepezil (Aricept) or rivastigmine (Exelon), both of which improve thinking functions. If these are not effective, your doctor may recommend metrifonate as the next conventional drug to take. And if none of these drugs helps, the next medication is phosphatidylserine, 100mg three times a day, which can improve mental performance, behavior, and mood in people who have dementia or Alzheimer's. A newer medication, galantamine, has shown benefit in Alzheimer's patients who also have cerebrovascular disease (hardening of the brain arteries).

Tacrine hydrochloride (Cognex) is a conventional drug that has been shown to delay the progression of Alzheimer's by six months. However, this drug causes liver toxicity, which must be monitored closely. Try this medication only if you're dealing with dementia that doesn't respond to other drugs and treatments.

Step 3: Enroll in Reality Orientation Therapy

Reality orientation therapy improves thinking functions. This is a process that strives to reorient the person to time, place, and person. It is often effective, in combination with the previous steps, in people who have moderate to severe dementia. Consult a doctor or clinic that specializes in Alzheimer's treatment for this type of therapy.

Step 4: Take Magnesium and Malic Acid

Because chronic aluminum exposure has been implicated as a cause of Alzheimer's, it may be helpful to take a combination of magnesium (200mg to 400mg daily) and malic acid (800mg to 1,200mg daily) if the previous steps don't help. Magnesium blocks the absorption of aluminum from the body, and malic acid binds and removes aluminum. You many have to take these supplements for several months before you see any benefit.

ANGINA

Angina is chest pain caused by the heart tissues not getting enough oxygen. This is usually a result of atherosclerosis, a buildup of cholesterol-containing material that blocks the heart arteries. The most common type of angina is called *stable angina*, characterized by chest pain primarily upon exertion (usually relieved by the drug nitroglycerin). In *unstable angina*, the symptoms are worse, more frequent, and pain may occur with light activities or even at rest, which is a sign of impending disaster. A rarer form of angina is called *Prinzmetal* or *variant angina*, occurs mostly in women, and is caused by spasm of the heart arteries rather than blockage.

Common Symptoms

- Squeezing or pressure-like pain in the chest that may radiate down the arm or to the jaw
- Indigestion-type symptoms
- Shortness of breath

What You Need to Know

Angina itself causes no permanent damage, but it is a sign that the heart is diseased. Not treating the angina and underlying heart disease can lead to heart attack and death. If you smoke cigarettes, stop, because the heart arteries cannot heal if you continue smoking (see the section on nicotine addiction on page 311 for helpful guidelines). Also avoid excessive coffee drinking, which can worsen angina. If you have high cholesterol, you must reduce it to normal to stop clogging your heart arteries (see the section on cholesterol on page 168 for guidelines).

General Recommendations

Diet: In addition to eating a balanced diet, you need to increase dietary fiber (eat more veggies) and eat at least two meals of fish per week (cold-water fish such as mackerel, salmon, halibut, tuna, herring, or cod) to reduce or prevent cholesterol buildup in the heart arteries. Avoid, or at least limit, saturated fats, foods high in cholesterol, and animal proteins, all of which increase cholesterol buildup in the heart arteries. I also recommend drinking one glass of wine daily with meals. Wine, especially red, has powerful antioxidant properties.

Exercise: Exercise is important because it helps you improve the ability of your cells to use oxygen efficiently, which reduces symptoms. Before starting an exercise program, however, you should have an exercise tolerance test (ETT) to determine your safe exercise level. On the basis of the test results, your doctor can advise you on a carefully graded, progressive aerobic exercise program.

Your Balanced Healing Action Plan for Unstable Angina

- **Unstable angina is considered an emergency and you should see a physician immediately.** Cardiac catheterization should be done, and if there is significant blockage of the heart arteries, the following steps are recommended:

Step 1: Procedures for Unstable Angina

There are three procedures that can be done for unstable angina if you have blockage of your heart arteries:

- *Angioplasty* involves using a catheter to clean out the artery.
- *Stenting* is a procedure that places a small device that holds the artery walls open to increase blood flow. This procedure is commonly used with specific drugs to improve survival rate. Additional external radiation is often used with this procedure to activate substances in the catheter/stent to prevent recurrences of the blockage.
- *Coronary artery bypass grafting* (CABG) involves major surgery to open the chest and replace clogged arteries with veins taken from the legs. A recent study showed that CABG may be slightly better than angioplasty to reduce symptoms, but only in the hands of a skilled surgeon.

The choice from these three procedures depends on the skills and experience of your cardiologist, the condition of your heart arteries, and other medical conditions that you may have. Even though these procedures will reduce your symptoms, they alone do not prolong life. Once your angina is stabilized, you should use the steps described under "Stable Angina" (below) and "General Recommendations" (above).

If you undergo angioplasty or stenting, your doctor will probably prescribe the medication clopidogrel (Plavix) with an aspirin every day to reduce your risk of heart attack. Also take B vitamins and fish oil to reduce the risk of the artery reclogging. Take the following:

- Fish oil, 1,000mg daily
- Folic acid, 1mg daily
- Vitamin B_{12}, 400mcg daily

- Vitamin B_6, 10mg daily

However, DO NOT TAKE antioxidant vitamins, C, E, and beta-carotene, because they interfere with the artery repair process following angioplasty.

Step 2: Take N-Acetylcysteine with Nitroglycerin

If you already have unstable angina, you probably have taken nitroglycerin to reduce your symptoms. Adding N-acetylcysteine (600mg three times daily) to transdermal nitroglycerin has been found to be very beneficial in stabilizing angina in many people. It can be tried if the above procedures are not done or do not fully reduce your anginal symptoms. However, headaches can occur with nitroglycerin and can become even more severe with the addition of N-acetylcysteine.

Step 3: Undergo Heparin Treatment

In the first 30 days of an unstable anginal attack, injecting the drug low-molecular-weight heparin (LMWH) is beneficial in preventing a heart attack, but beyond the 30 days, the benefit is less clear. You should consult your cardiologist to find out whether you are a candidate, and, if so, how much you should take and for how long.

Step 4: Take Aspirin and Vitamin C Daily

Aspirin reduces the risk of heart attack and death in unstable angina. You should take no more than 325mg per day because increased doses can cause harm, and they provide no additional benefit (81mg is a sufficient dose). Aspirin may cause bleeding complications if taken with LMWH. If you are sensitive or allergic to aspirin, your doctor may prescribe the drug ticlopidine instead for the same effect. Take vitamin C, 600mg per day, to maintain your body's stores of vitamin C (which aspirin depletes).

Caution: Ibuprofen blocks the blood-thinning effects of aspirin, so try not to take it if you are taking aspirin. If you must take ibuprofen, take the aspirin first, and wait at least an hour to take the ibuprofen, and take the lowest ibuprofen dose you can.

Your Balanced Healing Action Plan for Stable Angina

- Intravenous chelation therapy has been used by thousands of patients with angina, many of whom have reported resolution of most or all symptoms. Currently, there have been no definitive studies that prove intravenous chelation's benefits for angina, only these anecdotal reports. In fact, in a recent double-blind study, IV chelation was no better than placebo. The cost is approximately $2,500 to $4,000 and is not covered by insurance. I do not recommend this form of chelation at this time. If you desire chelation anyway, go to Step 7 for an alternative.

Step 1: Take the Appropriate Prescription Medications

Because angina can become unstable if not controlled properly, I recommend beginning with the conventional medications that have been proven effective. I would then try the following steps, and if your symptoms are improved, then it will be safer for you to decrease the dosages or stop taking these conventional drugs, with the guidance of your doctor.

- **For acute anginal symptoms that occur occasionally,** your doctor can prescribe nitrates, such as nitroglycerin tablets under the tongue (sublingual) or as a spray. Oral or transdermal (skin patch) nitrates can be used longer term, but you can develop a resistance, which decreases their effectiveness. This problem may be reversed by taking vitamin E (200 IU three times daily) so that you can continue using these medications.
- **For chronic angina,** your doctor may prescribe beta-blockers (such as propranolol, atenolol, metoprolol, or nadolol) or calcium channel blockers (such as dihydropy-ridine, diphenylalklylamine, or benzothiazepine), to provide long-term relief or prevention of your symptoms. These drug types may be used together, depending on the severity and frequency of the angina. The particular formulation and dosage should be determined with your physician.

These drugs should reduce anginal symptoms very quickly (usually within a few days), which is another reason I recommend them first. Beta-blockers can also help prevent heart attacks, so they serve two good purposes. But in some men, beta-blockers can cause HDL cholesterol to drop to harmfully low levels (less than 35mg/dl). If this side effect occurs, you should take chromium picolinate, 200mcg three times per day, which can increase HDL levels by 10 percent.

Step 2: Take L-Carnitine and Coenzyme Q10 (CoQ10)

If you still have anginal symptoms that Step 1 does not fully control, you can take L-car-nitine (500mg three times daily) and/or Coenzyme Q10 (CoQ10) (150mg to 300mg daily) in combination with prescription drug therapies. These supplements allow the heart to utilize oxygen more efficiently. It may take several weeks to notice improvement. If these supplements improve your symptoms, you may then be able to reduce the dosages of your prescription medications. However, consult with your doctor before doing so.

> Jason, a 55-year-old engineer, would get chest pain whenever he performed strenuous activities such as mowing his lawn, or his favorite hobby, wood-working. He was taking both a beta-blocker and a calcium channel blocker, which controlled his angina until he did something strenuous. When the angina occurred, nitroglycerin and rest relieved the pain, but he wanted to be able to perform his activities without having to stop all the time. I placed him on a Balanced Healing Diet, L-carnitine, and CoQ10. After one month, he was able to start walking up to five miles on a regular basis and do his wood-working without having to take nitroglycerin. After two months, Jason was able to discontinue the calcium channel blocker, but he did continue taking the beta-blocker, primarily to prevent heart attacks in the future.

Step 3: Take L-Arginine

If your symptoms continue after trying Step 2, you can take L-arginine (3g three times a day), which improves symptoms and cardiac function in patients with angina by augmenting nitric oxide in the blood (thus helping open their arteries). You can take this supplement along with the supplements in Step 2 to further improve your condition.

Step 4: Take Magnesium for Prinzmetal Angina

If spasm of the heart blood vessels (Prinzmetal angina) causes your symptoms, take magnesium, 200mg to 400mg three times daily.

Step 5: Take the Herbs Hawthorn and Khella for Heart Failure with Angina

Many people who have angina also have heart failure (see the section on heart disease for specific recommendations for treating heart failure). Once your heart failure is controlled by conventional medications, consider taking hawthorn, an herb that dilates coronary arteries and thus improves oxygen flow to the heart. Hawthorn can be beneficial if you have angina along with NYHA (New York Heart Association) Stage I or Stage II heart failure, in which you are comfortable at rest but ordinary physical activity results in fatigue, palpitation, breathing problems, or angina. However, if used with other conventional heart medications, hawthorn can possibly either increase the effect or interfere with these medications, so check with your doctor before taking it. The dosage is 100mg to 250mg of extract containing 1.8 percent vitexin-4'rhamnoside or 10 percent procyanidin content, three times a day.

Another herb, khella, dilates the coronary blood vessels. Khella may be beneficial if the above medications are not helpful, or in combination with them if they are only partially effective. Dosage is 100mg of powdered extract containing 12 percent khellin, three times daily. These herbs may take several weeks to reduce anginal symptoms, although you may observe results even sooner.

Step 6: For Continued Angina, Add Homeopathic Remedies

Homeopathic remedies, such as *Nux vomica* or *Arsenicum album*, can sometimes relieve angina that fails to respond to other measures. You should consult a qualified homeopathist for guidance on which remedies will be most beneficial and on proper dosages. Your symptoms should improve within one to two weeks. (See Appendix A, under "Homeopathy," for guidance on finding a qualified homeopathist.)

Step 7: Take Malic Acid or Cilantro for Prevention or Recurrence of Angina

Many alternative practitioners believe that various metals accumulate in our bodies and cause atherosclerosis and angina. They recommend intravenous chelation, a process in which a specific substance (called EDTA) is injected into your bloodstream and binds to these metals and helps the body dispose of them. However, intravenous chelation is expensive and has not been proven effective. If the previous steps are only partially effective, I recommend using herbs that can chelate. Although no studies have been done on these herbs, they are generally not harmful, so they're worth a try. Malic acid (800mg to 1200mg daily) is particularly useful for removing aluminum from the body.

Cilantro is excellent for cleaning all heavy metals out of the blood. Use the following recipe: Blend one cup of fresh cilantro with six tablespoons of olive oil until the cilantro is completely chopped. Add one clove of garlic, one-half cup of nuts (cashews or almonds are the best), and two tablespoons of lemon juice. Blend these into a paste (which will be lumpy), adding hot water if necessary. Take two to three teaspoons per day for two to three weeks, every few months. If you make large amounts, you can freeze the mixture for later use. You should see benefits within two to three weeks.

ANXIETY

Anxiety is an unpleasant emotional state that can range from mild unease to intense fear. When there is a threat of some type, anxiety is a normal response, but when there is no clear or realistic cause, anxiety is not normal. Serious anxiety disorders include panic attacks, phobias, obsessive-compulsive disorders, post-traumatic stress syndrome, "free floating" anxiety (an unexplainable feeling of apprehension that can last for months), and generalized anxiety disorder (GAD), defined as excessive worry on most days for at least six months, with some of the physical symptoms listed below. Chronic anxiety can underlie or worsen many diseases, including heart disease, hypertension, ulcers, headaches, irritable bowel syndrome, psoriasis, and insomnia, to name just a few. It can also worsen symptoms of most medical conditions.

Common Symptoms

- Heart palpitations
- Sense of impending doom
- Shortness of breath
- Inability to concentrate
- Muscle tension
- Diarrhea
- Chest pain
- Muscle aches
- Dry mouth
- Cold hands
- Trembling
- Excessive sweating
- Insomnia
- Irritability
- Restlessness
- Eating disorders

What You Need to Know

Identifying and eliminating any sources of stress is the ideal treatment for anxiety, but doing so is unrealistic in most cases because you may not have control over the stresses in your life. Therefore, it's important to cope with stress in a positive manner, and to protect your body from the harmful effects of stress.

General Recommendations

Diet: Good nutrition helps the body's cells to adapt better to stress, so a balanced diet is important to maintain balanced health in the face of stress. Increased lactic acid levels may be an underlying factor in anxiety and panic attacks, so eliminating nutritional factors that increase lactic acid may help reduce anxiety significantly. These factors include caffeine, alcohol, and sugar.

Exercise: Studies have shown that people who exercise are able to reduce their tensions and worries, improve their mood, and improve their ability to handle stressful life situations. I recommend both aerobic and anaerobic exercises. (See "Simple Healing Steps for All Health Conditions," on page 79, under "Exercise," for further information and guidance.)

Meditation: Any form of meditation is helpful to reduce anxiety. Not only does meditation relax you, it also helps prevent the harmful effects of anxiety on the body. And it allows you to better understand what is causing your stress—and how to deal with it more effectively. The more anxious you are, the longer or more frequently you should meditate. (See Appendix A, under "Mind-Body Techniques," and "Simple Healing Steps for All Health Conditions," on page 79, under "Meditation," for specific meditations and further information.)

Qigong: Qigong is very effective for reducing anxiety and relaxing the body through its breathing and movement exercises. (See "Simple Healing Steps for All Health Conditions," on page 79, under "Qigong" for more information.) There is a particular Qigong exercise that is excellent for reducing anxiety and can be completed in 16 minutes. (See Appendix C under "Qigong" for reference information.)

Your Balanced Healing Action Plan for Anxiety

- For moderately severe anxiety (anxiety that is significantly interfering with your daily activities), start with Step 1 in conjunction with Step 2 or Step 7, and then return to Step 2.
- Deficiency of several B vitamins, calcium, and/or magnesium can occur from the increased lactic acid caused by stress, so supplement these if your anxiety is chronic. I recommend taking a good multivitamin. (See Appendix B for further information on choosing multivitamins.)

Step 1: Use Interactive Imagery Techniques or Other Forms of Psychotherapy

Psychotherapy with a professional is essential for dealing with anxiety, especially if you cannot eliminate the sources of your stress and/or need to learn how to cope with them.

I also recommend interactive imagery, which uses both meditation and imagery to reduce and help you cope with anxiety. This is a mind-body method in which you mentally interact with images that represent your emotions. It's a powerful way to uncover and deal with subconscious psychological issues of which you may not be aware. (See Appendix A, under "Mind-Body Techniques," for a more detailed explanation.)

If interactive imagery is not available, other forms of psychotherapy are helpful, and I recommend using a licensed counselor, social worker, or psychologist, depending on your finances and the severity of your anxiety. Psychotherapy may take several months or even years to help reduce anxiety, but it's essential for long-term relief, because you have to understand and learn to deal with the underlying causes. The remaining steps can be used with psychotherapy.

Step 2: Take Appropriate Chinese Herbal Remedies

A Chinese herbal formula called *Ding Xin Wan*, one to three tablets three times daily, can be very helpful in controlling anxiety. Other formulas can be helpful as well. If you have mild depression along with your anxiety, I recommend trying a formula called *Gui Pi Wan*. Of the single Chinese herbs, American ginseng (200mg to 600mg capsules per day, or 1,600mg extract) enhances your resistance to stress and your ability to cope with both physical and mental stressors. It also gives you a general sense of well being. Ginseng can be taken with the above Chinese herbal formulas.

The advantages of Chinese herbs over conventional medications are that they have fewer side effects and they improve, not impair, your mental abilities. Consult a practitioner qualified in Chinese herbal medicine to determine which formulas are the best for your particular syndromes. You should notice improvement within three weeks (sometimes within a few days, depending on the formula), but you may need to take them longer, depending on your condition. (See Appendix A, under "Chinese Herbs," for further information.)

Step 3: Take the Western Herbal Remedies Kava Kava, Valerian Root, and/or St. John's Wort

If Chinese herbs are not helpful, try kava kava (45mg to 70mg of kavalactones three times daily). (See Appendix A for warnings about kava kava.) This herb is helpful for general anxiety. Valerian root (up to 400mg per night) can help both sleep at night and anxiety during the day, so it's recommended if anxiety keeps you from sleeping at night. If you have both anxiety and depression, there are some herbal combinations that include kava, Valerian and St. John's wort; they can be found in most health food stores. All these herbs work by stabilizing various neurotransmitters in the brain. These herbs (and combinations) should work within a few days.

Step 4: Undergo Massage

Massage is excellent for reducing mild anxiety states, and you can use it along with all other treatments. Swedish massage is the form with which most Americans are familiar, and uses gentle pressure to relax the muscles. Another popular form of massage is Shiatsu (from the Japanese words *shi*, "finger," and *atsu*, "pressure"). I recommend either one for general anxiety, but there are other forms that can be just as effective. (See Appendix A, under "Manual Therapy," for more information.) Massage can give you immediate relief, although it is usually short-lived.

Step 5: Use Hypnosis for Phobias and General Anxiety Disorder (GAD)

For phobias, and some general anxiety states, hypnosis is very effective. Two to six sessions are usually enough for you to know whether this method is bringing you relief, so it is worth a try, especially if the above steps have not been effective. (See Appendix A, under "Mind-Body Techniques," for more information on hypnosis.)

Step 6: Take Flaxseed Oil for Phobias

For some phobias, such as *agoraphobia* (fear of being alone or in public places), many people improve with flaxseed oil (two to six tablespoons daily for two to three months). Agoraphobia is thought to be due to a deficiency in alpha-linoleic acid (omega-3), which can also cause dry skin, dandruff, brittle fingernails, and nerve disorders in people who have agoraphobia. It may take several weeks to a few months to notice improvement.

Step 7: Take Prescription Antianxiety Medications

For anxiety that is more moderate to severe—or that has not responded to the previous steps—you need prescription antianxiety medications. Buspirone (BuSpar) has slower onset of action but fewer side effects than the benzodiazepines (such as Valium or Xanax); it's usually the first choice. For GAD, many antidepressants (Tofranil, Desyrel, or Paxil) have been shown to be superior to benzodiazepines. Your physician needs to determine which medications and what dosages are most likely to be effective for you. You should take medications in conjunction with counseling, not in place of it. Expect results within a few hours after taking antianxiety medications, but it may take up to three weeks if you take antidepressants.

> Becky, a 48-year-old airline executive, had recurrent anxiety caused by issues at work and with her family, as well as by going through menopause. She had taken kava kava, but it did not help. I put her on a Chinese herbal formula, *Ding Xin Wan*, but it helped only partially. So I then prescribed BuSpar, which controlled most of the symptoms, and I referred her for interactive imagery. After two months, she was able to stop taking the BuSpar and needed *Ding Xin Wan* only on an occasional basis.

Step 8: Take Appropriate Homeopathic Remedies

For specific causes of anxiety, homeopathy can be useful. If you're upset from a recent loss, try Ignatia. For stage fright or agoraphobia (fear of public places), use *Gelsemium*. You should consult a qualified homeopathist for guidance on which remedies will be most beneficial and for proper dosages. You should notice improvement in one to two weeks. (See Appendix A, under "Homeopathy," for guidance on finding a qualified homeopathist.)

Step 9: Use Other Natural Remedies Such as Flower Essences and Aromatherapy

Other natural treatments, including Bach flower remedies and aromatherapy, can help reduce anxiety. Bach remedies are designed to treat a particular emotional condition using essences from specific flowers. Aromatherapy uses your sense of smell to affect your emotions. The oils of lavender, jasmine, or blue chamomile are the most common aromatherapy products used for anxiety. Although these products can be found in health food and candle stores, there are practitioners who have been trained specifically in aromatherapy treatment and can give you more specific treatment with combinations of ingredients that cannot be found in stores. For flower remedies, most herbalists have this kind of expertise, and I recommend that you consult with them. Although you can expect to experience some benefits immediately, long-term relief may take several weeks. (See Appendix A, under "Aromatherapy" and "Flower Remedies," for further information.)

ARTHRITIS (see *Osteoarthritis* or *Rheumatoid Arthritis*)

ASTHMA

Asthma is primarily an allergic disorder, characterized by spasms of the bronchi (the large airway tubes of the lungs), swelling of the lining of these airways, and production of thick mucous. This results in obstruction of airflow and hyper-responsiveness of the airways. Asthma attacks can occur episodically, triggered by both environmental (allergic) and emotional triggers. It can also be brought on by exercise. Asthma can severely limit everyday activities and can lead to the inability to breathe. A severe asthma attack can be fatal.

Common Symptoms

- Shortness of breath
- Chest tightness
- Coughing
- Sputum production
- Wheezing

What You Need to Know

Because allergens are a source and cause of asthmatic attacks, make every effort to eliminate them from your environment. They include pollen, dander, dust mites, tobacco smoke, and some pets. Hypoallergenic bedding, air purifiers, and electrostatic filters help. Learn as much as you can about asthma because if you can manage your asthma, you significantly reduce the likelihood that you will need urgent or unscheduled medical care. Many local hospitals and pulmonary (lung) specialists provide asthma education programs.

Asthma can also be caused or initiated by acid reflux (GERD or heartburn). The acid in the esophagus can be inhaled into the lungs, causing irritation. If you have GERD, obtaining appropriate treatment can reverse or reduce asthmatic symptoms (see the section on heartburn on page 234 for treatment guidelines).

A recent initial study showed that hormone replacement therapy (primarily synthetic estrogen, but also synthetic progesterone) appears to worsen asthma, especially in women who had asthma before menopause. If you have severe or uncontrolled asthma that may have worsened with hormone replacement, stop taking the hormones to see whether your asthma improves, or replace them with natural hormones (see the section on menopause on page 279 for further guidelines).

General Recommendations

Diet: Studies have shown that a vegetarian diet, rich in vitamins E, A, and C, can provide significant relief for most asthma patients, but it takes at least one year to experience benefits. Broccoli contains selenium and magnesium, both of which are able to reduce asthma symptoms. Lycopene, found in tomatoes, autumn olives (an Asian fruit that tastes like cranberries), pink grapefruit, and watermelon may protect against asthma, especially exercise-induced asthma. Increased omega-3 fatty acids found in cold-water fish (mackerel, salmon, herring, trout, cod, tuna, and halibut) can also reduce the frequency of asthma attacks. If you are overweight, losing weight can significantly improve your asthma. Some food allergies can play a role in asthma, with immediate or delayed reactions. Foods commonly associated with immediate sensitivity include eggs, fish, shellfish, and nuts. Foods associated with delayed-onset asthma include milk, chocolate, wheat, citrus, and food colorings. Food additives should also be avoided. White wine has recently been shown to improve lung function due to its antioxidant effects. Red wine also helps, but not as much as white.

Exercise: Most people with asthma can safely exercise at intensities of 50 percent to 60 percent of maximum predicted heart rate (see "Simple Healing Steps for All Health Conditions" on page 79, under "Exercise" to determine your safe exercise heart rate). However, your safe level of exercise depends on your symptoms and the condition of your muscles (if you haven't exercised in a long time, you need to start much slower and build up). You should avoid exercise in polluted areas—don't jog along busy streets. Often, taking asthma medication (Step 1) before exercise is necessary. Some sports have differing triggering thresholds. For example, swimming triggers asthma attacks less than running or cycling. Consult a pulmonary specialist for individual recommendations.

Meditation: Meditation results in fewer and less severe episodes of shortness of breath through relaxation of the bronchial and chest muscles. (See Appendix A, under "Mind-Body Information," for more information.)

Your Balanced Healing Action Plan for Acute Asthma Attacks

■ **For severe asthma attacks that do not respond to your usual medications, go immediately to an emergency room.** You should seek care from a pulmonary specialist rather than a primary care physician. You may need to start with Step 13, and then return to Step 1 when your asthma stabilizes.

Your Balanced Healing Action Plan for Chronic Asthma

Step 1: Use Prescription Inhalers

Because asthma can be a life-threatening disease, you should always start with conventional medications to get it under control. Inhaled bronchodilators, called *beta-agonists*, open up the bronchiolar airways and are the mainstay of treatment for asthma. There are both short-acting inhalers (such as albuterol) and long-acting inhalers (such as salmeterol). If you have mild, intermittent asthma, short-acting inhalers are usually recommended only when you have an attack, not on a regular basis. If you have mild, *persistent* asthma, low-dose inhaled steroids are more effective than beta-agonists. However, they can be used together at the same time if either is not completely effective. (There is now a combination steroid/long-acting beta-agonist inhaler available for those who need both.) A long-acting inhaler is useful for nighttime asthma. Inhaled steroids used long term do cause bone loss, so take the lowest possible dose, and obtain bone scans to monitor for osteoporosis if you use them all the time (see the section on osteoporosis on page 326 for further guidelines if you already have this condition).

Step 2: Take Prescription Leukotriene Modifiers

Leukotriene modifiers (montelukast, zafirlukast, zileuton) are drugs that stabilize certain cells that, when irritated, can induce asthmatic attacks. They are usually the next line of treatment and are most often used with the two medications in Step 1. They are usually taken once or twice a day.

Oral medication to dilate the bronchial tubes, such as theophylline, can be used in place of or with inhaled bronchodilators if symptoms are not adequately controlled, but this is a fourth-choice medication. Blood levels of theophylline should be monitored on a regular basis to avoid toxicity (which is characterized by nausea, vomiting, headache, irritability, fast heart beat, and convulsions).

Step 3: Undergo Acupuncture for Long-Term Relief

After your asthma is stabilized, I recommend that you use acupuncture to reduce asthma attacks and your need for asthmatic medication. Principal points are usually found on the upper back, chest, hands, and wrists. There is also an effective ear acupuncture point called the Stop Wheezing (asthma) point. Always seek evaluation and treatment from a practitioner certified in acupuncture. (See Appendix A, under "Acupuncture," for guidance on finding a qualified acupuncturist and for further explanation of different acupuncture techniques.)

You should experience improvement within six acupuncture treatments, but you might need additional sessions for maximum benefits. If acupuncture is effective, you may be able to reduce or stop taking the prescription medications in Steps 1 and 2 (but consult with your physician first).

> When Deborah, a high school honor student, came to see me for her severe asthma, she was using two inhalers and taking two oral medications. I treated her using acupuncture. After four treatments, she was able to discontinue her oral medications and one inhaler. She needed to use the other inhaler only occasionally.

Step 4: Take Appropriate Chinese Herbal Remedies

Chinese herbal formulas are effective in reducing many symptoms of asthma, especially mucous production, coughing, and wheezing. They are often used in conjunction with acupuncture for faster results. The most common formula is *Ren Shen Ge Jie San*, but there are many others; the choice depends on the underlying pattern.

Consult a practitioner qualified in Chinese herbal medicine to determine which Chinese herbal formulas are the best for your particular syndromes (See Appendix A, under "Chinese Herbs"). Some practitioners use ephedra (Ma huang), which is a potent bronchodilator, but it can be dangerous in high doses and can worsen hypertension and angina. Chinese herbal formulas may take three to six weeks to have a beneficial effect.

Step 5: Take Vitamin C, Magnesium, B-Complex Vitamins, and Grapeseed Extract

If you still have asthmatic symptoms, take the following:

- Vitamin C, 10mg to 30mg daily for every two pounds of body weight
- Magnesium (200mg to 400mg three times per day)
- B-complex vitamins (Use a product that contains at least the Recommended Daily Amounts of all the B vitamins.)
- Grapeseed extract, 50mg to 100mg of 95 percent PCO content three times a day or green tea extract, 200mg to 300mg of 50 percent polyphenol content, three times a day

The benefits of these supplements derive from their antioxidant effects, with magnesium acting as a bronchodilator. They also inhibit formation and release of chemicals in the body that cause allergic reactions, such as histamine. You can take these supplements safely along with the medications in Steps 1 and 2. If you have exercise-induced asthma, add Lycopene, 5mg to 15mg daily. These supplements may take one to two months to provide benefits.

Step 6: Practice the Yoga Pigeon and Cobra Postures

Yoga can help you learn to breathe deeply and relax, helping you cope with stress factors that can initiate asthma attacks.

- The Pigeon posture may enhance breathing. Start at a kneeling position and slide your left leg straight behind you. Take a deep breath and stretch your torso while arching your back slightly. Hold this position for 20 to 30 seconds, breathing deeply during this time. Exhale and relax, and then repeat with the other leg.
- The Cobra posture can ease wheezing. Lie face down, placing both forearms on the floor, your elbows directly under your shoulders. Inhale and push your chest upward, straightening your arms, while keeping your pelvis against the ground. Hold this posture for 15 seconds, breathing deeply, and then slowly relax.

It may take several months to observe results from yoga. Consult a qualified yoga instructor for guidance on which postures are the best and how to perform them correctly. (See Appendix A for more information on yoga techniques.)

Step 7: Use Music Therapy to Improve Breath Control

Music therapy that involves blowing a wind instrument improves breath control and can be quite helpful to increase lung capacity and reduce asthmatic attacks. Consult with your doctor to see if there are such programs available in your area. Expect improvement within one to three months.

Step 8: Take Prescription Cromolyn Sodium

For continued asthma problems or increased severity, prescription cromolyn sodium is beneficial in stabilizing the lung membranes and is often used along with the above steps.

Step 9: Take the Ayurvedic Herbs Boswellia Serrate, Solanum Xanthocarpum, or Solanum Trilobatum

Ayurvedic herbs have also been used with some success in reducing asthmatic symptoms. The most common is *Boswellia serrate gum*. *Solanum xanthocarpum* or *Solanum trilobatum* improves breathing and can be used if symptoms are still present. Consult a qualified Ayurvedic practitioner for guidance on the best herbs for your condition and the proper dosages. (See Appendix A, under "Ayurvedic Medicine," for more information.) It may take three to six weeks to notice improvement.

Step 10: Take Appropriate Homeopathic Remedies

For certain factors that induce asthma attacks, you can use homeopathic remedies. For example, for symptoms that worsen at night or during cold weather, or that occur suddenly, take *Aconite* (6c). If your symptoms are made worse by dampness, *Natrum Sulphuricum* (6c) can be helpful. You should consult a qualified homeopathist for guidance on which remedies will be most beneficial and for proper dosages. You should notice improvement within a few hours for acute symptoms and a few weeks for chronic symptoms. (See Appendix A, under "Homeopathy," for guidance on finding a qualified homeopathist.)

Step 11: Use the Nambudripad Allergy Elimination Treatment (NAET)

Sometimes, allergies to food may be triggering your asthmatic attacks. If food allergies are thought to play a role in your asthma or attacks of asthma, I recommend that you undergo the Nambudripad Allergy Elimination Treatment. It combines acupuncture, kinesiology, chiropractic, herbs, and nutrition to desensitize you to foods to which you are allergic. It may take several months for its effectiveness to be observed, depending on how many allergens are sensitizing you. (See Appendix A, under "NAET," and the section on food allergies for a more detailed discussion.)

Step 12: Try Immunotherapy (Allergy Shots)

For asthma caused by identifiable allergens, immunotherapy is sometimes effective if the above steps are not. It works by injecting increasingly larger amounts of allergens into your body so that your system becomes desensitized to them and no longer overreacts in response to them. However, it may take two to five years for these shots to be effective, and they can lose their effectiveness. Not all people respond to immunotherapy, but you may not find out that you are one of them until you have taken them for years.

Step 13: Take Prescription Corticosteroids

For resistant asthma or severe attacks, corticosteroids may be necessary to decrease continued allergic and inflammatory responses. Corticosteroid use can increase levels of blood sugar (glucose), but this effect can be reversed by taking chromium, 200mcg three times daily. I recommend this as a last resort because steroids can be quite harmful to the body when used long term. These drugs can cause weight gain, osteoporosis, fatigue, suppression of the immune system, and a variety of other problems.

ATHEROSCLEROSIS (see *Cholesterol*)

ATTENTION DEFICIT DISORDER (ADD)

Attention Deficit Disorder, or ADD, is the inability to focus or concentrate for extended periods of time. People who have ADD have learning disabilities with inappropriately brief attention spans and poor concentration. A variation that includes hyperactivity is called ADHD (Attention Deficit and Hyperactivity Disorder). These conditions primarily occur in children and affect 10 times as many boys as girls. Without treatment, children are unable to learn appropriately, and this problem can have significant and long-term implications, even into adulthood. Adults also can have attention deficit disorders, but they are usually less intense and many do not discover that they have them until later in life.

Common Symptoms

- Continual failure to pay attention
- Difficulties with schoolwork
- Excessive distractibility
- Impulsiveness
- Disorganization
- Hyperactivity

What You Need To Know

A proper diagnosis is of the utmost importance. Many children are misdiagnosed and get unnecessary treatment with powerful medications. What causes ADD? We have a few answers. Frequent childhood infections, twice as common in children with ADD, may be a factor. So it's especially important to prevent and appropriately treat such infections, especially of the ear (*otitis media*). Exposure to high levels of heavy metals, such as lead, has also been linked to learning disabilities and attention deficit disorders. (There is a blood test available for determining lead levels; this test can tell you whether lead is a factor.) Adults also can have ADD. If you have learning problems, I recommend that you be tested and follow the same steps for treatment.

General Recommendations

Diet: Changing a child's diet may help immensely. It appears that hyperactivity in many children is associated with reaction to food additives, including artificial coloring, flavoring, and preservatives. Although this correlation is controversial, I recommend that you use fresh foods and eliminate refined sugars. It is worthwhile to try an elimination diet to discover whether there are any allergens affecting your child's behavior.

Your Balanced Healing Action Plan for ADD

- Be sure to have your child tested by a therapist trained in ADD/ADHD, to make sure other psychological problems are not causing the behaviors.
- If your child's symptoms are severe and interfere with social activities or school, go to Step 3 first.

Step 1: Take a High-Potency Multivitamin Supplement or Ginseng

I first recommend nutritional supplementation because so many children do not eat properly, and these supplements—necessary for brain function—can improve mental function in school-aged children. I recommend an optimum diet and supplementation with a high-potency multivitamin/mineral formula containing thiamine, niacin, vitamin B_6, B_{12}, copper, iodine, iron, magnesium, manganese, potassium, and zinc. (See Appendix B, under "Multivitamins," for further guidance on choosing a good multivitamin.)

In addition, I also suggest trying Siberian ginseng (400mg to 800mg extract daily), which has been used effectively in reducing the hyperactivity of ADHD, without the side effects of conventional drugs. It usually takes about four to eight weeks of treatment before you see benefits. **NOTE:** Discontinue ginseng for two to three weeks after every 60 to 90 days of use to avoid long-term side effects. See Appendix B for further information.

Step 2: Take Appropriate Homeopathic Remedies

Homeopathy works like the stimulants that are used to treat hyperactivity (see Step 3). It may take one to two weeks to be beneficial, and it's safer than drugs. Consult a qualified homeopathist for guidance as to which remedies will be most beneficial and at what dosages. (See Appendix A, under "Homeopathy," for guidance on finding a qualified homeopathist.)

Step 3: Take a Prescription Stimulant Such as Ritalin or Adderall, or Take Strattera

If nutritional supplements or homeopathy are not effective, or your child's behavior and symptoms are not well controlled, your doctor may prescribe stimulant drugs, the most common being Ritalin or Adderall. For reasons not thoroughly understood, stimulants are calming in children with attention deficit disorders. Although I prefer not to use high-powered, addictive medications in children, the alternative is either an out-of-control child or one who can't keep up in school, so I do recommend them. However, a new medication, atomoxetine (Strattera) is also effective and is not addictive. Atomoxetine is also beneficial for adults with ADD. You should see improvement almost immediately.

> When 13-year-old Joseph was diagnosed with ADHD, his doctor had to place him on a high dose of Ritalin to adequately control his symptoms. Even so, this did not completely control his behavior. I recommended the supplements in Step 1 and homeopathy. Within one month, Joseph's symptoms were totally controlled. Eventually he was able to decrease his dose of Ritalin to the minimum amount.

Step 4: Take Pyridoxine and Grapeseed Extract

Some children with attention deficit have low levels of serotonin, a brain neurotransmitter. Pyridoxine (300mg to 2g daily), which is necessary for the metabolism of serotonin, can reduce symptoms in such children. Anecdotally, grapeseed extract (75mg to 300mg daily for three weeks, then 40mg to 80mg daily) can also be beneficial in many patients. Both supplements may take one to three months to be effective.

BACK PROBLEMS

Back problems are the most common physical complaints in the United States and other developed countries. Although they can be caused by injury, many back problems are a result of lack of exercise, poor posture, use of vibratory tools, and psychological factors such as anxiety, depression, job dissatisfaction, and mental stress at work.

Acute low back pain is self-limiting, meaning that 90 percent of people recover in six weeks. But if recovery does not occur, chronic pain and disability are the primary results. In addition, if you have chronic low back pain, arthritis of the spine occurs much more quickly than otherwise and can be much more extensive than in normal aging. The spine can also become weaker, and this process can result in herniated (ruptured or slipped) discs, fractures, or spinal stenosis (narrowing of the spinal nerve outlets).

Common Symptoms

- Aching or stiffness anywhere along the lower spine
- Limited range of motion of the spine
- Pain after lifting, bending, or other activities
- Aching after prolonged sitting or standing
- Pain, numbness, or tingling down the arms or legs (radicular symptoms)
- Difficulty walking or climbing

What You Need to Know

Back braces are often prescribed for or used by people with low back pain. Although these braces can provide needed support and protection and lessen pain, they can also prolong healing and cause stiffness and loss of muscle tone. Use a back brace only when you need it for support, or when your doctor prescribes it for specific instability in your spine, or for prevention of further back injuries.

General Recommendations

Exercise: For **acute back pain**, formal exercises are often prescribed initially and can help some people, but they may make pain or inflammation worse for others. If your symptoms worsen with exercise, then postpone the exercises until symptoms decrease. Alternatively, I don't advise complete rest because it may cause more stiffness, loss of muscular tone, and disability. Continue doing as many physical activities as you can tolerate, but don't overdo them. Let your pain be your guide; some soreness is to be expected, but if you have severe pain, don't continue the activity.

In **chronic back pain**, exercise is a mainstay of both prevention and treatment. Exercise stimulates large neurons (brain cells) to help reduce the perception of pain and stimulate the production of natural pain-killers from the brain. Exercises are recommended for all patients with chronic back pain. Stretching and resistance exercises are the main forms, along with exercises specifically designed for the back. However, because your back pain may be caused by different underlying problems, you should consult a physical therapist to help you design an exercise program for your particular condition.

Meditation: Regular meditation reduces stress and relaxes muscles and tendons of the back and neck. This reduces the severity and duration of symptoms. (See "Simple Healing Steps for All Health Conditions" on page 79, for specific meditation exercises, and Appendix A, under "Mind-Body Techniques," for more information.)

Your Balanced Healing Action Plan for Recent Onset (Acute) Back Problems

- If you have severe and worsening back pain that extends down your leg, or paralysis, or inability to urinate or have a bowel movement, you may have a serious problem that requires emergency medical attention and diagnostic testing such as MRI or myelogram.
- There are several treatments for acute low back pain that I don't recommend: traction, prescription antidepressants, lumbar supports, and TENS units (small devices that conduct electricity to the superficial soft tissues).

Step 1: Take Over-the-Counter Pain Relievers or NSAIDs

Your first step is to relieve your pain and decrease inflammation, thus allowing your body tissues to heal themselves. I recommend analgesics, such as Tylenol, or over-the-counter nonsteroidal anti-inflammatories (NSAIDs), such as Advil, Aleve, and ibuprofen.

Step 2: Take Prescription Medications to Relieve Pain and Inflammation or Relax Muscles

If the above drugs do not control your pain, your doctor can prescribe stronger nonsteroidal anti-inflammatory medications (such as Naprosyn, Feldene, Daypro, Orudis, Mobic, Cataflam, Relafen, Arthrotec, and many more). However, these drugs may cause stomach irritation and bleeding. If this occurs, you can try Cox-2 inhibitors, which have less risk of these side effects. **NOTE:** Recent studies show an increased risk of heart attack in patients who use high-dose Cox-2 inhibitors along with naproxen (Aleve), so caution is advised. Also, if you have taken an NSAID (including ibuprofen) for a long time, it may precipitate a heart attack if you stop taking it suddenly. Obtain guidance from your doctor, especially if you have heart disease.

Muscle relaxants (such as Flexeril, Robaxin, Parafon Forte, Zanaflex, or Soma) are commonly prescribed and can reduce pain, but they cause drowsiness in many people. They are beneficial primarily in the first few days after an injury. Use prescribed narcotics for severe pain only a short period of time to avoid addiction, and avoid them altogether if possible.

The purpose of all these medications is to offer relief while healing is taking place, so you should take them only for a temporary period of time, until one (or several) of the following steps can work.

Step 3: Undergo Physical Therapy Modalities

Physical therapy modalities such as electrical current (applying low-voltage current to the area of pain), ultrasound (applying high-frequency sound that projects heat to the deep tissues), infrasound (low-frequency sound that increases local blood and lymph circulation and activity of the nervous system), hot/cold packs, and therapeutic massage can help accelerate the healing process. Use these treatments in combination for the best results. Ultrasound is sometimes helpful but can be irritating if there is inflammation.

These treatments can be provided by primary care doctors who have the necessary equipment, but if you are not improving, you should ask your doctor to refer you to a registered physical therapist. You should feel better after 6 to 12 treatments. If you don't, proceed with the next step.

Step 4: Undergo Osteopathic Mobilization Therapy (OMT) or Chiropractic Manipulation

Osteopathic mobilization or chiropractic manipulation is helpful in uncomplicated back problems (that is, if you don't have pre-existing back problems, such as severe arthritis, spinal stenosis, ruptured disc, or previous back surgeries). Manual therapy is helpful primarily if there are underlying structural problems (in other words, if bones, ligaments, tendons, joints, and/or muscles are not working correctly), which can be diagnosed via a chiropractic or osteopathic exam. If you have structural problems, then they must be corrected first, or your symptoms may recur. Your pain should start decreasing in 6 to 8 treatments, although additional treatments may be necessary to give you maximum benefit. If pain is still present after 10 to 12 treatments, structural problems are probably not the cause of your pain, and you may need further evaluation or a different method. (See Appendix A, under "Manual Therapy," for further information and guidance on finding a qualified practitioner.)

Step 5: Use Acupuncture

Acupuncture is effective for reducing pain, acute muscle spasms, and trigger points (small areas of muscle that become inflamed and are very painful when you push on them). In my clinic, we also have been able to relieve pain from bulging and herniated discs using acupuncture in combination with the low-energy laser. (Unfortunately, this laser is not yet readily available to most doctors, because it's a research device. See Appendix C for referral information.) However, acupuncture alone may be effective for reducing symptoms enough to avoid surgery. Principal points are usually found on the back, behind the knee, and on the ankles. You should always seek evaluation and treatment from a practitioner certified in acupuncture. (See Appendix A, under "Acupuncture," for guidance on finding a qualified acupuncturist and for further explanation on different acupuncture techniques.) You should feel better within six acupuncture treatments, but you might need additional sessions for maximum benefits.

Step 6: Undergo Diagnostic Testing to Discover More Severe Disc or Nerve Problems

If your back pain persists, leg symptoms worsen, or you develop urinary or bowel difficulties, you need diagnostic testing, such as MRI. This is the primary screening test for uncovering abnormalities that are not present on a physical exam. This test requires you to be placed in a narrow tube for 45 to 60 minutes, so, if you are claustrophobic, ask your doctor for Valium (10mg) to take before the test. There are also "open" MRI scanners available that do not cause claustrophobia.

Step 7: If the MRI Is Normal, Seek Counseling

If your pain continues despite normal test findings and continued treatment, underlying psychological factors may be occurring, even if you are not aware of them. Consider seeking an evaluation from a psychotherapist who treats pain symptoms. You should realize that when I advise you to do this, I am not suggesting that you are "crazy" or mentally ill. Many people simply do not realize that other psychosocial factors (such as job dissatisfaction, family problems, or financial difficulties) can prolong back pain, and once you are aware of these factors and how to deal with them, you can heal properly.

> When Jo Ann slipped and fell, hurting her back, her doctor prescribed physical therapy and gave her medications, but neither helped. Her MRI was normal. Jo Ann became frustrated and demanded that something be done. Her doctor sent her for epidural injections (despite her normal MRI), but they did not give her any relief. She was referred to me for acupuncture and laser. When I talked with Jo Ann, she revealed that her mother, whom she'd been taking care of for 10 years, had just died after an extended illness. During this time, Jo Ann also had been a full-time wife and mother. I sent her to a psychotherapist, who helped Jo Ann realize that she just wanted to be taken care of, after all these years of taking care of everyone else. After continued psychotherapy, her back pain went away.

Step 8: If the MRI Is Abnormal, Consider Epidural Steroid and Other Injections

If the previous steps have not helped you, then consider an epidural steroid injection (injection of cortisone into the lining of the spinal column). This procedure can relieve your symptoms if the MRI reveals disc or nerve abnormalities that correlate with the symptoms but do not yet require surgery—and if it has been less than two months since the start of your symptoms. If you get pain relief from the two initial injections, but it lasts only a few hours or days, further injections will usually not be beneficial, and I don't recommend proceeding with more. If these injections are effective, pain relief should last four to six months and as long as a year. Epidural injections are not beneficial if you have normal test findings, and they are used primarily if leg pain is present.

Other injections can also be tried, depending on your symptoms, physical findings, and MRI results. These include trigger-point injections (injection of cortisone into "tender" muscle areas), facet-joint injections (injection of cortisone in the joint[s] connecting the bones of the spine), or selective nerve root blocks (injections of cortisone around the nerves coming from the spinal cord and going to the legs). Like epidurals, these injections are usually effective only temporarily, but they may allow time for the body to heal itself.

Michael hurt his back lifting a heavy box. He had already been seen by an orthopedist and neurosurgeon, and MRI had shown a ruptured disc. He was prescribed physical therapy, had chiropractic treatment, and also underwent three epidural steroid injections, none of which were beneficial. Initially, his doctors did not recommend surgery because he was not having leg pain or other severe symptoms. However, they changed their minds because the therapy and injections had not helped, but Michael wanted to try other methods before surgery. After nine treatments with the low-energy laser and acupuncture in combination, his back pain was reduced 90 percent and he did not require surgery. Within six months, his back pain completely resolved.

Step 9: Undergo Additional Diagnostic Testing

If your symptoms continue, I recommend further tests. One possibility is a discogram, which is the injection of a dye into the disc spaces. If leakage of dye is detected by X-ray—*and* the injection causes the same pain that you have had shooting down your leg—you may have a disc rupture. Another test is the myelogram, in which dye is injected into the spinal column, outlining the spinal nerves as they leave the spinal cord and go to the leg. If the dye is seen to be obstructed, this may mean that the nerve is being compressed by a ruptured disc. Both of these tests can reveal abnormalities not observed on MRI, or they can confirm abnormalities that are seen on MRI.

Step 10: Consider Other Invasive Methods

Depending on what these further diagnostic tests show, there are other methods that can be useful for specific conditions. IDET (IntraDiscal ElectroThermal Therapy) is a procedure used when there is a tear in the covering of a spinal disc (an *annular tear*). IDET involves placing a wire around the disc and heating it, thus sealing the tear. IDET is most effective when you have only one or two damaged discs with a limited area of damage. Healing may take four to six months after the procedure, and physical activities must be severely restricted during this time. Long-term effectiveness is not known because IDET has been used only since 1997.

Step 11: Undergo Surgery as a Last Resort

Back surgery should be your treatment of last resort or when you have unrelenting leg pain or neurological signs (paralysis, or inability to urinate or have a bowel movement) that correlate with the results of the tests mentioned above. Surgery is often beneficial for reducing the pain that radiates into your legs, but it may not be as helpful for reducing the back pain. The optimum time for surgery is within three to six months of when the symptoms start, although beneficial results may still be achieved at longer intervals. In general, however, the longer the symptoms have been present, the poorer the results. In fact, surgery can sometimes predispose you to pain and other symptoms that become worse in the future, requiring additional back surgeries to relieve the additional symptoms.

Your Balanced Healing Action Plan for Chronic Back Pain

- Chronic back problems—those that last longer than three to six months—are very different from acute problems and do not usually respond to basic medications or physical therapy. Although stronger NSAIDs and other medications (such as the pain reliever Tramadol) can control the symptoms in many cases, I recommend proceeding with the following methods to eliminate the problems, which in turn can reduce or eliminate the need for medications. **NOTE:** Bed rest, biofeedback, long-term chiropractic manipulation, facet-joint injections, epidural steroid injections, lumbar supports, and traction have *not* been shown to be effective in improving *chronic* low back pain. At best, they may give temporary relief only, and I don't recommend them.
- Many doctors may tell you that there is nothing more they can do to relieve your pain, and that you will just have to learn to live with it. I do not believe this is true for most people, especially if you use the following steps. Overall, the goal should be elimination of the pain, but complete relief may not be possible. A more reasonable goal is to lessen the pain enough to be able to enjoy life and be able to participate in most activities of daily living. In my experience, that goal can indeed be accomplished.

Step 1: Go to Back School

Sitting, lifting, and performing other activities properly are very important factors in both preventing and treating back problems. For example, many people with back problems also walk hunched over or sit stooped over a computer. They might lift without using their legs. I think that anyone with chronic back pain should attend a back school. These schools teach you dozens of ways to keep your back pain from worsening and flaring-up, and to avoid further injuries. Many registered physical therapists and rehabilitation specialists teach at back schools, so inquire in your area or ask your doctor for a recommendation.

Step 2: Receive Low-Level Energy Laser Therapy

I recommend the use of low-level energy lasers as the next step because, in my studies, the laser appears to help heal the tissue, reduce inflammation, and give long-lasting relief for arthritic, nerve, and disc problems. These lasers are called "cold" lasers because they do not produce heat like the hot lasers used in surgical procedures do. Their primary side effect (in about 25 percent of patients) is that they cause a temporary increase in soreness, which may last from one to three days. You should observe a decrease in symptoms within six to nine treatments. Because this is currently a research device unavailable to most doctors, see Appendix C for reference information.

Step 3: Undergo Acupuncture

Acupuncture is very effective for chronic back problems. Principal points are usually found on the back, behind the knee, and on the ankles. You should always seek evaluation and treatment from a practitioner certified in acupuncture. (See Appendix A, under "Acupuncture," for guidance on finding a qualified acupuncturist and for further explanation on different acupuncture techniques.) You should notice improvement within six acupuncture treatments, but you might need additional sessions for maximum benefits. Occasional maintenance acupuncture may be necessary every 6 to 12 months.

Step 4: Undergo Osteopathic or Chiropractic Manipulation

Often, underlying structural problems (bones, ligaments, tendons, joints, and/or muscles not working correctly) are either causing your chronic back pain or not allowing proper healing to take place. I recommend osteopathic treatment to correct these underlying structural problems. This first requires an osteopathic exam. If structural problems are evident, then they must be corrected before you get other treatments, or your symptoms may keep coming back. With osteopathic treatment, your pain should start decreasing in three to six treatments, although you might need additional treatments for maximum benefit. If your pain is still present after 10 to 12 treatments, further evaluation or a different method may be necessary. (See Appendix A, under "Manual Therapy," for more information on osteopathic treatment and guidance in finding a qualified practitioner.)

Chiropractic manipulation can also be done and can help some people, but studies have not shown long-term effectiveness in most people. This is why I prefer osteopathic adjustments. If you choose chiropractic care, you should feel better within 6 to 8 treatments; occasional maintenance adjustments may be appropriate. I emphasize "occasional." I see many patients who have received chiropractic adjustments every week (sometimes several times a week) for years, with pain relief lasting only a few hours or days. These perpetual, frequent adjustments are not appropriate and can be harmful. (See Appendix A, under "Manual Therapy," for further explanation.) Do not continue with chiropractic manipulation after 10 to 12 treatments if you don't get long-term relief.

Step 5: Try a TENS Unit

The previous steps are designed to reduce your symptoms for a long time. For continued pain that cannot be relieved long term, there are some treatments designed to give you temporary relief.

Start with a TENS unit (Transcutaneous Electrical Nerve Stimulator). You wear a small electrical generator strapped to your belt. The generator is attached by wires to small pads placed around the area of pain. Turning up the amplitude will give you more stimulation. You can wear one of these units continuously to control pain, although in some cases it can lose effectiveness over time.

Step 6: *Apply Emu Oil, Long Crystal Menthol, Biofreeze, Capsaicin, Glucosamine/MSM, and Other Topical Solutions for Temporary Pain Relief*

If you still have residual pain or flare-ups of pain, there are numerous topical solutions that can give temporary relief when you apply them over the painful area. These include emu oil, long crystal menthol, Biofreeze, capsaicin, and glucosamine/MSM, as well as other herbal combinations. These topicals are not curative, but they may provide pain relief for two to eight hours, and they have minimal side effects (the most common is skin allergy or sensitivity). Some of these may work better than others on different people, so you may have to try several to find the best one. In my clinic, I apply samples to my patients so they'll know what works before they purchase it. Encourage your doctor or practitioner to do the same (for further information on these topicals, go to www.balancedhealing.com).

Other topicals use a mixture of prescription medications combined into a gel that is transported into the soft tissues. Some of these medications include gabapentin (Neurontin), ketoprofen, ketamine, clonidine, and amitriptyline (Elavil), but there are many others that can be helpful. A prescription from a doctor is required, but you can obtain the information from a pharmacist who mixes medications and bring it to your doctor for his approval.

Step 7: *Take Prescription NSAIDs for Temporary Pain Relief*

If the topical pain relievers are not helpful, then your doctor can prescribe stronger non-steroidal anti-inflammatory medications (such as Naprosyn, Feldene, Daypro, Orudis, Mobic, Cataflam, Relafen, Arthrotec, and many more). These medications may take three weeks to be effective and should be discontinued if there is no benefit or the side effects (such as stomach irritation and bleeding) become intolerable. If this occurs, you can try Cox-2 inhibitors, which have less risk of these side effects. **NOTE:** Recent studies show an increased risk of heart attack in patients who use high-dose Cox-2 inhibitors along with naproxen (Aleve), so caution is advised. Also, if you have taken an NSAID (including ibuprofen) for a long time, it may precipitate a heart attack if you stop taking it suddenly. Obtain guidance from your doctor, especially if you have heart disease.

Step 8: *Take Appropriate Chinese Herbal Remedies*

Several Chinese herbal formulations can reduce back pain and increase mobility, and you can safely take them with the previous steps. Formulas commonly used include *Wan Du Hua Yu Tang, Shu Jing Huo Xue Tang,* or *Huo Luo Xiao Ling Dan.* Consult a practitioner qualified in Chinese herbal medicine to determine which Chinese herbal formulas are the best for your particular syndromes. (See Appendix A, under "Chinese Herbs.")

Step 9: *Use Feldenkrais, Alexander, and Rolfing Forms of Bodywork*

Bodywork involves realigning, rebalancing, and retraining the structures of the body that have become dysfunctional due to pain, injury, disuse, or misuse. Bodywork can be helpful for chronic back pain that doesn't respond to other methods.

- The **Feldenkrais method** focuses on retraining the way you move your body; it interrupts unhealthy patterns of movement that have become habits.
- The **Alexander technique** concentrates on correcting faulty posture in daily activities (sitting, standing, and moving).
- **Rolfing** involves manipulating and stretching the body's fascial tissues (deep connective tissues that hold your body together), allowing correct realigning of the body.

Each of these bodywork methods requires a certified therapist. (See Appendix A, under "Bodywork," for more information and Appendix C to find a qualified therapist.)

Step 10: Undergo Prolotherapy or Sclerotherapy

If the previous measures don't relieve your pain, I recommend injections of natural substances to stimulate the growth of connective tissue to strengthen weak or damaged tendons and ligaments around the spine. In this technique, called reconstructive therapy, a mildly irritating solution (usually dextrose, glycerin, and phenol) is injected into the injured tissues, causing stimulation of the healing process. You should improve within six treatments, and you'll usually notice improvement during the first week. (For more information on this technique and guidance in finding a qualified practitioner, see Appendix A.)

Step 11: Practice Yoga Postures for Back and Neck

Yoga is often successful in reducing chronic back and neck symptoms. Yoga promotes relaxation and stretching, both of which are important in healing and preventing back pain. Because there are many different types of yoga, with some better for back pain than others, I recommend working with a qualified yoga instructor. (See Appendix A for more information on yoga and Appendix C to find a qualified yoga instructor.)

Step 12: Use Biomagnets

Biomagnets applied to the back (either taped or contained in a back brace) can reduce pain in some people. However, the relief lasts only while the magnet is in place. (See Appendix B for more information on biomagnets.)

Step 13: Practice Guided Imagery, Meditation, Biofeedback, and Hypnosis

Mind-body techniques such as guided imagery, meditation, biofeedback, or hypnosis may help when you use them along with the previous steps. (See Appendix A, under "Mind-Body," for further information.)

Step 14: Take Prescription Antidepressants

For some people, low-dose antidepressants, such as amitriptyline (Elavil) 25mg to 50mg daily, or trazodone (Desyrel) 50mg to 150mg daily, can decrease chronic back pain through effects on the pain center (hypothalamus) and neurotransmitters in the brain. However, they do not improve your ability to perform activities. You should try them if the previous steps are either ineffective or only partly effective in relieving your pain.

Step 15: Undergo Epidural Steroid Injections, Selective Nerve-Root Blocks, or Rhizotomy

If your pain is still present and is severe, you can try undergoing several types of spinal injections. Although very few people gain long-lasting relief from these procedures, they are worth a try before undergoing any surgery. Epidural steroid injections can occasionally benefit chronic back pain, but if two injections haven't given you long-term relief, additional injections won't either. Selective nerve root blocks can sometimes deaden a nerve, but again they may only give you temporary relief. Another procedure is called rhizotomy, in which your nerve root is destroyed by cutting it, using radio waves to destroy the nerve, or injecting a chemical that destroys the nerve. This interrupts the pain message going to your brain. Often, however, your nerve will grow back and the pain will return. I would recommend rhizotomy only for intractable, unrelenting pain that prevents you from participating in most activities.

Step 16: Enter a Multidisciplinary Pain Program

If the previous steps are not beneficial, I recommend that you enter a multidisciplinary pain program. Although such programs are not designed to reduce back pain specifically, they do improve your ability to function and to go back to work, and they teach you to cope better with your pain.

Step 17: Undergo Surgery

Surgeries should be avoided if at all possible. Most surgeries done for chronic low back pain are fusions—your spinal bones (vertebra) are fused together using bone from your hip or with instrumentation (rods, screws, and/or cages). Surgeries for chronic back pain should be done only for unrelenting pain with evidence of structural deterioration of the discs, and/or additional or worsening neurological signs. Surgery that involves a fusion at one or two levels exerts more pressure on the spinal disks above and below the fusion, typically causing them to deteriorate within two to five years. This is why many people have persistent or recurrent low back pain after these surgeries and end up undergoing many more surgeries.

> Jesse, a 30-year-old former rock climber, injured his back in a fall 15 years ago. He had four surgeries: The first was to repair a ruptured disc, the second to clean out scar tissue, the third to fuse two spinal levels, and the fourth because of another disc rupture above the fusion. Each surgery gave him relief for about four to eight months, and then his pain returned. Whatever treatments were available, Jesse tried them, including numerous epidural steroid injections, selective nerve root blocks, TENS unit, and narcotic medications. He had also tried chiropractic treatment, but he still had constant pain. I sent him first for an osteopathic exam, which revealed that part of his pain was from problems with his sacroiliac joint (which is part of the pelvis) and that his sacrum (the lowest bony part of the spine)

> was in an abnormal position (a condition called *sacral torsion*). Osteopathic treatment gave him considerable relief, but he still had pain. I then started him on acupuncture with low-energy laser. After 12 treatments, nearly all of his pain was gone, and he was able to stop taking his medications.

Step 18: Take Prescription Narcotics

Narcotic pain-relief medications are appropriate only for severe, unrelenting back pain that has not responded to any other treatment approaches. These drugs vary in potency from tramadol or propoxyphene (the mildest) to OxyContin or morphine (the strongest). They are highly addictive. A physician specializing in pain management should monitor you when you are taking these drugs for chronic back pain.

Step 19: Use a Dorsal Column Stimulator

Placement of a dorsal column stimulator (DCS) into the spine can control chronic, severe spine pain, but it is effective in only about 10 to 20 percent of people and has a high failure rate over time, even among those who do receive relief initially. It is usually done only if back surgeries fail (a situation known as *failed back syndrome*, or FBS). DCS should be used as a last resort—only for continued severe back pain not helped by other treatments.

BIPOLAR DISORDER (Manic-Depressive Illness)

Bipolar disorder is a psychological disturbance in which you may suffer from a *manic* state (impulsive, aggressive behavior) alone, or alternating manic and *depressive* states. The pattern of mood swings can vary widely. In some people, years can separate manic and depressive episodes. In other people, the cycles occur three or four times a year with respites in between. For still others, the cycles can rapidly and continuously alternate.

Often, this disorder is difficult to correctly diagnose, because its depression appears the same as other types of depression. Unless a therapist observes or knows about the manic phase, the true diagnosis may remain hidden. There are two types, *bipolar I* and *bipolar II*. In bipolar I, both phases (mania and depression) are very pronounced. In bipolar II, the mania is mild and the depression can be mild or severe. Bipolar II is more difficult to diagnose but is the most common form. It has fewer and shorter periods of remission, tends to run in families, and is less responsive to treatment. The origin of bipolar disorder is thought to be a genetic imbalance in brain chemicals.

Common Symptoms: Manic Phase

- Excessive self esteem or grandiosity
- Euphoria or irritability
- Excessive talk
- Racing thoughts

- Unusual energy with less need for sleep
- Impulsiveness with reckless pursuit of gratification (buying sprees, promiscuous sex, high-risk investments, fast driving, and so on)
- Hallucinations and delusion
- Inability to concentrate
- Increase in social or work activities

Common Symptoms: Depressive Phase

- Low self-esteem
- Apathy, inertia
- Sadness, loneliness, helplessness
- Fatigue
- Insomnia
- Slow speech
- Suicidal thoughts
- Substance abuse
- Guilt

What You Need to Know

It is important to eliminate other psychological disorders that can have similar symptoms, including school phobias, ADD/ADHD, dementia, schizophrenia, and psychotic states induced by drugs or alcohol. In addition, substance abuse is common in bipolar disorder, and any substance abuser should be evaluated for this disorder. Drugs and alcohol can interfere with the correct diagnosis (they also precipitate phase swings, so if you are diagnosed, you should avoid them for the rest of your life). *Hyperthyroidism* (elevated thyroid) can look like mania; some of the treatments for bipolar disorder (especially lithium) can lower thyroid hormone level, which can increase the hyperthyroidism; and bipolar patients can be very sensitive to variations in thyroid function, which means the effects of the hyperthyroidism can be even further exaggerated. I recommend that you undergo a thyroid profile (thyroxine index or FTI, and TSH) initially and then monitor your thyroid levels regularly. If you have low or borderline results, your doctor can prescribe thyroid medication (see the section on thyroid problems for further guidance).

Your Balanced Healing Action Plan for Bipolar Disorder

- For severe manic or depressive phases, hospitalization is usually required to protect you and others from harm.
- Do not take St. John's wort or SAMe for your depression because they can make you more manic or more depressive.

Step 1: Take Prescription Lithium or Depakote

Because bipolar disorder can be dangerous, you must get the symptoms under control as soon as possible by using prescription medications. The prescription drug lithium carbonate is usually the first choice, and it primarily controls the mania. Lithium blood levels must be monitored to ensure that you are receiving the proper dose of medication. Depakote is another prescription medication now used for this disorder, and your doctor must check blood levels as well for proper dosage.

Step 2: Take 5-HTP for Mild Depression

Because lithium primarily controls the mania, you need to take something for the depression phase. For mild depression, 5-HTP (200mg three times daily, along with the lithium) may be effective. It may take two to three weeks for you to notice improvement. **NOTE:** Be sure to use only products that are "peak X-free." Peak X is a contaminant that can cause significant side effects and even death.

Step 3: Take a Prescription SSRI Antidepressant Along with Lithium

If Step 2 is not effective or the depression is more severe, stop taking the 5-HTP. At this point, your doctor may prescribe an SSRI antidepressant (Prozac, Paxil, Zoloft, or others) with lithium. If SSRIs give you intolerable side effects, tricyclic antidepressants such as amitriptyline may be the ones to use next. (Do not take 5-HTP with an SSRI because side effects will increase.) One major side effect of SSRIs is decrease in sexual libido, both in men and women. To reverse or reduce this side effect, take gingko biloba, 60mg to 120mg per day.

Step 4: Use EEG Biofeedback

EEG biofeedback has been shown to be effective in helping control manic symptoms. In mild bipolar disorder, some people can stop taking lithium if EEG biofeedback is successful, so it is worth a try after you become stabilized by the above steps.

Step 5: Take Trace Minerals and Vitamins

A recent study has shown that taking a combination of trace minerals and vitamins significantly decreases symptoms and reduces the need for the medications in Steps 1 and 3. I recommend taking a good multivitamin containing one to two times the RDA values. Keep in mind that it may take four to six months to achieve maximum benefit. (See Appendix B, under "Multivitamins," for RDA values.)

Step 6: Take Vitamin C, Fish Oil, and/or Phosphatidylcholine (Lecithin)

If you still have symptoms after following the previous Steps, take vitamin C, 3g daily, and phosphatidylcholine, 15g to 25g per day, in pure form or as lecithin, to increase the brain levels of acetylcholine, a neurotransmitter that may cause symptoms of manic-depression if deficient in the brain. Fish oil (2g to 6g daily) can decrease depressive symptoms and increase remission times, but it doesn't help the mania.

After living most of her life taking prescription antidepressants, Ellie, a 55-year-old physical therapist, came to me looking for natural treatments for her depression. I referred her for interactive imagery, but the therapist surprisingly found Ellie not to be depressed at that time. Rather, she was hyperactive and aggressive, and testing showed that she was bipolar. She'd been misdiagnosed her entire life because every time she had seen a physician, she was depressed and not manic. I started her on lithium in combination with 5-HTP until she became stable. I then had her take a strong multivitamin with extra vitamin C and lecithin. After two months, she was able to reduce the dosages of her other medications.

Step 7: Use Light Therapy

If your bipolar depression becomes worse in winter, light therapy may be helpful. You sit for 20 to 30 minutes a day in front of a special light box that produces a full spectrum light of 10,000 lux. Ask your doctor where you can obtain one.

Step 8: Take Prescription Carbamazepine, Valproic Acid, or Haloperidol

If you are still suffering from manic episodes, and lithium and the above steps have not been effective, carbamazepine may be the next drug of choice. Other drugs that can be used as substitutes include valproic acid or haloperidol. These are all prescription medications and should be monitored by your doctor.

Step 9: Undergo Electroconvulsive Therapy

When bipolar disorder fails to respond to all other treatment measures, electroconvulsive (shock) therapy (ECT) is indicated, especially for people who are very depressed or suicidal. This is a last resort, but it may be necessary for uncontrolled bipolar disorder.

BLADDER INFECTION (Cystitis)

Cystitis is inflammation of the bladder caused by a bacterial infection. It occurs primarily in women and rarely in men. Bladder infections can lead to permanent damage in the urinary tract, which can lead to kidney damage and failure. Bladder infection also can be a sign of sexually transmitted disease that can affect other pelvic organs (uterus, ovaries, fallopian tubes) and cause sterility.

Common Symptoms

- Burning sensation when urinating
- Difficulty urinating
- Frequent urge to urinate
- Strong, foul odor
- Lethargy, incontinence (leakage of urine), and mental confusion (in older people)

What You Need to Know

If a man has a urinary tract infection, it always needs to be evaluated by a urologist for underlying structural problems. Women who have **recurrent** bladder infections (more than two or three in a year) should also be evaluated by a urologist. Some women develop infections after sexual intercourse, especially when not well lubricated. Proper lubrication and urinating after intercourse can help prevent these problems.

Over-the-counter antihistamines that contain Benadryl, chlorpheniramine, hydroxyzine, or cyproheptadine can underlie recurrent bladder infections in some women because they cause retention of urine. Stop taking them, and if these medications are causing your bladder infections, your symptoms should improve within a few weeks.

General Recommendations

Diet: Drinking large quantities of fluids, (water, juices, or tea are preferred) can help prevent bladder infections. Avoid fluids that irritate the bladder, including alcohol, coffee, black tea, peppers, chocolate milk, carbonated beverages, and citrus juices.

Your Balanced Healing Action Plan for Bladder Infection

- If bladder infection symptoms are moderate to severe, or have been present several days, go to Step 3.

Step 1: Increase Your Fluid Intake

After the first signs of bladder infection (within 24 hours), drinking lots of water (twelve 8-ounce glasses daily) or unsweetened cranberry juice (16 ounces daily) may alleviate the symptoms. Cranberry juice prevents bacteria from adhering to the walls of your bladder.

Step 2: Take a Chinese Herbal Remedy

Along with Step 1, there are Chinese herbal formulas that are very effective in reducing symptoms and helping to alleviate the infection. *Ba Zheng San* is a common formula, but there are several others, depending on the herbalist's diagnosis. Consult a practitioner qualified in Chinese herbal medicine to determine which herbal formulas are the best for your particular syndromes. (See Appendix A, under "Chinese Herbs," for more information.)

Step 3: Take Prescription Antibiotics

If you still have symptoms after 24 hours, you need to see your doctor for a prescription antibiotic to clear up the infection. There are many antibiotics that can be effective. Most doctors will prescribe one of the common ones, such as amoxicillin, sulfamethoxazole, or trimethoprim-sulfamethoxazole (Bactrim or Septra), which usually resolves the infection.

If your bladder infection comes back or does not respond to initial antibiotics, your urine needs to be tested for the type of bacteria and its resistance to various antibiotics. Then your physician can prescribe an antibiotic that will kill the specific bacteria causing the infection.

Your Balanced Healing Action Plan for Preventing Recurrent Bladder Infections

Step 1: Drink Cranberry Juice

Drink 16 ounces per day of unsweetened cranberry juice, to help prevent bacteria from adhering to your bladder's walls. Try to avoid sweetened juice because sugar can decrease resistance to the bacteria.

Step 2: Use Acupuncture

Acupuncture can reduce recurrent bladder infections for as long as a year or more. It takes four to eight treatments, on average, to obtain this effect. Principal points are usually found on the lower back, feet, and ankles. You should always seek evaluation and treatment from a practitioner certified in acupuncture. (See Appendix A, under "Acupuncture," for guidance on finding a qualified acupuncturist and for more information on different acupuncture techniques.)

> Dede, a 28-year-old actress, had urinary tract infections at least once a month, sometimes more often. She had been placed on long-term antibiotics, but this treatment caused vaginal yeast infections, so she wanted an alternative. She had been drinking cranberry juice, which had decreased the frequency of infections but did not eliminate them. I used 10 sessions of acupuncture to treat Dede, and she had only one infection during the next year and a half.

Step 3: Take the Western Herbal Remedy Uva Ursi (Bearberry)

If the previous steps do not keep your bladder infections from coming back, take Uva ursi (bearberry or upland cranberry), an herb that has antiseptic effects and has shown benefits in preventing recurrent bladder infections. Take it three times a day as a tea (2g to 4g), tincture (1:5, 4ml to 6 ml), or fluid extract (1:1 in 25 percent alcohol, standardized to 20 percent arbutin, 0.5ml to 4ml).

Step 4: Make Your Urine More Alkaline

In addition to Step 3, alkalinizing your urinary tract can sometimes fend off bladder infections. I recommend potassium or sodium citrate solutions, 125mg to 250mg orally three to four times per day. You can obtain these solutions at your local pharmacy.

Do not use this treatment if you have high blood pressure or heart failure because these solutions can make these conditions worse by causing fluid overload. Consult with your doctor if you want to explore this option.

Step 5: Take Long-Term Prescription Antibiotics

If your bladder infections still return despite the previous steps, then you and your doctor need to consider long-term treatment with antibiotics. There are several antibiotics that are used for this purpose, the major one being a sulfa drug combination (trimethoprim-sulfamethoxazole).

BONE SPURS

Bone spurs are abnormal growths at the ends of bones, usually caused by chronic inflammation. In response to the inflammation, the body deposits calcium in the area. Bone spurs most commonly occur in the spine or foot. If they continue to grow, they can put pressure on other tissues, causing additional medical problems.

Common Symptoms
- Stiffness or pain in the neck, back, or heel
- Pain radiating down the arm or leg (severe cases in the spine)
- Difficulty walking or running (heel spurs)

Your Balanced Healing Action Plan for Bone Spurs
- For neck spurs, start with Step 3.

Step 1: Wear Shoe Orthotics for Heel Spurs

Often, heel spurs are caused by weakness in your feet, especially the arches. A proper lift or insert for your shoes can often alleviate heel spur symptoms by correcting these underlying structural causes. Although basic arch supports/inserts purchased at a drug store may be helpful, you may need to obtain a more individualized insert at a specialized prosthetic or shoe shop because each foot is different, and molds may be necessary to determine your particular needs. Also, avoid wearing high heels and poorly supported shoes.

Step 2: Use Stretching and Apply Ice in Mild Heel Spurs

If your heel spur is mild, along with Step 1, you may be able to resolve the pain with stretching and ice. Hold on to something (such as a chair, table, or wall), and keep your entire foot on the ground. Keeping your knee locked straight, lean forward slowly. You will feel the stretch of your Achilles tendon (in back of your lower leg). Hold this for 5 to 10 seconds, and then stand again. Repeat this five times, and then apply ice to the back of your lower leg and heel for 20 minutes. Do this every day. You should feel better within a few weeks.

Step 3: Undergo Acupuncture for Long-Term Relief of Heel and Neck Spurs

Start with acupuncture for neck spurs, and add it if the previous steps are unsuccessful in relieving the pain and swelling of heel spurs. Principal points for the heel are usually found on the ankles and at the ear point representing the foot. Spinal points for neck spurs depend on the location of the spur, but they usually include points in the Urinary Bladder channel (on the upper back and neck), and points on the hands. Always seek evaluation and treatment from a practitioner certified in acupuncture. (See Appendix A, under "Acupuncture," for guidance on finding a qualified acupuncturist and for more information on different acupuncture techniques.) You should feel less pain within six acupuncture treatments, although you might need additional sessions for maximum benefits.

Step 4: Undergo Low-Energy Laser Therapy

Inflammation usually underlies spurs, so it's important to eliminate it to prevent further growth and recurrence of spurs. I recommend the low-level energy laser, which appears to help heal the tissue, reduce the inflammatory response, and give long-lasting relief. These lasers are called "cold" lasers because they do not produce heat like the hot lasers used in surgical procedures. Their primary side effect (in about 25 percent of patients) is that they cause a temporary increase in soreness, which may last one to three days. They can be used with acupuncture for faster results. This is a research device, not readily available in some areas of the country. (See Appendix C for referral information.)

Step 5: Undergo Shock-Wave Treatment for Heel Spurs

If you're still having problems with heel spurs, you can next try shock-wave treatment, called orthotripsy. In this medical treatment, sound waves—actually, a series of about 1,500 shocks—are transmitted through your heel. About 60 percent of people improve after three months.

Step 6: Undergo Osteopathic Mobilization Therapy (OMT)

If you continue to have recurrent problems from neck or back spurs, there may be an underlying structural problem (bones, ligaments, tendons, joints, and/or muscles not working correctly) that has not been corrected. I recommend osteopathic evaluation and mobilization (OMT), which is used to uncover and correct these underlying problems. Neck spurs in particular can result from structural abnormalities in the facet joints (the joints that connect the bones of the spinal column). Heel spurs can originate in abnormalities in the pelvis, which can cause you to walk incorrectly. OMT of the pelvis may be necessary to prevent recurrence.

With OMT, your pain should start to go away in 6 to 8 treatments, although you might need more to achieve maximum benefit. If you still have pain after 10 to 12 treatments, further evaluation or a different method may be necessary. (See Appendix A, under "Manual Therapy," for further information and guidance in finding a qualified practitioner.)

> Stephanie, a college tennis team captain, came to me with a heel spur on her left foot. She had previously had a heel spur on the right foot removed by surgery, but she still had some pain in that foot. She didn't want another surgery for the new bone spur on her left foot. An osteopathic evaluation indicated a problem with her pelvis that caused her to favor the left foot. She underwent four sessions of OMT to correct the underlying problem. At the same time, I gave her acupuncture with laser for the current pain and inflammation, which went away after six sessions. Stephanie has not had

> any further problems with her feet, but she does return every six months for an osteopathic recheck.

Step 7: Undergo a Cortisone Injection

If the previous steps don't help you, you can try an injection of cortisone into the heel. Some people get long-lasting relief from this, although other people experience very little relief at all. It's worth a try before proceeding with long-term medication or surgery (the following steps).

Step 8: Take a Prescription NSAID for Temporary Relief

Acetaminophen (Tylenol) can control pain in many people who have bone spurs. But if it doesn't do the trick, then your doctor can prescribe stronger nonsteroidal anti-inflammatory medications (such as Naprosyn, Feldene, Daypro, Orudis, Mobic, Cataflam, Relafen, Arthrotec, and many more), which can help relieve pain and inflammation. These medications may take three weeks to be effective and should be discontinued if there is no benefit or the side effects (such as stomach irritation and bleeding) become intolerable. If this occurs, you can try Cox-2 inhibitors, which have less risk of these side effects. **NOTE:** Recent studies show an increased risk of heart attack in patients who use high-dose Cox-2 inhibitors along with naproxen (Aleve), so caution is advised. Also, if you have taken an NSAID (including ibuprofen) for a long time, it may precipitate a heart attack if you stop taking it suddenly. Obtain guidance from your doctor, especially if you have heart disease.

Step 9: Have Surgery

Surgery should be the last resort, only for severe and unrelenting problems. Because pain from spurs usually comes from the inflammation, surgery may not relieve the pain unless the inflammation is also eliminated. Now you see why surgery does not always help. If you have surgery, it may take several months of recovery before your foot returns to normal.

BREAST PAIN OR LUMPS

Lumps and pain are the most common problems with women's breasts. Women's breasts usually change at puberty, during menstrual periods, and after menopause. These changes are usually normal, caused by hormonal changes. Persistent pain or lumps are abnormal, but they are most commonly caused by fibrous cysts (also known as *fibrocystic disease*). However, breast pain and lumps can be signs of infection or cancer, both of which can lead to damage of the breasts, spread of the infection or cancer, and death.

Common Symptoms

- Pain or feeling of fullness in one or both breasts
- Pain accompanied by warmth, redness, or discharge from the nipple
- A lump that you can see or feel (whether movable or not)

What You Need to Know

Every woman should examine her breasts every month starting at puberty (see box). If you find anything abnormal or anything that concerns you, have your physician evaluate it. The mammogram, a special type of x-ray of the breast, is an excellent screening tool for finding cancers that cannot be felt by hand, but controversy exists regarding when to start doing them and how often they should be done. Typically, most doctors recommend having a mammogram every one to two years beginning at age 40, then once a year after age 50.

HOW TO CHECK YOUR BREASTS

To check your breasts, first map out your breast so that you know you have checked the entire area. I recommend the *spiral method:* Begin at the top of your breast near your armpit, and make a circle around your breast. Repeat this, making smaller and smaller circles, until you end at your nipple. Using this "map," take the flat surface of your fingers and first apply light pressure over the entire breast, which enables you to feel tiny lumps near the surface. Then repeat, using deeper pressure. Be aware of any lumps or thickened tissue.

General Recommendations for Breast Cysts

Some doctors think that caffeine and saturated fat both contribute to breast cysts and should therefore be reduced, but studies have not been conclusive. To be on the safe side, reduce your caffeine and saturated fat; if your cysts don't shrink within about three months, these factors are not causing or contributing to your condition. If they do shrink, continue to reduce the foods and drinks that contain these ingredients (including most soft drinks, which contain caffeine).

Your Balanced Healing Action Plan for Breast Pain and Lumps

- Because breast pain and lumps can indicate life-threatening problems, you should always seek professional medical evaluation and diagnostics first. If an infection is causing the problem, your physician will prescribe antibiotics to treat it. Other treatment will be necessary if the lump turns out to be cancer; early diagnosis is critical for effective treatment.

Step 1: Take Vitamin E for Breast Pain

If breast pain is not caused by infection or a tumor, and there is no discharge, start with vitamin E at doses of 800 IU to 1,200 IU per day to reduce tissue inflammation. This is the easiest and least expensive treatment and is very effective as well. You may see benefits within a few weeks, although it can take one to two months for some women.

Step 2: Undergo Infrasonic Therapy for Breast Lumps

Infrasound, or low-frequency sound waves, works by increasing the local circulation of blood and lymph, which reduces fibrous breast tissue. I recommend it as the first practitioner-administered treatment because it may take just a few treatments to decrease or eliminate breast lumps. Numerous chiropractors, naturopaths, acupuncturists, and a few doctors use infrasound. (See Appendix C, under "Infrasound," for a reference source.)

Step 3: Apply Natural Progesterone Cream for Breast Pain and/or Lumps

Natural progesterone cream is especially beneficial for breast pain associated with the menstrual cycle because such pain may be caused by decreased levels of progesterone. Progesterone cream is also effective for fibrocystic disease because many cysts may occur because of an imbalance of hormones (usually too much estrogen and not enough progesterone).

Apply 20mg of progesterone cream once a day to your breasts during days 14 to 28 of your cycle to relieve pain and reduce lumps caused by cysts. The cysts should decrease in size within three to four months. (See Appendix B, under "Hormonal Supplements," for further guidance and information.)

> When she came to see me, 42-year-old Zelda, a restaurant manager, had been diagnosed with fibrocystic breast disease as a teenager. As an adult, she had several biopsies of breast lumps to make sure she did not have cancer. They were all negative. She has tried vitamin E and evening primrose oil, mistakenly thinking they would help breast lumps (they help breast *pain*). I placed her on natural progesterone cream, which she rubbed on her breasts, and within three months nearly all of her breast lumps were gone.

Step 4: Take Evening Primrose Oil or Chasteberry for Breast Pain

Evening primrose oil (500mg three times a day) works by inhibiting prostaglandins, natural substances in the body that cause inflammation. Chasteberry (solid extract, standardized to 0.5 percent agnuside, 175mg to 225mg daily), which works through its hormonal effects, can also reduce breast pain, especially if you have PMS. (Be aware, however, that chasteberry can decrease libido.) If these herbs are not effective in three months, they won't work, and you should stop taking them.

Step 5: Undergo Acupuncture for Breast Pain and Lumps

If the previous steps haven't helped you, I recommend acupuncture for either breast pain or breast lumps. Acupuncture is most effective when the breast pain first begins. Principal points can be found on the upper back, chest, arms, legs, and feet. Always seek evaluation and treatment from a practitioner certified in acupuncture. (See Appendix A, under "Acupuncture," for guidance on finding a qualified acupuncturist and for further explanation of the different acupuncture techniques.) You should notice improvement within six acupuncture treatments, but you might need additional sessions for maximum benefits.

Step 6: Take the Prescription Hormone Drugs Danazol or Bromocriptine

If the previous steps don't help you, your doctor can prescribe Danazol or Bromocriptine. These drugs are conventional hormones taken by mouth to control breast pain, but they do have various side effects. Consider them only if the previous steps do not provide relief.

BRONCHITIS

Bronchitis is an inflammation of the upper bronchial passageways of the lungs. Swelling from the inflammation can cause the smaller airways of the lungs to narrow or shut off. There are two forms of bronchitis, acute and chronic. Acute bronchitis is usually caused by infection, most often viral, and is most common in winter. It doesn't result in any long-term problems, although it can lead to pneumonia in some cases. Chronic bronchitis is more common in people who are physically inactive (sedentary), are overweight, or who smoke. Chronic bronchitis can cause permanent lung and heart damage.

Common Symptoms: Acute Bronchitis

- Hacking cough
- Productive yellow, white, or green phlegm
- Fever
- Chills
- Soreness and tightness of the chest

Common Symptoms: Chronic Bronchitis

- Persistent, productive cough for at least three months of the year
- Wheezing
- Shortness of breath

What You Need to Know

Although most doctors prescribe antibiotics for acute bronchitis, the medications don't work unless you have a bacterial infection, no matter how long you have been coughing. Colored sputum does not necessarily indicate bacterial infection. If coughing persists longer than three weeks, I recommend a chest x-ray to rule out pneumonia, TB, cancer, or some other underlying medical condition. Get tested immediately if you cough up blood from your lungs.

For chronic bronchitis, eliminating smoking is the most important factor in prevention and in effective treatment. If you have chronic bronchitis, you should have Pneumovax, a vaccine to prevent most pneumonias, and flu vaccine. Long-term antibiotics are not helpful, and you should not take them. Bronchitis can also be caused or initiated by acid reflux (also called *gastroesophageal reflux*, or *GERD*, or, more commonly, heartburn), a condition in which the acid in the esophagus is inhaled into the lungs, caus-ing irritation. If you have GERD, the appropriate treatment can reverse or reduce your bronchitis symptoms (see the section on heartburn on page 234 for treatment guidelines).

Your Balanced Healing Action Plan for Bronchitis

- Do not use cough suppressants! Sputum production is necessary to clear the lungs and avoid pneumonia.

Step 1: Take an Expectorant

An expectorant helps loosen and bring up secretions. It is the best treatment for both acute and chronic bronchitis. You can use either a conventional expectorant (guaifen-esin) or an herbal expectorant (glycerol guaiacolate, 200mg to 400mg three times daily for adults, 200mg three times daily for children). Both are available without a prescrip-tion and are equally effective. If these aren't helpful, another herbal expectorant to try is bromelain (80mg to 320mg per day), an herb that has expectorant abilities and also decreases bronchial secretions. You can take bromelain safely with the other expectorants.

Step 2: Take Vitamin C for Acute Bronchitis

Vitamin C can reduce symptoms of acute bronchitis through its antioxidant effects, but it is best started within two days of onset. Take 1,000mg daily.

Step 3: Use Heat and Postural Drainage for Both Chronic and Acute Bronchitis

Heat and postural drainage twice daily helps get rid of excessive mucus, and I recommend it for either acute or chronic bronchitis. Apply wet heat (hot towel or a heating pad that you can get wet) to your chest for 20 minutes, and then lie face down on a bed with the top half of your body off the bed. Maintain this position for 15 minutes, and try to cough mucus into a basin on the floor. Sometimes, lightly "drumming" (or tapping) on the chest can help break up the mucus.

Step 4: Take Appropriate Chinese Herbal Remedies

If you are still having symptoms of bronchitis, I next recommend Chinese herbals for both acute and chronic conditions, and these can be used with the previous steps. I recommend formulas such as *Ding Chuan Tang, Ching Fei Yi Huo Pian, Er Chen Wan,* or *Qing Qi Hua Tan Wan*. Consult a practitioner qualified in Chinese herbal medicine to determine which Chinese herbal formulas are the best for your particular syndromes You should see initial benefits from the herbs within three weeks (sometimes sooner), but you may need to take them longer, depending on your condition. (See Appendix A, under "Chinese Herbs," for further information.)

Step 5: Undergo Acupuncture for Chronic Bronchitis

If you continue to have chronic bronchitis symptoms, I recommend acupuncture in addi-tion to the Chinese herbals. Principal points are usually found on the upper back, wrists, and legs. Ear points include the bronchus, and the antiwheezing point (asthma). You should always seek evaluation and treatment from a practitioner certified in acupuncture. (See Appendix A, under "Acupuncture," for guidance on finding a qualified acupuncturist and for more information on different acupuncture techniques.) You should notice improvement within six acupuncture treatments, although you might need additional sessions for maximum benefits.

> Mitch, a 40-year-old TV repairman, came to see me after 11 years of chronic bronchitis. Besides his chronic cough and sputum production, he would have acute flare-ups that would always be treated with antibiotics and sometimes steroids. As a result, he had gained a lot of weight and also become resistant to several antibiotics. He had been instructed in postural drainage, but he did not do it regularly. I recommended bromelain as an expectorant and started him on Chinese herbs and acupuncture. Mitch began to improve almost immediately, and within two months, he was symptom free and off all his medications. Two years later, he had not had any flare-ups.

Step 6: For Persistent Cough, Take the Chinese Herbal Remedy Wen Dan Tang or a Conventional Inhaler

If you still have a persistent cough despite the above measures, I recommend trying another Chinese herbal formula, *Wen Dan Tang*, three times daily between meals. You should see benefits within 3 to 10 days. If this natural method does not reduce your cough, your doctor can prescribe a beta-agonist (albuterol) inhaler, which reduces spasm in the lung's passageways (these spasms may be causing the cough). Your coughing should diminish almost immediately. Do not use a drug to suppress the cough—you'll just mask the underlying cause, and it will take much longer for you to heal.

Step 7: Take Appropriate Homeopathic Remedies

If your symptoms are still not resolved, you might consider taking a homeopathic remedy. *Kali bichromicum* (6c) is used for loose, white phlegm, with cough and irritability; *Phosphorus* (6c) is used for loss of voice, cough, thirst, and sore throat. You should consult a qualified homeopathist for guidance on which remedies will be most beneficial and for proper dosages. You should feel better in one to two weeks. (See Appendix A, under "Homeopathy," for guidance on finding a qualified homeopathist and for further information.)

Step 8: Take N-Acetylcysteine for Recurrent Bronchitis

If you continue to have episodes of bronchitis that the previous steps don't control, take N-acetylcysteine (400mg-1,200mg daily), an amino-acid derivative that can break up mucus. You may have to take this supplement for four to six months before you see the benefits.

BURSITIS

Bursitis is inflammation of the bursa, a sac-like membrane pouch that lubricates joints. There are 150 different bursae sacs throughout the body. Bursitis is caused by strenuous activity, heavy lifting, repetitive motion, or extended working in unusual positions. The most common joints affected are the shoulder, elbows, hips, and knees. Most bursitis will improve and go away on its own (although it may last several months), but chronic bursitis can lead to the formation of calcium deposits, which can cause stiffness and decreased motion of the joint.

Common Symptoms

- Pain in the joint
- Occasional swelling
- Decreased range of motion

Your Balanced Healing Action Plan for Bursitis

- If you have bursitis for more than one month, or it is chronic, go directly to Step 4.

Step 1: Use the RICE Method

If you have recent onset or mild bursitis, use the RICE approach:

- **Rest** the joint: Avoid using it, especially for strenuous activities such as lifting (shoulder) or walking/climbing (knee, hip).
- Apply **ice** to the affected area: You can use commercial ice packs sold in drug stores or wrap a towel around some ice. Do not apply it for more than 20 minutes per hour.
- **Compress** the joint: Wrap the joint with an elastic bandage such as an ACE wrap, but don't tighten it so much that you cut off blood circulation.
- **Elevate** the affected limb. Keep the joint elevated; for example, put your knee on some pillows.

Step 2: Take Bromelain, Curcumin, and Citrus Flavonoids to Promote Healing

In addition to Step 1, start taking supplements of bromelain (250mg-750mg three times per day between meals) and curcumin (200mg to 400mg three times per day between meals), which can decrease inflammation and bruising. To cut healing time by half, add citrus flavonoids (5,600mg to 1,000mg three times daily) to these two supplements. You should feel better within one to three weeks.

Step 3: Take an NSAID If Pain and Swelling Continue

While the above measures are healing your bursitis, you may continue having pain and swelling. If so, take over-the-counter nonsteroidal anti-inflammatory drugs (NSAIDs), such as ibuprofen or naproxen (Aleve), which give you short-term pain relief and reduce inflammation while your tissues heal naturally. You should get some relief within a few days. If these are not effective, prescription NSAIDs (such as Naprosyn, Feldene, Daypro, Orudis, Mobic, Cataflam, Relafen, Arthrotec, and many more) may work. However, these drugs can cause stomach irritation and bleeding. If this occurs, try Cox-2 inhibitors, which have less risk of these side effects. **NOTE:** Recent studies show an increased risk of heart attack in patients who use high-dose Cox-2 inhibitors along with naproxen (Aleve), so caution is advised. Also, if you have taken an NSAID (including ibuprofen) for a long time, it may precipitate a heart attack if you stop taking it suddenly. Obtain guidance from your doctor, especially if you have heart disease. All these drugs should be used short term to relieve pain and swelling while the following steps have time to work.

Step 4: Undergo Physical Therapy

If your symptoms have not responded to the first three steps within a few weeks, add physical therapy treatments. These include electrical stimulation (passing direct or alternating low-voltage current through the painful joint), ultrasound (high-frequency sound that provides heat to the deep tissues), and iontophoresis (application of a topical steroid solution through the skin into the affected joint). I also highly recommend infrasound, or low-frequency sound. Infrasound works by increasing the local circulation of blood and lymph, thereby accelerating the healing process. It not only can reduce pain, it can also decrease swelling. Infrasound is used by numerous chiropractors, naturopaths, acupuncturists, and a few doctors. (See Appendix C, under "Infrasound," for a reference source.)

Wait until any inflammation subsides before performing exercises. If your symptoms improve, you can then discontinue or reduce the drugs from Step 3. You should start feeling better within one to two weeks.

Step 5: Undergo Acupuncture

If your bursitis persists after three to four weeks of physical therapy, I recommend acupuncture. Principal points depend on the particular joint involved. The Liver-Gall Bladder channels are important to treat because they control the tendons and sinews of the body. You should always seek evaluation and treatment from a practitioner certified in acupuncture. (See Appendix A, under "Acupuncture," for guidance on finding a qualified acupuncturist and for more information on different acupuncture techniques.) You should feel better within six acupuncture treatments, but you might need additional sessions to get maximum benefits.

Step 6: Undergo Low-Level Energy Laser Therapy

If acupuncture is not effective or only partially effective, I recommend low-level energy laser therapy, which appears to help heal the tissue, reduce the inflammatory response, and give long-lasting relief. These lasers are called "cold" lasers because they do not produce heat like the hot lasers used in surgical procedures do. Their primary side effect (in about 25 percent of patients) is that they cause a temporary increase in soreness, which may last one to three days. You should feel better within six to nine treatments. I often use this laser in conjunction with acupuncture for better and faster results. Because the low-level laser is currently a research device, it is unavailable to most doctors. (See Appendix C for information on doctors who are currently using the laser.)

> Nick, a 33-year-old concert violinist, had bursitis of his hip. He had undergone two steroid injections and physical therapy that had not helped. His doctor recommended bursectomy (removal of the bursa sac), but Nick wanted to avoid surgery. I treated him with acupuncture and low-level energy laser. His pain was gone within nine treatments.

Step 7: Undergo Corticosteroid Injections

If your bursitis is still giving you problems, your doctor can give you a local injection of corticosteroids. Sometimes these injections will resolve your symptoms, but often they will give only temporary relief (a few days or weeks). If they work, they can be repeated if the pain recurs, but you should not have more than three to four per year because the steroids can soften the bone and damage the joint. If one injection is not helpful, further injections won't work either, so discontinue the treatment.

Step 8: Surgery

Surgery to remove the offending bursa sac is a treatment of last resort. I have found surgery to help only a small percentage of people. It can cause permanent problems, such as decreased strength and range of motion.

CANCER

Cancer is an abnormal growth of cells that can grow and spread, interfering with normal bodily processes, crowding out healthy cells, and drawing nutrients from tissues. There are four main types of cancer, classified according to the tissues involved: *carcinoma* (solid tissue), *lymphoma* (lymph glands and system), *leukemia* (blood), and *sarcoma* (connective tissues). There are numerous causes of cancer, including viruses, genetic predisposition, environmental pollutants, poor diet, and poor general health. Often, the cause is a combination of several of these factors. Smoking is the most common environmental pollutant and can cause a variety of cancers, including lung, breast, stomach, throat, esophagus, and prostate. Cancers related to smoking are more likely to affect women than men. Diet is also a factor: Almost one-third of all cancers are related to being overweight or having a poor diet, especially cancers of the breast, colon, uterus, prostate, and gall bladder.

The four leading types of cancer are breast, prostate, lung, and colorectal. Although overall occurrences and deaths from cancer in the U.S. are decreasing, lung and breast cancers are increasing, especially in women. Lung cancer is the deadliest form of cancer in men and non-Hispanic women. Colorectal cancer occurrence has remained steady in the past decade. It is estimated that the incidence of cancer will doubled by 2050, primarily because there will be more people and people will be living longer.

Common Symptoms

Cancer has numerous symptoms, depending on where it is located and how it spreads. According to the American Cancer Society, there are seven main warning signs, listed under the acronym CAUTION:

- Change in bowel or bladder habits
- A sore that does not heal
- Unusual bleeding or discharge
- Thickening or lump
- Indigestion or difficulty swallowing
- Obvious change in wart or mole
- Nagging cough or hoarseness

In addition, unexplained weight loss is often a sign of cancer.

What You Need to Know

Prevention and early detection are the best ways of treating cancer. Everyone should have yearly physical exams. Additionally, for women, annual pap smears and breast exams are essential (see "Breast Lumps" on page 142 for information on how to examine your breasts), and mammograms should be done after age 40 to help detect and prevent breast cancer. For men, prostate exams and testing (for prostate specific antigen, or PSA) are important for prevention of prostate cancer (elevated PSA may indicate cancer, although it can also increase with other prostate conditions, such as prostatitis or benign prostatic hypertrophy; that's why an exam is essential along with the test). For both men and women, screening for blood in the stool should be done routinely, and a colonoscopy (placing a fiberoptic scope into the colon to look for polyps or cancer) should be done after the age of 50 to help detect and prevent colon cancer. Obviously, smoking should be eliminated to help prevent numerous types of cancer, especially of the lung.

Besides trying to destroy or slow the cancer itself, treatments are also directed at the symptoms caused by the cancer, and at the side effects of cancer treatment. The most common symptoms/side effects are fatigue and pain, with nausea and weight loss second. Some cancers are now curable. Spontaneous remission (sudden disappearance of the cancer) does occur, and conventional treatments can bring long-term remission. If you have not had a recurrence of your cancer within five years, you have a very good likelihood of survival and a low risk that it will return. For my patients, I try first to prolong life and second to improve quality of life. Both of these goals are achievable.

General Recommendations

Diet: There is no question that diet plays a significant role in both preventing and causing cancer. Animal fats and processed foods are the main foods that contain cancer-causing substances (called *carcinogens*) and should be limited. Citrus fruits and especially cruciferous vegetables are the main foods that protect against cancer, and you should try to eat more of them. Onions, garlic, berries, tomatoes, and autumn olives (which taste like cranberries) also have cancer-fighting properties. Various spices, including basil, rosemary, turmeric, ginger, and parsley all contain flavonoids that can help against cancer, but fresh herbs are preferred. There are no particular diets that will cure cancer, but limiting saturated fats, high-fat dairy, and processed foods, and increasing whole grains, fruits, and vegetables can help slow the progression of cancer as well as protect the body against toxic cancer treatments. Soy products can provide high-quality protein and *phytoestrogens* (natural estrogen produced by plants), and may be especially beneficial for hormonal-related cancers such as prostate and breast. (Do not exceed 30g to 35g per day or take less than 20g per day. (See Appendix B, under "Soy," for more information.) Soy and red grapes have *antiangiogenic* effects (that is, they reduce new blood vessel growth in tumors). Flaxseed (ground or oil) may be even better than soy at preventing breast cancer. Foods containing boron, such as wine, almonds, coffee, peanut butter, raisins, legumes, low-fat milk, and certain fruits and nuts, may help stave off cancer, especially prostate. Chemicals called *polyphenols*, which are antioxidants that you can get from red wine, have been found to keep prostate cancer cells from proliferating—and they may do the same for other cancers.

Exercise: Regular physical exercise helps protect against cancer of the breast, colorectal, and prostate. Once cancer occurs, exercise is invaluable for reducing fatigue, lessening anxiety and depression, increasing physical capacity, and helping to provide a better overall quality of life. I recommend all types of exercise. (See "Simple Healing Steps for All Health Conditions," on page 79, under "Exercise," for further guidance.)

Meditation: Meditation is excellent for reducing symptoms of anxiety and depression, and it also can reduce the side effects of cancer treatment and improve quality of life. (See "Simple Healing Steps for All Health Conditions," on page 79, under "Meditation," for further information and examples.)

Qigong: Qigong has been shown to reduce or eliminate the side effects of cancer treatments such as radiation and chemotherapy. In addition, because it improves immune function, Qigong may help to prolong survival. There are many Qigong exercises designed specifically for cancer patients. (See Appendix A, under "Traditional Chinese Medicine," for further information on Qigong exercises and guidance in finding a qualified instructor.)

Your Balanced Healing Action Plan for Cancer

- Each type of cancer has specific treatments. The following are general recommendations for all cancers, with additional recommendations for specific cancers.

Step 1: Undergo Proven Conventional Treatments

Always undergo the conventional approaches that have been proven effective, including radiation, chemotherapy, surgery, *hyperthermia* (elevating body temperature), and hormonal therapy. *Do not try alternative methods first to see whether they'll work because if they don't, it may be too late to treat your cancer with conventional means.* Proven conventional methods are your best bet for a cure. However, do not undergo these treatments if they have not been shown to be beneficial or if they are recommended just because "there is nothing else to do." These treatments can be toxic and impair your quality of life. So use them only if they are proven beneficial or hold promise of benefits. To find out whether they are potentially beneficial, ask your doctor what the research has shown specifically—and/or do your own research using the suggestions I gave you in Chapter 4.

Step 2: Take Supplements and Herbs During Conventional Cancer Treatment

Certain supplements and herbs may protect normal cells from specific chemotherapy agents, hyperthermia, or radiation damage and improve the outcome of these treatments. Specifically:

- If you undergo chemotherapy using **Adriamycin**, a drug used in many solid and blood cancers in which a small cell type is dominant, L-Carnitine (1g to 2g daily) and CoQ10 (50mg daily), can protect the heart against damage from the adriamycin.
- If you undergo chemotherapy using **Cisplatin**, a drug used in cancers of the testicles, bladder, and ovaries, there are three supplements that can be beneficial. Glutathione (600mg on days 2 to 5 of chemotherapy, intramuscularly) reduces the kidney and neurological toxicity of cisplatin. Quercetin (400mg to 500mg three times daily) increases the number of tumor cells killed when using cisplatin. It can also be given by IV, 420mg to 1400mg/m2, weekly or every three weeks. Selenium (200mcg daily) can increase the tumor-killing effects of cisplatin in the presence of EDTA (a chelating agent).
- If you undergo chemotherapy using **Interleukin-2**, consider taking melatonin (20mg to 50mg per day with chemotherapy, beginning one week before you start therapy), which may improve survival. Interleukin-2 is called a cytokine, a protein that helps regulate your immune system. It is used to treat cancers of the lung, GI (gastrointestinal) tract, liver, kidney, and breast, and melanoma.
- If you undergo chemotherapy using **triptorelin**, a drug used for prostate cancer, consider taking melatonin (20mg to 50mg per day with chemotherapy, beginning one week before you start therapy), which may improve survival.
- If you undergo chemotherapy with **interferon** (used in some kidney cancers), consider taking melatonin (20mg to 50mg per day with chemotherapy, beginning one week before you start therapy), which may improve survival.
- If **hyperthermia** is indicated for your cancer, Quercetin (400mg to 500mg three times daily) can increase the number of tumor cells killed when hyperthermia is performed. It can also be given by IV, 420mg to 1400mg/m2, weekly or every three weeks.
- If you undergo **radiation** therapy for any cancer, niacin (100mg to 300mg per day) can make radiation therapy more effective by depleting the oxygen used by cancer cells, thus killing them.

- If you undergo **radiation** therapy for **glioblastoma**, the most common malignant tumor of the brain, consider taking melatonin (20mg to 50mg per day with chemotherapy, beginning one week before you start therapy), which may improve survival.
- If you undergo chemotherapy using **Vincristine**, a drug used in leukemia, Hodgkin's, and other lymphomas, bromelain (80mg to 320mg per day for 10 days) can improve the effectiveness of this drug.
- If you undergo chemotherapy using **5-FU**, a drug used primarily in cancers of the gastrointestinal tract (stomach, colon, rectum, pancreas), bromelain (80mg to 320mg per day for 10 days) can improve the effectiveness of 5-FU.
- If you have any chemotherapy for **breast cancer**, take gingko biloba (240mg daily with the chemotherapy) because recent studies have shown that such chemotherapy impairs cognition (decreased memory, self-regulation, and planning functions). Gingko can protect the normal brain cells from being damaged by chemotherapy, and it stimulates the production of new nerve cells.
- If you undergo radiation therapy for **breast cancer** or chemotherapy for **lung cancer**, Astragalus (15g to 25g of powdered form daily) with ligustrum, a Chinese herb also known as Chinese privet (10g to 15g of powdered form daily or 3ml to 5ml of tincture three times daily) may increase survival rate.
- *Mucositis* (mouth and gum sores) can occur as a side effect of some radiation and most chemotherapy (except 5-FU). Taking German chamomile as a rinse (extracts or flowers standardized to 1.2 percent apigenin three to four times daily) can prevent mucositis.

Discuss these with your doctor before taking them.

Step 3: Take Chinese Herbal Remedies During Conventional Treatment

I also highly recommend using some Chinese herbal formulas while you are receiving any type of chemotherapy or radiation because they can help conventional treatment work better, and they can eliminate or reduce side effects of the treatment. There are several herbal formulas that can do either or both. My first choice is *Zuo Gui Wan/You Gui Yin*, which can strengthen the immune system, speed recovery from surgery, and reduce the side effects of chemotherapy and radiation. It should be started at least a week before cancer treatment is begun and continued throughout the treatment.

I also recommend Marrow Plus, a formula used in the Quan Yin Herbal Program in San Francisco for bone marrow suppression by chemotherapy or radiation. The bone marrow is responsible for making new blood cells, and chemotherapy shuts down these processes. If bone marrow suppression is severe, further treatments must be delayed until your blood count increases. Marrow Plus protects the bone marrow and helps it recover more quickly, allowing treatment to continue. Start taking this formula at least a week before you start cancer treatment, and continue until your strength returns and your blood count is normal. Because significant blood loss may occur in some cancer surgeries, you can also take it before and after surgery to help your body produce new blood cells more quickly. Another Chinese herbal formula that can be used for blood replacement is *Ba Zhen Tang*. (For further information on these herbal formulas, see Appendix C for referral information.)

Coriolus (Turkey Tail) is another herb that I highly recommend. It is a mushroom extract that Japanese research has shown to significantly prolong survival time (it may double it) in people with stomach, uterine, colon, lung, colorectal, prostate, breast and liver cancers, when taken with chemotherapy.

Step 4: Take Bovine Cartilage During Conventional Cancer Treatment

Bovine cartilage (3g three times a day) is a biological response modifier (in other words, it improves the functions of the immune system); it may also improve outcome when used with chemotherapy and radiation. Take it while you receive cancer treatment and for four months after your treatment ends. You can take bovine cartilage along with any of the other steps.

Step 5: Take Herbal Remedies After Conventional Cancer Treatment

There is some evidence that supplementation with high-potency vitamins, minerals, and antioxidants can inhibit cancer growth, improve immune function, and prevent cell or tissue damage. A few studies have shown that such combinations may help chemotherapy and radiation work more effectively while decreasing their side effects. On the other hand, some cancer authorities think that megadose antioxidant vitamins may interfere with the chemotherapy process because such treatment requires oxidation to kill the cancer cells. However, so far, no studies have proven this conclusively. At this time, I recommend taking a high-potency multivitamin along with the above steps, but not megadose vitamins. (See Appendix A, under "Multivitamins," for further information and recommended formulas.) In addition, I recommend several specific supplements to take after your cancer treatment has ended:

- Green tea (average of 4 cups per day, providing 240mg to 320mg of polyphenols, or standardized extracts containing up to 97 percent polyphenols) to inhibit the growth of cancer.
- Garlic (4g, or one clove, containing at least 10 percent alliin), and/or onions (50g fresh onion) daily to protect the liver from toxic damage.
- Quercetin (400mg to 500mg three times daily) may make abnormal cells return to normal and inhibit the growth of prostate cancer.
- Vitamin K (5mg) with vitamin C (250mg) twice daily may inhibit prostate and breast cancer. Vitamin K (45mg) alone has been shown to inhibit the progression of liver cancer. Because vitamin K affects how blood clots, take it only under supervision of a doctor.
- Flaxseed oil (2 teaspoonsful daily) may deter prostate cancer growth.
- Beta Glucans (mucopolysaccharides) may enhance the functioning of your immune system.

■ Elligatannins (from red raspberries) may prevent the development of cancer cells and slow their growth.

Step 6: Practice Guided Imagery, Interactive Imagery, Prayer, Meditation, and Other Mind-Body Techniques

Mind-body interventions, primarily guided imagery and interactive imagery, improve quality of life and can reduce the side effects of conventional cancer treatment. Meditation, prayer, and spiritual belief can also reduce side effects, anxiety, and depression. Use any or all of these methods along with the above steps. These techniques also benefit family members who are dealing with their own worries, fears, and concerns. (See Appendix A, under "Mind-Body Techniques," for further explanations and examples.) Interactive imagery can sometimes lead you to information that has eluded conventional detection.

When Diane, a 52-year-old social worker, was diagnosed with breast cancer, she was told that the cancer was very tiny and only in one spot. Her doctors recommended surgery, but she wondered whether she could cure the cancer by natural means and just watch it to make sure it didn't grow. She underwent interactive imagery, in which she saw the image of a wise man (her inner wisdom figure). He told her that she needed to undergo the surgery and that everything would be all right. Diane still didn't want to go through surgery, but she underwent interactive imagery two more times, again being told (by other images) that she needed to have surgery. She finally agreed to have surgery, at which time several more areas of cancer were found, as well as some in her lymph nodes. The surgery made the difference, and it's the reason Diane is alive today.

Step 7: Undergo Acupuncture for Adverse Effects of Treatment and Complications of Cancer

Acupuncture is excellent for preventing or treating nausea and vomiting, the typical side effects of chemotherapy. You can also treat yourself at home for nausea by using acupressure on the P6 acupuncture point in the forearm: Lay your middle three fingers across the palm side of your opposite wrist, with your ring finger against your wrist crease. The P6 point is next to the index finger, between the two tendons in the middle of your forearm. Massage this deeply. (Expect it to be tender.) You can also use Sea-Bands (tight bands containing a bead that presses on the P6 acupuncture point), which you can buy in most drug stores.

Acupuncture is also effective for other side effects—such as pain and fatigue—of either the cancer or cancer treatment. Side effects of radiation, such as salivary problems from head/neck irradiation (dry mouth, difficulty swallowing), GI problems (gas, bloating, nausea, diarrhea, constipation), breathing difficulties (shortness of breath), and incontinence (from bladder or prostate treatment) can all respond well to acupuncture.

Always seek evaluation and treatment from a practitioner certified in acupuncture. (See Appendix A, under "Acupuncture," for guidance on finding a qualified acupuncturist and for further explanation of different acupuncture techniques.) You should feel improvement within six acupuncture treatments, but you might need additional sessions for maximum benefits.

> Jeremy, a 60-year-old pharmacist, came to me after radiation had successfully treated his prostate cancer but had unfortunately burned his bladder, so he'd lost control over his urination. After just 2 acupuncture treatments, bladder function and control began to return. After 10 treatments, he only had occasional leakage.

Step 8: *Join a Support Group*

I urge you to join a support group during or after your cancer treatment. Such groups have been found to—in fact, at least double—survival time in most cancers, especially breast cancer and melanoma. Most hospitals have such support groups or can refer you to one.

Step 9: *Take Chinese Herbal Remedies After Conventional Treatment*

Several Chinese herbal formulas have anti-tumor effects and should be used after cancer treatment is ended. These include formulas called Regeneration and Power Mushrooms (a combination of Ganoderma, Tremella, Poria, and Shiitake mushrooms), both of which can also boost energy in addition to strengthening your immune systems. Maitake mushrooms also have a tumor-fighting compound (beta glucan) and can reduce cancer pain. Another Chinese herbal formula, called Cordyseng, combines several herbs that increase energy, improve immune function, and protect the liver and your digestion. It can decrease the fatigue that cancer and cancer treatment cause. It is a powder that can be mixed in any liquid, preferably ginger tea (which helps digestion) or green tea (which has an anti-tumor effect). You can take it at any time before, during, or after cancer treatment. (For further information on these herbal formulas, go to Appendix C for referral information.)

In a recent study, daily consumption of a traditional Chinese soup containing vegetables and herbs was associated with regression and prolonged survival in patients with small cell tumors of the lung. The soup has also been used successfully in many other cancers. See chart below for ingredients.

"CANCER SOUP" INGREDIENTS			
Soybean	Ginseng	Shiitake mushrooms	Sesame seed
Mung Bean	Red Date	Angelica Root	Hawthorn fruit
Scallion	Licorice	Dandelion Root	Parsley
Garlic	Senegal Root	Lentil Bean	Onion
Ginger	Leek	Olive	

(For further information on this soup, contact Alexander Sun, PhD, the Connecticut Institute for Aging and Cancer, 203-882-9672, or go to www.Sunfarmcorp.com.)

Anne, a 41-year-old college professor, was diagnosed with Stage III (advanced) colon cancer. She was scheduled for surgery to remove the mass, followed by chemotherapy. She came to me because she was worried about the side effects of the chemotherapy. I instructed her first in meditation and Qigong exercises, and then started her on *Zuo Gui Wan/You Gui Yin* Chinese herbal formula (Step 3). Following surgery, her surgeon was very surprised when she recovered twice as fast as expected and was able to start chemotherapy (5-FU) sooner. During chemotherapy, I started her on Bromelain (Step 2) to improve the effectiveness of the 5-FU, Coriolus to extend survival, and Marrow Plus for bone marrow support. She had no nausea or vomiting from the chemotherapy and lost so little hair that she didn't need a wig. She also maintained her energy level. Anne was able to complete all her chemotherapy treatments as scheduled. After her treatments were finished, she took *Fu Zheng* in Green Tea and Power Mushrooms (Step 9) for more than a year. She never had fatigue or other problems.

Step 10: Take PC-SPES for Prostate Cancer

A centuries-old herbal remedy, sold as PC-SPES (PC = "prostate cancer," *SPES* is Latin for "hope"), had shown excellent results in shrinking tumor size and reducing pain in prostate cancer. It is a combination of seven herbs: *Da Qing Ye*, licorice, *San Qi*, Reishi mushroom, Baikal skullcap, chrysanthemum, and saw palmetto. Unfortunately, PC-SPES has now been taken off the market due to contaminants. However, most qualified herbalists can prepare the same combination.

IMPORTANT: Cancer Treatments Not Proven Effective

There are many other treatments purported to cure or control cancer. None of these have yet been proven to do either one, although there are many testimonials that support each. These include:

- Essiac, based on an Ojibwa Indian formula, and containing four herbs: burdock root, sheep sorrel, slippery elm bark, and turkey (Indian) rhubarb.
- Antineoplastons, which are made from your own urine.
- Laetrile, derived from apricot seeds.
- 714X, a homeopathic camphor compound.
- Hydrazine sulfate, an *anticachexia* drug (prevents weight loss and debilitation), which ostensibly stabilizes or regresses tumors.
- Shark cartilage, which contains compounds that slow blood vessel growth in cancers.

- Gerson therapy, which uses a radical diet, nutritional manipulation, and coffee enemas.
- Contreras therapy, which includes Laetrile, a vegan diet, proteolytic enzymes, and antioxidant supplements.
- Pancreatic enzyme therapy, which uses numerous pancreatic enzymes to fight pancreatic cancer.
- Hoxsey therapy, which consists of two remedies: two external mixtures containing antimony trisulfide, zinc chloride, and bloodroot (red paste), and arsenic sulfide, sulphur, and talc (yellow paste), as well as an internal liquid mixture containing licorice, red clover, burdock root, stillingia root, barberry, cascara, prickly ash bark, buckthorn bark, and potassium iodide.

Many of these alternative therapies are currently under investigation by the National Center for Complementary and Alternative Medicine (NCCAM). In a recent study, Gerson and Contreras treatments were shown to be ineffective, but Hoxsey therapy showed promise. However, until the results of more research are available, I don't recommend them. In addition, some are very expensive, costing more than $50,000 per year.

CANKER SORES (Apthous Ulcers)

Canker sores are viral infections of the mouth. They can occur on the cheeks, lips, gums, tongue, or soft palate. Heredity plays a role: You have a 90 percent chance of having canker sores if your parents had them. They are more common in adolescents, and women are twice as likely as men to get them. Canker sores are thought to be a result of stress, an immune system defect, food sensitivities, or deficiencies in some vitamins or minerals. Canker sores generally go away on their own in 5 to 10 days. In this section, I'll show you how to eliminate them more quickly and sometimes prevent them from occurring.

Common Symptoms

- Tingling or burning in the mouth (6 to 24 hours before lesions appear).
- Small, painful craters, single or in clusters, that last 5 to 10 days.

General Recommendations

Diet: Certain foods may cause or promote canker sores, including coffee, spices, and citrus fruits. Milk and gluten (wheat) products may also be factors. To see whether specific foods in your diet are causing your canker sores, eliminate them from your diet, then reintroduce them to see whether sores come back. If they do, avoid the foods altogether, or try Step 4.

Your Balanced Healing Action Plan for Canker Sores

Step 1: Take Appropriate Chinese Herbal Remedies

Chinese herbal formulas work very quickly, healing sores usually in 12 to 24 hours. I recommend formulas called *Astra Isatis* (containing Isatis and Astragalus herbs) and Power

Mushrooms (containing Ganoderma, Tremella, Poria, and Polyporus) for their immune enhancement effects. (For further information on these herbal formulas, see Appendix C for referral information.) You can also use *Long Dan Xie Gan Wan*. Other beneficial herbal formulas include *Liang Ge San* or *Zhi Bai Di Huang Tang*. Consult a practitioner qualified in Chinese herbal medicine to determine which Chinese herbal formulas are the best for your particular syndromes. (See Appendix A, under "Chinese Herbs," for further information.)

> At 36, Robin, a graphic artist, had had canker sores since childhood. She would take nonprescription remedies as well as prescribed antiviral creams, but it would still take 7 to 10 days for the sores to clear. I recommended a formula containing Isatis and Astragalus herbs with Power Mushrooms. Within 48 hours, her canker sores had disappeared.

Step 2: Take Deglycyrrhizinated Licorice and Lysine

If Step 1 doesn't help or gives you only partial relief, take deglycyrrhizinated licorice, which is effective in reducing the severity and duration of canker sores because it helps the immune system work better. Most sores are healed within three days, at a dosage of 380mg tablets, one to two tablets twice daily. It can also be used as a mouthwash, which must be prepared by a pharmacist. For best effects, use licorice in combination with Step 1. Lysine (1,000mg three times daily) works against viral growth and can also be effective, either alone or in combination with licorice and/or Step 1.

Step 3: Take a High-Potency Multivitamin to Prevent Recurrent Canker Sores

Because nutritional deficiencies may play a role in canker sores, a high-potency multivitamin, especially one containing vitamins C and B complex, folic acid, zinc, and iron, can decrease the duration and frequency of outbreaks. Take three to six tablets per day. (See Appendix B, under "Multivitamins," for recommended formulas.)

Step 4: Follow the Nambudripad Allergy Elimination Treatment (NAET)

If your canker sores are a chronic problem that do not respond to the other measures, food allergies may be the underlying cause. I recommend the Nambudripad Allergy Elimination Treatment (NAET), which combines acupuncture, kinesiology, chiropractic, herbs, and nutrition to desensitize you to foods to which you are allergic. It may take several months for its effectiveness to be observed, depending on how many allergens are sensitizing you. (See Appendix A, under "NAET," and the section on food allergies for further explanation.)

CARPAL TUNNEL SYNDROME (Compressive Neuropathies)

Compressive neuropathy means that a peripheral nerve is being compressed by scarring or inflammation. The term *tunnel* identifies a compression that occurs where the nerve goes through a tunnel formed by ligaments and tendons. The most common compressive neuropathy is *carpal tunnel syndrome*, compression of the median nerve at the wrist. There are several others as well, including *radial tunnel* (radial nerve in the forearm), *cubital tunnel* (ulnar nerve at the elbow), and tarsal tunnel (posterior tibial nerve in the ankle).

Compressive neuropathies are most often caused by overuse of these areas or injury at work, occasionally by pregnancy or obesity, and—rarely—thyroid disorders. Repetitive stress injuries are more frequent in women, possibly because of hormonal differences or a predilection for lower B_6 levels, common in compressive neuropathies. Chronic pain and inability to use the area involved can cause significant disability and interfere with normal activities and work.

Common Symptoms

Pain, numbness, and tingling are the hallmarks of compressive neuropathies, and these symptoms are felt along the course of the affected nerve. For example, the median nerve goes to the thumb, first two fingers, and one-third of the ring finger, and this is where the numbness and tingling is usually felt in carpal tunnel. The ulnar nerve (cubital tunnel) goes to the inside part of the forearm and elbow and extends to two-thirds of the ring finger and the small finger. The posterior tibial nerve (tarsal tunnel) causes pain and tingling on the inside of the ankle and foot.

These symptoms are usually on and off at the beginning, but they eventually become constant. An important feature of carpal tunnel syndrome is that it tends to awaken you at night with the tingling and numbness. As the condition worsens, the symptoms may spread further up the affected arm or leg.

What You Need to Know

Many people are prone to developing compressive neuropathies and should avoid any type of repetitive work. But many who have been treated successfully for these syndromes often return to the same type of work that caused it in the first place, and as a result, find that their symptoms return.

Your Balanced Healing Action Plan for Carpal Tunnel Syndrome

- If your activities are causing the condition, you must stop performing them, or the symptoms will persist. If you must continue them, splints or braces are helpful in alleviating symptoms, especially at night and during work.
- If your symptoms are severe, or Nerve Conduction Velocity testing (which measures the speed at which electrical impulses travel down the nerve) shows decreased conduction time in the nerve, start with Step 2.

Step 1: Undergo Physical Therapy and Take an NSAID and Vitamin B_6

If you have just started having symptoms and they are mild (that is, they're intermittent and don't wake you at night), physical therapy using ultrasound (high-frequency sound that projects heat into the deep tissues) and iontophoresis (application of steroids through the skin using electrical current), NSAIDs, and vitamin B₆ (100mg daily) are your first course of action. You should notice improvement within four to six weeks, although vitamin B₆ may take three months to be completely effective.

Step 2: Undergo Acupuncture

The National Institutes of Health (NIH) supports acupuncture as effective for these syndromes, especially carpal tunnel, and I recommend it if Step 1 is not effective or the symptoms are already severe. Principal points for carpal tunnel are usually found on the arms and hands, and directly over the carpal tunnel. Acupuncture points for other nerves involved depend on their location. Always seek evaluation and treatment from a practitioner certified in acupuncture. (See Appendix A, under "Acupuncture," for guidance in finding a qualified acupuncturist and for further explanation on different acupuncture techniques.) You should feel improvement within six treatments, but you might need additional sessions for maximum benefits.

Step 3: Undergo Low-Level Energy Laser Therapy

I recommend the use of low-level energy lasers, which appear to help heal the tissue, reduce the inflammatory response, and give long-lasting relief for about half of those who have compressive neuropathies. This laser has recently been approved by the FDA for treatment of carpal tunnel syndrome. However, this treatment is not available everywhere. See Appendix C for information on how to find a doctor who uses it. I use the laser with acupuncture for even better results. You should observe a decrease in symptoms within six to nine laser treatments.

Step 4: Stretching Exercises During and After Treatment

Stretching exercises are helpful for some people during treatment, but I recommend these primarily for preventing the problem from recurring once your symptoms are reduced or eliminated and you've returned to work. The box gives some simple exercises that you can do.

STRETCHING EXERCISE 1

Extend one arm forward, palm up, while keeping your elbow straight. With the opposite hand, slowly pull down the fingers of your outstretched palm toward the floor, keeping the arm steady (don't pull the arm down). Hold the stretch for three seconds, and then stretch slightly further. Rotate the outstretched fingers as far right as possible—without rotating the rest of the arm—and hold for three seconds. Repeat, rotating to the left.

STRETCHING EXERCISE 2

1. Warm-Up

Massage the inside and outside of your hands with your opposite thumb and fingers. Grasp your fingers and gently bend your wrist backward. Hold for five seconds. Gently pull your thumb down and back until you feel the stretch. Hold for five seconds. Clench your fist tightly, and then release, fanning out fingers. Repeat this 5 times.

2. Wrist Rotation

Sit with your elbows close to your waist. Extend your forearms in front of you, parallel to the floor, with your palms facing down. Make fists with both hands and make circles with your fists to the right. Do this 10 times, and then make circles to the left 10 times. Open your hands, extend your fingers, and repeat the entire step.

3. Wrist Curl

Take the same position as with the wrist rotation. Then hold a one-pound dumbbell in each hand and slowly bend your wrists downward. Hold this position for five seconds, then repeat the curl 10 times.

4. Sideways Bend

Take the same position as before. This time, with the one-pound dumbbells, slowly bend your wrists sideways in and out. Repeat 10 times.

5. Wrist Twist

Take the same position as in Steps 3 and 4, and, with the one-pound dumbbell, slowly turn your wrists and forearms until your palms are face up, then turn them down again. Repeat 10 times.

Step 5: Undergo Corticosteroid Injections

Injection of corticosteroids just outside the specific "tunnel" might relieve your symptoms, but the relief is usually temporary. Try this only if the previous steps have failed to reduce your symptoms and before having surgery.

Elena, 34, developed both carpal tunnel and cubital tunnel syndromes from using her hands and arms repetitively at work on an automobile assembly line. She had already had surgery for carpal tunnel of her right wrist, but it didn't help. She went back to work, using splints, but pain and numbness returned in her right wrist and also developed in her left wrist. She tried physical therapy and injections, but these didn't help either. Several hand surgeons recommended surgery, but the first surgery hadn't helped, and Elena didn't want another. I recommended the low-energy laser with acupuncture. After eight treatments, Elena's pain and numbness were gone in both hands. I suggested that she then find another line of work, and do stretching exercises whenever she used her hands and arms a lot.

Step 6: Undergo Surgery

I recommend surgery only as a last resort. Although it's currently the most frequent treatment in this country for compressive neuropathies, surgery often is not beneficial, or it doesn't provide permanent relief. There are several different types of carpal surgery, the most recent one being a "mini-open" technique that takes 10 minutes to perform. I recommend that you consider surgery only if you have at least four out of six of the following conditions:

- The previous steps fail to provide relief.
- You are 50 years or older.
- You have had symptoms for more than 10 months.
- You have constant numbness and tingling.
- Your fingers "catch" when flexed (called trigger fingering).
- You have a positive Phalen's sign (tingling in the fingers when extending the wrist backwards for 30 seconds).

Even if you have surgery, there is no guarantee that it will provide permanent relief.

CEREBRAL VASCULAR INSUFFICIENCY (CVI) AND STROKE (CVA, or Cerebrovascular Accident)

Cerebral vascular insufficiency (CVI) means that there is not enough blood flow and oxygen to the brain. It's caused most frequently by atherosclerosis (hardening of the arteries), either in the arteries of the brain, or the carotid artery in the neck. *Stroke* (cerebral vascular accident, CVA) occurs when the blood supply is cut off completely and the brain cells die. Seventy-five per cent of the time, a stroke is due to a clot obstructing the artery. This condition is called *ischemic stroke*. The other major causes of stroke are a burst blood vessel (*aneurysm*) or bleeding or hemorrhaging of the arteries, usually due to high blood pressure. Mini-strokes, called TIAs (transient ischemic attacks), cause symptoms similar to stroke, but these symptoms disappear in 1 to 24 hours.

Half of all strokes occur in people who are over the age of 70. Women generally suffer more strokes than men but recover just as well, and men are twice as likely as women to die from a stroke. Stroke is the third leading cause of death and the leading cause of disability in this country.

Common Symptoms

TIA and CVI can cause

- Short-term memory loss
- Dizziness
- Headache
- Tinnitus (ringing in the ears)
- Blurred vision
- Confusion
- Double vision

- Weakness

CVA (stroke) can cause loss of

- Vision
- Strength
- Coordination
- Sensation
- Speech

What You Need to Know

Smoking and high blood pressure are two of the major causes of CVI and stroke. If you smoke, it is essential that you quit (see "Nicotine Addiction" on page 311 for treatment guidelines). Have your blood pressure checked every 6 to 12 months. If you have high blood pressure, the best antihypertensive medication to take for preventing strokes is a thiazide diuretic (such as Diuril, hydrodiuril, or HCTZ). If these do not control your blood pressure, see the section on high blood pressure for more specific recommendations. Other conditions that can cause stroke include uncontrolled diabetes and high cholesterol. (See the sections about these conditions, on pages 187, 168 respectively, for more information.)

General Recommendations

Diet: As with any blood vessel disease caused by atherosclerosis, diet plays a significant role in both causing and preventing stroke. A balanced diet, with not more than 30 percent of calories from fat and less than 10 percent of those fat calories from saturated fat (use monounsaturated fat preferably), can decrease blood cholesterol levels. If you have very high blood cholesterol levels, you should restrict your fat intake to 20 percent of calories, and even 10 percent for the best results. Also, avoid cholesterol-containing products. Use plant-based butter spreads, such as Take Control and Benecol, which can reduce cholesterol levels by an additional 10 percent. In addition, soy products are excellent at reducing cholesterol levels, as is black tea. Avocado is very potent at reducing cholesterol levels. Increasing the fiber in your diet can also decrease cholesterol levels. (See the section on cholesterol on page 168 for further information and guidelines.) I also recommend drinking one glass of wine daily with meals. Wine, especially red, has powerful antioxidant properties.

Exercise: Physical activity can significantly decrease the risk of stroke. Walking a brisk pace for 30 minutes a day is all that is required, although more strenuous aerobic exercise is even better.

Your Balanced Healing Action Plan for CVI and Preventing Strokes

Step 1: *Take an Aspirin a Day or Other Blood-Thinning Medications*

One aspirin a day (81mg) is quite effective for preventing ischemic stroke and is usually recommended by doctors if you have the above symptoms or are at high risk for ischemic stroke. Aspirin use can deplete body stores of vitamin C, so make sure you get at least 600mg of vitamin C per day through your diet or by taking a supplement. If aspirin bothers your stomach, your doctor may prescribe the drug ticlopidine instead. The prescription drugs dipyridamole (Persantine) or clopidogre (Plavix) are effective alternatives for those who cannot take either aspirin or ticlopidine. Your doctor should determine which medication is best for you.

Ibuprofen blocks the blood-thinning effects of aspirin, so try not to take it if you are taking aspirin. If you must take ibuprofen, take the aspirin first and wait at least an hour to take the ibuprofen, and take the lowest ibuprofen dose you can (three doses will negate 90 percent of aspirin's effects).

Step 2: Take Gingko Biloba

If you are having symptoms of CVI, take gingko biloba (160mg to 240mg per day, containing 24 percent gingko flavonglycosides). This herb can help reverse many symptoms, including impaired mental performance. It improves blood flow, oxygen flow, and glucose utilization, and it protects brain cells. I recommend taking it with aspirin. Gingko can also thin your blood, so be aware that you may bleed or bruise more easily when you take aspirin and gingko together.

Step 3: Take Aortic Glycosaminoglycans If You Have a TIA

If you have a transient ischemic attack (TIA), take aortic glycosaminoglycans (GAGs), which improve blood flow in both the brain and the extremities. Take them for at least six months after a TIA. Dosage is 100mg per day. You can combine them with the previous steps for the best results. They are available in health food stores.

Step 4: Take Low-Dose Estrogen Replacement (Post-Menopausal Women)

If you are a post-menopausal woman and your doctor recommends hormone replacement, I recommend taking very low-dose or natural estrogens because these have a very low risk of stroke. (On standard doses of estrogen, during the first year, you have an increased risk of stroke, especially if you smoke.) See the section on menopause for further information and treatment guidelines.

Your Balanced Healing Action Plan for Stroke

- The two main types of stroke, ischemic strokes and bleeding strokes, must be treated differently. Therefore, diagnostic testing (MRI or CAT scan of the brain) is crucial in determining which type of stroke has occurred.

For *Ischemic* Stroke:

Step 1: Take Thrombolytic Drugs

For ischemic strokes, your doctor may prescribe anticoagulants (blood thinners), which break up the blood clot (a process called *thrombolysis*). Studies show that these agents (urokinase, streptokinases, or recombinant tissue plasminogen activators [or rt-Pas]), taken shortly after ischemic stroke, will, over the long term, reduce overall death and disability. These drugs do have an increased risk of brain hemorrhage, but the benefits definitely outweigh this risk. We don't really know which patients are most likely to benefit from this therapy, which must be given within a few hours of stroke onset. These agents should not be used in bleeding strokes.

Step 2: Take Aspirin

If you do not receive the drugs in Step 1, your doctor may recommend taking aspirin within 48 hours. Don't take more than 325mg per day (81mg is enough to thin your blood). Aspirin use can deplete body stores of vitamin C, so make sure you replace it by diet or supplementation at 600mg per day. Ibuprofen blocks the blood-thinning effects of aspirin, so try not to take it if you are taking aspirin. If you must take ibuprofen, take the aspirin first, and wait at least an hour to take the ibuprofen, and take the lowest ibuprofen dose you can (three doses will negate 90 percent of aspirin's effects).

For *Bleeding* Stroke:

Step 1: Reduce Blood Pressure or Have Surgery

For stroke that results from hemorrhage (bleeding), you must reduce or eliminate the causes of the bleeding. If your blood pressure is elevated, it must be reduced to normal as quickly as possible. If the hemorrhage is caused by a burst artery (aneurysm), emergency surgery might be required. Blood-thinning medications (including aspirin) may need to be discontinued.

For Any Stroke:

Step 1: Enter a Specialized Stroke Rehabilitation Program

After a stroke occurs, intensive rehabilitation in a specialty stroke rehabilitation center is essential. The activities and exercises that you undergo in rehabilitation will re-educate healthy parts of your brain to take over the functions of the parts that have been damaged.

Step 2: Get Acupuncture Treatments

The National Institutes of Health supports acupuncture for aiding in recovery of function, sensation, and extremity strength after a stroke, as well as cognitive functions such as speech and vision. The sooner you begin acupuncture after the stroke, the more effective it is, although good results can be obtained even years afterward.

> Seventy-four-year-old Cathy's bleeding stroke four years ago left her with severe weakness and pain in her right arm and leg. She had a "claw" hand (meaning it was in a fist and the fingers could not be extended voluntarily). She walked with a limp and needed a cane. She also had memory and concentration difficulties. After 3 acupuncture treatments (using both body and ear points), her concentration and memory were restored almost completely. After 12 sessions, she could voluntarily open her hand and no longer needed a cane to walk. Her strength began returning and her pain resolved. She has continued receiving acupuncture on a monthly schedule and has kept getting better.

Principal points are usually found on the arms for the upper extremity and on the legs for the lower extremity. For facial paralysis, most points are found on the face and around the head and neck. For impaired speech due to tongue paralysis, points usually are found on the throat and wrists. To help you recover more quickly from an acute stroke, there are acupuncture points on several areas of the body. There are also several ear points corresponding to the extremities and the specific areas of brain damage.

Always seek evaluation and treatment from a practitioner certified in acupuncture. (See Appendix A, under "Acupuncture," for guidance in finding a qualified acupuncturist and for more information on different acupuncture techniques.) You should see improvement within six treatments, but you might need additional sessions for maximum benefits.

CHOLESTEROL (Atherosclerosis)

High cholesterol leads to atherosclerosis, a condition in which excess fat collects in the blood vessel walls, eventually causing clogging of the artery. The most common causes of high cholesterol are poor diet, especially eating foods high in fat and sugars, and lifestyle factors, such as being sedentary and smoking. Stress, worrying, and anxiety are other factors that can increase cholesterol. High cholesterol is a factor in numerous diseases, including peripheral vascular disease (which affects the arteries in the limbs), heart disease and heart attacks (which involve the coronary arteries), and cerebral vascular insufficiency and stroke (which are diseases of the cerebral arteries).

Common Symptoms

High cholesterol is exceedingly dangerous, because there are basically no symptoms—until complications occur in the heart, limbs, or brain (for example, a heart attack or stroke). Lab tests can tell you your blood cholesterol levels.

What You Need to Know

Cholesterol is a naturally occurring fat that contributes to vital bodily functions, such as producing hormones, protecting nerves, and building new cells. In the blood, cholesterol binds to proteins to form lipoproteins, of which there are several varieties. These include high-density lipoproteins (HDL), low-density lipoproteins (LDL), and very-low-density lipoproteins (VLDL). The HDL protects against heart disease, while high levels of LDL and VLDL are considered harmful. Lowering your overall cholesterol level helps prevent many devastating diseases and gives you a longer, healthier life.

General Recommendations

Diet: A balanced diet, with not more than 30 percent of calories from fat and less than 10 percent of those calories from saturated fat, can decrease blood cholesterol levels (use monounsaturated fat preferably). If you have very high blood cholesterol levels, you should restrict your total fat intake to 20 percent of calories, or 10 percent for best results. Also, avoid cholesterol-containing products. Use plant-based butter spreads, such as Take

Control and Benecol, which can reduce cholesterol by an additional 10 percent. In addition, soy products are excellent at reducing cholesterol levels, as is black tea. Avocado is very potent at reducing cholesterol levels. Increasing the fiber in your diet can also help. Almonds, walnuts, pecans, and pistachio nuts can lower LDL cholesterol levels if they are natural or dry-roasted (no added salts or oils).

People differ in their responses to cholesterol-lowering diets, and some may not respond at all. Just being overweight can prevent you from controlling your cholesterol by diet. If you change your diet but your cholesterol level doesn't budge, then you must follow the steps below for specific treatment.

If you want to follow a particular diet, the DASH diet reduces levels of LDL and total cholesterol (go to www.nhlbi.nih.gov/health/public/heart/hbp/dash/ to obtain a copy of the DASH diet). For highly elevated cholesterol levels, Dean Ornish, MD, has proven that a very low-fat diet, in combination with stress reduction from yoga, relaxation techniques, breathing techniques, "heart healing" imagery, meditation, aerobic exercise, and group support, can significantly lower cholesterol levels and even reverse diseases caused by high cholesterol. However, his method requires great motivation, which is why I'm recommending it if you have very high cholesterol levels. However, it can be used by anyone with elevated cholesterol levels. (For details of Dr. Ornish's diet, buy his book, *Reversing Heart Disease*, 1996, Royal Publications.)

Exercise: As important as diet, exercise can significantly lower blood cholesterol levels and raise the HDL component. High-volume aerobic exercise is the preferred form of activity; walking is the safest. Although resistance training does not increase HDL levels, it does decrease LDL, total cholesterol levels, and body fat, so it is also recommended. (For further information and description of exercises, see "Simple Healing Steps for All Health Conditions," on page 79, under "Exercise.")

Meditation: Meditation is effective in reducing cholesterol levels because it counteracts the cholesterol-increasing effects of stress. Even a five-minute meditation every day can help reduce cholesterol levels. (For more information and examples of meditation, see "Simple Healing Steps for All Health Conditions," on page 79, under "Meditation".)

Your Balanced Healing Action Plan for Reducing Cholesterol

- Your blood cholesterol level should be less than 200mg/dl, with LDL below 130mg/dl and HDL above 35mg/dl.
- A blood cholesterol level below 160mg/dl can be harmful, causing depression, anxiety, and increased risk of bleeding strokes.
- If your cholesterol level is between 200mg/dl and 300mg/dl, start at Step 1.
- If your cholesterol level is greater than 300mg/dl, go to Step 4, then return to Step 1.

Step 1: Try Cilantro Chelation

A very easy and simple way of reducing your cholesterol levels (and helping clean your arteries) is to use an herbal chelation recipe. Blend one cup of fresh cilantro with six tablespoons of olive oil until the cilantro is completely chopped. Then add one clove of garlic, half a cup of nuts (cashews or almonds are best), and two tablespoons of lemon juice. Blend these into a paste (which will be lumpy), adding hot water if necessary. Take one to three teaspoonfuls per day. If you make a large amount, you can freeze some of it for later use.

Step 2: Take Gugulipid, Policosanol, or Gamma-Oryzanol

I first recommend trying various herbs because they have very few, if any, side effects. An herb from India, Gugulipid, can decrease total cholesterol levels 14 percent to 27 percent and triglyceride and LDL levels 22 percent to 30 percent in 4 to 12 weeks. Dosage is 100mg to 500mg per day. Another beneficial supplement is Policosanol (10mg to 20mg once or twice daily), derived from the wax of the sugar cane or wax of honey bees. Policosanol can reduce cholesterol and triglyceride levels 15 percent to 25 percent in 6 to 8 weeks. A third supplement, Gamma-oryzanol (150mg twice daily) is derived from rice bran oil and is a prescription medication in Japan. It can reduce cholesterol, LDL, and triglyceride levels 12 percent to 15 percent. If one of these supplements does not lower your cholesterol levels to normal, you can safely take two or all three together.

Step 3: Take Flaxseed Oil, Niacin, Garlic, Ginger, and/or Calcium Citrate

If the previous steps do not lower your cholesterol to normal levels, I recommend adding a combination of flaxseed oil (one tablespoon daily), niacin (500mg to 1,000mg three times daily), and garlic (equivalent to 4,000mg of allicin daily; see Appendix B for precautions). This combination alone can reduce cholesterol levels 50mg/dl to 75mg/dl in about two months when your cholesterol level is 250mg/dl. If your cholesterol level is greater than 300mg/dl, it may take six months. If your cholesterol level has decreased but is still too high, add ginger (1,000mg per day), which contains antioxidants that can lower LDL and triglycerides. If you are a woman past menopause, you might find that calcium citrate supplements (1,000mg daily) can lower your total cholesterol, increase your HDL, and lower your LDL.

When your cholesterol level is controlled, the niacin dosage should be lowered because it has the most side effects (primarily flushing). You can also lower the dosages of the other supplements as long as your cholesterol levels stay normal.

Step 4: Take a Prescription Statin (Cholesterol-Lowering) Drug

If the previous steps fail to lower your cholesterol levels, or your cholesterol level is more than 300mg/dl initially, I recommend taking conventional prescription medications called *statins* (such as Lipitor, Mevacor, Zocor, and Pravachol). Statins have anti-inflammatory properties and have been shown to protect against heart attack if you have high cholesterol. Because these medications usually require taking only one pill a day, you may prefer this treatment to taking the natural supplements in Steps 1 and 2. On the other hand, most of these drugs are expensive and may have side effects. If you have muscle pain or weakness after starting these medications, you should stop them immediately. You should also have your liver enzymes checked yearly because these drugs can cause liver problems. Several statins may be allowed to go over-the-counter in the near future, so their prices may go down substantially. Studies have shown that a combination of niacin (Step 3) and statins is more effective than either one alone in lowering cholesterol levels and stopping the progression of atherosclerosis. So if you take a statin as your only treatment, I recommend adding niacin for an even better effect. Please note, however, that some people on this combination can have the side effect of muscle inflammation. If you take a statin, you should not take more than the RDA recommended amounts of antioxidants such as vitamins E, C, beta-carotene, and selenium. These antioxidants blunt the beneficial effect of statins, which is to raise your levels of HDL levels (the good cholesterol). Finally, most statins can cause a decrease in Coenzyme Q10 (CoQ10), which is important for proper heart and muscle function. I recommend supplementing with CoQ10 (30mg to 60mg daily) if you take a statin.

Step 5: Take Cholestin as a Less Expensive Alternative to a Statin Drug

If you want to take a statin but find it too expensive (most cost more than $120 per month), I recommend Cholestin, made from red yeast rice. The chemical structure and mechanism of Cholestin is similar to the statins, but it is about one-third of the cost (about $39). Cholestin is also available in combination with policosanol (Step 1) for better results. You can also add niacin to Cholestin to obtain lower cholesterol levels, as recommended in Step 4. Cholestin is manufactured by an MLM.

Step 6: Take Zetia

A new prescription drug called ezetimibe (Zetia) can lower cholesterol by inhibiting the absorption of intestinal cholesterol. It can be used alone if the above steps are not effective, or with statins to improve their effectiveness.

Step 7: Take Prescription Gemfibrozil or Cholestyramine

There are several other conventional medications that can lower cholesterol levels, including gemfibrozil (Lopid), and cholestyramine (Questran). These medications are also appropriate either when triglyceride levels alone are elevated or when both triglycerides and cholesterol levels are too high. Your doctor may prescribe these if your cholesterol level is not improving or if there are special circumstances regarding any other medical conditions you may have.

CHRONIC FATIGUE SYNDROME (CFS)

Chronic fatigue syndrome is exhaustion that doesn't result from overexertion and is not alleviated by rest or medications. Although described by conventional medicine as a new disease, references to similar conditions date back to the 1860s, and it has been known by many other names, including *chronic EBV syndrome (Epstein-Barr virus)*, *immune dysfunction syndrome*, and *post-infectious myasthenia syndrome*. CFS can last several years, during which time the symptoms can increase and decrease. Although symptoms don't seem to worsen over time, CFS can cause significant disability and interfere with most activities of daily living.

Common Symptoms

- Mild fever
- Painful lymph nodes
- Muscle weakness
- Muscle pain
- Prolonged fatigue after exercise
- Migrating joint pain
- Headaches
- Depression
- Sleep disturbance
- Recurrent sore throat
- Forgetfulness
- Confusion
- Difficulty concentrating

What You Need to Know

You may have chronic fatigue, but not Chronic Fatigue Syndrome. There are numerous causes of chronic fatigue besides CFS. For example:

- Diseases such as diabetes, heart disease, lung disease, rheumatoid arthritis, chronic inflammation, lupus, chronic pain, cancer, liver disease, multiple sclerosis.
- Drugs such as high-blood-pressure medications, anti-inflammatory agents, oral contraceptives, antihistamines, steroids, tranquilizers, and sleep medications.
- Emotional stress and depression.

These causes can be treated and corrected, so it is very important to undergo an extensive history, examination, and testing to rule them out.

General Recommendations

Exercise: Exercise can produce substantial improvement in fatigue and physical functioning. In fact, prolonged rest may actually be harmful in CFS. All three forms of exercise (stretching, aerobic, and resistance) are recommended for the best results (for more information, see "Simple Healing Steps for All Health Conditions," on page 79, under "Exercise"). I know—it's hard to be motivated to exercise when you feel fatigued all the time, but you'll notice almost immediate benefits.

Qigong: Qigong is very effective for both stimulating the immune system and increasing energy. Although you may feel too tired to practice Qigong, you will soon discover that it does increase your energy, so the effort is well worth the results. You can do Qigong even when you're sitting or lying down. (For further information and examples, see "Simple Healing Steps for All Health Conditions," on page 79, under "Qigong.")

Your Balanced Healing Action Plan for Chronic Fatigue Syndrome

Step 1: Take Appropriate Chinese Herbal Remedies

I start with Chinese herbal formulas because they are the most helpful in increasing energy, rebalancing the body, and strengthening the immune system. Some of the formulas that are commonly used include *Gan Cao (Licorice)*, *Cordyceps*, *Dong Chong Xia Cao*, or *Gui Pi Tang*. Herbal treatments must be based on accurate diagnosis from a qualified practitioner, who will determine which formula(s) will be best for you. You'll notice improvement within three weeks (sometimes sooner), but you may need to take the herbs for a longer period, depending on your condition(s). (See Appendix A, under "Chinese Herbs," for further information.)

Step 2: Undergo Acupuncture

I also recommend acupuncture along with the Chinese herbals. Acupuncture is effective for strengthening the immune system and increasing energy. Principal points are usually found in many areas of the body and are used in various combinations. *Moxibustion* (burning a specific herb to stimulate acupuncture points) can also be done to increase energy, and you can be taught to do it at home. Always seek evaluation and treatment from a practitioner certified in acupuncture. (See Appendix A, under "Acupuncture," for guidance on finding a qualified acupuncturist and for more information on the different acupuncture techniques.) You should feel improvement within six treatments, but you might need additional sessions to get the maximum benefit.

Step 3: Take Prescription Medications for Pain and Other Symptoms of CFS

If the previous steps don't help your pain, various prescription medications can help reduce it and other symptoms of CFS. They include nonsteroidal anti-inflammatory drugs (such as Naprosyn, Daypro, Feldene, Orudis, Mobic, and others) for muscle or joint aches and low-grade fever, and SSRI antidepressants (such as Prozac) to promote sleep, help depression, and relieve muscle pain. Consult your doctor for guidance.

Step 4: Take Coenzyme Q-10, Magnesium, and NADH

If you still have low energy, take Coenzyme Q-10 (CoQ10) (100mg per day) and magnesium (200mg to 300mg three times daily), which can help relieve chronic fatigue symptoms in some patients by increasing the production of energy molecules in the body's cells. If you still have fatigue, then add NADH (nicotinamide adenine dinucleotide), 10mg to 15mg daily, which increases energy molecules in the body.

Step 5: Try the Nambudripad Allergy Elimination Treatment (NAET)

If you haven't improved with the previous steps, food allergies may be playing a part in your chronic fatigue. I recommend using the Nambudripad Allergy Elimination

Treatment (NAET), which combines acupuncture, kinesiology, chiropractic, herbs, and nutrition to desensitize you to foods to which you are allergic. It may take several months to be effective, depending on how many allergens are sensitizing you. (See Appendix A, under "NAET," and the section on food allergies, for more information.)

Step 6: Take an Appropriate Homeopathic Remedy

If you still have fatigue, I next recommend trying homeopathy, which has been reported to help some people reverse CFS. There are several formulas, so consult a qualified homeopathist for guidance on which remedies will be most beneficial and for proper dosages. You should experience benefits within one to two weeks. (See Appendix A, under "Homeopathy," for guidance on finding a qualified homeopathist and for further information.)

COLDS AND FLU

Colds and influenza (flu) are infections of the upper respiratory tract. Most colds and all influenza cases are caused by viruses; a few colds are caused by bacteria (such as streptococcus). These contagious infections are spread mostly by skin contact and touching, as well as through the air. Influenza symptoms are more pronounced than cold symptoms (in other words, you are much sicker), and its complications are more severe. Colds are usually self-limited. They last about three days, although cough and congestion can continue for a week or more. Influenza can last longer, and in people who are debilitated or have heart or lung diseases, it can cause pneumonia and death.

Common Symptoms: Colds

- Head and chest congestion
- Sore throat
- Runny nose
- Sneezing
- Dry cough that may occur only at night
- Achiness
- Lethargy
- Chills
- Possible fever

Common Symptoms: Flu

- Higher fever
- Hacking cough
- Weakness
- Aching muscles
- Sore throat
- Headache
- Congestion

What You Need to Know

Because most colds and flu are caused by viruses, they do not require antibiotics unless testing clearly shows evidence of bacterial infection (the rapid antigen test is the most common test used to detect bacteria). If you take antibiotics for a virus, resistance to those antibiotics can eventually occur. Some people who always take antibiotics for a cold may think it is the antibiotic that gets rid of it, but in fact the cold usually goes away in the same period of time without antibiotics, as studies have documented again and again.

Everyone who's debilitated, elderly, or suffering from lung or heart diseases (including asthma), should get flu shots every year because influenza can be deadly for people who are weakened by other health conditions.

General Recommendations

Diet: Avoid milk products, which increase mucus production. Avoid sugar, which competes with vitamin C and decreases immune function. Chicken soup has been proven to help relieve sore throats and runny nose, and I highly recommended it (homemade is best). Eating garlic is also helpful because it helps prevent viruses from invading and damaging your tissues.

Also, drink lots of water, which improves the function of the white blood cells and keeps the respiratory tract moist, thus repelling viruses. Fruit juices containing vitamin C are helpful, but they should be taken undiluted because processed juices contain sugars that retard your white blood cells' ability to fight the infection. Making the juice in a juicer or eating the fruit itself is the best way to obtain the benefits.

Your Balanced Healing Action Plan for Colds and Flu

- If you have been diagnosed with influenza, start with Steps 1 and 9. If it is severe, go to Step 10.
- Do not give aspirin to a child with a cold because it can cause Reye's syndrome, a disease of the liver. Ibuprofen is the best analgesic to reduce fever and achiness. Avoid acetaminophen products (for example, Tylenol) because they can increase mucus. Do not treat low-grade fevers because this actually is a protective mechanism of the body to help fight the infection. For high-grade fevers, call your doctor.
- If you are elderly, **avoid** supplemental vitamin E because it might extend your recovery and increase symptoms.

Step 1: Rest and Drink Plenty of Fluids

Rest and fluids are the major treatments for both colds and flu. They allow your body to heal itself faster. I also recommend using a cool-air humidifier, which can help relieve congestion and loosen mucus. You can buy one in any drug store.

Step 2: Take Nonprescription Expectorants, Anise, or Bromelain to Reduce Mucus

In addition to Step 1, use an expectorant to break up and clear mucus. Many over-the-counter remedies contain guiafenesin, the most commonly used expectorant, but if you want to use a natural expectorant, anise (as a tea, or 50ml to 200ml of the essential oil, three times a day) is as effective. If these aren't helpful, another herbal expectorant to try is bromelain (80mg to 320mg per day), an herb that also decreases bronchial secretions. You can take bromelain safely with the other expectorants.

Step 3: Take Slippery Elm Bark or Use Aromatherapy for Sore Throat

I recommend slippery elm bark (alcohol extract, 1:1 in 60 percent alcohol, 5ml three times a day), if you have a sore throat. The inhalation of aromatic vapors from various herbs, such as sage or thyme (aromatherapy), can also reduce throat irritation and coughing and can be used with any of the previous or following steps.

Step 4: Take Appropriate Chinese Herbal Remedies

There are many Chinese herbal formulas that can be helpful, depending on your particular symptoms and how long you've had your cold. *Yin Chao Jin* is particularly effective in the early stages when you may have fever, headache, cough, or sore throat. *Xiao Qing Long Tang* is useful for colds that produce thin, watery drainage. *Gan Mao Ling* is a common formula that is antiviral, and there are several others that contain additional antiviral Chinese herbs that are used for more prolonged colds/flu. You can take any of them along with the previous steps. Consult a practitioner qualified in Chinese herbal medicine to determine which formulas are the best for your particular syndromes. You should begin to feel better within 12 to 36 hours. (See Appendix A, under "Chinese Herbs," for further information.)

Step 5: Take Echinacea to Speed Recovery

In addition to the previous steps, echinacea is an herb that can decrease the severity and duration of colds and flu through its antibacterial and antiviral properties. (There are numerous forms and dosages of echinacea, so see Appendix B for more information.) There is a combination of echinacea with two other herbs, wild indigo root and white cedar leaf (called Esberitox), which is even more potent than echinacea alone and has been used in Germany for several decades. (For more information on Esberitox, go to Appendix C for referral information.) Many of the Chinese herbal formulas in Step 4 may contain echinacea, so check the labels. Echinacea should not be used if you have systemic diseases, such as tuberculosis, collagen diseases (scleroderma, for example), or multiple sclerosis, and immune disorders, such as AIDS, HIV, and lupus, because it can make all of these conditions worse.

Step 6: Take Zinc to Speed Your Recovery

Although studies have been inconsistent, most show that zinc can reduce cold symptoms. Use the gluconate or acetate forms, containing 9mg to 24mg of elemental zinc, every two hours while awake. You must start within 48 hours of symptom onset for it to be effective. It can be taken with the previous steps.

Step 7: Take Appropriate Homeopathic Remedies to Reduce Symptoms and Speed Recovery

If your cold or flu persists, there are several homeopathic remedies that are effective, depending on the specific symptoms. These include *Gelsemium* for chills, aching, fatigue and sore throat; *Allium cepa* for burning, runny nose, sneezing, and eyes watering constantly; *Nux vomica* for a runny nose that becomes congested at night; and *Aconite* for a barking cough, burning sore throat, and a bitter taste in your mouth. *Pulsatilla*, *Hepar sulphuris*, *Lycopodium*, *Sulphur* and *Belladonna* are other remedies commonly used for upper respiratory illnesses. These are all given as a 12c dosage, every two hours for a maximum of four doses. Consult a qualified homeopathist for guidance as to which remedies and dosages will be most beneficial. You should feel better in one to three days. (See Appendix A, under "Homeopathy," for help in finding a qualified homeopathist and for further information.)

Step 8: Take High Doses of Vitamin C to Shorten Recovery Time

High dose vitamin C, 1g to 6g per day, can cut the length of a cold or flu by one day, and decrease the severity of symptoms, through its antioxidant effects. It is more effective if taken naturally through fruit and fruit juices, and can be taken along with the previous steps.

Step 9: Take N-acetylcysteine and Garlic for Flu Symptoms

If you have the flu (not a cold), I recommend taking N-acetylcysteine (600mg twice daily), which can reduce flu symptoms by breaking up mucus. Also take garlic (4g daily), which helps keep cold and flu viruses from invading and damaging your tissues, thus shortening the recovery period.

Step 10: Take Antiviral Medications If You Are at High Risk or to Prevent Flu from Spreading Among Household Members

For severe flu symptoms, or flu in high-risk patients—or to prevent flu from spreading among family members—your doctor may prescribe antiviral medications (such as Tamiflu). These medications are very effective in stopping the spread of the flu virus as well as killing the virus, thus speeding up your recovery.

Step 11: Take Appropriate Nonprescription Medications to Relieve Severe Symptoms

There are many over-the-counter remedies for reducing symptoms of colds and flus, such as decongestants and cough suppressants. I recommend them only for severe symptoms, and they should be used sparingly because they can make mucus thicker and harder after several days of use. Most of these conventional remedies are designed to suppress symptoms, rather than help your body to heal. Even if they improve your symptoms, they can actually prolong the duration of the cold.

Step 12: Take an Appropriate Chinese Herbal Remedy for Persistent Cough

Most persistent coughs are due to continued drainage and/or irritation of the lung passageways, a condition which can be helped by Chinese herbs. My first recommendation is an herbal formula called *Er Chen Tang*, but there are many other formulas; the choice depends on what's causing your cough. Consult a practitioner qualified in Chinese herbal medicine to determine which formulas are the best for your particular syndromes. You should see improvement within three to seven days (sometimes sooner), but you may need to take the herbs longer, depending on your condition(s). (See Appendix A, under "Chinese Herbs," for further information.)

Step 13: Take Prescription Medications for Persistent Cough

If Chinese herbs don't relieve your chronic cough, your doctor may prescribe beta-agonists (such as an albuterol inhaler), which are very effective in reducing chronic coughs caused by spasm in the lung passageways. You should experience almost immediate relief if your coughing is caused by spasm.

> Manny, a 35-year-old auto parts dealer, had a cold that ran its usual course; but after four weeks, he still had a tickle in his throat that made him cough. It became hard for him to speak, because talking made him cough even more. He saw a doctor in a clinic who prescribed an albuterol inhaler, but this helped only a little. I recommended a Chinese herbal formula. In five days, Manny's cough was completely gone.

CONSTIPATION

Constipation is an abnormal process of eliminating solid waste (stool) from the body, characterized by a slowing down and decreased frequency of bowel movements. It can occur at any time, to anyone, including children. The wastes from the food that you eat should be eliminated within two or three days, and the longer the fecal material stays in the colon, the worse the constipation becomes. Chronic constipation can lead to fecal retention and impactions, rectal distention, and loss of sensory and motor function in the lower bowels.

Common Symptoms

- Infrequent bowel movements (for adults, no bowel movement for more than three days; for children, four days)
- Hard, small feces
- Painful or difficult evacuation

What You Need to Know

Constipation has many causes that must be corrected to treat the condition effectively. Medical conditions that cause constipation include irritable bowel syndrome, diverticulosis, colorectal cancer, diabetes, Parkinson's disease, multiple sclerosis, pregnancy, and depression. Drugs that can cause constipation include most narcotics (morphine, codeine), aluminum-containing antacids, some iron and calcium supplements, and some antihistamines, diuretics, antidepressants, and blood-pressure medications. If you have constipation and are taking any medications, check the *Physician's Desk Reference* (*PDR*) to see whether constipation is a side effect, or ask your pharmacist.

General Recommendations

Diet: Fiber is the most important component of the diet for treating constipation because fiber increases water content and improves motility (movement) in the intestines. Increase your intake of foods that contain fiber, especially raw vegetables such as peas, beans, and broccoli, and fruits. Bran cereals, whole-wheat bread, and dried fruits, such as figs, prunes, and raisins, are also beneficial. You should also drink lots of water, about eight glasses a day, to improve the moisture content of the bowels. Carbonated water is especially beneficial for constipation.

Exercise: Walking for 20 to 30 minutes a day is very helpful for stimulating the colon and preventing constipation.

Your Balanced Healing Action Plan for Constipation

Step 1: *Take an Herbal Colon Activator*

In constipation, *peristalsis* (muscular movement of the colon) is slowed, and the colon becomes loaded with toxins and other harmful substances. I recommend an herbal formula that both cleans and activates the colon. Look for a formula that contains most or all of the following: cape aloe, cascara sagrada, barberry root, senna, ginger root, African bird pepper, and fennel. Expect results within one week, but start slowly and build up until your constipation is relieved.

Step 2: *Take Probiotics and Digestive Enzymes for Maintenance and Prevention*

Poor digestion and incomplete breakdown of food, which stagnates in your colon, can cause or worsen constipation. I recommend taking supplements that help break down the food you eat because the colon can excrete digested food much better than nondigested food. Start with digestive enzymes to help break down your food better. There are many products that contain digestive enzymes, and they should contain some or all of the following: protease, papain, amylase, lipase, bromelain, cellulase, and lactase.

I also recommend taking probiotics, which contain beneficial microorganisms that aid in digestion, absorption, and the production of vitamins and enzymes. *L. acidophilus* and *bifidobacteria* are the preeminent probiotics. Because the organisms in probiotics die off rapidly, make sure you purchase them as close to the manufacture date as possible (at least within 60 days), and keep them refrigerated. Because probiotics kill off harmful bacteria and yeast that are in your GI tract, you may have gas, bloating, and cramping for up to 10 days. If so, decrease the amount you are taking (one-half to one pill a day) and increase slowly. Yogurt contains beneficial microorganisms, but these are not the most important or potent. Also, many yogurt products are pasteurized to increase shelf life, but pasteurization destroys all the benefits. You should notice improvement in one to two weeks when taking probiotics and digestive enzymes.

> When Norlene, a 50-year-old nurse, came to me, she had suffered with constipation for many years. She had tried numerous conventional and nonprescription laxatives, but she'd become dependent on them and her constipation had continued. I recommended probiotics and digestive enzymes along with a colon activator. I also recommended that she drink more water, eat more fiber (vegetables), and start walking one mile a day. After three weeks, her constipation was completely relieved. She was able to discontinue the colon activator formula, and she continued taking digestive enzymes only.

Step 3: Take Appropriate Chinese Herbal Remedies

If the previous steps do not resolve your constipation problem, I next recommend Chinese herbs. Common formulas include *Fructus persica tea pills*, *Peach kernel tea pills*, *Ma Zi Ren Wan*, *Run Chang Tang*, and *Tiao Wei Cheng Qi Tang*. Consult a practitioner qualified in Chinese herbal medicine to determine which formulas are the best for your particular condition. You should see improvement within three weeks (sometimes sooner), but you may need to take the herbs for a longer period, depending on your condition. (See Appendix A, under "Chinese Herbs," for further information.)

Step 4: Undergo Acupuncture

Acupuncture is also effective in most people with chronic constipation, and it should be used in conjunction with the Chinese herbs. Principal points are usually found on the arms, legs, and abdomen. Ear points include Stomach, Small Intestines, Large Intestines, Sympathetic, and there is actually a Constipation point. Always seek evaluation and treatment from a practitioner certified in acupuncture. (See Appendix A, under "Acupuncture," for guidance in finding a qualified acupuncturist and for a more detailed explanation of the different acupuncture techniques.) You should notice improvement within six acupuncture treatments, but you might need additional sessions to get the maximum benefits.

Step 5: Practice Cobra and Knee-to-Chest Yoga Poses

Yoga exercises, such as the cobra position and the knee-to-chest pose, can activate and tone the abdominal organs and relieve gas. You can use yoga with any of the previous steps.

- For the Cobra position, lie on your stomach with the side of your head resting on the ground and your legs together. Place your hands palm down, just below your shoulders, and keep your elbows close to your body. As you inhale, lift your head and chest off the floor, keeping your face forward. Only your upper body should be raised. Your navel should still be touching the floor. Look up as high as you can and hold this position for five seconds. As you exhale, bring your head and chest back down. Repeat several times a day.

- For the Knee-to-Chest position, stand straight with your arms at your sides. Lift your right knee up, and grasp your right ankle with your right hand, and your right knee with your left hand. Pull your leg in as close as you can to your chest. Hold this position for six to eight seconds, and then do the same with the other leg. Repeat three to four times a day.

These poses activate the colon and are most effective for long-term prevention of constipation. It can take several weeks to several months to observe the benefits.

Step 6: Take Natural Laxatives

If the previous steps are not effective and you need to take a product to help relieve constipation, natural laxatives are very effective in controlling constipation. They work by attracting water into the colon. I recommend the previous steps first because they can give long-lasting relief for constipation, whereas the following give more short-term relief. I recommend that you try these natural laxatives in the order listed.

- Psyllium and Flaxseed Oil: Use one to two teaspoons of psyllium in cold water or juice; for best results, take with an equal amount of flaxseed oil.
- Bran: If psyllium and flaxseed oil do not help or give you only partial relief, try wheat bran or oat bran, both of which are high in fiber. However, they can cause gas for a few weeks until your system adjusts.
- Senna: Products containing senna can be beneficial if the previous steps are not effective or cause undesired side effects. There is a Chinese herbal formula, called Gentle Senna, that contains senna with fiber and other Chinese herbs (see Step 3 above).
- Lactulose: Lactulose, a nondigestible sugar solution, can be used safely on a regular basis to increase bowel motility, which decreases constipation.

The natural laxatives in this step can be used together if each provides only partial relief. But I recommend taking each step separately because all of them together can cause significant discomfort (gas, bloating) or diarrhea, and the combination may deplete minerals such as potassium and other nutrients. You should observe results within a few days.

Step 7: Take Conventional Laxatives

Only if the previous steps are not helpful should you consider conventional laxatives. These laxatives cause dependency and can also deplete your system of important nutrients, especially potassium. If you take laxatives, use them on an intermittent basis only. They should work within 12 to 24 hours.

Step 8: Take a Colon Detoxifier/Cleanser Intermittently for Prevention

After your constipation is relieved, take a formula that can cleanse and detoxify your colon by taking out old fecal matter and any poisons, toxins, or heavy metals that have accumulated. A good formula should contain most or all of the following: apple fruit pectin, slippery elm bark, bentonite clay (pharmaceutical grade), marshmallow root, fennel seed, activated willow charcoal, and psyllium seeds/husks. Take this formula for one week every three to four months. Because this formula may cause constipation as it works, take it with a colon activator (Step 1).

CROHN'S DISEASE (see *Inflammatory Bowel Disease*)

CUBITAL TUNNEL SYNDROME (see *Carpal Tunnel Syndrome*)

DEMENTIA (see *Alzheimer's Disease*)

DEPRESSION

Depression is an emotional disorder that can range from mild (depressive reaction) to severe (major depression). It is the most common psychological problem in this country, affecting nearly 20 million people. It can be caused by a particular event, it can be a side effect of medication, or it can be due to hormonal changes. A dysfunction or deficiency of *neurotransmitters* (chemicals that help the brain's cells communicate with each other)—doctors call it a *chemical imbalance*—also can cause depression. Depression can worsen cancer, asthma, diabetes, and heart disease, and it can even decrease bone density. At some time in life, we all feel depressed. But if your depression is prolonged, interferes with life's activities, or is present without any particular precipitating event, you have a health problem that needs medical attention and treatment.

Common Symptoms

If you have five or more of the following nine symptoms, you could have depression:

- Poor appetite accompanied by weight loss, or increased appetite accompanied by weight gain
- Insomnia or hypersomnia (too much sleep)
- Physical inactivity or hyperactivity
- Loss of interest or pleasure in your usual activities
- Fatigue
- Feelings of worthlessness
- Self-reproach or inappropriate guilt
- Diminished mental skills
- Recurrent thoughts of death or suicide

What You Need to Know

Because depression can be caused by numerous drugs (antihistamines, antihypertensives, anti-inflammatory agents, birth-control pills, steroids, and tranquilizers/sedatives) and environmental toxins (heavy metals, pesticides, herbicides, solvents), it is important to be fully evaluated physically to rule out these other causes. If you are depressed for no specific reason and are taking any medications, check the *Physician's Desk Reference* (*PDR*) to see whether depression is a side effect of your medication. Other causes of depression include alcohol, which is a brain depressant, and smoking, which increases your body's cortisol levels (elevated cortisol levels can contribute to depression). If you have depression, drinking alcohol and smoking will make it worse.

General Recommendations

Diet: I recommend eating more fruits and vegetables; they contain B vitamins and folate, both of which can fight depression. Omega-3 fatty acids found in cold-water fish (salmon, mackerel, tuna, sardines, trout, halibut, cod) can also boost your mood.

Exercise helps depression by improving blood flow to the brain, elevating mood, and relieving stress. All types of exercise are good. Aerobic is the best—it can actually relieve depression substantially faster than medications. Exercise at least three days a week for 30 minutes (see "Simple Healing Steps for All Health Conditions" on page 79, for more information and guidance).

Meditation is quite helpful in depression, especially if you also have stress and/or anxiety. Meditation promotes self-examination, problem solving, and spiritual support. It also decreases your body's output of cortisol, a chemical that negatively affects your mood. (See "Simple Healing Steps for All Health Conditions" on page 79, and Appendix A, under "Mind-Body Techniques," for further information and sample meditations.)

Qigong is also a very helpful treatment for depression. It stimulates the production of neurotransmitters in the brain, improves blood flow, and increases energy. (See "Simple Healing Steps for All Health Conditions" on page 79, and Appendix A, under "Qigong," for further information and examples.)

Your Balanced Healing Action Plan for Depression

- If your depression is severe, start with Steps 1 and 6.
- I recommend that you continue antidepressant therapy, whether conventional or natural, for four to six months after you are no longer depressed, to reduce the likelihood that your depression will return.
- Often, the most effective approach is to use more than one method.

Step 1: Undergo Interactive Imagery or Other Psychotherapy

Psychotherapy is the most important conventional step to identify and address the emotional basis of your depression. I recommend interactive imagery, if available, as the best psychotherapeutic approach to depression, because it works more quickly than most other approaches, and it adds the benefits of relaxation and meditation. It's a mind-body method in which you mentally interact with images that represent your emotions—so it's a powerful way to uncover and deal with subconscious psychological issues of which you may not be aware. (See Appendix A, under "Mind-Body Techniques," for a more detailed explanation.) If interactive imagery is not available in your area, then I recommend cognitive therapy and interpersonal therapy.

Psychotherapy is just as effective as drugs for treating depression, but you may need several months or more before you notice improvement. I recommend psychotherapy as the first step, however, because to get long-term benefit, you must uncover and treat the underlying reasons for your depression. While you're in psychotherapy, you can use the following steps for short-term control of your depression.

Step 2: Take St. John's Wort, Gingko Biloba, and/or Omega-3 Supplements

Natural antidepressants can be as effective as conventional drugs, but without their side effects. My first choice is St. John's wort (300mg containing 0.3 percent hypericin, three times a day), an effective herbal antidepressant for mild to moderate depression that works by re-balancing brain neurotransmitters. It takes from one to three weeks to be effective and is particularly helpful if you are under the age of 50.

If you are over 50, gingko biloba (160mg to 240mg containing 24 percent flavonglycosides per day) may be an effective antidepressant for you. Gingko works by increasing blood and oxygen flow to the brain, but it may take four to eight weeks to be effective. In addition, I recommend taking fish oil (4 grams daily, primarily containing EPA), or flaxseed oil (1 tablespoon to 2 tablespoons daily), which can be effective even in major depression that hasn't responded to conventional medications. It may take three weeks to notice improvement from these omega-3 fatty acid supplements.

Caution: Do not take St. John's wort with conventional prescription antidepressants, especially SSRIs, because these substances all increase serotonin levels. In combination, these substances can make your serotonin levels too high, which can cause a complication called *serotonin syndrome*. Symptoms of serotonin syndrome include confusion, itching, fast heartbeat, elevated blood pressure, muscle stiffness, restlessness, shaking, nausea, or sweating. If you are taking conventional antidepressants and want to change to St. John's wort, you should wean yourself off the conventional drugs first (slowly decrease the amount you take over at least two weeks), and then start St. John's wort. Do this only under a doctor's supervision.

Step 3: Take Appropriate Chinese Herbal Remedies

If natural antidepressants don't help you, or give you only partial relief, there are several excellent Chinese herbal antidepressant formulas. Because these formulas contain a variety of herbs (some even contain St. John's wort), they are often able to treat forgetfulness, phobias, anxiety, and nervous exhaustion along with depression. *Gui Pi Wan* and *An Shen Bu Xin Dan* are common formulas. Consult a practitioner qualified in Chinese herbal medicine to determine which Chinese herbal formulas are the best for your particular syndromes. You should notice improvement within three weeks. (See Appendix A, under "Chinese Herbs," for further information.)

Step 4: Undergo Acupuncture

If the Chinese herbs alone do not help your depression, I recommend acupuncture in conjunction with them. Acupuncture is thought to rebalance the brain neurotransmitters that are deficient in depression. Principal points are usually found on the back, chest, legs, and arms. Ear acupuncture is also effective; there actually are two specific antidepressant points and a "tranquilizer" point in the ear. Always seek evaluation and treatment from a practitioner certified in acupuncture. (See Appendix A, under "Acupuncture," for guidance on finding a qualified acupuncturist and for explanation on different acupuncture techniques.) You should notice improvement within six treatments, but you might need additional sessions for maximum benefits.

Step 5: Take 5-HTP

The supplement 5-HTP is converted to tryptophan, a precursor to serotonin, a brain neurotransmitter that is found to be deficient in many people with depression. 5-HTP can increase the levels of serotonin in your brain, thus reducing depressive symptoms. It is equal in effectiveness to most conventional antidepressants, with few side effects. Use it if the above steps are not effective. As with St. John's wort, however, do not take 5-HTP with conventional antidepressants, because of the risk of serotonin syndrome (see Step 2 for a description of this complication). Take 100mg to 200mg three times daily. You should observe benefits in two to four weeks.

Warning: Be sure to use only products that are "peak X-free." Peak X is a contaminant that can cause significant side effects and even death.

Step 6: Take a Prescription Antidepressant

Conventional antidepressants are useful and popular. In fact, 3 of the top 10 medications used in the U.S. are antidepressants. Unfortunately, these drugs can have many more side effects than the natural antidepressants, often making you feel emotionally "flat" or like a "zombie," so I recommend that you try the previous steps first. However, prescription antidepressants are very effective and sometimes are the best treatment, especially for severe depression.

They include several different classes of drugs:

- Serotonin reuptake inhibitors, or SSRIs (Prozac, Zoloft, Paxil, Celexa, Effexor, Luvox)
- Phenylpiperizine (Serzone)
- Trazodone (Desyrel)
- Tricyclics (Elavil, Pamelor, Sinequan, Anafranil)
- Bupropion (Wellbutrin, Zyban)
- MAO inhibitors (Parnate, Marplan, Nardil)

Within each of these classes of antidepressants, the drugs are generally equivalent to each other in effectiveness. However, you still may respond differently to different drugs (both in benefits and side effects), whether they are in the same or a different class. So you may have to try several before finding the one that is best for you.

For most antidepressants, it takes 2 to 3 weeks to see benefits. If you have severe depression and your doctor prescribes tricyclics, he can also prescribe thyroid supplements (triiodothyronine or T3) for a short period of time to speed up the response to the tricyclics. We don't know whether or not T3 will accelerate the response to other antidepressants.

One major side effect of SSRIs is decrease in libido (sexual interest), both in men and women. To reverse or reduce this side effect, take gingko biloba, 60mg to 120mg per day.

Warning: Stop taking St. John's wort or 5-HTP before beginning conventional antidepressants, due to the possibility of serotonin syndrome (see Step 2 for description). Do not abruptly stop taking any antidepressant—you run the risk of a wide range of unpleasant side effects. Instead, gradually take less of the drug (over several weeks), especially if your antidepressant is short-acting (such as Paxil and Luvox). Always consult your doctor before stopping your antidepressant.

Step 7: Take SAMe

SAMe (400mg daily for mild depression, 800mg to 1,600mg for moderate-to-severe depression), imported from Germany, can be an effective antidepressant. It affects several brain neurotransmitters and phospholipids that are essential for brain function. It also boosts antioxidants and protects DNA. I recommend SAMe if the previous steps are not effective or have intolerable side effects. SAMe can also improve the effectiveness of antidepressants, so you can take it along with them if the others are only partially effective.

Because SAMe starts working in half the time needed for tricyclics and does not cause the weight gain or sexual dysfunction that can be problems with other antidepressants, you may prefer to try it before Step 5. However, no studies have compared SAMe to SSRIs for effectiveness, the top-quality products are expensive, and many SAMe products contain subtherapeutic amounts or are poor quality. That's why I made it Step 7. As with most antidepressants, SAMe may take three weeks to have a beneficial effect.

> Tamara, a 42-year-old accountant, came to me with a history of several years of moderate depression, as well as some anxiety. She'd taken conventional antidepressants, but they made her anxiety worse and decreased her concentration and sexual desire, so she'd stopped taking them. I started her on the Chinese herbal formula *Gui Pi Wan*, which reduced her depression. I also gave her six acupuncture treatments, which gave her additional relief. At the same time, I referred her for interactive imagery, which uncovered physical abuse that she'd suffered during childhood. After several months of continued psychotherapy, she was able to reduce her herbs and eventually was able to stop taking them.

DIABETES

Diabetes is a disorder of blood sugar (glucose) metabolism, characterized by abnormal elevations of glucose in the blood. There are two types of diabetes. In *Type 1 diabetes*, also known as *insulin-dependent diabetes mellitus* (or *IDDM*), the body does not produce insulin and so cannot break down glucose in the blood. In type 2, also known as *non-insulin-dependent diabetes mellitus* (or *NIDDM*), the body produces insulin, but its cells don't respond to it. *Type 2 diabetes* is the most common (accounting for 90 percent of all cases) and is strongly related to obesity.

If your blood sugar is not well controlled, you can have both rapidly occurring and slowly occurring complications. The rapid problems occur when your blood sugar is too low or too high. When it's too low, you can develop *hypoglycemia*; symptoms include sweating, nervousness, tremor, hunger, or fainting. If left untreated, hypoglycemia can cause shock and death. Alternatively, when your blood sugar is too high, you can develop *ketoacidosis* (too much acid in your blood); symptoms include extreme fatigue, nausea, and vomiting. Ketoacidosis can also lead to coma and death if untreated. Diabetes is the seventh leading cause of death in the U.S.

Long-term complications of diabetes include the following:

- *Atherosclerosis*, especially of the heart and brain arteries.
- *Neuropathy* (loss of peripheral nerve function) and Charcot joints (osteoarthritis of the foot bones caused by the neuropathy).
- *Retinopathy* (serious eye disease and the leading cause of blindness in the country). About half of all people with diabetes will develop this complication within 10 years of diagnosis.
- *Nephropathy* (damage to the kidneys and the leading cause of death in people with diabetes).
- Foot ulcers, which are the leading cause of amputation.

Common Symptoms

- Increased thirst
- Increased urination
- Increased appetite
- Weight loss
- Fatigue
- Nausea
- Blurred vision
- Frequent vaginal infections

What You Need to Know

One-third of Americans who have diabetes are not aware that they have it, especially African-Americans, Hispanics, and Native Americans. There's also a strong correlation between diabetes and obesity. It is important to have your blood sugar checked regularly, especially if your ethnic heritage puts you at increased risk or you are overweight.

If you have diabetes, the most important action you can take is to monitor your blood sugar levels and keep those levels as close to normal as possible. This is your best strategy for avoiding the complications. Many physicians use blood glucose level to determine control, but the best and recommended test is called HbA_{1c}. If you aim for an HbA_{1c} (also called *glycosalated hemoglobin*) value of 6.5 percent or less (5 percent is the best), you'll significantly reduce your chances of diabetic complications.

Avoid alcohol, which interferes with your body's use of blood sugar, causing low blood sugar. Although this might seem to be an advantage, it actually creates a craving for more alcohol and high sugar foods, which eventually makes your diabetes worse. You should also stop smoking, because smoking increases the risk of diabetic complications, especially heart attack, stroke, neuropathy, and leg ulcers.

There are several herbs that can lower blood sugar as a side effect—and that can be dangerous if you're not aware of these effects, and your blood sugar goes too low (hypoglycemia). So if you're taking broom, buchu, dandelion, or juniper, monitor your blood sugar more closely. Some over-the-counter remedies contain ingredients that can cause additional problems with blood sugar levels. For example, aspirin can alter blood glucose levels if taken in large amounts. Respiratory products containing phenylephrine, ephedrine, or epinephrine can raise blood sugar levels. Appetite suppressants containing caffeine can do the same.

Finally, a recent study showed that 80 percent of people with diabetes who also have high blood pressure (*hypertension*) do not have their blood pressure under control, and may not even know they have hypertension. If you have diabetes, make sure you have your blood pressure checked, and, if it's high, get treatment. Otherwise, the above complications, especially heart disease and stroke, can become much worse.

General Recommendations

Diet: Eat a balanced diet that is low in refined sugars, fat, and animal products and high in plant fiber. Trans-fatty acids, found in commercially baked and deep-fried foods (processed and fast foods), are especially bad. The American Diabetes Association (ADA) diet is adequate and appropriate (go to www.diabetes.org and look under "Nutrition" for further information). However, I prefer the HCF diet (HCF stands for "high-complex-carbohydrate"—in other words, high fiber). As you plan your meals, follow the HCF daily guidelines: Eat 70 percent to 75 percent complex carbohydrates, 15 percent to 20 percent proteins, and only 5 percent to 10 percent fats. The HCF diet is plentiful in grains (bread, cereal, rice, and pasta), starchy vegetables (potatoes, corn, peas), and legumes (dried beans, peas, lentils), and is packed with vitamins, minerals, and fiber. You should consume at least 20 grams to 35 grams of fiber, but I recommend more if possible, because recent studies have shown that daily consumption of 50 grams of fiber leads to a 10 percent decrease in blood sugar.

Different carbohydrates can cause different increases in your blood sugar, and I recommend that you use the glycemic index to help guide you. This index tells you how quickly your blood sugar will rise when you eat a particular carbohydrate. (For more information about the glycemic index of common foods, go to www.glycemicindex.com.) You should eat those foods that have a low glycemic index. Be aware, however, that some low-glycemic foods, such as sausage and ice cream, are also high-fat and can make you gain weight.

The best way to obtain fiber is from food. Here are some good sources of fiber:

- Legumes (beans)
- Oat bran
- Psyllium seed husks
- Seeds
- Most vegetables
- Nuts
- Pears
- Apples

You can supplement fiber in your diet if you like. I recommend using 20 grams to 30 grams per day of guar, pectin, or oat bran.

As for protein, I recommend soy for several reasons. First, the protein from soy is the only protein from a plant source that is "complete," meaning that it contains food proteins that provide all the essential amino acids to maintain good health. Second, soy can help control blood sugar levels. Third, soy can help prevent or reduce complications of diabetes, especially atherosclerosis and nephropathy.

Cornstarch is absorbed slowly and is especially effective for Type 1 diabetics prone to low blood glucose levels overnight. Adding red wine vinegar (3 teaspoons) to your salad also can lower your blood sugar by up to 30 percent after meals by slowing digestion. Lemon juice works in the same way, so squeeze a fresh lemon into the water you drink. If you eat meat, chicken is better than red meat because chicken has lower saturated fats and a higher percentage of beneficial fatty acids.

If you have a high risk of diabetes or have a prediabetic condition (mildly elevated blood sugars), eating nuts may help keep you from actually getting the disease. I suggest eating one cup of nuts three to four times per week. Finally, onion and garlic lower your blood glucose and compete with insulin for liver sites, thus increasing the release of free insulin. I recommend incorporating them into your diet whenever possible.

Although you can follow these recommendations by yourself, planning well-balanced meals can be hard, especially if you have a busy schedule. No matter which diet you choose to follow, I recommend that you consult with a licensed dietician who can help you develop a good diet plan (for referral to a dietician specializing in diabetes, go to www.eatright.com, the Web site of the American Dietetic Association).

Exercise: My second important recommendation is exercise, which enhances insulin sensitivity, improves glucose tolerance, reduces serum cholesterol and triglycerides, lowers blood pressure, and helps in weight control. In general, aerobic exercise is the most effective. Exercise must be tailored to your individual needs, especially if you are insulin dependent, because exercise can significantly decrease your blood sugar levels. I recommend that you get advice from your doctor and/or a fitness trainer who has expertise in working with diabetics.

Before starting an exercise program, and especially if you have not exercised before, make sure you have a physical examination and exercise tolerance test, so that you can plan an appropriate program and avoid additional complications. And always monitor your blood sugar before and after exercise. Start your exercise slowly and build up gradually.

Caution: If you have complications of diabetes, avoid high-impact activities because they can cause further damage to the eyes and kidneys. Also, even small blisters that form on your feet can lead to chronic wounds or infection. Be sure to check your feet and treat any cuts, scrapes, or abrasions (use topical antibiotic ointment), and go to your doctor immediately if these do not heal or if they get worse.

Your Balanced Healing Action Plan for Type 1 Diabetes (Insulin-Dependent)

Step 1: Take Niacinamide and Vitamin D for Children at Risk for Developing Diabetes

For children who are at high risk of developing diabetes because of family history, give niacinamide, 25mg per kilogram of body weight (11.4mg per pound). This has been shown to prevent the development of Type 1 diabetes in many of these children. In addition, give your child Vitamin D supplementation in the form of cod liver oil (2,000 IU daily) during the first year of life. Make sure you see your pediatrician for further guidance and to monitor your child.

Step 2: Take Insulin Injections

Type 1 diabetes requires insulin replacement. Insulin can be taken only through injections. There are short-, intermediate-, and long-acting forms of insulin from several different sources (pork, humans, RNA), so consult with your doctor to find out which form is the best for you. A new form of insulin is now available that can be inhaled and helps reduce the number of injections required on a daily basis. However, it cannot be used if you have any problems with your lungs. Make sure you monitor and regulate your glucose regularly and under the guidance of a doctor.

Step 3: Begin Taking Niacinamide as Soon as You Are Diagnosed

If you have just been diagnosed as having Type 1 diabetes, take niacinamide, 25mg per kilogram of your body weight (11.4mg per pound) daily. If taken soon after onset of diabetes, niacinamide may slow the progression of—or possibly even reverse—the disease. You must still take insulin to control your blood sugar while the niacinamide has time to work. Monitor your blood sugar carefully and frequently during this time. If your blood sugar does not go down further after several weeks, then the niacinamide won't work, and you should stop taking it.

Step 4: Take Vitamin C, Vitamin E, Vitamin B₁₂, Vitamin B₆, Niacin, Magnesium, Mixed Flavonoids, Zinc, and Flaxseed Oil

Certain vitamins and minerals have been shown to help control and decrease blood sugar, and reduce complications from diabetes. In general, you should take the following amounts on a daily basis, from a combination of diet and supplementation:

- Vitamin C, 2,000mg
- Vitamin E, 800 IU to 1,200 IU
- Vitamin B_{12}, 1,000mcg
- Vitamin B_6, 100mg
- Niacin, 1200mg to 3,000mg
- Magnesium, 700mg
- Mixed flavonoids, 1,000mg to 2,000mg
- Flaxseed oil, 1 tablespoon
- Zinc, 30mg

A registered dietician can help you determine whether your diet provides the proper amounts of these nutrients.

Step 5: Take an Aspirin a Day to Help Prevent Heart Disease

If you have diabetes, you are at increased risk for heart disease, and you should take one aspirin daily to lower your risk. Take no more than 325mg per day for optimum benefit (81mg is sufficient to thin your blood). Take aspirin along with the previous steps.

Cautions: If you take aspirin, you should avoid taking ibuprofen, which blocks the blood-thinning effects of aspirin. If you must take ibuprofen, take the aspirin first, and wait an hour to take the ibuprofen so that the aspirin has time to take effect. Also, aspirin can deplete your body's stores of vitamin C, so you might need to replace this nutrient through your diet or by taking supplements (600mg per day).

Step 6: Take Gymnema Sylvestre, Bitter Melon, Defatted Fenugreek, Salt Bush, and/or Corosolic Acid (Queen's Crepe Myrtle)

Several herbs have been noted to decrease and help regulate blood sugar, as well as make the body's cells more responsive to insulin. The purpose of trying these herbs is to reduce your insulin dosage. In order of effectiveness, they are

- Gymnema sylvestre extract, 400mg daily
- Bitter melon, three to six ounces of fresh juice daily
- Defatted fenugreek powder, 50g daily
- Salt Bush, 3g daily

These herbs should decrease your blood sugar within one to two months, and you can take all of them together. If your blood sugar decreases, you then may be able to lower your insulin requirement, although you won't be able to discontinue the insulin completely. If your blood sugar hasn't decreased, there's no reason to continue taking the herbs. (There is a product that contains all four herbs along with the vitamins/minerals in Step 4. See Appendix C for referral information.)

Your Balanced Healing Action Plan for Type 2 Diabetes (Non-Insulin Dependent)

- You should have your liver enzymes and creatinine levels tested to assess your kidney function. If the levels are abnormal, insulin (Step 11) is usually recommended, and then return to Step 1.

Step 1: Lose Weight

Most people with Type 2 diabetes are overweight. If you are, you may be able to regulate your blood sugar levels with weight loss, diet, and exercise alone. A six-week trial will tell you whether the changes in your blood sugar are significant enough to forego medication, so it's certainly worth the effort.

Step 2: Take an Aspirin a Day to Help Prevent Heart Disease

If you have diabetes, you are at increased risk for heart disease. Take one aspirin daily to lower your risk. Take no more than 325mg per day for optimum benefit (81mg is sufficient to thin your blood). Take aspirin along with the previous steps.

Cautions: If you take aspirin, you should avoid taking ibuprofen, which blocks the blood-thinning effects of aspirin. If you must take ibuprofen, take the aspirin first, and wait an hour to take the ibuprofen so that the aspirin has time to take effect. Also, aspirin can deplete your body's stores of vitamin C, so replacement by diet or supplementation may be necessary (600mg per day).

Step 3: Take Vitamin C, Vitamin E, Vitamin B_{12}, Vitamin B_6, Niacin, Magnesium, Mixed Flavonoids, Zinc, and Flaxseed Oil

Certain vitamins and minerals have been shown to help control and decrease blood sugar, as well as reduce complications from diabetes. In general, you should take the following amounts on a daily basis, from a combination of diet and supplementation:

- Vitamin C, 2,000mg
- Vitamin E, 800 IU to 1,200 IU
- Vitamin B_{12}, 1,000mcg
- Vitamin B_6, 100mg
- Niacin, 1200mg to 3000mg
- Magnesium, 700mg
- Mixed flavonoids, 1000mg to 2000mg
- Flaxseed oil, 1 tablespoon
- Zinc, 30mg

A registered dietician can help you determine whether your diet provides the proper amounts of these nutrients. It may take one to two months before there are any glucose-lowering effects. But even if the nutrients don't lower your blood sugar, you should still take them, because they can help maintain your general health and prevent complications from your diabetes.

Step 4: Take Gymnema Sylvestre, Bitter Melon, Defatted Fenugreek, and Salt Bush

If your blood sugar is still elevated, I recommend trying several herbs that have been found to decrease and help regulate blood sugar, and make the body's cells more responsive to insulin. In order of effectiveness, these are

- Gymnema sylvestre extract, 400mg daily
- Bitter melon, 3 ounces to 6 ounces of fresh juice daily
- Defatted fenugreek powder, 50g daily
- Salt Bush, 3g daily

These herbs should decrease your blood sugar within one to two months, and you can take all of them together. But if your blood sugar does not decrease, there is no reason for you to continue taking the herbs. (There is a product that contains all four herbs along with the vitamins/minerals in Step 3. Go to Appendix C for referral information.)

If these herbs don't work for you or are only partially effective, you can try Corosolic Acid, also called Queen's Crepe Myrtle. Take 480 to 550 mcg, 1 to 2 tablets, 3 times a day. This recently discovered supplement has been shown to significantly decrease blood sugar in many Type II diabetics. It takes about two weeks to get the maximum benefit.

Step 5: Take Appropriate Chinese Herbal Remedies to Normalize Blood Sugar

If the previous steps do not bring your blood sugar to a normal level, or if you have fluctuations in blood sugar, I recommend taking Chinese herbs, such as *Zuo Gui Wan/You Gui Yin* in combination with *Zhi Bai Di Huang Wan*. These formulas can reduce and regulate blood sugar; they can reduce backache and excessive thirst and urination as well. Consult a practitioner qualified in Chinese herbal medicine to determine which Chinese herbal formulas are the best for your particular syndromes. You should see improvement in your blood sugar within three to six weeks (sometimes sooner), but you may need to take the herbs longer, depending on your condition. (See Appendix A, under "Chinese Herbs," for further information.)

Step 6: Undergo Acupuncture

Acupuncture has been used for centuries to reduce blood sugar, and it can be used in addition to the previous steps. You should use it especially with the Chinese herbs in Step 5. Principal points usually include M-BW-12 on the mid-back (called *pancreas hollow*, this point controls pancreatic function), with others found elsewhere on the back and on the legs and ankles. Always seek evaluation and treatment from a practitioner certified in acupuncture. (See Appendix A, under "Acupuncture," for guidance on finding a qualified acupuncturist and for explanation of the different acupuncture techniques.) You should notice improvement within six treatments, but you might need additional sessions for maximum benefits.

Step 7: Take Chromium to Lower Blood Sugar

If your blood sugar remains elevated, I recommend taking chromium (200mcg per day). Chromium has been shown to increase insulin sensitivity and binding, and it can lower blood sugar, especially if you are deficient in this mineral. You should see a decrease in blood sugar within one to two months. If your blood sugar does not decrease, stop taking the chromium.

Step 8: Take a Prescription Oral Medication

If the previous steps still have not controlled your blood sugar, then you should start on prescription medications. There are many different types of antidiabetic medications, so it is important to obtain guidance from your doctor or a diabetic specialist (*endocrinologist*). In general, your doctor may make these recommendations:

- If your liver and kidney tests are normal, and you are obese, your doctor may prescribe metformin, an oral antidiabetic medication that does not cause weight gain. Check your B12 level when taking this drug, and, if it's low, take a supplement.
- If your liver and kidney tests are normal, and you are normal weight, your doctor may prescribe a sulfonylurea medication (Glipizide, Glyburide). The major side effect is hypoglycemia (blood sugar that's too low). These medications can interact with trimethoprim (a kidney antibiotic), cimetidine (an antiulcer medication sold under the brand name Tagamet), alcohol, and anticoagulants (blood thinners), all of which can increase the chances of hypoglycemia if you take them with sulfonylureas.
- For some patients, the above two types of medication (Glipizide, Glyburide) can be used in combination for better glycemic control. Check with your doctor to see whether that's appropriate for you.
- If urine testing detects *microalbuminuria*, you should take an ACE inhibitor (such as captopril or analapril) along with the previous medications.

Nathan, a 43-year-old jeweler, was one of many people who have Type 2 diabetes and don't know it—but he saw marked improvements with the above steps when it was discovered. When Nathan came to see me, his blood sugar level was more than 300, and he was not following a good diet or getting exercise. He had fatigue and also numbness in his feet (mild neuropathy). Besides urging him to diet and exercise, I started him on a combination of vitamins, minerals, and herbals to decrease his glucose (Steps 3 and 4). His blood sugar levels decreased, but only to about 200. I next prescribed a combination of sulfonylurea and metformin, which brought his glucose levels to near normal. After much urging, he finally started an exercise program and an HCF diet. After three months, he started losing weight, and I was able to start reducing the dosage of his medications. He continued taking the vitamins and herbs, and, after one year, he was able to stop taking the conventional medications completely.

Step 9: Take an Alpha-Glucosidase Inhibitor

If the above prescription medications fail to lower your blood sugar or have intolerable side effects, then your doctor may prescribe an alpha-glucosidase inhibitor. These drugs can be used alone or in combination with a sulfonylurea. They frequently cause side effects such as flatulence, diarrhea, and abdominal cramps, which tend to go away with continued use (or if the medication is started in a low dose).

Step 10: Take an Insulin Sensitizer

The newest antidiabetic medications are thiazolidinediones (called glitazones for short). This class of drugs is designed as "insulin sensitizers"—they improve glucose control while lowering insulin levels. They may also reduce high blood pressure and cholesterol problems associated with insulin resistance. These drugs can be used alone, in place of Step 9, or in combination with metformin or a sulfonylurea (Step 8). However, glitazones may be associated with an increased risk of heart failure, so they need to be closely monitored by your doctor.

Step 11: Take Insulin Injections

If the previous steps don't control your blood sugar levels, you may need to take insulin. Some doctors prescribe insulin in combination with the oral medications, but this is more expensive and has no distinct advantage over insulin alone. There are short, intermediate, and long-acting forms of insulin and several different sources (pork, humans, RNA), so consult your doctor. A new form of insulin is now available that can be inhaled and helps reduce the number of injections required on a daily basis. However, it cannot be used if you have problems with your lungs. Be sure to monitor and regulate your glucose regularly and under the guidance of a doctor.

Your Balanced Healing Action Plan for Complications of Diabetes

- Prevention—by strictly maintaining healthy blood glucose levels—is the best way to avoid complications of diabetes. When complications do occur, the following treatments can help.

Treatments for Neuropathy (Nerve Problems)

Step 1: Undergo Acupuncture

Acupuncture can be very effective for reducing the symptoms of diabetic neuropathy. Principal acupuncture points usually are found on the legs. Ear point refers to the leg region.

Always seek evaluation and treatment from a practitioner certified in acupuncture. (See Appendix A, under "Acupuncture," for guidance on finding a qualified acupuncturist and for explanation of the different acupuncture techniques.) You should improve within six treatments, but you might need additional sessions for maximum benefits.

Step 2: Take a Low-Dose Prescription Tricyclic Antidepressant, Neurontin, or Pregabalin

If Step 1 is partially effective or not effective at all, your doctor can prescribe low-dose antidepressants such as amitriptyline, 25mg to 50mg per day, which can sometimes reduce pain. An alternative is Neurontin (gabapentin), 300mg to 2,400mg per day. Amitriptyline may cause dryness of the mouth, and both drugs may cause drowsiness. A newer drug, pregabalin, has recently been shown to be effective in 40 percent of people with diabetic neuropathy. It may take several weeks to notice improvement with any of these medications.

Step 3: Take Alpha-Lipoic Acid, Thiamine (Vitamin B_1), and/or Gamma-Linoleic Acid

Alpha-lipoic acid (ALA), considered a "super-antioxidant," has been used for 25 years in Germany to treat diabetic neuropathy. It has been demonstrated to decrease numbness and pain in neuropathy after three weeks of treatment, but this is with intravenous use. Unfortunately, I'm not aware of anywhere in the U.S. where you can receive this supplement intravenously, so you would have to go to Germany for this treatment. *Oral alpha-lipoic acid* (1,200mg to 1,800mg per day) can improve nerve conduction and decrease serum glucose, but it has not been shown to improve *symptoms* of neuropathy. I do think it is worth trying the oral form because it does have benefits for the nerves and for your diabetes, and it may slow the progression of your neuropathy. You should notice improvement in two to three months.

Supplements containing gamma-linoleic acid (GLA) can also improve neuropathy, although it may take several months for you to get any benefits from them. Evening primrose oil (480mg daily) is the most commonly used, but I recommend borage oil (1g daily) because it's less expensive and contains a greater percentage of GLA. Thiamine (vitamin B_1, 10mg to 30mg daily) has recently been found to improve neuropathy symptoms, and I recommend it, too. You can take all these supplements together.

Step 4: Use Transcutaneous Electrostimulation

Transcutaneous electrostimulation is sometimes successful in relieving some of the pain associated with neuropathy. This involves the use of a TENS unit, which is carried on a belt and connects electrodes to the leg areas. The unit is available through a doctor's prescription.

Treatments for Retinopathy (Eye Disease)

Step 1: Take Bilberry and Mixed Carotenoids

If your *retinopathy* is mild, supplements containing bilberry (160mg extract twice daily) may be very helpful. There are several products that combine bilberry with mixed carotenoids, which may be more effective than bilberry alone. These supplements protect the eye through their antioxidant effects. You should notice improved vision within one to two months.

Step 2: Undergo Photocoagulation

If your retinopathy is severe, *photocoagulation* will be necessary. This procedure uses high-energy laser to seal leaky blood vessels. If you are losing vision in your eyes despite Step 1, consult with an ophthalmologist (eye physician) regarding this procedure.

Treatments for Nephropathy (Kidney Disease)

- Have your urine checked for microalbuminuria every 3 to 6 months. This is the most sensitive test to detect early kidney problems. If the lab results are abnormal, you should have your creatinine, 24-hour protein, and creatine clearance checked every year.

Step 1: Make Dietary Changes to Support Kidney Health

In the early stages, nephropathy can be managed primarily by diet and nutrient balance. Although the Balanced Healing Diet (see "Simple Healing Steps for all Health Conditions," page 79) is appropriate for this purpose, I highly recommend consultation with a registered dietician first to help you understand and plan what you need to eat for optimum kidney health (see Appendix C for referral information). I also recommend adding soy products to your diet; they can provide needed protein, and they can improve kidney function (for further information and guidance on soy products, see Appendix B, under "Herbs.")

Step 2: Take Prescription ACE Inhibitors

If your urine tests show that you have *proteinuria* (excessive protein in your urine), your doctor may prescribe an ACE inhibitor (such as captopril or analapril) because these drugs reduce the risk of kidney failure. Some people may have coughing as a side effect. If you start coughing, take low-dose ibuprofen (200mg to 600mg per day), which, for many people, can block the cough. (Remember to take the ibuprofen several hours after taking aspirin.)

Step 3: Take Flaxseed Oil

I recommend taking flaxseed oil (1 tablespoon per day) with the previous steps. Flaxseed oil promotes kidney function, due to its effects in preventing artery disease and correcting defects in fatty acid metabolism seen in people with diabetes. Because of these effects, it also helps prevent heart disease.

Step 4: Undergo Dialysis

Severe nephropathy requires dialysis to take over the filtering functions of the damaged kidneys. Dialysis requires the creation of an *arteriovenous fistula* (surgical attachment of a vein to an artery, usually in the forearm), and then weekly or more frequent sessions in which your blood is cleaned of toxins through a dialysis machine. Because this process leaches many important nutrients from your system along with the toxins, your doctor will have these nutrients replaced in the dialysis solution.

Treatments for Atherosclerosis

See the section on cholesterol on page 168 for a full discussion and treatment of athero-sclerosis.

Treatments for Foot Ulcers

Step 1: Good Foot Care for Prevention

Good foot care and avoiding injury are the best approach to foot ulcers. If you do injure your feet, see your regular doctor or diabetes specialist immediately. Don't wear shoes or boots that squeeze or constrict your feet or that are otherwise uncomfortable.

Step 2: Undergo Conventional Wound Care

Appropriate conventional wound care is necessary if an ulcer starts forming. You may need wound *debridement* (removal of any dead tissue), appropriate antibiotics, and/or hyperbaric oxygen treatment. You will likely need surgery if the ulcer progresses into *gangrene*, in which the tissue dies and turns black. You can use the following steps along with conventional care to accelerate the healing process.

Step 3: Undergo Low-Energy Laser Treatment

I recommend the use of low-level energy lasers along with Step 2 because in my studies, the laser is very effective for healing ulcers by stimulating the damaged cells to heal and by increasing blood flow to the foot. These lasers are called "cold" lasers because they do not produce heat like the hot lasers used in surgical procedures do. Their primary side effect (in about 25 percent of patients) is that they cause a temporary increase in soreness, which may last from one to three days. You should observe results within two to three weeks. Because low-energy lasers are currently a research device and unavailable to most doctors, see Index C for reference information.

> Ethel, an art teacher, had diabetes most of her adult life, and at age 76 she developed dry gangrene (non-infectious death of tissue) in several of her toes. Her doctor told her she would need to have the toes amputated. This understandably frightened Ethel, because it meant she'd have to be in a wheelchair. She came to me, looking for other options. I started treating her with the low-energy laser, and after eight treatments, her circulation improved significantly, and most of the gangrenous tissue sloughed off, leaving normal tissue. We'd saved her toes, and she avoided amputation.

Step 4: Undergo Acupuncture

If your foot ulcers are still not healing or are slow to heal, I recommend acupuncture to stimulate blood flow and tissue healing. The acupuncture needles should be placed around the ulcer, but placement will also depend on your underlying Chinese diagnosis. (See Appendix A for more information on Chinese syndromes.) Always seek evaluation and treatment from a practitioner certified in acupuncture. (See Appendix A, under "Acupuncture," for guidance on finding a qualified acupuncturist and for explanation of the different acupuncture techniques.) You should see improvement within six treatments, but you might need additional sessions for maximum benefits. Acupuncture can be used with the laser in Step 3 for faster results.

DRUG ADDICTION

Drug addiction is the compulsive use of a drug, whether legal or illegal. The most commonly addicting drugs include cocaine, marijuana, heroin, benzodiazepines (such as Valium), narcotics (such as codeine, morphine, or Demerol), and stimulants (such as amphetamines). Drug addiction has many causes, including genetic predisposition; environmental and social factors, such as poverty and family dysfunction; and peer pressure. Tolerance to various drugs increases with use, so more of the drug is required for the same effects as time goes by. Addictive drugs make users believe that they are immune to addiction, and that belief makes the addiction very difficult to treat. Most drugs will also cause physical dependence—if you suddenly stop taking them, you will have withdrawal symptoms. Drug abuse can lead to permanent brain damage, thoughts of suicide, violence, coma, and heart and liver disease.

Common Symptoms

- Changes in appearance and behavior that affect performance.
- Changes in mood or attitude.
- Depending on what type of drugs are involved—sedatives, stimulants, cocaine, opiates, psychedelics, or marijuana—a wide variety of other symptoms can occur.
- Drug withdrawal can cause pain, anxiety, insomnia, headache, and nausea and vomiting.

What You Need to Know

The most important factor in treating addiction is the desire to stop. Once the motivation is present, treatments are much more effective. However, one type of treatment alone usually is not effective because of the many factors involved, so treatments should be used in combination. Many times, family members and friends may contribute to the perpetuation of the drug addiction by denying its occurrence or defending the addicted person (making themselves co-dependent). Thus, efforts to treat drug addiction successfully must involve these other participants.

Drug addiction may be part of or even caused by *bipolar disorder,* and you should be tested to make sure you don't have this disorder. It's characterized by bouts of hyperactivity followed by bouts of depression (see the section on bipolar disorder on page 134 for further information).

General Recommendations

Diet: Most people with drug addictions suffer from nutritional deficiencies, and they often have problems processing sugar and carbohydrates, so they crave these substances. You should eat three meals a day, avoid sugars, limit carbohydrates (especially processed), and increase your protein intake.

Your Balanced Healing Action Plan for Drug Addiction

Step 1: Receive Professional Help

The best action you can take for drug addiction is to obtain professional help. There are excellent professional programs to help you withdraw and end addiction, and this is the best way to start. Just seeing a doctor does not usually resolve drug addiction, so organized programs are essential. Many hospitals have drug addiction programs, and there are many private or community programs as well. These programs differ primarily in how they are funded, some requiring insurance and others supported by private foundations or government programs. Although you can enter most of these programs without a doctor's referral, you should ask your doctor for guidance on the best programs in your area.

Step 2: Take the Herb Milk Thistle

I recommend that you take the herb milk thistle (200mg to 400mg of a standardized 70 percent silymarin extract, daily) if you use drugs or have used them in the past. This herb helps protect the liver from the toxic effects of drugs and helps the liver regenerate new liver cells to replace those damaged by drugs. You should continue taking milk thistle for two to three months after you discontinue drugs to obtain maximum repair of your liver.

Step 3: Take a Good Multivitamin

Along with Step 2, you should also take a good multivitamin, especially if your diet is poor, to protect the rest of your body's cells from damage. Take three to six capsules a day. (See Appendix B, under "Multivitamins," for a recommended formula.) As with Step 2, continue taking the supplement for two to three months after you have discontinued drugs.

Step 4: Undergo Acupuncture to Help Reduce Cravings While You Discontinue Drugs

Acupuncture is excellent for reducing cravings, so it will help you get off the drugs. Use it along with the previous steps. Acupuncture can also speed up the withdrawal process and make it much more effective and longer lasting.

Ear acupuncture is the preferred form. It uses press tacks or needles in the following ear points: Shenmen, liver, lung, kidney, and sympathetic (some acupuncturists add the zero point to help balance the system and reduce anxiety). There is a point for drug addiction in the *tragus*, the flap in front of the ear. You massage these points several times a day to stimulate the points. These needles remain in the ear for three to seven days and then are replaced weekly until they're not needed any longer (that is, until you have no more desire or cravings for drugs).

You should always seek evaluation and treatment from a practitioner certified in acupuncture. (See Appendix A, under "Acupuncture," for guidance in finding a qualified acupuncturist and for explanation of the different acupuncture techniques.) The ear tacks should decrease the desire for drugs within hours or days.

Step 5: Take an Appropriate Chinese Herbal Remedy to Prevent Withdrawal Symptoms

Along with acupuncture, I recommend the Chinese herbal formula, *Chai Hu Mu Li Lung Gu Tang* to reduce withdrawal symptoms as well as cravings during withdrawal (take three tablets three times daily between meals). Consult a practitioner qualified in Chinese herbal medicine to guide you. You should observe initial benefits within three to seven days (sometimes sooner). Take them until you no longer have cravings or withdrawal symptoms. (See Appendix A, under "Chinese Herbs," for further information.)

> Kevin is a 20-year-old college student who was addicted to smoking marijuana. He came to me for help in quitting. I gave him the Chinese herbal formula *Chai Hu Mu Li Lung Gu Tang* and placed acupuncture press tacks in his ear points. Much to Kevin's surprise, after just two days he had no desire for marijuana. I replaced the needles on two more occasions during the next month, after which he had no desire for marijuana even without the needles. To prevent relapses, I urged Kevin to see a psychotherapist to discuss the underlying reasons for his addictive personality characteristics.

Step 6: Take Prescription Medications for Withdrawal Symptoms

For withdrawal symptoms that do not respond to the Chinese herbs, your doctor can prescribe several medications, such as tricyclic antidepressants (amitriptyline) or clonidine. There are other medications used for specific drug addictions (such as Naloxone for narcotic drugs and methadone, LAAM, or buprenorphine for opioid addiction). See your physician or drug counselor for specific recommendations and dosages.

Step 7: Practice Meditation and Other Mind-Body Interventions During and After Drug Withdrawal

Because drug addiction is so powerful, you may get very anxious and have sleep problems during withdrawal and afterward. Mind-body interventions such as meditation can help reduce anxiety and improve sleep (see "Simple Healing Steps for All Health Conditions," page 79, under "Meditation," for further information and examples). To unlock underlying psychological causes, I highly recommend interactive imagery. This is a mind-body method in which you mentally interact with images that represent your emotions. It is a powerful method to uncover and deal with subconscious psychological issues of which you may not be aware. (See Appendix A, under "Mind-Body Techniques," for further explanation and examples.)

Step 8: Organ- or System-Specific Treatments (Complications of Drug Use)

Drug addictions can cause a variety of other conditions involving almost any organ of the body. For complications of addictions involving particular organ systems, please see the sections for those conditions.

ECZEMA (Atopic Dermatitis)

Eczema is a form of *dermatitis* (or irritation of the skin). Many cases of eczema are related to allergies and/or asthma. The condition can arise from—or be made worse by—physical stress (injury, repetitive use of the area), chemical sensitivity (anything from perfumes to solvents), or emotionally induced stress. Eczema can alter natural pigmentation, making the affected area either lighter or darker. It occurs most frequently on the face, wrists, elbows, and knees.

Common Symptoms

- Dry, itchy, thickened, and scaly skin
- Skin lesions and patches of redness

What You Need to Know

Certain environmental *allergens* (substances that the body recognizes as "foreign" and thus tries to destroy) can cause your eczema. If you know anything that does cause a flare-up, the best treatment is to avoid it. Because dust mites may be a factor, use bedding covers. Contact with animals, detergents, or underlying vaccinations do not seem to affect eczema symptoms, so don't worry about avoiding them.

General Recommendations

Diet: Increase the amount of fatty fish (such as mackerel, tuna, trout, halibut, cod, sardines, or salmon) you eat; the omega-3 fatty acids they contain can decrease your symptoms. Sometimes food allergies (especially to milk, eggs, and, in children, peanuts) cause eczema. (See the section on food allergies on page 210 for more information and treatment recommendations.)

Your Balanced Healing Action Plan for Eczema

Step 1: Apply Topical Steroids for Temporary Relief of Mild Eczema

Topical steroids are the most effective and quickest treatment for reducing mild skin lesions. An over-the-counter cortisone cream (such as Cortaid) works well for some people. If it isn't effective for you, your doctor can prescribe a more potent cream. Which one? That depends on where your eczema is because some creams might cause harmful effects if used on certain areas of the skin, such as the face. The cream should be used for two to four weeks, and then discontinued until lesions reoccur. In addition to the steroid cream, I recommend an emollient (a moisturizing cream), which can further reduce your symptoms.

Step 2: Take Zinc and Omega-3 Fatty Acids to Correct Underlying Deficiencies

People who have eczema often have zinc and fatty acid deficiencies. If you're deficient in these nutrients, zinc supplementation will help because zinc is essential to the proper metabolism of fatty acids. Get a blood test to measure your zinc level, and, if it's low, take a supplement. Use up to 45mg to 60mg per day, and then decrease to 30mg a day when your skin clears. It may take one to two months to notice an effect.

Omega-3 fatty acid supplements are helpful to correct underlying fatty acid deficiencies, especially if you don't eat fish (see diet recommendations above). In this case, there's no blood test; you can find out if you're deficient only by seeing whether the supplements decrease your symptoms. I prefer flaxseed oil (1 tablespoon daily). A second alternative is fish oil (540mg EPA and 360mg DHA daily). If you don't respond in three months to either of these supplements, continue with the next step.

Step 3: Receive Acupuncture for Long-Term Relief

If any underlying nutritional deficiencies have been corrected and you still have symptoms of eczema, I recommend acupuncture as the next step. Principal points usually are found on the neck, arms, and wrists. Always seek evaluation and treatment from a practitioner certified in acupuncture. (See Appendix A, under "Acupuncture," for guidance in finding a qualified acupuncturist and for explanation of the different acupuncture techniques.) You should see improvement within six treatments, although you might need additional sessions to get the maximum benefits.

> Larry, a 22-year-old waiter, had eczema on his hands. It got worse when he was exposed to outside elements, especially cold weather and yard work. He had used topical steroids, which helped at first but then had no effect. He took fish oil supplements and underwent acupuncture. After two months of treatment, his eczema completely cleared up.

Step 4: Take Digestive Enzymes and Probiotics

If your digestive tract does not work well, your food will be incompletely broken down. Incomplete dissolved proteins can cause an allergic response, so improving your digestion may help. Start with digestive enzymes to help break down your food more thoroughly. There are many products that contain digestive enzymes, and they should contain some or all of the following: protease, papain, amylase, lipase, bromelain, cellulase, and lactase.

I also recommend taking probiotics with the enzymes. *Probiotics* are live cultures of organisms (the "good" bacteria) that help digest food properly. Of the beneficial microorganisms in probiotics, *L. acidophilus* and *bifidobacteria* are the best. Other beneficial bacteria include *L. salivarius, L. rhamnosus, L. plantarum, streptococcus thermophilus, L. bulgaricus, L. casei,* and *L. sporogenes.* You should notice improvement in three to six weeks.

Many people believe that yogurt contains beneficial microorganisms that can take the place of probiotics. Yogurt products do contain beneficial microorganisms, but they are not the most important or potent. Also, many yogurt products are pasteurized to increase shelf life, but this process kills most of the good bacteria, thus destroying all the benefits. Don't rely on yogurt to re-colonize your GI tract.

Step 5: Try the Nambudripad Allergy Elimination Treatment

If you suspect food allergies could be contributing to your eczema and Step 4 hasn't helped, I recommend the Nambudripad Allergy Elimination Treatment. This method uses a combination of kinesiology, chiropractic, acupuncture, herbs, and nutrition to resolve allergies to food. However, it may take several months to get results—it all depends on how many foods are causing you problems. (See Appendix A, under "NAET," and the section on food allergies for further information.)

Step 6: Use the Prescription Ointment Protopic or Elidel

If the above steps are not beneficial, your doctor may prescribe Protopic, a topical ointment, which can help clear eczema in people who don't get relief from other treatments. It won't cure your eczema, but it can give you temporary relief. Another new nonsteroidal cream is Elidel, which can be used for mild to moderate eczema on a short-term or intermittent long-term basis. But don't use these products if you have skin infections; they can make them worse.

Step 7: Take Licorice, Grapeseed Extract, Quercetin, and/or Glutathione

If all else fails, try licorice (Glycyrrhiza glabra) which can help control eczema symptoms because it has antiinflammatory and antiallergic effects. However, it may take a long time (several months to a year) to be effective, so try the previous steps first. Use the deglycyrrhizinated (DGL) form, one or two 380mg chewable tablets before meals. You can also apply a licorice salve to the eczema lesions (your pharmacist must concoct the salve). Other supplements that may have beneficial effects include the following:

- Grapeseed Extract (50mg to 100mg of 95 percent procyanidolic oligomers content)
- Quercetin (400mg to 500mg three times daily)
- Glutathione (250mg daily)

As with licorice, it may take months to observe benefits. The supplements can be taken together.

EPILEPSY (Seizures)

Epilepsy is a group of disorders caused by the erratic discharge of neurons (nerve cells) in the brain. Epilepsy is divided into two general categories, *general* and *partial,* which in turn are divided into several subtypes. The most common subtypes include *generalized, focal/partial, absence,* and *psychomotor seizures. Febrile seizure* is another subtype that usually occurs in sick children who have a sudden fever. A seizure can usually be controlled and doesn't cause permanent problems, although it can be very dangerous if it occurs while a person is driving or is in some other potentially hazardous situation.

Common Symptoms

Symptoms vary according to the part of the brain that is affected.

- **Generalized (formally called "grand mal") seizures** typically last up to 30 minutes and may include such symptoms as loss of consciousness, rhythmic jerking movements, incontinence, and an aura (that is, a warning sign before the seizure, such as nausea, or a particular taste or smell). Myoclonus seizures are a subclass of generalized seizures; they involve only muscle contractions.
- **Absence (formerly known as "petit mal") seizures** are typically brief, and the person (and others) may not even know they are occurring. Typical symptoms include staring straight ahead and immobility lasting a few seconds.
- **Psychomotor (formerly known as "temporal lobe") seizures** may include such symptoms as repetitive lip smacking, fiddling movements, and a sense of detachment from surroundings.
- **Focal/Partial (such as Jacksonian) seizures** typically involve a rhythmic twitching of the hand, foot, or face, followed by a period of weakness or paralysis.

What You Need to Know

Seizures can have many causes, including lead poisoning, head injury, brain tumor or infection, alcohol or drug addiction, organ disease, and medications. So it's important to be thoroughly evaluated and tested by a physician to detect and correct any underlying problems. There are some controversies about the treatment of seizures, especially the question of whether to treat someone who has only had one seizure. Studies have shown that treatment with seizure medication reduces further seizures by half, but 60 percent of untreated people will not have another seizure anyway. There is also possible long-term harm from seizure medication. Doctors also disagree over how long to continue seizure medication when a patient has been seizure-free on medication. Because these controversies are complex and the decisions are individualized, you should discuss them with your neurologist.

Your Balanced Healing Action Plan for Epilepsy

Step 1: Take Prescription Antiseizure Medication

Antiseizure medication is the first step for any seizures, especially if they reoccur. The most common seizure medications are carbamazepine, lamotrigine, gabapentin, phenytoin, valproate, primidone, and phenobarbital. Your seizures may not be completely controlled on just one of these medications, and you may need a combination of them.

Step 2: Receive Acupuncture

Acupuncture can be effective in reducing the frequency of chronic seizures, and it may help reduce the dosage of conventional medications necessary to control them. Principal points usually are found on the neck and head. **Use acupuncture ONLY in addition to conventional methods.** Always seek evaluation and treatment from a practitioner certified in acupuncture. (See Appendix A, under "Acupuncture," for guidance in finding a qualified acupuncturist and for explanation of the different acupuncture techniques.) You should experience improvement within six treatments, but you might need additional sessions to get the maximum benefits.

> When Sydney, a 34-year-old attorney, came to see me, she'd had generalized seizures for more than 10 years. She'd been on various combinations of antiseizure medications and was taking two of them at the time I saw her, yet she still had intermittent "breakthrough" seizures every few months. I gave her acupuncture treatments, and after 12 sessions, she was able to take just one medication and had no more breakthrough seizures.

Step 3: Take N-Acetylcysteine for Myoclonic Seizures

For myoclonus (muscle-contracting) epilepsy, I recommend taking N-acetylcysteine (4 grams to 6 grams daily), an amino acid derivative that's been shown to reduce the severity and frequency of attacks.

FIBROMYALGIA

Fibromyalgia is characterized by widespread inflammation of your muscles and joints. Although several factors may cause this condition, low levels of serotonin and dysfunction of your immune system may also be involved. It commonly occurs along with Chronic Fatigue Syndrome, and the co-occurrence of the two ailments makes it even more difficult to treat fibromyalgia successfully (see the section on chronic fatigue syndrome on page 171).

Diagnosis

Fibromyalgia is often mistakenly diagnosed in people who have chronic pain. A correct diagnosis is very important, because many symptoms that appear to be due to fibromyalgia may be due to other, reversible, causes. Before a definitive diagnosis can be made, your doctor must document 11 out of 18 specific trigger points (tender areas of the body). Also, you must have a history of generalized aches or stiffness in three areas of the body for at least three months, as well as four of the following eight symptoms:

- Sore throat
- Muscle pain

- Pain in multiple joints
- Tender lymph nodes
- Headaches
- Impaired memory or concentration
- Unrefreshed sleep
- Postexertional malaise (extreme tiredness and lack of motivation after exertion)

Common Symptoms

The previous symptoms are the primary ones that help diagnose this condition, but other symptoms and factors are common in fibromyalgia:

- Muscular pain, aching, stiffness, especially in the morning
- Symptoms worse in cold or wet weather
- History of injury up to one year before other symptoms appear
- Depression
- Irritable Bowel Syndrome
- Headaches (migraine and non-migraine)
- Raynaud's phenomenon (fingers turn colors and are painful when cold)

What You Need to Know

Fibromyalgia is a very difficult condition to treat, and most conventional methods have been unsuccessful in reducing its symptoms. Alternative methods have had some success but usually cannot cure the condition. Sleep quality is one of the most important aspects of fibromyalgia, and correlates with the severity of pain: The less sleep you get, the more pain you have.

General Recommendations

Diet: Saturated animal fats and arachidonic acid from red meats and dairy products can increase the inflammatory response, so reducing these foods may help reduce your pain. It may also be helpful to eat a more vegetarian diet with oils high in omega-3 fatty acids (olive and canola oils, for example). Eating cold-water fish (such as salmon, trout, mackerel, cod, tuna, halibut, sardines, and swordfish) can supply you with natural omega-3 fatty acids and can lessen your body's inflammatory and allergic responses.

Exercise: Aerobic exercise can significantly reduce fibromyalgia symptoms over a course of 12 weeks. You should start out slowly and increase time and intensity slowly. Although it may be difficult to undergo exercise when you're hurting, once you start doing it, your symptoms will improve.

Meditation: Because insomnia, anxiety, and depression are all involved with fibromyalgia, meditation is helpful in reducing these symptoms and improving your overall condition. (See "Simple Healing Steps for All Health Conditions," page 79, and Appendix A, under "Mind-Body Techniques," for further information and sample meditations.)

Qigong: Qigong is very beneficial for anyone with fibromyalgia because it enhances the immune system, requires movement (which helps reduce pain and stiffness), and reduces anxiety and insomnia. (See Appendix A, under "Qigong," for further information and examples.)

Your Balanced Healing Action Plan for Fibromyalgia

Step 1: Undergo Acupuncture

I recommend acupuncture as the first step because I've seen it work better and more consistently than any other treatment. Principal points usually are found on the arms and legs, but you may require additional points specific to your underlying Chinese diagnosis (see Appendix A, under "Traditional Chinese Medicine," for further information on Chinese diagnosis). Always seek evaluation and treatment from a practitioner certified in acupuncture. (See Appendix A, under "Acupuncture," for guidance in finding a qualified acupuncturist and for explanation of the different acupuncture techniques.) You should notice improvement within six treatments, but you'll probably need additional sessions to get the maximum benefits.

Step 2: Take 5-HTP, St. John's Wort, Magnesium, and Malic Acid

Serotonin levels are usually deficient in people with fibromyalgia, so supplements that raise serotonin levels often can relieve symptoms. Along with the acupuncture, I recommend taking 5-HTP (50mg to 100mg daily), in combination with St. John's wort (300mg containing 0.3 percent hypericin content three times a day), magnesium (150mg to 250mg three times daily), and malic acid (1,200mg daily). You should notice improvement within one to two months.

> Hilary, a 52-year-old social worker, had fibromyalgia for 12 years, with pain throughout her body that never let up. Her pain kept her from participating in most activities—even shopping—for more than a few minutes at a time. She had taken numerous conventional medications, had undergone trigger-point injections and physical therapy, and also had tried various topical creams and ointments. I started her on acupuncture as well as the combination supplements in Step 2. After two months, nearly all of her symptoms had gone away, and she felt better than she had in years. She has continued to get an acupuncture treatment every few months for flare-ups.

Step 3: Take Appropriate Chinese Herbal Remedies

If the previous supplements do not help, there are several Chinese herbal formulas that can be used together to help reduce symptoms. Helpful formulas include *Du Huo Luo Dan* in combination with either *Gui Pi Tang* or *Huo Luo Xiao Ling Dan*. Consult a practitioner qualified in Chinese herbal medicine to determine whether these formulas are the best for your particular problem. You should feel better within three to six weeks, but you may need to take the herbs longer, depending on your condition. (See Appendix A, under "Chinese Herbs," for further information and guidance.)

Step 4: Take a Conventional Medication to Help You Sleep

Because people with fibromyalgia typically have difficulty sleeping, or they do not sleep restfully, a conventional sleep medication is often beneficial. This can be an actual sleep medication, such as Ambien, Restoril, or Sonata, or a mild antidepressant such as amitriptyline (Elavil) or trazodone (Desyrel). Use sleep medications in addition to the previous steps if your sleep is disturbed.

Step 5: Take Valerian or Melatonin to Help Sleep

If you prefer a natural sleep aid, I recommend Valerian (200mg to 400mg) or melatonin (0.3mg to 1.0mg). I have not found these natural aids to be as effective as the conventional medications in fibromyalgia patients, which is why I recommend them at this step. However, if you don't want to take conventional medications, or those drugs have not worked, these remedies are worth a try.

Step 6: Take Prescription Medications for Other Fibromyalgia Symptoms

If you still have considerable pain and other symptoms, conventional medications may help. Start with amitriptyline (Elavil) or cyclobenzaprine (Flexeril) in small doses to improve pain and sleep. Pregabalin (450mg dose) can reduce pain and increase sleep in 30 percent of patients. The next step is a mixed-neurotransmitter reuptake inhibitor, such as Effexor or Wellbutrin. (Do not take these medications with 5-HTP or St. John's wort (see Step 2) because of increased side effects.) For continued pain, I suggest Ultram, because it's not as addicting as narcotic medication. If you also have restless legs syndrome (your legs jerk spontaneously, usually at night), I recommend Klonopin, 0.5mg at night. For anxiety, buspirone (BuSpar) is my first choice.

Step 7: Take SAMe

If you still have pain or only partial relief, try SAMe, a compound from Germany. You can take it with the other supplements at a dosage of 800mg to 1600mg per day, but the top-quality brands are expensive, which is why I don't recommend it sooner. It may be four to six weeks (sometimes less) before you see benefits.

Step 8: Use the Nambudripad Allergy Elimination Treatment (NAET)

Sometimes, food allergies may be playing a role in causing fibromyalgia symptoms or making them worse. If the previous steps haven't helped you, I suggest undergoing the Nambudripad Allergy Elimination Treatment. It combines acupuncture, kinesiology, chiropractic, herbs, and nutrition to desensitize you to foods to which you are allergic. It may take several months to work, depending on how many foods are causing you problems. (See Appendix A and the section on food allergies for further information and for help in finding a practitioner who uses NAET.)

Step 9: Take Bovine Cartilage and/or Colustrum to Enhance Your Immune System

If you still have symptoms, take bovine cartilage (2g to 3g three times a day) and/or colustrum (500mg to 2000mg daily). These are immune system modulators that reregulate the immune system and help it work better. Colustrum is a nutrient-rich milk precursor that contains immunoglobulins (antibodies that counteract allergens), antimicrobial proteins, and carbohydrates. You can use them in addition to the previous steps, or take them alone if the previous steps haven't helped. However, they may take several months to work.

Step 10: Take Guaifenesin

Guaifenesin (such as Humibid), an expectorant used in many over-the-counter cough remedies (such as Robitussin), is supposed to help reduce the symptoms of fibromyalgia. But if you decide to try it, you must take high doses, and it usually takes several months to be effective. Unfortunately, it can—and usually does—cause a much more severe increase in pain in the initial few weeks or months of treatment. You'll need a prescription for 600mg twice daily. (For more information on the treatment protocol for guifenesin, go to www.csusm.edu.)

FOOD ALLERGIES

A food allergy is an adverse reaction that occurs when you eat a particular food. It can be caused by any component of the food, including protein, starch, fat, food coloring, flavorings, stabilizers, or preservatives. Many studies have indicated that food allergies may cause or contribute to numerous medical conditions, including gastrointestinal, urinary, musculoskeletal, skin, and respiratory.

Common Symptoms

- Puffiness and dark circles under the eyes
- Fluid retention
- Swollen glands
- Stomach aches
- Diarrhea
- Stiffness, pain, or swelling of joints

What You Need to Know

Conventional skin-prick or blood tests such as ELISA/Act, IgG ELISA, or RAST tests measure the antibodies that are directed at specific food and chemical allergens. However, the tests are expensive and can be unreliable in diagnosing many food allergies. They are often misleading if you're taking prednisone, aspirin, antihistamines, and other drugs. I recommend the following elimination diet to find the foods to which you are allergic:

Step 1: Discontinue commonly eaten foods and replace them with hypoallergenic foods, or special hypoallergenic formulas. The standard diet consists of lamb, chicken, potatoes, rice, banana, apple, and cabbage, broccoli, or Brussels sprouts. There are many companies that sell hypoallergenic foods, and I suggest that you ask a registered dietician about them. (To find a qualified dietician, go to www.eatright.com, the Web site of the American Dietetic Association.)

Step 2: Stay on this diet for one to four weeks. If your symptoms are caused by a food that you were previously eating, they'll disappear, usually within one week. If they don't disappear, you may be allergic to one of the foods in the elimination diet, and you will have to restrict even further the foods you eat.

Step 3: After the elimination period, reintroduce foods individually. You can either reintroduce a single food every two days or every two meals. If the food is causing your symptoms, they'll reoccur or get worse.

Your Balanced Healing Action Plan for Food Allergies

If you can identify the foods that are causing your allergies, eliminating them from your diet can end your symptoms. This can be a time-consuming process, but it's ultimately successful. However, even if you can't detect the foods responsible for your allergies—or can't or don't want to eliminate the foods you eat—the following steps should give you significant improvement.

Step 1: Try Probiotics and Digestive Enzymes First

If your digestive tract does not work well, your food will be incompletely broken down. Incomplete proteins can cause an allergic response, so improving your digestion is of the utmost importance. Start with digestive enzymes to help break down your food better. There are many products that contain digestive enzymes; get one that contains some or all of the following: protease, papain, amylase, lipase, bromelain, cellulase, and lactase.

I also recommend taking probiotics with the enzymes. These consist of live cultures of organisms (the "good" bacteria) that help digest food properly. Of the beneficial microorganisms in probiotics, L. acidophilus and bifidobacteria are the best. Other beneficial bacteria include L. salivarius, L. rhamnosus, L. plantarum, streptococcus thermophilus, L. bulgaricus, L. casei, and L. sporogenes.

You should notice improvement in two to six weeks. During the first week, you may initially have increased gas, bloating, or cramping; if so, reduce your dosage, and then gradually increase it as the side effects diminish. Contrary to common belief, yogurt is not a good choice for supplying probiotics. Yogurt products do contain beneficial microorganisms, but they are not the most important or potent. Also, many yogurt products are pasteurized, but this process kills most of the good bacteria and eliminates their benefits.

Step 2: Use the Nambudripad Allergy Elimination Treatment (NAET)

If Step 1 does not help or gives you only partial relief, I recommend the Nambudripad Allergy Elimination Treatment, or NAET, which has been shown to be an effective way of reducing or eliminating food allergies. This system combines acupuncture, chiropractic, kinesiology, herbs, and nutrition to eliminate food allergies permanently. However, NAET can take several months to work, depending on how many allergies you have, which is why I recommend this step second. (See Appendix A for further information and suggestions for finding a practitioner who uses NAET.)

> Kaye, a bright, easygoing teenager, had numerous food allergies and was underweight because there were so many foods that caused her to react. She had tried elimination diets, but there were too many foods that caused symptoms. I started her on probiotics and digestive enzymes (Step 1), and she then underwent NAET (Step 2). She was allergic to almost everything, but especially eggs and wheat. After three months of treatment, she was able to eat 90 percent of all foods without any reaction, and she started gaining weight.

Step 3: Take Appropriate Chinese Herbal Remedies

If you still have problems with food allergies after trying the previous two steps, try Chinese herbs next. I recommend the 900-year-old formula, *Ping Wei San*. Consult a practitioner qualified in Chinese herbal medicine to determine whether other formulas are appropriate for your particular problems. You should start seeing benefits within three weeks (sometimes sooner), but you may need to take the herbs longer, depending on your condition(s). (See Appendix A, under "Chinese Herbs," for further information.)

Step 4: Try the Rotary Diversified Diet

If the previous steps don't help you, then I recommend trying the rotary diversified diet, developed by Dr. Herbert Rinkle. This diet requires you to eat a highly varied selection of foods in a defined rotation. The goal is to prevent the formation of new allergies and control existing ones. In this diet, if you eat a particular food on one day, you cannot eat that food again for four to seven days.

GALL BLADDER DISEASE

The gall bladder stores bile, a juice made by the liver; bile breaks down fats. Gall bladder disease often originates with dietary and digestive problems (poor diets, low stomach acid, low fiber, and so on), which cause liver dysfunction, which in turn causes bile to be thicker in consistency and to harden more quickly. The resulting crystal-like deposits are called gallstones. Gallstones often cause no problems, and you can have them for as long as 25 years before you develop symptoms. But when a gallstone moves into the bile duct and gets lodged there, it causes significant symptoms. Even if you don't have gallstones, your gall bladder can be dysfunctional. It may not be working well, or it may be producing a thickened secretion called *sludge*; in either case, you may have symptoms. Chronic obstruction of the bile duct can lead to infection, problems with the pancreas, liver, and small intestine, and cancer of the gall bladder and bile duct.

Common Symptoms

- Severe and sudden pain in the upper right portion of the abdomen, often after eating a fatty meal
- Indigestion
- Nausea and vomiting
- Jaundice in severe cases

What You Need to Know

Although gall bladder attacks can be quite severe and painful, almost one-third of those who have their first one will not have another. And many people can have recurrent attacks over several years, without any particular damage or need for surgery.

Synthetic estrogen taken after menopause can increase your risk of gallstones. I recommend that you take natural hormones instead. (See the section on menopause and Appendix A, under "Hormonal Supplements," for further information and guidance.)

General Recommendations

Diet: Because gall bladder disease is more frequent in overweight people, weight reduction is important. If you reduce your intake of fats, fried foods, and sugar, and increase your intake of fruits, vegetables and fiber, you can alleviate and reverse gall bladder disease. However, very low-fat diets (less than 10 percent of calories from fat) can also cause gallstones, and you should avoid them. Moderate consumption of olive oil is also beneficial in reversing this condition; use it preferentially when you cook. Drinking coffee has been shown to prevent symptoms of gallstones, but it doesn't prevent the gallstones themselves.

Your Balanced Healing Action Plan for Gall Bladder Disease

- If you have unrelenting abdominal pain, fever, abdominal swelling, or continuous vomiting, go to Steps 7 or 8.

Step 1: Cleanse Your Liver and Blood

Start with herbal formulas to clean and detoxify your liver. You'll not only protect the liver from further toxic damage, you'll also help reduce or reverse your symptoms because you'll be producing normal bile. Follow with an herbal formula that cleanses the blood, because toxins will be released from the liver into the blood.

Take a liver-cleansing formula that contains all or some of the following: milk thistle, dandelion root, Picrorhiza kurroa root, and artichoke or beet leaf. Some formulas may contain burdock root, cinnamon bark, licorice root, cardamom seed, Uva ursi, ginger, parsley root, and clove buds. After taking this formula for one to two weeks (see label for specific directions; some products may need to be taken for a longer period of time), take a blood-cleansing formula that contains some or all of the following: chaparral, red clover, burdock root, goldenseal, yellow dock, Oregon grape root, bloodroot, mistletoe, periwinkle flowers, lobelia seeds, sheep sorrel, and cayenne. Again, different products will have different recommendations for length of use, but most take one to three weeks.

Because liver and blood cleansing may release toxins, you may undergo a "healing crisis" in which your symptoms suddenly worsen. This can occur at any time—or even several times—during the course of treatment, but it should last only two to three days. Also, if you become constipated, you may need to undergo a colon detoxification as well. (See Appendix A, under "Detoxification Therapy," for further details.)

Step 2: Take Peppermint Oil and Milk Thistle

After the cleansing is finished, take peppermint oil (one to two enteric-coated capsules containing 0.2/ml per capsule, three times a day) and milk thistle (200mg to 400mg a day as 70 percent silymarin extract) to help dissolve the remaining gallstones and protect your liver. Take these together. It may take three to six weeks to see the benefits. Continue taking peppermint oil and milk thistle for several months after your symptoms go away, to make sure the gallstones are fully dissolved.

Step 3: Take Appropriate Chinese Herbal Remedies

If the previous steps do not completely resolve your symptoms, then take Chinese herbal formulas to help dissolve small gallstones and reduce abdominal pain. *Chuan Lian Zi, Da Chai Hu Tang, Si Ni Wan,* and *Long Dan Xie Gan Wan* are common formulas used to reverse gall bladder disease. Consult a practitioner qualified in Chinese herbal medicine to determine which Chinese herbal formulas are the best for you. You should notice improvement within three weeks (sometimes sooner), but you may need to take the herbs longer, depending on your condition. (See Appendix A, under "Chinese Herbs," for further information.)

Before she came to see me, Devin, a 47-year-old concert violinist, had had pain in her right upper abdomen off and on for several years, but recently it had become more frequent. She noticed that the pain was worse when she ate certain foods, especially cabbage, ice cream, and fried foods. Her doctor ordered gall bladder tests, which revealed that her gall bladder was working at only 20 percent of normal function and contained sludge. The doctor recommended surgery, but Devin wanted to try other alternatives first. I suggested liver and blood cleansing, followed by maintenance on milk thistle and peppermint oil, as well as the Chinese herbal formula *Chuan Lian Zi*. After two weeks, Devin's pain started easing, and within two months, it was gone. I then instructed her on a proper diet to prevent recurrences.

Step 4: Undergo Acupuncture in Conjunction with Chinese Herbs

Along with the Chinese herbs, I recommend starting acupuncture, especially if your symptoms are severe or you continue having flare-ups. Principal acupuncture points usually include M-LE-23 on the legs (called the gall bladder orifice), with other points elsewhere on the legs, as well as the mid-back and upper abdomen. Ear points include the gall bladder point. Always seek evaluation and treatment from a practitioner certified in acupuncture. (See Appendix A, under "Acupuncture," for guidance in finding a qualified acupuncturist and for explanation of the different acupuncture techniques.) You should notice improvement within six acupuncture treatments, but you might need additional sessions to get the maximum benefits.

Caution: Acupuncture can precipitate an acute gall bladder attack if there is a gall-stone ready to enter the duct. If this happens, you may need surgery.

Step 5: Take an Appropriate Homeopathic Remedy

If your symptoms still continue, I recommend trying homeopathy next. The most common homeopathic remedies are *Carbo vegetabilis* or *Lycopodium*. You should notice improvement within one to two weeks. Consult a qualified homeopathist for guidance as to which remedies will be most beneficial and for proper dosages. (See Appendix A, under "Homeopathy," for further information.)

Step 6: Take Lecithin and Vitamin C

If you still have symptoms after trying the previous steps, take phosphatidylcholine (lecithin) (1.2g to 2.4g per day). This supplement may help prevent gallstones if you have chronic gall bladder problems, but it is not effective alone, so take it with the above steps. If you are a woman, you should also take vitamin C (1,000mg daily), which may help prevent gallstones by countering the effects of estrogen on the gall bladder.

Step 7: Undergo Surgery

The previous steps are recommended to help prevent gallstones from forming or to help dissolve them. However, you may have stones that have already formed and won't dissolve, so they need to be removed if they are causing severe symptoms. Surgery to remove the gall bladder is the definitive treatment for gallstones or a dysfunctional gall bladder. It's appropriate when you have attacks that involve infection of the abdomen, persistent and disabling pain, recurrent attacks, or damage to the gall bladder or other organs. The procedure can be done through a laparoscope, which requires only a small incision and allows you to recover quickly.

Many gall bladder surgeries are done if the doctor finds gallstones or sludge when investigating abdominal pain or other symptoms, yet pain continues after the surgery. A test may show that you have gallstones, but they may not necessarily be causing your symptoms. Unless your symptoms are severe or there are other signs of danger, such as fever, chills, and vomiting, it's best to try nonsurgical treatments first, to see whether they relieve your symptoms, before you have surgery. Most people with gall bladder problems can reverse their disease without surgery.

Step 8: Have Gallstones Removed by Lithotripsy

For patients who do not want surgery or cannot undergo surgery, *lithotripsy* (high-frequency sound waves that break up the stone) can be effective, with the least side effects. *Contact dissolution* is another conventional method that uses the injection of a drug through a catheter into the gall bladder, but it's more invasive. You can also take bile salts to dissolve the stone, but this can take several months.

GERD (Gastroesophageal Reflux Disorder) (see *Heartburn*)

GLAUCOMA

Glaucoma is caused by degeneration of the optic nerve, which controls vision. The most common forms are *primary open-angle glaucoma*, caused by increased pressure within the eye (increased intraocular pressure), and *low-tension* (normal pressure) *glaucoma*. Glaucoma can be caused by cataracts, uveitis (inner eye inflammation), eye tumor, injury, or diabetes. About one-fourth of those who have glaucoma don't know it, because they may not be aware of the initial symptoms. This situation is worrisome because glaucoma is one of the leading causes of blindness. The older you are, the greater your risk. The higher your intraocular pressure, the greater the rate of vision loss.

Common Symptoms

Acute glaucoma is a medical emergency that requires immediate treatment. Its symptoms include the following:

- Nausea and vomiting
- Seeing rainbow halos around objects, especially lights
- Dilated pupils

Chronic glaucoma may have no symptoms until it is well established, at which point these symptoms are common:

- Peripheral vision loss
- Difficulty moving from a bright room to a darker room
- Difficulty judging steps and curbs
- Headaches
- Need for new glasses
- Tearing
- Aching or throbbing pain
- Visual field abnormalities (blurred vision and loss of peripheral vision)

What You Need to Know

Because glaucoma may occur without obvious symptoms, it is very important that you get routine eye exams, either by an ophthalmologist or an optometrist, to measure the pressure in your eyeball. In this painless test, drops are placed in your eyes to deaden any feeling, and then a device is placed against your eye to measure the pressure. Normal pressure is 21mm/Hg. You should start having your eye pressure checked when you're over 40—or sooner, if you have eye problems.

General Recommendations

Diet: Vitamin C and omega-3 fatty acids are very important in reducing intraocular pressure and improving glaucoma. Fresh fruits and vegetables, and cold-water fish (such as herring, salmon, halibut, mackerel, cod, sardines, and tuna) are the best sources.

Your Balanced Healing Action Plan for Glaucoma

- Acute glaucoma is an emergency and you should go to an emergency room if you have any of the symptoms previously listed.
- For chronic glaucoma, if your peripheral vision is poor (you can't see things on each side of you, only straight ahead), go to Step 7, then restart at Step 1.

Step 1: Use Conventional Prescription Medications

If you already have glaucoma, you should first be treated with conventional medications, which may include beta blockers, carbonic anhydrase inhibitors, miotics (pilocarpine), α-2 agonists, or prostaglandin analogues, all of which decrease intraocular pressure. Because these medications all have different side effects and may interfere with other medications, your ophthalmologist should prescribe the specific drug or combination of drugs that is most appropriate for you. These medications do not protect against loss of peripheral vision, but they do decrease the pressure in your eyes and prevent the other complications and dangers of glaucoma, so they should be used first.

Nonsteroidal anti-inflammatory drugs (NSAIDs)—both over-the-counter (such as ibuprofen and Aleve) and prescription (Naprosyn, Relafen, Orudis, Feldene, Daypro, Mobic, and others)—may interfere with some of these medications, so you should tell your doctor if you are taking any of them.

Step 2: Take Vitamin C, Flaxseed Oil, Bilberry with Bioflavonoids, and Chromium

Along with the previous step, I recommend you take supplements that can improve vision and can decrease intraocular pressure. These include the following:

- Vitamin C, minimum of 2,000mg daily
- Magnesium, 200mg to 400mg daily
- Flaxseed oil, 1 tablespoon daily
- Bilberry with bioflavonoids, 80mg (containing 25 percent anthocyanidin content) three times daily
- Chromium 200mcg to 400mcg

Step 3: Undergo Infrasonic Treatment

Along with the previous steps, I recommend undergoing *infrasound* treatment, or low-frequency sound waves. Infrasound works by increasing the local circulation of blood and lymph, and it can decrease intraocular pressure in many patients. It may take 6 to 20 treatments before you see improvement. Numerous chiropractors, naturopaths, acupuncturists, and a few doctors use infrasound. (See Appendix C, under "Infrasound," for a reference source.)

Step 4: Undergo Acupuncture

Acupuncture can reduce intraocular pressure and improve vision, and I recommend it along with the previous steps. Principal acupuncture points usually are found on the face, head, arms and legs. Ear points include vision 1 and vision 2. Always seek evaluation and treatment from a practitioner certified in acupuncture. (See Appendix A, under "Acupuncture," for guidance in finding a qualified acupuncturist and for further explanation of the different acupuncture techniques.)

You should notice improved vision within six treatments, but you might need additional sessions to get the maximum benefits. If your intraocular pressure decreases after acupuncture, you can then decrease the dosage of medications in Step 1 under the guidance of your doctor.

> Ron, a 48-year-old dentist, had been struggling with glaucoma for 10 years. Although he was taking both beta-blockers and carbonic anhydrase inhibitors (see Step 1), his symptoms worsened. I recommended flaxseed oil plus a supplement formula containing bilberry, carotenoids, and vitamin C. After one month, his vision (especially night vision) had improved, but his intraocular pressure had decreased only minimally. So I started him on acupuncture treatments. After 10 sessions, his eye pressure had dropped to normal, his vision improved even more, and he was able to stop taking one of his medications completely.

Step 5: Take Gingko Biloba

If your vision or intraocular pressure remains abnormal, try gingko biloba (240mg daily). This herb has only a mild effect on decreasing intraocular pressure, but it may be helpful along with the other steps.

Step 6: Evaluate Medicinal Marijuana

Marijuana has been shown to lower intraocular pressure and may help glaucoma patients who don't respond to other treatments. However, the use of marijuana for medicinal purposes remains illegal in most states and violates federal law nationwide.

Step 7: Undergo Surgery

If the previous steps fail to stop the progress of your symptoms, or if you have loss of peripheral (side) vision, you most likely will need surgery to preserve your vision. Either surgical trabeculectomy or laser trabeculoplasty, or both, can be done to protect further visual loss and decrease intraocular pressure. Consult an ophthalmologist (eye physician) to determine which procedure is the best for you.

GOUT

Gout is a form of arthritis caused by an increased amount of uric acid (a breakdown product of protein) that becomes deposited as crystals in joints (commonly the big toe), tendons, kidneys, and other tissues. The increase in uric acid is either brought on by too much uric acid in your system or not enough excretion of uric acid through the kidneys. Chronic gout can lead to joint and tendon destruction, damage to the bones and cartilage, kidney stones, and even kidney failure, and it can shorten your life.

Common Symptoms: Acute Gout Attack

- Sudden, intense joint pain, most commonly in the big toe, less frequently in the knee, ankle, or wrist.
- Swelling of the joint

Common Symptoms: Chronic Gout

- Joint swelling
- Joint inflammation
- Hot feeling in the joint
- Tiny, hard lumps (called tophi) accumulating in the soft tissues of the hands, feet, or ear lobes

What You Need To Know

Men who are overweight, have high blood pressure, or take thiazide diuretics (such as diuril and HCTZ) are more prone to gout. A gout attack can be precipitated by alcohol, a high-protein meal, trauma, or certain drugs (chemotherapy, diuretics, and niacin), so you should avoid these factors if you have gout.

General Recommendations

Diet: Avoid foods with high purine content (which breaks down into uric acid in the body). These include red meats in particular, as well as shellfish, yeast, herring, sardines, mackerel, and anchovies. Alcohol can precipitate attacks of gout, so avoid it also. Complex carbohydrates (fruits and vegetables) can reduce the symptoms of gout, and increasing your intake of clear fluids can help flush out uric acid from the kidneys. Eating fresh or canned cherries, up to eight ounces per day, lowers uric acid and can prevent acute attacks. Blueberries are also helpful but are not as potent as cherries.

Your Balanced Healing Action Plan for Gout

Step 1: Take Colchicine or Nonsteroidal Anti-Inflammatory Drugs (NSAIDs)

For an acute attack, your doctor may prescribe colchicine (1mg to 1.2mg at first sign of attack, then 0.5mg to 0.6mg every hour until the symptoms stop). Usually, this medication resolves your symptoms within 8 to 24 hours. As an alternative, nonsteroidal anti-inflammatory drugs (NSAIDs)—Naprosyn, Daypro, Orudis, Relafen, Mobic, and others—can also help relieve the pain of acute attacks quickly.

Step 2: Take Folic Acid and Flaxseed Oil After the Acute Attack

Once the acute attack is over, first take folic acid (10mg to 40mg daily) to inhibit the enzyme responsible for producing uric acid. Also take flaxseed oil (1 tablespoon daily) to prevent tissue damage from uric acid. Check your uric acid level every few weeks, and if it has returned to normal, continue these supplements to keep the uric acid normal. If your uric acid remains elevated, go to the next step.

Step 3: Take Allopurinol or Probenicid

If the previous supplements do not lower your uric acid levels to normal, then get a prescription from your doctor for allopurinol (100mg daily). Have your uric acid levels tested until they are normal. Probenicid (500mg twice daily) is another medication to lower uric acid.

HEADACHES (Tension, Migraine, Cluster)

A headache is any type of pain in your head. Headaches can have many causes. The most common type is tension headache, caused by muscle contractions that pinch nerves or blood vessels. Muscle tension headaches are very common and usually result from stress, eyestrain, poor posture, or nighttime grinding of teeth. Vascular headaches, particularly migraine, are caused by changes in the blood vessels of the head, first tightening (constriction), then relaxing (dilatation), although there may be nerve dysfunction involved as well. About half of those who have migraine headaches have a family history of migraines. Migraines can be triggered by many factors, including various foods, wind, excessive caffeine, emotional upheaval, sex, cold foods, hormonal fluctuations, exercise, or changes in altitude. No one knows what causes cluster headaches, but they may be triggered by certain foods, alcohol, or smoking.

Muscle tension and migraine headaches can occur together, or one can trigger the onset of the other. Migraines are usually more long lasting than tension headaches, but the latter can last for days at a time and be chronic as well.

Common Symptoms: Muscle Tension Headache

- Dull, steady pain
- Squeezing or band-like feeling around the head
- Entire head hurts

Common Symptoms: Migraine Headache

- One-sided.
- Pounding or throbbing.

- Nausea and vomiting.
- Auras may precede migraines: visual phenomena (flashing lights, zigzag or jagged lines, blind spots, focusing problems), speech difficulties, numbness and tingling, or psychological disturbances (disturbed thinking).

Common Symptoms: Cluster Headache

- Occurs in groups.
- Severe, piercing.
- Located around red, watery eye.
- Nasal congestion.
- Intermittent attacks with remissions: The typical headache lasts 30 to 45 minutes and occurs one to two times per day for one to four months.

What You Need to Know

Almost every conventional medication can cause headaches or make them worse as a side effect, so it is important to rule out medications as a cause before taking additional medications to treat the headaches. If you have headaches and are on a medication, check the *Physician's Desk Reference* (*PDR*) to see whether that medication can cause headaches, or consult with your pharmacist.

General Recommendations

Diet: Food allergies are not known to play a role in tension headaches, but they may be involved in migraines and cluster headaches. Food allergy testing and elimination diets may be helpful in determining which foods play a part (see the section on food allergies). Certain foods, including chocolate, cheese, beer, and wine, can also trigger migraine attacks and should be avoided if they do.

Meditation: Relaxation and stress reduction are essential in the treatment of muscle tension headaches and can also be very beneficial in migraine or cluster headaches. Meditation is the best means to relax and reduce stress. (For further information, see Appendix A, under "Mind-Body Techniques.")

Your Balanced Healing Action Plan for Muscle Tension Headaches

Step 1: Take Acetaminophen for Occasional Headaches

For mild, intermittent muscle tension headaches, take acetaminophen (Tylenol) or ibuprofen, which should relieve your headache within 20 to 45 minutes. If these don't seem to be strong enough, your doctor can prescribe a medication containing butalbital (such as Fiorcet).

Step 2: Use Massage and Acupressure for Occasional Headaches

Massage or acupressure also can relieve acute headaches by applying pressure directly to the trigger points or tense muscles, usually around the neck, forehead, and temples.

Applying pressure on the acupuncture point LI-4 often quickly relieves headaches. This point is located in the web between the thumb and index finger, and it is usually quite tender. Apply firm pressure on this point and massage it for several minutes.

Step 3: Take Appropriate Chinese Herbal Remedies

Use the previous steps if you have occasional headaches. If your headaches occur more often or are constant, I recommend Chinese herbal formulas, which can work better than conventional medications and with fewer side effects. *Ding Xin Wan, Qiang Huo Sheng Shi Tang,* or *Chai Hu Mu Li Long Gu Tang* are formulas that are helpful in treating tension headaches. Consult a practitioner qualified in Chinese herbal medicine to determine which Chinese herbal formulas are the best for your particular condition. You should notice improvement within a few days to a week, although it may take three weeks to get the full effect. (See Appendix A, under "Chinese Herbs," for further information.)

Step 4: Undergo Acupuncture for Long-Term Relief

Acupuncture is very effective for reducing the frequency of or eliminating tension headaches, and I recommend it if the previous steps have not given you long-lasting relief. Principal points for *frontal* headaches (on the forehead) are usually found on the face and toes; for *occipital* headaches (back of the head), on the hands, ankles and head; and for *parietal* headaches (sides of the head), on the face, head, and ankles. Always seek evaluation and treatment from a practitioner certified in acupuncture. (See Appendix A, under "Acupuncture," for guidance in finding a qualified acupuncturist and for further explanation of the different acupuncture techniques.) You should notice improvement within six treatments, but you might need additional sessions to get the maximum benefits.

Step 5: Undergo Interactive Imagery or Other Psychotherapy

If the previous treatments don't relieve your headaches, anxiety or underlying emotional problems may be the reason. At this point I recommend psychotherapy to help resolve these factors. I especially recommend interactive imagery, which I think works faster than regular psychotherapy. This is a mind-body method in which you mentally interact with images that represent your emotions. It's a powerful way to uncover and deal with subconscious psychological issues that you may not be aware of. (See Appendix A, under "Mind-Body Techniques," for a more detailed explanation and for help in finding a qualified practitioner.) If interactive imagery is not available, then you should seek other forms of psychotherapy.

Step 6: Take Magnesium and 5-HTP

If you continue to have chronic or recurrent tension headaches, the next step to try is supplements of magnesium (250mg to 400mg three times a day) and 5-HTP (100mg three times daily). These supplements can prevent muscle tension headaches in many people, but it may take one to two months before they start to work.

Step 7: Try Botox Injections

Injections of botulinum toxin (Botox) can help reduce the frequency of tension headaches. One to four injections are given at three-month intervals. The Botox is injected into various muscle groups, depending on the location of your headache.

Step 8: Take a Low-Dose Prescription Tricyclic Antidepressant for Chronic Tension Headaches

If your chronic tension headaches continue despite the previous steps, your doctor can prescribe low-dose antidepressants, such as amitriptyline (Elavil). These medications may take at least three weeks to work.

Step 9: Undergo Chiropractic Manipulation

If you still are having headaches, especially coming from your neck, chiropractic manipulation can be effective in relieving muscle tension and cervicogenic headaches (those starting in the back of your head/neck). You should feel relief within four to six treatments. Don't continue these treatments unless your headaches are becoming less frequent and less severe.

Step 10: Use Biofeedback

If you still have tension headaches, I recommend trying biofeedback. (For an explanation of biofeedback, see Appendix C.) For some people, biofeedback can be an effective treatment for reducing the frequency and severity of muscle tension headaches when other treatments have failed.

Your Balanced Healing Action Plan to Stop an Acute Migraine Headache

Step 1: Undergo Acupuncture

I recommend acupuncture first for an acute migraine attack, because it is very effective—it usually takes only 15 to 30 minutes to relieve most symptoms. With continued acupuncture, the severity and frequency of migraine attacks can be reduced and even eliminated. Principal points usually are found on the face, head, legs, and hands. You should always seek evaluation and treatment from a practitioner certified in acupuncture. (See Appendix A, under "Acupuncture," for guidance in finding a qualified acupuncturist and for further explanation of the different acupuncture techniques.)

> By the time Daniel, a 34-year-old food marketing executive, came to see me, he had a long history of migraine headaches. They would occur once or twice a month and would be very severe, often accompanied by nausea and vomiting and lasting for hours or even days. He had taken many different types of medication that helped reduce the symptoms, but he would still feel bad for several days. During one of these attacks, he came to the

> clinic. He looked ashen, and he could barely tolerate any light or sound. I performed acupuncture, and, within 20 minutes, most of his pain was gone. An hour later, he was able to return to work.

Step 2: Take an NSAID

If acupuncture has not eliminated your migraines and they are mild, your doctor can prescribe nonsteroidal anti-inflammatory drugs (such as Naprosyn, Daypro, Relafen, Mobic, or Orudis), or a combination of aspirin, acetaminophen, and caffeine (the migraine formulas of Advil, Motrin, or Excedrin). These drugs often can give you relief until the migraine passes. If you cannot take medications because of gastrointestinal symptoms from your migraine, you can try a new form of aspirin called *oral dispersible*; you take it without water and let it dissolve in your mouth.

Step 3: Take a Prescription Triptan Medication

If the milder medications do not help your migraines, or your migraines are severe, your doctor can prescribe drugs called triptans (Imitrex, Maxalt, Relpax, Axert, Amerge, Zomig, Frova). Imitrex was the first and is the standard triptan used by doctors. It's available in nasal spray and injectable, in addition to oral, forms. The other triptans can be just as beneficial or even better. Zomig is about the same as Imitrex. You take it via a nose spray, and it works faster than the pill forms. Axert and Amerge have fewer side effects than Imitrex but may be less effective. Frova lasts the longest (26 hours, versus 5 hours for the others) and is recommended for menstrual migraines. Relpax is more effective than Imitrex at higher dosages (80mg) but has more side effects. Maxalt can be dissolved on the tongue and can alleviate migraines within 30 minutes. It's more effective than Imitrex and is the most consistently effective of all the triptans. Basically, all the triptans can be equally beneficial. When one fails, another one may work, so you may have to try several to see which one is the best for you.

Step 4: Take an Ergotamine Medication

If the drugs in Step 3 are not effective, the next ones to try are ergotamine-containing medications (both oral and nasal spray). These include Ergotamine tartrate, and D.H.E. These drugs usually work better if you have warning signs that the migraine is going to happen or are in the early stages of migraine. There are more restrictions on using ergotamine medications because they cause blood vessels to contract.

Step 5: Receive a Narcotic Injection

If the above steps do not relieve your migraine, an injection of Stadol or Demerol may be necessary. These drugs can "break" the migraine, but you will probably have side effects of drowsiness and not be able to return to normal activity for several hours or even several days. In addition, you may need a repeat injection if your headache lingers.

Your Balanced Healing Action Plan to Prevent Migraines

Step 1: Avoid Trigger Factors

An important way to prevent migraines is to avoid anything that triggers them—for example, stressful events, bright lights, flying, changes in barometric pressure, and various foods.

Step 2: Undergo Regular Acupuncture Treatments

Each time you undergo acupuncture, it can reduce the severity and frequency of your migraine attacks. Principal points are on the face, head, legs, and hands. Acupuncture works better if it is applied when you have the headache, rather than when you are symptom free, but it can be successful either way. Always seek evaluation and treatment from a practitioner certified in acupuncture. (See Appendix A, under "Acupuncture," for guidance in finding a qualified acupuncturist and for further explanation of the different acupuncture techniques.) You should have improvement within six treatments, but you might need additional sessions to get the maximum benefit or to relieve occasional flare-ups.

Step 3: Take Appropriate Chinese Herbal Remedies

In Chinese medicine, there are many underlying causes of migraine headaches, and thus numerous herbal combinations may help. *Chai Hu Mu Li Long Gu Tang*, *Long Dan Xie Gan Wan*, *Tian Ma Gou Teng Yin Wan*, or *Qiang Huo Sheng Shi Tang*, can all help reduce the severity and frequency of migraine headaches. An advantage of Chinese herbs over conventional medications and supplements is that, once your migraines are under control, you can reduce or discontinue them. You should notice improvement within three weeks, but you may need to take the formulas longer for complete relief. Consult a practitioner qualified in Chinese herbal medicine to determine which Chinese herbal formulas are the best for your particular condition. (See Appendix A, under "Chinese Herbs," for further information.)

Step 4: Take Riboflavin, Magnesium, Vitamin B₆, 5-HTP, CoQ10, and/or Feverfew

If the previous steps don't totally reduce the frequency or severity of your migraines, take riboflavin (vitamin B_2, 400mg per day). If riboflavin alone is not effective, use it with a combination of magnesium (250mg to 400mg daily), vitamin B_6 (100mg daily), 5-HTP (100mg to 200mg three times daily), and the herb feverfew (freeze-dried leaf at 50mg to125mg per day, standardized to contain 0.2 percent parthenolide). The combination product Migra-Lieve contains feverfew with riboflavin and magnesium, which may give you adequate relief. CoQ10 (120mg daily) may also help prevent migraines and can be taken with the other supplements. Take these supplements along with your acupuncture treatments. You should see improvement within one to two months.

Step 5: Use the Nambudripad Allergy Elimination Treatment (NAET)

Foods trigger migraines in some people. In addition, food allergies can be a possible cause of your migraines. The Nambudripad Allergy Elimination Treatment, or NAET, combines acupuncture, kinesiology, chiropractic, herbs, and nutrition to desensitize you to foods to which you are allergic. It may take several months to notice improvement, depending on how many foods are causing you problems. (See Appendix A and the section on food allergies for further information and help in finding a practitioner who uses NAET.)

Step 6: Use Biofeedback for Children with Migraines

In children, biofeedback is very effective in reducing the severity and frequency of migraines, but it's not as effective for adults. (For further information and help in finding a biofeedback practitioner, see Appendix C, under "Biofeedback.")

Step 7: Take Botox Injections

Injections of botulinum toxin (Botox) sometimes help reduce the frequency of migraine headaches. One to four injections are given at three-month intervals and are applied at several different muscle groups, depending on the location of your headaches.

Step 8: Take an Appropriate Prescription Medication to Prevent Migraines

If you are still having persistent or recurrent migraines, your doctor may prescribe beta-blockers (such as propranolol or timolol) or the ACE inhibitor lisinopril (Prinivil, Zestril) to reduce migraine severity and frequency. If these drugs are not effective, amitriptyline, divalproex sodium (Depakote), or gabapentin (Neurontin) are the next conventional medications to try. Each medication may have different results for different people, so you may need to try several to find the one that is most effective for you, with the least side effects. It may take several weeks to see improvement.

> Joan, a bank vice-president, was 38 years old when I first saw her. She'd suffered from migraines for more than 20 years. She got a headache at least twice a week, with each episode lasting for hours and sometimes days. She had tried numerous medications that helped dull her headaches but did nothing to diminish the frequency or severity of the attacks. I gave her eight acupuncture treatments and suggested that she also take the Chinese herbal formula *Chai Hu Mu Li Long Gu Tang*. The combination worked, and Joan has not had any migraines for more than two years—the longest period of relief in her adult life!

Step 9: Take Combinations of Medications

Some migraines are stubborn, and success requires diligence and experimentation. If the previous treatment steps are not effective, try the following in various combinations: aspirin, multiple NSAIDs, gabapentin (Neurontin), verapamil, other beta-blockers, and the herb feverfew. Again, each medication may have different effects on different people, so you may need to try several to find the one that is most effective for you, with the least side effects.

Your Balanced Healing Action Plan to Stop Cluster Headaches

Step 1: Receive Oxygen Inhalation Treatment

Oxygen inhalation during an acute attack is effective and safe and is the first treatment for cluster headaches. Your doctor needs to prescribe this treatment, which involves breathing oxygen through a face mask at a rate of 7 to 8 liters/min for 10 to 15 minutes, in a sitting position.

Step 2: Undergo Acupuncture

If oxygen doesn't help, I recommend acupuncture as the next step. Principal points usually are found on the face, head, legs, and hands. Acupuncture during the headache gives the best results; you should get relief within 20 to 30 minutes. Always seek evaluation and treatment from a practitioner certified in acupuncture. (See Appendix A, under "Acupuncture," for guidance on finding a qualified acupuncturist and for further explanation of the different acupuncture techniques.)

Step 3: Take Melatonin

If your cluster headaches continue, take the supplement melatonin (10mg), which sometimes can abort the attack.

Step 4: Take an NSAID

Nonsteroidal anti-inflammatory drugs (NSAIDs), especially the drug Naproxen, can be effective for headaches that last longer than 45 minutes. Unfortunately, many cluster headaches do not last that long, so you must take the NSAID as soon as you have a headache to get any relief from it.

Step 5: Take a Prescription Triptan Medication

If your cluster headaches continue after you have tried the previous steps, your doctor can prescribe drugs called triptans (Imitrex, Maxalt, Relpax, Axert, Amerge, Zomig). Imitrex was the first and the standard triptan used by doctors, but the others can be just as beneficial, or better. Zomig is about the same as Imitrex. Imitrex is available in nasal spray and injectable, in addition to oral, forms. Zomig is given through a nose spray, and works faster than the pill forms. Axert and Amerge have fewer side effects than Imitrex, but they may be less effective. Frova lasts the longest (26 hours versus 5 hours for the others). Relpax is more effective than Imitrex at higher dosages (80mg), but it has more side effects. Maxalt can be dissolved on the tongue and can alleviate migraines within 30 minutes. It has better effectiveness than Imitrex and is the most consistently effective of all the triptans. Basically, all the triptans can be equally beneficial. When one triptan fails, another one may work, so you might have to try several to see which one is the best for you.

Your Balanced Healing Action Plan to Prevent Cluster Headaches

Step 1: Undergo Acupuncture

Acupuncture is very effective for reducing the severity and frequency of cluster headaches over the long term. Principal points usually are found on the face, head, legs, and hands. You should have acupuncture when you have the headache for best results, but preventive acupuncture is also helpful. Always seek evaluation and treatment from a practitioner certified in acupuncture. (See Appendix A, under "Acupuncture," for guidance on finding a qualified acupuncturist and for further explanation of the different acupuncture techniques.) You should experience improvement within six treatments, but you might need additional sessions for maximum benefits.

Step 2: Take Magnesium, Vitamin B₆, and 5-HTP

For cluster headaches that continue to recur, take a combination of magnesium (250mg to 400mg daily), vitamin B_6 (100mg daily), and 5-HTP (100mg to 200mg three times daily). Magnesium prevents overexcitability of nerve cells and maintains the tone of blood vessels, vitamin B_6 helps prevent histamine release (which can trigger headaches), and 5-HTP increases brain neurotransmitters, especially serotonin. It may take one to two months to notice improvement.

Step 3: Use the Nambudripad Allergy Elimination Treatment (NAET)

Foods and food allergies may trigger cluster headaches. The Nambudripad Allergy Elimination Treatment, or NAET, combines acupuncture, kinesiology, chiropractic, herbs, and nutrition to desensitize you to foods to which you are allergic. It may take several months to experience improvement, depending on how many allergens are sensitizing you. (See Appendix A and the section on food allergies for further information and ways to find a practitioner who uses NAET.)

Step 4: Take Prescription Medications

If the above treatments fail to relieve your cluster headaches, several prescription medications might help. You'll need to take them long term to keep the headaches at bay. Talk with your doctor about possible side effects, which vary. These include the following:

- A combination of verapamil (240mg/day) and prednisone (60mg to 80mg/day), but use the prednisone for only 7 to14 days.
- Methysergide (2mg three times a day).
- Lithium, or valproic acid (Depakene), or both together.

Step 5: Undergo Surgery

There are some surgical procedures that can relieve cluster headaches when all other treatment approaches fail, but there may be serious risks. Glycerol injection is the least risky. Surgery should be a treatment of last resort.

HEART DISEASE

Heart disease is a term that encompasses several types of heart problems and is the number one killer in this country. Its primary cause is atherosclerosis, otherwise known as hardening of the arteries. Other factors causing atherosclerosis and/or heart disease include smoking, high cholesterol, hypertension, obesity, poor diet, infections, toxins, genetic abnormalities, and other diseases of the body's organs. Heart disease also can lead to diseases of and damage to the body's organs. It can result in significant disability, as well as death from heart attack or heart failure. The major forms of heart disease are:

- Congestive heart failure, in which the heart is unable to pump blood effectively
- Arrhythmias, in which there are abnormal heartbeats or rhythm
- Valvular diseases, in which there is poor functioning of the four heart valves that regulate the flow into and out of the heart
- Cardiomyopathy, which is disease of the heart muscle itself

Common Symptoms

- Shortness of breath
- Breathing difficulties when lying flat
- Chest pain (see the section on angina for further explanation and treatment guidelines)
- Fluttering, thumping, pounding, or racing sensation in the chest
- Fluid retention in the legs, ankles, abdomen, or lungs
- Light-headedness or dizziness
- Weakness
- Fatigue

What You Need to Know

One of the major causes of heart disease is smoking, including second-hand inhalation. If you smoke, stop (see the section on nicotine addiction for treatment guidelines). High cholesterol is a key contributor to heart disease, so you should have your blood cholesterol level checked regularly. (If you have high cholesterol, see the section on cholesterol for treatment guidelines.)

Recent studies have shown that chronic inflammation is also a cause of heart disease. The above factors can cause inflammation, but you may never be aware that you have this underlying problem. Measuring your C-reactive protein level (CRP) can indicate whether you are having chronic inflammation in your body. Following the general recommendations that follow may reverse this inflammation.

If you are a woman who is past menopause and you already have heart disease, be very cautious about taking synthetic hormone replacement therapy (HRT or synthetic estrogen). Recent studies show an increased chance of death, heart attack, or unstable angina when you are taking estrogen, especially during the first few years. Although this risk decreases with long-term use, it is doubtful that synthetic estrogen has any long-term benefits for women who already have heart disease. (See the section on menopause for recommendations for alternate hormone replacement using natural hormones.)

General Recommendations

Diet: Eating habits and nutrition are major factors in causing, preventing, and reversing heart disease. High fat content, processed and fried foods, fast foods, and high-cholesterol foods all worsen the atherosclerotic process. Even minor improvements in diet can help a great deal. Increasing your fiber is recommended for decreasing the risk of heart disease, especially if you are a woman. Eating three to five servings of fruits and vegetables daily can increase your fiber intake and also provide other ingredients that protect the heart, such as antioxidants. Green leafy vegetables and vitamin-C-rich fruits and vegetables are especially protective against heart disease and its progression. One meal per week of cold-water fish (mackerel, tuna, herring, salmon, cod, trout, sardines, or halibut) can reduce the risk of heart attack by half, by increasing HDL (the "good" cholesterol) and decreasing LDL (the "bad" cholesterol).

I recommend drinking one glass of wine daily, which has been shown to help prevent the development of atherosclerosis due to its antioxidant and anti-inflammatory properties. Red wine is the best choice because it contains antioxidants called polyphenols; but beer, white wine, and grape juice can also provide benefit. To avoid weight gain from drinking alcoholic beverages, drink them during meals. Drinking black or green tea has also been shown to help prevent heart disease as well as heart attacks because of its antioxidants, anti-inflammatories, and blood-thinning ingredients. A recent study showed that eating lots of dairy products, such as milk, yogurt, cheese, or ice cream, may reduce the risk of heart disease, even when the dairy products are high fat (although low fat is the better choice).

There are several diets that can prevent heart disease and stop the progression of atherosclerosis. The Balanced Healing Diet, American Heart Association Diet, DASH diet, and Mediterranean Diet are all beneficial. The diet designed by Dean Ornish, MD, has been proven to actually reverse heart disease (see Step 3 below).

Exercise: In conjunction with diet, exercise is essential in preventing and reversing heart disease. Aerobic exercise is the primary form necessary to do so. I recommend the American Heart Association guidelines, which includes a minimum of 30 to 60 minutes of moderate intensity activity, three to four times a week, supplemented by an increase in daily lifestyle activities, such as gardening, walking the stairs, or doing household chores. However, if you have not exercised before, have your doctor order an Exercise Tolerance Test (ETT) to evaluate your heart condition and help you plan a graded exercise program.

Meditation/Relaxation: Meditation and relaxation reduce factors that accelerate atherosclerosis, including stress and emotions such as anger, anxiety, and frustration; these emotions are more prevalent and harmful in certain personality types (See Appendix A, under "Mind-Body Techniques," for more information and examples.)

Your Balanced Healing Action Plan for Heart Disease

- For treating symptoms of angina (heart pain), see the section on angina.
- Vitamins E, C, and beta-carotene, and intravenous chelation therapy have not been shown to be beneficial for heart disease and are not recommended at this time.

Step 1: Take the Appropriate Prescription Medications for Symptoms of Heart Disease

If you have symptoms of heart disease, first get them under control and stabilize your heart with conventional medications. Otherwise, your condition may worsen and you may have serious complications. If you have had a heart attack, your doctor may prescribe beta-blockers (such as atenolol, propranolol) because these drugs significantly reduce the risk of death from heart disease.

Caution: Beta-blockers can sometimes reduce HDL-cholesterol levels to levels that are so low they're harmful. If your blood tests indicate an HDL cholesterol level lower than 35mg/dl, I recommend taking chromium picolinate, 200mcg three times per day, which can increase the levels by 10 percent.

Many other conventional medications can control various symptoms of heart disease and prevent complications. These include ACE inhibitors, calcium channel blockers, angiotensin-receptor blockers, nitrates, diuretics, digitalis, and antiarrhythmic drugs. The choice of which class of drugs and which particular medication is most beneficial for you depends on your particular heart condition and other diseases that you also may have. Some of these medications can interfere with the actions of each other. **NOTE:** NSAIDS (Nonsteroidal anti-inflammatory drugs, used for arthritis and pain) can worsen or precipitate heart failure or detract from the benefit of ACE inhibitors in some people, so they should be used with caution in these circumstances. Consult with your doctor about the benefits and side effects of any heart medication.

Once your symptoms are stabilized, you can then try the following steps. If they help, you can then reduce the dosage or discontinue your prescription medications under your doctor's direction and supervision.

Step 2: Take an Aspirin a Day to Prevent Heart Attack

An aspirin a day is important in slowing the progression of atherosclerosis and preventing heart attack because of both its blood-thinning and anti-inflammatory effects. Take aspirin after a heart attack to decrease the risk of sudden death and further progression of atherosclerosis. Take no more than 325mg per day (81mg is sufficient to thin the blood). Be aware that ibuprofen blocks the blood-thinning effects of aspirin. If you must take ibuprofen, take the aspirin first, and wait at least two hours to take the ibuprofen so that the aspirin has time to exert its beneficial effects. Take the lowest dose of ibuprofen necessary. Aspirin use can deplete body stores of vitamin C, so make sure you get 600mg a day through diet or by taking a supplement. **NOTE:** In some people, aspirin can worsen or precipitate heart failure or detract from the benefit of ACE inhibitors (see Step 1), so they should be used with caution and under your doctor's guidance in these circumstances.

Step 3: Follow the Dean Ornish Program to Reverse Heart Disease

I recommend the Dean Ornish, MD, program for heart disease no matter what other steps you take. Dr. Ornish has proven that a very low-fat diet, coupled with other methods that I recommend (stress reduction from yoga, relaxation techniques, breathing techniques, "heart healing" imagery, and/or meditation, aerobic exercise, and group support), can actually reverse heart disease. His method requires great motivation, but it will help you to feel much better, to significantly or completely reduce your symptoms, and to live a normal life span. If you are not willing to follow the entire program, just following parts of it will lead to improvement. (To learn the Ornish program, buy the book, *The Dean Ornish Program for Reversing Heart Disease*, Royal Publications, 1996.) It usually takes several months to a year to reverse your condition, although you may see reduction of your symptoms much sooner.

Step 4: Take Flaxseed Oil, Vitamin E, Garlic, Niacin, Folic Acid, Vitamin B_6, and Vitamin B_{12}

In addition to the previous steps, I recommend taking several supplements to help prevent the progression of atherosclerosis and its complications. These include flaxseed oil (1 tablespoon daily) or fish oil (4g per day), which help prevent deposition of fats into the arteries. I prefer flaxseed oil (or ground flaxseed) because fish oil in high doses can decrease HDL cholesterol (the good cholesterol) in some people. If you take fish oil and your HDL level is reduced to below normal, take vitamin E (200 IU daily) and garlic (4,000mg daily) or niacin (1g to 3g daily) to raise HDL.

Also take daily vitamin B_6 (25mg), vitamin B_{12} (400mcg), and folic acid (400mcg) if your homocysteine levels are elevated. Elevated homocysteine levels are correlated with a higher risk of heart disease, and these vitamins can lower the levels. You can take all these supplements in combination with the other treatments.

Step 5: Undergo Acupuncture for Heart Failure or Arrhythmias

A recent study shows that acupuncture decreases overstimulation of the heart, helping to minimize the symptoms of heart failure. Acupuncture can also be effective in reducing arrhythmias. Principal points usually are found on the arms, legs, and back in various combinations. Always seek evaluation and treatment from a practitioner certified in acupuncture. (See Appendix A, under "Acupuncture," for guidance on finding a qualified acupuncturist and for further explanation of the different acupuncture techniques.) You should notice improvement within six treatments, but you might need additional sessions for maximum benefits.

Step 6: Use a Sauna to Reduce Arrhythmias in Congestive Heart Failure

Daily sauna therapy, consisting of 15 minutes lying on your back in a 60-degree (Centigrade) dry sauna, followed by 30 minutes under blankets at room temperature, can reduce irregular heart beats, fatigue, shortness of breath, insomnia, and other symptoms in congestive heart failure. It takes only two weeks to see the benefits.

Step 7: Undergo Sleep Apnea Evaluation and Therapy for Congestive Heart Failure

Sleep apnea is a condition in which you do not breathe in enough oxygen while sleeping. About one-third of people with congestive heart failure also have sleep apnea. If you have heart failure, you should be tested in a sleep lab, and, if the findings are abnormal, use a breathing device at night called a CPAP machine.

Step 8: Take Coenzyme Q10 (CoQ10) for Various Heart Conditions and Before Heart Surgery

Coenzyme Q10 (CoQ10) (1mg for each pound of body weight, daily) can be very effective in reducing symptoms of *congestive heart failure, mitral valve prolapse, cardiomyopathy,* and *arrhythmias*. It works by increasing ATP, the body's energy molecule, and through its antioxidant properties. You can take CoQ10 with any of the previous steps. If CoQ10 is effective in reducing your symptoms, you can then reduce the dosages of the medications in Step 1, under your doctor's guidance. You should notice improvement within a few weeks. I also recommend that you take CoQ10 if you are having heart surgery because it has been shown to help prevent complications. Take 120mg daily starting a week before your surgery.

Step 9: Take Other Herbs and Supplements for Various Heart Conditions

Several herbs and supplements may be beneficial for various heart conditions if your symptoms continue. You can take all of them with the previous steps.

- **Congestive heart failure and minor arrhythmias:** Take hawthorn extract (100mg to 250mg containing 10 percent procyanidin content, three times daily) and L-carnitine (300mg three times daily). Hawthorn improves all the functions of the heart muscle, and L-carnitine increases energy production in heart tissue. If your symptoms are not reduced or not completely resolved, add L-arginine (2g to 5g, three times daily), which improves circulation and quality of life. If your symptoms improve with these supplements, you can then reduce the dosages of the medications in Step 1, under your doctor's guidance. **Caution:** Take hawthorn *only for NYHA (New York Heart Association) stage II heart failure*, defined as heart disease with no resulting limitations of physical activity (you are comfortable at rest, but ordinary physical activity results in fatigue, palpitation, breathing problems, or angina). Hawthorn taken with conventional heart medications can possibly intensify the effect or interfere with successful treatment, so check with your doctor before taking it.
- **Arrhythmias:** Magnesium is very important in stabilizing the heart's electrical system; take 200mg to 400mg three times per day.
- **Congestive heart failure:** Take creatine, 20g per day for 5 to 10 days to increase your strength and endurance.

> At age 68, Peter, a retired electrician, had high cholesterol and high blood pressure. He had suffered two heart attacks in the past 10 years. He took medications to lower his blood pressure and cholesterol, and he took one aspirin daily as well as beta-blockers. He was prescribed a balanced diet but did not follow it very well. He developed congestive heart failure, with swelling in his ankles and difficulty breathing. He started taking diuretics and an ACE inhibitor, which helped but did not eliminate his symptoms. The amount of blood he was pumping from his heart (called *ejection fraction*) was only 25 percent of normal. I started him on CoQ10, hawthorn, and flaxseed oil. After three months, his ejection fraction had risen to 45 percent, his swelling and shortness of breath went away, and he was able to stop taking some of his medications.

Step 10: Undergo Cardiac Resynchronization

The FDA has recently approved a new device, called a biventricular pacemaker, that boosts the heart's pumping ability for people with severe heart failure who do not respond to the previous steps, and before heart transplant is considered. The device works by synchronizing the heart muscles to contract more efficiently and increase the blood flow. Some people are even taken off the transplant list when this device works for them.

Step 11: Receive a Heart Transplant

The treatment of last resort for a failing heart is heart transplant, performed in numerous medical centers throughout the country. To be considered, you have to meet the following criteria: be less than 69 years old, stop smoking and drinking alcohol (forever), not have arterial disease in your arms or legs or have cancer, and must have insurance coverage. You must be unresponsive to other treatment, and your other vital organs must be in good shape. Donor hearts last six hours outside the body, so surgery must be done quickly. There is a 70 percent survival rate for heart transplantation. After heart transplant, you must be on drugs to suppress your immune system, and you must follow a healthy lifestyle. I would also recommend taking the supplements in Step 4 to protect your new heart.

HEARTBURN/GASTROESOPHAGEAL REFLUX DISORDER (GERD)

Heartburn (GERD) is a condition caused by a weakness in the muscular valve between the stomach and esophagus (the *lower esophageal sphincter*, or LES), resulting in stomach acid leaking into and irritating the esophagus. There are two types, non-erosive and erosive; erosive involves inflammation of the esophagus and can eat away the lining.

The major cause of heartburn is overeating, but other factors include obesity, cigarette smoking, and consuming certain foods (see "Diet" below), which causes increased pressure on the stomach from the abdomen or directly weakens the LES. Some authorities believe too much stomach acid is a factor, but most nutrition-oriented practitioners believe that too little acid is the actual problem. Occasionally, heartburn can be a sign of a hiatal hernia (outpouching of the esophagus above the LES).

In some people, GERD can cause strictures, *Barrett's esophagus* (a precancerous change in cell structure), esophageal cancer, irritation and scarring of the vocal cords, and a variety of lung problems, including asthma and bronchitis.

Common Symptoms

- Burning feeling in the chest (behind the breastbone), usually after eating. This discomfort can also occur when bending over or lying on your back.
- Burning in the throat, with a hot, sour, or salty taste.
- Belching.
- Chest pain.

What You Need to Know

The symptoms of GERD can often imitate those of a heart attack. You should obtain a heart evaluation if you have any chest pain, especially if you have symptoms of shortness of breath, dizziness, pain in the jaw, or the pain is not relieved by antacids. Cigarette smoking causes heart disease and also relaxes the LES, so stopping this habit can help both conditions. In addition, numerous medications can cause heartburn as a side effect, especially aspirin, nonsteroidal anti-inflammatory drugs (NSAIDs), and some antibiotics. Changing to a different medication may relieve the symptoms and prevent the need for additional measures. If you have GERD and are taking medications, check the *Physician's Desk Reference* (*PDR*) to see whether your medication can cause these symptoms, or consult your pharmacist.

General Recommendations

Diet: Foods that cause relaxation of the LES include tomatoes, citrus fruits, garlic, onions, chocolate, coffee, alcohol, and peppermint. Foods high in fats and oils also cause increased heartburn. If you have GERD, avoid these foods.

Meditation and Qigong: Stress is a major factor that causes and worsens heartburn, so meditation and Qigong are both valuable adjuncts to reduce stress. (For further information and examples, see Appendix A, under "Mind-Body Techniques.")

Your Balanced Healing Action Plan for GERD

Step 1: Elevate the Head of Your Bed

For many people, GERD symptoms worsen when they go to bed. To relieve nighttime symptoms, elevate the head of your bed. Do this by elevating the frame of your bed (as with blocks) rather than by sleeping with cushions or more pillows, which have a tendency to shift while you sleep.

Step 2: Take Probiotics and Digestive Enzymes

When you have GERD, the acid production in your stomach often is not correctly balanced. This can occur as a result of improper digestion. As a result, your food is not broken down completely, which can itself cause more symptoms. I recommend that you take digestive enzymes to help break down your food better. There are many products that contain digestive enzymes, and they should contain some or all of the following: protease, papain, amylase, lipase, bromelain, cellulase, and lactase.

I also recommend taking probiotics with the enzymes. These consist of live cultures of organisms (the "good" bacteria) that help digest food properly. Of the beneficial microorganisms in probiotics, *L. acidophilus* and *bifidobacteria* are the best. Other beneficial bacteria include *L. salivarius*, *L. rhamnosus*, *L. plantarum*, *streptococcus thermophilus*, *L. bulgaricus*, *L. casei*, and *L. sporogenes*.

You should start to feel better in two to six weeks when using digestive enzymes and probiotics. If you have increased gas, bloating, or cramping during the first week of this treatment (which is common), reduce your dosage and then gradually rebuild it as these side effects lessen. Yogurt is not a good source of beneficial microorganisms to take the place of probiotics. Although yogurt products do contain beneficial microorganisms, they are not the most important or potent. Also, many yogurt products are pasteurized after they are made to increase their shelf life, but this kills most of the good bacteria and destroys the benefits.

Step 3: Take Appropriate Chinese Herbal Remedies

If the previous steps don't help, next try Chinese herbal formulas that reduce the symptoms of heartburn and strengthen the LES. *Kang Ning Wan*, *Ping Wei San*, and/or *Yue Ju Wan* can all be helpful. Consult a practitioner qualified in Chinese herbal medicine to determine which Chinese herbal formulas are the best for your particular syndromes. You should feel better within three weeks, but you may need to take the herbs longer for complete relief. (See Appendix A, under "Chinese Herbs," for further information.)

Step 4: Receive Acupuncture

Along with the Chinese herbs, acupuncture helps with long-term reduction of symptoms and also can strengthen the LES. Principal points usually are found on the arms, legs, and abdomen. Ear points include Stomach, and Esophagus. Always seek evaluation and treatment from a practitioner certified in acupuncture. (See Appendix A, under "Acupuncture," for guidance on finding a qualified acupuncturist and for further explanation of the different acupuncture techniques.) You should notice improvement within six treatments, but you might need additional sessions for maximum benefits.

Step 5: Take Ginger or Licorice for Immediate Relief

The previous steps are directed at giving you long-term relief. When you need immediate relief, start with ginger. You can take ginger by drinking the tea three times a day (do not exceed 4g per day), taking 2ml of tincture daily, taking 250mg tablets three times a day, or taking it in extracts standardized to 20 percent gingiol and shogaol, 100mg to 200mg four times a day. Expect relief within a few hours. You can also take licorice, (deglycyrrhizinated form (DGL) one or two 380mg chewable tablets before meals) alone or with ginger. Licorice has antispasmodic, anti-inflammatory, and soothing properties.

Step 6: Take Antacids for Immediate Relief

Antacids can give you immediate relief if the ginger is not helpful. However, don't take antacids regularly or long term because they can cause other medical problems, such as kidney stones or aluminum toxicity.

Step 7: Take an Appropriate Homeopathic Remedy

Several homeopathic remedies are useful for specific situations. These include *Nux vomica* after eating spicy foods, *Carbo vegetabilis* after eating rich foods, and *Arsenicum album* for burning pain. These remedies are used in a dosage of 6c, taken every 15 minutes up to three times. The series can be repeated once, if needed. You should consult a qualified homeopathist for guidance on which remedies will be most beneficial and for proper dosages. You should notice improvement within one to two weeks. (See Appendix A, under "Homeopathy," for guidance on finding a qualified homeopathist and for further information.)

Step 8: Take a Prescription Proton Pump Inhibitor Medication

If you continue to have discomfort, your doctor can prescribe a drug called a *proton pump inhibitor* (such as Nexium, Prevacid, Prilosec, or Aciphex). These drugs are very effective in controlling the symptoms of GERD, but they don't cure the problem and they are expensive. You are likely to need additional methods of relief because these drugs don't stop all symptoms. In addition, the absorption of many medications and vitamins can be decreased when you're using these drugs.

> Candace, a 32-year-old math teacher, got heartburn every time she ate and at night when she tried to sleep. She took the prescription drugs Prevacid and Prilosec, but neither completely reduced her symptoms. I started her on probiotics and digestive enzymes, which brought about nearly immediate relief of most of her discomfort. I added a Chinese herbal formula and started her on acupuncture to correct her underlying syndromes (stagnant Liver Qi with Damp Heat). After seven acupuncture sessions, Candace had only an occasional episode of heartburn every month or so. She takes her probiotics every few months for a few weeks to make sure her digestion stays normal, and she takes digestive enzymes whenever she does have an episode of heartburn.

Step 9: Take an H_2 Blocker Medication

If the proton pump inhibitors don't work for you, try one of the H_2 acid blockers (Zantac, Pepcid, Tagamet). However, because these drugs work by blocking acid production, they can cause decreased absorption of other medications and especially fat-soluble vitamins (vitamins A, D, E, and K), and vitamin B_{12}. (If your B_{12} is low on blood testing, take cranberry juice, which increases the absorption of B_{12}.) Also, if low acid is contributing to your reflux, these drugs can make it worse. They are not as effective as proton pump inhibitors for GERD.

Step 10: Undergo a Stretta Procedure

A new, minimally invasive procedure is available in some areas to relieve persistent GERD. Called the *Stretta procedure*, it uses high-frequency radio waves to tighten the LES, thus reducing acid reflux. After this procedure, many people are able to stop taking their acid-blocking medications. However, because this is a new procedure, we don't yet know how long the benefits will last.

Step 11: Undergo Surgery

If all else has failed, laparoscopic surgery may be necessary to repair the LES if symptoms are severe and do not respond to other treatments. Surgery doesn't eliminate the need for medications in 75 percent of patients, and it has side effects (diarrhea and bloating) in at least 15 percent; thus it should be done only as a last resort. Surgery is more effective than low-dose proton pump inhibitors, but not more effective than high-dose inhibitors.

HEMORRHOIDS

Hemorrhoids are abnormally large or painful collections of blood vessels, supporting tissues, and mucous membranes in the anal-rectal area. They can be either internal or external. They are caused by genetic weakness of the veins and/or excessive pressure on the veins due to straining, diarrhea, pregnancy, liver disease, prolonged sitting or standing, and heavy lifting. Hemorrhoids can clot, causing severe pain and requiring surgical correction.

Common Symptoms

- Bright red bleeding from the rectum, seen on stool or toilet tissue
- Tenderness or pain during bowel movements
- Itching
- Painful swelling
- Mucous discharge

What You Need to Know

The best treatment for hemorrhoids is prevention. Avoid prolonged standing or sitting, heavy lifting, or straining during defecation, and eat a high-fiber diet.

General Recommendations

Diet: A high-fiber diet is the most important component in the prevention of hemorrhoids. An increase of vegetables, nuts, fruit, and whole grains can help reduce the symptoms.

Your Balanced Healing Action Plan to Relieve Acute Hemorrhoidal Swelling and Pain

Step 1: Take Psyllium or Guar Gum

Start by taking natural bulking agents, particularly psyllium (Metamucil) and guar gum

(5g per day before or with meals, with at least eight ounces of water). These are both inexpensive and effective in reducing the symptoms of hemorrhoids. You should notice improvement within a few days.

Step 2: Use Topical Preparations Containing Cortisone for Pain and Swelling

If you continue to suffer pain and/or swelling from your hemorrhoids, use a local topical preparation containing cortisone (such as Anusol HC), which can shrink the hemorrhoid. You can use a topical product with the previous step. Topicals should give you relief in one to three days, but they may have only temporary effects.

Step 3: See Your Doctor for Medical Intervention

If your pain is severe or you are still bleeding, or if your hemorrhoids are prolapsed (bulging outside the anal area), more invasive methods might be necessary. Injection, banding, cauterization, and surgery are all viable options. I recommend starting with the least invasive (which is the order in which they are listed).

Your Balanced Healing Action Plan to Prevent or Control Hemorrhoids

Step 1: Cleanse and Detoxify Your Colon

Certain combinations of herbs can cleanse and detoxify the colon, which can correct and prevent underlying problems that cause hemorrhoids. Start with an herbal formula that both cleans and activates the colon. Look for a formula that contains all or most of the following: cape aloe, cascara sagrada, barberry root, senna, ginger root, African bird pepper, and fennel. Take this combination for about a week, and then add an herbal formula to detoxify the colon. I recommend a formula that contains most or all of the following: apple fruit pectin, slippery elm bark, marshmallow root, fennel seed, activated willow charcoal, psyllium seeds and husks, and pharmaceutical grade bentonite clay. Take this formula for another one to two weeks. (See Appendix A, under "Detoxification Therapy," for more information.)

Step 2: Take Aortic Glycosaminoglycans (GAGs) or HER

For persistent hemorrhoids, several supplements can give you relief. Aortic glycosaminoglycans (GAGs), 100mg per day, give the best results. If they're not helpful, try a combination of bilberry, rutin, and hydroxyethylrutosides, called HER. HER (1,000mg to 3,000mg per day) is especially useful for hemorrhoids caused by pregnancy. These supplements may take one to three weeks to have a beneficial effect.

Step 3: Take Appropriate Chinese Herbal Remedies

If the previous step doesn't help, try Chinese herbal formulas, which can give long-lasting relief from hemorrhoids. *Bai Tou Weng Tang* is one of the formulas effective in stopping bleeding and reducing the inflammation of hemorrhoidal tissues. Consult a practitioner qualified in Chinese herbal medicine to determine which Chinese herbal formulas are the best for your particular syndromes. You should notice improvement within three weeks, but you may need to take the herbs longer for complete relief. (See Appendix A, under "Chinese Herbs," for further information.)

Step 4: Undergo Acupuncture

Along with Chinese herbals, I recommend acupuncture to relieve hemorrhoid pain and swelling for prolonged periods of time. Principal points usually are found on the low back, tailbone area, and legs. There is an ear acupuncture point specific for hemorrhoids. Always seek evaluation and treatment from a practitioner certified in acupuncture. (See Appendix A, under "Acupuncture," for guidance on finding a qualified acupuncturist and for further explanation of the different acupuncture techniques.) You should notice improvement within six treatments, but you might need additional sessions for maximum benefits.

> The hemorrhoids that Edie, a 32-year-old personal trainer, developed during her second pregnancy continued after her baby was born. Topical preparations helped to some degree, but her job involved prolonged standing and lifting, which caused the hemorrhoids to recur. She had one surgery, but the hemorrhoids came back when she returned to her job. I started her on a colon detoxification program, followed by the Chinese herbal formula *Bai Tou Weng Tang*, and four sessions of acupuncture. Within one month, her symptoms went away. She has had no problems with hemorrhoids in more than a year.

Step 5: Take an Appropriate Homeopathic Remedy

There are more than a dozen homeopathic remedies that can help with hemorrhoids that persist despite the previous steps. Some examples include *Hamamelis* for soreness, bruising and bleeding; *Aesculus* for sharp, spiking pain worsened by bowel movements; and *Sulphur* for burning and itching aggravated by warmth. These remedies are used at a dose of 12x. Consult a qualified homeopathist for guidance on which remedies will be most beneficial and for proper dosages. You should notice improvement in one to two weeks. (See Appendix A, under "Homeopathy," for guidance on finding a qualified homeopathist and for further information.)

HEPATITIS

Hepatitis is inflammation of the liver. The most common causes are viruses, but it can also be due to alcohol, toxins, or drugs (including acetaminophen). Hepatitis can be acute or chronic; you can have chronic hepatitis for many years before there are symptoms. Hepatitis A is contacted through contamination, and 99 percent of the cases resolve completely. Hepatitis B is caused primarily by sexual contact, needles, and blood transfusions; 10 percent of people who get hepatitis B become chronic carriers. Hepatitis C is transmitted through needles or blood and accounts for 16 percent of cases in the U.S. Hepatitis B, C, and the non-viral forms can lead to liver cirrhosis, liver cancer, and death.

Common Symptoms

Many cases of hepatitis are unrecognized, causing only mild flu-like symptoms or no symptoms at all. When symptoms are present, they can include the following:

- Flu-like symptoms
- Loss of appetite
- Mild fever
- Fatigue
- Muscle or joint aches
- Nausea and vomiting
- Abdominal pain
- Jaundice
- Dark urine
- Enlarged liver

What You Need to Know

It is most important to prevent infection. The virus that causes hepatitis A stays in your system and can infect other people for about seven weeks. If a close friend, relative, or co-worker has hepatitis A, a gamma globulin injection may protect them. For medical workers and other high-risk people, a series of vaccines can prevent hepatitis B infection. If you have hepatitis B or C, you can become a carrier (you have the infection but no symptoms) and can infect another person through blood, needle sharing, or sex. Blood tests measure liver function and the degree of damage, if any, that has already occurred.

General Recommendations

Diet: Nutrition is very important in both acute and chronic hepatitis. In acute infections, replacing fluids by means of vegetable broths, vegetable juices, or herbal teas is recommended. In chronic hepatitis, good nutrition is essential, especially eating fruits and vegetables. Alcohol can damage the liver, so do not drink alcohol if you have hepatitis.

Your Balanced Healing Action Plan for Acute Hepatitis

Step 1: Rest, Drink Fluids, and Get Good Nutrition

Rest, fluids and good nutrition are the hallmarks of treatment for any type of acute hepatitis. You don't have to stay in bed; simply restrict your activities when you feel tired or weak. Also follow the Balanced Healing Eating Guidelines (see "Simple Healing Steps for All Health Conditions") and drink plenty of clear fluids. Depending on the type of hepatitis you have and how your body responds to it, your symptoms may last from a week to several months.

Step 2: Hospitalization for Severe Cases

Viral hepatitis rarely requires hospitalization; but toxic, drug, or alcoholic hepatitis may require intravenous fluids and parenteral nutrition (food and other nutrients given through a vein) if you cannot eat or drink or have continuous vomiting.

Your Balanced Healing Action Plan for Chronic Hepatitis

- If you have chronic hepatitis that is severe (significant elevation of liver enzymes), or unstable (worsening symptoms), go to Step 8 first, then restart at Step 1 when your liver enzymes are stable.

Step 1: Liver and Blood Cleansing

Because one of the liver's functions is to remove toxins, disease that affects the liver allows toxins to build up in the liver as well as in the blood, causing more damage to both the liver and other organ systems. I recommend starting with herbal formulas to clean and detoxify the liver and the blood, which will not only protect the liver from further toxic damage but also help reduce your symptoms and rebuild the liver. Use a liver-cleansing formula that contains all or some of the following: milk thistle, dandelion root, Picrorhiza kurroa root, and artichoke or beet leaf.

Follow this with a blood-cleansing formula that contains some or all of the following: chaparral, red clover, burdock root, goldenseal, yellow dock, Oregon grape root, blood-root, mistletoe, periwinkle flowers, lobelia seeds, sheep sorrel, and cayenne. Various health food store products will have different instructions, but you should observe benefits within a few weeks.

If you have colon problems (disease or constipation), you should undergo a colon detoxification process before liver and blood detoxification, because toxins that are removed from the liver and blood are deposited in the colon for excretion. If the colon is not functioning correctly, these toxins will not be eliminated and will be reabsorbed into the body. Colon detoxification will prevent this from occurring. (See Appendix A, under "Detoxification Therapy," for further information.)

Step 2: Take Milk Thistle

Once you are through with cleansing your liver and blood, continue on milk thistle (silymarin) to both protect and regenerate new liver cells. Take 140mg to 210mg, containing at least 70 percent silymarin content, three times a day. It may take one to three months to see your symptoms improve and your liver enzymes decrease.

Step 3: Take Licorice

If your liver enzymes remain elevated or you still have symptoms of hepatitis, next add licorice extract. Use the deglycyrrhizinated (DGL) form, one or two 380mg chewable tablets before meals. You can use licorice with the previous steps. Licorice can raise blood pressure in some people (primarily the non-DGL forms), so monitor your blood pressure levels if you have hypertension.

Step 4: Take Appropriate Chinese Herbal Remedies

Several Chinese herbal formulations are helpful when the previous steps do not control your symptoms or your liver enzymes remain elevated. *Long Dan Xie Gan Wan* is a helpful formula, but there are many more that contain herbs that benefit the liver, including *Han Lian Coa*, *Wu Wei Zi*, and *Huang Qi*. Consult a practitioner qualified in Chinese herbal medicine to determine which Chinese herbal formulas are the best for your particular syndromes. You should see improvement within three to six weeks, but you will probably need to take them longer for maximum benefits. (See Appendix A, under "Chinese Herbs," for further information.)

Step 5: Take an Appropriate Homeopathic Remedy

If your symptoms continue or your liver enzymes remain elevated, several homeopathic remedies can be useful for reducing liver inflammation and relieving some of the specific symptoms of hepatitis. These include *Phosphorus*, *Taraxacum officianale*, *Lycopodium*, and *Chelidonium*. Consult a qualified homeopathist for guidance on which remedies will be most beneficial and for proper dosages. You should see improvement in one to three months. (See Appendix A, under "Homeopathy," for guidance on finding a qualified homeopathist and for further information.)

Step 6: Take Vitamin E and N-Acetylcysteine

If your liver enzymes continue to be elevated, add vitamin E (800mg daily) and N-acetylcysteine (600mg twice daily), which protect against toxin-induced liver injury through their antioxidant effects.

Step 7: Take Liver Extract and Bovine Thymus Extract

If the above steps still do not return liver enzyme blood levels to normal, I recommend trying liver extracts (500mg to 1,000mg per day) and/or bovine thymus extracts (120mg pure polypeptide). Both types of extract may lower liver enzymes and can be used together, although I recommend taking one at a time to observe the response. You should see improvement in one to three months.

Step 8: Take Interferon and Phosphatidylcholine

For chronic, progressive hepatitis (worsening condition), you should receive prescription medications that work quicker than the previous steps because you can develop severe and even fatal complications. Alpha-interferon and ribavirin given together have been the drugs of choice. However, they have numerous side effects (nausea, fever, joint pain, and flu-like symptoms). A new drug, peginterferon alpha-2b, requires just one injection a week. Both treatments are expensive ($1,500 a month for alpha-interferon and $1,000 for peginterferon). An even newer variety of peginterferon, called PEG-IFNs, can be taken once a month and is especially effective when combined with ribavirin. If you take any of these forms of interferon, also take phosphatidylcholine (15g to 25g daily) to increase the effectiveness of interferon. You can use this step with the previous steps for better long-term results.

> Brenda, a 45-year-old veterinarian, contracted hepatitis C through a blood transfusion. She had a progressive form of the disease and was taking interferon, which improved her liver enzymes, but she still felt weak and fatigued, with occasional nausea and muscle aches. She had no interest in social activities and stayed in her home most of the time. I recommended phosphatidylcholine, which further improved her enzymes, but still her symptoms continued. I started her on liver and blood cleansing for one month, then continued her on milk thistle, licorice, and a specially formulated Chinese herbal formula. After three months, her liver enzymes decreased to just above normal limits, and most of her symptoms went away. She was able to return to her normal social activities and became fatigued only when she did too much.

Step 9: Receive a Liver Transplant

Hepatitis that continues to progress ultimately destroys the liver, leaving a liver transplant as the only hope. There are strict guidelines for liver transplant candidates. Survival rates are 60 percent to 75 percent in adults and 80 percent to 90 percent in children. After liver transplant, you must be on drugs to suppress your immune system, and you must follow a healthy lifestyle.

HIGH BLOOD PRESSURE (Hypertension)

Blood pressure is a measurement of the pressure blood exerts against the wall of your arteries. There are two numbers that are important. The *systolic* (top number), is the peak force of the blood against the artery wall when the heart contracts. The *diastolic* (the bottom number), is the force of blood against the artery wall as the heart is filling. Both are important, and elevation of either or both can cause heart, kidney, and brain damage, strokes, dementia, heart attacks, heart failure, kidney failure, vision problems, and death.

The levels of high blood pressure (in mm/Hg) are

- Borderline: 140/90
- Mild: 140 to 159/90 to 99
- Moderate: 160 to 179/100 to 109
- Severe: 180/110

Common Symptoms

Most often, high blood pressure has no symptoms. When symptoms are present, they can include the following:

- Headaches
- Chest pain
- Nosebleeds

- Numbness
- Tingling
- Palpitations
- Muscle cramps
- Weakness

What You Need to Know

For years, the diastolic measurement was considered the most important blood pressure measurement, but we now recognize that the systolic component is as important as—or more important than—the diastolic. Often, your blood pressure will be falsely elevated in the doctor's office (*white coat hypertension*), and the best way to determine your blood pressure is to take several measurements during the day at home. Changes in lifestyle (especially exercise) and diet can control blood pressure in 80 percent of people who have borderline to moderate hypertension. Smoking is a key contributor to high blood pressure; if you smoke, it will be nearly impossible to control your blood pressure without medication.

Controlling hypertension is one of the easiest and most significant ways to prevent heart disease, stroke, circulation problems, and death. Unfortunately, this is not as simple as it sounds. One in four of those who have high blood pressure don't know it, and more than half of those who do know they have high blood pressure don't take their medications. Untreated hypertension is certain to lead to other health problems and even death.

General Recommendations

Diet: I first recommend following the DASH (Dietary Approaches to Stop Hypertension) diet, which is specifically designed to reduce blood pressure. This diet emphasizes fruits, vegetables, and low-fat dairy and includes whole grains, poultry, fish, and nuts. (For a copy of the DASH diet, go to www.nhlbi.nih.gov/health/public/heart/hbp/dash/.) If you don't follow this diet, any of the following dietary recommendations will still be helpful.

Increase your vegetable intake (three cups per day), and decrease your animal meats (less than 4 to 6 ounces daily). Using extra virgin olive oil can lower your blood pressure after six months. Certain foods can help lower blood pressure, including celery, garlic, onions, nuts and seeds, cold-water fish (mackerel, cod, trout, shark, salmon, tuna, herring, sardines, or halibut), whole grains, and legumes. Tomatoes and tomato products are also beneficial in lowering blood pressure due to their lycopene content, and eating them with oil (especially olive) increases this effect. A berry called autumn olives eaten in Asia (and tasting like cranberries) has up to 18 times the amount of lycopene found in tomatoes. Reducing salt content of the food you eat (to 1.5mg per day) is also extremely important, because most hypertensive people are salt sensitive. This is especially true in postmenopausal women, who can lower blood pressure up to 16mm by limiting their intake of salt to one teaspoon a day. Foods with high vitamin C content are also beneficial for reducing high blood pressure. I also recommend drinking one glass of wine a day; red is the best, but white wine is also beneficial. Women with hypertension SHOULD NOT eat a very low-fat diet (less than 10 percent saturated fat) because this can increase a type of hemorrhagic stroke.

Exercise: Moderate exercise can reduce blood pressure by an average of 7mm. I recommend primarily aerobic exercise, but resistance exercise can be done at 30 percent to 60 percent of maximum heart rate (see "Exercise," under "Simple Healing Steps for All Health Conditions," page 79, for guidance on how to calculate your maximum heart rate). Be aware, however, that resistance exercise can initially increase blood pressure, but this phenomenon goes away as you continue the exercise program. Be sure to undergo a thorough physical exam from your doctor and ask for his guidance before beginning an aggressive exercise program, especially if you have not exercised previously or for more than a year.

Meditation: Most mind-body techniques, including biofeedback, meditation, progressive muscle relaxation, and hypnosis can all reduce high blood pressure by relaxing the blood vessel walls and offsetting the effects of stimulant substances in the body such as adrenalin and cortisol. (See Appendix A, under "Mind-Body Techniques," for further information and examples.)

Qigong: I strongly recommend both Qigong and Tai Chi, which have been shown in studies to reduce blood pressure 8mm to 10mm over a course of 12 weeks. (For further information and examples, see Appendix A and "Simple Healing Steps for All Health Conditions," page 79, under "Qigong.")

> Overweight and a 20-year smoker when he came to see me, Ted, a 42-year-old government worker, had mildly elevated blood pressure. He did not want to take blood pressure medications, but he was willing to change his lifestyle to try to control his blood pressure. First, he stopped smoking by using acupuncture and Chinese herbs (see the section on nicotine addiction). I placed him on the DASH diet, and he began an exercise program, primarily walking (he gradually increased to four miles per day). He also practiced Qigong, although not as regularly as instructed. After several months, he had lost nearly 30 pounds, and his blood pressure returned to normal.

Your Balanced Healing Action Plan for Hypertension

- For moderate to severe hypertension, start with Step 4, and then return to Step 1.

Step 1: Take Calcium, Magnesium, Lycopene, Flaxseed Oil, Coenzyme Q10 (CoQ10), Hawthorn, and/or Olive Leaf

There are several nutritional supplements that can lower your blood pressure if it is borderline or mild. You can take these alone or together. If you are already on blood pressure medications, these supplements may help you reduce your dosage (do so under the guidance of your doctor). You should observe the lowering of your blood pressure within one to three months using these nutrients. These include the following:

- Calcium (800mg per day) and magnesium (800mg per day) have both been found to be effective in reducing blood pressure in many patients. Try one at a time for one month to see if it is effective, although they can be taken together.
- Lycopene, an antioxidant found in tomatoes and tomato products, can reduce blood pressure by 7mm to 9mm in people with mild hypertension. This effect can be obtained by taking lycopene extracts containing at least 15mg of lycopene. (Lyc-O-Mato is the product used in the study.)
- Flaxseed oil (1 tablespoon per day) or fish oil (4g/day, providing 2.04g DHA and 1.4g EPA) are very effective in reducing mildly elevated blood pressure.
- Garlic (containing 4,000mm allicin daily) has been reported to lower blood pressure up to 20mm to 30mm systolic and 10mm to 20mm diastolic, but this effect varies greatly among people.
- Coenzyme Q10 (CoQ10) (30mg to 75mg per day for mild, 120mg to 150mg per day for moderate high blood pressure) can reduce hypertension through its bioenergetic effects on the heart. Hypertension tends to deplete your body's supply of this nutrient.
- Hawthorn (100mg to 250mg, containing 10 percent procyanidins, three times daily) can also reduce high blood pressure in much the same way as CoQ10 does. Caution: If taken with other conventional heart medications, hawthorn can possibly heighten the effect or interfere with successful treatment, so check with your doctor before taking it.
- Olive Leaf (containing 20 percent olueropein, twice daily) has also been found to help lower blood pressure.

Step 2: Undergo Acupuncture

Acupuncture has been used quite successfully to reduce blood pressure and is most effective when you have borderline to mild hypertension. The earlier you start acupuncture after being diagnosed, the more successful it will be. There are at least five possible underlying causes for hypertension in Chinese medicine, so acupuncture points will vary. However, general principal points usually are found on the head, arms, legs, and feet. There is an ear acupuncture point called Lower Blood Pressure Groove (or Hypotensive point). Always seek evaluation and treatment from a practitioner certified in acupuncture. (See Appendix A, under "Acupuncture," for guidance on finding a qualified acupuncturist and for further explanation of the different acupuncture techniques.) You should notice improvement within six treatments, but you might need additional sessions for maximum benefits. However, the longer you have been on antihypertensive medication, the less the likelihood that acupuncture will help reduce your blood pressure.

Step 3: Practice Biofeedback

If your blood pressure has not decreased to normal and/or your blood pressure fluctuates, especially when you are stressed or anxious, try biofeedback (which teaches you how to relax and lower blood pressure using your mind). This method is most effective for borderline to mild hypertension. (For more information and guidance on how to find a practitioner qualified in biofeedback, see Appendix A, under "Mind-Body Techniques.")

Step 4: Take Prescription Antihypertensive Medications

The most important factor in high blood pressure is returning it to normal. If the above steps do not do so, you should seek prescriptive medication from your doctor. Numerous and varied medications for high blood pressure are available. Your blood pressure should be lowered within a few days to a week when taking these medications. Other health conditions may dictate the choice of antihypertensive medications appropriate for you, but in general, you should try them in this order:

- Start with a **diuretic** (such as HCTZ) and/or a **beta-blocker** (such as atenolol or propranolol), which are the least expensive and are very effective. In some people, beta-blockers can sometimes reduce HDL cholesterol to low levels that are harmful. This side effect can be reversed by taking chromium picolinate, 200mcg three times per day. If you take a diuretic, your potassium excretion through the urine is increased (and your blood potassium level drops), so you should also take potassium (10mEq to 20mEq per day), and eat more vegetables that contain potassium (primarily green, leafy vegetables).
- **ACE inhibitors** (such as captopril or enalapril) may be considered next, to replace or combine with diuretics and beta blockers. ACE inhibitors are also commonly used as a first choice in hypertensive diabetics (those who have high blood pressure) with protein in their urine; they may also be used with a diuretic in people with congestive heart failure. Cough is sometimes a side effect of ACE inhibitors, but it can be reduced by taking ibuprofen.
- **Central a–antagonists** (such as clonidine or methyldopa) may be the next choice.
- **Calcium channel blockers** (such as nifedipine, verapamil, or diltiazem) are effective but can cause an increased risk of heart disease compared to the other medications.

Controlling blood pressure often requires multiple approaches. Barbara, a 52-year-old executive, has had hypertension for more than 15 years. Medications had controlled her blood pressure, but she didn't like the side effects so she stopped taking them, which caused her blood pressure to go up. I recommended the DASH diet, and she began exercising. I prescribed calcium, magnesium, flaxseed oil, and a lycopene supplement. These efforts brought Barbara's blood pressure to mildly elevated. I then recommended Qigong, which further reduced her blood pressure. But it was still borderline high. At that point, I prescribed a mild diuretic, which did not have any side effects. Finally, all of these efforts brought Barbara's blood pressure back to normal.

Step 5: Undergo Interactive Imagery or Other Forms of Psychotherapy

Interactive imagery or other forms of psychotherapy have been successful at reducing blood pressure in some people by helping to release the repressed emotions and reduce the stress and anxiety that may be underlying the condition. Interactive imagery is a mind-body method in which you mentally interact with images that represent your emotions. It is a powerful method to uncover and deal with subconscious psychological issues of which you may not be aware. (See Appendix A, under "Mind-Body Techniques," for a more detailed explanation and to help find a qualified practitioner.)

Step 6: Practice Appropriate Yoga Postures

Yoga has been shown to help lower blood pressure by reducing stress, and I recommend it if your blood pressure goes up when you are anxious. Consult a qualified yoga instructor for guidance on which postures are the best and how to perform them correctly. It may take several months to see results with yoga. (See Appendix A for further information on yoga techniques.)

HIVES (Urticaria)

Hives are welts in the skin that are caused by an allergic reaction. When an *allergen* (a substance that is recognized as "foreign" by your immune system) enters your body, certain cells (mast cells) are stimulated and break open, releasing a chemical called histamine, which causes the hives to form. In the most extreme form of this allergic reaction, angioedema, hives develop in the tissues under the skin. Any type of allergen can cause hives, including foods and medications. Stress, extreme cold or heat, strep throat in children, hepatitis B in adults, insect bites, and blood transfusions can also cause hives.

Common Symptoms

- Raised and swollen welts with blanched centers
- Itching
- Burning under the skin

What You Need to Know

The best treatment for hives is prevention. Common allergens include milk products, strawberries, eggs, chocolate, beans, tomatoes, fish, nuts, food additives, flavorings, or preservatives, and drugs such as penicillin and aspirin. If you can identify the allergen that causes your hives, elimination of that allergen is the best treatment.

Your Balanced Healing Action Plan for Acute Hives

Acute angioedema is a medical emergency that can be life-threatening. It requires immediate care.

Step 1: Take OTC Antihistamine Medications

Initially, take an over-the-counter antihistamine, such as Benadryl, when the hives appear, or if you know you've been exposed to an allergen that will cause hives. Because hives are a direct result of histamine release, antihistamines counteract this chemical and can negate its effects. If you can't take Benadryl, hydroxyzine is an alternative.

Step 2: Take Vitamin C, Vitamin B₁₂, and Quercetin

If Step 1 is not effective in reducing your hives, try a combination of vitamin C (1,000mg three times a day), vitamin B_{12} (1,000mcg pr day), and quercetin (200mg to 400mg 20 minutes before each meal). These supplements lower or inhibit histamine release; you can take them along with an antihistamine.

Step 3: Take an Appropriate Homeopathic Remedy

If the previous steps don't help, there are several homeopathic remedies available that can be beneficial. *Urtica urens* (12x) is for stinging and itching. Apis (12x) is for redness and swelling. They are taken every two to three hours, up to four doses per day. Consult a qualified homeopathist for guidance on which remedies will be most beneficial and for proper dosages. You should experience relief in 12 to 36 hours. (See Appendix A, under "Homeopathy," for guidance on finding a qualified homeopathist and for further information.)

Step 4: Take Prescription Antihistamines

If you continue to have recurrent hives despite the previous steps, your doctor can prescribe stronger antihistamines to control them when they occur. Desloratadine (Clarinex) has a 50-fold greater ability to block histamine than other antihistamines currently in use.

Step 5: Take an H₂ Blocker Medication

If your hives persist, your doctor can prescribe an H_2 blocker such as Tagamet, Zantac, or Pepcid. Not all people respond to these drugs, however. Because these drugs work by blocking acid production, they can cause decreased absorption of other medications and especially fat-soluble vitamins (vitamins A, D, E, and K), as well as vitamin B_{12}. (If your B_{12} is low on blood testing, take cranberry juice to increase the absorption of B_{12}.)

Your Balanced Healing Action Plan for Prevention of Hives

Step 1: Take Appropriate Chinese Herbal Remedies

For recurrent hives, I recommend taking Chinese herbal formulas to correct the underlying causes. Some formulas include *Kai Yeung* Pills (for skin rash and itching) and *Lian Qiao Bai Du Pian* (for red, inflamed rashes). Consult a practitioner qualified in Chinese herbal medicine to determine which Chinese herbal formulas are the best for your particular syndromes. You should see improvement within one to three weeks. (See Appendix A, under "Chinese Herbs," for further information.)

Step 2: Undergo Acupuncture

Along with Chinese herbs, acupuncture is very effective for chronic urticaria. Principal points usually are found on the legs and arms. There are also ear acupuncture points specific for skin disorders. Always seek evaluation and treatment from a practitioner certified in acupuncture. (See Appendix A, under "Acupuncture," for guidance on finding a qualified acupuncturist and for further explanation of the different acupuncture techniques.) You should see improvement within six treatments, but you might need additional sessions for maximum benefits.

> Ralph, a 35-year-old bus driver, had episodes of hives several times a month, sometimes so severe that he couldn't go to work or even get dressed. Allergy testing showed moderate to severe allergies to environmental allergens. He was taking numerous antihistamines, but they gave him only partial and temporary relief. He had taken allergy shots for five years, but they had not helped at all. I placed him on Chinese herbs and performed five acupuncture treatments. He has had no further hives in more than two years.

Step 3: Nambudripad Allergy Elimination Treatment (NAET)

If food allergies are a possible cause of your hives, I recommend the Nambudripad Allergy Elimination Treatment (NAET). It combines acupuncture, kinesiology, chiropractic, herbs, and nutrition to desensitize you to foods to which you are allergic. It may take several months to notice improvement, depending on how many allergens are sensitizing you. (See Appendix A, under "NAET," and the section on food allergies for further explanation.)

HYPERTENSION (see *High Blood Pressure*)

IMPOTENCE (Erectile Dysfunction)

Impotence is the inability to attain or maintain an erection of the penis for satisfactory sexual performance. Physical factors are the primary cause (especially atherosclerosis) 90 percent of the time. Smoking, diabetes, and increasing age are all contributing factors.

Common Symptoms

Inability to become erect can be occasional (normal), develop gradually (as a physical problem), or occur sometimes but not at others (in which case it may have a psychological basis). It is normal to have an erection during sleep (primarily with dreams), so, if this occurs, you probably do not have a physical cause for erectile dysfunction and should seek counseling. The steps that follow address physical causes of impotence.

What You Need to Know

Atherosclerosis of the penile artery is present in more than half the men over the age of 50 who have erectile dysfunction. Efforts to prevent or treat atherosclerosis are the best methods of preventing impotence (see the section on cholesterol for further treatment recommendations). In addition, alcohol and tobacco use can both inhibit sexual function and should be avoided.

General Recommendations

Diet: A diet rich in whole foods and adequate protein can help improve erectile function. The best protein sources are fish, chicken, turkey, and lean cuts of meat. Special foods recommended for enhanced virility include liver, oysters, nuts, seeds, and legumes because of their zinc content.

Exercise: Sexual enhancement is noted in men who regularly exercise and is correlated with the degree of individual improvement in fitness. I recommend aerobic exercise, which improves oxygen flow to the genitalia and may also stimulate production of sex hormones.

Your Balanced Healing Action Plan for Impotence

Step 1: Take Appropriate Chinese Herbal Remedies

I first recommend taking Chinese herbal formulas, which have the advantages that you do not need to plan your sexual activity and they have little to no side effects. A common formula is *You Gui Wan.* Consult a practitioner qualified in Chinese herbal medicine to determine which Chinese herbal formulas are the best for your particular syndromes. You should notice improvement within three weeks, but you may need to take them longer for full benefit. (See Appendix A, under "Chinese Herbs," for further information.)

> Fifty-three year-old Jay, a pharmacist, was able to get an erection, but he could not keep it hard enough to complete intercourse. He had been prescribed Viagra, but it hadn't helped. I prescribed a Chinese herbal formula to increase his Kidney Yang, and within one week his wife was pleased to report that their sex life had improved dramatically.

Step 2: Undergo Acupuncture

Along with Chinese herbs, I recommend acupuncture. Acupuncture takes longer to obtain benefits, but it can give you longer lasting results and decrease or eliminate the need to take drugs or supplements. Principal points usually are found on the chest, back, abdomen, legs, and ankles. Ear points include External Genitalia, and Testicles. Always seek evaluation and treatment from a practitioner certified in acupuncture. (See Appendix A, under "Acupuncture," for guidance on finding a qualified acupuncturist and for further explanation of the different acupuncture techniques.) You should notice improvement within six treatments, but you might need additional sessions for maximum benefits.

Step 3: Take an Herbal Product Containing Ginseng, Saw Palmetto, Wild Oat, Stinging Nettle, Damiana, Yohimbe, Sarsaparilla, Kola Nut, and/or Puncture Weed

Several herbs can be effective in improving erectile function. Look for a product that contains some or all of the following herbs: ginseng, saw palmetto, wild oat, stinging nettle, damiana, yohimbe, sarsaparilla, kola nut, and puncture weed. You should experience improvement within one to three months.

Step 4: Take L-Arginine or DHEA

If you still have erectile problems due to atherosclerosis, try L-arginine (5g per day), which increases blood flow to the penis, thus improving sexual function. DHEA (50mg daily) has also been shown to improve all aspects of sexual function, but it may take three to six months to become effective.

Step 5: Take Prescription Viagra

If the previous steps have not improved your condition, your doctor can prescribe Viagra (sildenafil) or vardenafil. These drugs are very effective, but you must take them an hour before sex. Vardenafil has been shown to improve erectile function, regardless of the cause, in 85 percent of men. **Caution:** Viagra or vardenafil can cause heart attacks and death in men who have heart disease and/or are taking nitrates, so take it only under a physician's direction.

Step 6: Take Yohimbe, Panax Ginseng, and/or Gingko Biloba

If your erectile dysfunction persists, you can try yohimbe, which is the Chinese herbal equivalent of Viagra. Look for a product that contains a standardized 15mg content of yohimbine (the active ingredient), and take it two to three times per day. (There is a prescription form of 5.4mg tablets.) The advantage of yohimbe is that you don't have to plan your sexual encounters. However, yohimbine can negate the effects of hypertensive medications and can enhance tricyclic antidepressants such as amitriptyline and nortriptyline. Do not use yohimbe if you have heart disease or angina (its effects are much like Viagra), have kidney disease, or are a woman. Yohimbe can also lower blood glucose, so use it with caution if you have diabetes.

Panax Ginseng (5mg content of ginsenosides) and gingko biloba (160mg to 240mg per day) can also be effective for some men. You can take all of these herbs together.

Step 7: Try More Invasive Treatment Options

If you are still having impotence problems, there are several more invasive techniques that can adequately help you attain erections. The choice of which method to use is a personal one and you should discuss this with a urologist. These include the following:

- **Vacuum Pump:** You insert your penis into a plastic tube and use a hand-held vacuum pump to draw blood into the penis. A constriction device placed around the base of the penis prevents blood from leaking out. You then remove the plastic tube for intercourse. You must remove the constriction device within 30 minutes.

- **MUSE intraurethral suppository:** You insert an ultra-thin applicator into the tip of your penis and gently push a plunger that releases a small, rice-size pellet of Prostaglandin E1 (Alprostadil). This medication dilates the blood vessels, causing an erection within 10 to 15 minutes. The primary, and most bothersome, side effect is penile aching.
- **Injection Therapy:** You inject Alprostadil directly into your penis. Erection again occurs within 10 to 15 minutes and lasts 45 to 60 minutes. A rare side effect is priapism (an erection lasting more than four hours), which can damage your penis and requires prompt medical attention.
- **Surgical Implants:** There are several mechanical devices that can be implanted into the penis. The most popular is an inflatable implant that is activated by squeezing a pump in the scrotum. These implants are not visible and are much like breast implants. This method requires a surgical procedure, which is covered by Medicare.

INCONTINENCE

Incontinence is the involuntary loss of urine. There are three main types: *stress incontinence,* caused by weakness of the muscles surrounding the opening of the urethra (the tube from the bladder); *urge incontinence,* due to uncontrolled contractions of the bladder; and *overflow incontinence,* caused by decreased sensation of the bladder. Besides embarrassment and inconvenience, leakage of urine can lead to bladder or urinary tract infections. Incontinence is eight times more common in women than men.

Common Symptoms

- **Stress incontinence:** A cough, sneeze, or laughing can cause leakage.
- **Urge incontinence:** Leakage occurs as soon as the bladder is full.
- **Overflow incontinence:** Unexpected, sudden leakage.

What You Need to Know

Incontinence is a potential side effect of many medications, including diuretics, sedatives, antidepressants, antihistamines, and many forms of synthetic estrogen. If you take any of these medications, check the *Physician's Desk Reference* (PDR), and if the medication you take can cause incontinence, change to another one. Urinating at specified times during the day can also help increase bladder tone and train the bladder to function better.

General Recommendations

Diet: Discontinuing beverages that contain caffeine, including coffee, tea, and soft drinks, can often reduce incontinence.

Your Balanced Healing Action Plan for Incontinence

■ Injectable devices, artificial slings, and tension-free vaginal tape have not been thoroughly researched and cannot be recommended at this time.

Step 1: For Women: Practice Kegel and Pelvic Floor Exercises

Kegel exercises increase the strength and tone of the pubococcygeus muscle, the one that controls your urine flow. When urinating, stop the flow to feel this muscle; however, do not exercise the muscle during urination. You can also place your finger inside your vagina and squeeze down; the muscle will tighten. Once you learn which muscle it is, you can voluntarily contract and relax this muscle whenever you want. The more you exercise it, the stronger it will become. There are other, more specific exercises to strengthen the pelvic floor muscles, but you must learn these from registered physical therapists specifically trained in these techniques (check with your state physical therapy association). These exercises are especially valuable after childbirth, for preventing stress incontinence.

Step 2: Receive Acupuncture

Acupuncture is very effective in reducing or resolving incontinence by increasing the tone of the bladder muscles and improving bladder sensation. It is beneficial for both men and women. Principal points usually are found on the back, abdomen, and legs. Acupuncture can be used as an adjunct to Step 1. Always seek evaluation and treatment from a practitioner certified in acupuncture. (See Appendix A, under "Acupuncture," for guidance on finding a qualified acupuncturist and for further explanation on different acupuncture techniques.) You should notice improvement within six treatments, but you might need additional sessions for maximum benefits.

Step 3: Practice Biofeedback

If you still have incontinence problems, biofeedback can lead to improved or complete bladder control, so I recommend trying this method next. (For more information and guidance on how to find a qualified biofeedback practitioner, see Appendix A and/or Appendix C, under "Mind-Body Techniques.")

Step 4: Take an Appropriate Prescription Medication

For continuing leakage, your doctor can prescribe various medications for the different types of incontinence. Estrogen has been shown to lessen the irritation of incontinence in some women, but it can worsen incontinence in others. If you're taking hormone replacement, I recommend taking natural estrogen, or Raloxiphene, the only synthetic estrogen that does not cause incontinence problems. (See Appendix B, under "Sex Hormones," for further information.) Long-acting tolterodine (Detrol) or oxybutynin (Ditropan) are effective for both overactive bladder and urge incontinence. Duloxetine can be beneficial for stress incontinence.

Step 5: Take Appropriate Chinese Herbal Remedies

If you are still having incontinence problems, there are several Chinese herbal formulas that can be helpful. *Zuo Gui Wan/You Gui Yin* can reduce frequent urination, especially at night. *Jin Suo Gu Jing Wan* can help with urge incontinence. Consult a practitioner qualified in Chinese herbal medicine to determine which Chinese herbal formulas are the best for your particular syndromes. You should notice improvement within three weeks, but you may need to take them longer for complete relief. (See Appendix A, under "Chinese Herbs," for further information.)

> Frances, a 51-year-old jewelry store owner, had urge incontinence with overactive bladder, a combination that made it especially difficult for her to enjoy social activities. Her urologist had placed her on Detrol, but this drug had not controlled all of her symptoms. I referred her to a physical therapist, who taught Frances various exercises to strengthen her pelvic muscles. I then performed acupuncture. After one month, her remaining incontinence had gone away, but when Frances tried to stop taking the Detrol, she still had intermittent leakage. I prescribed the Chinese herbal formula *Jin Suo Gu Jing Wan*, continued acupuncture treatments, and had Frances continue her exercises. Within three months, her leakage stopped completely, and Frances was once again able to go to the movies, go shopping, and enjoy spending time with her friends without worry.

Step 6: Receive Collagen Injection Treatments

If you still have incontinence symptoms, you may need an invasive procedure to correct any structural problems. Collagen injection can be beneficial for stress incontinence, but it usually breaks down over time. A new injectable, called Durasphere, is as effective as collagen but is longer lasting.

Step 7: Use Devices

Some women obtain relief from using pessaries and cone-shaped vaginal weights when the previous steps don't help. Consult a urologist for specific recommendations.

Step 8: Undergo Surgery

As a last resort, surgery may be necessary to repair weakened or damaged pelvic muscles (often the result of pregnancy or childbirth). Suspension and sling procedures are the most effective. Consult a urologist for further information and recommendations.

INFERTILITY

Infertility is the inability to conceive a child after one year of unprotected sex. It can occur in couples who have never conceived (*primary infertility*) and in couples who have previously conceived (*secondary infertility*). There are several causes of infertility, including ovulation disorders, polycystic ovary disease, endometriosis, tubal damage, and low sperm count.

Common Symptoms

The only symptom of infertility is inability to conceive.

What You Need to Know

There are many physical causes that prevent conception, so it is important for both partners to be thoroughly evaluated. Many of these physical problems can be successfully treated and conception made possible. In addition, certain factors can contribute to infertility. Smoking decreases sperm count and mobility. Many drugs, especially antihypertensives, as well as herbal products, including selenium, melatonin, echinacea, gingko, and St. John's wort, may contribute to infertility. You should not take these medications or products if you are trying to have a baby.

General Recommendations

Diet: Increase the amount of vegetables (8 to 10 servings per day), fruits (2 to 4 servings per day), and legumes, especially soy, that you eat. These foods contain antioxidants and/or *phytoestrogens* (plant estrogens) that can help promote fertilization, especially in women.

Your Balanced Healing Action Plan for Infertility

Step 1: Wear Loose-Fitting Clothing

To be viable, sperm must be below body temperature. Infertile men should wear boxer shorts, and take a cold shower or apply ice to the scrotum on a daily basis.

Step 2: Have Intercourse During Ovulation

Less frequent intercourse and waiting for intercourse at the time of ovulation is essential, so that the sperm count can build and be available at the best time for fertility. The woman should take basal temperature readings as soon as she wakes in the morning. Ovulation causes an increase in temperature of one to two degrees.

Step 3: Men Should Take Zinc Sulfate, Folic Acid, Vitamin E, Vitamin C, and Beta-Carotene

In addition to the previous steps, I recommend men taking daily zinc sulfate (65mg), folic acid (5mg), vitamin E (800 IU), vitamin C (1,200mg), and beta-carotene (100,000 IU). Zinc is essential in every aspect of male reproduction, folic acid can increase sperm count by up to 74 percent, and the other vitamins negate oxidation damage that may harm sperm. It may take several months before conception occurs.

Step 4: Take the Appropriate Chinese Herbal Remedies

Chinese herbal formulas have had success at improving fertility in both men and women and can be used if the above steps are not helpful. There are several formulas that have been used, including *You Gui Wan* for men, and *Yi Guan Jian*, *Fu Ke Zong Zi Wan* or *Yang Rong Wan* for women. These formulas are not known to harm a fetus if you do become pregnant. Consult a practitioner qualified in Chinese herbal medicine to determine which Chinese herbal formulas are the best for your particular syndromes. You should notice improvement within one to three months, but you may need to take them longer. (See Appendix A, under "Chinese Herbs," for further information.)

Step 5: Undergo Acupuncture

If you still have not conceived, use acupuncture next or in addition to taking Chinese herbals. Principal points for men usually are found on the back, legs, and ankles, and ear points include external genitalia, testis, and endocrine. Principal points for women usually are found on the abdomen, back, and legs, with ear points including uterus, ovary, genital control, and endocrine. Always seek evaluation and treatment from a practitioner certified in acupuncture. (See Appendix A, under "Acupuncture," for guidance on finding a qualified acupuncturist and for further explanation of the different acupuncture techniques.) It may require 6 to 12 sessions to help you conceive.

> Irene, 35, and Bill, 38, were married and co-owners of a small business. They had one child two years after they were married, but then they were unable to conceive for the next six years. Thorough medical evaluations turned up no structural problems or abnormalities. They had tried the usual methods of basal temperature-taking and avoiding heat, and had only weekly intercourse, but without success. I recommended zinc, vitamin C, vitamin E, and beta-carotene for Bill, as well as a prescribed Chinese herbal formula to increase his Kidney Yang. I recommended *Yi Guan Jian* for Irene and also performed several acupuncture treatments on both of them. After three months, Irene became pregnant and subsequently delivered a healthy baby boy.

Step 6: For Men: Take L-Carnitine and Arginine

If you still have not conceived, start taking L-carnitine (300mg to 1000mg three times daily), which can improve sperm motility, but it is expensive. Arginine (4g per day) is essential for sperm formation, and can be helpful if your sperm count is more than 20 million. You can take these supplements with the previous steps.

Step 7: For Women: Take Chasteberry

If you have still not conceived, take chasteberry (solid extract, standardized to 0.5 percent agnuside, 175mg to 225mg daily), which works through its hormonal effects. However, it may take three to seven months to be effective. Chasteberry may decrease sexual libido.

Step 8: For Women: Take Prescription Fertility Medications

Only if the previous steps have failed should you consider taking prescription medications such as Clomiphene, human menopausal gonadotropin, or follicle stimulating hormone. Although these drugs can increase fertility, they are expensive and can cause multiple conceptions. Consult with your gynecologist.

Step 9: For Women: Undergo Surgery

If structural problems are detected and thought to be a cause of your infertility, surgical methods, including laparoscopic ovarian drilling, tubal catheterization, and lysis of tubal adhesions may be beneficial. Consult with your obstetrician for further information.

Step 10: Undergo Assisted Fertilization Methods

Artificial insemination and in vitro (test tube) fertilization are sometimes successful for couples who have not achieved fertilization by the other methods. Consult with your obstetrician for further information.

INFLAMMATORY BOWEL DISEASE (IBD); CROHN'S DISEASE; ULCERATIVE COLITIS

IBD is a general term describing a group of chronic inflammatory disorders of the intestines. *Crohn's disease* involves inflammation throughout the entire thickness of the bowel wall, usually involving the end of the small intestines and/or the colon. *Ulcerative colitis* is limited to the lining of the colon. Both diseases share a number of features, but each has specific symptoms. The cause of IBD is unknown, but the disorder may be a result of immune dysfunction. People with Crohn's disease can develop *fistulas* (openings that channel through the intestines and can cause obstruction in the GI tract) and nonintestinal problems, including inflammation of the eyes, skin, joints, and kidney stones. The development of fistulas means that other organs next to the bowels can become involved. Women often have gynecological involvement symptoms such as vaginal bleeding, discharge, or cramping, which may occur before bowel involvement is noted. With *ulcerative colitis,* abscesses and *fissures* (deep cracks) can develop, also causing bowel obstruction. Both diseases can predispose to colorectal cancer.

Common Symptoms: Crohn's Disease

- Severe abdominal pain
- Diarrhea
- Cramps in the right lower abdomen
- Loss of appetite
- Low-grade fever
- Fatigue
- Weight loss
- Arthritis in some cases

Common Symptoms: Ulcerative Colitis

- Bloody diarrhea
- Cramping in the lower abdomen
- Weight loss
- Fever

What You Need to Know

People with IBD, especially Crohn's disease, may have to undergo multiple surgeries to repair fistulas and relieve obstructions. If you smoke cigarettes, stopping this habit will significantly reduce your risk for recurrent surgeries. (See "Nicotine Addiction" for help on quitting smoking.) Aspirin and nonsteroidal anti-inflammatory drugs (NSAIDs) increase the risk of relapse and should be avoided.

General Recommendations

Diet is very important, both in helping reduce symptoms and in supplementing lost nutrients caused by the inflammation. I recommend a high-complex carbohydrate, high-fiber diet (HCF). This diet asks you to follow these daily guidelines in planning your meals:

- 70 percent to 75 percent complex carbohydrates
- 15 percent to 20 percent proteins
- 5 percent to 10 percent fats

The HCF diet is plentiful in grains (bread, cereal, rice, and pasta), starchy vegetables (potatoes, corn, peas), and legumes (dried beans, peas, lentils), and is packed with vitamins, minerals, and fiber. You should consume at least 20 to 35 grams of fiber. (Also, consult with a registered dietician for further guidance. Go to www.eatright.org, the Web site of the American Dietetic Association, to find a qualified dietician.)

Use caution if you eat wheat bran, which can be difficult to handle in IBD. Because IBD may also be linked to food allergies, a rotation diet can be used in conjunction (see "Food Allergies" for more information). To reduce the incidence of kidney stones, a low oxalate diet is recommended. Again, I recommend that you consult with a certified nutritionist to help you plan your meals.

Meditation and imagery methods can reduce stress, help control symptoms, and prevent recurrences; everyone with these conditions should use these techniques. (For further information and examples, see "Meditation," under "Simple Healing Steps for All Health Conditions," page 79, and Appendix A, under "Mind-Body Techniques.")

Your Balanced Healing Action Plan for Inflammatory Bowel Disease

Step 1: Take Appropriate Prescription Medications

Because these diseases can cause significant problems, it is essential that you get them under control by first using prescription medications. For Crohn's disease, sulfasalazine is the primary treatment. If needed, corticosteroids may be necessary for short periods of time to reduce acute inflammation, along with the sulfasalazine. For ulcerative colitis, azathioprine, sulfasalazine and salicylates (Pentasa, Rowasa) are often used, as well as corticosteroids to reduce and control the inflammation. Loperamide (Imodium) or codeine derivatives to control diarrhea should be taken only with a doctor's approval. The drug 6–mercaptopurine can be beneficial for both Crohn's and ulcerative colitis by inducing remission.

Step 2: Detoxify Your Colon and Take Probiotics

After your symptoms have stabilized, I recommend a one-to-two-week detoxification of the colon using herbal supplements. The inflammation in your colon may be caused or made worse by toxins, chemicals, and old fecal matter that have been retained, and detoxification will remove these substances and soothe your colon. Look for a product that contains some or all of the following: apple pectin, slippery elm bark, marshmallow root, licorice root, fennel seed, activated willow charcoal, and montmorillonite clay. This combination can be taken with the medications in Step 1. (See Appendix A, under "Detoxification Therapy," for further information and cautions.)

When the disease is under control, I also recommend taking probiotics with the colon detoxification. These consist of live cultures of organisms (the "good" bacteria) that help digest and excrete food properly. A good probiotic will re-establish the good bacteria and improve function of the entire GI tract. Of the beneficial microorganisms in probiotics, *L. acidophilus* and *bifidobacteria* are the best. Other beneficial bacteria include *L. salivarius*, *L. rhamnosus*, *L. plantarum*, *streptococcus thermophilus*, *L. bulgaricus*, *L. casei*, and *L. sporogenes*. You should notice improvement in two to six weeks. You may have increased gas or bloating initially and should reduce your dosage if this occurs.

You might think that yogurt contains beneficial microorganisms that can take the place of probiotics. Yogurt products do contain beneficial microorganisms, but they are not the most important or potent. Also, many yogurt products are pasteurized after they are made to increase shelf life, but this kills most of the good bacteria and destroys all the benefits. Don't rely on eating yogurt to re-colonize your GI tract.

Step 3: Undergo Acupuncture

Acupuncture can provide long-term relief of IBD, especially in decreasing the frequency and severity of flare-ups. Principal points usually are found on the legs, abdomen, and arms. Ear points include large intestine and small intestine. If acupuncture is effective, you can then reduce the medications in Step 1, under your doctor's guidance. Always seek evaluation and treatment from a practitioner certified in acupuncture. (See Appendix A, under "Acupuncture," for guidance on finding a qualified acupuncturist and for further explanation on different acupuncture techniques.) You should notice improvement within six treatments, but you might need additional sessions for maximum benefits, as well as maintenance sessions for flare-ups.

Step 4: Take Vitamins, Minerals, and Antioxidants

There are many nutrients that can help reduce symptoms of IBD, and I recommend that you take them along with the previous steps. I especially recommend omega-3 fatty acids, found in flaxseed oil (1 tablespoon daily) or fish oil (2g to 4g daily), to reduce inflammation. A good multivitamin/mineral formulation is also helpful, especially one that contains zinc, folic acid, and vitamin B_{12}, because these vitamins/minerals are commonly found to be deficient in IBD. (See Appendix B for a recommended multivitamin formula.)

Certain antioxidants might decrease colon inflammation, although this has not yet been proven conclusively. These include glutathione and N-acetylcysteine (one of the components of glutathione). Doses are 250mg daily for glutathione and 600mg two to three times daily for N-acetylcysteine. These supplements have minimal side effects and may be very helpful. You can take all of these supplements together, and you should notice improvement in one to three months.

Daniel, a 48-year-old dermatologist, has had Crohn's disease for several years. He takes sulfasalazine and has been on several rounds of corticosteroids for flare-ups, which have occurred five or six times a year. He has had three surgeries for fistulas and obstructions. Despite the medications, he still had cramping and diarrhea. I recommended colon detoxification using an herbal formula, and then I placed him on fish oil. After one month, his diarrhea and cramping stopped. Daniel did well for a few months but then had a flare-up, for which his gastroenterologist wanted him to take steroids. However, Daniel didn't want to take the drugs because of the side effects (swelling, nausea, weight gain) so he came back to see me. I started him on acupuncture, which ended the flare-up within a few days. He completed one course (10 treatments) of acupuncture and has not had another flare-up in more than a year.

Step 5: Take an Appropriate Homeopathic Remedy

If the previous steps do not reduce or eliminate your symptoms, try homeopathy. To relieve diarrhea, there are several remedies, to be taken every 30 minutes, up to four doses per day. These include *Podophyllum* (6c) for green, painless diarrhea with stomach cramps or gurgling, worst in the morning; *Arsenicum album* (6c) for profuse diarrhea with anxiety, chills, and burning or crampy stomach; and *Mercurius corrosivus* (6c) for blood and mucus in the stool and a feeling of not being emptied. Consult a qualified homeopathist for guidance on which remedies will be most beneficial and for proper dosages. You should notice improvement in one to two weeks. (See Appendix A, under "Homeopathy," for guidance on finding a qualified homeopathist and for further information.)

Step 6: Use the Nambudripad Allergy Elimination Treatment (NAET)

If your symptoms or flare-ups continue, the underlying cause may be food allergies. If this is a possibility, I recommend undergoing the Nambudripad Allergy Elimination Treatment (NAET) program. It combines acupuncture, kinesiology, chiropractic, herbs, and nutrition to desensitize you to foods to which you are allergic. It may take several months for you to experience improvement, depending on how many allergens are sensitizing you. (See Appendix A, under "NAET," and the section on food allergies for further explanation.)

Step 7: Take the Prescription Drug Remicade

For *refractory disease* (not responsive to other treatments), a drug given intravenously, infliximab (Remicade), often reduces symptoms and can be used if the previous steps have not been effective.

Step 8: Undergo Surgery

As a last resort, surgery may be necessary if you develop fistulas, abscesses, fissures, or obstructions that are not relieved quickly by the above methods. Surgery may involve taking out parts of the small intestine in Crohn's disease, and the entire large intestine in ulcerative colitis. After surgery, you might develop a vitamin B_{12} deficiency, so have your blood levels checked every six months, and take a supplement if they are low.

INSOMNIA

Insomnia is difficulty falling asleep or staying asleep. Sleep is a very important aspect of health, and insomnia can lead to many health problems, including mental dysfunction (memory, concentration), depression of your immune system, and psychological problems. Causes of insomnia include physical illnesses (such as pain, heartburn, breathing disorders, hot flashes, diabetes, acid reflux, ulcers, Parkinson's disease, kidney disease, and hyperthyroidism), stress, excessive caffeine, irregular sleeping patterns (naps), anxiety or depression, alcohol, drugs, and many prescription medications.

Common Symptoms

- Persistent trouble falling asleep
- Waking up during the night with inability to go back to sleep
- Waking up earlier than usual

What You Need to Know

Psychological factors, especially anxiety, tension, and depression, are often the cause of insomnia, so these need to be addressed if you have them (see the sections on depression or anxiety for further treatment recommendations). Drugs that commonly cause insomnia include alcohol; beta-blockers; caffeine; some antidepressants; decongestants; some cold, asthma, and allergy medications; drugs for digestive disorders; and thyroid medications. If you are on any of these drugs, consult your doctor about changing to another drug that does not cause insomnia.

General Recommendations

Exercise: Moderate exercise, both aerobic and resistance, can help you sleep better. Although some authorities advise no exercise just before sleep, recent studies have disproved this (for recommendations on exercise, see "Simple Healing Steps for All Health Conditions," page 79).

Meditation: Because stress and tension are major factors in insomnia, meditation is very beneficial, whether done during the waking hours or at bedtime. I recommend listening to a meditation tape specifically designed for sleep when you go to bed.

Your Balanced Healing Action Plan for Insomnia

Step 1: Change Your Lifestyle

There are several lifestyle suggestions that may help you sleep better, which include the following:

- Limit the time you spend in bed not sleeping (don't read or watch TV).
- Don't substitute a nap for a good night's sleep.
- Limit your intake of caffeine-containing foods and beverages; don't drink coffee after 2:00 p.m.
- Think warmth, such as keeping your extremities warm with socks or mittens.
- Don't drink warm milk.
- Don't go to bed hungry. A small snack helps; a large meal doesn't.
- Don't smoke for at least two hours before bedtime.
- Face your alarm clock away from the bed.
- Maintain a regular sleep schedule seven days a week.

Step 2: Take Valerian, 5-HTP, and/or Passion Flower

If you have anxiety that is keeping you up at night or waking you at night, Valerian (up to 400mg per night) is very effective for both insomnia and anxiety. If you have depression that is keeping you awake, take 5-HTP (100mg to 300mg per night), which can also help if you have anxiety with your depression. You can combine either of these herbs with Passiflora incarnata (Passion Flower; 6ml to 8ml of the tincture or as a tea) for better results.

Step 3: Take Appropriate Chinese Herbal Remedies

Chinese herbal formulas containing Schizandra fruit can be very effective if the previous steps don't work. Formulations that can be helpful include *An Mien Pian, An Shen Bu Xin Wan, An Shui Wan, Bai Zi Yang Xing Wan, Suan Zao Ren Tang,* or *Tian Wang Bu Xin Dan.* Consult a practitioner qualified in Chinese herbal medicine to determine which Chinese herbal formulas are the best for your particular syndromes. You should notice improvement within three days to a week, but you may need to take them longer for complete benefit. (See Appendix A, under "Chinese Herbs," for further information.)

Step 4: Undergo Acupuncture

If the previous steps fail to lead you to a good night's sleep, I recommend acupuncture, which can address both the insomnia and underlying factors. Principal points usually are found on the legs, arms, and feet. Ear points include insomnia 1, insomnia 2, and pineal gland (which controls biorhythms).

Ear tacks placed in the insomnia points can be very effective as well. These are small needles that are embedded in an adhesive bandage and then are pressed in specific points in the ear. You can massage these needles several times a day for added stimulation. These needles remain in the ear for as long as possible, (on the average, one week) and are replaced when they fall out. For improved results, you can tap on the needle at nighttime to stimulate the point.

You should always seek evaluation and treatment from a practitioner certified in acupuncture. (See Appendix A, under "Acupuncture," for guidance on finding a qualified acupuncturist and for further explanation of the different acupuncture techniques.) You should sleep better within a few nights, but additional sessions may be necessary for maximum benefits.

Edna, a 27-year-old photographer, was healthy and active, but she started having trouble falling asleep at night. She had tried various herbal remedies as well as prescription drugs, but they were either not effective or made her too drowsy the next day, so she really didn't like taking them. I placed ear tacks in the two insomnia points in her ear; they remained in her ear for two weeks. She reported no problem falling or staying asleep during that time, and she had only occasional insomnia when the tacks eventually fell out.

Step 5: Take Melatonin

If the previous steps have not helped you sleep, try melatonin (0.3mg to 1.0mg per night), which is effective for insomnia primarily when body melatonin levels are low. You should notice improvement within a few days.

Step 6: Take Prescription Sleep-Aid Medications

If all else fails to put you to sleep, there are several prescription medications that are very effective, including benzodiazepines (Halcion, Dalmane), Ambien, and Sonata; the latter medication has a short duration of action and can be taken if you wake up in the middle of the night. However, these drugs can cause drowsiness the next day and in the long term can cause abnormal sleep patterns and dependence. Do not take prescription sleep medications for more than 14 days at a time.

IRRITABLE BOWEL SYNDROME (IBS); SPASTIC COLITIS

Irritable bowel syndrome (IBS) is a disorder of the intestines in which *peristalsis* (wavelike movements that move food) becomes irregular and uncoordinated. IBS is the most common of all digestive disorders. The cause is unknown, but stress and food sensitivities are important factors.

Common Symptoms

- Abdominal pain with diarrhea or constipation
- Flatulence
- Nausea
- Bloating

General Recommendations

Diet: Often, increasing dietary fiber will help control the symptoms of IBS. Food allergies may also play a role, so an elimination diet may be necessary to determine which foods may be causative factors (for further information, see the section on Food Allergies on page 210). Foods high in refined sugar and fats also can contribute to IBS, and you should avoid or decrease them.

Exercise: Walking at an aerobic pace for 20 to 30 minutes has been shown to reduce symptoms, and I definitely recommend it.

Meditation: Stress and anxiety can contribute to (or even cause) the symptoms of IBS, so meditation is valuable to relieve these factors. (For further information and examples, see "Meditation," under "Simple Healing Steps for All Health Conditions," page 79.)

Your Balanced Healing Action Plan for Irritable Bowel Syndrome

Step 1: Detoxify Your Colon and Take Probiotics

The dysfunction of your colon may be caused or made worse because of toxins, chemicals, and old fecal matter that have been retained. I first recommend that you undergo a one- to two-week detoxification of the colon, using herbal supplements to remove these substances and soothe your colon. Look for a product that contains some or all of the following: apple pectin, slippery elm bark, marshmallow root, licorice root, fennel seed, activated willow charcoal, and montmorillonite clay. (See Appendix A, under "Detoxification Therapy," for further information and precautions.)

I also recommend taking probiotics with the enzymes. These consist of live cultures of organisms (the "good" bacteria) that help digest and excrete food properly. Of the beneficial microorganisms in probiotics, *L. acidophilus* and *bifidobacteria* are the best. Other beneficial bacteria include *L. salivarius, L. rhamnosus, L. plantarum, streptococcus thermophilus, L. bulgaricus, L. casei,* and *L. sporogenes.* You should notice improvement within two to six weeks. You may have increased gas or bloating initially and should reduce your dosage if this occurs.

You might think that yogurt contains beneficial microorganisms that can take the place of probiotics. Yogurt products do contain beneficial microorganisms, but they are not the most important or potent. Also, many yogurt products are pasteurized after they are made to increase shelf life, and this kills most of the good bacteria and destroys all the benefits. Don't rely on eating yogurt to recolonize your GI tract.

Step 2: Take Appropriate Chinese Herbal Remedies

After colon cleansing, if you still have symptoms of IBS, I recommend taking Chinese herbal formulas. I recommend the formula *Bo He Wan*, but there are several others that are beneficial, such as *Mu Xiang Shun Qi Wan*. Consult a practitioner qualified in Chinese herbal medicine to determine which Chinese herbal formulas are the best for your particular syndromes. You should notice improvement within three weeks, but you may need to take them longer for complete relief. (See Appendix A, under "Chinese Herbs," for further information.)

Step 3: Undergo Acupuncture

Along with Chinese herbs, or if these herbs have not helped, I recommend undergoing acupuncture, which can eliminate the symptoms of IBS for long periods of time. Principal points usually are found on the feet, legs, and abdomen. Always seek evaluation and treatment from a practitioner certified in acupuncture. (See Appendix A, under "Acupuncture," for guidance on finding a qualified acupuncturist and for further explanation of the different acupuncture techniques.) You should notice improvement within six treatments, but you might need additional sessions for maximum benefits.

Step 4: Undergo Interactive Imagery or Hypnosis

If your symptoms are still present, your IBS may have an underlying psychological component that needs to be unearthed and resolved. Interactive imagery and hypnosis are both effective means of treating IBS. Interactive imagery is a mind-body method in which you mentally interact with images that represent your emotions. It is a powerful method to uncover and deal with subconscious psychological issues of which you may not be aware. (See Appendix A, under "Mind-Body Techniques," for a more detailed explanation and help in finding a qualified practitioner.) The mechanism of action for hypnosis is unknown, but some studies report a 96 percent success rate in reducing IBS symptoms.

Lorraine is a 34-year-old sculptor and a patient of mine who had had irritable bowel syndrome since 4th grade. She always had to be near a bathroom due to sudden cramping and diarrhea. Over the years, different doctors had tried her on various conventional medications, but none ever worked very well. I started her on the Chinese herbal formula *Bo He Wan*, which eliminated most of her symptoms. However, every time she tried to stop taking the Chinese herbs, her symptoms came back. At that point, I began acupuncture and also interactive imagery. The imagery revealed that in 4th grade, another student stayed home a lot because of sickness (nausea and vomiting), and she began doing the same. Her parents also divorced that year; the divorce caused many repressed negative feelings, which all came out during the imagery sessions. Within two months, her symptoms went away completely and have not returned.

Step 5: Take Enteric-Coated Peppermint Oil, Flaxseed Oil, or Five-Herb Formula

If the previous steps fail to provide complete relief of your symptoms, try enteric-coated peppermint oil (0.2ml to 0.4ml twice a day) or flaxseed oil (1 tablespoon daily), which can help bulk up your stool and reduce diarrhea. Or take a five-herb formula consisting of chamomile flower, peppermint leaf, caraway fruit, licorice root, and lemon balm leaves. (This formula is a modification of Iberogast, an herbal preparation now available in health food stores.) You should notice improvement within one to three months.

Step 6: Use the Nambudripad Allergy Elimination Treatment (NAET)

Food sensitivities can be a cause of IBS or make symptoms worse. If this is a possibility or your symptoms still persist despite following the previous steps, I recommend undergoing the Nambudripad Allergy Elimination Treatment (NAET). It combines acupuncture, kinesiology, chiropractic, herbs, and nutrition to desensitize you to foods. It may take several months for its effectiveness to be observed, depending on how many allergens are sensitizing you. (See Appendix A, under "NAET," and the section on food allergies for further explanation.)

Step 7: Take an Appropriate Homeopathic Remedy

If your IBS symptoms are still causing you discomfort, try homeopathic remedies such as *Mercurius vivus, Nux vomica,* and *Ignatia.* You should consult a qualified homeopathist for guidance on which remedies will be most beneficial, and for proper dosages. You should notice improvement in one to two weeks. (See Appendix A, under "Homeopathy," for guidance on finding a qualified homeopathist and for further information.)

Step 8: Take Hyoscamine, Diclyclomine, or Loperamide

If nothing else has worked, your doctor can prescribe medications such as hyoscamine (Levsin), diclyclomine (Bentyl), or loperamide (Imodium), all of which can offer temporary relief. BuSpar, an antianxiety medication, can also be helpful for some people. Another drug called Lotronex was found to be effective for IBS, but due to several deaths and adverse gastrointestinal side effects, it was withdrawn from the market by the FDA. It has now been reapproved for IBS with severe diarrhea, but only under strict regulations; it can be prescribed only by approved physicians. Zelnorm is a new medication for women with IBS who have constipation.

KIDNEY STONES

Kidney stones are collections of calcium, *struvite* (a combination of ammonia, magnesium, and phosphorus), or uric acid that clump together in the kidney or ureter (the tube that passes from the kidney to the bladder). Various diseases can cause kidney stones, including gout, inflammatory bowel disease (IBD), sarcoidosis, and chronic urinary tract infections. Other causes include dehydration, vitamin D excess, and antacids that contain calcium. Kidney stones usually do not lead to harmful effects, but they can indicate underlying diseases that need evaluation and treatment.

Common Symptoms

- Excruciating or sharp pain that begins in the flank (side) and can go to the groin
- Nausea and vomiting
- Profuse sweating
- Blood in the urine
- Decreased urine output
- Abdominal distention
- Fever and chills (if infected)

What You Need to Know

The major purpose of treatment is to prevent recurrences of kidney stones. Because there are several types of kidney stones, it is helpful to strain your urine and collect the stone so that its composition can be determined.

General Recommendations

Diet: Kidney stone formation is directly associated with several dietary factors, including low fiber intake, high refined carbohydrates, high alcohol consumption, increased animal protein, high fat intake, and high calcium/low vitamin D/magnesium-enriched milk products. Reversing these dietary habits will help you prevent kidney stones. In addition, I also recommend high intake of fluids (36 to 48 ounces per day). Contrary to popular belief, calcium supplementation DOES NOT increase the frequency of stones; on the contrary, restricted calcium does. If your stones are made of uric acid, you should avoid foods with high purine content (which breaks down into uric acid). These include red meats in particular, and shellfish, yeast, herring, sardines, mackerel, and anchovies.

Your Balanced Healing Action Plan for Acute Kidney Stones

Step 1: Wait It Out

If your symptoms are not severe, you can wait until the kidney stone passes, although this can take several weeks. I have found it effective to take a very hot bath or soak in a hot tub, while flushing the kidneys with fluids, including beer.

Step 2: Take Prescription Pain Medications

If your pain is severe and urination is decreased, you may require narcotic medications (Demerol or codeine derivatives) until the stone passes. If your urine output does not increase and/or you become dehydrated, you may need to be hospitalized for intravenous fluids. When urination improves, you can take oral fluids.

Step 3: Undergo Lithotripsy to Break Up Stones That Don't Pass

If your kidney stones have not passed and you continue having severe pain, I recommend lithotripsy. This method uses sound waves to break up kidney stones that are too large to pass on their own or that cause complete obstruction.

Step 4: Undergo Surgery

The last resort for kidney stones that cause significant problems is surgical removal. Surgery is usually done through an endoscope, but open surgeries occasionally are required.

Your Balanced Healing Action Plan to Prevent Kidney Stones

Step 1: Take Vitamin B₆, Vitamin K, Magnesium, and Calcium Citrate

To prevent recurrent kidney stones, I first recommend taking nutritional supplements containing 25mg of vitamin B_6, 2mg of vitamin K, and 600mg of magnesium. Calcium citrate (300mg to 1000mg per day) is also very effective for reducing stones, and it can be taken with the other nutrients. These supplements inhibit oxalate stone formation by reducing oxalate production and increasing its excretion. Take these supplements together for the best results, although you can take them separately if blood testing reveals a deficiency in a particular supplement.

Step 2: Drink Cranberry Juice

Along with the previous step, drink eight ounces a day of cranberry juice to reduce the amount of ionized calcium in the urine. Some juice products have a high sugar content, so look for unsweetened products. Cranberry concentrates or capsules (300mg to 400mg twice daily) are also effective.

> The first time 54-year-old Horace, a freelance writer, had a kidney stone, he was on vacation in Hawaii and spent an afternoon planned for the beach instead in the hospital emergency department. Fortunately, the stone passed and Horace was able to enjoy the rest of his vacation. Over the next four years, though, he had 10 more episodes of kidney stones. Most of the time, the stones would pass after a few days, but several times, he had to be hospitalized and undergo lithotripsy. His stones were of various compositions. I placed him on a low purine diet and increased his vegetable (fiber) intake, prescribed a good multivitamin containing vitamins B_6, K, magnesium, and folic acid, and had him increase his fluids, especially having him drink at least one glass of unsweetened cranberry juice a day. For the past three years, he has not had another kidney stone.

Step 3: Take Folic Acid

If you have been able to have your stones analyzed and they are made of uric acid, take folic acid (5mg per day), which inhibits an enzyme responsible for producing uric acid.

LUPUS ERYTHEMATOSUS

Lupus is a chronic autoimmune disease in which your immune system makes cells (called *antibodies*) that attack the connective tissue of your body. *Discoid lupus* affects only the skin, and *systemic lupus erythematosus* affects the skin and many of the vital organs (heart, lungs, brain, and especially the kidneys). Lupus can have recurrent flare-ups and remissions, and it can vary in intensity and duration. Lupus can be very debilitating, and it can cause diseases of the vital organs listed above. It can inflame and damage the connective tissue in the joints, muscles, and skin, and can cause inflammation of the blood vessels, resulting in ulcers or lesions.

Common Symptoms

- Severe fatigue
- Low-grade fever
- Severe muscle aches
- Joint pain
- Skin rash on face or body
- Sun sensitivity
- Weight loss
- Mental confusion
- Ulcers in the nose, mouth, or throat
- Poor circulation
- Enlarged lymph nodes
- Pain in the chest during inhalation
- Urinary difficulties

What You Need to Know

DO NOT USE echinacea or any other product that stimulates the immune system if you have lupus. Stimulating the immune system will worsen lupus, because more destructive cells are produced. The herbs and supplements listed below as treatments help the immune system normalize (called *immunoregulators*), instead of stimulating it.

General Recommendations

Diet: Cutting down on red meats and dairy may help, because these foods can increase inflammation. Increasing consumption of fish may reduce inflammation. Alfalfa can cause a worsening of lupus and should be avoided. Lupus may be a result of or be aggravated by food allergies, so an elimination diet may be necessary to detect offending foods (see the section on "Food Allergies" for further guidance).

Qigong is excellent for strengthening and regulating the immune system, and I recommend it highly if you have lupus. You should notice improvement within three months. (For further information and examples, see "Simple Healing Steps for All Health Conditions," page 79, and Appendix A, under "Mind-Body Techniques.")

Your Balanced Healing Action Plan for Lupus

- If your symptoms are severe (life-threatening problems such as severe anemia, widespread bruising/bleeding, water on the lungs or around the heart, kidney damage, inflammation of blood vessels, or brain dysfunction), start with Step 7, and then return to Step 2 when your symptoms are stabilized.

Step 1: Take NSAIDs and Use Topical Hydrocortisone Cream

If your inflammation and pain symptoms are mild, you can take NSAIDs (nonsteroidal anti-inflammatory medications). Start with non-prescription drugs such as ibuprofen or Aleve (naproxen). If they don't help, your doctor can prescribe stronger NSAIDs. You can also use topical hydrocortisone creams to relieve mild skin rashes (again, over-the-counter medications such as Cortaid or stronger prescription steroid creams). You should receive relief within a few hours to a few days.

Step 2: Take DHEA

I also recommend taking DHEA (50mg to 200mg per day) to reduce fatigue, arthritis symptoms, and triglyceride levels, and to improve your quality of life. However, DHEA can lower HDL cholesterol, so take flaxseed oil (1 tablespoon daily) or niacin (2g to 3g daily; see Appendix B for precautions) to offset this effect. Because DHEA may have many other side effects at this dosage, see Appendix B, under "Hormonal Supplements," for further information. You should notice improvement within one to two months.

Step 3: Undergo Acupuncture to Decrease Symptoms and Prevent Flare-Ups

Along with the previous steps, I recommend that you undergo acupuncture, which can effectively reduce your symptoms of fatigue, muscle aches, and joint pain, and prevent flare-ups. Principal points usually are found on the back, legs, and arms. You should always seek evaluation and treatment from a practitioner certified in acupuncture. (See Appendix A, under "Acupuncture," for guidance on finding a qualified acupuncturist and for further explanation of the different acupuncture techniques.) You should feel improvement within six treatments, but you might need additional sessions for maximum benefits.

Step 4: Take Mucopolysaccharides

I next recommend trying mucopolysaccharides (such as Beta 1,3/1,6 glucan, once daily). These are special carbohydrates that can trap harmful antibodies, helping to prevent destruction of the body's tissues. Mucopolysaccharides are not absorbed into the body, but they bind harmful substances in the GI tract that adversely affect the immune system.

Step 5: Take Appropriate Chinese Herbal Remedies

If your symptoms continue, or along with acupuncture, I recommend Chinese herbal formulas to rebalance the immune system so that it works properly. Lithospernum is a specific formula designed for lupus, and a formula in the Quan Yin Herbal program in San Francisco (called Enhance) is also useful. (Go to www.HealthConcerns.com for further information on these formulas.) Consult a practitioner qualified in Chinese herbal medicine to determine which Chinese herbal formulas are the best for your particular syndromes. You should notice improvement within three to six weeks, but you may need to take them longer depending on your condition. (See Appendix A, under "Chinese Herbs," for further information.)

> Becca is a 37-year-old woman who has had systemic lupus for 10 years. She had recurrent flare-ups and remissions, which occurred every few months (four to six times a year). Becca had some pain in her joints all the time. She also complained of muscle aches and severe fatigue. For her previous flare-ups, she had been placed on steroids and azathioprine, which she would need to take for several months before her symptoms would resolve. She would then take prescription NSAIDs and antimalarial drugs for her joint pain, which helped reduce the pain, but they did not eliminate it. She also took low-dose steroids, but she gained a lot of weight and had other side effects as a result. I placed her on a good multivitamin, containing high levels of vitamins C and E, and 200mcg of selenium. I also suggested that she take DHEA, which increased her energy, decreased her arthritic symptoms, and helped her feel better in general. I then started a course of acupuncture (10 sessions). She had only two flare-ups the following year, and both were mild (they had been severe before). During the flare-ups, she underwent acupuncture, which resolved the symptoms within two to three sessions. Best of all, she was able to discontinue the steroids and antimalarial drugs.

Step 6: Take Vitamin C, Vitamin E, Selenium, and Beta-Carotene

If your symptoms still persist, take vitamin C (1,000mg daily), vitamin E (800 IU daily) and selenium (200mcg daily) in combination. Beta carotene (25,000 IU to 50,000 IU per day) may help clear up skin rashes of discoid lupus. You can take these nutrients with the previous steps. You should notice improvement within one to two months.

Step 7: Take Prescription Medications

For severe lupus or acute flare-ups with fever, conventional medications are required. High-dose corticosteroids are usually necessary for a short period of time (one to three months), along with immunosuppressive drugs such as azathioprine. Corticosteroid use can increase levels of blood sugar (glucose), but this effect can often be reversed by taking chromium, 200mcg three times daily. DHEA (Step 2) can decrease the dosage of steroids required. For more chronic, moderate symptoms, or after flare-ups have abated, antimalaria drugs (such as hydroxychloroquine or chloroquine) can be beneficial and can be combined with lower-dose steroids. Antimalarials can cause eye problems, so you need to have your eyes checked every six months while taking them. Always consult with an arthritis specialist if your symptoms are moderate or severe.

Step 8: Take Prescription Cyclophosphamide

If you have a severe case of lupus with kidney involvement, you may need to take prescription cyclophosphamide, another immunosuppressant drug. Consult with an arthritis specialist (*rheumatologist*) for guidance.

MACULAR DEGENERATION (AMD)

Macular degeneration is scarring of the *macula*, a small area at the back of the eye that is necessary for focused, straight-ahead vision such as reading, watching TV, driving, and sewing. There are two types of degeneration, *exudative* and *dry* (*atrophic*), the latter being the most common. It is commonly referred to as age-related macular degeneration (AMD) because it is a result of the free-radical damage and decreased blood and oxygen supply to the eye that occurs with aging. Atrophic macular degeneration is slowly progressive, taking about 5 to 10 years to cause legal blindness. Exudative macular degeneration is responsible for 90 percent of sudden, severe visual loss in people with AMD.

Common Symptoms

- Dim or distorted vision
- Difficulty reading
- Gradual loss of central vision
- Blank spots when looking straight
- Straight lines that appear wavy

What You Need to Know

The major risk factors for macular degeneration are smoking, aging, atherosclerosis, and high blood pressure, so these conditions must be treated to prevent or slow the progress of AMD. (See the sections on "Nicotine Addiction," "Cholesterol," and "High Blood Pressure" for further treatment guidelines if you have these conditions.)

General Recommendations

Diet: Nutrition designed to reduce atherosclerosis and increase antioxidants will help if this is the cause of your macular degeneration. If you increase the amounts of fruits and vegetables you eat, you can lower your risk for macular degeneration, as well as slow down its progression.

Your Balanced Healing Action Plan
for Exudative Macular Degeneration (AMD)

- For exudative AMD, studies have not shown benefit from external beam radiation, submacular surgery, or subcutaneous interferon a–2A.

Step 1: *Undergo Laser Photocoagulation Surgery or Photodynamic Treatment*

Exudative macular degeneration is an emergency situation and requires immediate laser surgery to coagulate leaking blood vessels in the eye. Laser photocoagulation is a surgical procedure commonly used for exudative macular degeneration, and it decreases the rate of severe visual loss. Photodynamic treatment with verteporfin reduces the risk of moderate and severe visual loss and can be used with photocoagulation.

Your Balanced Healing Action Plan for Dry Macular Degeneration

Step 1: Undergo Acupuncture

I recommend starting with acupuncture, which can give you long-term improvement in vision. Principal points usually are found on the back, legs, head, and face. Ear points include the Eye point. You should always seek evaluation and treatment from a practitioner certified in acupuncture. (See Appendix A, under "Acupuncture," for guidance on finding a qualified acupuncturist and for further explanation of the different acupuncture techniques.) You should notice improvement within six treatments, but you might need additional sessions for maximum benefits.

Step 2: Undergo Infrasonic Treatment

Along with the previous steps, I recommend undergoing infrasound treatment, or low-frequency sound waves. Infrasound works by increasing the local circulation of blood, thus increasing the oxygen delivery to the eye. It can help reverse the condition or slow the rate of degeneration. It may take 6 to 20 treatments to see improvement. Numerous chiropractors, naturopaths, acupuncturists, and a few doctors use infrasound. (See Appendix C, under "Infrasound," for a reference source.)

Step 3: Take Bilberry with Carotenoids

Take bilberry extract with carotenoids (40mg to 80mg, containing 25 percent anthocyanidin content per day), which is very effective at halting and even reversing dry macular degeneration. These supplements increase blood flow to the retina and improve visual processes. You should notice improvement within one month. You should take these supplements with the previous steps.

> Josh's uncle and grandfather both had macular degeneration, and Josh, a 31-year-old graphic designer, developed the same condition at age 14. He was denied a driver's license because he could not pass the eye exam. I started him on a formula containing bilberry and carotenoids. After two months, he was able to pass the eye test and was given his driver's license.

Step 4: Take Gingko Biloba

Gingko biloba (160mg to 240mg, containing 24 percent gingko flavonglycosides, per day) is also very effective in slowing the progression of this condition. You can take it along with the previous steps. Gingko acts similarly to bilberry by increasing blood flow. It may take up to two months to see the benefits.

Step 5: Take Zinc, Fish Oil, and Antioxidant Vitamins

You can improve poor vision by taking zinc in doses of at least 80mg per day (as zinc oxide). Zinc helps reduce symptoms and may be able to halt the progression of macular degeneration, especially in combination with vitamin E (800 IU per day), vitamin C (500mg), and beta-carotene (15mg). Too much zinc, however, can interfere with copper absorption and immune function (see "Zinc Side Effects" in Appendix B), so add copper, 2mg daily (as cupric oxide). Recent studies have also shown benefits from fish oil (1000mg daily) in age-related macular degeneration. It may take several months to observe benefits. You can take these supplements with the above steps.

Step 6: Take Grapeseed Extract

If you are having problems with poor night vision or photophobia (increased sensitivity to bright light), add grapeseed extract (150mg to 300mg per day, containing 95 percent procyanidolic content) to the previous steps. It may take one to two months to notice improvement.

MENIERE'S DISEASE

Meniere's disease is a disorder of the inner ear in which there is too much *endolymph*, the fluid that fills the inner ear. Anxiety or excessive salt intake can trigger the vertigo attacks characteristic of this condition, and some people have an abnormally shaped middle ear that predisposes to this disease. Eventually, vertigo and other symptoms clear up in 60 percent to 80 percent of people, although it may take years. Meniere's disease can cause hearing loss, poor job performance, accidents, and psychological disorders.

Common Symptoms

- Intermittent vertigo, which is rotatory dizziness (spinning) that can last from less than an hour to two days
- Nausea
- Exhaustion
- Hearing problems
- Tinnitus (ringing in the ears)
- Fullness in the ear
- Headache

General Recommendations

Diet: Some nutritionists recommend increasing calories, fat, and protein, but this has not been proven effective and can have harmful effects. Another recommendation is restricted salt intake, which lessens the frequency and number of attacks in some people.

Meditation: Stress and anxiety can precipitate attacks of Meniere's disease, and they can also be a result of the disease. Meditation can help prevent attacks and recurrences by decreasing your stress and anxiety level. (See Appendix A, under "Mind-Body Techniques" for further information and examples.)

Your Balanced Healing Action Plan for Meniere's Disease

Step 1: Take Meclizine, Valium, or Diuretics for Initial Short-Term Relief

The first treatment goal is to get your symptoms under control, and conventional medications are the best choice. Your doctor can prescribe Meclizine (Antivert), the first drug of choice for dizziness, and some doctors use Valium. Diuretics (such as HCTZ) can decrease swelling in the inner ear. You should feel relief within a few hours to a few days.

Step 2: Undergo Acupuncture for Long-Term Relief

Along with Step 1, I also recommend acupuncture, which is very effective for reducing the symptoms and resolving the disease over the long term. Once the acupuncture works, you can then decrease or discontinue the medications in Step 1. Principal points usually are found on the head, feet, legs, and arms. Always seek evaluation and treatment from a practitioner certified in acupuncture. (See Appendix A, under "Acupuncture," for guidance on finding a qualified acupuncturist and for further explanation of the different acupuncture techniques.) You should notice improvement within six treatments, but you might need additional sessions for maximum benefits.

Step 3: Take Appropriate Chinese Herbal Remedies

Chinese herbal formulas are effective at controlling symptoms of dizziness and are most effective when you take them along with acupuncture. Helpful formulas include *Wen Dan Tang, Ba Zhen Wan, Du Zhong Pian, Si Wu Tang,* and *Tian Ma Gou Teng Yin.* Consult a practitioner qualified in Chinese herbal medicine to determine which Chinese herbal formulas are the best for your particular syndromes. You should notice improvement within three weeks, but you may need to take the herbs longer for complete relief. (See Appendix A, under "Chinese Herbs," for further information.)

> Jeff, a 52-year-old stockbroker, had Meniere's disease for 15 years. He had a nearly constant feeling of "fullness" in his ears, as if they were plugged, as well as ringing in his ears and dizziness. He had taken Meclizine and diuretics, but these medications gave him no relief. I started him on the Chinese herbal remedy *Wen Dan Tang,* which cleared up the "ear fullness" symptoms. I then provided acupuncture, and after five sessions, the rest of his symptoms also went away.

Step 4: Take Vitamin C, Vitamin B₁, Vitamin B₂, Vitamin B₆, and Zinc

For symptoms that continue, I next recommend taking daily vitamin C (2,000mg), vitamins B_1, B_2, and B_6 (50mg each), and zinc (20mg). You can use these along with the previous steps.

Step 5: Take an Appropriate Homeopathic Remedy

Several homeopathic remedies can reduce or control persistent symptoms. These include the following:

- *Bryonia* for headache, dizziness, and a roaring in the ears
- *Conium* for sensitivity to light and increased symptoms when lying down or turning over
- *Cocculus* for dizziness and nausea

Consult a qualified homeopathist for guidance on which remedies will be most beneficial and for proper dosages. You should notice improvement in one to two weeks. (See Appendix A, under "Homeopathy," for guidance on finding a qualified homeopathist and for further information.)

Step 6: Practice Yoga and Receive Massage for Stress Relief

Because stress and anxiety can bring on acute attacks of Meniere's—and can be caused by the disease itself—I recommend undergoing massage and/or practicing yoga, both of which provide relaxation and stress relief (see Appendix A, under "Yoga" and "Mind-Body Techniques," for more information and ways to find a qualified practitioner).

Step 7: Take the Prescription Medications Promethazine or Dimenhydrinate

If the previous steps don't work, your doctor can prescribe medications such as promethazine or dimenhydrinate. These drugs help reduce symptoms of vertigo for some people, but will not cure the condition. Other drugs that that have been used include betahistine and trimetazidine, but benefits are questionable.

MENOPAUSE AND PERIMENOPAUSE

Menopause is the cessation of menstruation (i.e., when it has been 12 months since your last menstrual period); it also occurs as a result of a complete hysterectomy (removal of your uterus and ovaries). *Perimenopause* is the time period before menopause, in which women can have irregular menstruation and many of the symptoms of menopause. Menopause occurs around age 50 on average, but it can be as early as age 40 and as late as age 60. Perimenopause can last from 1 to 10 years. Symptoms of menopause will usually go away on their own but may take several years to do so. Menopause can lead to deterioration of various organ systems, especially the heart, brain, and bones.

Common Symptoms

- Hot flashes
- Night sweats
- Irritability
- Increased urination
- Headaches

- Depression
- Palpitations
- Insomnia
- Back pain
- Constipation
- Painful intercourse
- Lowered sex drive
- Restless Legs Syndrome

What You Need to Know

Before menopause, your sexual, reproductive, and many other organ systems (primarily heart, brain, and bone) require a balance of two basic sex hormones, estrogen and progesterone. In the past, doctors recommended hormone replacement therapy (called HRT) after menopause to protect these organ systems, prescribing synthetic estrogen primarily, and synthetic progesterone only if you still had your uterus, to prevent the increased risk of uterine cancer caused by the synthetic estrogen. However, recent studies have shown HRT to be potentially harmful, and current conventional recommendations are to take HRT only for a short time to control symptoms, if at all. Unfortunately, this leaves your organs vulnerable to deterioration. The following steps are designed to both decrease symptoms and protect your organ systems, without using synthetic hormones.

General Recommendations

Diet: A balanced diet can help all the symptoms of menopause, especially foods that contain plant estrogens (phytoestrogens), particularly soy and lima beans. Other beneficial foods include nuts and seeds, fennel, celery, and parsley. These foods can increase the levels of estrogen in your body, although they may not be enough to prevent all menopausal symptoms (they contain "weak" estrogens). A diet low in saturated fat can help prevent post-menopausal heart disease. If you are a post-menopausal woman, you can be especially sensitive to salt, and limiting salt intake to one teaspoon daily can significantly reduce your blood pressure if it is high. HRT can deplete your body's stores of vitamin B_6 and folic acid, which you can replace or supplement by eating more vegetables and fruits or fortified food products.

Exercise: Many menopausal or perimenopausal women gain weight, especially around the midsection. Exercise is the primary method of reducing this particular type of weight gain (diet alone has not been shown to be effective unless accompanied by exercise). Aerobic exercise can help prevent post-menopausal heart disease (it increases HDL cholesterol) and improve brain function. Resistance (strength-training) exercises can help prevent bone loss and make new bone, and decrease LDL cholesterol, total cholesterol, and body fat. Strength training will also increase your metabolism. I recommend at least 30 minutes of strength training three times per week and 30 minutes of aerobic activity every day (see "Simple Healing Steps for All Health Conditions," under "Exercise," for further guidelines and recommendations).

Your Balanced Healing Action Plan for Perimenopause and Menopausal Symptoms

- If you are going through perimenopause or menopause but do not have any symptoms, there is no benefit from following the treatment steps.
- If you are post-menopausal, go to the next section, "Your Balanced Healing Action Plan for Post-Menopause."

Step 1: Take Appropriate Chinese Herbal Remedies

I first recommend taking Chinese herbs because they are very effective at reducing perimenopausal and menopausal symptoms. I recommend *Er Xian Tang*. If hot flashes persist, and there is evidence of Yin deficiency, you can add *Zhi Bai Di Huang Wan*. *Gan Mai Da Zao Wan* is also commonly used for perimenopausal symptoms. Consult a practitioner qualified in Chinese herbal medicine to determine which Chinese herbal formulas are the best for your particular syndromes. You should notice improvement within three weeks but may need to take them longer for complete or ongoing relief. (See Appendix A, under "Chinese Herbs," for further information.)

Step 2: Take Black Cohosh, Flaxseed Oil, Gamma-Oryzanol, Soy Extract, or Red Clover

If Step 1 is not completely effective, I next recommend black cohosh (20mg daily, standardized to contain triterpene glycosides calculated as 27-deoxyactein), which helps reduce many menopausal symptoms through its phytoestrogen (plant-estrogen) content. If black cohosh does not eliminate your symptoms, flaxseed oil (one tablespoon per day) is also very effective for this purpose, and you can take it along with black cohosh.

Gamma-oryzanol (150mg twice daily), derived from rice bran oil, has been used primarily in Japan for hot flashes, but it also can lower cholesterol. If you don't want to use soy in your diet, taking a soy extract (250mg twice daily, standardized to 10 percent isoflavones) can often reduce symptoms.

Red clover (liquid extract, 1:1 in 25 percent alcohol, taken 1.5ml to 3ml three times a day, or tincture, 1:10 in 45 percent alcohol, 1ml to 2ml three times a day) contains phytoestrogens as well, but they are weaker than those in black cohosh. If one of these supplements is not totally effective, you can combine any of them together for better results.

Step 3: Undergo Acupuncture

For symptoms that continue, I recommend acupuncture. Principal points usually are found on the ankles, feet, legs, back, wrists, and arms. Ear points include endocrine, ovary, and uterus. Always seek evaluation and treatment from a practitioner certified in acupuncture. (See Appendix A, under "Acupuncture," for guidance on finding a qualified acupuncturist and for further explanation of the different acupuncture techniques.) You should notice improvement within six treatments, but you might need additional sessions for maximum benefits.

Step 4: Take Natural Progesterone and Natural Estrogen

If your symptoms still persist, I recommend that you start using natural progesterone 50mg to 200mg once daily if in oral form, or 20mg to 40mg daily as a cream, days 7 to 27 of your menstrual cycle if you are perimenopausal. If you still have symptoms after one to two months of taking the natural progesterone, your doctor can prescribe natural estrogens (Tri-est or Bi-est, 0.625mg to 2.5mg daily for the first 21 days of your cycle, or every 25 days with a five-day rest if your periods have stopped). Do not take natural estrogen if you are at a high risk or have had breast cancer. Some doctors also include natural testosterone (0.25mg to 2mg daily) if you feel your sex drive is low or have fatigue, or DHEA (12.5mg to 25mg daily) to increase your energy and well-being. DHEA breaks down into estrogen and androgens (such as testosterone), but doses greater than 50mg can cause masculinizing effects. Although long-term studies have not been done, so far, natural hormones have not been found to have the harmful side effects found with synthetic hormones. You must consult with a doctor because a prescription and adjustment of dosages are necessary.

Natural hormones (except progesterone alone) must be *compounded* (mixed together) by a compounding pharmacist trained in these techniques. You can take natural hormones in several forms, including creams, capsules, troches, and suppositories. Dosage adjustments can be based on saliva testing of hormones (rather than blood tests), which is available at the compounding pharmacies. (See Appendix B, under "Sex Hormones," for further information.)

> Margaret, a 48-year-old fashion designer, still has regular periods but began having perimenopausal symptoms, including night sweats, fatigue, weight gain, lowered sex drive, and depression. Low-dose estrogen had controlled the symptoms, but she stopped taking the hormones because of the dangers, so her symptoms returned. I recommended *Er Xian Tang* as well as natural progesterone cream. Within two months, all of her symptoms had gone away.

Step 5: Take Synthetic Estrogen

If all else fails to control your symptoms, then your doctor can prescribe synthetic estrogen. Some doctors prescribe oral contraceptives, and others recommend taking low-dose estrogen, which can decrease symptoms with a lessened risk of cancer, blood clots, and gall stones than is seen with higher doses. Raloxiphene is a new type of estrogen called a *selective estrogen receptor modulator* (SERM) that also demonstrates less of a risk of cancer or blood clots. You should take synthetic hormones for as short a time as possible. Do not take synthetic estrogen if you are at a high risk of or have had breast cancer.

Your Balanced Healing Action Plan for Post-Menopause

- If you have vaginal bleeding after you are menopausal, you should seek gynecological care immediately to rule out uterine or cervical cancer.

Step 1: Take Natural Estrogens and Progesterone

For all post-menopausal women, I recommend natural estrogens (1.25mg to 2.5mg, one to two times per day), which is a combination of two or three estrogens (estriol and estradiol, with or without estrone), and natural progesterone (50mg to 100mg twice daily in oral form, 20mg to 40mg daily if in cream). If you have a high risk of cancer, you can use estriol alone, but ask your gynecologist for guidance.

These natural hormones are referred to as bioidentical hormones because they are biologically identical to the hormones made in your body before menopause. Because they are natural, they appear to relieve post-menopausal symptoms and provide long-term protection against heart, brain, and bone diseases without the risks and side effects of synthetic hormones. Some doctors also include natural testosterone (0.25mg to 2mg daily) if your sex drive is low, or DHEA (12.5mg to 25mg daily) to increase your energy and well-being. DHEA breaks down into estrogen and androgens (such as testosterone), although doses greater than 50mg can cause masculinizing effects.

You can take these hormones in several forms, including creams, capsules, troches, and suppositories; they should be taken for the remainder of your life. You should consult with a doctor because a prescription and adjustment of dosages may be necessary. Natural hormones must be *compounded* (mixed together) by a compounding pharmacist trained in these techniques. Dosage adjustments can be based on saliva testing of hormones or blood tests. Saliva tests are available at the compounding pharmacies. (See Appendix B, under "Sex Hormones," for further information.)

Step 2: Take Appropriate Chinese Herbal Remedies for Short-Term Post-Menopausal Symptoms

If the above step does not completely relieve your menopausal symptoms, I recommend taking Chinese herbs because they are very effective at reducing post-menopausal symptoms. I recommend *Er Xian Tang*. If hot flashes persist, and there is evidence of Yin deficiency, you can add *Zhi Bai Di Huang Wan*. Consult a practitioner qualified in Chinese herbal medicine to determine which Chinese herbal formulas are the best for your particular situation. You should notice improvement within three weeks, but you may need to take them longer for complete or ongoing relief. (See Appendix A, under "Chinese Herbs," for further information.)

Step 3: Take Black Cohosh, Flaxseed Oil, Gamma-Oryzanol, Soy Extract, or Red Clover for Short-Term Post-Menopausal Symptoms

If the previous steps are not completely effective for reducing your post-menopausal symptoms, or you prefer not to take any hormones (Step 1), I recommend black cohosh (20mg daily, standardized to contain triterpene glycosides calculated as 27-deoxyactein), which helps reduce the symptoms through its phytoestrogen (plant-estrogen) content. If black cohosh does not eliminate your symptoms, flaxseed oil (one tablespoon per day) is also very effective for this purpose, and you can take it along with black cohosh.

Gamma-oryzanol (150mg twice daily), derived from rice bran oil, has been used primarily in Japan for hot flashes, but it also can lower cholesterol. If you don't want to use soy in your diet, taking a soy extract (250mg twice daily, standardized to 10 percent isoflavones) can often reduce symptoms.

Red clover (liquid extract, 1:1 in 25 percent alcohol, taken 1.5ml to 3ml three times a day, or tincture, 1:10 in 45 percent alcohol, 1ml to 2ml, three times a day) contains phytoestrogens as well, but they are weaker than those in black cohosh. If one of these supplements is not totally effective, you can safely combine any of them together for better results.

Step 4: Take Calcium, Magnesium, and Vitamin D

Because post-menopausal women lose bone from aging, as well as from estrogen loss, I recommend that you take calcium supplementation. You should combine calcium (1,200mg/day through supplementation and/or food) with magnesium (400mg to 800mg daily) and vitamin D (400 IU daily), the latter two of which are important for helping calcium get into the bone and strengthening the bone. There are numerous forms of calcium, some more absorbable than others, and some that contain the magnesium and vitamin D in the same formulation (see Appendix B, under "Calcium," for further details and recommendations).

Step 5: Use Natural Estrogen, Oral Progesterone, and/or Vitamin E Intravaginal Creams for Vaginal Dryness

For vaginal dryness that does not respond to the above steps, your doctor can prescribe an intravaginal natural estrogen cream rather than the oral or body cream form. The cream should contain primarily estriol, which works the best and has the least risks of all the estrogen forms. If that does not work, micronized progesterone is helpful in place of the cream form of natural progesterone. Intravaginal vitamin E is also very effective for vaginal dryness, and you can use it with either of the other two products.

Step 6: Undergo Acupuncture

If the natural hormones do not alleviate your post-menopausal symptoms, I recommend acupuncture. Principal points usually are found on the feet, legs, arms, and head. For problems with sex drive, principal acupuncture points usually are found on the feet and low back. There is also an effective ear acupuncture point called the "sexual desire" point.

Always seek evaluation and treatment from a practitioner certified in acupuncture. (See Appendix A, under "Acupuncture," for guidance on finding a qualified acupuncturist and for further explanation of the different acupuncture techniques.) You should notice improvement within six treatments, but you might need additional sessions for maximum benefits.

> Rena, a biology professor, had stopped having periods at age 50. She had hot flashes, but they went away. But three years later, Rena started having depression, trouble sleeping, weight gain, decreased sex drive, and vaginal dryness. I started her on an exercise program, acupuncture, and a combination of natural estrogens and natural progesterone. After three months, the majority of her symptoms were gone, but she still had some vaginal dryness. I suggested that she take the estrogens as a vaginal cream, along with vitamin E vaginal cream, which eliminated her vaginal dryness.

Step 7: Take Testosterone to Increase Libido and Energy

If you are still having a problem with decreased libido (sex drive) and fatigue, your doctor can prescribe testosterone supplementation by pill, patch, or injection. There are both synthetic and natural forms, and I prefer the natural to begin (0.25mg to 2mg daily). Natural testosterone can be combined with natural estrogen and progesterone in one formulation. However, testosterone can have some masculinizing effects, so most women prefer to take it separately so they can adjust the dose more easily. Testosterone supplements require a doctor's prescription, whether you use the synthetic or natural forms. It may take several months to obtain a maximum response.

Step 8: Take Synthetic Estrogen Only for Unresponsive Symptoms

If nothing else works to reduce your post-menopausal symptoms, your doctor can prescribe the synthetic forms of estrogen. Take a very low dose of synthetic estrogen, which has a lower risk of cancer and blood clots yet can provide necessary protection to the body's tissues. I also recommend Raloxiphene, a new type of estrogen (called a *selective estrogen receptor modulator*, or SERM) that also demonstrates less of a risk of cancer, blood clots, and gallstones. However, if you do not have any symptoms of post-menopause, it may not be advisable to take synthetic hormones because recent studies revealed that taking them when you don't have such symptoms can actually cause those symptoms (especially more fatigue and decreased physical functioning).

If you take synthetic estrogen and still have your uterus, you will need to take progesterone in some form (natural or synthetic) to negate the increased risk of uterine cancer caused by the synthetic estrogen. I recommend taking the natural form because synthetic progesterone can negate the beneficial effects of estrogen and can cause many undesirable side effects (see Appendix B, under "Sex Hormones," for more information and recommendations on dosage). Current recommendations are that synthetic hormones should be taken only until your menopausal symptoms resolve.

MENSTRUAL PROBLEMS (Amenorrhea, Dysmenorrhea, Menorrhagia, Irregular Menstruation)

Four main menstrual problems can occur to a woman during her childbearing years:

- *Amenorrhea* is lack of periods (not caused by pregnancy). It can signal an underlying hormonal imbalance and an increased risk of uterine cancer, and it can prevent pregnancy. It can also occur in athletes, especially long-distance runners, and those with anorexia nervosa (extreme underweight), both of which cause suppression of estrogen production.
- *Dysmenorrhea* is painful periods or cramps, and is usually due to an excess in prostaglandins, substances that cause contraction of the uterus during your periods. It can also be caused by endometriosis, or infection. Often, cramps will diminish after you have had a baby.
- *Menorrhagia* is excessively prolonged or excessive bleeding during your period and can signal several underlying conditions, including endometriosis, fibroids, infection, or cancer. It can cause iron deficiency anemia, and it may also signal lack of ovulation, low levels of progesterone, or an excess of prostaglandins.
- *Irregular menstrual* periods are due to hormonal fluctuations and are usually not serious.

What You Need to Know

There are many causes of menstrual problems that are easily correctable but require proper diagnosis. For example, over-exercise can cause amenorrhea, intrauterine devices (IUDs) can cause dysmenorrhea, and stress can cause menorrhagia and irregular menstruation. If you have menstrual problems, always start with a complete history and exam by a gynecologist or your primary care doctor so you can get a proper diagnosis.

Your Balanced Healing Action Plan for Amenorrhea (Lack of Menstrual Periods)

Step 1: *Receive Acupuncture*

I recommend starting with acupuncture first, once known causes are corrected or ruled out. The primary acupuncture points usually are found on the legs, back, and abdomen. Always seek evaluation and treatment from a practitioner certified in acupuncture. (See Appendix A, under "Acupuncture," for guidance on finding a qualified acupuncturist and for further explanation of the different acupuncture techniques.) Your period should start within four to six treatments, but you might need additional sessions to restore your cycles to normal.

Step 2: *Take Appropriate Chinese Herbal Remedies*

Along with acupuncture, I recommend that you take Chinese herbal formulas. A combination that has been effective is a tincture consisting of one part chaste tree (Vitex), two parts blue cohosh, and two parts mugwort leaf. Take 2 ml three times daily until menstrual flow begins. Other formulas include *Ba Zhen Tang*, *Si Wu Tang Wan* and *Tao Hong Si Wu Tang Wan*. Consult a practitioner qualified in Chinese herbal medicine to determine which Chinese herbal formulas are the best for your particular syndromes. Your periods should return within one to two months, but you may need to take the formulas longer to fully restore your cycles. (See Appendix A, under "Chinese Herbs," for further information.)

Step 3: Take Prescription Hormones

If the above steps do not work, then hormonal treatment using estrogen and/or progesterone may be necessary to start your period. Often, progesterone will be given by injection to jump-start your period. Consult your gynecologist for determination of the best method for your situation.

> At age 28, Angela, a court reporter, had not had a period in eight months. She was not athletic or anorexic, two conditions that commonly cause amenorrhea. Her doctor had given her two shots of progesterone, but they had not started her period. He also recommended a procedure to clean out her uterus (D & C), but she preferred natural methods. I started her on *Ba Zhen Tang* and also acupuncture. After one month, her periods restarted and have continued to be regular.

Step 4: Take Zinc and Vitamin B Complex

If you are still not getting your period, take supplements of zinc (20mg to 40mg daily) and vitamin B complex, deficiencies of which can contribute to amenorrhea. These nutrients are essential elements necessary for growth, development, and reproduction.

Step 5: Take Deglycyrrhizinated Licorice

If your period still has not started, I recommend trying licorice root (deglycyrrhizinated (DGL) form, one or two 380mg chewable tablets before meals). Licorice rebalances the hormonal system by decreasing estrogen metabolism when estrogen levels are too high, and it promotes estrogen production when estrogen levels are too low. You can take licorice with the preceding steps.

Your Balanced Healing Action Plan for Dysmenorrhea (Cramps)

Step 1: Take Ibuprofen or Naproxen for Mild Cramps

Nonsteroidal anti-inflammatory drugs (NSAIDs) such as ibuprofen and naproxen (Aleve) are often the most effective treatment for painful menstrual cramps and are available in over-the-counter formulas. Mefenamic acid (Ponstel) is a fast-acting prescription NSAID that can be prescribed by a doctor if the over-the-counter NSAIDs don't work. Begin taking one or the other the day before your period, and continue through your period.

Step 2: Undergo Acupuncture

For more severe cramps, I recommend acupuncture next. Principal acupuncture points usually are found on the abdomen, feet, and legs. *Moxibustion* (heating the acupuncture points) can also be done at points on the abdomen. Always seek evaluation and treatment from a practitioner certified in acupuncture. (See Appendix A, under "Acupuncture," for guidance in finding a qualified acupuncturist and for further explanation of the different acupuncture techniques.) You should notice improvement within six treatments, but you might need additional sessions for maximum benefits.

Step 3: Take Appropriate Chinese Herbal Remedies

Chinese herbal formulas are the next course of treatment and are excellent for reducing painful periods. You can take them in conjunction with acupuncture for faster benefits. Recommendations include *Tong Jing Wan, Dan Zhi Xiao Yao Wan, Corydalis Yan Hu Suo Pian,* or *Yan Hu Suo Wan. Tong Jing Wan* contains the herb crampbark, which is often used alone for menstrual cramps, but this formula is more effective with the additional Chinese herbs. Consult a practitioner qualified in Chinese herbal medicine to determine which Chinese herbal formulas are the best for your particular syndromes. You should notice improvement within one or two periods. (See Appendix A, under "Chinese Herbs," for further information.)

> Elaine, a 26-year-old ballet dancer, had bad cramping before and during her periods. The pain would get so severe that she could not work or participate in her usual activities. She had tried various nonsteroidal anti-inflammatory drugs (NSAIDs) as well as pain medication, but she continued to have problems. I suggested that she take the Chinese herbal formula *Tong Jing Wan*, which decreased the cramps enough that she could work, although she still had pain. I then gave her two acupuncture treatments at the start of her next period, and her cramps went away completely. During her next period, her cramps were much less severe. I gave her two more acupuncture treatments, and again her cramps went away. Since then, she has had only very mild cramps that last a few days, which she can control by taking ibuprofen.

Step 4: Take Vitamin B Complex, Vitamin C, and Magnesium

If you are still having cramps, a multivitamin containing vitamin B complex, calcium (300mg daily), and magnesium (300mg daily) may relieve your symptoms. You also can take vitamin B_6 alone, 50mg twice a day.

Step 5: Take Low-Dose Birth Control Pills

If all else fails, then your doctor can prescribe low dose contraceptives (birth control pills), the preferred form of synthetic hormones for this purpose.

Your Balanced Healing Action Plan for Menorrhagia (Excessive Menstrual Bleeding)

- You should first always obtain a gynecological consultation and examination to rule out correctable physical causes of your bleeding.
- Studies have not shown hormonal therapies (oral synthetic progesterone, oral contraceptives, or gonadotropin-releasing hormone) to be effective for menorrhagia.

Step 1: Take Iron and Folic Acid

Because excessive bleeding can cause an iron-deficiency anemia, take iron (300mg daily) and folic acid (400mcg daily) to treat and prevent anemia, until the bleeding is decreased. Two-thirds of women with menorrhagia have iron deficiency anemia.

Step 2: Take Appropriate Chinese Herbal Remedies

If you have mild to moderate excessive menstrual bleeding, certain Chinese herbal formulas can rebuild your blood as well as correct underlying problems causing the excessive bleeding. I recommend *Ba Zhen Tang* or *Qing Re Zhi Beng Tang*. Consult a practitioner qualified in Chinese herbal medicine to determine which Chinese herbal formulas are the best for your particular syndromes. You should notice improvement within one to two periods, but you may need to take the formulas longer for complete relief. (See Appendix A, under "Chinese Herbs," for further information.)

Step 3: Undergo Acupuncture

If the Chinese herbals alone do not slow your bleeding, add acupuncture. Principal acupuncture points usually are found on the feet, ankles, legs, and back. Always seek evaluation and treatment from a practitioner certified in acupuncture. (See Appendix A, under "Acupuncture," for guidance in finding a qualified acupuncturist and for further explanation of the different acupuncture techniques.) You should notice improvement within six to eight treatments, but you might need additional sessions for maximum benefits.

Step 4: Take Prescription Naproxen, Meclofenamic Acid, or Diclofenac

If your excessive bleeding is still not controlled, your doctor can prescribe the non-steroidal anti-inflammatory drugs (NSAIDs) naproxen, meclofenamic acid, or diclofenac. These drugs decrease the effects of prostaglandins that may be causing the bleeding. Begin taking one of these drugs several days before your period, and continue through your period. Ibuprofen has not been found to be effective for menorrhagia.

Tonya, a 39-year-old hair stylist, came to me because she was having severe fatigue and dizziness. Blood testing revealed a severe iron-deficiency anemia that required a blood transfusion. This corrected the anemia, but Tonya still had fatigue. She also had excessive menstrual bleeding, which had gradually increased over the previous two years and was the cause of her anemia. Her gynecologist prescribed NSAIDs, but they hadn't worked. He then recommended hysterectomy, but she felt that she was too young, and she didn't know whether she wanted to have more children. I suggested that she take *Ba Zhen Tang*, and I also started acupuncture. After four sessions, her energy returned, and after six more sessions, her excessive menstrual bleeding was reduced to normal levels.

Step 5: Take Shepherd's Purse or Chasteberry

If your menorrhagia continues despite the previous steps, try the Western herb shepherd's purse. The dosage is three times per day in the following forms: 4ml to 6ml of the tincture (1:5), 0.5ml to 2.0ml of the fluid extract (1:1), or 250mg to 500mg of the solid powdered extract (4:1). You can also take chasteberry (solid extract, standardized to 0.5 percent agnuside, 175mg to 225mg daily), which works through its hormonal effects. It may take eight weeks or more to be effective. Keep in mind that chasteberry can cause decreased libido.

Step 6: Undergo Dilatation and Curettage (D&C)

If your excessive bleeding is not controlled with the above noninvasive steps, your gynecologist can perform *dilatation* and *curettage* (*D&C*), an outpatient surgical procedure that cleans out the inner lining of the uterus.

Step 7: Take Prescription Danazol

If your menorrhagia is still uncontrolled or very severe, your doctor might prescribe Danazol, a male hormone that temporarily stops the menstrual cycle. Danazol does have several side effects, such as hot flashes, acne, and weight gain, so use it as a last resort before considering major surgery.

Step 8: Undergo Hysterectomy or Endometrial Destruction

The treatment of last resort is *hysterectomy* or *endometrial destruction* (*laser ablation* or *resection*), which can be done for uncontrolled bleeding or severe endometriosis, or for other uncontrollable conditions. Endometrial destruction has short-term advantages, including shorter operating time and hospital stay, fewer complications, faster recovery, and less need for pain medication. However, 30 percent to 90 percent of women will have continued bleeding, although not severe, and 40 percent will require repeat surgery within four years. Most women report higher satisfaction with hysterectomy. These procedures are suitable only for women who no longer want to become pregnant.

Your Balanced Healing Action Plan for Irregular Menstruation

Step 1: Undergo Acupuncture

I recommend acupuncture as the first step, to avoid the need to take hormones. The principal acupuncture points usually are found on the legs, feet, and ankles. Always seek evaluation and treatment from a practitioner certified in acupuncture. (See Appendix A, under "Acupuncture," for guidance on finding a qualified acupuncturist and for further explanation on different acupuncture techniques.) You should notice improvement within one to two periods, but you might need additional sessions to keep your cycles regular.

Step 2: Take Appropriate Chinese Herbal Remedies

Chinese herbal formulas can effectively regulate menstruation, and they should be used with acupuncture for faster results. Suggested formulas include *Ba Zhen Tang* or *Wen Jing*

Tang. Consult a practitioner qualified in Chinese herbal medicine to determine which Chinese herbal formulas are the best for your particular syndromes. You should notice improvement within your first two periods, but you may need to take the formulas longer to completely restore your cycles to regularity. (See Appendix A, under "Chinese Herbs," for further information.)

Step 3: Take Birth Control Pills (Hormone Therapy)

If the previous steps don't regulate your periods, your doctor can prescribe hormonal therapy, usually oral contraceptives (birth control pills). I recommend the previous steps first because they have less potentially harmful side effects than oral contraceptives. However, if you want regular periods and birth control, oral contraceptives give you both.

MIGRAINE (see *Headaches*)

MOTION SICKNESS

Motion sickness is nausea and dizziness that occur during traveling in a vehicle or on a boat. You feel motion sickness when your brain receives conflicting information from your senses, including your eyes, inner ear, and nervous system.

Symptoms

- Sweating
- Dizziness
- Paleness
- Nausea

Your Balanced Healing Action Plan for Motion Sickness

Step 1: Apply Acupressure

Massaging the acupuncture point (acupressure) on Pericardium 6 (P6) in the anterior forearm is an excellent way to relieve motion sickness. P6 is located in the forearm (palm side), two Chinese units from your wrist crease (one unit is the width of your thumb joint). Massage the point deeply to get an effect. It may feel tender or sore. You can also purchase bands that contain a hard nodule (Sea-Bands) that can stimulate this point by positioning the nodule over the P6 point.

Step 2: Take Ginger

If acupressure doesn't help, I recommend taking ginger. The dosage is 2g of powdered root with water, ginger tea, or in capsules, 250mg four times a day.

Jordan, a 44-year-old bank vice-president, would not get on a boat because she would always get motion sickness. She was getting married and wanted to take a cruise, so she wanted some method to prevent the motion sickness. She had tried Dramamine and scopolamine previously, but these drugs only partially helped. I showed her how to use acupressure on the P6 acupuncture point and also suggested that she take ginger in combination with long-acting scopolamine. She was able to enjoy her seven-day cruise without any motion sickness.

Step 3: Take Dimenhydrinate or Use Scopolamine Patches

If you are still having symptoms, you can try over-the-counter dimenhydrinate (Dramamine), a conventional drug that is quite effective for motion sickness. For a long trip, your doctor can prescribe scopolamine patches for long-term relief. Be sure to wash your hands after placing the patch behind your ear, because any drug remaining on your fingers can cause your pupils to dilate (causing double vision) if any of it gets into your eyes.

Step 4: Take an Appropriate Homeopathic Remedy

Homeopathic remedies that are effective for motion sickness include *Petroleum, Ipecac, Nux vomica,* or *Cocculus,* depending on your symptoms. You should consult a qualified homeopathist for guidance on which remedies will be most beneficial and for proper dosages. You should feel better within a few minutes to an hour of taking these remedies. (See Appendix A, under "Homeopathy," for guidance on finding a qualified homeopathist and for further information.)

MULTIPLE SCLEROSIS (MS)

Multiple sclerosis (MS) is an immune-system dysfunction in which your body makes cells that destroy the protective covering (called *myelin*) of nerves, causing conduction abnormalities in the nerve. There are several types of MS, from occasional attacks to chronic and progressive. The resulting symptoms vary in severity and frequency. Although there is no cure for MS, life expectancy is not affected.

Common Symptoms

- Motor and sensory nerve disturbances
- Blurred or double vision
- Pain
- Cognitive (thinking) problems
- Dizziness
- Muscle weakness
- Tingling sensations

- Weakness
- Stiffness
- Spasticity and tremors
- Instability and lack of balance or coordination
- Bladder or bowel leakage
- Constipation
- Fatigue
- Depression

General Recommendations

Diet: Nutrition is especially important in MS because an imbalance of fatty substances has been noted in people with MS. I recommend the Swank diet, designed by Dr. Roy Swank of Oregon State University; this diet increases your intake of fatty acids and decreases saturated fats. It's basically a low-fat diet supplemented with fish oil. The following changes are recommended in this diet:

- You don't eat red meat for the first year, including dark meat from chicken and turkey.
- You can eat 3 ounces of red meat once a week after the first year.
- Do not partake of dairy products containing 1 percent butterfat or more.
- Do not eat any processed foods containing saturated fats.
- Saturated fat intake should not exceed 15g per day.
- Unsaturated oils should be kept between 20g and 50g daily.
- Take fish oil, flaxseed oil, or cod liver oil supplements, along with a multivitamin.

(For further information on the Swank diet, and recipes, you can buy the book, *The Multiple Sclerosis Diet Book: A Low-Fat Diet for the Treatment of* M.S.)

The only other diet that I recommend is the MacDougall diet (gluten- and fructose-free with megavitamins), also referred to as the *Paleolithic* diet because it was used by our ancestors. Roger MacDougall was a playwright who had MS, and he developed this diet to control his disease. (For more information on the MacDougall Diet, go to www.direct-ms.org or www.paleodiet.com.)

Exercise can reduce and help prevent some of the muscular disturbances in MS. I recommend gentle stretching, swimming, and low-impact aerobics. Don't exercise strenuously or during an attack.

Your Balanced Healing Action Plan for Multiple Sclerosis

- If your MS is already severe or progressive, start with Step 2, and then return to Step 1 when your symptoms are stable.

Step 1: Take Vitamin E, Selenium, Vitamin B$_{12}$, and Flaxseed or Fish Oil

Nutritional supplements are valuable for improving symptoms of MS. I recommend vitamin E (800 IU), selenium (200mcg to 400mcg), vitamin B_{12} (1,000mcg daily), and fish oil (2g to 4g daily) or flaxseed oil (1 tablespoon per day). Vitamin E and selenium detoxify free radicals that are thought to play a role in MS. Vitamin B_{12} is often deficient in MS patients and is essential for proper nerve function. Flaxseed or fish oil increases fatty acids (which are deficient in MS) and improves immunity. It may take one to three months to notice improvement.

Step 2: Take Prescription Interferon

If your symptoms are severe or progressive, you may need a prescription for β-1A/B-interferon (Avonex, Betaseron), which has been the primary treatment to decrease the severity and frequency of attacks. Another form of Interferon, α-interferon, appears to be more promising but is still being tested.

Step 3: Take Other Appropriate Prescription Medications for Short-Term Relief of Various Symptoms

Various conventional medications can reduce specific symptoms of MS. Although these medications provide only temporary relief, they are fast acting and can relieve your symptoms while you try the remaining steps. If the following steps work well, you may be able to reduce or discontinue these medications. These medications include the following:

- Corticosteroids, intravenous followed by oral, for **blurred or double vision** (caused by optic neuritis, inflammation of the vision nerve of the eye)
- Baclofen, botulinum toxin, diazepam, tizanidine, for **spasticity**
- Muscle relaxants, for **stiffness**
- Amantadine, fluoxetine, methylphenidate, pemoline, for **fatigue**
- Oxybutynin, tolterodine, propantheline bromide, imipramine, for **bladder problems**
- Bulking agents (such as psyllium seeds), anticholinergics, for **fecal incontinence**
- Benzodiazepines (Valium, Xanax), gabapentin (Neurontin), for **tremor**
- Cladribine, for general stabilization and improvement

Step 4: Receive Acupuncture for Long-Term Relief of Various Symptoms

I highly recommend acupuncture for long-term relief of various MS symptoms, including pain, spasticity, stiffness, and fatigue. You can take the above medications while undergoing acupuncture, and if and when the acupuncture is beneficial, you may then be able to decrease or discontinue those medications, under your doctor's guidance. Principal points depend on the areas affected, such as arm, leg, or vision, and on your particular symptoms.

You should always seek evaluation and treatment from a practitioner certified in acupuncture. (See Appendix A, under "Acupuncture," for guidance in finding a qualified acupuncturist and for further explanation of the different acupuncture techniques.) You should notice improvement within six treatments, but you might need additional sessions for maximum benefits.

> Shirley, a 43-year-old office manager, had chronic progressive multiple sclerosis, which gave her severe fatigue, extreme spasticity and stiffness, and pain. Despite aggressive treatment with interferon and other conventional medications, she was unable to perform any activities. She would have such severe spasms that, for hours at a time, she could not extend her hips and legs. I prescribed nutritional supplements and started her on acupuncture. After the first session of acupuncture, her energy and flexibility increased remarkably, and she spent an entire day cleaning her house. She continued to have pain and spasm, but with more acupuncture, the severity and frequency of her spasm attacks, and all her other symptoms, decreased significantly.

Step 5: Take Pancreatin

If you are still suffering symptoms, I recommend taking Pancreatin (pancreatic enzymes), which is helpful in reducing the severity and frequency of flare-ups involving visual disturbances, sensory disturbances, and bladder and bowel function, but not tremor, dizziness, or spasticity. These enzymes work by decreasing immune complexes (antigens that attack the nerve bound to antibodies that fight them) that may cause some of the symptoms of MS.

Step 6: Take Lecithin

If the previous steps only partially help your symptoms, take lecithin (5g to 15g per day), which can strengthen nerve sheaths. It may take one to three months to notice improvement.

Step 7: Receive Feldenkrais Method and Proprioceptive Neuromuscular Facilitation (PNF) to Help Muscle Function

Bodywork is very helpful in preventing muscle deterioration and improving coordination and balance. I recommend the *Feldenkrais method* and *PNF* (*Proprioceptive Neuromuscular Facilitation*). These techniques improve the structure and functioning of the body using manual therapy techniques to rebalance and recondition the body. However, they are quite distinct from massage, chiropractic, and osteopathic methods. They require "hands-on" treatment by therapists trained in the particular technique (see Appendix A, under "Bodywork," for further information and suggestions for finding a qualified practitioner.)

Step 8: Undergo Bee Venom Therapy

Apitherapy, or *bee venom therapy* (BVT), has anecdotally given relief to some people with MS. You allow yourself to be stung by live bees. Caution is necessary if you have an allergy to bee venom, and you might consider this method only when all else has failed and your symptoms remain intolerable. Undergo this treatment only with a practitioner who is knowledgeable and experienced in this technique.

NAUSEA DURING PREGNANCY
(Hyperemesis of Pregnancy: Morning Sickness)

Nausea and vomiting are common during pregnancy in a pattern known as morning sickness because, most of the time, these symptoms occur in the morning only. However, many women have nausea and vomiting throughout the day. Nausea usually goes away after the first trimester (first three months of pregnancy), but it continues throughout pregnancy in some women.

What You Need to Know

Morning sickness is usually mild and causes no harmful effects unless you can't keep food down long enough for your body to digest it. If this happens, you need to see your obstetrician to make sure you are receiving adequate nutrition and hydration.

General Recommendations

Diet: It is difficult to maintain a good diet when you have nausea. If possible, try to eat dry toast immediately after rising and small, frequent meals throughout the day.

Your Balanced Healing Action Plan for Nausea During Pregnancy

Step 1: Undergo Acupuncture

Acupuncture works quickly to reduce and eliminate morning sickness for the duration of the pregnancy, and I recommend it as the first course of treatment. Often, only two to four treatments are necessary. Principal points usually are found on the arms, legs, feet, and abdomen. **Caution:** Several acupuncture points are considered forbidden points in pregnant women because they may induce spontaneous miscarriage. Always seek evaluation and treatment from a practitioner certified in acupuncture. (See Appendix A, under "Acupuncture," for guidance in finding a qualified acupuncturist and for further explanation of the different acupuncture techniques.)

Mandy, a 33-year-old full-time mom, was pregnant for the third time. She had mild nausea during the first trimester of her first pregnancy, and more nausea and some vomiting that lasted into her second trimester during her second pregnancy. She started having both nausea and vomiting all day long with her third pregnancy, and for a week she had not been able to retain fluids or food. Her obstetrician told her she would have to go into the hospital if the problems continued another few days. After her first acupuncture treatment, her vomiting stopped, and she was able to drink some fluids. After two more acupuncture treatments, her nausea occurred only for a few hours in the morning, and she was able to eat and drink. After two additional acupuncture sessions, her nausea went away entirely and did not return during the remainder of her pregnancy.

Step 2: Take Ginger

If acupuncture doesn't work, or while you're waiting for it to work, ginger can be effective in reducing and preventing hyperemesis during pregnancy. Use 1g to 2g of dry powder (you can make it into a tea as well), or 100mg to 200mg of extracts, standardized to contain 20 percent gingerol and shogaol, on a daily basis.

Step 3: Take Vitamin B$_6$

If the previous steps fail to provide relief or give you only partial relief, take vitamin B$_6$ (25mg two to three times per day).

Step 4: Undergo Counseling

Studies have shown that certain circumstances can increase and/or prolong morning sickness—for example, the pregnancy is unplanned or undesired, or the woman has a negative relationship with her mother. Counseling is recommended if this is a possibility.

NECK PAIN

Neck pain is the second-most-common health complaint in the United States. There are several categories of neck pain: uncomplicated pain (sprain), whiplash (caused by sudden thrust backward and forward), and pain with *radiculopathy* (radiating down the arms). Many factors can cause neck pain, including injury, poor posture, occupational problems, and arthritis (degenerative disc disease).

What You Need to Know

Neck pain can be a result of poor posture, stress, depression, and anxiety. These factors can, in turn, make neck pain worse and even prevent treatment from being effective. It is important to consider these factors in looking for ways to relieve your neck pain.

General Recommendations

Exercise: For acute neck pain, many practitioners start by prescribing formal exercises. Although these help some people, they also may make your pain or inflammation worse. If your pain worsens, postpone these exercises until you feel better. On the other hand, I don't advise complete rest, because it may cause more stiffness, loss of muscular tone, and disability. I recommend that you continue doing as many physical activities as you can tolerate.

In **chronic neck pain** (pain lasting more than three to six months), exercise is more important. Exercise stimulates large neurons (brain cells) to help reduce the perception of pain and stimulate the production of natural pain-killers from the brain. Stretching and resistance exercises are the main forms, along with exercises specifically designed for the neck (a registered physical therapist can teach you these). Rest makes pain and disability worse, so you need to keep moving.

Meditation can lessen the severity and duration of chronic neck pain when you do it regularly, especially when stress or anxiety is involved. Meditation also can relax the neck muscles, allowing increased blood and oxygen flow (see "Meditation," under "Simple Healing Steps for All Health Conditions," page 79, for more information and examples).

Your Balanced Healing Action Plan for Acute Neck Pain

- For severe neck pain with radiation down your arm, or neurological signs such as reflex loss, weakening, or paralysis of your arms, seek emergency treatment.
- Neck collars are often provided in emergency rooms or by primary care doctors if you've been injured, but prolonged use can cause additional problems and slows healing. They should not be used for more than a few days, or very intermittently.
- Treatments that have been shown to be ineffective for acute neck pain include bed rest and traction. Treatments that have doubtful effectiveness include antidepressants, behavioral therapy, neck braces, biofeedback, spray and stretch, and TENS units.

Step 1: Take Over-the-Counter Pain Relievers

If your neck pain is mild to moderate, I recommend that you start with pain relievers such as Tylenol, or over-the-counter nonsteroidal anti-inflammatory drugs (NSAIDS), such as Advil, Aleve, and ibuprofen. These medications relieve discomfort temporarily while your body has time to heal itself.

Step 2: Take Prescription Medications for Short-Term Relief

If the OTC medications don't control your pain, your doctor can prescribe stronger NSAIDs, such as Daypro, Relafen, Orudis, Mobic, Naprosyn, or Cataflam. These are all equally effective, although one may work better for you than another. You may have to try several to see which is the most effective for you (ask your doctor for samples). However, stomach irritation or bleeding may occur. If you have such side effects, then try Cox-2 inhibitors, which have less risk of these problems. **Caution:** Recent studies show an increased risk of heart attack in patients who take high-dose Cox-2 inhibitors along with naproxen (Aleve), so caution is advised if you have heart disease.

Muscle relaxants (Flexeril, Robaxin, Parafon Forte, or Soma) are commonly prescribed for acute neck pain and can reduce spasm but can cause drowsiness. You should take them primarily during the first few days of neck pain. After that, they lose their effectiveness. Avoid taking narcotics if possible, but if your pain is not relieved by prescription NSAIDs, you can use narcotics for a short period of time (longer use can cause addiction). All these medications should be used for a temporary period of time, until the other steps have time to work.

Step 3: Undergo Physical Therapy Modalities

Along with the previous steps, I recommend physical therapy modalities such as therapeutic massage and electrical current (both direct current and alternating current can be applied to the painful areas; I prefer alternating, which can project deeper into the tissues without burning the skin). These methods increase blood flow and oxygen delivery to the damaged tissues, helping them heal faster. Other modalities include hot packs (dilate blood vessels and increase blood flow to the damaged area), and cold packs (decrease swelling and spasm). Ultrasound (high-frequency sound that projects heat into the deep tissues) can be used for some patients, but it can be irritating if there is inflammation. I also highly recommend infrasound, or low-frequency sound therapy. In distinction to ultrasound, infrasound works by increasing the local circulation of blood, lymph, and the activity of the nervous system to accelerate the healing process. Not only can it reduce pain, but it can also decrease spasms and swelling. Numerous chiropractors, naturopaths, acupuncturists, and a few doctors use infrasound. (See Appendix C, under "Infrasound," for a reference source.)

You should feel better in 6 to 12 treatments from physical therapy modalities, but you might need additional treatments depending on the severity of your condition. Primary care doctors who have the necessary equipment can provide physical therapy treatments, but if you are not improving, you should ask your doctor to refer you to a registered physical therapist who is more specifically trained in using these modalities and usually has more advanced equipment. If you do not notice improvement in your condition after 6 to 12 treatments, proceed with the next step.

Step 4: Receive Osteopathic Mobilization or Chiropractic Manipulation

If physical therapy modalities do not help, osteopathic mobilization or chiropractic manipulation can improve uncomplicated neck and whiplash problems, particularly if structural problems (bones, ligaments, tendons, joints, and/or muscles not working correctly) are causing your neck pain. If structural problems are evident, then they must be corrected, or your symptoms may continue or reoccur. You can combine either of these treatments with physical therapy modalities for faster results. Your pain should improve in 6 to 8 treatments; if it does not, proceed with the following steps. If you are improving, continue the treatments until your improvement levels off or your symptoms resolve. However, if you still have pain after 15 to 20 treatments, you need further evaluation or different treatment.

Step 5: Undergo Acupuncture

Acupuncture is especially effective for reducing muscle spasms and trigger points (small areas of muscle tenderness). Principal points usually are found on the neck and arms, and at specific *Ah Shi* points (areas that are painful to pressure). Always seek evaluation and treatment from a practitioner certified in acupuncture. (See Appendix A, under "Acupuncture," for guidance on finding a qualified acupuncturist and for further explanation of the different acupuncture techniques.) You should notice improvement within six treatments, but you might need additional sessions for maximum benefits.

Step 6: Undergo Psychotherapy If Diagnostic Testing Is Normal

If your symptoms still persist, or if arm symptoms and/or neurological signs worsen, diagnostic testing, such as MRI or CT scan, is indicated. If disc or nerve abnormalities are *not* noted, underlying psychological factors may be prolonging your pain, even if you are not aware of them. You should seek evaluation from a psychotherapist who treats pain syndromes. You should realize that this does not mean that you are "crazy" or have a mental problem. Many people simply do not realize that other psychosocial factors can prolong pain, and once you are aware of these factors, you can heal properly.

Step 7: Receive Epidural Steroid Injections If the Testing Is Abnormal

An epidural steroid injection may relieve your symptoms if the testing reveals disc or nerve abnormalities that correlate with your symptoms but do not yet require surgery, if arm pain is present, and if it has been less than two months since the start of your symptoms. If two initial injections relieve your pain for only a few hours or days, further injections will usually not be beneficial. If effective, pain relief should last at least from four to six months up to a year. Epidural injections usually don't help if you have normal test findings.

Other injections can also be tried as well, depending on your symptoms, physical findings, and MRI results. These include trigger-point injections (injection of cortisone into tender muscle areas), facet-joint injections (injection of cortisone in the joints that connect the bones of the spine), or selective nerve-root blocks (injections of cortisone around the nerves coming from the spinal cord and going to the legs). Like epidurals, these injections may be effective only temporarily, but they might give you pain relief while your body has time to heal itself.

> Alexis, an 18-year-old college student, injured her neck when she slipped and fell on a patch of ice. She had constant neck pain, with pain and numbness in her arms. Her doctor prescribed pain medications, muscle relaxants, and NSAIDs, but she continued to have pain, so her doctor sent her for physical therapy. This involved exercises, which made her worse. She underwent an MRI scan, which showed mildly bulging discs. She was sent for three epidural steroid injections, but the first relieved her pain for a week, and the other two did not provide any relief. I started her on osteopathic manipulation as well as acupuncture for the pain and spasm. She started improving after one week, and she was pain free after one month.

Step 8: Undergo Additional Diagnostic Testing

If your symptoms continue, I recommend further testing, such as a *discogram*, which is the injection of a dye into the disc spaces. If leakage of dye is detected by x-ray and the injection causes the same pain that you have had shooting down your arm, you may have a disc rupture. Another test is the *myelogram*, in which dye is injected into the spinal column, outlining the spinal nerves as they leave the spinal cord and go to the arm. If the dye's flow is obstructed, this may mean that the nerve is being compressed by a ruptured disc.

Both of these tests can reveal abnormalities not observed on MRI—or confirm abnormalities that are seen on MRI.

Step 9: Undergo IDET

IDET (*IntraDiscal Electrothermal Therapy*) is a procedure that is used when there is a tear in the covering of a spinal disc (*annular tear*). IDET involves placing a wire around the disc and heating it, thus sealing the tear. The ideal patient for IDET has only one or two damaged discs with a limited area of damage. Healing may take four to six months following the procedure, during which time your activities must be limited. There are no serious complications, but long-term effectiveness is not known because IDET has been in use only since 1997.

Step 10: Undergo Surgery

Surgery should be the last resort or used if you have unrelenting arm pain and/or neurological signs that correlate with MRI or myelogram findings. Surgery may reduce radiating pain but may not be as helpful for reducing the neck pain. The optimum time for surgery is within three to six months of when your pain begins; the optimum time can be as long as a year. In general, however, the longer the symptoms have been present, the poorer the results. In fact, surgery can worsen your pain and other symptoms in the future, requiring additional neck surgeries to relieve the recurrent symptoms. This occurs especially if only one or two levels are fused together, which causes more pressure to be exerted on the discs above and below. This can accelerate the deterioration of these discs over the next few years, resulting in additional or recurrent problems.

Your Balanced Healing Action Plan for Chronic Neck Pain

- Chronic neck problems (lasting longer than three to six months) are very different from acute problems and do not usually respond to basic medications or physical therapy. Although stronger NSAIDs and pain medications (such as tramadol) can control the symptoms in many cases, I recommend proceeding with the following methods to correct the underlying cause, and thus reduce or eliminate the need for medications.
- Many doctors may tell you that there is nothing more they can do to relieve your pain and that you will just have to learn to live with it. In most cases, I do not believe that, especially if you use the following steps. Although the goal is always to eliminate pain, sometimes complete relief may not be possible. A more reasonable goal is to lessen the pain enough to be able to enjoy life and participate in most activities of daily living.
- Bed rest, biofeedback, chiropractic manipulation, facet-joint injections, epidural steroid injections, neck supports, and traction have not been shown to give long-term relief in most people who have chronic pain.

Step 1: Go to Back School

Sitting, lifting, and performing other activities properly are very important in both preventing and treating neck problems. Back school teaches you dozens of ways to avoid worsening and flare-ups of neck pain and help prevent further injuries. Many registered physical therapists teach at back schools, so inquire in your area or ask your doctor for a recommendation.

Step 2: Undergo Low-Level Energy Laser Treatment

I first recommend the use of low-level energy lasers because, in my studies, the laser appears to help heal the tissue, reduce the inflammatory response, and give long-lasting relief for arthritic, nerve, and disc problems. These lasers are called "cold" lasers, because they do not produce heat like the hot lasers used in surgical procedures. You should notice improvement within six to nine treatments (two to three weeks). Because this is currently a research device unavailable to most doctors, see Appendix C for a reference source.

Step 3: Undergo Acupuncture

If you are still having pain, I next recommend acupuncture. At my clinic, I usually combine acupuncture with the laser for better results, but acupuncture alone can also provide significant decrease in your pain. Principal points usually are found on the neck, upper back, shoulder, and wrists. Always seek evaluation and treatment from a practitioner certified in acupuncture. (See Appendix A, under "Acupuncture," for guidance in finding a qualified acupuncturist and for further explanation of the different acupuncture techniques.) You should feel better within six treatments, but you might need additional sessions for maximum benefits.

Step 4: Receive Osteopathic Mobilization Therapy or Chiropractic Manipulation

If the previous steps fail to bring you relief, underlying structural problems (bones, ligaments, tendons, joints, and/or muscles not working correctly) may be either causing your chronic neck pain or not allowing proper healing to take place. I recommend osteopathic treatment to correct these underlying structural problems. This first requires an osteopathic exam. If structural problems are evident, then they should be corrected before other treatments are done, or your symptoms may continue to reoccur.

With osteopathic treatment, your pain should start decreasing in 3 to 6 treatments, although you might need additional treatments for maximum benefit. If your pain is still present after 10 to 12 treatments, you need further evaluation or a different treatment method. (See Appendix A, under "Manual Therapy," for more information on osteopathic treatment and guidance in finding a qualified practitioner.)

Chiropractic manipulation is also commonly performed and can help some people, but studies have not shown long-term effectiveness for most chronic neck pain, which is why I prefer osteopathic adjustments. If you choose chiropractic care, you should observe improvement within six to eight treatments, although you might need occasional maintenance adjustments.

I see many patients who have received chiropractic adjustments every week (sometimes several times a week) for years, with pain relief lasting only a few hours or days. These perpetual, frequent adjustments are not appropriate and can be harmful (see Appendix A, under "Manual Therapy," for further explanation.) Do not continue with chiropractic manipulation after 10 to 12 treatments if this method fails to give you long-term relief.

Step 5: Undergo Feldenkrais Method, Alexander Technique, or Rolfing

If you are still suffering from chronic neck pain, the *Feldenkrais method, Alexander technique,* and *Rolfing* are all forms of bodywork that may be effective for chronic neck pain that doesn't respond to other treatments. Bodywork involves realigning, rebalancing, and retraining the structures of the body, which have become dysfunctional due to pain, injury, disuse, or misuse. The Feldenkrais method focuses on retraining the way you move your body, to interrupt unhealthy patterns of movement that have become habits. The Alexander technique concentrates on correcting faulty posture in daily activities (sitting, standing, and moving). Rolfing involves manipulating and stretching the body's fascial tissues (deep connective tissues that hold your body together), thus allowing correct realigning of the body. These bodywork methods require a therapist certified in these techniques. (See Appendix A for further information on bodywork; see Appendix C to help find a qualified therapist.) It may take several months (sometimes less) to observe benefits from these methods.

Step 6: Practice Appropriate Yoga Postures

For neck pain that continues, I recommend practicing yoga. Yoga promotes relaxation and stretching, both of which are important in healing and preventing further neck pain. Because there are many different types of yoga, with some better for neck pain than others, I recommend working with a qualified yoga instructor. (See Appendix A for further information on yoga, and Appendix C to find a qualified yoga instructor.) It may take several months to notice improvement.

Step 7: Try a TENS Unit

The previous steps are designed to reduce your symptoms for a long time. For continued pain that cannot be relieved long term, there are some treatments designed to give you temporary relief.

Start with a *TENS* unit (*Transcutaneous Electrical Nerve Stimulator*), which involves wearing a small electrical generator strapped to your belt; the generator is attached by wires to small pads placed around the area of pain. Turning up the amplitude will give you more stimulation. This unit can be worn continuously to control pain, although sometimes it can lose effectiveness over time.

Step 8: Apply Emu Oil, Long Crystal Menthol, Biofreeze, Capsaicin, Glucosamine/MSM, or Prescription Topical Compounds to the Painful Area

For residual pain or flare-ups of pain, there are several topical solutions that can give temporary relief when applied over the painful area. These include emu oil, long crystal menthol, Biofreeze, capsaicin, glucosamine/MSM, as well as other herbal combinations. These products won't cure the source of your pain, but they may provide pain relief for two to eight hours or longer and have minimal side effects (most commonly, skin allergy or sensitivity). Some of these may work better than others, so you may have to try several to find the best one. In my clinic, I apply samples to my patients so they'll know whether the product works before they buy it. Encourage your doctor or practitioner to do the same.

Other topicals use a mixture of prescription medications that are combined into a gel that is absorbed into the soft tissues. Some of these medications include gabapentin (Neurontin), baclofen, ketamine, clonidine, or amitriptyline (Elavil). A prescription from a doctor is required, but you can obtain the information from a pharmacist who prepares the medications and bring it to your doctor for his approval.

Step 9: Take Prescription NSAIDs

If the topical pain relievers are not helpful, then your doctor can prescribe stronger non-steroidal anti-inflammatory drugs (NSAIDs), such as Naprosyn, Feldene, Daypro, Orudis, Mobic, Cataflam, Relafen, Arthrotec, and many more. These medications may take three weeks to be effective and should be discontinued if there is no benefit or the side effects (such as stomach irritation and bleeding) become intolerable. If this occurs, you can try Cox-2 inhibitors, which have less risk of these side effects. **NOTE:** Recent studies show an increased risk of heart attack in patients who use high-dose Cox-2 inhibitors along with naproxen (Aleve), so caution is advised. Also, if you have taken an NSAID (including ibuprofen) for a long time, it may precipitate a heart attack if you stop taking it suddenly. Obtain guidance from your doctor, especially if you have heart disease.

> Judy, a 48-year-old owner of a dry-cleaning establishment, had an automobile accident 15 years ago. It left her with chronic neck pain. Each doctor would prescribe the same treatments (physical therapy, NSAIDs, epidural steroid injections, and other injections), even though these treatments never worked. She had seen a chiropractor, who told her she would need treatment twice a week for at least a year; but after 20 treatments, her pain was not improved. She had seen an osteopathic physician, and his treatment had helped, but only a minimal amount because there were only minor structural problems. She had tried numerous topical solutions, both prescribed and from health food stores, and some gave her one to two hours of relief. When she came to me, I started her on acupuncture. After only three treatments, she was able to return to golf and tennis, favorite activities she had long ago given up because of her pain. After five more treatments, her pain was nearly gone.

Step 10: Take Appropriate Chinese Herbal Remedies

If you are still suffering from neck pain, my next suggestion is to try these Chinese herbal formulations:

- For chronic pain: *Shu Jing Huo Xue Tang, Qi Li San,* or *Huo Luo Xiao Ling Dan*
- For muscle tension: *Chai Hu Gui Zhi Tang* or *Chai Hu Mu Li Long Gu Tang*
- For muscle spasm: *Shao Yao Gan Cao Tang*

Consult a practitioner qualified in Chinese herbal medicine to determine which Chinese herbal formulas are the best for your particular condition. You should notice improvement within three weeks, but you may need to take the herbs longer for complete relief. (See Appendix A, under "Chinese Herbs," for further information.)

Step 11: Use Biomagnets

Biomagnets applied to the neck (either taped or contained in a neck brace) are worth a try if you still have pain after following the previous steps. However, any relief biomagnets provide disappears when the magnet is removed. There are many different types and strengths of magnets, as well as unipole, dipole, and north- or south-directed, all of which can make a difference in whether they are effective for your condition. Biomagnets should help relieve your pain almost immediately. (See Appendix B for more information on biomagnets.)

Step 12: Take Low-Dose Prescription Antidepressants

If your pain still persists, your doctor can prescribe low-dose antidepressants such as amitriptyline (Elavil) 25mg to 50mg daily or trazodone (Desyrel) 50mg to 150mg daily. These drugs can decrease chronic neck pain through effects on the pain center (hypothalamus) and neurotransmitters in the brain, but they are effective in only some people.

Step 13: Undergo Guided Imagery, Biofeedback, and Hypnosis

For pain that continues, I recommend mind-body techniques such as guided imagery, biofeedback, and hypnosis in combination with the previous steps (for more information and help finding qualified practitioners, see Appendix A, under "Mind-Body Techniques").

Step 14: Enter a Multidisciplinary Pain Program

If your chronic neck pain still continues, I recommend entering a multidisciplinary pain program. Although such programs are not designed to reduce neck pain specifically, they do improve functional and back-to-work ability, and they teach you how to cope better with your pain. They usually include evaluation and treatment by pain-management specialists, physical and occupational therapists, and psychologists or psychiatrists.

Step 15: Undergo Epidural Steroid Injection, Nerve-Root Block, or Rhizotomy

If your pain is still present and is severe, you can try undergoing several types of spinal injections. Although these procedures don't often provide long-lasting relief, they are worth trying before undergoing any surgery. *Epidural steroid injections* can occasionally benefit chronic neck pain, but if two injections haven't given you long-term relief, additional injections won't either. Selective *nerve-root blocks* can sometimes deaden a nerve, but again they may give you only temporary relief.

Rhizotomy destroys the nerve root either by cutting, using radio waves, or injecting a chemical into it. Success is defined as greater than 50 percent pain relief that lasts an average of six months. There are side effects possible, including numbness, sensation loss, and difficulty in bladder or bowel control. Often, your nerve will grow back and the pain will return. I recommend rhizotomy only for intractable, unrelenting pain that prevents you from participating in most activities.

Step 16: Undergo Surgery

Surgeries should be avoided if at all possible in chronic neck pain. Most surgeries done for chronic neck pain are fusions, with or without instrumentation (placing rods, screws and/or cages), and should be done only for unrelenting pain with evidence of structural deterioration of the discs, and/or additional or worsening neurological signs. Many of these surgeries are done to prevent further deterioration, but be aware that if surgery involves a fusion at one or two levels, more pressure becomes exerted on the spinal disks above and below the fusion, commonly causing them to deteriorate within two to five years. This is why many people have recurrent neck pain and end up undergoing multiple surgeries.

Step 17: Take Long-Term Prescription Narcotics

If nothing else has worked, the only way for you to obtain pain relief is with drugs. Narcotic medications are appropriate *only* for severe, unrelenting neck pain that has not responded to any other treatments. They vary in potency from propoxyphene to OxyContin to morphine. These drugs are highly addictive and should be monitored by a specialist in pain management.

NEURALGIA (Trigeminal, Post-Herpetic)

Neuralgia is nerve pain caused by irritation or damage to a nerve. The most common forms include *trigeminal neuralgia*, which involves a nerve in the face (the trigeminal nerve, or the 5th cranial nerve), and *post-herpetic neuralgia*, which involves nerves primarily in the torso (along rib margins) but also the face. Pressure from a blood vessel or trauma to the face can cause trigeminal neuralgia. Post-herpetic neuralgia is caused by the chickenpox virus (*herpes zoster*), which, after initially causing chickenpox, has remained dormant until some factor causes it to reappear (such as stress or trauma). The acute infection is more commonly known as *shingles*.

Common Symptoms

Severe pain in the distribution of the nerve, which can be sharp, stabbing, burning, or shooting; the pain can be intermittent or unrelenting, and you can be hypersensitive to touch in that area. The pain can occur in paroxysms that last a few seconds to a few minutes.

What You Need to Know

With trigeminal neuralgia, you can have hundreds of attacks a day—or go long periods (sometimes years) with no attacks. Touch or specific activities such as eating, talking, washing your face, or brushing your teeth can trigger attacks. In some people, the pain becomes more severe and less responsive to treatment over time.

Your Balanced Healing Action Plan for Neuralgia

Step 1: Undergo Acupuncture

I recommend acupuncture first, because it provides the fastest relief of any treatment. The sooner you start acupuncture after the onset of the pain, the more effective it is. For *intercostal neuralgia* (post-herpetic involving the ribs), principal points usually are found on the arms, legs, and over the ribs. For *trigeminal neuralgia*, principal points usually are found on the face, with supplemental points depending on the specific branch affected (there are three branches). Press tacks can be placed in the trigeminal nucleus point in the posterior ear, providing relief in many people. Press tacks are small needles that are embedded in an adhesive bandage and then are pressed in specific points in the ear. These needles remain in the ear for as long as possible, (on the average, one week) and are replaced when they fall out, or until the pain is gone. For better results, you can tap on the needle several times a day to stimulate the point.

Always seek evaluation and treatment from a practitioner certified in acupuncture. (See Appendix A, under "Acupuncture," for guidance in finding a qualified acupuncturist and for further explanation of the different acupuncture techniques.) You should notice improvement within six treatments (often fewer), but you might need additional sessions for maximum benefits.

> Earl, a 33-year-old Marine recruiter, had trigeminal neuralgia for several years. He had been prescribed numerous medications, none of which had helped. Because he lived more than 200 miles away, I placed press tacks in the trigeminal area points of both ears. These completely relieved his pain. He returned on two more occasions (three weeks apart) to have them replaced, but, after that, his pain went away for good.

Step 2: Take Appropriate Chinese Herbal Remedies

Along with acupuncture, you can also use a Chinese herbal formula to speed up the healing and rebalancing process. I often use the formula *Shao Yao Gan Cao Tang*, but there are others. Consult a practitioner qualified in Chinese herbal medicine to determine which Chinese herbal formulas are the best for your particular syndromes. You should observe initial benefits within one to two weeks, but you may need to take them longer for complete relief. (See Appendix A, under "Chinese Herbs," for further information.)

Step 3: Undergo Low-Energy Laser Treatment

If the previous steps fail to end your pain, I recommend undergoing treatment with a low-level energy laser because, in my studies, the laser reduces inflammation, heals the nerves, and gives long-lasting pain relief. These lasers are called "cold" lasers, because they do not produce heat like the hot lasers used in surgical procedures do. You should notice improvement within six to nine treatments (two to three weeks). Because the laser is currently a research device unavailable to most doctors, see Appendix C for a reference source.

Step 4: Apply Emu Oil, Long Crystal Menthol, Biofreeze, Capsaicin, or Prescription Compounds to the Painful Area

The previous steps target long-term relief. If they don't work, however, you should at least try to obtain short-term relief. I recommend starting with topical pain-relieving creams or lotions. Natural topicals include emu oil (usually with aloe vera and MSM), long crystal menthol, Biofreeze, capsaicin, and other herbal combinations.

If the natural topicals don't work, your doctor can prescribe topicals made from conventional drugs and mixed in a gel that is absorbed into the soft tissues. The topical forms of these drugs usually don't have the side effects that can occur if you take them orally. These drugs include gabapentin (Neurontin), amitriptyline, baclofen, ketamine, ketoprofen, and others. Whether natural or conventional, some topicals may work better than others, so you may have to try several to find the best one. You can also mix several different topicals for better results.

In my clinic, I apply samples to my patients so they'll know whether the product works before they purchase it. Encourage your doctor or practitioner to do the same. These topicals should give you pain relief in just a few minutes. They don't cure the underlying causes of pain, but may provide pain relief for two to eight hours or longer and have minimal side effects (most commonly, skin allergy or sensitivity).

Step 5: Take Prescription Carbamazepine, Baclofen, and/or Dilantin

If the previous steps still have not been fruitful, your doctor can prescribe various conventional drugs. Carbamazepine (Tegretol) is usually the first choice, but it can cause sedation. If carbamazepine is not effective, baclofen (Lioresal) is usually the next step. If your pain is still present, you can then try phenytoin (Dilantin). If these are not effective, you can substitute additional drugs, such as gabapentin (Neurontin), valproic acid, or clonazepam (Klonopin). You should notice improvement within one to three weeks.

Step 6: Take Prescription Amitriptyline

If the above drugs don't help, your doctor can prescribe tricyclic antidepressants, particularly amitriptyline (Elavil), which can be helpful in reducing chronic neuralgic pain in some people, and it can be added to the previous steps if pain continues. It usually takes three weeks for antidepressants to have a beneficial effect.

> Although the sores from a shingles outbreak healed after a few months, Dana, a 58-year-old guidance counselor, continued to have severe pain in her face and chest (where the outbreak occurred). She had seen several doctors who had prescribed Tegretol, Neurontin, and Elavil, none of which helped. The pain was so severe, Dana became very discouraged and felt like it wasn't worth living anymore. I first gave her an herbal topical, which gave her temporary relief for four to six hours. I gave her the Chinese herbal formula *Shao Yao Gan Cao Tang* and also performed acupuncture, which started working almost immediately. She needed only five acupuncture sessions to completely end her pain. Now Dana enjoys her life to the fullest!

Step 7: Take Prescription Narcotics

The medications of last resort are narcotics, which are indicated only for severe, unrelenting neuralgia that has not responded to any other treatments. They are used only to control your pain, but are highly addictive and have many side effects. They vary in potency from propoxyphene to OxyContin or morphine. A specialist in pain management should monitor your use of these drugs.

Step 8: Undergo Rhizotomy, Glycerol Injection, Microvascular Decompression, or Gamma-Knife Radiosurgery

As a last resort, there are some surgical procedures that sometimes improve trigeminal neuralgia. These include the following:

- *Radiofrequency rhizotomy* (90 percent effective, but you can have sensation loss, weakness, and eye sensitivity, and the pain can return after six months)
- *Glycerol injection* (85 percent effective, but with similar side effects)
- *Microvascular decompression* (90 percent effective, but it requires opening the skull)
- *Gamma-knife radiosurgery* (gives 70 percent of patients complete relief after one year, but after five to six years, only 56 percent of patients still have complete or partial relief)

NEUROPATHY, PERIPHERAL (Non-Diabetic)

Peripheral neuropathy is a degeneration of the nerves in your limbs, particularly the legs, but sometimes the arms. When it occurs, it usually starts at the toes or fingers and spreads up the lower legs or arms, usually stopping at the level of your knees or elbows. We don't know how many patients have peripheral neuropathy, but the condition becomes more common with advancing age. We also don't know what causes peripheral neuropathy, but it may be caused by environmental toxins. Peripheral neuropathy can be a progressive disease, gradually worsening, but it does not usually result in other complications.

Common Symptoms

- Tingling
- Numbness
- Burning
- Loss of function of limbs
- Pain
- Muscle weakness

What You Need to Know

Although symptoms of diabetic and non-diabetic neuropathy are similar, the cause is different, and thus the treatment also differs. (See the section on "Diabetes," page 187 for information on the treatment of diabetic neuropathy.)

Your Balanced Healing Action Plan for Peripheral Neuropathy (Non-Diabetic)

Step 1: Undergo Acupuncture

I first recommend acupuncture, which I have found to be the best method for reducing the symptoms of neuropathy, although it may work in only 50 percent of people. Principal acupuncture points are on the legs, but there are many miscellaneous and specialized points that are used by various schools of acupuncture. Ear points refer to the leg region. Always seek evaluation and treatment from a practitioner certified in acupuncture. (See Appendix A, under "Acupuncture," for guidance in finding a qualified acupuncturist and for further explanation of the different acupuncture techniques.) You should notice improvement within 6 to 8 treatments, but you might need additional sessions (sometimes 15 to 20) for maximum benefits.

Step 2: Use Infrasound

The use of low-frequency sound (infrasound) has been found to help reduce symptoms and can be used with acupuncture. It can be used in a sweeping motion down the legs and/or over specific acupuncture points. In distinction to ultrasound, infrasound works by increasing the local circulation of blood, lymph, and the activity of the nervous system to accelerate the healing process. Not only can it reduce pain—it can also decrease spasms and swelling. Numerous chiropractors, naturopaths, acupuncturists, and a few doctors use infrasound. (See Appendix C, under "Infrasound," for a reference source.)

Step 3: Take Appropriate Prescription Medications

If the previous steps are not effective, then I recommend conventional prescription medications. Neurontin (gabapentin) (300mg to 2400mg per day) is usually the primary drug recommended, and it can reduce symptoms to acceptable levels, but it might have intolerable side effects at higher doses (drowsiness, fatigue, dizziness). Other medications that may be used for neuropathic pain include low dose amitriptyline (25mg to 50mg per day), ketamine, amantadine, orphenadrine, haloperidol, carbamazepine, valproic acid, phenytoin, mexiletine, prazosin, baclofen, and nifedipine. These drugs can be given orally, by injection, and in some situations, sublingual (under the tongue), rectally, nasally, and in the buccal (cheek) region. Most of these drugs can reduce pain in one to three weeks. If they're not effective in this period of time, you should try another medication. Consult with your doctor for guidance on choosing the best drug for you.

> Regina, a 62-year-old postal worker, had progressive neuropathy for 10 years, with constant pain and numbness in both legs that became worse at night. She was taking large doses of Neurontin (2,400mg per day), which helped, but it caused fatigue and drowsiness. I started her on acupuncture. She required about 15 treatments but was able to decrease the dose of her Neurontin to 300mg daily, and this controlled her pain without side effects.

Step 4: Take Borage Oil

In some people, gamma linoleic acid (GLA) may help reduce pain, and this can be added to the previous steps. The best source of GLA is borage oil (1,500mg daily). It may take two months to observe benefits. If it is beneficial, you can then decrease the medications in the previous step, under the guidance of a doctor.

Step 5: Apply Emu Oil, Long Crystal Menthol, Biofreeze, Capsaicin, or Prescription Compounds to the Painful Area

If oral medications don't help your pain or give you only partial relief, I recommend trying topical pain-relieving creams or lotions. Natural topicals include emu oil (usually with aloe vera and MSM), long crystal menthol, Biofreeze, capsaicin, and other herbal combinations.

If the natural topicals don't work, your doctor can prescribe topicals made from conventional drugs and mixed in a gel that is absorbed into the soft tissues. The topical forms of these drugs usually don't have the side effects that can occur if you take them orally. These drugs include gabapentin (Neurontin), amitriptyline, baclofen, ketamine, ketoprofen, and others. Whether natural or conventional, some topicals may work better than others, so you may have to try several to find the best one. You can also mix several different topicals together for better results.

In my clinic, I apply samples to my patients so they'll know whether a product works before they purchase it. Encourage your doctor or practitioner to do the same. These topicals should provide you with pain relief in just a few minutes. They don't cure the underlying problem, but they might provide pain relief for one to eight hours or longer and have minimal side effects (most commonly, skin allergy or sensitivity).

Step 6: Receive Transcutaneous Electrostimulation

If you still have neuropathy pain, the last step to try is transcutaneous electrostimulation, which is sometimes successful in relieving some of the pain associated with neuropathy.

This method is performed by registered physical therapists, under prescription from your doctor.

NICOTINE ADDICTION (Smoking)

Nicotine is an addictive drug found in tobacco. Although the nicotine itself may not cause a great deal of damage, its addiction leads to continued smoking and damage to your body from the other 200 chemicals that cigarettes contain. Because the body develops a need for nicotine, withdrawal symptoms will occur when you stop. Cigarette smoking can cause major damage to the body, including atherosclerosis, dementia, heart disease, emphysema (*chronic obstructive pulmonary disease*, or *COPD*), peripheral blood vessel disease, strokes, cancer (lung, breast, stomach, and prostate), ulcers, bladder dysfunctions, and many other health problems.

Common Symptoms with Smoking Addiction

- Angina
- Claudication (pain in legs when walking)
- Shortness of breath
- Ulcers, stomach pain
- Brain dysfunction: memory, concentration
- Bladder/prostate problems
- Poor recovery from surgical procedures
- Prolonged wound healing
- More frequent illnesses, such as colds/flu
- Yellow staining of skin and clothing

Common Nicotine Withdrawal Symptoms

- Headache
- Nausea
- Constipation or diarrhea
- Insomnia
- Fatigue
- Irritability
- Anxiety or depression
- Concentration difficulties
- Decreased heart rate
- Increased hunger and resultant weight gain

What You Need to Know

The causes of smoking and nicotine addiction are a complex combination of hereditary predisposition and a variety of social, environmental, physical, and psychological factors. The most important factor in treating addiction of any kind is the desire to stop. Once the motivation is present, treatments are much more effective.

General Recommendations

Diet: Most people who smoke can have nutritional deficiencies. In addition, they can have problems processing sugar and carbohydrates, and they may crave these substances. If you smoke, you should eat three meals a day, avoid sugars, limit carbohydrates (especially processed), and increase the amount of protein you eat. You should also take a good multivitamin/mineral complex (see Appendix B, under "Multivitamins," for a recommended formula).

Meditation: Stress and anxiety can not only perpetuate your smoking habit—they can also occur when you try to quit. Meditation is excellent for reducing stress and anxiety, helping you to successfully eliminate this habit (see "Simple Healing Steps for All Health Conditions," page 79, under "Meditation," for further guidance and examples).

Your Balanced Healing Action Plan for Reducing or Preventing Nicotine Withdrawal

- Withdrawal symptoms may prevent you from following through on your commitment to stop smoking. The following steps help ease these symptoms while you are discontinuing the habit.

Step 1: Take Appropriate Chinese Herbal Remedies

I first recommend Chinese herbal formulas that reduce cravings during withdrawal. I recommend the formulas *Chai Hu Mu Li Long Gu Tang* or *Chai Hu Gui Zhi Tang*. Consult a practitioner qualified in Chinese herbal medicine to determine which Chinese herbal formulas are the best for your particular syndromes. You should get relief from your symptoms within three to seven days, but you will need to take the formulas until you no longer have withdrawal symptoms or crave cigarettes. (See Appendix A, under "Chinese Herbs," for further information and ways to find a qualified practitioner.)

Step 2: Take Vitamin C

In addition to Step 1, take vitamin C, 500mg to 1000mg per day. Most people who smoke are deficient in vitamin C. You can get this amount in both food (fruits and green leafy vegetables) and supplements.

Step 3: Use Nicotine Patches

If the above natural treatments fail to relieve your withdrawal symptoms, I recommend using nicotine patches. These prevent withdrawal by giving your body the nicotine to which it is accustomed. The patches are designed to gradually reduce over several weeks the amount of nicotine that you absorb, allowing you to decrease your body's need for nicotine until your body no longer craves it. The first two weeks are the most critical. Increase the dosage if you are experiencing withdrawal symptoms or if you still have the need to smoke. A starting dose of 21mg or 22mg is usually effective for mild to moderate smokers. You can use nicotine patches along with the previous steps for better results.

Do not use nicotine patches long term because nicotine itself can stimulate angiogenesis (the formation of new blood vessels), a key feature of both cancerous tumors and atherosclerosis. Do not exceed the directions on the label.

Step 4: Take Prescription Clonidine

If your withdrawal symptoms persist, your doctor can prescribe Clonidine. You can take this drug while using nicotine patches.

Your Balanced Healing Action Plan to Stop Smoking

- One step alone may not be enough for you to stop smoking permanently, so you may require several steps at the same time to obtain the most benefit.
- **Do not take beta-carotene**, which may increase your risk of lung cancer.

Step 1: Undergo Hypnosis

I first recommend hypnosis, which is a fast and effective tool because it addresses the multiple underlying reasons why you continue to smoke, including habit, tension reduction, stimulation, pleasure, emotional need, and cravings. Usually only one to three sessions are necessary (see Appendix A, under "Mind-Body Techniques," for further information and guidance in finding a qualified hypnotherapist).

Step 2: Undergo Acupuncture

As the next step, I recommend acupuncture, which you can use along with hypnosis for faster results. Acupuncture is effective in reducing the cravings and desire to smoke, and it also helps reduce or prevent withdrawal symptoms. Ear acupuncture is the preferred form, using tacks or press needles in the following ear points: Shenmen, liver, lung, kidney, and sympathetic (some acupuncturists add the zero point to help balance the system and reduce anxiety). There is a specific point called the Nicotine Point or the Stop Smoking Point in the tragus, the flap in front of the ear.

These needles remain in the ear for three to seven days and then are replaced weekly until you no longer need them (that is, you have no more desire or cravings for cigarettes). For better results, you can tap on the needle several times a day to stimulate the point. Always seek evaluation and treatment from a practitioner certified in acupuncture. (See Appendix A, under "Acupuncture," for guidance in finding a qualified acupuncturist and for explanation of the different acupuncture techniques.) You should experience relief from cravings and withdrawal symptoms almost immediately with ear tacks.

Step 3: Take Prescription Bupropion or Nortriptyline

If you have not succeeded at quitting your smoking habit, your doctor can prescribe bupropion (Wellbutrin, Zyban), an antidepressant that also is very effective in reducing the desire for smoking. The most common side effects are dry mouth and insomnia, and you can take it while you are using nicotine patches. Take the bupropion on a daily basis for at least seven weeks. Nortriptyline is another antidepressant that can also be effective if you cannot tolerate the bupropion. If bupropion helps you quit smoking, but you later restart, it may not be beneficial the second time.

Harold, a tavern owner, had smoked for more than 40 years and had a two-pack-a-day habit. Just 56 years old, he had already suffered two heart attacks and a small stroke, and his doctor told him that if he didn't quit smoking, he'd be dead before the age of 60. Harold quit once with the help of nicotine patches and bupropion, but after 10 months he started smoking again. When he tried to quit a second time, the patches and drugs had no effect. I placed press tacks in his ears, gave him the Chinese herbal formula *Chai Hu Mu Li Long Gu Tang*, and performed hypnosis. I also gave him a hypnosis tape to use at home to reinforce the office hypnosis. He immediately was able to stop smoking and did not have any withdrawal symptoms. I replaced the press tacks on two occasions during the next three weeks, and Harold was able to stop taking the Chinese herbs. Over the next two years, Harold had only occasional urges to smoke (when he was under stress), but he was able to overcome them simply by playing the hypnosis tape.

Step 4: Use Nicotine Gum, Nasal Spray, or Inhaler

If you are still having withdrawal symptoms or cravings, or you are having unpleasant reactions to other methods, I recommend taking a nicotine substitute. Substitutes include nicotine gum, nasal spray, or nicotine inhaler. Again, these drugs work by replacing the nicotine that your body still may crave, allowing you to stop smoking cigarettes. Consult with your doctor on the best form for you. As with nicotine patches, it is very important not to use other nicotine substitutes long term because nicotine itself can stimulate angiogenesis (formation of new blood vessels), a key feature of both cancerous tumors and atherosclerosis. Do not exceed the directions on the label.

OBESITY

Obesity is defined as a body-fat percentage greater than 30 percent for women and 25 percent for men (measured by various instruments), or as weighing 20 percent more than your ideal body weight (based on insurance charts). At present, the most reliable definition uses the Body Mass Index (BMI), a calculation using your height and weight (see below for calculation). A BMI of 25 to 29 is considered overweight, and greater than 30 indicates obesity. To find your BMI from a chart, go to www.consumer.gov/weightloss/bmi.htm or www.nhlbisupport.com/bmi/bmicalc.htm).

The major reasons for obesity are diets high in fats and sugars, and lack of exercise. Obesity places you at much greater risk for developing a variety of diseases, including cancer (especially of the pancreas, breast, uterus, gall bladder, and colon), heart disease, hypertension, gallstones, stroke, and diabetes, not to mention a premature death.

BODY MASS INDEX CALCULATION

Step 1: Multiply your weight (in pounds) by 703.
Step 2: Multiply your height (in inches) by your height (in inches) (inches squared).
Step 3: Divide your answer in Step 1 by your answer in Step 2.

What You Need to Know

All diets that reduce calories, regardless of their composition, result in weight loss. What matters more is that you *maintain* the weight loss and establish eating habits that are healthy for you in the long run. There are three important considerations that you must incorporate into your life if you want to lose weight and maintain that loss, and be healthy for the rest of your life.

- **Make a long-term commitment to change your lifestyle.** Short term dieting ("yo-yo" dieting) not only doesn't work for long—it is also unhealthy for the body. Also, you regain lost weight quickly and usually put on even more. The only proven way to lose weight and keep it off is to make permanent lifestyle changes.
- **Focus more on calories than categories of food.** The bottom line is that if you eat less, you'll lose more. It's really that simple.
- **Set realistic goals.** Losing one to two pounds per week is the best way to lose weight and keep it off.

Although obesity results in various diseases and increased mortality, it is not the extra fat cells alone that are harmful to your body. It is what you eat or don't eat and what activity you do or don't do that determines whether your body's tissues are harmed. Those are the factors that not only cause you to gain weight in the first place, but that also damage your body at the same time. Just losing weight, without changing those lifestyle factors, does not protect your body from damage.

General Recommendations

Diet: The balance of foods you eat, both in quality and quantity, affects whether you will lose weight. The Balanced Healing basic weight-loss plan makes these recommendations:

- Follow the Healthy Eating Pyramid, a guide to balancing your meals developed by Dr. Walter Willett at the Harvard School of Public Health. When you follow a food pyramid as a guide to eating, you eat more foods from the bottom of the pyramid and less as you go up to the top. In the Healthy Eating Pyramid, equal weight is given at the bottom level to whole grain foods and plant oils (including olive, canola, soy, corn, sunflower, peanut, and other vegetable oils), which you can eat at almost every meal. The next level of the pyramid includes vegetables and fruits, which can be eaten 2 to 3 times a day. Above that level are nuts and legumes, which can be eaten 1 to 3 times a day, followed by fish, poultry, and eggs, which can be eaten no more than 2 times a day. The next level of the pyramid includes dairy products, which can be eaten 1 to 2 times a day. At the top of the pyramid, you'll find red meat, butter, white rice, white bread, potatoes, pasta, and sweets—which should all be eaten sparingly. For more information about the Healthy Eating Pyramid, read Dr. Willett's book, *Eat, Drink, and Be Healthy.*

- Women, restrict calories to 1,200 per day, and men, to less than 1,500 per day. Get a good calorie-counting book and use it!
- Of total calories, for the best balance, less than 30 percent should come from fat, 20 percent from protein, and 50 percent from carbohydrates.
- When eating fat, use monounsaturated, which does not elevate your cholesterol levels. You should not exceed 10 percent saturated fats, because these elevate your blood cholesterol level. Also, avoid trans fats, which are contained in processed (packaged) and fried foods. Trans fats are even worse for your health than saturated fats. In fact, the Institute of Medicine reported that NO level of trans fatty acids is safe to consume.
- When eating carbohydrates, fresher is better. Fresh fruits and vegetable and whole grains are absorbed better into your system, are more nutritious, contain more fiber, and do not put more weight on you.
- When eating protein, restrict animal fats, which increase cholesterol. If you eat animal protein, consume more fish, chicken, and turkey than red meat. Eat more plant protein (legumes, beans) than animal protein.
- When eating grains, choose whole rather than refined grains. The refining process removes most of the beneficial nutrients and vitamins in the grains. If you eat refined grains, make sure they are enriched.
- Consume 30g to 40g of fiber daily. You can obtain this amount by eating lots of fruit, vegetables, and whole grains.
- Total cholesterol intake should be less than 300mg per day. Use vegetable spreads (such as Benecol or Take Control) instead of butter or margarine.
- When using oils, use olive preferably, with canola oil second. These oils are monounsaturated so they don't elevate cholesterol levels as other oils do.
- Take a multivitamin while dieting, to make sure you are receiving all the essential nutrients (see Appendix B, under "Multivitamins," for recommended formulas).

Do you think that eating low-fat products will help you lose weight? Not always! In fact, they may have the opposite effect. Many low-fat products contain as many calories as their regular-fat counterparts. People tend to eat larger amounts of low-fat products, thinking they won't do any harm, yet again adding to their weight problem. In addition, beneficial fats (primarily fatty acids, such as omega-3) are eliminated in low-fat products. Be sure to read the labels on low-fat products to check the calories, added ingredients, and serving size.

Other Lifestyle Changes: The manner in which you eat can also help you lose weight. Here are some additional recommendations:

- Plan your meals every morning.
- Eat more frequent meals. People who have been most successful losing weight and keeping it off average five mini-meals per day. This is because the more meals you

eat, the less total fat is absorbed into your body.

- When you eat a meal, do not engage in another activity. Studies show that watching TV or reading while eating definitely increases weight gain, because your digestion slows down, allowing more fat to be absorbed into your body.
- Drink lots of water.

Exercise: Other than your diet, exercise is the most important factor in losing weight. If you are overweight but fit, you can often live longer than if you are normal weight but not fit. You will lose more weight and be much healthier if you combine exercise with diet. And without exercise, 95 percent of all people on weight loss diets regain the pounds they lose. I recommend aerobic and resistance exercise, at least four days per week, for 30 to 60 minutes. Resistance exercise (weight lifting) is crucial if you want to lose body fat (see "Simple Healing Steps for All Health Conditions," page 79, for more information and guidance on exercise).

Your Balanced Healing Action Plan for Obesity

- Many popular dietary aids and treatments can have harmful side effects. There are numerous products (pills, powders, and liquids) that may help you lose weight, but not in ways that are healthy. Many of these products contain a combination of ephedra and guarana, the herbal counterparts of the conventional drug combination ephedrine and caffeine. Most are effective at reducing weight using the "fat burner" approach (called thermogenesis) in addition to suppressing appetite.

I DO NOT recommend these products because they're marketed with the false premise that you can lose weight without needing to exercise, reduce calories, or eat healthy foods. **This is exceedingly dangerous** because, as I mentioned before, eating unhealthy foods and not exercising causes long-term harm to your body tissues. Losing weight with these products gives you a false sense of security. In addition, they are all expensive, rebound weight gain is common once you stop them, and they may contain other ingredients that are harmful.

Of particular danger are these products:

- Conventional appetite suppressants such as phentermine, amphetamines, caffeine, or ephedrine, which can have serious side effects and provide only short-term weight loss.
- Thyroid-related weight loss aids, such as those containing tiratricol or triac, which can cause heart attacks and strokes.

Step 1: Recommended Diet Programs

The previous diet recommendations will help you safely lose weight and keep it off. However, it is often easier and more helpful to follow a designed diet plan. I recommend any of the following (your choice depends on which diet fits your lifestyle):

- The Balanced Healing Eating Guidelines (See "Simple Healing Steps for All Health Conditions" on page 79.)
- Mediterranean Diet (Go to your local bookstore; there are numerous cookbooks on the Mediterranean diet.)

- The John MacDougall program (Buy the book *The MacDougall Program for Maximum Weight Loss,* or go to www.rightfoods.com.)
- Weight Watchers (For more information, go to www.weightwatchers.com.)

Fad diets, such as the high protein/low carbohydrate, Sugar Busters, and the Zone Diet, are not recommended because of potential harm and long-term ineffectiveness. For example, the latter two are semi-starvation diets. And the high-protein/low-carbohydrate diet can lose important nutrients that cannot be replaced by supplementation. Also, this diet may result in cravings for high-carbohydrate and high-fat foods, result in poor athletic performance, and cause kidney stones and/or long-term osteoporosis. Finally, the weight loss does not come from fat loss alone, but also from loss of salts and minerals. Again, balance is the key.

Step 2: Use Acupuncture and Hypnosis in Combination

Along with the diet plans, I recommend undergoing acupuncture and hypnosis; the combination is very helpful in decreasing your desire to eat unhealthy foods. Either method alone is not nearly as beneficial, and both must be combined with a good diet and exercise. For acupuncture, ear acupuncture using press tacks is usually the most effective and easiest form. Small needles are embedded in an adhesive bandage and then pressed in specific points in the ear.

The points generally used are mouth, esophagus, stomach, small intestines, point zero, Shen Men, and the hunger point (or Appetite control). These needles remain in the ear for as long as possible (on the average one week) and are replaced when they fall out. For better results, you can tap on the needle several times a day to stimulate the point. (For hypnosis, see Appendix A, under "Mind-Body Techniques," for more information and how to find a qualified practitioner.)

Step 3: Take 5-HTP

If you still have trouble controlling your eating urges, I recommend taking 5-HTP, which reduces appetite and promotes weight loss, and reduces carbohydrate cravings. Dosage is 50mg to 100mg 30 minutes before meals. If you don't lose one pound per week, increase the dosage to 200mg to 300mg. This supplement can cause nausea initially, but this side effect will resolve within six weeks. 5-HTP can be used with the above steps for better results.

Step 4: Take Appropriate Chinese Herbal Remedies

If you still have trouble losing weight, take Chinese herbal formulas (not those containing primarily ephedra), which can help curb appetite and improve digestion. According to Chinese medicine, obesity can be a result of Dampness, Phlegm, Qi deficiency, Heat, and/or food stagnation. (See Appendix A, under "Traditional Chinese Medicine," for further explanation of Chinese syndromes.) I recommend *Fang Feng Tong Sheng San.* Consult a practitioner qualified in Chinese herbal medicine to determine which Chinese herbal formulas are the best for your particular condition. You should observe initial benefits within three weeks (sometimes sooner). (See Appendix A, under "Chinese Herbs," for further information.)

Step 5: Take Bupropion

An antidepressant used to help quit smoking has now been shown to help you lose weight. Bupropion (Wellbutrin, Zyban) can help you lose up to 10 percent of your body weight, when given with exercise and proper diet, by reducing the flow of certain hormones in the brain that affect behavior. I recommend taking it if the previous steps have not helped you reduce weight.

Step 6: Prescription Weight-Loss Medications

If you are still having difficulty losing weight, your doctor can prescribe an appetite suppressant. Sibutramine (Meridia) is the first choice and can be used long term. Because of possible adverse effects on blood pressure and heart rate, frequent monitoring is recommended. Intermittent use (weeks 1 to 12, 19 to 30 and 37 to 48) is just as effective as continuous use.

Orlistat (Xenical) can also be used long term. Unlike other weight-loss drugs, it works on the digestive tract, not the central nervous system, preventing about one-fourth of the fat you eat from being absorbed. However, it does have several GI side effects that occur if you eat too much fat. If you adhere to eating less than 30 percent fat, you are less likely to have the side effects, and you will lose more weight.

If your child is obese, your doctor can prescribe metformin, a drug normally used for people with diabetes. If your child has normal blood sugar, metformin will significantly increase weight loss if used with a low-calorie diet.

Sandy is a 34-year-old executive administrator who had gained more than 60 pounds during her two pregnancies but was never able to lose the weight easily. She had tried most of the fad diets, including the Zone Diet, Atkins, and Sugar Busters, as well as several "fat burner" formulas. She did lose weight with almost all of these, but she had various side effects, she was unable to continue following the diets, or she gained most or more weight back when she stopped following them. She did try Orlistat but had increased gas and bloating. I suggested that she follow the Balanced Healing Diet, I placed acupuncture press tacks in her ears, and I gave her a hypnosis tape. I encouraged her to start exercising, which she did three times a week for 30 to 45 minutes. I also gave her the Chinese herbal formula *Fang Feng Tong Sheng San.* The hypnosis and acupuncture press tacks decreased her appetite and also stopped her from snacking. The Chinese herbs helped improve her digestion and decreased her appetite. She lost 10 pounds in the first two weeks, and then an average of 1 to 2 pounds per week after that (about 10 to 12 pounds per month). Within six months, she was back to her pre-pregnancy weight and felt great. Two years later, she was still exercising. Every so often (mainly when stressed), she would start eating more and would gain 5 to 8 pounds. At those times, she would listen to the hypnosis tape and take the Chinese herbal formula, and she would lose those extra pounds within two to three weeks.

Step 7: Undergo Surgery

If you are severely obese and have failed to lose weight, or you have metabolic dysfunction, or your weight causes significant physical or health problems, you may require a surgical method to reduce your weight. The first way surgery promotes weight loss is by decreasing food intake. Gastric banding and *vertical banded gastroplasty* (VBG) are surgeries that limit the amount of food the stomach can hold by closing off or removing parts of the stomach. VBG is the most commonly used. Thirty percent of patients achieve normal weight, and 80 percent achieve some degree of weight loss. The second type of surgery causes food to be poorly digested and absorbed. Gastric bypass is the primary surgery that provides this malabsorption. Most patients undergoing bypass lose two-thirds of their weight within two years.

With surgery, most patients lose weight rapidly and continue to do so until 18 to 24 months after the procedure. Most patients then start to regain some of the lost weight, but few regain it all. Ten to 20 percent of patients require follow-up operations to correct complications, one-third develop gall stones, and 30 percent develop nutritional deficiencies (and must take vitamin and mineral supplementation).

OSTEOARTHRITIS

Arthritis is inflammation of a joint (*arth* = "joint", and *itis* = "inflammation"), and osteoarthritis is the most common type (*osteo* = "bone"). Another name for osteoarthritis is *degenerative joint disease*. Primary osteoarthritis is caused by a wear-and-tear degeneration of the joint, either from advancing age, overusing the joint, or putting it under a great deal of stress (such as performing jobs that require repetitive lifting). *Secondary* osteoarthritis is caused by some predisposing factor, such as trauma, inherited abnormalities, and other diseases that affect joints. Osteoarthritis can affect any joint in the body, but the hands, hips, knees, and spine are the most commonly involved. If arthritis progresses, it can limit and actually destroy the joint.

Common Symptoms

- Pain that worsens with use of the joint
- Swelling
- Stiffness, especially early morning
- Bony swelling or protuberances
- Restricted mobility
- Heberden's nodes (small masses on finger joints)

General Recommendations

Diet: Some people with osteoarthritis can have flare-ups of pain when eating shrimp, milk, or nitrates. Some people obtain pain relief by eliminating foods from the nightshade family, including tomatoes, potatoes, eggplant, peppers, and tobacco. Other people have obtained significant relief by eliminating red meat, fruit, dairy products, additives, preservatives, herbs, spices, or alcohol. It is worth eliminating some of these foods to see whether they affect your arthritis. However, some spices, such as turmeric and ginger, have anti-inflammatory effects and may help reduce pain. Some people have done well on a vegetarian diet rich in *lactobacilli,* although this can cause side effects of nausea and diarrhea.

Exercise: It is important for you to be active. Your osteoarthritic joints are like rusty hinges; if you don't use them, they stiffen up until they freeze altogether. There are particular exercises (both aerobic and resistance) that are beneficial, especially for knee and back arthritis. If your joints are unstable, you need to exercise with caution or use braces. I recommend that you consult with your doctor or a registered physical therapist, who can teach you the best exercises for the joints involved in your particular condition. I do not recommend running because runners are prone to develop osteoarthritis.

Your Balanced Healing Action Plan for Osteoarthritis

Step 1: Undergo Low-Level Energy Laser Treatment and Infrasound

I first recommend the use of low-level energy lasers because, in my studies, the laser appears to help heal the tissue, reduce the inflammatory response, give long-lasting relief, and prevent further deterioration of the joint. These lasers are called "cold" lasers, because they do not produce heat like the hot lasers used in surgical procedures do. You should feel better within six to nine treatments (two to three weeks). Because this is currently a research device unavailable to most doctors, see Appendix C for a reference source.

Along with laser treatment, I also recommend infrasound, or low-frequency sound. Infrasound works by increasing the local circulation of blood and lymph; it also stimulates the production of hyaluronic acid, which lubricates joints. It not only can reduce pain, but it can decrease stiffness and swelling as well. Numerous chiropractors, naturopaths, acupuncturists, and a few doctors use infrasound (see Appendix C, under "Infrasound," for a reference source).

Step 2: Undergo Acupuncture

If laser and infrasound are not available in your area, or if they haven't helped you, I next recommend acupuncture for long-lasting relief. Which joint or area of the spine is involved determines the acupuncture points. Always seek evaluation and treatment from a practitioner certified in acupuncture. (See Appendix A, under "Acupuncture," for guidance on finding a qualified acupuncturist and for further explanation on different acupuncture techniques.) You should notice less pain, stiffness, and swelling within 6 to 7 treatments, although you might need 10 to 12 treatments followed by maintenance treatments once or twice a year for maximum and long-lasting benefits.

As a young man, Paul, a police officer, played football during his early years, sustaining numerous injuries to his knees. He always had some swelling in his knees, and they cracked and popped all the time. Now 57 years old, he had tried various anti-inflammatory drugs, and he'd had several surgeries on both knees. He tried to exercise but couldn't because his pain and swelling would get worse. I started him on low-level energy laser treatment. After just three treatments, his swelling was completely gone. After nine treatments, nearly all of his pain was gone, too. He was able to return to almost all activities that he had stopped (golf, tennis, skiing). To eliminate the remainder of his pain, I performed acupuncture, which took only eight treatments to give Paul something he hadn't experienced for decades: pain-free knees.

Step 3: Apply Emu Oil, Long Crystal Menthol, Biofreeze, Capsaicin, Glucosamine/MSM, or Prescription Compounds to the Affected Areas

The previous two steps are designed to give you long-lasting relief. If they are not effective, then you should focus on obtaining short-term relief. I recommend starting with natural topical solutions that reduce pain and inflammation. Natural topicals include emu oil (usually with aloe vera and MSM), long crystal menthol, Biofreeze, capsaicin, glucosamine/MSM, and other herbal combinations. If the natural topicals don't work, your doctor can prescribe topicals made from conventional drugs and mixed in a gel that is absorbed into the soft tissues. The topical forms of these drugs usually don't have the side effects that can occur if you take them orally. The drugs include gabapentin (Neurontin), amitriptyline, baclofen, ketamine, ketoprofen, and others.

Whether natural or conventional, some topicals may work better than others, so you may have to try several to find the best one for you. You can also mix several different topicals for better results. In my clinic, I apply samples to my patients so they'll know whether the products work before they purchase them. Encourage your doctor or practitioner to do the same. These topicals should provide you with pain relief in just a few minutes. Although they don't cure the underlying problem, these products can provide pain relief for two to eight hours or longer.

Step 4: Take Glucosamine, Chondroitin, MSM, Cetyl Myristoleate, and/or Sea Cucumber

If your arthritis affects joints other than your spine, and your discomfort continues, take glucosamine sulfate, 1,500mg per day. Glucosamine also slows the progression of osteoarthritis, which is why I recommend it before conventional medications. You should notice improvement in pain or stiffness within four to eight weeks; if you don't, you are either taking a poor quality brand (see Appendix B, under "Glucosamine," for more information) or it won't work for you. There is no reason to take it longer than eight weeks if it isn't working. Glucosamine is often combined with other supplements, including the following:

- Chondroitin (200mg to 400mg, two to three times daily) is the most common supplement added to glucosamine, but it takes at least two to four months to be effective, and has a much weaker effect.
- Methylsulfonylmethane (MSM) (1,000 to 3,000mg per day). MSM is itself an anti-inflammatory, but it also may help glucosamine get into the joints. However, marketing claims have not yet been substantiated by research.
- Cetyl myristoleate (1,000mg twice daily) is an immuno-modulator, which shuts off production of immune-system cells that irritate the tissue. Its advantage is that you take it only for one to three months but its effects are long-lasting.
- Sea cucumber (500mg, two to four times per day) has anti-inflammatory properties and is effective within four to six weeks.

You can take any of these supplements individually or in various combinations with or without glucosamine. See Appendix B for further information.

Step 5: Take an Over-the-Counter NSAID

If the previous steps are not effective, start taking over-the-counter nonsteroidal anti-inflammatory drugs (NSAIDs). These include ibuprofen and naproxen (such as Aleve). Even at their low doses, these drugs may still cause stomach irritation. NSAIDs may take several days to a week to achieve pain relief.

Step 6: Apply Biomagnets

If the previous steps are still not beneficial, before trying stronger drugs, you should try biomagnets, which are applied to the affected joint (either taped or contained in a brace). Like conventional drugs, biomagnets can relieve your pain symptoms but they can't cure the underlying cause of them. Their relief disappears when the magnet is removed. There are many different types and strengths of magnets, as well as unipole, dipole, and north- or south-directed, all of which can make a difference in whether they are effective for your condition. (See Appendix B for more information and guidance on biomagnets.) Biomagnets should give you relief almost immediately.

Step 7: Take a Prescription NSAID

If your joints remain stiff and/or painful, your doctor can prescribe a stronger NSAID, such as Naprosyn, Feldene, Daypro, Relafen, Orudis, Mobic, Cataflam, and Arthrotec. These drugs are all equally effective, although one may work better for you than another. You may have to try several to see which one is the most effective for you (ask your doctor for samples). Prescription NSAIDs are stronger than over-the-counter products, but they also have a higher risk of side effects, primarily stomach irritation and bleeding. If these side effects occur, NSAIDs known as Cox-2 inhibitors have less risk of stomach problems.

However, they are more expensive, not covered by some insurance plans, and may increase your risk of heart attack if you already have heart disease, especially if you are also taking naproxen (Aleve). Prescription NSAIDs may take three weeks or longer to give you full relief. Often, one product will work for several months and then stop being effective. Usually, switching to another brand will continue to provide pain relief.

> Louise, a retired nurse, had pain from osteoarthritis in her fingers, knees, hips, and shoulders. She had been placed on numerous medications, including prescription NSAIDs, and had been given several steroid injections in her hips and knees. She had also undergone Hyalgan injections (Step 13), which also failed to relieve her pain. Her doctor recommend joint replacements of her hips and knees (Step 14), but because she was 78 years old, Louise was afraid of undergoing surgery. I suggested that she try a combination of glucosamine and sea cucumber, along with cetyl myristoleate. Within six weeks, most of her pain was gone, and she actually went out dancing for the first time in 15 years.

Step 8: Take Appropriate Chinese Herbal Remedies

If you are still suffering from arthritis pain, the next treatment for you to use is Chinese herbal formulas. Recommended formulas include *Shu Jing Huo Xue Tang* and *Huo Luo Xiao Ling Dan*. Consult a practitioner qualified in Chinese herbal medicine to determine which Chinese herbal formulas are the best for your particular syndromes. You should feel better within three weeks, but you may need to take the formulas longer for full relief. (See Appendix A, under "Chinese Herbs," for further information.)

Step 9: Take SAMe

If your pain continues to this point, try taking SAMe (200mg three times a day). SAMe is a supplement imported from Germany; it has been shown to be effective for reducing symptoms of osteoarthritis, but the high-quality brands are very expensive. You can take it in combination with some of the herbs or drugs in the previous steps, and you should notice improvement within three to four weeks.

Step 10: Take Phlogenzym or Guggal

For osteoarthritis of the knee that hasn't been completely relieved by the previous steps, I recommend a combination product (called Phlogenzym), containing rutin (100mg), trypsin (48mg), and bromelain (90mg). A recent study has shown guggal (500mg three times daily), an herb from India, is also helpful in reducing arthritic symptoms. You can take these in combination with other treatments.

Step 11: Take Vitamin E and Niacinamide

For pain that continues, take vitamin E (600 IU to 800 IU), and high-dose niacinamide

(3,000mg per day). Such a high dose of niacinamide can cause side effects such as flushing and liver toxicity, so use a non-flushing product and have your doctor check your liver enzymes after three months (see Appendix B for further guidance).

Step 12: Receive Corticosteroid Injections

A corticosteroid solution injected directly into the painful joint can provide relief that lasts several weeks to several months. However, you can receive these injections only three to four times a year because of their potential side effects, which include softening of the bone and weight gain.

Step 13: Undergo Viscosupplementation

Viscosupplementation is the injection of hyaluronic acid derivatives (Synvisc or Hyalgan), which replaces the normal fluid in the joints (synovial fluid) that lubricates and maintains the joint. This fluid is usually deficient in osteoarthritic joints. Although these derivatives do not retard the progression of the arthritis, they may delay the need for surgery for years. However, they require three to six injections and the benefits may last only six months to a year. You can receive repeat injections when your symptoms return, but they tend not to be as effective as the first time. Recent studies have shown that these injections offer no better relief than placebo injections, so their effectiveness is questionable.

Step 14: Undergo Surgery

If all else fails, joint-replacement surgery is the last resort. Such surgery is necessary if your joint has been completely worn down by arthritis and none of the previous steps have helped you. The most common joints replaced are the knee and hip. Some surgeons attempt to delay joint replacement by using arthroscopy to clean out the joint, but this is simply a temporary fix at best and can worsen your pain. In fact, a recent study shows that this surgery is no better than placebo, so I don't recommend it. At present, artificial joints last 8 to 12 years on average, but some can last much longer. A joint can be replaced a second or third time, but it is not as effective, so the longer you can avoid the first surgery, the better. That is why most surgeons recommend waiting until you are 65 to 70 years old.

OSTEOPOROSIS

Osteoporosis means "porous bones," and it is the thinning and weakening of your bones. It occurs as a consequence of aging and is more frequent in women than men. In women, it is primarily due to estrogen loss following menopause (estrogen in women helps prevent bone loss). In men, 50 percent to 70 percent of cases are caused by other diseases (especially liver and endocrine) or medications (such as steroids, antiseizure drugs, and even tobacco or alcohol). All bones can be affected by osteoporosis. The most harmful (and potentially fatal) complication of osteoporosis is bone fracture, which occurs most frequently in the spine, hip, and wrist. Men with fractures have a much worse outcome than women; 30 percent to 50 percent die within a year of fracture, versus 20 percent of women.

Common Symptoms

There are usually no symptoms of osteoporosis until a bone fracture occurs. There can be back pain, loss of height, and loss of bone in the jaw (seen on x-ray).

What You Need to Know

Some medications typically prescribed for other diseases also can reduce bone loss. These include thiazide diuretics for swelling or hypertension and statins for high cholesterol. These are the preferred medications to take if you have these diseases and have osteoporosis as well.

General Recommendations

Diet: Vegetarians have a lowered risk of osteoporosis in the later decades of life, so increased intake of vegetables is recommended for helping prevent and treat osteoporosis. Dairy products and calcium-fortified juices and cereals are important sources of calcium and vitamin D. Carbonated beverages increase the risk for osteoporosis and should be avoided.

Exercise: One of the most important methods for preventing osteoporosis is exercise. Weight-bearing (resistance) exercises are recommended because they stress the bone, which stimulates new bone formation. I recommend walking, running, tennis, stair climbing, and weight lifting. Swimming and bicycling are not helpful for osteoporosis because they do not put enough stress on the bones.

Your Balanced Healing Action Plan for Osteoporosis

Step 1: Take Calcium, Magnesium, and Vitamin D

I recommend starting with a combination of calcium (800mg to 1200mg daily), magnesium (400mg to 800mg daily), and vitamin D (400 IU daily). Calcium alone is not enough; it requires the presence of vitamin D to be deposited in bone. Magnesium is also essential for bone formation, and not taking it with calcium and vitamin D can intensify the risk of heart disease. Take these products all together, in a form that is highly absorbable. (See Appendix B for recommended formulations.)

A recent study demonstrated that sustained-release sodium fluoride significantly reduces the risk for spine fractures by stimulating new bone formation, whereas the above nutrients primarily prevent loss of bone. A sodium-fluoride medication is awaiting FDA approval at this writing and should be included with the above nutrients when approved.

Step 2: Take Natural Progesterone and Natural Estrogen

Natural progesterone (50mg to 100mg twice daily in oral form, 20g to 40g daily if in cream) can increase bone density, while natural estrogen (1.25mg to 2.5mg daily) can prevent bone loss after menopause. I recommend that all post-menopausal women take these natural hormones. However, do not take natural estrogen if you are at a high risk of or have had breast cancer. For men who have osteoporosis, I recommend taking the natural progesterone, which will increase bone density without any feminizing side effects. You should see improvement in bone density within three to six months (see section on menopause and/or Appendix B, under "Sex Hormones," for further information on natural hormones).

Step 3: Take Ipriflavone, Fish Oil, and Evening Primrose Oil

If you still have osteoporosis after following the previous steps, take Ipriflavone, 600mg daily. This synthetic isoflavone (plant estrogen) has been shown to significantly reduce or prevent post-menopausal bone loss. In addition, you can take a combination of fish oil (1,000mg daily) and evening primrose oil (1mg to 2.5mg daily). These oils, when taken with calcium, have been shown to decrease bone turnover and increase bone density.

Step 4: Take Low-Dose Synthetic Estrogen Replacement

If you are a woman and the previous steps have not increased your bone density, your doctor can prescribe low-dose synthetic estrogen replacement. Because estrogen can increase your risk of breast cancer and blood clots, you should use only low-dose estrogen or a selective estrogen receptor modulator (SERM), such as Raloxiphene, an estrogen that has minimal risk of breast cancer. Because synthetic estrogen use can increase the risk of heart attack during the first few years of use, consult with your doctor if you have heart disease.

Step 5: Take Prescription Biphosphonates

If your osteoporosis continues to progress, your doctor can prescribe biphosphonates (such as Fosamax), which can help slow bone loss and prevent fractures. Calcitonin-salmon nasal spray is also effective for preventing the progression of osteoporosis and preventing fractures and is commonly used with biphosphonates. Use it if you have had a fracture, because it also helps reduce pain while your fracture is healing. **Important note:** Calcium can decrease the absorption of biphosphonates, so take your calcium at least two hours before or after the biphosphonates.

> Because Paula, a piano teacher, had been diagnosed with and treated for breast cancer when she was 60, she was told not to take any estrogen after menopause, and instead she was prescribed calcium. However, her bone-density tests showed worsening of her osteoporosis. She then was prescribed Fosamax, but she had gastrointestinal side effects, and it only minimally slowed her bone loss. I recommended a resistance-exercise program to start, and I also gave her natural progesterone cream. She reported seeing her calcium pills still intact in her stool, so I changed her to a more absorbable form. I also advised her to take magnesium and vitamin D along with her calcium. After six months, her bone density had improved measurably, and after one year it was normal.

Step 6: Receive Parathyroid Hormone Injections

If you are a woman who has had bone fractures from osteoporosis, your doctor may prescribe daily injections of parathyroid hormone (a natural hormone that regulates calcium in the body) to increase bone density and help prevent future fractures.

PAIN (Chronic)

This section addresses general pain that is located throughout the body. For specific areas of pain, or *fibromyalgia*, see the sections on those topics. Pain is considered chronic if it has been present for more than three to six months. Numerous factors can cause pain, including injury, disease, poor posture, aging, and psychological problems. Having chronic pain can also cause many psychological disturbances such as anxiety, depression, anger, and stress. We don't know why pain becomes chronic, but we do know that chronic pain is very different from acute pain, both in how the body reacts to it and how it is treated.

Common Symptoms

There are dozens of ways to describe pain but the most common are sharp, dull, aching, burning, stabbing, or tearing. Pain can be constant or intermittent, with flare-ups that can last a few hours to several weeks. Muscle spasms, stiffness, or swelling can accompany chronic pain.

What You Need to Know

When pain becomes chronic, many changes occur in the brain and body tissues that can perpetuate the pain. These include a heightened sensitivity to pain in both the spinal nerves and brain, and an increase in particular chemicals (NMDA, Substance P) that increase the pain messages going to the brain. In addition, receptors in your soft tissues that usually detect non-painful stimuli (such as wetness, heat, cold, light touch) are converted into pain receptors, which is why such stimuli often cause your pain to worsen. There are also many nonphysical factors that play a role in pain, such as stress, mood, emotion, and motivation. Treatment for chronic pain involves much more than just giving pain medication. In fact, pain medication can perpetuate and even worsen chronic pain.

General Recommendations

Diet: Many foods can affect pain both positively and negatively. Foods that contain tryptophan can increase a brain neurotransmitter, serotonin, which can block pain. Foods high in tryptophan include turkey, chicken, cheddar cheese, halibut, eggs, peanuts, and nuts. Foods containing omega-3 fatty acids, such as cold-water fish (e.g., mackerel, tuna, sardines, salmon, herring, cod, trout, and halibut), have natural anti-inflammatory properties. Foods high in calcium and magnesium, such as dairy products, salmon, and whole grains, can relax muscles. Avoid saturated fats because they contain prostaglandins, which increase the inflammatory response.

Exercise: Regular exercise is very important in reducing chronic pain. Exercise stimulates large neurons (brain cells) to help reduce the perception of pain and stimulate the production of natural pain-killers from the brain. Inactivity causes increased stiffness and loss of muscle tone, which can increase and perpetuate the pain. Aerobic, resistance, and stretching exercises are all important, and you should perform all three types at least three times a week. You may feel that you cannot perform exercises because of the pain, but you will find out that exercise will decrease your pain. Even with disabilities, there are exercises that you can do (see "Exercise," under "Simple Healing Steps for All Health Conditions," page 79, for further guidelines).

Meditation: Because anxiety and stress can increase pain, meditation is invaluable in helping reduce these factors (see Appendix A, under "Mind-Body Techniques," for further guidance on and examples of meditation).

Your Balanced Healing Action Plan for Chronic Pain

Step 1: Undergo Acupuncture

I always recommend acupuncture first for chronic pain, because it can address both the area of pain and the part of the brain that perceives pain (the hypothalamus). Acupuncture also can address factors that may be underlying the pain. Principal points depend on the area affected, as well as specific syndromes that underlie your pain, which must be determined by traditional Chinese medicine tongue and pulse diagnosis (see Appendix A, under "Traditional Chinese Medicine," for further explanation). Always seek evaluation and treatment from a practitioner certified in acupuncture. (See Appendix A, under "Acupuncture," for guidance in finding a qualified acupuncturist and for further explanation of the different acupuncture techniques.) You should notice improvement within 6 treatments, but you might need up to 12 or 15 additional sessions for maximum benefits.

Amy, a 28-year-old lab technician, began having pain on the left portion of her face, which then spread to her left arm, left leg, and eventually her entire body, over the course of several months. She had been evaluated by numerous doctors, including physiatrists, neurologists, anesthesiology pain specialists, and a psychiatrist, none of whom could tell her why she was hurting. She was eventually diagnosed as having polyneuritis, a widespread inflammation of the nerves throughout her body. After two years, the pain had worsened to the point that Amy was unable to engage in any activity. She had to quit her job, could not maintain a sexual relationship, and could not engage in any social activities. She literally became an invalid. I performed acupuncture based on her underlying Chinese diagnoses. After the first acupuncture, she was pain free for the first time in two years—and she went out partying to celebrate. The pain did return within a few days, but it was not as severe. She continued acupuncture on several more occasions, and eventually her pain went away for good.

Step 2: Undergo Psychological Counseling

Chronic pain can cause a variety of psychological problems, especially anxiety, frustration, anger, and depression. These in turn can make the pain worse. I recommend counseling with a therapist who works with chronic-pain patients to help you learn to cope better with your chronic pain, so you can participate in more activities and generally feel better. Counseling also helps improve your relations with family, friends, and work. This does not mean that you are "crazy," simply that you need help in dealing with the changes that are inevitable with chronic pain. Often, your pain will also decrease as a result of dealing with your emotions.

Step 3: Undergo Feldenkrais Method, Alexander Technique, or Rolfing

If you are still suffering from chronic pain, the Feldenkrais method, Alexander technique, and Rolfing are all forms of bodywork that might relieve chronic pain that doesn't respond to other treatments. Bodywork involves realigning, rebalancing, and retraining the structures of the body, which have become dysfunctional due to pain, injury, disuse, or misuse. The Feldenkrais method focuses on retraining how you move your body, to interrupt unhealthy patterns of movement that have become habits. The Alexander technique concentrates on correcting faulty posture in daily activities (sitting, standing, and moving). Rolfing involves manipulating and stretching the body's fascial tissues (deep connective tissues that hold your body together), thus allowing correct realigning of the body. These bodywork methods require a therapist certified in these techniques. (See Appendix A for further information on bodywork and Appendix C to help find a qualified therapist.) It may take several months to notice improvement from these methods. You can use them in combination with the first two steps.

Step 4: Undergo Hypnosis, Guided Imagery, and/or Interactive Imagery

If your pain continues, I recommend trying some mind-body methods. Hypnosis can reduce pain by addressing the emotional and psychological factors that can either cause pain or make it worse. Hypnosis can work quickly, often in two to three sessions. Guided imagery can influence the *amygdala*, the area of the brain that receives pain messages, teaching the brain not to perceive the pain. This method may take several weeks to months to be effective. Interactive imagery is a mind-body method in which you mentally interact with images that represent your emotions. It is a powerful way to uncover and deal with subconscious psychological issues of which you may not be aware, but that may be causing your pain. It may take several weeks to a few months to notice improvement in your pain using interactive imagery. (See Appendix A, under "Mind-Body Techniques," for further information and examples.)

Kathy is a 48-year-old guidance counselor and a patient of mine who would develop pain in different areas of her body at different times (what doctors call "migrating pain"). She had been prescribed pain medications, which did control the pain but did not resolve her problems. I felt that there was an underlying psychological basis for the pain, and I performed interactive imagery. After several sessions, she began having repressed memories revealing that her father had abused her physically, mentally, and emotionally. Each time a particular memory occurred, she would report pain in some area of her body, which correlated with the abuse (for example, she would have pain in her arm, and remember her father twisting her arm). The pain would continue or worsen until she dealt with the memory, at which time the pain would disappear. She is still undergoing interactive imagery and continues to make good progress.

Step 5: Practice Appropriate Yoga Postures

If you are still suffering from chronic pain, I recommend practicing yoga. Yoga promotes relaxation and stretching, both of which are important in healing and preventing pain. Because there are many different types and different levels of yoga, with some better for chronic pain than others, I recommend working with a qualified yoga instructor. (See Appendix A for further information on yoga and Appendix C to find a qualified yoga instructor.) It may take several months (sometimes sooner) to notice improvement.

Step 6: Take Appropriate Chinese Herbal Remedies

If your pain continues despite the above measures, I recommend trying Chinese herbal formulas to address the syndromes that may be perpetuating or underlying your pain. Consult a practitioner qualified in Chinese herbal medicine to determine which Chinese herbal formulas are the best for your particular syndromes. You should notice improvement within three weeks, but you may need to take the formulas longer for complete relief. (See Appendix A, under "Chinese Herbs," for further information.)

Step 7: Take Naproxen or Ibuprofen

If you are still hurting, you can take nonprescription medications to control your chronic pain. Over-the-counter naproxen and ibuprofen are the safest long term and should be tried first when other methods fail to relieve your pain, but they may not be effective if your pain is severe or has been present a long time. Avoid acetaminophen long term because it can cause liver problems.

Step 8: Take Prescription Amitriptyline or Trazodone

For some people, low-dose antidepressants, such as amitriptyline (Elavil) 25mg to 50mg daily or trazodone (Desyrel) 50mg to 150mg daily, can decrease chronic pain through effects on the pain center (hypothalamus) and neurotransmitters in the brain. Your doctor can prescribe them if the previous steps don't help you, but it may take four to six weeks for your pain to decrease.

Step 9: Take a Prescription NSAID

For continued pain, your doctor can prescribe nonsteroidal anti-inflammatory drugs (NSAIDs), such as Naprosyn, Feldene, Daypro, Orudis, Mobic, Cataflam, Relafen, and Arthrotec. Prescription NSAIDs are more powerful than over-the-counter products, but they also have a higher risk of side effects, primarily stomach irritation and bleeding. If these side effects occur, NSAIDs known as Cox-2 inhibitors have less risk of stomach problems. However, they are more expensive and may increase your risk of heart attack if you already have heart disease, especially if you are also taking naproxen (Aleve). All NSAIDs are equally effective, although one may work better for you than another. You may need to try several (ask your doctor for samples), and it can take three weeks or longer for any of these drugs to decrease your pain.

Step 10: Take Tramadol, Propoxyphene, or Narcotic Prescription Pain Relievers

If prescription NSAIDs fail to relieve your pain, a stronger pain reliever may be necessary. However, these drugs do have side effects, can be addictive, and can cause your pain to continue. You should use them only if the other methods are not effective and your pain prevents you from engaging in your usual activities. Your doctor may first prescribe tramadol (Ultram), which is a non-narcotic and so has less addiction potential. The next option may be propoxyphene, which has an addictive potential, although less than codeine-containing narcotics. However, taking more than six to eight per day can have harmful effects (to kidney and liver) when used long-term.

Next are codeine-containing drugs, which range in potency from Tylenol with codeine (Tylenol 3) to hydrocodone (Lortab) to oxycodone (Percodan, OxyContin). These drugs can cause stomach irritation and constipation when used long term, and they are highly addictive. You may be able to decrease your dosage of these narcotics by taking acetaminophen (Tylenol) or ibuprofen with them or between doses. Highly potent narcotics (morphine, Demerol) should be reserved for the worst cases. Some pain medications (kappa opiates) are far more effective in relieving pain in women than in men. There are several devices, including the morphine pump, which can allow easy control of pain for people who require potent narcotics.

For medication management of chronic pain, I highly recommend that you be evaluated and treated by a physiatrist, a specialist in medical pain management, especially if controlling your pain requires more potent pain medications.

Step 11: Enter a Multidisciplinary Pain Program

For chronic pain that continues, I recommend entering a multidisciplinary pain program. Although such programs are not designed to reduce pain specifically, they do improve functional and back-to-work ability, and they teach you how to cope better with your pain. Treatment in these programs includes evaluation and treatment by pain-management specialists, physical and occupational therapists, and psychologists or psychiatrists.

Step 12: Enter a Drug Addiction Treatment Program If Addicted to Narcotic Pain Relievers

Unfortunately, many people with chronic pain become addicted to medications they take for pain relief. Pain medications, especially narcotics, can actually cause an increase of your pain perception through their effect on the brain, making you feel more pain, not less. Reducing the amount of medication you take can often reduce your pain, but this can produce psychological difficulties and physical withdrawal. If you are dependent on or addicted to pain medication, I recommend that you enter a drug addiction treatment program (see the section on "Drug Addiction," page 199, for further treatment guidelines).

> Now 45 years old, Ed, a bus driver, had suffered with chronic arthritic pain for more than 15 years. Conventional therapies had not given him any relief. During the 3 years before he came to see me, only large doses of hydrocodone, a narcotic, could control his pain. I treated Ed with acupuncture, which totally relieved his pain within 10 treatments. However, he had been so used to taking the hydrocodone he could not stop taking it because of psychological addiction, even though he knew he didn't need it anymore. I tried to wean him off the drugs and gave him withdrawal medications, but he felt that he "needed" more. I referred him to an outpatient addiction center, and, with extensive counseling, he was finally able to stop taking the medications in six weeks.

PREMENSTRUAL SYNDROME (PMS)

PMS is a physical condition that typically recurs during a particular phase of your menstrual cycle, usually 7 to 14 days before your period. We don't know what causes PMS, but hormonal imbalance, dietary deficiencies, and genetics may be involved. There may also be a deficiency in serotonin, a brain neurotransmitter. Often, PMS occurs after you experience a major hormonal change, such as after childbirth, miscarriage, abortion, or tubal ligation. PMS is quite common, with 30 percent to 40 percent of menstruating women having the condition and 10 percent having severe symptoms.

Common Symptoms

- Tension
- Irritability
- Moodiness
- Fatigue
- Depression

- Headache
- Acne or cold sores
- Breast pain and swelling
- Back aches and joint or muscle aches
- Swelling of the fingers and ankles
- Abdominal bloating
- Altered sex drive
- Food cravings, especially sweet or salty foods
- Nausea, constipation, or diarrhea
- Insomnia

General Recommendations

Diet: Nutrition is very important in PMS and can help reduce symptoms. Vegetarian diets are the most beneficial, and you should reduce your fat intake, eliminate sugar and caffeine, and reduce salt. Soy products are very beneficial in reducing symptoms and providing high-quality protein (see Appendix B, under "Soy," for further information). Acidophilus and other probiotics are helpful as supplements to your food by increasing absorption of nutrients (see Appendix B, under "Probiotics," for recommended products). Eating cold-water fish (such as salmon, tuna, halibut, herring, cod, trout, mackerel) twice a week can provide essential fatty acids that can reduce PMS symptoms.

Exercise: Regular exercise can reduce PMS symptoms by improving mood and decreasing stress levels; it also has a positive effect on hormonal balance. Aerobic and resistance exercises are both beneficial (see "Exercise," under "Simple Healing Steps for All Health Conditions," page 79, for further information and guidance).

Meditation: Stress and anxiety can both be caused by PMS and can make the symptoms worse. Meditation can be helpful in reducing the tension, moodiness, and irritability associated with PMS (see Appendix A, under "Mind-Body Techniques," for further information and examples of meditation).

Your Balanced Healing Action Plan for PMS

Step 1: Take a Multiple Vitamin Supplement with Vitamin B6 and Magnesium

Because dietary deficiencies may cause or contribute to PMS, start with a good multivitamin/mineral complex, with at least 100mg of B6 daily. Magnesium is very important and you should supplement it at 4mg to 6mg for each pound of your body weight. I also recommend flaxseed oil (one tablespoon daily). Take these supplements together as the first step (see Appendix B, under "Multivitamins," for recommended formulas).

Step 2: Take Appropriate Chinese Herbal Remedies

Along with the nutritional supplements, I recommend that you take Chinese herbal formulas. *Xiao Yao San, Xiao Yao Wan, Bu Tiao, Hsiao Wan, Dang Gui Wan,* or *Jia Wei Xiao*

Yao Wan can all be beneficial for PMS. Consult a practitioner qualified in Chinese herbal medicine to determine which Chinese herbal formulas are the best for your particular syndromes. You should notice improvement within three weeks, but you may need to take the formulas longer for full relief. (See Appendix A, under "Chinese Herbs," for further information.)

Step 3: Undergo Acupuncture

Along with Chinese herbs, I recommend undergoing acupuncture. Principal points usually are found on the legs, abdomen, and feet. Always seek evaluation and treatment from a practitioner certified in acupuncture. (See Appendix A, under "Acupuncture," for guidance on finding a qualified acupuncturist and for further explanation of the different acupuncture techniques.) You should notice improvement within six treatments, but you might need additional sessions for maximum benefits.

Step 4: Take Natural Progesterone

If you are still having symptoms of PMS, I next recommend trying natural progesterone cream 20mg to 40 mg, or 200mg to 1200mg orally, one to two times daily from days 12 to 27 of your menstrual cycle. Often with PMS, you have too much estrogen in your system, and the natural progesterone will rebalance your hormones. I do NOT recommend synthetic progesterone because it has more side effects and is not as effective in PMS.

Step 5: Take Chasteberry Extract, Licorice, or Black Cohosh

These herbal remedies can provide relief from specific symptoms of PMS that are still bothering you:

- *Chasteberry extract* (fluid extract, 2ml, or dry powdered extract with 0.5 percent agnuside content, 175mg to 225mg, daily) for PMS-associated breast pain, infrequent periods, or a history of ovarian cysts. Keep in mind that chasteberry can decrease libido.
- *Licorice* (deglycyrrhizinated (DGL) form, one or two 380mg chewable tablets before meals, to reduce swelling and bloating.
- *Black cohosh* (20mg, containing 27-deoxyacteine, twice daily) to shrink uterine fibroids.

Step 6: Take Prescription Selective Serotonin Reuptake Inhibitors (SSRIs)

If the previous steps are not beneficial, your doctor can prescribe selective serotonin reuptake inhibitors, (SSRIs), such as Prozac, Sarafem, Zoloft, Luvox, or Celexa. These antidepressants increase serotonin levels in the brain, which may be deficient in some women who have PMS.

Cindy, a 32-year-old financial planner, had suffered from PMS since she was a teenager. She had irritability, insomnia, anxiety, bloating, abdominal and breast swelling, and nausea that had gotten worse over the years, to the point that she was almost incapacitated during the 14 days before her period. Various doctors had prescribed SSRIs, which didn't help, and she had tried different herbs, such as chasteberry, *Dong Quai,* and black cohosh, which only partly relieved her discomfort. I placed her on a strong multivitamin (containing magnesium and vitamin B$_6$) and flaxseed oil, as well as the Chinese herbal formula *Dan Zhi Shao Yao San.* After just one month, she had significant improvement. I added acupuncture, and, over the next three months, Cindy's symptoms nearly disappeared.

Step 7: Take Hydrochlorothiazide or Wu Ling San for Fluid Retention

If you have fluid retention that is not reduced by the above steps, your doctor can prescribe hydrochlorothiazide (HCTZ), a mild diuretic. A natural alternative is a Chinese herbal formula, *Wu Ling San.* Consult a practitioner qualified in Chinese herbal medicine to determine whether this formula would be beneficial for you. With either option, you should see benefits within a week.

Step 8: Take Prescription Bromocriptine for Breast Tenderness

If the previous steps are not helpful, your doctor can prescribe bromocriptine for breast tenderness, but side effects are common, including involuntary movements, GI upset, confusion, dizziness, drowsiness, insomnia, and visual disturbances.

Step 9: Take Danazol or Gonadotropin-Releasing Hormone to Suppress Ovulation

If you still have severe PMS, your doctor can prescribe ovulation suppression with Danazol or a gonadotropin-releasing hormone. However, these drugs can have significant adverse effects, and you should consider them as a last option before surgery.

Step 10: Undergo Surgery

If nothing else works, you may consider undergoing a complete hysterectomy with *oophorectomy* (removal of the uterus and ovaries), which does eliminate PMS symptoms. Hysterectomy is major surgery that should be your last resort, only for symptoms that do not respond to any other step.

PROSTATE ENLARGEMENT (Benign Prostatic Hypertrophy or BPH)

The prostate gland is responsible for producing seminal fluid, which contains nutrients for sperm. *Prostate enlargement* is quite common with advancing age and typically starts appearing after the age of 45. The cause of prostate enlargement is hormonal; as you age, your testosterone levels decrease, but other hormone levels increase, resulting in an increase of a more powerful derivative of testosterone. This derivative causes prostate cells to grow and enlarge, thus constricting the *urethra* (the tube that leads from your bladder through your penis). Symptoms of BPH can wax and wane. BPH can cause blockage of the urinary tract, which can lead to infection, bladder failure, and kidney problems.

Common Symptoms

- Nocturia (having to urinate at night)
- Difficulty in urination
- Increased frequency of urination
- Straining to urinate
- Dribbling of urine
- Inability to empty the bladder

What You Need to Know

Because BPH symptoms can be the same as prostate cancer, it is important that you have a prostate examination and PSA (Prostate Specific Antigen) blood level. **Never diagnose and treat yourself!** If your prostate exam and PSA are negative for cancer, you can then follow the next steps.

Over-the-counter antihistamines containing Benadryl, chlorpheniramine, hydroxyzine, and cyproheptadine can cause prostate enlargement in some men because they cause retention of urine. Conventional medications including narcotics and anticholinergic drugs can also cause more urine retention. If these medications are causing your prostate enlargement, your symptoms should improve within a few weeks after discontinuing the medications.

Your Balanced Healing Action Plan for BPH

Step 1: Take Saw Palmetto, Cernilton, and/or Herbal Prostate Formulas

Start with the herb saw palmetto (160mg twice a day, standardized to contain 85 percent to 95 percent fatty acids and sterols), which is very effective for mild to moderate BPH. Many herbal prostate formulas also contain pumpkin seed (5g twice daily) and pygeum (100mg to 200mg of standardized lipophilic extract twice daily, containing 0.5 percent docosanol and 14 percent triterpenes), which are also effective at reducing prostate enlargement. If these are not helpful, try cernilton (60mg to 120mg, two to three times daily), an extract of flower pollen, which has been used in Europe for 35 years and reduces symptoms in 70 percent of men who have BPH. You should notice improvement within three to four weeks.

> Joe is a 72-year-old retired carpenter who complained of increased urination, especially at night, as well as difficulty starting urination and dribbling after he was through. He went to a urologist who ruled out prostate cancer but did diagnose an enlarged prostate. Joe was prescribed an α-blocker, but he stopped taking it because of side effects. He was placed on finasteride, but it only partially relieved his symptoms. I placed him on a combination of saw palmetto with pumpkin seed and pygeum and flaxseed oil. His symptoms soon vanished, and he was eventually able to discontinue the finasteride.

Step 2: Take Zinc, Flaxseed Oil, or Amino Acids

If your symptoms continue, I recommend several nutritional supplements that have been shown to decrease prostatic enlargement, increase urine flow, and decrease most symptoms of BPH. They include the following:

- *Zinc* (45mg to 60mg per day)
- *Flaxseed oil* (one tablespoon daily)
- *Amino acids* (a daily combination of 200mg each of Glycine, Glutamic Acid, and Alanine)

Each of these nutrients alone can be helpful, but you can take them together if one does not completely eliminate your symptoms. You should notice improvement within four to six weeks.

Step 3: Take Prescription Doxazosin, Terazosin, Tamsulosin, or Finasteride

If your symptoms continue, your doctor may prescribe an α-blocker (doxazosin, terazosin, or tamsulosin). These drugs have possible side effects of dizziness, weakness, rhinitis (runny nose), and postural hypotension (dizziness when standing up). If this drug does not work, your doctor may prescribe a 5α-reductase inhibitor (finasteride) as the next step, for mild to moderate prostate enlargement.

Step 4: Undergo Surgery

As a last resort, you can have surgery to remove part or all of your prostate gland. *Transurethral prostatectomy* (TURP) is the standard procedure and usually does not increase the risk of erectile dysfunction or incontinence. However, there are several newer minimally invasive procedures that are done internally, including laser, balloon dilatation, stents, *transurethral needle ablation* (TUNA), *transurethral microwave thermotherapy* (TUMT), and high-intensity ultrasound. These procedures have not been fully researched in comparison to each other or to TURP. It is important to evaluate whatever procedure you are considering and obtain second opinions. Open prostatectomy is the surgery of last resort, involving the removal of the prostate externally.

PSORIASIS

Psoriasis is a chronic inflammatory skin disorder caused by rapid replication of skin cells, almost 10 times normal. It also can affect the nails and can cause joint pain. Psoriasis can be triggered by physical trauma, infection, some medications (ibuprofen, lithium salts, and beta-blockers), and especially stressful or emotional events. Severe psoriasis can substantially affect quality of life. The lesions are most commonly on the scalp, elbows, and knees, but there is a form called *plantar* or *palmar* psoriasis that affects only the feet or hands.

Common Symptoms

- Raised, pink patches of skin with white or silvery scales
- Pitting, thickening, or discoloration of the nails
- Cracked, scaly skin on the palms or soles of the feet
- Painful, swollen joints

What You Need to Know

Lifestyle factors, including cigarette smoking, alcohol use, and obesity, can all contribute to psoriasis. Eliminating them can improve the symptoms.

General Recommendations

Diet: Animal meats especially make psoriasis worse, and a diet high in protein and low in fiber can also make psoriasis worse. Foods containing omega-3 fatty acids, especially cold-water fish (such as mackerel, salmon, tuna, cod, sardines, halibut, herring), are helpful.

Meditation: Anxiety and stress are major factors in precipitating psoriasis, so meditation is very beneficial. One study showed that using meditation with ultraviolet light (UV) treatment heals skin four times faster than UV light without meditation (see Appendix A, under "Mind-Body Techniques," for further information and examples of meditation).

Your Balanced Healing Action Plan for Psoriasis

- For severe psoriasis, start at Step 9, then return to Step 1 when your symptoms are stable.

Step 1: Take Flaxseed Oil, Vitamin A, Zinc, Vitamin D, Selenium, and Vitamin E

Start with supplements of flaxseed oil (one tablespoon daily), vitamin A (10,000 IU per day), and zinc (30mg daily) because many people with psoriasis are deficient in these nutrients. Vitamin A and zinc are also essential for healthy skin. Vitamin D (400 IU daily), selenium (200mcg daily), and vitamin E (400 IU daily) can also help reduce the symptoms, so a good multivitamin may be your best bet to include all of these nutrients (see Appendix B for recommended multivitamin formula). It may take several months before you notice improvement from these nutrients.

Step 2: Undergo Colon, Liver, and Blood Detoxification

Toxins from bacteria and yeast in the gastrointestinal tract may contribute to the development of psoriasis. Poor liver function can also make psoriasis worse, because a weak liver cannot clean these toxins out of the blood. For these reasons, I recommend a series of detoxifications, including colon, liver, and blood.

Start with colon detoxification. To cleanse and detoxify the colon, first use a formula that cleanses the colon (called an *activator*), which should contain most or all of the following: cape aloe, cascara sagrada, barberry root, senna, ginger root, African bird pepper, and fennel. After a week on an activator, you should then take a formula that detoxifies your colon (i.e., takes out old fecal matter and any poisons, toxins, or heavy metals that have accumulated), which should contain most or all of the following; apple fruit pectin, slippery elm bark, bentonite clay (pharmaceutical grade), marshmallow root, fennel seed, activated willow charcoal, and psyllium seeds/husks. A good colon cleansing and detoxification program should take about two to three weeks.

I then recommend liver and blood detoxification. A good liver detoxification formula should include all or some of the following: milk thistle, dandelion root, artichoke or beet leaf, and an herb called Picrorhiza kurroa root. Following liver detoxification, you can take a blood-cleansing formula that contains some or all of the following: red clover, burdock root, chaparral, periwinkle, and goldenseal. This detoxification process takes about two more weeks to complete. (See Appendix A, under "Detoxification Therapy," for more information and possible side effects.)

Step 3: Undergo Acupuncture for Long-Term Relief

If the previous steps are not helpful or give you only partial relief, I recommend acupuncture as the next step. Principal points are usually found on the neck, back, arms, and legs. Always seek evaluation and treatment from a practitioner certified in acupuncture. (See Appendix A, under "Acupuncture," for guidance in finding a qualified acupuncturist and for further explanation of the different acupuncture techniques.) You should notice improvement within six treatments, but you might need additional sessions for maximum benefits.

> Troy is a 38-year-old computer technician who has had psoriasis for 25 years. He came to me because of a severe flare-up of joint pain and swelling. I performed acupuncture on three occasions, which greatly reduced his joint pain and swelling, although it did not clear up his lesions. I then recommended detoxification and nutritional supplements, which reduced his lesions and prevented further flare-ups of his joint pain.

Step 4: Take Bovine Cartilage

If your psoriasis still isn't controlled, take bovine cartilage (10g to 25g daily). It can be taken orally, subcutaneously (injected under the skin), or even topically (this form must be compounded by a pharmacist). New lesions can occur in the first few weeks as the bovine cartilage begins working, but eventually they will stop appearing. Expect it to take one to three months to see benefits.

Step 5: Apply Calcipotriol, Coal Tar, Capsaicin, Gotu Kola, or Glycyrrhetinic Acid

The previous steps are designed to give you long-lasting relief, but if they haven't, you should use measures designed to give you short-term relief. There are several topical salves and ointments that may help, both prescription and natural. These include the following:

- *Calcipotriol*, a prescription compound that is related to vitamin D
- *Coal tar* solutions and shampoos
- *Capsaicin* (0.025 percent), derived from cayenne peppers (must be mixed by a compounding pharmacist)
- *Gotu Kola* (must be mixed by a compounding pharmacist)
- *Glycyrrhetinic acid*, a derivative of licorice (must be mixed by a compounding pharmacist)

People respond differently to these products, so you may need to try more than one to obtain the best results. You should notice improvement within one to three weeks.

Step 6: Apply Steroid Creams and Tazarotene

If the topicals in Step 4 do not reduce your lesions, you can try topical steroid creams, which are beneficial at reducing symptoms and scales in mild to moderate psoriasis. If you add a topical retinoid (tazarotene), it will improve the response rate to steroids. Over-the-counter steroids (such as Cortaid) can work on mild psoriasis, but if your condition is more severe, you will need a prescription from your doctor for a more potent form (as well as for the tazarotene). You should notice improvements within a few weeks.

Step 7: Undergo Interactive Imagery

Because psychological factors can play a significant part in both causing psoriasis and its flare-ups, I recommend interactive imagery. You can use this along with any other step. This is a mind-body method in which you mentally interact with images that represent your emotions. It is a powerful method to uncover and deal with subconscious psychological issues of which you may not be aware, and which may be causing your condition. (See Appendix A, under "Mind-Body Techniques," for a more detailed explanation.)

Dolores, a 35-year-old flight attendant, had psoriasis since she was a teenager. She had tried many topical solutions but continued to have flare-ups, persistent lesions, and joint involvement. I recommended interactive imagery, which brought out a great many underlying psychological issues related to childhood circumstances of abandonment and adoption, and resulting repressed anger. Remarkably, after just two sessions of interactive imagery, most of her skin lesions and her joint pain went away. Her family and friends commented that she had made a significant and sudden change in her personality—and she wasn't even aware of it. With continued imagery work, more of her psoriasis cleared up, and topical ointments easily controlled the remainder.

Step 8: Take an Appropriate Homeopathic Remedy

If the previous steps have not reduced your lesions or symptoms completely, I recommend trying homeopathy. Remedies that may be of benefit include *Sulphur, Graphites, Lycopodium,* and *Arsenicum album.* Consult a qualified homeopathist for guidance on which remedies will be most beneficial and for proper dosages. You should notice improvement within one to two weeks. (See Appendix A, under "Homeopathy," for guidance in finding a qualified homeopathist and for further information.)

Step 9: Undergo Phototherapy

If your psoriasis persists or is severe to begin with, you may need to undergo *phototherapy* (light therapy). This conventional method has been found to be beneficial in many people with psoriasis, both short term and for maintenance. One type uses ultraviolet B radiation, which carries a risk of nonmelanoma skin cancer. The other type (PUVA) uses a combination of Ultraviolet A in conjunction with a conventional medication, psoralen. Long-term treatment with PUVA carries a risk of squamous-cell cancer. You should consult with a dermatologist for further guidance. Using meditation along with phototherapy improves your condition four times faster than with phototherapy alone.

Step 10: Receive Anthralin Applications

If phototherapy is not effective, your doctor may use anthralin topically, which is reserved for severe cases of psoriasis. Only a properly trained therapist should apply anthralin.

Step 11: Take Prescription Methotrexate or Cyclosporin

If all else fails, there are many potent immune-suppressing drugs that can improve psoriatic lesions. The main drugs used for this purpose are methotrexate or cyclosporin. You should use these as a last resort only. Methotrexate can cause liver fibrosis, and cyclosporin has significant toxicities. You should be under the care and guidance of a dermatologist or rheumatologist when using these potent drugs.

If you're taking methotrexate, you should supplement with folate, which reduces its toxicity. In addition, methotrexate lowers blood levels of folate, but folate also decreases the effectiveness of methotrexate, so you must take higher doses of this drug.)

REFLUX (ACID) (see *Heartburn*)

RHEUMATOID ARTHRITIS (RA)

Rheumatoid arthritis (RA) is a chronic inflammatory disease primarily affecting your joints. It is caused by dysfunction of the immune system, which makes cells (antibodies) that destroy your joints and other tissues. This disease can be variable and unpredictable, causing flare-ups and remissions, or it can be progressive. Rheumatoid arthritis can cause significant structural damage to your joints (making them gnarled and misshapen), and it can have systemic effects leading to damage of other organ systems, including heart, lungs, eyes, nerves, and muscles.

Common Symptoms

- Inflammation and tenderness of joints, especially fingers, toes, wrists, elbows, and ankles
- Stiffness of joints, especially in the morning or after inactivity
- Afternoon fatigue
- Low-grade fever
- Thickening of joints
- Nodules under the skin
- Deformation of joints, especially hands and fingers (late manifestation)

General Recommendations

Diet: Food allergies have been implicated as a possible cause of RA, and an elimination diet is helpful for determining whether any foods are contributing to your condition (see the section on food allergies). The most common foods causing inflammation are wheat, corn, milk, and foods from the nightshade family, such as potatoes, eggplant, tomatoes, peppers, and tobacco. Beef protein especially may be implicated. Foods that help reduce RA symptoms include vegetables, fruits (especially flavonoid-containing berries— cherries, blueberries, blackberries), and cold-water fish (such as mackerel, herring, halibut, trout, cod, sardines, and salmon). Olive oil (three tablespoons per day) is also excellent at reducing inflammation and symptoms of rheumatoid arthritis. When cooking, the use of ginger and turmeric also aids in decreasing joint inflammation.

Qigong is excellent at reducing joint pain and also has a beneficial effect on the immune system, and I highly recommend it. It may take three months for maximum effects, but you should see initial results in two to four weeks (see "Qigong," under "Simple Healing Steps for All Health Conditions," page 79, for more information and examples).

Your Balanced Healing Action Plan for Rheumatoid Arthritis

■ For moderate to severe rheumatoid arthritis, go to Steps 11 through 13, and then return to Step 3 when your symptoms stabilize.

Step 1: Take Aspirin for Mild Symptoms

The first purpose of treatment in RA is to control your symptoms and inflammation of the joints. Salicylates (aspirin compounds) are the primary drugs to control pain and stiffness in mild rheumatoid arthritis. If you take aspirin, you should avoid taking ibuprofen, which blocks the blood-thinning effects of aspirin. If you must take ibuprofen, take the aspirin first, and wait at least two hours to take the ibuprofen so that the aspirin has time to exert its beneficial effects. Take as few ibuprofen as you can because three doses will negate 90 percent of aspirin's effects, even if taken after the aspirin dose. You should also take vitamin C (600mg daily) as a supplement because aspirin can deplete vitamin C levels in the body.

Step 2: Take Prescription NSAIDs for Mild to Moderate Symptoms

If aspirin is not helpful, then your doctor can prescribe stronger nonsteroidal anti-inflammatory drugs (NSAIDs), such as Naprosyn, Feldene, Daypro, Orudis, Mobic, Cataflam, Relafen and Arthrotec, to relieve pain and inflammation. These medications may take three weeks to be effective and should be discontinued if there is no benefit or the side effects (such as stomach irritation and bleeding) become intolerable. If this occurs, you can try Cox-2 inhibitors, which have less risk of these side effects. **NOTE:** Recent studies show an increased risk of heart attack in patients who use high-dose Cox-2 inhibitors along with naproxen (Aleve), so caution is advised. Also, if you have taken an NSAID (including ibuprofen) for a long time, it may precipitate a heart attack if you stop taking it suddenly. Obtain guidance from your doctor, especially if you have heart disease.

Step 3: Take Flaxseed Oil or Fish Oil

If your symptoms continue, I recommend trying omega-3 fatty acid supplements. I recommend either flaxseed oil (one tablespoon daily) or fish oil (containing 1.8g of EPA daily), which also have anti-inflammatory properties. Both have been shown to enhance the effect of NSAIDs and decrease the need for NSAIDs. It may take about one to two months to observe an effect with flaxseed or fish oil. You can take these with any of the previous steps.

> For a long time, Hannah, a 55-year-old French teacher, was able to control her mild rheumatoid arthritis with aspirin. But then her symptoms began worsening, and she was prescribed several NSAIDs that did not relieve her pain and swelling. I placed her on sea cucumber and flaxseed oil, and then gave her cold-laser treatments. Within one month, all her symptoms were gone. I continued her on the flaxseed oil and recommended a good multi-vitamin. I advised her that she might have flare-ups, which should respond to additional laser treatment and sea cucumber.

Step 4: Undergo Acupuncture

For rheumatoid arthritis that affects multiple joints, acupuncture can address the entire body and the immune-system dysfunction. Principal points are usually found on the hands, arms, and legs. Always seek evaluation and treatment from a practitioner certified in acupuncture. (See Appendix A, under "Acupuncture," for guidance in finding a qualified acupuncturist and for further explanation of the different acupuncture techniques.) You should notice improvement within six treatments, but you might need additional sessions for maximum benefits.

Step 5: Undergo Low-Level Energy Laser Treatment and Infrasound for Longer-Term Relief

If the previous steps haven't worked, I recommend the use of low-level energy lasers next because, in my studies, this laser reduces swelling and stiffness and gives long-lasting pain relief in many patients. These lasers are called "cold" lasers because they do not produce heat like the hot lasers used in surgical procedures do. They should be used if you have only a few joints involved because multiple joints require too much laser energy, which then becomes ineffective. You should notice improvement within six to nine treatments (two to three weeks). Because this is currently a research device unavailable to most doctors, see Appendix C for a reference source.

Along with the laser, I recommend infrasound, or low-frequency sound. Infrasound works by increasing the local circulation of blood and lymph, and it also stimulates the production of hyaluronic acid, which lubricates the joints. It can not only reduce pain, but it can also decrease stiffness and swelling. Numerous chiropractors, naturopaths, acupuncturists, and a few doctors use infrasound. (See Appendix C, under "Infrasound," for a reference source.)

Step 6: Take Sea Cucumber, Mucopolysaccharides, and/or Borage Oil

If your symptoms still persist, I recommend taking sea cucumber (500mg), which has been shown in Australian studies to be very effective in reducing symptoms in most people with rheumatoid arthritis. You should take four per day for the first two weeks, and then two a day. You should notice improvement within one to two months. You can also take *mucopolysaccharides* (such as Beta 1,3/1,6 glucan, once daily), special carbohydrates that can trap antibodies and thus help prevent destruction of the joints. Another supplement that can be beneficial is borage oil (1,500mg daily), an omega-6 fatty acid that has anti-inflammatory properties. You can take all three supplements together for better results. Mucopolysaccharides and borage oil may take six to eight weeks to be beneficial.

Step 7: Take Vitamin E, B Vitamins, and a Multivitamin Containing Boron

For continued symptoms, you should take other supplements that may help reduce symptoms, including vitamin E (400 IU daily) and B vitamins, and a general multivitamin containing boron. (See Appendix B for recommended multivitamin formulation.) You can take these with any of the previous steps.

Step 8: Take Appropriate Chinese Herbal Remedies

If you continue to suffer from pain and stiffness, Chinese herbals can be beneficial in treating the underlying immune dysfunction and some of the symptoms of rheumatoid arthritis, and they can be used along with acupuncture. *Shu Jing Huo Xue Tang* or *Du Huo Luo Dan* may be helpful. Consult a practitioner qualified in Chinese herbal medicine to determine which Chinese herbal formulas are the best for your particular condition. You should notice improvement within three weeks, but you may need to take the herbs longer for full relief. (See Appendix A, under "Chinese Herbs," for further information.)

Step 9: Take Digestive Enzymes and Probiotics

Food allergies may contribute to rheumatoid arthritis. Often, food allergies are caused by incomplete breakdown of the food that you eat, which produces fragments of proteins that can cause an allergic response. If the previous steps have not been effective, I recommend taking digestive enzymes to help break down your food more completely. There are many products that contain digestive enzymes, and those you take should contain some or all of the following: protease, papain, amylase, lipase, bromelain, cellulase, and lactase.

I also recommend that you take probiotics. These consist of live cultures of organisms (the "good" bacteria) that help digest food properly. Of the beneficial microorganisms in probiotics, *L. acidophilus* and *bifidobacteria* are the best. Other beneficial bacteria include *L. salivarius*, *L. rhamnosus*, *L. plantarum*, *streptococcus thermophilus*, *L. bulgaricus*, *L. casei*, and *L. sporogenes*. Yogurt is not a good substitute for probiotics. Although yogurt does contain beneficial microorganisms, they are not the most important or potent. Also, many yogurt products are pasteurized to increase shelf life, but this process kills most of the good bacteria and destroys the benefits.

You should notice improvement within two to six weeks. If you experience increased gas, bloating, or cramping during the first week, reduce your dosage and then gradually build the dose back up as these side effects lessen.

Step 10: Use the Nambudripad Allergy Elimination Treatment (NAET)

If you suspect food allergies but Step 9 hasn't helped, I recommend using the Nambudripad Allergy Elimination Treatment (NAET). This method combines acupuncture, kinesiology, chiropractic, herbs, and nutrition to desensitize you to foods to which you are allergic. It may take several months to notice improvement, depending on how many allergens are sensitizing you (see Appendix A and the section on food allergies for further information and to find a practitioner who uses NAET).

Step 11: Take Low-Dose Prednisolone

If your symptoms have still not been controlled, or if they are moderate to severe to begin with, your doctor can prescribe low-dose corticosteroids (prednisolone, 7.5mg to 15mg daily). Steroids can reduce inflammation in the short term and reduce joint destruction in the long term, but they may have long term side effects as well. Corticosteroid use can increase levels of blood sugar (glucose), but you can reverse this effect by taking chromium, 200mcg three times daily.

Step 12: Take Prescription DMARD Medications

The latest weapons in the medical arsenal for moderate to severe or progressive rheumatoid arthritis are medications called DMARDs (disease-modifying antirheumatic drugs). Doctors usually prescribe these in combinations, either with each other or preferably with NSAIDs and/or steroids. Methotrexate, minocycline, hydroxychloroquine sulfate, sulfasalazine, and auranofin (oral gold) are all beneficial and have similar effects. A recent study showed that another DMARD, leflunomide, is more effective than methotrexate, which has been the usual first choice for treatment. These powerful and toxic drugs should be used under the supervision of a rheumatologist, and they may need to be the first step (within the first year) if you have moderate to severe disease at the onset.

If taking methotrexate, you should supplement with folate, which reduces its toxicity. In addition, methotrexate lowers blood levels of folate, but folate also decreases the effectiveness of methotrexate, so you must take higher doses of this drug.

Roxanne, 72 years old, had severe rheumatoid arthritis for more than 45 years. Over the years, she had been prescribed steroids and numerous DMARDs, which would give her only moderate relief from her pain and stiffness, and to which she would become resistant after a year or two. She had significant destruction of her finger joints and was unable to pick up a piece of paper. I placed her on flaxseed oil and a multivitamin, and I provided cold-laser treatment. After just seven treatments, she was able to not only pick up a piece of paper, but also to open jars. Her deformities could not be corrected, but her pain and stiffness were reduced significantly.

Step 13: Receive Etanercept or Infliximab by Injection

Drugs called *tumor necrosis factor antagonists* (etanercept, infliximab), given intravenously, can prevent erosion of your joints when your rheumatoid arthritis is severe. You must use these along with methotrexate (or one of the other DMARDs) to avoid the formation of cells (antibodies) that can destroy these drugs. These are powerful drugs with potentially serious side effects, so discuss them with your doctor.

Step 14: Take Stronger DMARDs

If your arthritis continues and progresses, your doctor can prescribe stronger DMARDs. Because of their possible side effects, you should use these drugs only if the previous medications are ineffective. These include penicillamine, azathioprine, cyclophosphamide, and cyclosporine.

Step 15: Undergo Surgery

Rheumatoid arthritis may continue to progress, causing destruction of your joints. If you have significant erosions of your bones, you can undergo replacement of the joint by a qualified orthopedic surgeon.

SCIATICA

Sciatica is inflammation of the sciatic nerve, a large nerve that comprises several nerves from the lower lumbar and sacral levels of the low back. These nerves combine together in the pelvic region, enter the leg, and then branch out into separate nerves once again. Sciatica can be caused by local injury, spinal disc problems, poor posture, muscle strain, pregnancy, obesity, wearing high heels, or sleeping on a mattress that is too soft. It can be an acute or a chronic problem. If it's caused by a herniated disc, permanent injury to the nerve can occur.

Common Symptoms

Sciatica is characterized by pain radiating (shooting) through your buttock and down the back portion of your leg. The pain can be sharp, achy, or burning, and it can be intermittent or continuous. It can be made worse by coughing, sneezing, bending, or lifting.

What You Need to Know

Often, sciatica occurs in older people who have degenerative disc disease (arthritis of the spine), and doctors may conclude that it is your disc deterioration that is causing your symptoms, and they may sometimes recommend invasive treatments (such as surgery). However, this nerve can be irritated by other causes, and it may not be the disc disease causing your symptoms. It is important to follow the steps below and not rush into an invasive procedure that may not help—or that may make you worse.

Your Balanced Healing Action Plan for Acute Sciatica

- If you have worsening severe back pain with radiation down the leg, or paralysis, or inability to urinate or have a bowel movement, you should obtain emergency medical attention and diagnostic testing such as MRI or myelogram (start with Step 7).
- For acute sciatica, many treatments are given that are not helpful and thus not recommended. These include traction, prescription antidepressants, lumbar supports, and TENS units (small devices that conduct electricity to the superficial soft tissues).

Step 1: Take NSAIDs for Temporary Relief While Your Nerve Heals

If your symptoms are mild, start with nonsteroidal anti-inflammatory medications (NSAIDs), which can help control your symptoms while the body has time to heal the nerve itself. Begin with over-the-counter NSAIDs (ibuprofen, naproxen), but if these are not helpful, your doctor may prescribe stronger NSAIDs, such as Naprosyn, Feldene, Daypro, Orudis, Mobic, Cataflam, Relafen, and Arthrotec. Prescription NSAIDs are more powerful than over-the-counter products, but they also have a higher risk of side effects, primarily stomach irritation and bleeding. If these side effects occur, NSAIDs known as Cox-2 inhibitors have less risk of stomach problems. However, they are more expensive, not covered by many insurance plans and may increase your risk of heart attack if you already have heart disease, especially if you are also taking naproxen (Aleve). All NSAIDs are equally effective, although one may work better for you than another. You may need to try several (ask your doctor for samples), and it can take three weeks or longer for any of these drugs to decrease your pain.

These medications are used to control your pain while the body heals itself, and they may not help if the condition is more severe. If your pain continues after several weeks, or if these products are ineffective, proceed with the next steps.

Step 2: Take Prescription Pain Medications or Muscle Relaxers

If NSAIDs do not control your pain, your doctor can prescribe pain medication temporarily until your symptoms improve. Tramadol (Ultram) is a common choice of doctors, and if that isn't effective, propoxyphene is another option. Muscle relaxers (such as Flexeril, Soma, Parafon Forte, or Robaxin) can be used in conjunction with these medications for extra relief, but they may make you drowsy. As with Step 1, the purpose of these medications is to allow time for your body to heal itself, but if the pain continues, proceed with the next steps. You can become addicted to some of these medications, so you don't want to take them long term.

Step 3: Take Prescription Narcotics for More Severe Pain

If your pain is still not controlled or is more severe, you may require narcotic medication to control the pain. The most common include Tylenol with codeine, hydrocodone, and oxycodone (listed in order of increasing potency). They should be used only in combination with the remaining steps, and these stronger narcotics should not be used long term because of their addiction potential.

Step 4: Receive Physical Therapy Modalities

Along with taking the above medications, I recommend undergoing physical therapy modalities to help your nerve heal faster. Treatments that can help include therapeutic massage and electrical current (both direct current and alternating current can be applied to the painful areas; I prefer alternating, which can project deeper into the tissues without burning the skin). These modalities increase blood flow and oxygen delivery to the damaged tissues, thus helping them heal faster.

Other modalities include hot packs (which dilate blood vessels and increase blood flow to the damaged area), and cold packs (for swelling and spasm). Ultrasound (high-frequency sound that projects heat into the deep tissues) can be used for some patients, but it can be irritating if there is inflammation present. A physical therapy modality which I also highly recommend is infrasound, or low-frequency sound. Infrasound works by increasing the local circulation of blood, lymph, and the activity of the nervous system to accelerate the healing process. It can not only reduce pain, but it can decrease spasms and swelling as well. Numerous chiropractors, naturopaths, acupuncturists, and a few doctors use infrasound. (See Appendix C, under "Infrasound," for a reference source.)

Primary care doctors who have the necessary equipment can provide these treatments, but if you are not improving, you should ask your doctor to refer you to a registered physical therapist who has more expertise and usually has more advanced equipment. If you do not observe improvement in your condition after six to eight treatments with physical therapy, proceed with the next step. Many doctors prescribe exercises, but in acute sciatica, this can make your symptoms worse.

Step 5: Undergo Acupuncture

If the previous steps don't help, I recommend that you undergo acupuncture to reduce your pain and inflammation and help heal the nerve. Principal points usually are found on the back, hip, and legs. Always seek evaluation and treatment from a practitioner certified in acupuncture. (See Appendix A, under "Acupuncture," for guidance in finding a qualified acupuncturist and for further explanation of the different acupuncture techniques.) You should notice improvement within six treatments, but you might need additional sessions for maximum benefits.

> Wayne, a 38-year-old shop foreman, had acute sciatic pain from lifting a heavy object. He had tried various NSAIDs and mild pain relievers, which helped control the pain. However, when he tried to stop taking the medications, his pain would return. His doctor sent him for physical therapy, but he was given only exercises and traction, which made his symptoms worse. I started him on several physical therapy modalities, and I also performed acupuncture. His pain steadily decreased and was totally gone in three weeks.

Step 6: Undergo Osteopathic Mobilization for Structural Problems

If the previous treatments are not effective, it may mean that you have an underlying structural problem (your bones, ligaments, tendons, joints, and/or muscles are not working correctly) that is causing your pain or not allowing proper healing to take place. Because the sciatic nerve passes through the pelvis, structural problems involving your pelvis, sacrum, or sacroiliac joint can be pinching, stretching, or irritating the nerve. I recommend osteopathic treatment to correct these underlying structural problems. This first requires an osteopathic exam. If structural problems are evident, then they must be corrected, or your symptoms may continue or reoccur. With osteopathic treatment, your pain should start decreasing in 3 to 6 treatments, although additional treatments may be necessary to achieve maximum benefit. If your pain is still present after 10 to 12 treatments, further evaluation or a different method may be necessary. (See Appendix A, under "Manual

Therapy," for further information and guidance in finding a qualified practitioner.)

Chiropractic manipulation may also be helpful for acute sciatica. With chiropractic treatment, you should notice improvement of your pain within six to eight treatments. If not, continued treatment is unlikely to be of benefit.

Step 7: Undergo MRI Scan

If the previous steps are not helpful, I recommend that you undergo an MRI scan of the low back to determine whether a ruptured disc(s) may be the cause of your sciatica. If the MRI detects that a disc is compressing a nerve, then more invasive methods (as follows) may be necessary.

Step 8: Undergo Epidural Injections

If a herniated or bulging disc is causing the sciatica, an epidural steroid injection may be helpful in the first six to eight weeks after onset. The purpose of the injection is to reduce the inflammation and allow the nerve to heal. If the first injection is not beneficial (if relief doesn't last several months), you can repeat the procedure once or twice, but additional injections are unlikely to be of benefit if the initial ones are not effective.

Step 9: Undergo Surgery

Surgery may be necessary if your nerves are being pinched by a ruptured disc and the previous steps are ineffective, and/or if you have neurological symptoms (loss of knee reflex, paralysis of the leg, loss of bladder or bowel control). Surgery may also be necessary if you have intolerable pain going down your leg or can't use your leg. If MRI does not show a significant disc problem correlated with neurological signs (such as leg weakness, sensory loss, or reflex loss), have further testing (discogram, myelogram) before you consider surgery.

Your Balanced Healing Action Plan for Chronic Sciatica

- Chronic sciatica is very different than acute sciatica, and it does not usually respond to basic medications or physical therapy. Although stronger NSAIDs and other medications (such as the pain reliever tramadol) can control the symptoms in many cases, I recommend the following methods so that you won't need medications.
- I do not recommend bed rest, biofeedback, long-term chiropractic manipulation, facet-joint injections, traction, or lumbar supports. None of these methods have been shown to be beneficial in chronic sciatica.

Step 1: Undergo Low Level Energy Laser Therapy and Infrasound

I first recommend the use of low-level energy lasers because, in my studies, the laser appears to help heal the tissue, reduce the inflammatory response, and give long-lasting relief for many nerve problems. These lasers are called "cold" lasers, because they do not produce heat like the hot lasers used in surgical procedures do. You should notice improvement within six to nine treatments (two to three weeks). Because this is currently a research device unavailable to most doctors, see Appendix C for a reference source.

I also highly recommend infrasound, or low-frequency sound therapy. In distinction from ultrasound, infrasound works by increasing the local circulation of blood, lymph, and the activity of the nervous system to accelerate the healing process. It not only can reduce pain, but it can also decrease spasms and swelling. Numerous chiropractors, naturopaths, acupuncturists, and a few doctors use infrasound (see Appendix C, under "Infrasound," for a reference source).

Step 2: Undergo Acupuncture

If the laser and infrasound do not relieve your symptoms, I next recommend that you undergo acupuncture, which can be very effective in reducing your pain and inflammation and healing the nerve. Principal points usually are found on the back, hip, and legs. Always seek evaluation and treatment from a practitioner certified in acupuncture. (See Appendix A, under "Acupuncture," for guidance in finding a qualified acupuncturist and for further explanation of the different acupuncture techniques.) You should notice improvement within six treatments, but you might need additional sessions for maximum benefits.

Step 3: Undergo Osteopathic Mobilization to Correct Underlying Structural Problems

If the first two steps do not help, you may have underlying structural problems (bones, ligaments, tendons, joints, and/or muscles not working correctly) that are either causing your chronic sciatica or not allowing proper healing to take place. I recommend osteopathic treatment to correct these problems. First you need an osteopathic exam. If structural problems are evident, then they must be corrected before other treatments can be effective, or your symptoms may continue to recur. With osteopathic treatment, your pain should start decreasing in 3 to 6 treatments, although you might need additional treatments to achieve maximum benefit. If your pain is still present after 10 to 12 treatments, further evaluation or a different method may be necessary. (See Appendix A, under "Manual Therapy," for further information and guidance to help find a qualified practitioner.)

Chiropractic manipulation has not been found to be effective for chronic sciatica, and I do not recommend it for this purpose. At best, it may give you temporary (a few hours' or days') relief.

Step 4: Undergo Feldenkrais Method, Alexander Technique, or Rolfing

If the previous steps have been only partially effective or not beneficial, I recommend that you try bodywork, using the Feldenkrais method, Alexander technique, or Rolfing. Bodywork involves realigning, rebalancing, and retraining the structures of the body, which have become dysfunctional due to pain, injury, disuse, or misuse. The Feldenkrais method focuses on retraining the way you move your body, to interrupt unhealthy patterns of movement that have become habits. The Alexander technique concentrates on correcting faulty posture in daily activities (sitting, standing, and moving). Rolfing involves manipulating and stretching the body's fascial tissues (deep connective tissues that hold your body together), thus allowing correct realigning of the body. Each body-work method requires a therapist certified in that particular technique. (See Appendix A for further information on bodywork and Appendix C to find a qualified therapist.) It may take you several months to observe benefits from these techniques.

Step 5: Practice Appropriate Yoga Postures

Yoga may be successful in reducing chronic sciatica symptoms when the previous steps have not been effective. Yoga promotes relaxation and stretching, both of which are important in healing and preventing sciatic pain. Because there are many different types of yoga, I recommend working with a qualified yoga instructor. (See Appendix A for further information on yoga and Appendix C to find a qualified yoga instructor.) It may take you several months to observe benefits from yoga.

Step 6: Receive Epidural Steroid Injections

Although epidural steroid injections generally are not effective in chronic sciatica, some people may receive relief for a few months. However, if one or two injections have not given you more than a week's relief, then further injections will not help and are not recommended.

Step 7: Apply Emu Oil, Long Crystal Menthol, Biofreeze, Capsaicin, Glucosamine/MSM, or Other Topical Solutions for Pain Relief

For residual pain or flare-ups of pain, several topical solutions can give temporary relief when applied over the painful area. These include emu oil (usually combined with MSM and aloe vera), long crystal menthol, Biofreeze, capsaicin, glucosamine/MSM, as well as other herbal combinations. If natural topicals don't work, you can try topicals made from prescription medications that are combined into a gel that is transported into your soft tissues. Some of these medications include gabapentin (Neurontin), ketoprofen, ketamine, clonidine, baclofen, and amitriptyline (Elavil). A prescription from a doctor is required, but you can obtain the information from a pharmacist who compounds medications (mixes them himself) and bring it to your doctor for his approval.

These topicals are not curative, but they may provide pain relief for one to eight hours and have minimal side effects (most commonly, skin allergy or sensitivity). Some of these may work better than others on different people, so you may have to try several to find the best one. In my clinic, I apply samples to my patients so they'll know whether a product works before they purchase it. Encourage your doctor or practitioner to do the same.

Step 8: Use Biomagnets for Short-Term Relief

If the topicals in Step 7 do not provide you with pain relief, you can try biomagnets applied to the sciatic area, either taped or contained in a back brace. As with the topicals, biomagnets provide only symptomatic relief, which disappears when the magnet is removed. (See Appendix B for more information on biomagnets.) You should feel better almost immediately when using biomagnets.

Step 9: Take Low-Dose Prescription Antidepressants

For some people, low-dose antidepressants, such as amitriptyline (Elavil) 25mg to 50mg daily or trazodone (Desyrel) 50mg to 150mg daily, can decrease chronic sciatic pain through effects on the pain center (hypothalamus) and neurotransmitters in the brain. Your doctor may prescribe these drugs if the previous steps fail to completely relieve your pain. It may take several weeks to a month before you notice improvement.

Step 10: Take Prescription Narcotic Medications

Narcotic pain-relief medications are appropriate only for severe, unrelenting sciatic pain that has not responded to any other treatment approaches. They vary in potency from propoxyphene (the mildest) to OxyContin or morphine (the strongest). Although these drugs give you immediate relief, they are highly addictive and should be monitored by a physician specializing in pain management.

Step 11: Undergo Surgery

Surgery should be a treatment of last resort for chronic sciatica, and should be done only if there is definitive evidence (through testing) that the sciatic nerve is being compressed by a disc rupture or structural abnormality that can be corrected by the surgery. Most often, surgery is not helpful in chronic cases of sciatica. You should consider it only if you have severe, unrelenting pain, or if you have worsening neurological signs such as loss of reflex, paralysis, or loss of bladder or bowel control.

> Teresa, a 17-year-old gymnast, injured her back several years ago, causing sciatica. After she tried several conservative measures (medications and physical therapy), an MRI scan showed a bulging disc that was touching a nerve, and she underwent surgery. She had relief for about a year, but the pain came back. She was told that she had developed scar tissue and underwent another surgery to remove the scarring and fuse the bone. This surgery helped for only about a month, at which time she was told that there was nothing else that could help. Her doctor placed her on low-dose antidepressants and narcotic pain relievers. She had tried biomagnets and several topical salves, but these gave her relief for only an hour or two. I recommended osteopathic mobilization because I felt that her sacroiliac joint (SI joint) was dysfunctional. Sure enough, the exam showed not only SI joint dysfunction, but also facet joint dysfunction in her entire lumbar area. After five osteopathic treatments, her pain was much improved but still present. I then performed a combination of acupuncture and cold laser, which ended her remaining pain in seven treatments.

SEIZURES (see *Epilepsy*)

SHINGLES (see *Neuralgia, Post-Herpetic*)

SINUSITIS

Sinusitis is an inflammation of the sinus cavities, air-filled areas in the facial bones. There are four pairs of sinuses, extending from the cheeks, along the nose, and up to the forehead, any of which can be involved with inflammation. Sinusitis can be acute, usually caused by infection, or chronic, caused by continued inflammation, scarring, allergies, or obstruction of the sinus openings (called *ostia*). Although it has been reported that 90 percent of people with chronic sinusitis have fungi in their sinuses, it is not known whether the fungi are a result—or a cause—of sinusitis. When sinusitis becomes chronic, breathing problems and nasal polyps can develop.

Common Symptoms: Chronic Sinusitis

- Fullness in the sinuses
- Pressure behind the eyes
- Nasal obstruction
- Nasal drainage
- Foul smell in the nose

Additional Common Symptoms: Acute Sinusitis

- Fever and chills
- Frontal headaches

Your Balanced Healing Action Plan for Acute Sinusitis

- If symptoms are severe, persist for at least seven days and include any of the following symptoms (purulent nasal drainage, facial pain, or tooth pain/tenderness), proceed to Step 6.

Step 1: *Apply Wet Heat and Take Vitamin C, Bioflavonoids, and Bromelain*

Start with local application of wet heat in combination with vitamin C (500mg every two hours), bioflavonoids (100mg per day), and bromelain (250mg to 500mg between meals). Vitamin C and bioflavonoids work through their antioxidant effects, and bromelain is an expectorant. This combination is very effective in reducing symptoms and healing the inflammation.

Step 2: *Take an Over-the-Counter Decongestant*

If your symptoms are not completely reduced with Step 1, add over-the-counter decongestants (such as Triaminic, Dimetapp), which can reduce swelling and help unclog the sinuses.

Step 3: Take Appropriate Chinese Herbal Remedies

If your symptoms continue, I recommend taking Chinese herbs, which can be very effective in reducing or resolving acute sinusitis. Formulas are determined based on the color of your sputum (phlegm). *Qing Bi Tang* and *Long Dan Xie Gan Tang* are commonly used for heat, and *Xiao Qing Long Tang* for cold. Consult a practitioner qualified in Chinese herbal medicine to determine which Chinese herbal formulas are the best for your particular condition. You should notice improvement within a few days to a week, but you may need to take the formulas longer for full relief. (See Appendix A, under "Chinese Herbs," for further information.)

Step 4: Take an Appropriate Homeopathic Remedy

If your sinusitis is still present, I recommend homeopathy as the next step. Homeopathy uses several different remedies to control and resolve acute sinusitis. *Mercurius vivus* (30c) is twice daily used for facial pain, yellow-green discharge, and alternating chills and sweats. *Nux vomica* (30c) is used twice daily for clear, thin discharge, sneezing, headache, and nasal stuffiness at night. *Kali bichromicum* (30c) is used one to two times daily for thick, stringy mucous, and pain in the cheeks or nose. *Pulsatilla* (30c) is used twice a day for light yellow or green discharge accompanied by lack of thirst and low spirits. Consult a qualified homeopathist for guidance on which remedies will be most beneficial and for proper dosages. You should notice improvement within one to three days. (See Appendix A, under "Homeopathy," for guidance on finding a qualified homeopathist and for further information.)

Step 5: Take Echinacea

Along with the above steps, you can use echinacea (2ml to 4ml of tincture (1:5) or fluid extract (1:1) three times daily), which is helpful in reducing symptoms and the duration of the condition if infection is involved. Do not use echinacea if you have any immune or systemic diseases (such as tuberculosis, lupus, multiple sclerosis, scleroderma, or AIDS).

Step 6: Take Prescription Antibiotics

If the previous steps are not effective, your symptoms continue after seven days, and you have purulent nasal drainage, facial pain, or tooth pain/tenderness, your doctor can prescribe antibiotics. Do not use antibiotics unless you have these conditions because otherwise the drugs will not help, and you can develop antibiotic resistance. Narrow-spectrum antibiotics, such as amoxicillin, doxycycline, or trimethoprim-sulfamethoxazole are the most commonly prescribed. If you are allergic to penicillin, erythromycin or a cephalosporin (Keflex, Ceclor) is the next choice.

Your Balanced Healing Action Plan for Chronic Sinusitis

- Although your drainage may be colored, antibiotics are not indicated in chronic sinusitis and should be avoided.

Step 1: Take Appropriate Chinese Herbal Remedies

I recommend starting with Chinese herbal formulas, which are excellent at reducing the symptoms, as well as the underlying causes, of chronic sinusitis. *Qing Bi Tang, Xiao Qing Long Tang,* and *Wen Dan Tang* are both beneficial. There are several other formulas that address allergic causes, such as *Yu Ping Feng San.* Consult a practitioner qualified in Chinese herbal medicine to determine which Chinese herbal formulas are the best for your particular condition. You should notice improvement within one to three weeks, but you may need to take the herbs longer for complete relief. (See Appendix A, under "Chinese Herbs," for further information.)

Step 2: Undergo Acupuncture

Acupuncture is very effective for resolving chronic sinusitis, whether it's due to allergies or other causes, and I usually use it with Step 1. Principal points usually are found on the face. Always seek evaluation and treatment from a practitioner certified in acupuncture. (See Appendix A, under "Acupuncture," for guidance in finding a qualified acupuncturist and for further explanation of the different acupuncture techniques.) You should notice improvement within three to four treatments, but you might need additional sessions for maximum benefits.

Step 3: Use the Nambudripad Allergy Elimination Treatment (NAET)

If the above treatments are not effective, and if allergies are a suspected cause (either food and/or airborne), the Nambudripad Allergy Elimination Treatment (NAET) method should be tried next. It combines acupuncture, kinesiology, chiropractic, herbs, and nutrition to desensitize you to substances to which you are allergic. It may take several months for its effectiveness to be observed, depending on how many allergens are sensitizing you (see Appendix A and the section on food allergies for further information and help in finding a practitioner who uses NAET).

Step 4: Undergo Cranial-Sacral Manipulation for Structural Problems

If the previous steps have not been effective or give you only partial relief, you may have underlying structural problems causing your continued symptoms. If the bones in your face and cheek are not aligned correctly, they can cause obstruction of the sinuses. At this point, I recommend that you undergo osteopathic evaluation. If structural problems are evident, then they must be corrected before you get any other treatments, or your symptoms may continue to reoccur. A specific type of osteopathic treatment, called *cranial-sacral manipulation,* is necessary. With osteopathic treatment, you should notice relief in three to six treatments. (See Appendix A, under "Manual Therapy," for further information and guidance to help find a qualified practitioner.)

> Jenna, a 25-year-old veterinary student, came to my clinic for treatment of constant migraine headaches. Several neurologists had treated her for years, but nothing relieved her symptoms. Because migraine headaches are rarely present all the time, I evaluated her further and found that her problem was not migraines but instead chronic sinusitis, caused by allergies. The sinus inflammation was causing her headaches. Because one of the standard Chinese herbal formulas contains cinnamon, to which she was allergic, a specific formula was designed for her. She also underwent 12 acupuncture sessions. These two methods significantly decreased her symptoms and her flare-ups, but she still had some residual problems. I suggested that she undergo osteopathic evaluation, and she underwent cranial-sacral manipulation. She did receive additional benefit from this technique and her remaining symptoms are now easily controlled by the Chinese herbal formula alone.

Step 5: Take Inhaled Steroids

If your chronic symptoms continue despite the previous steps, your doctor can prescribe inhaled steroids, which can be helpful in reducing chronic inflammation. It may take one to three weeks for inhaled steroids to be effective.

Step 6: Undergo Surgery

For chronic, persistent sinusitis that does not respond to the previous measures, endoscopy to clean the sinuses may be indicated. Other surgeries are done to remove polyps and open up "windows" for drainage. Surgery should be the last resort, and it does not always resolve your sinusitis.

SMOKING CESSATION (see *Nicotine Addiction*)

SPASTIC COLITIS (see *Irritable Bowel Syndrome*)

STOMACH INFLAMMATION (Gastritis, Ulcers)

Both *gastritis* and *ulcers* are characterized by an irritation of the stomach lining, with ulcers also causing erosion of the lining. Ulcers can also occur just beyond the stomach, in the duodenum (called *duodenal* rather than *gastric* ulcers). Gastritis and ulcers can be caused by smoking, excessive alcohol use, and a variety of medications, especially aspirin and nonsteroidal anti-inflammatory drugs (NSAIDs). A bacterium, *Helicobacter pylori* (called *H. pylori*) is responsible for up to 95 percent of duodenal ulcers and more than 80 percent of gastric ulcers. Chronic gastritis can lead to deficiency of B_{12} (a condition called *pernicious anemia*).

Common Symptoms

- Abdominal distress
- Pain (often relieved by eating food or taking antacids)
- Nausea
- Vomiting
- Loss of appetite

What You Need to Know

It is important to be tested for H. *pylori* before proceeding with any treatment because various antibiotics can kill this bacterium and cure the ulcer. The best tests to detect H. *pylori* are the urea breath or stool antigen tests (if positive, see Step 1). NSAIDs can cause irritation of the stomach, so if you are predisposed to stomach problems and must take them, try the newer NSAIDs, called Cox-2 inhibitors. These drugs usually have fewer side effects on the stomach than the older NSAIDs. But recent studies show an increased risk of heart attack in patients who use Cox-2 inhibitors, especially when taken along with naproxen (Aleve), so caution is advised. Obtain guidance from your doctor, particularly if you have heart disease. Smoking causes inflammation and ulcers, so stopping this habit is also essential in preventing and treating these conditions.

General Recommendations

Diet: Increasing the fiber in your diet has been shown to reduce the rate of ulcers and gastritis. Raw cabbage is also very effective in both preventing and treating stomach inflammation and ulcers. Contrary to popular belief, milk does not prevent or cure ulcers, and it can make them worse. Honey and yogurt both protect your stomach against H. *pylori*.

Meditation: Stress is a factor in both causing and worsening stomach inflammation and ulcers in many patients. Meditation is effective in reducing negative reactions to stress, and thus reducing symptoms and preventing recurrences (see Appendix A, under "Mind-Body Techniques," for further information and examples of meditation).

Your Balanced Healing Action Plan for Stomach Inflammation

Step 1: Take Prescription Triple Antibiotic Therapy for H. Pylori Infection

If testing indicates that you have H. *pylori* infection, you should take triple antibiotic therapy. There are several different combinations, currently the best of which is lansoprazole (Prevacid), clarithromycin (Biaxin), and amoxicillin. Other combinations using bismuth (Pepto Bismol) tetracycline, amoxicillin, and/or metronidazole (Flagyl) are less expensive, but may not be as effective. Three-drug regimens are taken for a week; but recently, four-drug regimens have been tested that take only 5 days of treatment and are less expensive overall (amoxicillin, metronidazole, clarithromycin with either Prevacid or Zantac). If H. *pylori* is not a factor, or if this therapy does not reduce your symptoms, then proceed with the next steps.

If you take antibiotics, they can destroy your beneficial digestive bacteria. After finishing your antibiotics, you should take probiotics, which consist of live cultures of organisms (the "good" bacteria) that help digest food properly. Of the beneficial microorganisms in probiotics, *L. acidophilus* and *bifidobacteria* are the best. Other beneficial bacteria include *L. salivarius*, *L. rhamnosus*, *L. plantarum*, *streptococcus thermophilus*, *L. bulgaricus*, *L. casei*, and *L. sporogenes*. It will take about two to three weeks for a probiotic to re-establish the good bacteria (see Appendix B, under "Probiotics," for further information and help in finding a good probiotic). Yogurt is not a good substitute for probiotics. Although yogurt does contain beneficial microorganisms, they are not the most important or potent. Also, many yogurt products are pasteurized after they are made to increase shelf life, but this process kills most of the good bacteria and destroys the benefits.

Step 2: Take Over-the-Counter Antacids

If you have occasional and mild to moderate symptoms, you can take over-the-counter antacids. Bismuth-containing products (Pepto Bismol) are effective at reducing symptoms and also inhibiting *H. pylori*, and they can be used instead of antacids. Antacids should be used intermittently because they can cause long-term side effects (aluminum- or magnesium-based antacids can impair kidney function; calcium-based antacids can cause decreased parathyroid gland function; all types can decrease absorption of various drugs and antibiotics).

Step 3: Take Digestive Enzymes and Probiotics

Because poor digestion both causes and is a result of stomach inflammatory conditions, I recommend that you take digestive enzymes. Such enzymes help break down your food in the stomach and duodenum, thereby reducing irritation of your stomach. There are many products that contain digestive enzymes, and they should contain some or all of the following: protease, papain, amylase, lipase, bromelain, cellulase, and lactase. If you haven't taken antibiotics (Step 1), take probiotics with the enzymes.

You should notice improvement within two to six weeks. If you have increased gas, bloating, or cramping in the first week, reduce your dosage and then gradually build the dose up as these side effects lessen.

Step 4: Take Appropriate Chinese Herbal Remedies

If you continue to have stomach irritation, I recommend taking Chinese herbal formulas as the next step. *Ping Wei San* and *Sai Mei An* are both beneficial formulas. Consult a practitioner qualified in Chinese herbal medicine to determine which Chinese herbal formulas are the best for your particular condition. You should notice improvement within three weeks, but you may need to take the herbs longer for complete relief. (See Appendix A, under "Chinese Herbs," for further information.)

Step 5: Undergo Acupuncture

If your stomach problems resist the previous methods, I recommend that you undergo acupuncture, which also can give you long-lasting relief and prevent recurrences. For gastritis, principal points usually are found on the legs, arms, and abdomen. For ulcers, principal points usually are found on the back, abdomen, arms, and legs. Always seek evaluation and treatment from a practitioner certified in acupuncture. (See Appendix A, under "Acupuncture," for guidance in finding a qualified acupuncturist and for further explanation of the different acupuncture techniques.) You should notice improvement within six treatments, but you might need additional sessions for maximum benefits.

Step 6: Take Deglyrrhizinated Licorice

If you still are having stomach problems, next take deglyrrhizinated licorice (DGL), a special form of licorice, which is as effective in controlling inflammation and ulcers as conventional medications but without the side effects of these drugs. It works by stimulating mucous secretion in the stomach. Dosage is two to four chewable tablets (380mg) between or 20 minutes before meals. Take it for at least 6 to 18 weeks. Take it before meals because it needs saliva to be effective.

Step 7: Drink Raw Cabbage Juice and Take Vitamin A, Vitamin E, and Zinc

If your symptoms persist, I recommend drinking raw cabbage juice, which is as effective as raw cabbage. In addition, supplement with vitamins A (5,000 IU daily), vitamin E (100 IU three times a day), and zinc (20mg to 30mg daily). These supplements can increase mucin, which protects the lining of your stomach. You should notice improvement within three to six weeks.

Step 8: Take Over-the-Counter Zantac, Tagamet, or Pepcid

If you are still suffering from stomach inflammation, I recommend trying over-the-counter H2-receptor antagonists (Zantac, Tagamet, Pepcid), which work by reducing acid production in your stomach. However, be aware that stomach acid is necessary for proper absorption of many medications (especially antibiotics), iron, and fat-soluble vitamins, so you may have to increase the dosage of these other substances to obtain their benefits. You should obtain relief within a few days using these medications.

Step 9: Take Prescription Proton Pump Inhibitors

If nothing has worked so far, or the previous steps have given you incomplete symptom relief, your doctor can prescribe proton pump inhibitors, which also work by decreasing stomach acid. These medications work better than the H_2-receptor antagonists, but they are much more expensive. The most common ones include Prilosec, Prevacid, and Aciphex. In general, they have a low risk of side effects. However, like the H_2-receptor antagonists, the absorption of many medications and vitamins can be decreased by these drugs. You should obtain relief within a few days, although some people do not obtain complete relief. Prilosec is available over-the-counter and is less expensive than the prescription variety.

> Marvin, a 58-year-old clothing store owner, had chronic stomach pain for 10 years. The diagnosis was ulcer disease. Over the years, he had been hospitalized several times and given numerous medications, including antacids, H$_2$-receptor antagonists, and proton pump inhibitors. These medications helped but did not completely eliminate his symptoms, and he continued to have severe flare-ups. He was in a very stressful job, which made the symptoms worse. He had been tested for *H. pylori*, and even though he had this infection, treatment did not alleviate his symptoms. I taught him some simple meditations and urged him to eat more cabbage (which he liked). I then placed him on digestive enzymes and probiotics, which did reduce his symptoms, but not completely. I recommended the Chinese herbal formula *Ping Wei San* and started acupuncture. After seven sessions, he was symptom free and had only occasional pain, which was relieved by taking the Chinese herbal formula for a day or two.

Step 10: *Take Panax Ginseng*

If you are still having residual symptoms, try Asian (Panax) ginseng (1,200mg to 1,800mg extract daily), which can reduce ulcer symptoms and inflammation in some patients. You should observe results within two to four weeks.

Step 11: *Undergo Surgery*

If ulcer disease persists, causing severe symptoms, or the ulcer eats a hole in the stomach, causing a perforation, surgery is usually necessary. Most surgeries are designed to take out the portion of your stomach that contains the ulcer. However, this does not correct the underlying causes of your ulcers, which must be addressed, or you will continue to have stomach problems.

STROKE (see *Cerebral Vascular Insufficiency*)

TARSAL TUNNEL SYNDROME (see *Carpal Tunnel Syndrome*)

TENDONITIS

Tendonitis is inflammation of a tendon, the fibrous tissue that connects muscles to bones. The most common tendons affected include the Achilles (heel), elbow (*tennis elbow or lateral epicondylitis*), and wrist (*DeQuervain's tenosynovitis*). The most common cause of tendonitis is repetitive use of the tendon, but disease and injuries also can cause tendon inflammation. Most tendonitis is self-limited, lasting only a few weeks. However, it can last from six weeks to a few years, especially if you keep reirritating the tendon by continued use. In some cases of chronic tendonitis, calcium deposits will occur in the tendon.

Common Symptoms

- Tenderness where the tendon inserts into a bone
- Stiffness
- Decreased range of motion
- Occasional swelling

General Recommendations

Exercise: Stretching properly before sports activities or exercise is the primary method of preventing tendonitis.

Your Balanced Healing Action Plan for Tendonitis

- If tendonitis has been present for more than two weeks, or is chronic, go to Step 3.

Step 1: Use the RICE Method

If you have recent onset of your pain, or your symptoms are mild, start with the RICE program:

- Rest
- Ice (not more than 20 minutes per hour)
- Compress the joint (elastic bandage such as ACE wrap)
- Elevate the limb

You should notice improvement in your inflammation and pain within a few days to a week.

Step 2: Take Over-the-Counter Ibuprofen or Naproxen

Along with Step 1, take over-the-counter NSAIDs (ibuprofen, naproxen), which are helpful short term to reduce inflammation and pain, and allow your body to heal itself. If your symptoms persist after a few weeks, proceed with the following steps.

Step 3: Undergo Acupuncture

For persistent tendonitis, the most effective and fastest resolution is from acupuncture. Usually only three or four sessions are required to obtain substantial relief, although more treatments may be necessary for long-lasting resolution. Principal points depend on the particular tendon involved. The Liver-Gall Bladder channels are important to treat because they control the tendons and sinews of the body. Acupuncture can work even if you are still using the tendon in various activities. Always seek evaluation and treatment from a practitioner certified in acupuncture. (See Appendix A, under "Acupuncture," for guidance in finding a qualified acupuncturist and for further explanation of the different acupuncture techniques.)

Step 4: Undergo Low-Level Energy Laser Therapy

If your symptoms continue, I recommend using low-level energy lasers because, in my studies, the laser appears to help heal the tissue, reduce the inflammatory response, and give long-lasting relief. I commonly use the laser in conjunction with acupuncture for better and faster results. These lasers are called "cold" lasers, because they do not produce heat like the hot lasers used in surgical procedures do. You should notice improvement within six to nine treatments (two to three weeks). Because this is currently a research device unavailable to most doctors, see Appendix C for a reference source.

Step 5: Undergo Physical Therapy Modalities

If your symptoms persist, your doctor can refer you for physical therapy modalities, including electrical stimulation (both direct current and alternating current can be applied to the painful areas; I prefer alternating, which can project deeper into the tissues without burning the skin), ultrasound (high-frequency sound that produces heat deep in the tissues), and iontophoresis (injection of steroids through the skin into the tendon). A physical therapy modality that I also highly recommend is infrasound, or low-frequency sound. Infrasound works by increasing the local circulation of blood and lymph to accelerate the healing process. It not only can reduce pain, but it can decrease swelling as well. Numerous chiropractors, naturopaths, acupuncturists, and a few doctors use infrasound. (See Appendix C, under "Infrasound," for a reference source.)

You can receive physical therapy along with the previous steps, and you should feel improvement in your pain within six to eight treatments.

Step 6: Take Bromelain, Curcumin, and Citrus Flavonoids

If the previous steps have not helped or have been only partially beneficial, take supplements of bromelain (250mg to 750mg three times per day between meals) and curcumin (200mg to 400mg three times per day between meals). These supplements can decrease inflammation, as well as bruising. To decrease healing time by half, you can add citrus flavonoids (5,600mg to 1,000mg three times daily) to these two supplements.

Step 7: Learn and Practice Counterstrain

If your tendonitis has not been resolved yet, I suggest trying an osteopathic technique called *counterstrain*. In tendonitis, your nerves may be overstimulating your tendons in certain positions, causing your pain. Counterstrain is used to "re-wire" your nerve-tendon communications to reduce the stimulation. This is done by first finding the area that has the most tenderness and the position that causes the most pain. Then you use your other surrounding muscles to find a position that immediately relieves the pain. You then repeat that position as often as you can, thus establishing a different pattern of nerve firing, which doesn't cause pain. You can be taught this technique by an osteopathic physician and perform it at home.

Step 8: Undergo Corticosteroid Injections

If nothing else has worked, your doctor can give you a local injection of corticosteroids. Steroids can help some people, but they should not be repeated often because they can cause softening of your bone and long-term damage to your tendon. If one injection is not helpful, repeat injections won't be helpful and are not recommended.

> Jerry, a 40-year-old furniture store employee, injured his elbow while doing repetitive lifting eight months before I examined him. He could work only on light duty, and he wasn't able to lift anything heavier than 10 pounds without having pain. He had been prescribed anti-inflammatory medications, had undergone physical therapy, and had received three steroid injections by three different doctors, even though none of the treatments ever worked. I started him on acupuncture. By the third treatment, he had significant improvement, and, by the fifth treatment, his pain was completely gone.

Step 9: Undergo Surgery

Some physicians perform surgery for chronic tendonitis, especially in the elbow or wrist. I have found surgery to help only a small percentage of people, and it can cause permanent problems such as decreased strength and limited range of motion. Surgery should be your last resort and be done only if you have severe unrelenting pain or cannot use the affected limb.

THYROID PROBLEMS

The *thyroid gland* regulates your body's metabolism, and the most common problems involve irregular production of thyroid hormones. Too much hormone results in *hyperthyroidism,* and too little results in *hypothyroidism.* Hyperthyroidism can be caused by dysfunction of your immune system (Grave's disease), or by formation of small tumors that produce too much thyroid hormone (*toxic adenomas*). Hypothyroidism is caused by underproduction of the thyroid, as a result of autoimmune disorders (*Hashimoto's thyroiditis*), or being exposed to excessive amounts of iodine.

Common Symptoms of Hyperthyroidism

- Weight loss despite increased activity
- Fast heart rate
- High blood pressure
- Nervousness with perspiration

- Increased frequency of bowel movements, diarrhea
- Muscle weakness
- Trembling hands
- Insomnia
- Menstrual problems
- Bulging eyeballs

Common Symptoms of Hypothyroidism

- Slowed mental processes
- Lethargy, fatigue
- Depression
- Dry skin
- Slower heart rate
- Weight gain
- Increased cold sensitivity
- Tingling or numbness of the hands

What You Need to Know

The diagnosis of thyroid hormone imbalances is based on measuring blood levels of thyroid hormones, but some results can be misleading because of interference from other medical conditions or medications (for example, one thyroid hormone, T_4, can be falsely elevated if you take birth control pills). The TSH (thyroid stimulating hormone, a pituitary hormone that stimulates production of thyroid hormones) level is a more reliable test: Below-normal levels indicate hyperthyroidism, and above-normal levels indicate hypothyroidism.

However, many alternative practitioners believe that some people can have low thyroid even if the TSH is normal. They recommend that you take your basal body temperature (your temperature first thing in the morning), which reflects your metabolic rate. If low, these practitioners recommend taking thyroid hormones. However, the metabolic rate is not solely dependent on thyroid hormones, so other factors may be causing the lowered body temperature, as well as your symptoms.

Another important aspect of thyroid function is iodine. The main function of iodine in the body is for thyroid hormone production. Too much or too little iodine can cause symptoms of both hypothyroidism and hyperthyroidism. If your TSH is normal but you have the above symptoms, I recommend buying a bottle of tincture of iodine (it costs about 87 cents) and placing it on a patch of skin (thigh is best) about one inch square. If the iodine disappears in 24 hours, you are not obtaining enough iodine. If it lasts much longer than 24 hours, you may be taking too much iodine, either in food or supplements.

General Recommendations

Diet: Cabbage, peaches, soybeans, spinach, peanuts, and radishes can all interfere with the production of thyroid hormones. They should be avoided in hypothyroidism, but taken in hyperthyroidism.

Exercise stimulates the production of thyroid hormones and increases tissue sensitivity to the hormones. It is especially important to exercise if you are overweight and hypothyroid because dieting can cause a slowing of your metabolic rate, thus making your symptoms worse. But exercise will prevent this from occurring by stimulating your metabolic rate.

Your Balanced Healing Action Plan for Hyperthyroidism

Step 1: Take Radioactive Iodine, Propylthiouracil, or Methimazole

Depending on the cause of your hyperthyroidism, your doctor may prescribe radioactive iodine or antithyroid medication (propylthiouracil or methimazole). These methods shut down thyroid hormone production. If you take the antithyroid medication, your symptoms will decrease in about six to eight weeks, but you will need to continue the drugs for a year. Sometimes, this will cure your condition, and it will not reoccur when you stop taking the drugs. If you undergo radioactive iodine treatment, your gland will usually be destroyed, and you will eventually need to take thyroid hormone replacement.

Step 2: Take the Appropriate Chinese Herbal Remedies

Chinese herbs can help relieve symptoms of hyperthyroidism but are not a cure. They can be taken with Step 1. Most formulas use a mixture of baked licorice, bupleurum, dragon bone, and/or peony. They can be used with conventional medications for better results. Consult a practitioner qualified in Chinese herbal medicine to determine which Chinese herbal formulas are the best for your particular syndromes. You should notice improvement within two to three weeks, but you may need to take the herbs longer for maximum benefit. (See Appendix A, under "Chinese Herbs," for further information.)

> Emily, a 42-year-old basketball coach, came to my clinic with numerous problems, including feeling hot and stinging inside her body, yet feeling cold outside her body, as well as insomnia, headaches, muscle weakness and soreness, and trembling hands, all of which had been worsening over the past two years. Her family and primary doctor thought her symptoms were psychological, even though her mother and aunt both had a history of thyroid problems. Lab tests revealed that her thyroid hormones were significantly elevated and a thyroid scan was consistent with Grave's disease. I put her on antithyroid medication and a Chinese herbal formula, and her symptoms gradually went away over the next four to five weeks.

Step 3: Undergo Surgery

Surgery is usually recommended when you are under age 45 and if you have toxic adenomas because these do not usually respond to the previous steps. After removal of the tissue, your thyroid hormone levels should return to normal within a few weeks.

Your Balanced Healing Action Plan for Hypothyroidism

- If you are hypothyroid, you must take thyroid hormone supplementation.
- Health food stores sell thyroid extracts that are milder forms of dessicated thyroid. They can ease symptoms of mild hypothyroidism, but I don't recommend them because their purity and potency are not consistent from product to product, and from bottle to bottle, even when you use the same brand.

Step 1: Take Dessicated Thyroid

Most physicians prescribe synthetic thyroid hormones (see Step 2), but most of these medications usually contain only one form of thyroid hormone. Dessicated thyroid contains all forms of thyroid hormone, which is what I recommend. These are available only by prescription. (Armour thyroid, Westhroid.)

Step 2: Take Synthetic Thyroid Hormone Supplement

Synthetic thyroid hormones (such as Synthroid, Levoxyl, Levothroid) are the most commonly prescribed medication for hypothyroid states. However, they usually contain only one form of thyroid, and recent studies show that they may increase the risk of prostate cancer. However, overall they are relatively safe, have been used for decades, and are very effective.

TINNITUS (Ringing in the Ears)

Tinnitus is a noise heard inside your ear caused by damage to the *cochlea,* a small organ in the internal ear. The most common cause of tinnitus is chronic and loud noise exposure. It can also be associated with other diseases, such as *Meniere's disease* (see section on Meniere's), and it often occurs with hearing loss—but it is not caused by it. Other causes of tinnitus include wax blockage, infection, and tumor of the auditory nerve.

Common Symptoms

The noise can be several varieties, including buzzing, ringing, crickets, roaring, hissing, or whistling. It can be intermittent or continuous, and it is usually more prominent at night.

What You Need to Know

Treatable causes of tinnitus (infection, tumor) should be ruled out by an examination or testing. In addition, there are more than 200 medications (including nonprescription) that can cause tinnitus, especially aspirin, some antibiotics, and quinine. If you are taking any medications, check the *Physician's Desk Reference* (PDR) to see whether that medication can cause tinnitus. Because noise exposure is the primary cause of chronic tinnitus, always wear hearing protection. Loud music increases the risk, so those who listen to rock music or other music at high decibel levels should be warned of the risks.

General Recommendations

Diet: Salt, caffeine, alcohol, and smoking can make tinnitus worse and should be reduced or eliminated.

Your Balanced Healing Action Plan for Tinnitus

Step 1: Undergo Acupuncture

Acupuncture can resolve or reduce tinnitus long term, and I recommend it first. The longer the tinnitus is present, the more difficult it is for acupuncture to be effective. Principal points usually are found on the face, head, and hands, with supplemental points on the legs and feet. Always seek evaluation and treatment from a practitioner certified in acupuncture. (See Appendix A, under "Acupuncture," for guidance in finding a qualified acupuncturist and for further explanation of the different acupuncture techniques.) You should notice improvement within six treatments, but you might need additional sessions for maximum benefits.

Step 2: Take an Appropriate Homeopathic Remedy

If your symptoms persist, I recommend trying homeopathy. Homeopathic remedies differ, depending on the type of sound being heard. *Chininum sulphuricum* is used for buzzing or hissing. *Salicylium acidum* is used for roaring sounds with hearing loss. *Kali iodatum* is used for ringing sounds. *Barboneum sulphuratum* is used for roaring sounds accompanied by feeling that your ears are blocked and tingling sensations. You should consult a qualified homeopathist for guidance on which remedies will be most beneficial and for proper dosages. You should notice improvement within one to two months. (See Appendix A, under "Homeopathy," for guidance in finding a qualified homeopathist and for further information.)

Step 3: Take Vitamin B₁₂ and Vitamin A

If your tinnitus continues despite the above methods, then take vitamin B_{12} (1,000mcg daily) and vitamin A (5,000 IU to 10,000 IU). These vitamins are necessary for normal ear function and hearing and may help in some cases. Beneficial results may take several months.

Step 4: Take Feverfew or Gingko Biloba

If you continue to have ringing in your ears, take feverfew (50mg to 125mg whole leaf standardized to contain 0.6 percent to 0.7 percent cardenolide). If feverfew is not helpful, try gingko biloba (160mg to 240mg daily), which is effective when a circulation problem is causing your tinnitus. It may take several weeks to two months to be effective.

Step 5: Undergo Cranial-Sacral Manipulation

Some people have structural problems involving the bones of the face and surrounding the ear. If the previous steps have not helped you, I recommend that an osteopath evaluate you to determine whether such a structural problem exists. If so, you can undergo an osteopathic technique called cranial-sacral manipulation, in which the bones of the face and skull are realigned. You should notice improvement within three to four treatments. (See Appendix A, under "Manual Therapy," for further information and guidance in finding a qualified practitioner.)

> Joshua, a 33-year-old rock musician, had constant tinnitus, which he described as "crickets" in his ears all the time. The tinnitus had worsened over 15 years and was worse in the right ear than the left. I started him on acupuncture, as well as some of the herbal remedies (Step 4), and the tinnitus in his left ear improved, but not in the right ear. I wondered whether there might be a structural problem with the right ear, and he underwent osteopathic evaluation. My questioning prompted Joshua to remember an accident 20 years before in which he struck the right side of his head and sustained a concussion. I recommended treatment using cranial-sacral techniques, and after only three sessions, the tinnitus in his right ear was completely gone.

Step 6: Undergo Hypnosis

If you are still bothered by tinnitus, I recommend that you undergo hypnosis, which might help you to "turn off" the sound for days or weeks at a time. You can use hypnosis in addition to the previous steps (see Appendix A, under "Mind-Body Techniques," for further information and guidance on how to find a qualified hypnotist).

Step 7: Use a Sound-Masking Device

If nothing has helped by now, there are several devices, such as tinnitus maskers, that are available. These devices are designed to block out the tinnitus by making different sounds, but sometimes they can be worse than the tinnitus. Another method, called auditory habituation, uses a device that generates "white noise," teaching the brain to ignore the tinnitus. Consult an ear specialist (*otologist*) for further information and guidance.

TMJ (Temporomandibular Joint) Syndrome

TMJ syndrome is a dysfunction of the joint that connects the jawbone to the skull. This joint is one of the busiest joints of the body because it is instrumental in speaking and eating. TMJ has many causes, the most common of which is strain of your jaw muscles, usually from clenching or grinding your teeth. It can also be a result of injury, a displaced disk (in the joint), or degenerative joint disease.

Common Symptoms

- Pain in the joint in front of the ears
- Pain in the face muscles

- Clicking or popping of the joint when opening the mouth
- Difficulty opening the mouth
- Headaches

General Recommendations

Meditation: TMJ is often associated with stress, so meditation is very helpful at relaxing the face muscles. Some people unconsciously grind their teeth (called *bruxism*), which also responds well to meditation (see Appendix A, under "Mind-Body Techniques," for further information and examples of meditation).

Your Balanced Healing Action Plan for TMJ

Step 1: Take Over-the-Counter Pain Relievers

More than 90 percent of us may have some problem with our TMJ during our lives, such as when yawning widely or eating something chewy. Your jaw may pop or hurt for a few hours or days. If your problem is of recent onset and mild, just taking over-the-counter analgesics (acetaminophen or ibuprofen) and massaging the TMJ may be sufficient to resolve the problem.

Step 2: Undergo Physical Therapy

If your symptoms persist, I next recommend undergoing physical therapy, using electrical stimulation, ultrasound (high-frequency sound producing deep heat), massage, and moist heat. These modalities can relieve pain and stiffness in mild cases of TMJ by decreasing inflammation. You will need a referral to a physical therapist from your doctor or dentist.

Step 3: Undergo Treatments to Stop Grinding (Bruxism)

If the cause of your TMJ is bruxism, your dentist can prescribe a splint or bite guard. In addition, I recommend that you undergo hypnosis, which is very effective in preventing your grinding in just a few sessions (see Appendix A, under "Mind-Body Techniques," for further information and guidance in finding a qualified hypnotist).

Step 4: Use Biofeedback If You Have Stress

If the cause of your TMJ syndrome is stress (clenching your jaw), I recommend biofeedback in addition to meditation. Biofeedback teaches you how to relax your jaw when you become anxious (see Appendix A, under "Mind-Body Techniques," for further information and guidance in finding a qualified biofeedback practitioner).

Step 5: Undergo Osteopathic Mobilization for Structural Causes

If you've been in an accident, there is a good possibility that your TMJ is caused by a structural abnormality in your facial or skull bones. If so, I recommend being evaluated by an osteopathic physician, who can perform cranial-sacral techniques, in which the facial and skull bones are realigned properly. With osteopathic treatment, your pain should start decreasing in three to six treatments, although additional treatments may be necessary to achieve maximum benefit. (See Appendix A, under "Manual Therapy," for further information and guidance in finding a qualified practitioner.)

Step 6: Undergo Low-Level Energy Laser Therapy

If x-rays and examination show that you have degenerative (wear and tear) changes that are causing your TMJ symptoms, I recommend treatment using a low-level energy laser, which can effectively decrease the chronic inflammation. These lasers are called "cold" lasers, because they do not produce heat like the hot lasers used in surgical procedures do. You should notice improvement within six to nine treatments (two to three weeks). Because this is currently a research device unavailable to most doctors, see Appendix C for a reference source.

Step 7: Undergo Acupuncture for Degenerative or Inflammatory Causes

If the cause of your TMJ is not structural, and you have a degenerative or inflammatory condition, acupuncture can be very effective at reducing your symptoms. I often use acupuncture with the cold laser for faster results in such conditions, but acupuncture alone can be beneficial. Principal points usually are found on the face and feet. Always seek evaluation and treatment from a practitioner certified in acupuncture. (See Appendix A, under "Acupuncture," for guidance in finding a qualified acupuncturist and for further explanation of the different acupuncture techniques.) You should notice improvement within six treatments, but you might need additional sessions for maximum benefits.

Sari, a 20-year-old college student, developed TMJ syndrome two months after being involved in a rear-end car collision, in which her jaws "snapped" from the force of the collision. She had been treated by a dentist who specialized in TMJ problems, and she had been given various medications and a splint to wear at night. These measures helped to a minimal degree. Because she had been in an accident, I suspected an underlying structural problem, and she underwent cranial-sacral manipulation. This helped her a great deal, but she still had soreness and stiffness in the joints caused by chronic irritation and scarring. I treated her with the cold laser in conjunction with acupuncture, which ended her remaining symptoms.

Step 8: Undergo Rolfing

If you are still suffering from TMJ problems, I recommend that you undergo Rolfing, a form of bodywork that involves manipulating and stretching the body's fascial tissues (deep connective tissues that hold your body together), thus allowing a rebalancing of the tissues. If your TMJ is caused by a combination of structural abnormalities and scar tissue that has not responded to osteopathic treatment, Rolfing may be of benefit (see Appendix A, under "Bodywork," for further information and ways to find a qualified practitioner).

Step 9: Undergo Surgery

Surgical intervention is the last resort, but it is effective in severe cases that do not respond to other treatments. If no other method has worked, you have constant pain, or your jaw is "frozen" or does not work correctly, you may be a candidate for surgery.

TRIGEMINAL NEURALGIA (see *Neuralgia*)

ULCERATIVE COLITIS (see *Inflammatory Bowel Disease*)

ULCERS (see *Stomach Inflammation*)

VARICOSE VEINS/VENOUS INSUFFICIENCY

Varicose veins are swollen veins that protrude beneath the skin. Veins have valves that normally keep blood from backing up, but when those valves become damaged, your blood then pools in the veins, causing the bulging. Varicose veins occur primarily in the legs, due to gravitational pull when standing. Varicose veins can become ulcerated, inflamed, and prone to bleeding, and they can cause swelling of the extremity in severe cases. In venous insufficiency, the blood flow is also backed up, but this occurs in the deeper veins. It is also caused by the valves not working properly, as well as from blood clots. Venous insufficiency can cause varicose veins, but not vice versa. Complications and treatments are similar for both conditions.

Common Symptoms of Varicose Veins

- Prominent, dilated, tortuous, superficial veins
- Heaviness
- Pain

Common Symptoms of Venous Insufficiency

- Leg swelling
- Aching in calf
- Stasis dermatitis (skin inflammation)
- Nighttime cramps
- Leg discoloration

General Recommendations

Diet: Because obesity is one of the primary predisposing factors for varicose veins, a balanced diet for weight management is important (see the section on obesity for further treatment guidelines). In addition, because excessive pressure from straining can worsen or cause varicose veins, a high-fiber diet is beneficial in making bowel movements easier.

Foods high in antioxidants, especially berries, garlic, onions, ginger, and cayenne, are very helpful in maintaining the structure of the veins.

Exercise is very important to prevent and treat varicose veins. Aerobic exercises such as walking, biking, and jogging are especially beneficial because they help contract the leg muscles, which then squeeze the veins and push the blood up your legs. Resistance exercises can help as well, as long as you don't overstrain (see "Exercise," under "Simple Healing Steps for All Health Conditions," page 79, for more information).

Your Balanced Healing Action Plan for Varicose Veins/Venous Insufficiency

Step 1: Take Horse Chestnut, Gotu Kola, Butcher's Broom, Bilberry with Flavonoids, Bromelain, Aortic GAGs, HER, and/or Grapeseed or Pine Bark

I recommend a number of herbal extracts that are effective in enhancing the structure, function and tone of veins. They can be used alone or together. They include the following:

- Horse Chestnut (extracts containing 50mg escin, daily)
- Gotu kola (30mg to 60mg of triterpenic acids daily)
- Butcher's broom (100mg containing 9 percent to 11 percent ruscogenin, three times a day)
- Aortic GAGs (100mg daily)
- HER (1,000mg to 3,000mg daily)
- Bilberry with flavonoids (80mg to 160mg, containing 25 percent anthocyanosides, three times daily)
- Bromelain (500mg to 750mg, containing 1,200mcu to 1,800mcu, two to three times a day between meals)
- Grapeseed or pine bark extract (150mg to 300mg, containing at least 95 percent procyanidolic oligomers, daily)

Step 2: Wear Support Stockings

Along with the herbal remedies, you can use elastic support stockings, which can help the blood circulation in the legs. These stockings should fit snugly, but if they are too tight, they can cause more discomfort and restrict the veins even more.

Step 3: Take an Appropriate Homeopathic Remedy

If your varicose veins continue to cause symptoms, try homeopathic remedies. *Pulsatilla* is one that is often prescribed for long-term relief. For short-term symptoms, you can try over-the-counter remedies, including the application of *Hamamelis* cream (6x to 15c) to bruised or bluish areas that are sore and *Belladonna* (12x or 12c) four times daily for red, hot, swollen, and tender veins. You should consult a qualified homeopathist for guidance as to which remedies will be most beneficial and for proper dosages. You should notice improvement in one to two months. (See Appendix A, under "Homeopathy," for guidance in finding a qualified homeopathist and for further information.)

Step 4: Drink Noni Juice

Anecdotal reports indicate that Noni juice is beneficial in reducing varicose veins, but no studies have been conducted to support these reports. However, I feel that it is worth a try if the previous steps are not helpful. You should notice improvement within two to three weeks.

Step 5: Undergo Surgery

For severe varicose veins that are very painful and swollen, the last resort is surgery. There are several surgeries that may help. The most common uses a high-energy ("hot") laser. The next-best surgery is vein stripping, followed by the injection of sclerosing agents into the veins.

WEIGHT LOSS (see *Obesity*)

Alternative Methods and Procedures

Chapter 2 gives a few examples of several alternative methods and procedures used today and their benefits. Scientific research supports many of these, while others are backed up by nothing more than tradition or unproven concepts. This appendix summarizes the basic premises behind the most commonly used methods and procedures and tells you what you need to know to use them effectively.

MOST COMMONLY USED METHODS SUPPORTED BY RESEARCH

Manual Therapy

- Chiropractic
- Massage
- Osteopathic

Mind-Body Techniques (Psychoneuroimmunology)

- Attitude and Emotion
- Biofeedback
- Hypnosis
- Imagery
- Meditation
- Prayer, Spiritual Belief, and Organized Religion
- Relaxation

Traditional Chinese Medicine

- Acupuncture
- Chinese Herbs
- Nutrition
- Qigong

OTHER METHODS SUPPORTED BY RESEARCH

- Ayurvedic Medicine
- Homeopathy
- Naturopathic Medicine
- Self-Help Groups
- Yoga

ALTERNATIVE METHODS BASED IN TRADITION OR UNPROVEN CONCEPTS

- Applied Kinesiology
- Aromatherapy
- Bodywork
- Chelation
- Detoxification Therapy (Colon; Liver and Blood)
- Energy Healing
- Flower Remedies
- Iridology
- Light Therapy
- Music Therapy
- Nambudripad Allergy Elimination Treatment (NAET)
- Reconstructive Therapy (Sclerotherapy)

MOST COMMONLY USED METHODS SUPPORTED BY RESEARCH

Manual Therapy

Manual therapy is a vast field with hundreds of different techniques including chiropractic, osteo-pathic, massage, reflexology, Rolfing, and acupressure to name just a few. Each technique can differ substantially from the others, and each can benefit different types of medical conditions.

Chiropractic

Chiropractic is a rapidly growing profession and the most common form of manual therapy. There are more than 50,000 chiropractors in North America, with more than half having graduated since 1977. The original theory behind chiropractic is that, since all bodily systems are connected by the nervous system, any misalignment of the spinal column can cause disease by impinging on or stretching nerves. By correcting the abnormal spinal alignment and taking pressure off the nerves, the medical condition can be controlled or cured. This "single cause" concept of disease has now been abandoned by most modern chiropractors, who limit their practice to musculoskeletal disorders and make no claims about their ability to prevent all diseases or cure other organic illnesses.

Chiropractic manipulation (or "adjustment") usually employs a sudden, quick thrust, the purpose of which is to adjust the spine into its proper alignment. There are two basic types of thrust: the *short-leverage*, which uses contact with one spinal vertebra, and the *long-leverage*, which focuses on two or more vertebrae at the same time. In the long-leverage technique, the spinal joints are manipulated slightly beyond the normal range; this usually produces a pop-ping sound thought to be a result of gas bubbles being released in the tissue surrounding the vertebra. (This also is what happens when you "pop" your knuckles.)

Chiropractic treatment has been shown to be safe and effective during the first month or two that you have *uncomplicated* low back pain and neck pain (that is, without the pain radi-ating down your arms or legs, and without pre-existing problems such as degenerative arthritis, ruptured discs, or spinal stenosis). In fact, several studies have shown chiropractic treatment to be more cost-effective and beneficial than conventional treatment for many acute back problems. However, if your symptoms have lasted longer than a month or two, the effective-ness of chiropractic manipulation is unproven.

In *acute* conditions (the problem or pain is recent), chiropractic treatment should give some relief from neck, back, or headache pain within 6 or 7 treatments. If you are receiving benefit, continue the treatment until you no longer see improvement. Long-term continuous treatment (more than 15 to 20 treatments) without substantial pain relief is not necessary or recommended. If you get only temporary relief, or you are told that it might take more than 20 treatments to even begin to see results, or that it might take six months to obtain maximum benefits, I advise that you stop and seek other therapies.

Many people with *chronic* neck and low-back pain undergo chiropractic treatment, but studies have so far not shown any long-term benefit, and I don't recommend it. Most people can receive short-term relief of their chronic pain through chiropractic manipulation, but the pain makes a prompt return, sometimes within hours or days. In such situations, chiropractic does not provide a cure for chronic neck or back pain, and it can manage the pain at a tolerable level only as long as patients receive frequent treatments. Unfortunately, this can be costly, and there may be other methods that are more cost-effective and longer lasting.

Another concern with long-term chiropractic manipulation is that it can create a different set of problems for you. Each time your back is "popped," it stretches the ligaments that hold your spinal vertebra. With repeated stretching, the ligaments no longer hold your spine in place for very long, and it quickly slips out of alignment once again. Certainly, another chiropractic treatment can put it back in place, but the result will not last. That is why many people with chronic conditions may get only a few hours or days of relief from chiropractic treatments. Unless chiropractic treatment gives you pain relief that lasts for several weeks or months at a time, I do not recommend it in chronic conditions.

Many chiropractors also use roller tables, activators, and other devices. None of these have undergone thorough research, although they may be of some benefit with short-term use. If you don't see beneficial results in four to six treatments using these devices, you most likely won't with additional treatments. Chiropractors often also sell vitamins, supplements, homeopathic remedies, and glandular substances. The same cautions are advised with these products as mentioned elsewhere in this book. Many chiropractors use acupuncture along with manipulation, but they may have minimal training (about 100 hours). To know whether your chiropractor is qualified, see the section on acupuncture.

Finally, although most chiropractors practice within the modern definition of their discipline as treatment for musculoskeletal problems related to the spine, some chiropractors portray themselves as being primary care specialists who can diagnose and treat any and all illnesses through spinal manipulation. They can't. These individuals typically have very little knowledge or training in medicine, and they should be avoided. For further information on chiropractic and how to find a qualified practitioner, see Appendix C, under "Manual Therapy."

Massage

Massage is the second-most-common, and can be one of the most effective forms of manual therapy. Massage increases the level of *serotonin*, a chemical substance used by the brain that is abnormally low in various conditions, especially depression. Massage also lowers the levels of stress hormones, reducing anxiety. Massage also can stretch connective tissue and relieve tension in muscles.

There are numerous types of massage, ranging from gentle touching to intensely therapeutic. Many techniques are named for the individuals who have promoted them: Trager, Rolfing, Alexander, Feldenkrais, Hanna, Aston-patterning, Hakomi, Hellerwork, Rubenfield Synergy, and the Pesso system. Other names describe the technique: Swedish, manual lymph drainage, ideokinesis, continuum movement, kinetic awareness, cranio-sacral, shiatsu, authentic movement. Also included are techniques such as reflexology and acupressure. All of these forms are variations of the five basic types of massage: effleurage, petrissage, percussion, kneading, and friction.

One of the most common and well-known forms of massage is Swedish massage, developed more than 150 years ago. This is the form with which most Americans are familiar, and it uses gentle pressure to relax the muscles. Another popular form of massage is shiatsu (shi = "finger," atsu = "pressure"). This Japanese form of massage focuses on unblocking "energy flow" by targeting several of about 75 active "points" on the body. The appropriate points for specific diseases are massaged in a circular motion by the thumb or forefinger for half a minute. Rolfing is a more aggressive form of massage that is used to stretch and loosen connective tissue, rather than focusing on muscles and ligaments. Because it involves massaging structures down to the bone, Rolfing is used on the deep tissues and can be painful. To perform Rolfing requires a bachelor's degree followed by seven months of training at a Rolfing center.

Reflexology utilizes pressure points on the feet and in the hands. There are more than 7,000 sensory nerve endings in the feet that correlate to all organ systems of the body. Reflexologists can diagnose medical conditions by finding which points are tender, and then massage those points to reduce the symptoms. Acupressure is similar to reflexology in that it utilizes acupuncture points, but throughout the entire body. All organs, glands, and nerves in your body have corresponding pressure points. Pain or tenderness in any of those areas is a sign of congestion or malfunction in the corresponding organ or gland, and massaging these areas can help relieve the condition. A great advantage of acupressure is that you do not have to rely on practitioners; you can learn how to apply it yourself with the same beneficial results (in fact, there are numerous books on acupressure that can teach you how to do it).

The experience and skill of the practitioner is very important in obtaining benefits from massage. Especially when using the more aggressive or complicated forms of massage, you should make sure your practitioner is certified in that method. Like most other alternative methods, you should obtain some benefits after four to six treatments. Be aware that certain forms of massage worsen acute joint inflammation, and there also have been reported cases of burns and broken bones from massage therapy.

For further information on massage and to help find a qualified practitioner, see Appendix C, under "Manual Therapy."

Osteopathic

Doctors of osteopathy (DOs) are the only other health care providers who are taught a body of knowledge as broadly based as that taught to MD physicians. There are more than 36,000 osteopathic physicians practicing in the United States, most of whom in fact practice standard medical specialties, such as family practice, internal medicine, obstetrics and gynecology, orthopedic and general surgery, cardiology, and others. However, osteopathic training emphasizes a more holistic approach than that taught in medical schools.

In addition, osteopaths are taught a hands-on approach referred to as *Osteopathic Mobilization Therapy*, or OMT. This is a type of manipulation that is similar in theory to chiropractic, but it is performed much differently. Whereas both treat the misalignment of the spine, the osteopath also treats the underlying cause of the misalignment. Osteopaths rarely "pop" the back, preferring to use more subtle maneuvers, and they provide additional therapies such as myofascial release, counterbalancing, and neuromuscular re-education. These techniques take a much longer time to perform than chiropractic manipulation, often requiring more than an hour for each treatment. Osteopathic manipulation usually heals faster and is longer lasting than chiropractic manipulation, and it has fewer long-term problems. It is my preferred form of manipulation for *chronic* spine conditions, but it is also beneficial for acute problems. It may take from two to eight treatments to notice improvement, and occasional re-adjustments may be necessary.

The osteopathic approach can often diagnose muscle and skeletal problems that cannot be determined by conventional means. This was the case for Wende, who injured her back in a car accident and still had pain several years later, not only in her back but also toward her neck. She was having some breathing problems as well. Conventional physicians had told her that the back pain was caused by a bad disc, the neck pain was not related to the back injury, and the breathing difficulties were psychological. On osteopathic exam, it was obvious that her back pain was actually caused by misalignment of her pelvis and sacrum, and her neck pain was due to her upper body compensating for the injuries to her lower body. She was also diagnosed as having a frozen rib cage, which can cause breathing difficulties. Osteopathic mobilization was done on four occasions, which put an end to Wende's back and neck pain, as well as to her breathing problems.

Although osteopathy is based on a more holistic foundation than conventional medicine, most osteopaths do not perform osteopathic manipulation nor might they use a holistic approach. Most practice medicine just like their MD counterparts do. To learn more about osteopathic mobilization and/or find an osteopath who performs OMT, you should contact your state's osteopathic association or see Appendix C for reference information.

Mind-Body Techniques (Psychoneuroimmunology)

Mind-body techniques are the most commonly used alternative methods, and for good reason. The mind is a powerful tool of healing. By harnessing and channeling the power of your mind, you can reduce symptoms and even reverse some diseases, as well as prevent health problems from occurring in the first place. Conversely, your mind can contribute to the development of disease. More than 85 percent of all medical conditions are caused or complicated by underlying stress or emotional factors.

Although you might think of your body and your mind as separate, recent research reveals that they are intimately and inextricably connected. Thousands of chemical substances control the myriad bodily functions that sustain life. When you are healthy, your body releases these chemicals in amounts that have beneficial effects. Positive emotions influence the balance of chemical transmitters in your body, either reducing the high levels that can cause damage or stimulating production when low levels jeopardize your health. Studies demonstrate, for example, that patients undergoing surgery heal better and faster if their anesthesiologists simply talk with them before surgery. Listening to relaxing music during surgery has shown the same results.

Sometimes, the outcome of a positive outlook is nothing short of amazing. When 36-year old Marcy discovered she had advanced breast cancer, she was determined to beat it. The typical course of disease for Marcy's diagnosis is quite poor, with most women living only a few years. But Marcy was adamant that she must live until her sons, youngsters at the time of her diagnosis, were out of college. She believed that she *would* live and held firm to her optimism. Amazingly enough, her cancer went into remission for 15 years—long enough for her youngest son to graduate from college.

Negative emotions such as fear, anger, depression, and frustration, as well as environmental factors such as stress, can have the opposite effect, causing an imbalance of chemical substances that results in disease. For example, cortisol is a hormone that helps the body adapt to stress. But high levels of stress cause your body to produce excessive cortisol, which can damage vital organs such as the stomach, heart, and brain. Another well-known connection is that between depression and low levels of serotonin, a chemical messenger in the brain that influences mood and emotion. Negative emotions and stress cause more harm when they are persistent. We all experience negative emotions and stress during our lives. If they are only temporary, the imbalances are easily reversed. When these emotions are prolonged or occur frequently, however, the imbalances remain longer and disease is more likely to occur.

How we *react* to negative emotions and stress can also determine what occurs to our bodies. Some people react to stress calmly, letting their natural response mechanisms function as designed to restore balance and maintain health. Other people react to stress with agitation, creating imbalance and a higher risk of disease or death.

When I was an intern, I diagnosed early lung cancer in a 35-year-old woman. Although the cancer was incurable, I explained to her that she could live for a few more years with proper treatment. She became terribly distraught and told me she did not want to go through all those treatments and just wanted to die. Despite wonderful support from her family, she was so despondent that she died in just two weeks.

If physical illness can be caused or made worse by emotional factors, then it is logical to assume that the mind can be used purposefully to reverse or control these ailments. That is the purpose of mind-body interventions. Commonly used mind-body techniques include those discussed in the following sections.

Attitude and Emotion

Attitude and emotion influence disease significantly because they are essential parts of the mind-body connection. Positive emotions and a positive attitude alone can provide numerous medical benefits. It is not just having certain emotions, however, but also the *expression* of those feelings that have a healing effect. Studies of women with breast cancer and melanoma have shown that women in support groups live twice as long and have fewer side effects of treatment than those who do not participate. This is due to the process of allowing their emotions to be expressed freely.

Most frequently, it is negative emotions that must be released because these are the ones that may cause disease. But it is equally important to express positive emotions, which can neutralize the effects of the negative emotions. Unfortunately, many of us dwell on the negative and do not allow the positive to surface, but it would do wonders for us to look around and feel happy about the good things in life as well.

Biofeedback

Biofeedback uses technology to teach you how to consciously influence bodily functions. Electrodes that can register the electrical energy of your muscles connect you to a machine that signals how your body is reacting to various events and then the biofeedback process teaches you techniques to change those reactions. If you have tension headaches, for example, skin monitors measure the tenseness of your forehead muscles, and you are taught how to relax these muscles. A sound signals how tense these muscles are, with the sound being louder with high tension and becoming softer and finally disappearing as you relax more. You focus on using the relaxation techniques you've learned to lower the sound intensity, which relaxes your muscles and stops your headaches.

Any number of people, from medical technicians to psychiatrists, can provide biofeedback, so make sure that the professional you choose is certified to perform this technique. For more information on biofeedback and to find a qualified practitioner, see Appendix C, under "Biofeedback."

Hypnosis

Hypnosis is a mind-body technique that physicians have used for years. The American Medical Association approved hypnosis as a medical treatment in 1958, and since then more than 15,000 doctors have been trained in its use. Numerous psychologists and social workers also perform this technique. Hypnosis involves placing you in a deeply relaxed and focused state, referred to as a *hypnotic trance*. While you are in a trance, the hypnotist makes positive suggestions regarding your emotions, habits, and bodily functions. Your unconscious mind "hears" these suggestions and carries them out after the trance ends.

There are two types of trances. *Superficial* is a semi-awake state, in which you can remember and accept the suggestions given to you. When Stacey came to me for help losing weight, I placed her in a superficial trance. When she awoke, she told me she had heard everything I had said, and she did not feel like she had really been in a trance. In fact, she also had been distracted by noises outside the room. But over the next week, she realized that she had no desire whatsoever for any midday or evening snacks, which was one of the hypnotic suggestions. *Somnambulistic* places you into a much deeper unconscious state in which you don't remember the suggestions, but, nevertheless, you carry them out after you awaken.

You cannot be hypnotized against your will. About 10 percent of people cannot be hypnotized at all, and, in fact, only 20 percent to 30 percent of people can be placed in a somnambulistic trance. Nor will you carry out any suggestion after awakening that is counter to your values or take any actions that you don't want to do. The hypnotist cannot influence you unless you are willing to allow the influence. Often the fear of being hypnotized comes from watching stage hypnosis, in which volunteers are placed in a trance and are told to perform various acts, many of which appear quite ridiculous or embarrassing. In reality, stage hypnotists learn how to choose subjects who are easy to place into a somnambulistic trance and who already expect and are willing to perform such acts. This does not happen in clinical or therapeutic hypnosis.

When you're seeking out a hypnotist, the practitioner's experience is the most important factor. You want a practitioner who does hypnosis as a major part of his or her practice. To find a practitioner qualified in hypnosis, see Appendix C for reference information.

Imagery

Have you ever had a dream in which you have been running or falling and when you wake up, your heart is pounding and you are sweating? The images in our minds can definitely induce physical reactions, and research has corroborated this. This technique is the most recent of the mind-body methods, but it holds promise as the most powerful to induce changes in the body.

When you picture an image in your mind, the visual portion of your brain is activated; when you imagine hearing something, the auditory portion becomes active; and so on. Just creating an image in your mind is enough to elicit actual bodily reactions. The key to using imagery techniques to control or reverse your medical condition is to create specific images that will induce a healing response in your body.

There are two main types of imagery, *guided* and *interactive*. In guided imagery, you create a picture in your mind of your medical condition and then you create other pictures to counteract the condition. When George came to me for treatment of his chronic pain, I placed him in a relaxed state and asked him to create a picture of his pain. He described his pain as "burning" and pictured a raging fire. I then had him picture himself dousing this fire with cold water. I instructed him to do this exercise every day, and, after several weeks, his pain was diminished substantially.

In interactive imagery (also called *creative visualization*), instead of creating specific images, you allow your mind to spontaneously present images to you. These images represent your symptoms, illness, or emotions. By mentally talking with these images, you can gain understanding of why you are ill and how you can heal yourself.

Remember in the mid-1980s when the saga of baby Jessica gripped Americans and indeed the entire world? Jessica was three years old and had fallen into an abandoned well in Texas. During this time, a patient of mine, Mary, felt as if she could not catch her breath. She had never had any lung problems, and the several lung tests I ordered were all normal. I felt that there was a psychological basis for this sudden occurrence and that she needed interactive imagery to discover the source.

After she was deeply relaxed, an image of a cave appeared to Mary. In the cave were many candles and a man who looked like Methuselah, who represented her "inner guide." Mary mentally asked the man what this cave represented and heard him say, "This is your cave of remembrance, and now you will remember." At that moment, a picture came to her mind of when she was very young. Her mother would often be too busy to pay attention to Mary's demands and would become frustrated. So she placed Mary in a small crawl space underneath the floor. Mary recalled feeling that she could not catch her breath in this stuffy little space. When Baby Jessica had fallen into the well, it activated the same physical reaction that she had experienced when her mother placed her in the crawl space. It was only when the inter-active imagery allowed these memories to surface that Mary's breathing returned to normal.

Interactive imagery can directly uncover and confront repressed emotions and use sub-conscious resources to both discover what is causing your illness and what can be done to reverse it. This method is just in its infancy, but it holds great promise for a number of lethal diseases such as AIDS and cancer, and it can also be used for other chronic diseases. Keep in mind, however, that the images that appear with this form are spontaneous and symbolic, and they require interpretation, much like interpreting the underlying meaning of a dream.

Certainly, many repressed memories and emotions can be discovered and then examined through this technique. However, there also have been many instances in which apparent events such as prior sexual abuse were revealed, but no abuse actually had taken place. In such cases, the images were created by the mind to symbolize a different meaning. Unfortunately, many parents and relatives nevertheless have been falsely accused of such actions as a result. It is therefore very difficult to know whether the interpretation is true, unless the others who were involved corroborate it.

The unconscious mind is powerful, and suddenly releasing long-repressed emotions can be very frightening and difficult to deal with. Always obtain the guidance of practitioners well trained in this technique to help interpret such images. For further information on imagery work and to find a qualified practitioner, see Appendix C, under "Imagery."

Meditation

Meditation is a formalized, purposeful form of relaxation. Meditation keeps your attention pleasantly anchored in the present, without reacting to memories of the past or being preoccupied with the future. While similar in mechanism to relaxation, meditation does more than just relax you. It also enables you to observe and explore the workings of your own mind. As a result, meditation changes you psychologically, giving you more insight into your life and allowing you more control over your emotions. In addition, most people who meditate commonly notice growth in their spirituality. Physically, meditation decreases the blood levels of various body chemicals such as cortisol, epinephrine, and norepinephrine, which can be harmful to tissues if high levels are maintained for long periods of time. Stress causes high production of these substances, and so such techniques as meditation prevent and reverse the harmful effects of stress.

There are two major types of meditation. The first is called *concentrative*, in which you focus on your breath, an image, or a sound (mantra). The objective is to "still" your mind and allow greater awareness and clarity of your emotions and behaviors to emerge. *Transcendental meditation* (TM) is the most well-recognized form of concentrative meditation. TM is practiced 15 to 20 minutes morning and evening, while you are sitting comfortably with your eyes closed and concentrating on a mantra. During the practice, you experience a unique state of restful alertness as the mind gradually gains its most settled state and the body becomes deeply relaxed. The profound bodily rest gained from this type of meditation dissolves accumulated stress and fatigue.

The second type of meditation is called *mindfulness*. Here, you simply become aware of passing feelings, sensations, images, thoughts, sounds, smells, and so on, without actually thinking about them. In other words, it is as if you are an observer of your own mind. The purpose of this type of meditation is to become fully aware of internal and external events occurring in your life from moment to moment. As a result, those who practice mindfulness meditation feel less stressed and more in charge of their lives.

There are several forms of mindfulness meditation, including these:

- The *body scan*, which is done lying down and involves paying attention to different parts of your body, moving slowly from one part to the next and becoming aware of sensations in each part.
- In *sitting meditation*, you sit upright, either cross-legged on a cushion or in a straight-back chair, and focus on a particular bodily activity such as breathing.
- In *mindful hatha yoga*, you place your focus on awareness of breathing and on sensations of stretching, lifting, and balancing in specific areas of the body. You can do this form of meditation in various positions, including lying prone or supine, sitting, and even standing.

You can also practice mindfulness meditation simply by deeply relaxing and just observing what spontaneously comes to your mind. For examples of meditation, see the section "Meditation" in "Simple Healing Steps for All Health Conditions," page 79. For more information on meditation and to find qualified practitioners or schools, see Appendix C.

Prayer, Spiritual Belief, and Organized Religion

Prayer and spiritual belief are not often recognized as actual alternative medical treatments, but they do involve the mind-body connection, they are of great benefit to your health, and they are seldom included in conventional treatment. Prayer and spiritual belief appear to be similar but are really based on different mechanisms. Prayer is an action that you take, while spiritual belief is a passively felt emotion that comes from your inner "being."

How *spiritual belief* provides physical benefits is not fully understood, but it has been proven in many studies. Both the relaxation response and religious experience affect a part of the brain's *limbic system* called the *amygdala*, which controls emotions, sexual pleasure, and deeply felt memories. As with meditation and hypnosis, the beneficial effects of spiritual belief may also be correlated with the relaxation response.

Attending *religious services* is a subcategory of spiritual belief and is also correlated with health benefits. You don't have to attend a religious house of worship to obtain the benefits of prayer or spiritual belief, but there are added benefits from doing so. These extra benefits are obtained from socialization with others, which provides support, warmth, and purpose. These factors contribute significantly to wellness because they also help to properly balance the body's chemical substances. Being alone or in isolation, alternatively, can cause a decrease or over-production of these chemical substances to negatively affect your health.

There are two types of *prayer—intercessory*, in which you ask for divine intervention, and *petitionary*, in which you ask for something specifically. As with other mind-body techniques, prayer also has a relaxation and meditative component, but it must entail much more because positive effects have been noted even when the beneficiaries are not aware that they are being prayed for! (called *remote healing*) Most authorities consider such effects to be the influence of subtle healing energies. Research called the *Spindrift study* supports this theory. In this investigation, prayers were made for mold seeds to germinate more quickly. The results showed that the seeds did germinate quicker if they were prayed for, compared to the controls that were not prayed for.

Relaxation

Taking even 15 minutes a day to relax has profound positive effects on both health and aging. Relaxation does not necessarily mean inactivity. You can also relax through various activities. Any activity that makes you feel relaxed is beneficial, whether it is gardening, fishing, golfing, reading, or any number of hobbies. Relaxation works by opposing or reducing the harmful chemical substances that negative emotions and stress cause, and these effects persist long after the relaxation session is finished.

When you are not relaxed, your muscles tense up and restrict movement, balance, and fluidity. Even your organ systems become tense (every organ has muscles, too). Circulation becomes sluggish, and the millions of chemical messengers, hormones, and cells of your body become unbalanced. A major problem for many people is that when they have time to relax, they engage in activities that are not relaxing at all, trying to cram in as much as possible during time available. How often have you gone on a vacation and when you return, you realize that you are now so tired that you need a vacation to recover from your vacation? Regular relaxation, done consistently over time, is what achieves the beneficial results. Balance cannot be hit-or-miss, and neither can your efforts to maintain it.

Traditional Chinese Medicine

Traditional Chinese medicine (TCM) both views and treats illness very differently than conventional medicine does. TCM has the premise that, in the normal state, the body and mind are naturally in harmony with the environment. In this balanced state, we all have vital energy, called Qi (pronounced "chee"), which flows freely along defined but invisible pathways in our bodies, called *meridians*. However, various factors, such as stress, injury, emotions, or environmental factors such as radiation or pollutants, can disrupt or block this flow of energy. When that occurs, an imbalance results, causing disease somewhere along that meridian. TCM techniques then are used to restore the normal flow, which rebalances the body to restore health and well-being. A good analogy for this energy flow through the meridians is that of blood circulating through the blood vessels. A blockage in blood flow can cause organ damage and disease, but by removing the blockage, nutrients and oxygen can once again be supplied to the organs, restoring health.

There are 12 primary meridians, 10 of which are represented by an organ. The "organs" in Chinese medicine not only include the anatomical organs in our bodies, but also other tissues, as well as emotional factors. The major TCM organ meridians and some of their functions follow (see the following pages for definitions of some terms).

- **Liver (Lv):** Spreads and regulates the Qi throughout the body, stores blood (at rest). Includes the tendons, ligaments, external genitalia; regulates the flow of emotions.

- **Gall Bladder (GB):** Stores and excretes gall (bile), which is made by the Liver. Includes the function of decision-making.
- **Heart (H):** Controls the blood vessels and moving the blood through them, as well as stores the Spirit (Shen). Includes complexion, tongue, external ear, and functions of awareness in the conscious mind.
- **Small Intestine (SI):** Includes the function of separating out the useful components of food (and sending them throughout the body), and transmitting wastes to the organs of elimination (Large Intestine).
- **Kidney (K):** Stores Essence, has a primary role in water metabolism, and holds the body's most fundamental Yin and Yang. Includes the adrenal glands, ovaries, testes, brain, spinal column, bones, teeth, anus, urethra, and inner ear, as well as fluid balance, fertility, and growth/development.
- **Urinary Bladder (UB):** Transforms fluids into urine and excretes it from the body. Includes the bone and marrow; helps control the spine.
- **Lung (Lu):** Takes Qi from the air, is responsible for the energy state of the Qi in the body, and controls liquid metabolism of the skin. Includes the skin and hair; maintains rhythm, and defends the surface of the body from toxic external influences.
- **Large Intestine (LI):** Includes the processes of elimination of solid wastes; extracts water from waste and sends it to the Bladder. Also includes psychological release.
- **Spleen (Sp):** Principle organ of digestion; transports nutrients, produces and regulates the Blood, and transforms food into nourishment. Includes the pancreas, lymphatics, large muscles, flesh, lips, and eyelids.
- **Stomach (ST):** Receives and "ripens" foods and fluids. Includes the process of preparation of food to be digested by the Spleen, and sends waste to the Small Intestine.

The two non-organ meridians are

- **Triple Burner or San Jiao (TF originally, now SJ):** This meridian ties together the organs that regulate Water (Lungs, Kidney, and Spleen), making these organs a complete system.
- **Pericardium (P):** This meridian is the outer protective shield of the Heart system.

There are also eight Extra Meridians, six of which have no acupuncture points of their own but instead share points from the major meridians. The use of these six meridians requires a much deeper level of understanding by experienced TCM practitioners. The other two Extra Meridians do have their own points, and they are as commonly used as the major meridians. They are

- **Governor Vessel or Du Mai (Gv originally, now Du):** This meridian represents the confluence of all the Yang meridians, and thus "governs" these channels. It influences the brain and spinal column. (The Yang meridians are the "hollow" organs: Stomach, Gall Bladder, Bladder, Small Intestines, Large Intestines, and San Jiao.)
- **Conception Vessel or Ren Mai (Co originally, now Ren):** This meridian represents the confluence of all the Yin meridians, and, as its name implies, it influences the female organs. (The Yin organs are the "solid" organs: Spleen, Liver, Kidney, Heart, Lungs, and Pericardium.)

TCM doesn't approach medical conditions in terms of a particular disease, but rather in terms of particular syndromes that affect these meridians and organ systems during a disease.

The word *syndrome* is used very differently in each type of medical approach. In conventional medicine terms, a syndrome is the disease, but in TCM terms, syndromes represent the imbalances that *underlie* the disease.

High blood pressure is a good example of how this difference plays out. To conventional doctors, hypertension represents one disease, and standard medications are used to lower it. In TCM, high blood pressure can be seen in a variety of syndromes, including Liver Fire, Deficient Yin/Excessive Yang, Phlegm, Liver Wind, or Deficient Yin and Yang. So the TCM physician will treat someone with hypertension based on which of these syndromes is occurring, with each treatment being very individualized.

This approach can explain observations that conventional medicine cannot. For example, conventional medicine recognizes that people with the same disease can have different symptoms, but it cannot explain why. TCM can explain how this can occur because different symptoms indicate different underlying syndromes. Also, in conventional medicine, if all people with the same disease are treated with the same medication, some improve, some don't, and some get worse or have intolerable side effects. In TCM, the syndrome concept again offers an explanation, because each syndrome reacts in a different way to each medication.

The syndromes of TCM can occur in any of the meridians or organ systems and can overlap each other, manifesting in a variety of illnesses and symptoms. The following are basic terms and syndromes used in TCM practice. These descriptions are very simplified and are given primarily for illustration. To more fully understand the basis of TCM, see Appendix C for reference sources.

- **Blood Stagnation, Blood Stasis:** the Chinese concept of blood not only includes the thick fluid that conventional medicine recognizes, but also subtle patterns that involve mental and emotional life. With stasis, the Blood moves slowly, congeals, or forms clots, resulting in symptoms such as bruising, menstrual irregularities, or pain. With stagnation, the blood doesn't move.
- **Cold:** This is a condition of reduced metabolic activity, and it includes intolerance of cold, desire for heat, or sleepiness.
- **Damp:** This involves watery accumulations in organs or cavities, often resulting from weakness of the Spleen. Symptoms may include heavy feelings, swelling, bloating, discharges of phlegm, nodular masses, or watery stool.
- **Damp Heat:** A combination of excess Damp and excess Heat, it usually affects the GI tract or Spleen organ/meridian.
- **Deficiency:** A condition of reduced function or capacity of an organ or process. It also includes decreased resistance to infection or stress. The most common deficiencies are of Blood, Qi, Essence, Yin, or Yang.
- **Essence (Jing):** The subtle substance that underlies all organic matter, and the source of change. It is the basis of reproduction and development of the organism. Congenital disorders and old age are both a result of Essence deficiencies.
- **Excess:** A condition of heightened function or obstruction of an organ system or process. It also includes hyper-reactivity to stress or infection.
- **Heat:** Increased metabolic activity, inflammation, and sensations of heat and warmth.
- **Phlegm:** Defined as Congealed Damp, it can be found in Heat or Cold conditions. It may accumulate in any acupuncture channel or organ system, and it may be deposited

throughout the body in the form of nodules, lumps, or tumors. It may also represent fatty deposits (atherosclerosis) in the heart and blood vessels.

- **Qi:** Vital energy that is necessary to run the body and its organ systems.
- **Shen (spirit):** Includes the mind, consciousness, and spiritual connection. Symptoms of disturbed Shen include manic states, insomnia, anxiety, restlessness, and poor memory.
- **Toxin:** Includes viral or bacterial infections, external pollutants, or accumulated metabolic toxins.
- **Wind:** An acute occurrence; includes symptoms of tremors, twitching, migratory pain, spasm, seizures, itching, and conditions caused by exposure to the elements (such as colds or flu).
- **Yang:** Translated as "vital function," it relates to the functional aspects of the body and organs, and generation of metabolic heat. Characteristics include fire, day, rising tendency, movement outward, lightness, male, excitement, acute, and strong.
- **Yin:** Translated as "vital essence," it relates to the material aspects of the body, and functions to cool and moisten the organs. Characteristics include water, night, falling tendency, movement inward, heaviness, female, quiescence, chronic, and weak.

The meridian system also explains symptoms that conventional medicine cannot. Consider *angina* (heart pain), for example, in which pain travels down the arm and up to the jaw. Conventional medicine does not have a good explanation for why heart pain radiates to these areas. But from the TCM perspective, this symptom makes perfect sense: The Heart meridian travels down the arm and is connected to the Small Intestine meridian, which ends in the jaw area.

TCM *Diagnosis*

Because TCM concepts are very different from conventional concepts, TCM uses diagnostic techniques that are also very different. One technique is that of examining the tongue. Conventional doctors totally ignore the tongue, while TCM practitioners examine the tongue's shape, contour, size, color, texture, cracks, crevices, and coatings, with all of these factors providing valuable clues about the body's energy balance and meridian and organ dysfunctions. Pulse diagnosis is even more complex and is considered the most important Chinese diagnostic tool. Conventional physicians take the pulse simply to measure the heart rate. TCM practitioners may examine 18 pulses, 9 at each wrist, and then further determine specific characteristics of those pulses. These pulses reflect the condition of the internal organs and meridians, in terms of their deficiencies, excesses, heat, cold, and so on. All of the identified syndromes usually can be diagnosed on the basis of pulse and tongue examination, although other TCM diagnostics, such as history and looking/smelling, may also be used.

Although unfamiliar to most conventional doctors, such diagnostic techniques provide important information that often cannot be found with conventional testing and can lead to natural treatments that are quite effective even after all conventional treatment has been exhausted, as they did for two of my patients, Andy and Cathy.

Andy had complained of indigestion problems for several years, which he said started after a sinus infection. From a conventional medical viewpoint, this does not make sense, but in TCM, the sinuses and stomach are connected by the stomach meridian. Andy's TCM diagnosis was Phlegm syndrome. Following TCM treatment to resolve the phlegm put an end to Andy's indigestion problem. Cathy had abdominal pain that conventional medicine treated by removing her gall bladder. Yet she continued to have the pain, and she also developed severe fatigue and a myriad of other symptoms. After extensive testing and consultations for six months, her doctors could not find the source of her problems and referred her to me. I diagnosed her as having Liver Qi stagnation, and I treated her with several Chinese herbs specific for this syndrome. Her pain went away in two weeks, her fatigue faded over the next few months, and Cathy finally felt like herself again.

TCM *Treatment*

Of all the Chinese treatment approaches, most Americans think first of acupuncture and utilize it the most often. In China, however, acupuncture is only one of many methods to reverse disease. The other important methods include nutrition, Chinese herbal medicine, and Qigong.

Acupuncture

Acupuncture is the most commonly used form of TCM in the United States, although it is not the major technique of TCM used in China (nutrition, herbs, and Qigong are done more often). Also, most acupuncture performed in this country is done for pain, even though the technique can be even more effective for other diseases.

According to TCM, placing a needle in acupuncture points can remove obstructions in that meridian, which restores energy flow and rebalances the body. Because the meridians connect the external surface to the internal organs, treatment from the outside of the body can heal the inside. Western medicine is skeptical of this explanation, so researchers are conducting their own studies. So far, these studies reveal that acupuncture works by stimulating various types of nerves, as well as important structures in the brain. In fact, it has been proven that activation of separate acupuncture points activates separate areas of the brain, stimulating the brain to heal the body. Acupuncture also appears to inactivate the brain regions involved in the transmission and perception of pain.

Acupuncture often benefits conditions that conventional medicine is unable to improve. Pete had injured his shoulder and, in the two years since the initial injury, he had developed loss of muscle and sensation in his arm. He did not have enough strength even to shake my hand. His neurologist diagnosed injury to the *brachial plexus*, a group of nerves that travels through the shoulder before going into the arm. This doctor told Pete that it might take years for the nerves to re-grow, if ever. After 10 electro-acupuncture treatments, however, Pete regained 65 percent of his muscle mass and strength.

Four-year-old Samantha, who was born with a congenital defect that caused her to vomit almost continuously, also found relief through acupuncture. The first year of her life was spent in the hospital, and the vomiting was not controlled by any conventional means. After a series of acupuncture treatments, she has not had further vomiting problems in three years.

Acupuncture involves inserting tiny needles (the thickness of a hair) into specific meridian points. However, light (laser), low-frequency sound, and electrical impulses can also be used to stimulate the points, with or without the needles. Another variation of acupuncture is *moxibustion*, which involves the burning of an herb, *Artemisia vulgaris*, a member of the daisy family, on the acupuncture points. It is the heat and chemicals produced by this herb that stimulate these points. Another variation is *cupping*, which uses suction cups to withdraw excess toxins from specific acupuncture points.

There are actually many different forms of acupuncture, and they are practiced differently depending in which country it is performed. The traditional form practiced in China is body acupuncture (placing needles in the meridian points on the body). There are approximately 360 major body acupuncture points, with 120 of those being the most commonly used.

However, there are actually more than 1,200 acupuncture points in all. Other body acupuncture forms include the Japanese style, which is more gentle (the needles are not manipulated after being placed). The French have a form called *energetics*, which is very effective for deep neurological pain, such as from a herniated disc or peripheral neuropathy. Another school teaches a *5-element approach*, which is particularly useful for problems with underlying emotional disturbances.

Still other forms of acupuncture rely on the premise that all meridians can be accessed through one small part of the body, such as the scalp (*Yamamoto scalp acupuncture*), the hand (*Korean Hand acupuncture*) or the ear (*auricular acupuncture*). Auricular acupuncture is the most common of these, with various points on the ear directly corresponding to specific body parts. Acupuncture points in the ear are very superficial (just below the surface) and can be detected by a device that measures skin resistance/sensitivity. The acupuncturist probes the ear with a detector, and when an acupuncture point is activated, a sound is heard. The acupuncturist then places a needle in that point for about 15 minutes. Often, electrical current is applied to those needles for more stimulation. These ear acupuncture points can also be stimulated by electrical current only, without the use of needles.

Because of all these variations in acupuncture treatment, the training and skill of acupuncturists are very important in achieving beneficial results. In fact, I have had a large number of patients who have not received benefit from other acupuncturists, but they have responded in my clinic. There are several reasons for this, the first of which is training. For example, most chiropractors have only 100 hours of acupuncture training, whereas standard training for physicians is 260 hours. To receive a degree as a Doctor of Oriental Medicine in the U.S. requires three to four years of training and exam certification, and in China requires four to eight years of study and apprenticeship. Even in China, there are different schools, each of which may teach different patterns of acupuncture points for the same condition. So the results you receive may depend greatly on where and how thoroughly your practitioner was trained.

Second, in China, acupuncture is almost always used in conjunction with Chinese herbs or Qigong, but this is not always the case in this country. Many of the acupuncturists practicing in the United States (especially doctors) have not been adequately trained in these TCM aspects, or they simply don't spend the time to use them. This is unfortunate because many conditions will not respond to acupuncture alone, but they will respond to a combination of these TCM treatments.

When 26-year-old Anna came to see me about her dysmenorrhea (painful menstrual periods), she had already seen another practitioner who had given her acupuncture treatments. But she received only partial relief. I performed the same type of acupuncture but also gave her a Chinese herbal formula, which in combination gave her complete and long-lasting relief.

Third, acupuncture effectiveness may depend on proper diagnosis using TCM principles, not conventional medicine diagnoses. Although there are standard acupuncture points for most diseases that have been used for centuries, each person responds differently depending on the underlying TCM syndromes that are present. If these underlying imbalances are not corrected, the body cannot heal as effectively. Acupuncture points used incorrectly won't harm you, but the treatments won't benefit you, either.

Justin had severe sinus allergies. Like Anna, he had been treated by another acupuncturist, but he had only partial relief. His tongue was swollen, which represents a Phlegm syndrome. I acupunctured two additional points, which finally put an end to his symptoms. Treatment using acupuncture is very individualized, and an acupuncturist should always use tongue and pulse diagnosis before every acupuncture treatment. If your acupuncturist doesn't, you may not receive the optimum benefits because the underlying causes are not being addressed.

Finally, the effectiveness of acupuncture and response time may depend on manipulation of the acupuncture needle after it is placed in an acupuncture point. For example, depending on the syndrome(s), the needle must be twirled in a specific direction and both inserted and removed at specific speeds. Even more importantly, the practitioner must obtain the "de qi" response from the patient to be assured that the acupuncture point and meridian has been stimulated. The *"de qi" response* is a reaction in which you feel a pinching, pressure, aching, burning, tingling, or electrical shock sensation upon manipulation of the needle. If the acupuncturist fails to elicit this response in you, then you may not obtain all the benefits of acupuncture. This is important to know because many acupuncturists, even some who have learned in China and practiced for years, do not obtain the "de qi" response. Sadly, some just place the needles as fast as possible and go on to the next patient.

When searching for a good acupuncturist, you should always choose one who takes your pulse, looks at your tongue, takes a thorough history, manipulates the needles, and obtains the "de qi" response. (For further information on acupuncture and to find a qualified practitioner, see Appendix C).

Chinese Herbs

Treatment using Chinese herbs is very important in China. It is not only the primary treatment for most medical conditions, but it is commonly used in times of good health as well, to prevent disease from occurring in the first place. Chinese herbs are quite different from standard herbs and conventional medications in several respects. First, Western herbs and drugs are most frequently used only to treat symptoms, whereas the purpose of Chinese herbs is to help the body restore its natural balance by correcting the underlying disharmony. Second, because Chinese herbal formulas focus on correcting the underlying cause of disease, most are not designed to be taken forever for chronic conditions. Often, in fact, you might be on certain Chinese herbs for a few weeks and then change to other herbs as your condition improves or changes as a result of the herbal treatment. Often, you can eventually discontinue or reduce the dosage of the herbs without the condition recurring, in contrast to conventional drugs, which you usually need to take in the same dosage for the rest of your life.

Third, Chinese herbs are usually given in the form of formulas that contain numerous types of herbs, with some formulas having as many as 25 separate herbs. Many of these formulas have been used for more than 2,000 years. There are four components to a Chinese herbal formula.

- The **Emperor** herbs address the root cause of the disease.
- The **Minister** herbs reinforce the benefits of the emperor herb or address a coexisting pattern of disease.
- The **Assistant** herbs either treat some of the symptoms of the disease or moderate the harshness or balance the tropism of the Emperor and Minister herbs.
- The **Servant** herbs either guide the action of the formula to a specific organ or meridian or harmonize the other ingredients together, reducing toxicity and protecting digestion.

Used alone, each herb in a formula may not be potent enough to have a great effect, but when used together, they work synergistically to provide significant results. This is in contrast to conventional medications, which contain primarily one active ingredient in its most potent form. In addition, because these herbs are of low potency, they have fewer side effects than conventional medications.

Many common medical conditions respond well to Chinese herbs. At age 76, Steve could achieve an erection but could not maintain its hardness. He had tried Viagra, but it had not helped. His TCM diagnosis was a deficiency in Kidney Yang, which can cause such problems. I gave him a Chinese herbal formula that cured his problem in only one week. Esther came to me with bloating, gas, and poor digestion. She had tried numerous conventional drugs, including Prevacid, Prilosec, Zantac, and Tagamet, all without benefit. Based on tongue and pulse diagnosis, Esther had Spleen Qi deficiency, for which I gave her an herbal formula called Six Gentlemen. This formula resolved her symptoms.

In China, TCM practitioners prescribe combinations of herbs based on each individual presentation (individualized formulas). However, there are also formulas that contain a standard set of the same ingredients and that are beneficial for certain syndromes common in many patients. These are called *patent formulas*, many of which have been used for thousands of years. The following lists some of these patent Chinese herbal formulas and their most common uses, as examples. Here, and in Part Two of the book, I refer to the Chinese herbal formulas by their Chinese names, called *Pinyin*, so that you will have a standard reference name to discuss with your TCM practitioner.

These formulas are the type usually found in Chinatown areas of major cities, and many companies also sell these worldwide. It is important to know that some of these formulas can

COMMON PATENT CHINESE FORMULAS	
Pinyin	**Common Uses**
Bai Tou Weng Tang	Candida infection (vaginal yeast, gastrointestinal problems)
Chai Hu Gui Zhi Tang	Nervousness, insomnia, emotional distress; addiction withdrawal symptoms
Ding Xin Wan	Anxiety, depression
Du Huo Luo Dan	Degenerative diseases, fibromyalgia, injuries
Fang Feng Tong Sheng San	Eating disorders, weight control
Huo Luo Xiao Ling Dan	Pain relieving and relaxant properties
Jiu Wei Qiang Huo Tang	Headaches, TMJ syndrome
Kang Ning Wan	Gastrointestinal disorders
Long Dan Xie Gan Tang	Inflammatory conditions
Ping Wei San	Improves digestion, food allergies
Qi Li San	Pain and swelling
Qing Bi Tang	Acute and chronic sinus congestion
Ren Shen Ge Jie San	Chronic lung conditions
Shu Jing Huo Xue Tang	Chronic arthritis, inflammation
Si Jun Zi Tang	Immune system enhancement
Su He Xiang	Cardiac and cerebral blockage
Xiao Qing Long Tang	Acute lung and upper respiratory conditions
Zuo Gui Wan You Gui Yin	Degenerative conditions, strengthens immune system, speeds recovery from illness

be adulterated or contain impurities, such as bugs, twigs, steroids, benzodiazepines (such as Valium), anti-inflammatories (such as ibuprofen); and many herbs are sprayed with DDT in China. In addition, patent formulas don't allow variation for individual patient needs. You should avoid any Chinese herbal formula that doesn't say "manufactured in the U.S." on the label, because these are the most likely to contain impurities. In addition, if a formula does not list the ingredients, or it lists a "secret" or "special" ingredient, avoid it, because these ingredients are usually illegal or conventional drugs. There are several companies that import Chinese herbs, and only after checking the herbs thoroughly for purity and potency do they put them together in formulas in the U.S. (See Appendix C for reference information).

Not all TCM practitioners have expertise in Chinese herbal medicine, which is a separate specialty from acupuncture. Because Chinese herbs can make your condition worse if the correct Chinese diagnosis is not made, it is essential to find a qualified herbal practitioner. For further information on Chinese herbs and to help find a qualified practitioner, see Appendix C.

Nutrition

Nutrition is the basis of health in Chinese medicine. In TCM belief, there are specific foods and liquids that should be eaten only during certain seasons of the year, and they should be avoided at other times. In the same manner, all foods are thought to have specific properties, such as producing hot or cold reactions, and having yin or yang energies. Depending on the characteristics of the person, some of these foods should be eaten and some should be avoided. For example, if you have an internal heat syndrome, you must avoid foods that are internally warming and eat those that are cooling. If you have an excess of yin energy, you should avoid yin foods and eat more yang foods, to balance the energies.

This theory may seem odd, but in reality, it correlates well with conventional medical recommendations. For example, if you have gall bladder disease, conventional doctors advise you to avoid fat, greasy food. In TCM, gall bladder disease usually represents too much damp-heat and yang in the system, and greasy, fatty foods are warming and yang-producing, which overloads the system and causes symptoms of bloating and pain.

Qigong (Chi Kung)

Qi means "energy" and *Gong* means "ability"; Qigong means the ability to build up your own vital energy. It relies on the same principles as acupuncture to heal disease—that is, it stimulates and rebalances energy flow through the meridians to reverse disease. Qigong is relatively new to this country, but Chinese research has demonstrated beneficial effects from this TCM method in every system of the body, and so it can be helpful in treating any disease process. Studies using Qigong demonstrate positive effects in every organ system, including regulating blood pressure, increasing lung volume, increasing efficiency of immune cells, decreasing osteoporosis, regulating lipid and sugar metabolism, improving the function of endocrine glands such as thyroid and pituitary, and strengthening digestion.

There are two forms of Qigong, *qi emission* and *qi gong prescriptions/self-practice Qigong*. The latter is the most common form and is used to teach you how to do certain movements that will stimulate your meridian channels, and thus benefit your particular condition. Sometimes the results astound patients and doctors alike. When 75-year-old Douglas learned he had pancreatic cancer, his doctor told him he might live another four months. Douglas started practicing a specific Qigong exercise and he lived another four years!

There are more than 3,000 Qigong prescriptions, some designed for specific illnesses, others meant for particular seasons of the year, and still others for specific meridians. Most are easily performed, even if you are elderly or in a weakened condition, and some exercises may take only 15 minutes. You will usually feel improvement and a sense of well-being within a few days or weeks of doing Qigong, although for more chronic conditions, major benefits may take three months of daily practice. Performing Qigong movements requires discipline on your part because you must take responsibility for your own healing. By doing the Qigong exercises daily, the results are more effective and longer lasting.

It is important that you learn the basics of Qigong from an experienced practitioner. There are many videos purporting to teach you these exercises, but many of them demonstrate incorrect techniques or forms that will not benefit you. Just because a video is produced by a well-known martial arts star doesn't mean that the person is an expert in Qigong! (For more information and examples of self-practice Qigong, see the section "Simple Healing Steps for All Diseases" and Appendix C, under "Qigong.")

Qi emission is the other form of Qigong. It first requires a proper TCM diagnosis, including an "off-the-body" scanning of your Qi field. The therapist then taps into his personal or a universal energy field, which is focused and radiated into you. This alters the energetic matrix of your meridians, causing your physical body to be rebalanced. When this is accomplished, you may feel a gentle warmth or tingling begin to flow in various parts of your body. Depending on the healer's skill, Qi emission can be used on almost any condition, including headaches, broken bones, sexual dysfunction, cancer, and so on. In China, this form of treatment is used when all other methods have failed. In this form of TCM, it is again important to find a practitioner who is well-trained and experienced in the technique. In China, it takes from four to six years to learn Qi-emission, and you are not considered an expert until you have been thoroughly tested by several masters.

Most Americans are more familiar with Tai Chi than with Qigong. Tai Chi is actually a martial arts form, but it does have health benefits. Qigong is the basis of Tai Chi, and both are commonly practiced together.

For more information on Qigong and to find a qualified practitioner, see Appendix C, under "Traditional Chinese Medicine/Qigong."

OTHER METHODS SUPPORTED BY RESEARCH

The previous methods are the primary alternative approaches used in this country. There are several other methods that are also used and have been supported by research, yet they are not as common. These include those discussed in the following suggestions.

Ayurvedic Medicine

Practiced in India for 5,000 years, *Ayurvedic* means "science of life." It places equal emphasis on body, mind, and spirit, and it strives to restore the innate harmony of the individual, much like traditional Chinese medicine. Ayurvedic bases diagnosis on three metabolic body types, called *doshas*. Each person has one predominant dosha, but all three are present in varying degrees in every cell, tissue, and organ of the body. The three basic types are the following:

- **Vata:** The primary characteristic of this type is changeability. Vatas tend to be thin with prominent features, joints, and veins, with cool, dry skin. They are also prone to anxiety, insomnia, PMS, and constipation.
- **Pitta:** The primary characteristic is predictability. Pittas tend to be of medium build, strength, and endurance. They tend to perspire heavily, are warm, and often thirsty. They are prone to acne, ulcers, hemorrhoids, and stomach ailments.
- **Kapha:** The primary characteristic is relaxed. The Kapha body type is solid, heavy,

and strong. They tend to be slow in everything, procrastinate, and are obstinate. They are prone to high cholesterol, obesity, allergies, and sinus problems.

Ayurvedic utilizes pulse and tongue diagnosis, as does TCM, but it additionally evaluates the eyes and nails. Ayurvedic medicine uses four main methods for treatment:

- **Cleansing and Detoxifying:** To rid the body of toxins, Ayurvedic physicians have patients release material from their stomach, nasal sinuses, and bowels. They induce this by inserting herbs in the nose and anus, and through the skin.
- **Palliation:** This stage focuses on the spiritual dimension of healing, using a combination of herbs, fasting, chanting, yoga, breathing exercises, meditation, and lying in the sun for a limited time.
- **Rejuvenation:** This is a tonifying stage, to enhance the body's inherent ability to function, much like a body "tune-up." This is accomplished using special herbs prepared as pills, powders, jellies, and tablets; mineral preparations specific to a patient's dosha and condition; and yoga and breathing exercises.
- **Mental Hygiene and Spiritual Healing:** The last stage is designed to release psychological stress, emotional distress, and unconscious negative beliefs. It does so through sound (mantra) therapy, concentrating on geometric figures (yantra), directing energies through the body (tantra), meditation, and using the subtle vibratory healing powers of gems, metals, and crystals.

There are currently 108 Ayurvedic colleges in India that grant degrees after a five-year program. As with other alternative medicine techniques, you should seek a practitioner with the proper training and credentials. To obtain more information on Ayurvedic Medicine and to find a qualified practitioner, see Appendix C.

Homeopathy

Homeopathy was one of the primary approaches doctors used in this country in the early twentieth century. It is now currently undergoing a renaissance in the U.S. and Europe. Worldwide, 500 million people utilize homeopathy as their primary form of medical diagnosis and treatment. Homeopathy is based on the principle that a disease is best treated with a remedy that would produce a similar set of symptoms in a healthy volunteer. For example, if a certain homeopathic substance causes a healthy person to develop diarrhea, then, if you really have diarrhea, that substance will stop it. Homeopathy further assumes that through repeatedly diluting and shaking the remedies (*succussion*), they become more powerful (called *potentization*). So the smaller the amount present of the active ingredient, the more powerful the remedy. In fact, analyses of many homeopathic remedies have found no evidence of the actual substances used to make the solution.

Because of these unusual premises, homeopathy represents a system of healing quite distinct from conventional methods. To most physicians, the basis of homeopathy makes no sense whatsoever and is thought to be largely a placebo effect. However, an analysis of all homeopathic research studies reveals that the majority show benefits. In addition, many homeopathic principles actually are observed in conventional medicine. For example, conventional physicians routinely prescribe low doses of digitalis to manage certain kinds of irregular heartbeat. Yet at higher doses, digitalis actually *causes* irregular heart rhythms.

Homeopaths choose among a variety of remedies for the individual patient, with the choice being influenced by the specific pattern of symptoms and related findings. For example, these are some remedies for the common cold:

- *Aconitum napellus* (**monkshood**)**:** For cold symptoms following exposure to a cold, dry wind, with the patient being anxious and chilly.
- *Allium cepa* (**red onion**)**:** Patient has profuse, watery nasal discharge and burning, watery eyes.
- *Pulsatilla* (**windflower**)**:** Patient has thick, yellow-green nasal discharge.
- *Arsenicum album* (**trioxide of arsenic**)**:** Restless, anxious, chilly, and thirsty patient with worsening of symptoms in the open air and after midnight.
- *Kali iodatum* (**potassium iodide**)**:** Patient with profuse, watery nasal discharge, headache between the eyes, and who awakens at night.
- *Mercurius vivus* (**quicksilver**)**:** Patient with alternating fever and chills, with thick and foul-smelling nasal discharge.

Homeopathic remedies for acute conditions should work within a few hours to days. For chronic problems, expect a few weeks to a month to start observing benefits, although it may take several months to achieve maximum benefit. As for dosage, you may see a description such as "6c" or "12c." This indicates the number of dilutions that were done to obtain the remedy; the higher the number, the more dilutions and the more powerful the remedy. However, do not think the more potent remedy, the better the results; there may be adverse effects if too powerful a remedy is used in some conditions.

There are many different homeopathic schools and many disputes over the correct way to prescribe a remedy. Some homeopathists prescribe based on the totality of symptoms, some on acute presentations; others consider constitutional types or essential features of the condition, while others use *isopathy* (using the "disease agent" itself in dilute form) to treat the disease. Because of this, results may vary depending on which approach your practitioner uses. There is licensing for homeopathists in only four states, and training varies widely, so check your practitioner's credentials. Find out how and where the practitioner was trained, and whether the training requires certification. For further information on homeopathy and to find a qualified practitioner, see Appendix C.

Naturopathic Medicine

The naturopathic approach to medical care includes disease prevention, encouragement of the body's inherent healing abilities, natural treatment of the whole person, personal responsibility for one's health, and education of the patient in health-promoting lifestyles. Not only do naturopaths use a holistic approach, they also are trained to offer a variety of alternative methods, including clinical nutrition, herbal medicine, homeopathy, acupuncture, Ayurvedic, hydrotherapy, physical medicine (exercise, massage, and manipulation), lifestyle modification, and minor surgeries. If you're interested in finding a practitioner who is trained in several different alternative approaches, you might consider a naturopath. However, not all naturopaths use all the above methods in clinical practice, so you should inquire about which ones they use before beginning treatment. For further information on naturopathy and to find a qualified practitioner, see Appendix C.

Self-Help Groups

Many illnesses are quite prevalent, and support groups have been formed for both patients and their families. The most prominent group is Alcoholics Anonymous, but there are hundreds of other smaller groups for a variety of problems, from pain and cancer, to *torticollis*, a disease that causes severe spasm in various muscle groups.

Research has borne out the fact that support groups are very worthwhile and can definitely improve health. Studies done with cancer and AIDS patients, for example, have demonstrated significant reduction of symptoms, as well as improved quality of life and perhaps even prolonged survival. The reasons for these results are unknown but are probably derived from mind-body effects. It is thought that in such groups, the participants are able to arrive at a deeper level of understanding regarding their illnesses and better able to express emotions that may be underlying or complicating the condition. A second explanation is socialization, the benefits that we have already noted associated with attending religious services regularly. It is well recognized that being alone is commonly associated with depression, which in turn is a negative influence on health. So any social contact with others can definitely be beneficial.

Yoga

Yoga is a meditative exercise that originated in India more than 5,000 years ago. In this mindfulness exercise, participants assume postures in conjunction with specific breathing exercises, referred to as *pranayama*. There are several forms of yoga, and each can differ in many ways. "Soft" forms, such as *hatha yoga*, are recommended for general wellness. *Ayengar* and *kundalini* forms can sometimes be more stressful for the body and are recommended for more advanced participants. Research has shown yoga to be helpful for several specific conditions, such as carpal tunnel syndrome, neck and back pain, hypertension, headaches, chronic fatigue, and asthma. It also decreases stress, helps develop and maintain physical balance, provides isometric toning, and promotes flexibility.

As with other alternative methods, your practitioner is the most important factor in whether you will receive benefit. Always start slowly and gradually increase your participation, under the practitioner's guidance. There are also many yoga videos available; but again, learn the basics from an instructor before trying it on your own. To obtain more information on yoga and find a qualified practitioner, see Appendix C, under "Yoga."

ALTERNATIVE METHODS BASED IN TRADITION OR UNPROVEN CONCEPTS

There are many other methods that are not as frequently utilized as those already discussed in this chapter and that also have not been well researched by conventional means. This does not mean that they are ineffective, only that they are not yet supported by research. Some of the following methods are recommended or otherwise discussed in the Balanced Healing Action Plans because I have had specific experience using them or I have been familiar with patients who have been treated with them.

Applied Kinesiology

This technique identifies weaknesses in specific muscles to identify health imbalances in the body's organs and glands. The kinesiologist then diagnoses and attempts to resolve a variety of health problems by stimulating or relaxing these key muscles. Kinesiology is also used to determine whether you are allergic to a substance, or whether an herb or medication will be effective. For example, the practitioner asks the patient to hold his arm up and resist the practitioner pulling the arm down. Then various substances are placed in the patient's other hand and the practitioner again pulls on the arm. If the arm is pulled easily (you seem weaker), the substance is not beneficial or can be causing problems. If you remain strong, the substance is beneficial.

This therapy was originated in 1964, and it is commonly used for testing in other alternative methods (such as NAET below). However, because this is a subjective test (requires active participation of the patient), psychological and other factors can play a part. In addition, the skill of the practitioner and the diagnostic conclusions he makes are significant, and it takes years of experience to become expert. For more information and guidance on how to find a qualified practitioner, contact the International College of Applied Kinesiology, 6405 Metcalf Ave., Suite 503, Shawnee Mission, Kansas 66202-3929; (913) 384-5336.

Aromatherapy

Essential oils are extracted from plants and herbs in this technique, and it is their aroma that stimulates the brain through the sense of smell. Aromatherapy is used to treat conditions such as infections, skin disorders, immune deficiencies, stress, arthritis, and muscle spasm. (See chart "Common Aromatherapy Oils" for common essences and their benefits). Aromatherapy can be applied through diffusers, through the skin, from floral waters (hot bath), and from candles. Although these products can be found in health food stores and candle stores, there are aromatherapy essences that are very complex and much stronger, and that are used for more serious conditions. These essences must be prescribed by a trained practitioner. For further information and practitioners, go to the Internet at www.naha.org.

COMMON AROMATHERAPY OILS	
Oil	**Application**
Eucalyptus	Antiviral, expectorant
Everlast	Sports injuries, bruising
Mandarin	Anxiety
Peppermint	Nausea, motion sickness
Lavender	Burns, insect bites
Geranium	Antifungal, antiviral

Bodywork

Bodywork involves manual therapy techniques to realign, rebalance, and retrain the structures of the body, which have become dysfunctional due to pain, injury, disuse, or misuse. However, these techniques are quite distinct from massage, chiropractic, and osteopathic methods. Some of the most common bodywork techniques include the Feldenkrais method, the Alexander Technique, and Rolfing (structural integration). Less common techniques include Aston-patterning, Hellerwork, and the Trager Approach. The Feldenkrais method focuses on retraining how you move your body, to interrupt unhealthy patterns of movements that have become habits. The Alexander technique concentrates on correcting faulty posture in daily activities (sitting, standing, and moving). Rolfing involves manipulating and stretching the body's fascial tissues (deep connective tissues that hold your body together), thus allowing correct realigning of the body. These methods require "hands-on" treatment by therapists trained and certified in the particular technique. For further information on each technique and to find a qualified practitioner, see Appendix C, under "Manual Therapy."

Chelation

In *chelation*, certain substances (primarily sodium EDTA, along with various minerals, vitamins, amino acids, and even herbs) are injected into the body to bind toxins, minerals (including lead, mercury, iron, copper, arsenic, aluminum, and calcium), and metabolic wastes, and then remove them from the body. These chelating agents are administered intra-venously and are promoted to prevent heart attacks and strokes, reverse atherosclerosis, and reduce pain from diseases such as arthritis and lupus. Chelation can, however, deplete the blood of important nutrients, which must be supplemented. Other side effects include high blood pressure, headaches, rash, low blood sugar, and leg clots. Double-blind studies have so far failed to show any benefit for intravenous chelation. Treatment is usually 20 to 30 sessions, one to three times a week, and each session lasts three to four hours. It is also expensive, cost-ing an average of $4,000.

If you want lower-cost chelation, there are options available using herbs that can chelate. Malic acid (see Appendix B) is particularly useful for removing aluminum from the body. Cilantro is excellent for cleaning heavy metals out of the blood. Use the following recipe: Blend one cup of fresh cilantro with six tablespoons of olive oil until the cilantro is completely chopped. Then add one clove of garlic, one-half cup of nuts (cashews or almonds are the best), and two tablespoons of lemon juice. Blend these into a paste (which will be lumpy), adding hot water if necessary. Take two teaspoons to three teaspoons per day for two to three weeks, every few months. If you make large amounts, you can freeze them for later use.

Detoxification Therapy

We are all affected by environmental pollutants, such as radiation exposure, exhaust from vehicles, pollution in the air we breathe, chemicals and antibiotics in our food, chemicals in our water, and so on. Our bodies try to handle these pollutants, but they become overwhelm-ing. These toxins can build up in our bodies and can manifest themselves in decreased immune function, toxicity of the nervous system, hormonal disruption, psychological disturbances, GI disturbances, cancer, and probably many more diseases. Detoxification Therapy is a process used to rid the body of these chemicals and pollutants, thus facilitating a return to health.

The forms of detoxification that I recommend include the following:

Colon detoxification, which is important to rid the body of wastes and toxins that have not been eliminated. Because the colon is the "dumping ground" for the solid wastes that we pro-duce, a clean colon is essential for health. It is estimated that a sluggish bowel can retain 10 to 20 pounds of old toxic and fecal matter, some of which is resorbed back into the body. To cleanse and detoxify the colon, first use a formula that cleanses the colon (called an *activator*), which should contain most or all of the following: cape aloe, cascara sagrada, barberry root, senna, ginger root, African bird pepper, and fennel. After a week on an activator, you should then take a formula that detoxifies your colon (take out old fecal matter and any poisons, toxins, or heavy metals that have accumulated), which should contain most or all of the fol-lowing: apple fruit pectin, slippery elm bark, bentonite clay (pharmaceutical grade), marshmallow root, fennel seed, activated willow charcoal, and psyllium seeds/husks. A good colon cleansing and detoxification should take about two to three weeks.

I also recommend *liver and blood detoxification*, especially for digestive problems, low energy, allergies/hay fever, and liver or gall bladder conditions. Some authorities recommend it for sys-temic conditions such as arthritis, diabetes, infertility, and high blood pressure, feeling that toxins in our blood cause or contribute to these conditions. A good liver-detoxification formula should include all or some of the following: milk thistle, dandelion root, artichoke or beet leaf, and an herb called Picrorhiza kurroa root. Afterward, you can take a blood-cleansing formula that contains some or all of the following: red clover, burdock root, chaparral, periwinkle, and goldenseal. This detoxification process takes about two to three weeks to complete.

Although you can cleanse your liver and blood only, I recommend that you cleanse and detoxify your colon first because the toxins and wastes from the liver/blood detoxification must be eliminated through the colon, and a sluggish colon will decrease the effectiveness.

NOTE: As your body is detoxified, there will be a release of toxins, drug residues, fat cells, and other debris. When these are released into the body, they can cause a temporary increase in your symptoms, until they are excreted. This is referred to as a "healing crisis." Depending on how long you have had your condition, this healing crisis can occur once or several times during the detoxification process. It usually occurs a few days after you start the detoxification and often after you have started feeling better. But it will pass, and signifies that you are healing. Some of the symptoms of a healing crisis include joint/muscle pain, headaches, diarrhea, fatigue, sleeplessness, nausea, sinus congestion, low-grade fever, skin break-outs, cold-like symptoms, or general ill feeling. The healing crisis usually lasts for one to three days, but it will pass. To help it resolve faster, drink plenty of fluids (juices, water, or herbal teas) and take ground flaxseed.

Energy Healing

There are several alternative techniques whereby practitioners impart healing energy to you or "reshape" your energy patterns. Although research is lacking to document the nature of this energy, these methods are quite popular. These techniques are referred to as "hands-on healing," but they do not necessarily require physical contact. Qi emission Qigong (see "Qigong," under "Traditional Chinese Medicine") is one such technique, but several others are based on similar principles.

Reiki, which means "universal life energy," is designed to "bring back into balance what is not balanced." It is an ancient Japanese form in which energy is channeled from a divine energy source, through the practitioner, and into you, similar to Qigong. Unlike the other forms, however, various symbols and a set of hand positions are used to promote healing; and once an individual is "attuned" to Reiki, he/she then is able to channel Reiki energy through their body and into others. Advanced practitioners are able to perform remote healings, which is actually quite similar to the mechanism and benefits of remote praying. I have not found any particular studies to support the claims of Reiki healing, but it is based on the same principles as the other forms of energy healing. (For more information and guidance on how to find a practitioner, go to www.reiki.org, the Web site for the International Center for Reiki Training.)

Therapeutic touch (*healing touch*) is another form of energy healing and in fact is the most common of these methods in this country. It utilizes the hands to clear, energize, and balance the human and environmental energy field, which can be disrupted by any number of factors (stress, injury, and so on). It is practiced by thousands of practitioners in this country and worldwide, primarily nurses (more than 30,000 nurses in this country). This technique is taught in more than 100 colleges and universities in 75 countries. In this form of energy healing, practitioners spend a few minutes with you to become "centered." Then they move their hands over you to sense disruptions in your energy field, which are signs and symptoms of disease. Finally, they "normalize" the disturbed fields, usually by touching you.

There have been studies that both support and negate the benefits of therapeutic touch. Benefits have been documented for healing of burns and surgical wounds, improved breathing and circulation after surgery, and enhanced growth rate in premature infants. Proponents recommend it for use with any other chronic disease, as well as for grief management and rehabilitation. The major problem is that some practitioners receive only a few hours or days of training, which is simply not adequate to teach the detection of energy fields. With Qigong emission, for example, practitioners train for a minimum of four years. Although training standards have been established for therapeutic touch, there are no requirements or certification. (For further information and guidance on how to find a qualified practitioner, go to www.heal ingtouch.net, the Web site for Healing Touch International.)

Because a healing energy capable of healing has not yet been documented, benefits are primarily anecdotal. Other studies have demonstrated that just providing positive attention or physically touching patients in a reassuring manner promotes the healing process, so energy healing techniques may well involve this factor.

Flower Remedies

Flower remedies are promoted to address your emotional state, to help both psychological and physiological well-being. First developed at the turn of the 20th century by the British homeopath Edward Bach, these remedies are used to treat a variety of psychological states. There are 38 basic Bach remedies, each specific for a particular emotional condition. The remedies are made by soaking flowers on the top of a bowl in the sun for several hours. This then releases the flowers' energy into the water.

There are now other sources of flower remedies besides the Bach remedies, and additional Bach remedies have been developed by his followers. Although the remedies are available in most health food stores, I advise you to consult with a qualified herbalist who has training in these remedies. If you desire to self-treat, there are a number of books on flower remedies. I recommend *The Bach Remedies: A Self-Help Guide*, by Leslie Kaslof.

To use these remedies, put 1drop to10 drops in a beverage, or 1 drop directly on or under your tongue. You can use them as often as needed.

Iridology

Used as a preventive tool, *iridology* involves evaluating abnormal markings and color changes in the iris of the eye to detect stresses and weaknesses in the body's systems. With this information, you can then make decisions regarding lifestyle and eating habits to strengthen your body. Some iridologists have minimal training (a few weekends at a seminar), but to be an expert takes years of experience. For further information or guidance on how to find a qualified practitioner, go to www.iridologyassn.org, the Web site for the International Iridology Practitioners Association.

Light Therapy

Full-spectrum, ultraviolet, colored, or laser light is used for a range of conditions, from chronic pain and depression, to immune disorders and cancer. Light therapy is especially important if you live in latitudes that do not provide enough light (which can cause vitamin D deficiency), for bipolar patients who suffer more during the winter months, and for seasonal affective disorder (SAD). Specific types of light (ultraviolet) used along with medications are helpful for the treatment of diseases such as psoriasis. Unfortunately, there is not much information available that discusses light therapy comprehensively. However, books on specific types of light therapy are available in most bookstores.

Music Therapy

Different types of music and sounds have been shown to have a profound effect on healing. Such therapy has been used in hospitals, schools, corporate offices, and mental institutions for reducing stress, lowering blood pressure, alleviating pain, overcoming learning disabilities, improving movement and balance, and promoting endurance and strength. For more information or guidance on how to find a qualified practitioner in your area, go to www.musictherapy.org, the Web site of the American Music Therapy Association.

Nambudripad Allergy Elimination Treatment (NAET)

This is a technique that combine principles of kinesiology, chiropractic, acupuncture, herbs, and nutrition to treat food allergies, which may be the underlying cause of many chronic diseases and chronic pain. Efforts are made to isolate and remove energy blockages caused by food allergens. Depending on the severity and extent of your allergies, it may take several weeks to months to observe maximum benefits. This is because each allergen must be treated separately, followed by a 24-hour period in which you must avoid the particular food. There are many practitioners throughout the country using this technique, although some try to use shortcuts, which are not nearly as effective. It is helpful for you to know what to expect so that you are not short-changed. For more information on NAET and to find a qualified practitioner, see Appendix C.

Prolotherapy or Sclerotherapy (Reconstructive Therapy)

Using injections of natural substances to stimulate the growth of connective tissue, reconstructive therapy is designed to strengthen weak or damaged tendons and ligaments. In this technique, a mildly irritating solution (primarily dextrose [sugar water] in combination with a variety of substances, such as glycerin, phenol, sodium bicarbonate, and/or local anesthetic) is injected into the injured or weak tissues, causing a localized inflammation that increases the blood supply and flow of nutrients and stimulates that tissue to repair itself. This technique has been used for degenerative arthritis, low back pain, carpal tunnel syndrome, migraine headaches, and injuries to ligaments and cartilage. It is also used for joint dysfunction and TMJ syndrome, and many other chronic conditions. Most people should improve within six treatments, and they usually will notice improvement during the first week of treatment. For more information on this technique and guidance on how to find a qualified practitioner, go to www.acopms.com, the Web site of the American College of Osteopathic Pain Management and Sclerotherapy.

BALANCING ALTERNATIVE WITH CONVENTIONAL MEDICINE

Each of the major alternative methods described has benefits in various disease processes and/or for preventive medicine. As you may have noted, however, many medical conditions are more successfully treated using combinations of these alternative methods or a combination of alternative with conventional approaches. In my clinic, for example, we might use acupuncture along with manual therapy for pain, in addition to using conventional medications and standard physical-therapy modalities. For a disease such as acid reflux, we commonly utilize acupuncture with Chinese herbs and mind-body techniques. So, although single methods or procedures may be effective for various medical conditions, achieving the best health possible often requires a balance of several approaches, both alternative and conventional.

Alternative Medicine Products

Many herbs, vitamins, minerals, and other supplemental substances are commonly used either to treat medical conditions or prevent them from occurring in the first place. This appendix lists and discusses the most common ones. Many do offer health benefits, but before you use any of them, you should keep these precautions in mind:

There are no easy roads to better health, and no magic pills. You might feel that all you have to do to become healthier on your own is take vitamins and supplements. Certainly some alternative products can be beneficial, but they alone cannot replace years of neglect and bad habits. The best health is achieved by actively changing your lifestyle and diet, which does require effort on your part.

Many of the ingredients in these products have been isolated from other sources or chemicalized, and thus they may not work the same way they do in their natural forms. To be effective, they may need other ingredients that are contained in the natural form but are not included in the supplement. Some of these other ingredients may be necessary for proper absorption or use of the nutrient within the body.

Obtain an accurate medical diagnosis before taking herbs, vitamins, or supplements to help combat various diseases. Although such products may help, a misdiagnosis is at best a waste of money and at worst could cause you harm. For example:

- Symptoms of prostate cancer can be similar to benign prostate enlargement; just taking saw palmetto may delay early intervention that could prevent complications and even save your life.
- Symptoms of depression can be very similar to those of anxiety; taking St. John's wort may make anxiety symptoms worse.
- Congestive heart failure patients often self-treat with hawthorn, an herb with blood-pressure-lowering effects. Accurate blood pressure measurements are essential to avoid unforeseen complications from this product.

Alternative products are not quality controlled or regulated in any way, and for most of them, the amounts needed to achieve various benefits have not been determined. More and more analyses of these products are showing them to contain percentages of the ingredients that are too small to have an effect on the body, or that they simply don't even contain the actual ingredients they advertise.

Even when research has shown alternative products to be beneficial, the products you purchase in a store may not have the same effects as those reported from the research. Most of the herbs used in research are of higher quality and potency than you find in stores, or they are blended specifically for the study. For example, the echinacea used in studies in Germany is not the same as the echinacea products sold in the U.S. Because of this, you may not receive the benefits that have been reported from these studies.

HOW TO USE THIS APPENDIX

The list that follows includes the most commonly used Alternative Medicine Products. Each one is described, and its main actions and common uses, established by research studies, are given.

Each description also includes:

- The product's most common side effects
- Any known interactions with other products or prescription drugs (negative, neutral, or beneficial)
- Specific precautions that may apply to the product
- Laboratory tests that can show false results when the product is used
- The dosage and form or strength of the product most often recommended or reported in research studies

Because adequate research has not been done on most of these products, dosages can only be approximated, and there may be additional side effects and interactions that have not yet been fully described or listed. Always obtain guidance from a doctor or practitioner who is knowledgeable in herbal medicine before taking these products.

Many of the herbs and supplements recommended in Part Two of this book are included in this appendix. For more information on these, as well as products not included in Part Two, check the Web site references in Appendix C.

BIOMAGNETS

Most alternative products are obviously "food" substances that are taken orally or applied to the skin. There is one other popular alternative product, however, which is not a food but still is considered an alternative product: the biomagnet. Biomagnets have been used since the time of Aristotle, but very little has been known about how they work. They have been shown to increase blood flow, and they cause minute electrical disturbances known as *Eddy currents*. These currents may mimic or trigger sympathetic nerve impulses, which in turn can affect pain and circulation in the small blood vessels (capillaries).

The major physiological responses attributed to magnetic fields include the following:

- Reduced inflammation and pain relief in muscles and joints.
- Relaxation of tense muscles, tendons, and connective tissue.
- An anesthetic or pain-blocking phenomenon.

Many professional athletes use magnets and report that they work well. Many of my patients report no long-lasting benefit, although others have obtained excellent pain relief. The differences in response may be due to several factors. To begin with, there are *static magnets* and *dynamic magnets*; the latter induce greater capillary flow. Second, magnets differ in construction and strength; magnetic intensity is measured in gauss, and different materials produce different energy levels:

- Barium Ferrite: 2,550 gauss

- Strontium Ferrite: 3,950 gauss
- Neodymium: 12,300 gauss

Third, magnets can differ in terms of *unipole* (north or south) and *multipole*. The application of the correct magnetic field with respect to pole selection can be very important to the outcome of treatment. For example, applying the negative pole to a fracture can aggravate the condition, whereas the positive pole can alleviate the symptoms.

COMPARISON OF NORTH/SOUTH POLE ENERGY EFFECTS	
North (Treat)	**South (Stimulate)**
Reduces swelling	Increases blood circulation
Acts to sedate pain	Expands or dilates
Draws fluid	Dispenses fluid
Dissolves cholesterol	Increases biochemical reactivity
Arrests protein activity	Increases protein synthesis
Increases alkalinity	Increases acidity
Decreases abnormal calcification	Strengthens protein molecules
Relieves arthritic pain	
Controls spread of infection	

There are no major side effects to magnets, but each individual has a specific tolerance for magnetic energy. Once you reach yours, you might feel tingling, or more pain can result. You shouldn't use magnets if you have a pacemaker.

Shop around before you purchase magnets; many companies make biomagnets, and costs vary greatly. Some MLMs (multi-level marketers) sell magnets that produce the very lowest energy yet are among the most expensive. Those that are sold already in wraps and braces are preferable over those that have to be taped in place. When buying bracelets or other jewelry that contains magnets, check the energy they produce; some are so weak they have little therapeutic effect.

HERBS

Herbs can be very beneficial, but the manner in which they are manufactured and distributed can determine whether or not those benefits will be present. You must realize that raw herbs contain numerous ingredients, which may need to interact with each other to produce the most benefits. Scientists have tried to identify the main "active" ingredient(s) and the percentage of that ingredient needed to have an effect, so the products can be standardized or made more consistent. Standardization is a start, but it is not perfect, simply because we do not really know how *all* the ingredients work together. There may be some ingredients that are not considered to be active, yet they are essential for the active ingredient to work.

The best way to take herbs is to consult an experienced herbalist who can guarantee the quality of fresh, raw herbs and mix them professionally for the greatest benefits. Unfortunately, there are not that many experienced herbalists, so the next best thing is to make sure the herbal products you take have been tested by independent labs for quality, purity, and potency (see Appendix C for reference information).

Whatever type of herbal product you purchase, you can test it yourself in these ways:

1. **Look at the herb.** Any sign of raw herb fiber or varying color or texture indicates a high percentage of bio-inactive material.
2. **Taste the herbs.** A gritty texture may indicate a high concentration of sand, fiber, or foreign substances.
3. **Dissolve the herb in warm water.** Tablets should get soft and disintegrate. If they don't, they won't be absorbed in your body, either. If the herbs dissolve well but leave a sugary taste, the product has a high concentration of added sugar.
4. Request a Certificate of Analysis (COA) from the manufacturer.

Aloe Vera (Juice/Latex, Gel)

The juice and latex from this cactus plant causes increased mucous production and movement of the muscles in the colon when taken orally. When used topically, it inhibits *bradykinin*, a pain-producing substance; inhibits *histamine*, which causes itching; and speeds healing of wounds.

Used For: Laxative when taken orally (dried juice from leaf, latex); topically to relieve pain and inflammation; help heal burns, skin ulcerations, psoriasis, frostbite; dermabrasion (gel only).

Side Effects: Oral: abdominal pain and cramps (requires dose reduction). If used long term: decreased potassium levels, blood in urine. Gel: None known.

Drug Interrelationships: Overuse of the oral form can increase the toxicity risk of drugs used for heart arrhythmias or heart failure. It can cause increased potassium loss when used orally with diuretics and corticosteroids, and also may decrease blood sugar.

Disease Cautions: Oral formulations should not be used in intestinal obstruction, abdominal pain of unknown cause, hemorrhoids, and GI inflammatory conditions, such as Crohn's disease and ulcerative colitis. It should be used with caution in diabetes because it can decrease blood sugar.

Dosage: Take the minimal amount necessary to produce a laxative effect, beginning at about one ounce for oral laxative use or 20mg to 30mg hydroxyanthracene derivatives per day, calculated as anhydrous aloin. Oral use should be short term only (1 to 2 weeks). Topically, you can use it liberally.

Anise

Because of its sweet taste, anise is often used to flavor food and alcoholic beverages, and it is used in bath products. The oil smells like licorice.

Used For: Anti-spasmodic that relieves indigestion; expectorant to bring up mucous in conditions such as bronchitis.

Side Effects: Allergic reactions of the skin, respiratory tract, and GI tract; sensitivity to light.

Drug Interrelationships: High doses can interfere with blood thinners, hormone therapy, and MAO inhibitor antidepressants (such as Nardel, Parnate).

Disease Cautions: None known.

Dosage: 50ml to 200ml essential oil or 1g dried fruit three times daily. It can be used as a tea.

Astragalus

The root of this herb is used widely in China because it is an antioxidant and potent immune-system enhancer. It also can dilate the blood vessels of the heart and increase blood flow.

Used For: Common cold and upper respiratory tract infections; angina; chronic hepatitis; adjunct therapy with radiation for breast cancer and with chemotherapy for lung cancer.

Side Effects: None known at recommended doses.

Drug Interrelationships: It may reduce the effects of certain immunosuppressive drugs, including cyclophosphamide, cyclosporine, azathioprine, and methotrexate.

Disease Cautions: Should avoid in organ-transplant patients and autoimmune disorders (such as lupus, rheumatoid arthritis, sarcoidosis), because of increased immune system stimulation.

Dosage: 9g to 25g per day in powder form. Common cold, 5g daily. More than 25g per day may not offer any additional benefits and may cause suppression of the immune system.

Bilberry (Dried Ripe Fruit, Not Leaf)

Bilberry is the European cousin of the blueberry. It contains tannins, which are useful in GI problems, as well as antioxidants. It is often used in combination with mixed carotenoids for enhanced antioxidant effects.

Used For: Non-specific, acute diarrhea; mild inflammation of mouth and throat mucous membranes; diabetic or hypertensive retinopathy (eye disease).

Side Effects: None known.

Drug Interrelationships: None known.

Disease Cautions: None known.

Dosage: Bilberry extract, 40mg to 80mg three times daily, containing 25 percent anthocyanosides. External use: 10 percent concoction.

Bitter Melon

Also known as balsam pear and looking like an ugly cucumber, the fruit and seeds of this tropical fruit have insulin-like properties.

Used For: Type II diabetes.

Side Effects: None known.

Drug Interrelationships: Should use with caution with other diabetic medications, including insulin, because it can reduce blood sugar.

Disease Cautions: Should monitor blood sugar levels in diabetes. Can worsen reactive hypoglycemia (low blood sugar).

Dosage: 15g aqueous extract daily, or hold your nose and take a two-ounce shot (it doesn't taste very good).

Black Cohosh

The American Indians introduced this forest plant into medicine. The rhizome and root of this herb have estrogenic and possibly other hormonal effects. In the past, black cohosh was known as bugbane because it was used as an insect repellant.

Used For: Menopausal symptoms (such as hot flashes); premenstrual discomfort and dysmenorrhea (painful periods).

Side Effects: Nausea; diarrhea; dizziness.

Drug Interrelationships: May have additive antibreast cancer effects in combination with tamoxifen.

Disease Cautions: None known.

Dosage: 2mg of triterpene glycosides per 20mg tablet, calculated as 27-deoxyacteine, 40mg to 80mg twice daily; or 40 percent to 60 percent alcohol extracts corresponding to 40mg of herb, or 300mg to 1,800mg dried rhizome or root tip.

Black Currant Seed Oil: see *Oils*

Borage Oil: see *Oils*

Bromelain

Derived from pineapple, bromelain uses an enzyme factor to produce its effects.

Used For: Osteoarthritis (in combination with rutin and trypsin); post-operative and post-traumatic swelling, especially of the nasal and paranasal sinuses; varicose veins.

Side Effects: GI disturbances or diarrhea; occasional allergic reaction.

Drug Interrelationships: Zinc inhibits bromelain activity, and magnesium activates bromelain. Bromelain can increase blood levels of tetracyclines and may improve your response to other antibiotics (penicillin, erythromycin, chloramphenicol). Improves effectiveness of some chemotherapy drugs (vincristine, 5-FU).

Disease Cautions: None known.

Dosage: 100mg to 300mg (containing 1,200mcu to 1,800mcu, or 200 to 800 FIP units), per day for 10 days.

Butcher's Broom

Derived from the holly bush, the rhizome and root induce constriction of certain blood vessels; butcher's broom has been used since the first century.

Used For: Hemorrhoids (itching and burning); varicose veins; chronic venous insufficiency (pain, heaviness, leg cramps, swelling, and/or itching).

Side Effects: GI disturbances.

Drug Interrelationships: None known.

Disease Cautions: None known.

Dosage: Equivalent to 7 percent to 11 percent of total ruscogenin per day, 100mg three times daily. Available in suppositories, ointments, and capsules.

Capsicum (Cayenne or Red Pepper)

The fruit of this pepper contains substances that stimulate digestion and also deplete substance P, a factor that increases nerve pain when released in high amounts. Applied topically, it is a rubefacient; that is, an agent that reddens the skin, causing a counterirritant effect.

Used For: Topically for temporary relief of pain from rheumatoid arthritis, osteoarthritis, post-herpetic neuralgias, or diabetic neuropathy; used orally protects the stomach from aspirin damage; indigestion, fibromyalgia.

Side Effects: Topically: burning; itching. Orally: GI irritation; sweating; flushing.

Drug Interrelationships: Topical capsicum can contribute to the coughing side effects that can occur with ACE inhibitors.

Disease Cautions: Should not be used orally with infectious or inflammatory GI conditions (Crohn's disease, ulcerative colitis). Do not apply topically to damaged skin.

Dosage: Oral: tincture, 0.3ml to 1ml three times daily. Topically, 0.025 percent to 0.075 percent, apply a maximum of 3 to 4 times daily, and wash hands after application. Do not use this herb near eyes or sensitive skin. It can be removed by a diluted vinegar solution. It may take three days to have an effect on chronic pain.

Cat's Claw

The root and bark of this vine can stimulate the immune system, and so it is being studied in diseases such as AIDS and viral infections.

Used For: Immune system stimulant; knee osteoarthritis (during physical activity only).

Side Effects: Orthostatic hypotension (dizziness when standing); loose stools with increased dosages.

Drug Interrelationships: May potentiate blood pressure medications. Do not use in chronic progressive diseases such as tuberculosis, lupus, MS, or AIDS because of its immune-stimulating effects.

Disease Cautions: May reduce blood pressure.

Dosage: Immune system, 500mg to 1,000mg one to three times per day. Osteoarthritis, 100mg freeze-dried aqueous extract. Can be taken as tea.

Chasteberry (Vitex)

This fruit is derived from a small tree or shrub that grows in the Mediterranean. It is known to inhibit the secretion of a hormone, prolactin, from the pituitary gland. It was once chewed by monks to decrease libido and thus maintain celibacy.

Used For: Menstrual irregularity, breast pain, infertility; amenorrhea (no menstrual period), PMS; acne (may take six months).

Side Effects: Headaches; increased menstrual flow; decreased libido; itching.

Drug Interrelationships: May interfere with oral contraceptives and hormone therapy.

Disease Cautions: Caution is advised during pregnancy and breastfeeding.

Dosage: Fluid extract (1:1), corresponding to 30mg to 40mg of the herb, daily; solid extract, standardized to 0.5 percent agnuside, 175mg to 225mg daily.

Cranberry

It was once thought that the cranberry fruit works by acidifying the urine and through antibiotic properties, but this is not the case. Instead, it contains an antioxidant and fructose, which prevent bacteria from adhering to the wall of the bladder.

Used For: Preventing and treating urinary-tract infections; urinary deodorizer for incontinent patients; prevents bacteria growth in children with neurogenic bladder.

Side Effects: GI symptoms if take more than 3 liters to 4 liters per day.

Drug Interrelationships: May increase absorption of vitamin B_{12} in patients taking Prevacid, Prilosec, or Aciphex.

Disease Cautions: Take cautiously if you have diabetes, because of its sugar content (use unsweetened if possible). It has not been shown to cure urinary-tract infections once they are present, but it can decrease symptoms and shorten the duration of infection.

Dosage: Three ounces cranberry juice cocktail (33 percent pure cranberry juice) daily for prevention; 16 to 32 unsweetened ounces per day for infection (with antibiotics). Cranberry powder is also available, but juice is recommended.

Echinacea

Known as the cone flower, echinacea grows wild in the central U.S. It was initially introduced into medicine by a Nebraska physician in 1871 as a "blood purifier." The entire plant has anti-inflammatory and immune-stimulant abilities; it also affects the pituitary and adrenal glands. However, after eight weeks of use, it can suppress the immune system.

Used For: Wound healing; colds and flu (severity and duration); poorly healing skin wounds and ulcers; prevention of vaginal yeast infections (with antifungal cream).

Side Effects: Allergic reactions (ragweed and marigold family).

Drug Interrelationships: None known.

Disease Cautions: Echinacea can worsen progressive systemic diseases, such as tuberculosis, collagen diseases (such as scleroderma), or multiple sclerosis, and immune disorders, such as AIDS, HIV, and lupus. It also may worsen infertility problems.

Dosage: Variable, depending on which parts are used, which form of delivery, and which concentration. Examples include the following (all three times daily):

- Dried Root (or tea), 0.5g to 11g
- Tincture (1:5), 2ml to 4ml
- Fluid Extract (1:1), 2ml to 11ml
- Solid Extract (6.5:1) or 3.5 percent echinacoside, 150mg to 300mg
- Expressed juice, 6ml to 9ml

Evening Primrose Oil: see *Oils*

Fenugreek Seed

This herb resembles maple syrup in both odor and taste and has been used to mask the taste of medicines. It is considered a vegetable in India, where it has been used for centuries to decrease blood sugar.

Used For: Type II diabetes; loss of appetite (oral); local inflammation (topical).

Side Effects: Gas; diarrhea; allergic reactions.

Drug Interrelationships: Because it can decrease blood sugar, oral diabetes drugs and insulin requirements may need adjustment.

Disease Cautions: Can alter blood-sugar control in diabetics.

Dosage: 3g to 6g daily in divided dosages; 50g powdered drug with ¼ liter water for poultice (topical).

Feverfew

Although known as a medicine since the first century AD, feverfew's use began in the 1970s. The leaf of this plant interferes with production of *prostaglandins*, chemical mediators that can contribute to many medical problems.

Used For: Prevention and reduction of severity in migraine headaches; allergies; arthritis (initial inflammatory stages); tinnitus.

Side Effects: Mouth ulceration; GI symptoms. If you take large amounts, "post-feverfew" syndrome can occur, characterized by tension headaches, anxiety, insomnia, joint pain, and tiredness.

Drug Interrelationships: None known.

Disease Cautions: Has cross-allergenicity to the ragweed, marigold family.

Dosage: Freeze-dried leaf at 50mg to 125mg per day with or after food; extract, 50mg to 100mg daily. Make sure the product contains at least 0.2 percent parthenolide.

Caution: A recent study showed that only 1 out of 32 feverfew products in a health food store contained enough of the active ingredient to be effective.

Fish Oils: see *Oils*

Flaxseed Oil: see *Oils*

Garlic

People have used garlic for food and medicine since the earliest recorded history. It has numerous beneficial properties, including antibacterial, anthelminthic (parasites), antiviral, and antifungal. It affects high blood pressure and high cholesterol, reduces spasm, thins blood, stimulates the immune system, and is an expectorant.

Used For: Elevated blood cholesterol and triglyceride levels; preventive for colorectal, stomach, prostate cancers (in food form, not supplement); atherosclerosis in large arteries (in food form, not supplement); inflammation of mouth and pharynx; respiratory tract infections; tick repellant.

Side Effects: GI symptoms in high doses; increased bleeding tendency; allergic reactions (rare).

Drug Interrelationships: Can interfere with blood thinners, aspirin, and diabetic drugs. Can reverse decreased LDL-cholesterol caused by fish oil.

Disease Cautions: Use with caution in diabetes, bleeding disorders, surgery (discontinue two weeks prior to surgery); and gastrointestinal irritation. Garlic should not be taken if you take saquinavir (a protease inhibitor) for AIDS, because it can significantly reduce the blood levels of this drug.

Dosage: To achieve the benefits linked to garlic requires the equivalent of 4,000mg of fresh garlic per day, roughly four cloves. If using fresh, you must cut it open and allow it to stand for 10 minutes to activate its beneficial ingredients. If you are using a supplement, it should provide a daily dose of at least 10mg of alliin; or use standardized garlic powder extract at 1.3 percent alliin. Alliin is the component of garlic that converts to allicin, the major therapeutic ingredient. Alliin is odorless while allicin has the usual garlic odor. Fresh garlic supplements contain threefold the amount of alliin as aged garlic extracts. For fungal skin infections, use a cream containing 0.6 percent to 1 percent ajoene (a sulphur compound derived from allicin).

Ginger Root

Known in China 2,500 years ago for its medicinal value, ginger has multiple effects on the GI tract, as well as on the respiratory and circulatory systems.

Used For: Dyspepsia (indigestion); motion sickness, seasickness, morning sickness (safety not clearly established); post-operative nausea and vomiting; joint pain in rheumatoid arthritis.

Side Effects: Dermatitis in sensitive individuals.

Drug Interrelationships: May cause increased bleeding when used with aspirin or anticoagulants.

Disease Cautions: Can worsen gall-bladder disease.

Dosage: Extracts standardized to contain 20 percent gingiol and shogaol, at 100mg to 200mg four times a day. Dry powder, 250mg four times a day. For motion sickness, 1g dried powder one to two hours before travel. Also available in tea form.

Caution: Do not use more than 4g of ginger root per day.

Gingko Biloba (Leaf Extract)

The gingko tree has survived unchanged in China for more than 200 million years and was first brought to Europe in 1730 for use as an ornamental tree. It is the oldest living tree species in existence. The fruits and seeds have been used in China since 2800 BC, but the effects of its leaves were discovered only 20 years ago. Gingko stimulates populations of nerve cells that are still working and protects nerve cells from toxic and environmental damage.

Used For: Organic brain syndrome; dementia: multi-infarct (stroke), Alzheimer's (mixed form); age-related memory loss; vertigo (dizziness); claudication (pain in the legs when walking); memory and concentration enhancement in normal people; tinnitus (ringing in the ears); altitude sickness; premenstrual syndrome (PMS); macular degeneration; color vision in diabetic retinopathy; antidepressant-caused sexual dysfunction; impotence.

Side Effects: GI complaints; headache; dizziness; palpitations; allergic skin reactions.

Drug Interrelationships: Can cause excessive bleeding when used with other herbs or medications, such as Coumadin and heparin, that have antiplatelet or blood-thinning side effects. Can increase blood pressure when used with thiazide diuretics (water pills).

Disease Cautions: May worsen infertility, and heighten seizure activity.

Dosage: 80mg of extract containing 24 percent gingko flavonglycosides, three times daily in Organic Brain Syndrome; 120mg to 160mg in other conditions. It may take at least eight weeks before you might experience a benefit.

Ginseng Root

Almost everyone over the age of 40 in the Far East takes ginseng on a daily basis, and it has been used for medical conditions for more than 2000 years. It is referred to as a "tonic," which invigorates and fortifies you, especially in times of fatigue or debility. There are three primary varieties of ginseng: Panax (Asian), Siberian, and Quinquefolius (American); the latter is the most utilized in this country but has the least research data. Of all these types, Siberian is considered the safest, and Panax and Quin are not recommended for the very weak, elderly, and infirm because these types of ginseng are the strongest.

Used For: General tonic, to improve energy and well being; *adaptogen* (helps the body adjust to emotional or physical stress); abstract thinking, selective memory, mental skills; boosts memory function after stroke, diabetes; improve immune response; congestive heart failure; speed, quality, capacity of physical work; high blood pressure; atherosclerosis; cancer; edema (swelling); ulcers; viral illnesses; ADHD; anorexia.

Side Effects: American ginseng has no known side effects. Siberian ginseng has rare side effects, but long-term use can cause inflamed nerves (most often sciatica) and muscle spasms. Panax ginseng can cause muscle soreness, breast pain, insomnia, fast heart rate, mania, itching, decreased appetite, palpitations, headache, dizziness, and swelling of limbs. These occur more frequently when ginseng is taken in combination with other herbs. It may have some estrogenic effects, such as excessive menstrual bleeding, and gynecomastia (enlarged breasts) in men. It can lower blood sugar.

Drug Interrelationships: Can increase the stimulant effects of caffeine (coffee, tea), and long-term use with caffeine ingestion can increase blood pressure.

Disease Cautions: Should not be used in conditions of hemorrhage, and should be used with caution in patients with cardiac disorders. Use with caution in diabetes because it can lower blood sugar.

Dosage: Each type of ginseng varies in potency, quality, and purity, and there is a great variability in commercial ginseng products, with many preparations differing significantly from what is on the label. In general, 1,500mg to 1,800mg of ginseng root in tea bag or liquid extract, and 200mg to 600mg per day in capsule form (standardized to 4 percent to 7 percent ginsenoside content) are taken one to two times daily. You should stop taking ginseng after three months for a rest period of two to three weeks before restarting. Some authorities use ginseng cyclically for a period of 15 to 21 days, followed by a two-week rest period. Siberian ginseng is the safest type, with Asian Panax (Chinese or Korean) being the strongest, and American (Quinquefolius) being in between. You should always start with a low dose and increase gradually.

Gotu Kola

Found in swampy areas of India, Sri Lanka, and South Africa, this herb was thought to slow aging because elephants, which are noted for their longevity, ingest it extensively.

Used For: Improved memory and intelligence; chronic venous insufficiency; skin disorders including psoriasis; wound healing; prevention of keloid/hypertrophic scarring; *schistosomiasis* (an amoebic disease not usually seen in the U.S. but extensively noted worldwide).

Side Effects: Can cause body itching and light sensitivity. Topical application can cause an allergic or skin disorder.

Drug Interrelationships: None known.

Disease Cautions: May elevate blood pressure in high doses; can cause abortion; can elevate blood sugar levels, cholesterol, and triglyceride levels.

Dosage: Extract containing daily dose of 30mg to 60mg triterpenic acids. Venous insufficiency, 120mg daily.

Grapeseed/Pine Bark (Pycnogenol)

Seeds of certain grapes and an extract from pine trees in coastal France contain *proanthocyanidin*, a very potent antioxidant said to have 30 to 50 times the antioxidant effects of vitamins C and E.

Used For: Venous insufficiency; night vision; eye stress from glare; poor vision; immune enhancement; eczema, diabetic neuropathy; ADHD (Attention deficit/Hyperactivity); exercise enhancement; high cholesterol.

Side Effects: None.

Drug Interrelationships: None known.

Disease Cautions: None known.

Dosage: Grapeseed extract, 50mg to 80mg daily as preventative; 150mg to 300mg daily for therapeutic; for eczema, 50mg to 100mg of 95 percent procyanidolic oligomers content. Pycnogenol, 100mg three times daily for therapeutic; retinopathy, 50mg three times daily; high cholesterol, 120mg three times daily; exercise enhancement, 200mg daily. Grapeseed extracts contain 10 percent more proanthocyanidin and are less expensive than Pycnogenol.

Green Tea

Green tea contains twice as many antioxidants as its cousin, black tea, the form most commonly used in this country. Green tea is made directly from harvest and is nonfermented, whereas black tea is fermented.

Used For: Cognitive performance (brain function); high cholesterol; oral *leukoplakia* (white patches on mouth membranes); diuretic; diarrhea; cancer preventive (breast, bladder, esophagus, pancreas).

Side Effects: Indigestion; constipation; contains caffeine, so high doses can cause caffeine side effects.

Drug Interrelationships: Green tea can increase the effect of aspirin, acetaminophen, asthma drugs (Proventil, Ventolin, Alupent), ergotamine, and theophylline. Several drugs can increase the adverse effects of caffeine in green tea, including Tagamet, Antabuse, ephedrine, oral contraceptives, phenylpropanolamine, quinolone antibiotics (such as Cipro), and Verapamil. Other drugs can decrease the effect of caffeine in green tea, including barbiturates, benzodiazepines (such as Valium, Xanax), and Dilantin. Green tea may enhance the effects of blood thinners.

Disease Cautions: None known.

Lab Test Interference: Green tea can decrease bleeding time, and creatine levels in the blood.

Dosage: Average is 3 cups per day. To obtain cholesterol-lowering effects, 10 cups per day are required. Tablets and capsules are available, containing up to 97 percent polyphenols, equivalent to 4 cups per day.

Guar Gum

Guar gum is a dietary fiber source that can swell up to 20 times when in water.

Used For: Laxative; fiber source; high cholesterol; high triglycerides.

Side Effects: Gastrointestinal disturbances for the first few days; can also cause small bowel obstruction.

Drug Interrelationships: May decrease absorption of some drugs, including aspirin, blood thinners, digoxin, penicillin, and metformin (Glucophage). Can reduce the absorption of vitamins and minerals.

Disease Cautions: May reduce blood-sugar levels in diabetics. Should not be used in cases of gastrointestinal obstruction.

Dosage: Start with 2g to 3g per day with at least eight ounces of water. May increase to 5g per day. Do not take if you have problems swallowing.

Guggal

Derived from the mukul myrrh tree, this herb has been used for centuries in India for heart disease.

Used For: Lowering cholesterol and triglycerides; nodulocystic acne; osteoarthritis pain.

Side Effects: GI upset; belching; headache; mild nausea; hiccups.

Drug Interrelationships: Can decrease effects of propranolol (Inderal), and Cardizem.

Disease Cautions: None known.

Dosage: For cholesterol, an extract containing 50mg of guggulsterone per 500mg tablet three times per day. For acne, 25mg once daily.

Gymnema Sylvestre

This plant is native to the tropical forests of India, and originally (and erroneously) was marketed as allowing sugar to pass through the GI tract unabsorbed. When applied to the tongue, extracts block the sensation of sweetness.

Possibly Beneficial For: Diabetes mellitus (Types I and II); high cholesterol and triglycerides in Type II diabetes.

Side Effects: None known.

Drug Interrelationships: Some preparations can decrease iron absorption; enhances blood-sugar-lowering effect of insulin and oral antidiabetic drugs.

Disease Cautions: Diabetes, as above.

Dosage: 200mg extract twice daily.

Hawthorn (Leaf With Flower Extract)

The medicinal properties of this smallish tree was known as far back as the first century A.D. It has a direct effect on the heart; it also dilates blood vessels.

Used For: Heart disease: improves heart flow, exercise ability, and reduces symptoms. Useful for NYHA Stage II heart failure.

Side Effects: Headache; nausea; insomnia; dizziness; agitation; palpitations and circulatory disturbances; rash; fatigue.

Drug Interrelationships: Might interfere or potentiate other drugs used for angina, heart failure, hypertension, and arrhythmias. Might potentiate effects of digitalis, requiring dose reduction.

Disease Cautions: None known.

Dosage: 100mg to 250mg of extract containing 1.8 percent vitexin-4'rhamnoside or 10 percent procyanidin content, three times a day, or 160mg to 900mg native water-ethanol extract corresponding to 30 to 168.7 procyanidins or 3.5 to 19.8 flavonoids. Also comes in tincture (1:5 in 45 percent alcohol) or powder (200mg to 500mg three times daily).

Horse Chestnut (Seed Only)

Adults in many countries superstitiously carry the large brown seeds of the horse chestnut tree to prevent or cure arthritis and rheumatism. The key ingredient, escin, primarily affects the venous system, not the joints.

Used For: Chronic venous insufficiency; varicose veins; tiredness, swelling of the legs, night leg cramps.

Side Effects: GI irritation; kidney damage.

Drug Interrelationships: May decrease blood sugar.

Disease Cautions: You should not use this herb if you have inflammatory or infectious GI problems (Crohn's disease or ulcerative colitis). Don't use it if you have liver or kidney disease. It can also lower blood sugar in diabetes.

Dosage: 250mg to 315mg extract, one to three times per day. If labeled, should have 16 percent to 21 percent escin, or 100 mg escin content daily.

Kava Kava

Meaning "intoxicating pepper," this herb derives from an area of the Pacific Ocean islands that used it in a drink for ceremonies and celebrations because of its calming effect and ability to improve socialization. It is commonly combined with St. John's wort and other herbs.

Used For: Short-term anxiety disorders; to prevent diazepam (Valium, Xanax) withdrawal.

Side Effects: GI symptoms; dilated pupils; disturbances of eye movement and focusing; headache; drowsiness; dizziness; long-term use can cause dry, flaking skin; reddened eyes; yellow discoloration of skin, hair and nails; liver toxicity (see below).

Drug Interrelationships: Because of its potentiating effects, you should not use Kava with other psychotropic medications, such as valium, barbiturates, or sedatives. Use it with caution if you take levodopa (for Parkinson's) because it may reduce the benefits of levodopa.

Disease Cautions: Do not use it if you have severe depression (caused by chemical imbalance) because it can make that type of depression worse. It should not be taken at all if you are pregnant or nursing.

Dosage: 45mg to 70mg of kavalactones three times daily.

Caution: You should not use kava kava for more than three months at a time because it can adversely affect your health. Stop taking it if a skin disorder occurs (see side effects above). **NOTE:** There have been 70 reports of liver damage worldwide in patients using Kava; however, these have been linked to processes involving acetone extraction or ethanol extraction, the use of synthetic kavain, use of the stem (which is more toxic than the root or rhizome), interaction with alcohol (including in other extracts), long-term use, or when used along with conventional medications that can cause liver toxicity.

Licorice (Root)

Licorice contains more than 400 phytochemicals. Most imported licorice is used to flavor tobacco products, making them sweet and pleasant tasting (from its glycyrrhizin content). Licorice candy and other products are popular but in fact do not contain any of the root, and they derive their flavor from anise, not licorice.

Used For: Heartburn; gastric or duodenal ulcers; upper respiratory tract inflammation; prostate cancer (as combination in PC-SPES).

Side Effects: Can cause amenorrhea (no menstruation); large amounts can cause salt and water retention, and potassium loss.

Drug Interrelationships: Simultaneous use with thiazide diuretics can increase potassium loss and increase sensitivity to *digoxin* (a drug used in heart failure). It should not be administered with *spironolactone* or *amiloride* (other diuretics). May cause hypertension and swelling if used with oral contraceptives.

Disease Cautions: Can cause or worsen hypertension due to the glycyrrhizin content, can interfere with blood sugar control, and can worsen cirrhosis. Do not use in pregnancy.

Dosage: Deglycyrrhizinated licorice (DGL) is a form that does not elevate blood pressure. The standard dose of DGL is one or two 380mg chewable tablets before meals.

Milk Thistle (Silymarin; Fruit, Seed)

Used for centuries in liver diseases, milk thistle was almost totally discontinued in the early twentieth century. In the early 1980s, however, German scientists isolated its main component, silymarin, which has been shown to not only protect liver cells but make new ones as well.

Used For: Toxic liver damage (including from drugs and alcohol); dyspepsia (stomach ache); hepatitis; cirrhosis; bile-duct inflammation.

Side Effects: Occasional laxative effect.

Drug Interrelationships: May increase risk of bleeding with blood thinners. May help antihypertensive medications lower blood pressure. Can reduce cyclosporin-induced high blood pressure after heart transplants, and can protect against kidney damage if cisplatin is used for chemotherapy.

Disease Cautions: Mild allergy (ragweed/marigold family); should be used with caution in aspirin-sensitive individuals. Can interfere with blood sugar control in diabetes. Can lower blood pressure.

Dosage: 200mg to 400mg per day using a standardized extract containing 70 percent silymarin. There is a tea available, but the active ingredients may not dissolve.

Oils: Black Currant, Borage, Evening Primrose, Fish, and Flaxseed

Although not specifically herbs, there are many oils that are derived from herbs and that are very popular as supplements. They all contain essential fatty acids, of which there are two main types, omega-3 and omega-6, which benefit the cardiovascular system.

It is important to understand the difference between these fatty acids because they compete against each other for binding sites in the body and so can negate each other's benefits. Several combination supplements contain both types; these supplements are less effective because the ingredients may simply cancel each other out. *Omega-3 fatty acids* are the best because they decrease total cholesterol and LDL cholesterol, the "bad" cholesterol, while increasing HDL, the "good" cholesterol. *Omega-6 fatty acids* decrease total cholesterol and LDL cholesterol, but they also decrease HDL. With this in mind, you will better understand what each oil does as compared to the others.

Black Currant Seed Oil (contains 6 percent to 17 percent GLA, an omega-6 fatty acid)

Not used as much as EPO or borage oil (see below), black currant seed oil is usually used with other herbal oils as a combination product.
Used For: Improves immune function in elderly.
Side Effects: None known.
Drug Interrelationships: None known.
Disease Cautions: None known.
Dosage: 500mg to 1,000mg daily, up to 4,500mg.

Borage Seed Oil (contains 24 percent to 27 percent gamma-linoleic acid, or GLA, an omega-3 fatty acid)

The leaves and flowers of this herb have been used since the first century A.D. and were added to wine to make people happy and content. The seeds are now used as a source of essential fatty acids. This oil was added to honey in the second century to help treat sore throats. Natural food enthusiasts eat it like spinach. Some borage products contain pyrrozolidine alkaloids, which can cause liver damage.
Used For: Rheumatoid arthritis; atopic dermatitis; peripheral neuropathy.
Side Effects: Can prolong bleeding time; ataxia (loss of balance).
Drug Interrelationships: Caution if you take blood thinners.
Disease Cautions: Contraindicated in liver disease unless certified free of unsaturated pyrrolizidine alkaloids (UPA-free).
Dosage: 1g one to two times per day with meals, certified UPA-free.

Evening Primrose Oil (EPO) (contains 9 percent to 12 percent GLA, an omega-6 fatty acid)

Considered a noxious weed, evening primrose is native to North America, where native Americans and early European settlers used it for medicinal purposes. It is the most commonly used source of GLA.
Used For: Mastalgia (breast pain); rheumatoid arthritis; PMS-associated irritable bowel syndrome; osteoporosis (with fish oil and calcium).
Side Effects: GI disturbances; headaches; loose stools.
Drug Interrelationships: Can cause seizures when used with phenothiazines in schizophrenia.
Disease Cautions: None known, except above.
Dosage: For mastalgia, 3g to 4g daily. For rheumatoid arthritis, 1g to 2.5g daily for six months. For PMS, 2g to 4g daily.

Fish Oil (contains two other varieties of omega-3 fatty acids, called EPA [eicosapentaenoic acid] and DHA [docosahexaenoic acid])

This oil is derived from cold-water fish (including mackerel, herring, tuna, salmon, trout, halibut, cod liver, whale, and seal blubber), which have been shown to protect against heart disease and reduce damage from heart attacks when eaten once per week.

Used For: High triglycerides; reduce risk of dying after heart attack; morning stiffness in rheumatoid arthritis; bipolar disorder; eczema; psoriasis; depression; mild hypertension; diabetic nephropathy; night vision in dyslexic children; migraine headaches in adolescents; weight loss; age-related maculopathy (macular degeneration); osteoporosis (with evening primrose oil and calcium); reduced risk of stroke; Raynaud's disease; dysmenorrhea (painful menstrual periods); high cholesterol (with garlic); prostate cancer prevention; osteoporosis (with evening primrose oil and calcium).

Side Effects: Heartburn; belching; nosebleeds; and halitosis (bad breath). High doses (greater than 3g per day) may depress the immune system.

Disease Cautions: Primarily in high doses, it may deplete certain antioxidant nutrients and increase the levels of harmful lipid peroxidases in the body, causing increased blood lipids and poor diabetes control. Eating garlic and taking vitamin E with fish oil can negate most of these effects.

Dosage: For lowering blood pressure, 4g per day. For lowering triglycerides and all other conditions, 1g to 2g per day. The DHA is better for hypertension and at lowering heart rate than EPA, but most supplements contain more EPA.

Caution: In diabetes, do not take more than 1,800mg daily because blood sugar control is worsened and cholesterol increases at these dosages.

Flaxseed Oil (contains primarily alpha-linoleic acid, ALA, which is an omega-3 fatty acid)

This oil contains both omega-3 and omega-6 fatty acids, but because they are combined naturally, they do not negate each other's effects. This oil is the richest source of omega-3 fatty acids in the world and is my preferred form.

Used For: High cholesterol and triglycerides; anticancer; chemotherapy side effects; breast cancer proliferation; kidney function in lupus.

Side Effects: None known.

Drug Interrelationships: May delay the absorption of drugs taken simultaneously, due to its mucilage content.

Disease Cautions: There may be a delay in glucose absorption in diabetic patients.

Dosage: One to two teaspoons mixed with liquid or used as salad dressing. It can spoil quickly, so check the expiration date on the bottle. Some manufacturers put the oil into capsules, which may last longer.

Olive Leaf

The leaf of the olive tree contains several substances that have antioxidant and antibacterial properties.

Used For: Hypertension; infections from viruses, fungi, yeasts, protozoa, and some bacteria.

Side Effects: The pollen may cause seasonal respiratory allergies.

Drug Interrelationships: None known.

Disease Interactions: None known.

Dosage: Can be used as a tea (two teaspoons of the dried leaf boiled in water for 30 minutes, and then strained). Extracts are available and should contain 20 percent Oleuropein, 500mg one to two daily.

Peppermint Oil

This oil differs from the previous oils because it does not contain essential fatty acids. It is actually not a natural plant but an accidental hybrid that sprouted in a field of spearmint in England in 1696 and is now cultivated. Its oils contain a complex mixture of ingredients that increase salivation, suppress the cough reflex, and relax the muscles (and spasms) of the esophagus and stomach. Its main ingredient is menthol.

Used For: Coughs and colds (topical, inhalation); esophageal spasm; myalgia (topical); neuralgia (topical); muscle and nerve irritation (topical); tension headaches (topical); inflammation of mouth and respiratory tissues (topical); irritable bowel syndrome; postoperative nausea; spasm of bile ducts, stomach, and esophagus.

Side Effects: Heartburn; headache; flushing.

Drug Interrelationships: It can cause increased side effects if used with H2 acid-blocking drugs (such as Tagamet, Zantac, Pepcid). Take only in enteric-coated capsules if used along with these medications.

Disease Cautions: You should not use if you have gallstones or gall-bladder disease, bile duct obstruction, severe liver disease, or if you have no stomach acid.

Dosage: For gastrointestinal problems, 0.2ml to 0.4ml (6 to 12 drops) twice daily between meals, or lozenge; topically, it can be used in several forms. Inhalation, 3 to 4 drops in hot water.

Quercetin

A bioflavonoid found in many plants (including St. John's wort and gingko), quercetin has anti-inflammatory and antioxidant effects.

Used For: Prostatitis (nonbacterial); cancer prevention; asthma; canker sores; eczema; gout; hives.

Side Effects: Headache; tingling in arms and legs.

Drug Interrelationships: It may interfere with quinolone antibiotics (such as Cipro).

Disease Cautions: None known.

Dosage: 400mg to 500mg three times per day.

Red Clover

Using the flower top, red clover has more than 100 chemical constituents. It is active as an expectorant and antispasmodic, it has estrogenic properties from its isoflavones (such as genistein, found in soy), and it also has some anticancer compounds.

Used For: Post-menopausal spinal bone loss; menopausal symptoms; osteoporosis; prostate hypertrophy; prevention of hangovers.

Side Effects: Rash.

Drug Interrelationships: None known.

Disease Cautions: Large amounts can cause blood thinning, so use with caution if you are on anticoagulants.

Dosage: Tea, using 4g three times per day; liquid extract or tincture (1:1 in alcohol) is 1ml to 3ml three times daily. For hangovers, use several drops in one-half glass of water before sleep.

Saw Palmetto

Derived from a common palm tree, this herb is frequently combined with pygeum, an African herb, and pumpkin seed, both of which have been shown to potentiate its benefits.

Used For: Benign prostatic hyperplasia (BPH); prostate cancer (used with seven other herbs); breast enlargement.

Side Effects: Headache; rare stomach problems.

Drug Interrelationships: May interfere with oral contraceptives and hormone therapy.

Disease Cautions: None known, but do not self-treat until proper diagnosis is made.

Dosage: 320mg of lipophilic extract, or 1g to 2g of whole berries daily. The extracts should contain 80 percent to 90 percent fatty acids. Saw palmetto can be used safely in combination with pygeum and pumpkin seed, herbs that also benefit the prostate.

Slippery Elm

Native Americans and early settlers of North America used the bark of the slippery elm as a medicinal centuries ago.

Used For: Sore throat.

Side Effects: Can cause abortion; contact dermatitis.

Drug Interrelationships: None known.

Disease Cautions: None known.

Dosage: Powdered inner bark (1:8 decoction), 4ml to 16ml three times a day. Alcohol extract, 5ml three times a day.

Soy

The soybean is a legume that contains high-grade protein, carbohydrates, oils, fatty acids, and a variety of vitamins, amino acids, fiber, and minerals. Soybeans are prized for their high protein content of 38 percent. They also contains phytoestrogens (plant estrogens) called isoflavones that can have an anti-estrogenic effect in pre-menopausal women and a weak estrogenic effect in post-menopausal women. In addition, these isoflavones can mimic estrogen's effects in some tissues and block the effects in other tissues. The major isoflavones are genistein and daidzein.

Used For: Cholesterol reduction; hot flashes; osteoporosis; prostate cancer risk; hypertension in pre-menopausal women; kidney failure; nutritional liver disease; chronic hepatitis.

Side Effects: Allergic reactions including skin rash, itching (cross-allergy to peanuts), GI complaints.

Drug Interrelationships: None known.

Disease Cautions: Asthma and allergic rhinitis may worsen if allergy to soy is present; soy can inhibit thyroid hormone synthesis. Controversy exists whether soy can increase breast cancer risk or can have protective effects. It appears that low-dose soy may stimulate cell growth (at least in the test tube), but high doses may inhibit breast cancer growth. Most animal studies show a protective effect against cancer when the animals are eating soy. Nonfermented soy products (such as soymilk and tofu) tend to be more protective than fermented varieties (such as miso). If you have breast cancer or are at high risk for breast cancer, you are advised to take soy with caution and monitor any breast growths. According to most studies, taking more than 20g is safe.

Dosages: Cholesterol-lowering: 20g to 50g per day, containing at least 6.25g of soy protein. Osteoporosis, hot flashes, prostate cancer risk: 40g per day, containing 2mg to 2.5mg of isoflavones per gram of protein.

NOTE: Soy supplements may not contain a natural mix of isoflavones, fiber, or carbohydrates. If you are using supplements, genistein is the most potent isoflavone. The best source is protein isolate powder that you can mix in a beverage ("Supro" sources are the best of these). Although soy foods are healthier for you, many soy foods do not contain the essential nutrients (they are removed in processing); these include soy burgers, hot dogs, cheeses, and sauce. Tofu, soy milk, roasted nuts, and raw beans are recommended; the firmer the tofu, the more protein and calcium it provides.

Stinging Nettle (Above-Ground Parts or Root)

The above-ground parts of the stinging nettle are used as an anti-inflammatory and local anesthetic, and they have antimicrobial properties, while the root is used for urinary problems.

Used For (above-ground parts): Allergic rhinitis; urinary tract (flushing); kidney stones; arthritic disease; **(root):** Benign prostatic hypertrophy, stages I and II.

Side Effects: Diarrhea; other GI symptoms.

Drug Interrelationships (above-ground parts): Stinging nettle has vitamin K, which can interfere with clotting, and thus blood thinners; it can enhance the anti-inflammation properties of diclofenac (Cataflam, Voltaren), an NSAID; **(root):** None known.

Disease Cautions: Above-ground parts should not be used in heart or kidney failure if you have edema (swelling of ankles).

Dosage: For flushing the urinary tract, use a tea of 8g to 12g per day; fresh juice is 10ml to 15ml three times daily. For other conditions, extract of 300mg to 600mg daily. For allergic rhinitis, use the freeze-dried (cryogenic) form of the herb, 300mg, three times daily.

Tea Tree Oil

This Australian tree oil, used for centuries by the aborigines, contains substances that have antimicrobial properties. It was used commonly in the 1920s by surgeons and dentists to prevent infection.

Used For: Acne; fungal skin and nail infections; antiseptic; cuts, burns, bites, and stings; athlete's foot.

Side Effects: May cause local allergic irritation of skin (contact dermatitis).

Drug Interrelationships: None known.

Disease Cautions: None known.

Dosage: 70 percent to 100 percent applied topically two to three times a day for nail infections (may take six months); athlete's foot, 10 percent gel; acne, 5 percent gel.

Uva Ursi

The leaf of this herb, the bearberry or upland cranberry, has antiseptic effects.

Used For: Urinary tract inflammatory disorders.

Side Effects: Nausea; tinnitus; shortness of breath; vomiting.

Drug Interrelationships: None known.

Disease Cautions: Should not use in kidney disorders or GI irritation.

Dosage: As a tea, one to two teaspoons (1.5g to 4g), fluid extract (1:1 in 25 percent alcohol, standardized to contain 20 percent arbutin), 1.5ml to 2.0ml three times daily. Do not exceed 15g because of side effects.

Valerian Root

Legendary tales relate that Valerian was used by the Pied Piper to lure rats from the town of

Hamelin because the odor is attractive to rats. It has been used for more than 1,000 years for its sedative effects.

Used For: Insomnia; mood improvement; anxiety; migraine; muscle spasms; neuralgia; stomach cramps, concentration.

Side Effects: Uneasiness; insomnia; headache; cardiac disturbances; excitability; morning drowsiness.

Drug Interrelationships: None documented.

Disease Cautions: None known.

Dosage: Extract containing 400mg to 800mg. Also available in tincture, one-half to one teaspoon (1ml to 3ml), one to three times per day; extract or tea equal to 2g to 3g per day.

Caution: You should use Valerian for only two to four weeks at a time.

Yohimbe

This Chinese herb dilates the blood vessels in the genital area and stimulates sacral nerves (which promote sexual function). It is the Chinese equivalent of Viagra.

Used For: Impotence (erectile dysfunction).

Side Effects: Tremor; insomnia; anxiety; fast heart beat; increased blood pressure; nausea.

Drug Interrelationships: Yohimbe may interfere with blood-pressure medication; it can heighten the effect of MAO inhibitors (antidepressant drugs such as Parnate, Nardil). Yohimbe should not be taken if you have heart disease or angina. It can cause manic reactions in patients with depression or bipolar disorder. It can trigger acute symptoms in post-traumatic stress disorder (PTSD); it may cause *hypoglycemia* (low blood sugar) in patients with diabetes. Avoid in patients with kidney failure or liver disease.

Dosage: Products should contain 15mg yohimbine content, taken two to three times per day. There is a prescription formulation of 5.4mg tablets.

HORMONAL SUPPLEMENTS

In the past few years, the media and manufacturers have deluged us with claims that various hormonal supplements are the "magic pills" that can allow you to live practically forever. There have even been many books written about these substances, most of them bestsellers. Yet, so far, research in humans has not corroborated most of these claims.

Hormones are essential components of the endocrine system, which regulates your bodily functions. However, whether hormones that are taken as supplements are beneficial or harmful in the long run is not known and probably will not be known for decades. The "age-reversing" claims of these hormonal products are theorized on the observation that these hormones decrease as you age. However, it has now been noted that some of these hormones do not in fact decrease with age; and, furthermore, the purpose of these hormones may not have anything to do with aging, but rather simply with maintenance of the body.

Androstenedione

This hormone is chemically related to DHEA and was made famous by baseball's home-run record-breaker, Mark McGwire.

Used For: Increase testosterone levels.

Side Effects: May increase the risk of pancreatic cancer, liver problems; may cause breast enlargement in men and increased facial hair in women.

Drug Interrelationships: None known.

Disease Cautions: Should not be taken if you have liver disease, and can worsen or initiate prostate cancer. It was recently thought that androstenedione might help heart disease, but recent studies show that it increases the risk of heart disease.

Dosage/Caution: This product is not recommended.

Dehydroepiandrosterone (DHEA)

A precursor of male and female sex hormones as well as steroids, DHEA is the most abundant hormone in the bloodstream. There is no question that DHEA declines with age, with an 80- to 90-year-old having 10 percent to 20 percent of the peak lifetime level. However, that does not mean that by supplementing DHEA, you will reverse aging or any other medical condition. In fact, levels of DHEA also plunge during childhood, a time of growth rather than deterioration.

Used For: Erectile dysfunction; depression; systemic lupus erythematosus (SLE); vaginal atrophy (applied vaginally); bone density; skin grafting; AIDS; vaccination; increases bone density; improves immune function; increases HDL cholesterol; improves well-being and sexuality in women with adrenal insufficiency; increases insulin sensitivity; rheumatoid arthritis.

Side Effects: Acne; oily skin; facial hair; mood changes; possibly heart disease in women; decreases HDL cholesterol.

Drug Interrelationships: Can increase triazolam (Halcion) concentrations. May also increase levels of drugs metabolized in the Cytochrome P450 3A system (similar to St. John's wort), although studies have not been done on these drugs. Some of the more common of these drugs include Xanax, BuSpar, Elavil, Zoloft, Celexa, Prevacid, Mevacor, Meridia, and Viagra.

Disease Cautions: Can interfere with the effectiveness of insulin in diabetes, can worsen liver disease, and can increase the risk of prostate and breast cancer.

Dosage: For SLE, 200mg per day (pharmaceutical grade, GL701); for depression, 30mg to 90mg per day; for adrenal insufficiency or rheumatoid arthritis, 50mg per day; other conditions, 25mg to 50mg daily. The wild yam extract (sometimes called "natural DHEA") does not produce DHEA in the body and should be avoided.

Cautions: If you are under 30, you should avoid DHEA because it can suppress your body's natural hormone production. If you take DHEA, protect yourself if you are a man by having prostate exams and PSA levels; if you are a woman, perform bi-annual breast exams and undergo mammograms more often.

Human Growth Hormone (HGH)

HGH is a pituitary hormone that affects protein, carbohydrate, and lipid metabolism. HGH is very expensive, costing from $15,000 to $20,000 per year, and it must be taken for the rest of your life. A nasal spray that purports to stimulate HGH production in the body costs $1,300 per year, but no studies have shown either effectiveness or long-term side effects. Unlike DHEA, HGH does not automatically decline with age; only one-third of those over age 65 have decreased levels. Furthermore, HGH is released in pulses by the body; supplemental HGH cannot release this way and hence affects the body differently.

Used For: Human growth hormone deficiency (short stature, pituitary disease); lean body mass, central obesity (subcutaneous injection); ischemic myocardiopathy.

Side Effects: Carpal tunnel syndrome; gynecomastia (breast enlargement in men); fluid retention; enlargement of organs and joints.

Drug Interrelationships: None known.

Disease Cautions: Can trigger heart failure and worsen diabetes.

Dosage: For deficiency, individualized depending on weight, and must be **medically supervised**. It is not recommended for any other conditions.

Melatonin

Produced by the pineal gland, a tiny gland in the brain, melatonin is responsible for regulating rhythms and patterns of the body.

Used For: Jet lag; insomnia (primarily in the elderly); sleep disorders in mental retardation and autism; *thrombocytopenia* (decreased platelets) from cancer and its treatment; cancer survival (in combination with interleukin-2 or radiotherapy for specific cancers); benzodiazepine withdrawal in elderly people with insomnia (controlled-release form); skin protectant (topically); tardive dyskinesia; sunscreen; cluster headache; nicotine withdrawal symptoms.

Side Effects: Grogginess; headaches; nausea; mild depression; nightmares and vivid dreams; daytime fatigue; dizziness; abdominal cramps; irritability; reduced alertness. It also may adversely affect the reproductive system and cause decreased libido in both men and women.

Drug Interrelationships: Might interfere with immune-suppressant drugs (used in organ transplant). Can enhance the effects of INH (tuberculosis) and reduce the insomnia side effects of beta blockers (such as propranolol, atenolol) and Prozac. It can cause increased sedation when used with other psychotropic drugs, including alcohol and benzodiazepines (Valium, Xanax).

Disease Cautions: May worsen dysphoria in some people with depression. Should use with caution in liver disease and seizure disorders. Can worsen high blood pressure.

Lab Test Interference: Can decrease levels of luteinizing hormone (LH) and increase levels of oxytocin and vasopressin.

Dosage: For insomnia, 0.3mg to 5mg (start with lowest dose possible); for jet lag, 5mg at bedtime for one week beginning three days before the flight; for cancer, 20mg to 50mg in combination with chemotherapy or radiation; for benzodiazepine withdrawal, 2mg at bedtime for the first week, 1mg for the second week, and 0.5mg during weeks three and four. For nicotine withdrawal, 0.3mg two to three hours after last cigarette.

Sex Hormones

Estrogen and Progesterone

Before menopause, women undergo cycles that balance estrogen and progesterone. After menopause, women are at higher risk to develop heart, brain, and bone disease due to decreased production of these hormones, and therefore hormone replacement had previously been recommended. However, conventional medicine replacement recommendations (called HRT, or hormone replacement therapy) are inadequate for the following reasons:

- Most doctors usually prescribe only estrogen, ignoring the benefits of progesterone. Progesterone is prescribed only to counteract the cancer-causing effects of estrogen in women who still have their uterus. Yet progesterone does have beneficial effects that estrogen does not have.
- It is the synthetic versions of these hormones that have been prescribed. Although there are some benefits, these synthetic versions have many side effects because of the synthetic portion, which is foreign to the body. This is especially true with synthetic progesterone. A recent major study showed that taking a combination of synthetic estrogen and progesterone had more risks than benefits and cannot be recommended long term.

Beneficial effects of post-menopausal estrogen (both synthetic and natural): Menopausal symptoms: hot flashes, irritability, depression, insomnia; osteoporosis (prevents hormone-related bone loss); brain function; lower cholesterol levels.

Beneficial effects of post-menopausal *synthetic* progesterone: Helps prevent uterine cancer, when taking synthetic estrogen.

Beneficial effects of *natural* progesterone: Stimulates osteoclasts (builds bone); may protect cardiac function; facilitates thyroid hormone action; natural antidepressant; natural diuretic; restores libido; protects against breast cysts; may help prevent breast, uterine cancer, and BPH, prostate cancer in men.

Side effects of *synthetic* estrogens: Increased risk of breast, uterine, and ovarian cancer; blood clots; breast tenderness; liver dysfunction; gall stones; increased risk of stroke and post-menopausal asthma; can also cause dry-eye syndrome.

Side effects of *natural* estrogens: Breast tenderness.

Side effects of *synthetic* progesterone: Bloating; weight gain; GI disturbances; changes in appetite; fluid retention; fatigue; drowsiness; acne; insomnia; allergic reactions; headache; depression; breast discomfort or swelling; PMS symptoms and irregular bleeding. It can also decrease HDL cholesterol (the "good" cholesterol) and increase LDL cholesterol (the "bad" cholesterol).

Side effects of *natural* progesterone: Spotting.

Again, current conventional recommendations are to NOT take synthetic hormones except for short term to reduce menopausal symptoms. Unfortunately, this does not help protect you from deterioration of your bones, heart, and brain, which was one of the original reasons for HRT. To protect these organ systems, I recommend hormone replacement, but using natural estrogen and progesterone rather than synthetic. Natural hormones are referred to as *bioidentical* hormones, because they are biologically identical to your actual hormones. Although studies are lacking, natural hormones have not been noted to have the side effects found with synthetic hormones and have not yet been determined to be harmful. However, do not take natural estrogen if you are at high risk for breast cancer or have had breast cancer.

Dosages: These vary depending on whether you are pre-menopausal, peri-menopausal, or post-menopausal (see sections on menopause and menstrual problems in Part Two for specific recommendations). Tri-estrogens (natural estrogens) usually contain 10 percent estrone, 10 percent estradiol, and 80 percent estriol, at dosage usually twice that of synthetic estrogens. (For example, the equivalent of 0.625mg of Premarin is1.25mg of Tri-estrogen). If you are at a high risk for breast cancer, you can take estriol alone, which is considered the safest estrogen, but do so under your doctor's direction. Progesterone cream is usually started at 20mg per day in alternating sites, or micronized progesterone at 100mg per day. It normally takes three to four months before your hormone levels will be balanced.

Some doctors may recommend taking DHEA (25mg to 50mg) or testosterone (0.25mg to 5mg) for certain symptoms, along with your estrogen and progesterone, and these can be combined together in one formulation. DHEA is added to increase energy and improve mood. (See the section below for testosterone indications.)

More than 100 companies manufacture natural progesterone, which does not require a prescription. If you buy a cream, it should contain at least 480mg of progesterone per ounce. Mexican yam products are advertised as providing natural progesterone, but they must be processed to become active, and most aren't. If you do use a natural progesterone product from a health food store, carefully read the concentrations and use the appropriate amount suggested above. Because natural estrogens and testosterone are considered drugs, and dosage must be individualized, you must obtain a prescription for these hormones from a physician.

NOTE: Natural hormones can be combined together as topical creams, troches, vaginal suppositories, or capsules by a compounding pharmacist (pharmacists especially trained to formulate and mix these natural compounds). Because each form may vary in absorption, blood hormone levels may be necessary to individualize your intake. Saliva testing is recommended for a more accurate determination than blood levels provide.

For more extensive information and guidance on using natural hormones, see Appendix C, under "Women's Health."

Testosterone (Natural)

Testosterone is thought of as a male hormone, but, in actuality, women also require it. Forty percent of the testosterone in women is made in the ovaries, with the remainder from the adrenal glands. Besides its hormonal effects, testosterone is important for the strength and integrity of muscles, skin, and bones. As with estrogen and progesterone, testosterone can be made synthetically, but it also occurs in the natural form, which I prefer.

In men, testosterone is given for lowered testosterone levels, impotence, and low libido. In women, it is prescribed for decreased libido, energy, to improve mental abilities, increase calcium retention, and protect the heart.

Synthetic testosterone comes in injections and a skin patch (transdermal), but these dosages can be too powerful for women and can cause masculinizing effects, such as facial hair, weight gain, lowered voice, and so on. Natural testosterone is weaker and may not cause these side effects.

If you want to take testosterone for one of the above reasons, I recommend taking it separately from estrogen and progesterone, so that you can monitor side effects and more easily fine-tune your dosage. You can use a cream that contains 2 percent per gram. Apply 1g to the vaginal area or thigh every night for up to two weeks (when it should start working), and then take testosterone "pearls," which are small pellets of 0.25mg to 5mg, which you can take daily. Because natural testosterone is considered a drug, it must be prescribed by a physician.

MINERALS

Minerals are very important for the enzymatic reactions that occur in our bodies. If the body requires more than 100 milligrams of a mineral each day, the substance is labeled a mineral; if the requirement is less than 100mg, the mineral is labeled a trace element. Mineral deficiencies have been blamed for many diseases, and supplementation has been recommended for these and other medical conditions. However, some minerals have been touted as being necessary or beneficial even if individuals do not have such deficiencies. Various studies support some of these claims but refute many others. Like vitamins, there is a plethora of mineral products in health food stores, drug stores, groceries, and even gas stations. Once again, the quality of these products, and their absorption, varies greatly, so beware.

Minerals are also manufactured in several forms. Most tablet forms of minerals come from salt- or metallic-based sources (sea clay- or oyster shell-derived) but there is another form called *colloidal*, which is derived from plants. Proponents of colloidal minerals claim that they are much more absorbable than metallic or salt-based minerals, but colloidal minerals are also a lot more expensive. So far, there have been no specific comparative studies that have determined how well these various forms are absorbed and whether colloidal forms have any advantage. Another form of minerals is called *chelated*, which is also promoted to be better absorbed. Although these minerals may be better absorbed, many chelated minerals are in a form that the body cannot use.

The best way to get your minerals is through food, especially fruits and vegetables. Most mineral supplements may achieve an absorption rate of only 5 percent, but most minerals in food are completely absorbed. If you must take a mineral supplement, you should take it with vitamins and other nutrients. Refer to the section on multivitamins for specific recommendations.

Medical science has determined that several minerals should be supplemented for various conditions. However, there are other minerals for which supplementation is questionable, at best. The following are the most commonly promoted minerals.

Calcium

Calcium is necessary for muscle contraction as well as for bone health. It is lost from the body faster as we age, and the body replaces it by taking it out of bones. You might be concerned that taking calcium will predispose you to developing kidney stones. It has now been shown, however, that people on *low-calcium* diets have increased production of oxalate, which is one of the major factors that increase the risk of producing stones. So taking calcium might actually prevent kidney stones.

Used For: Antacid; kidney failure; bone loss and fractures in post-menopausal women; prevention of osteoporosis; PMS; colorectal cancer risk reduction; chronic renal failure; hypertension; corticosteroid use; pre-eclampsia; ischemic stroke prevention; high cholesterol; heart disease risk; hot flashes, pregnancy-induced leg cramps.

Side Effects: Gastrointestinal symptoms and gas. Calcium chloride can cause GI hemorrhage, and calcium carbonate can cause an increase in stomach acid.

Drug Interrelationships: It can decrease the absorption of biphosphonates (such as Fosamax), fluoroquinolones (such as Cipro), levothyroxine (Synthroid), and tetracyclines. Calcium use can decrease the absorption of supplemental zinc, iron, and magnesium. These drugs and minerals should be taken two hours before or after ingestion of calcium. Drugs that decrease calcium absorption or increase its excretion include loop and thiazide diuretics (HCTZ, Lasix), aluminum and magnesium salts, mineral oil, tetracyclines, stimulant laxatives, corticosteroids, and synthetic thyroid hormones (Synthroid). Vitamin D decreases the absorption of calcium.

Disease Cautions: Smoking decreases calcium absorption. Sarcoidosis and kidney insufficiency increase calcium absorption.

Lab Test Interference: Calcium carbonate increases serum gastrin and insulin levels and can decrease serum magnesium levels, lipase concentrations, glucose levels, and uptake of Iodine 131 (used in thyroid gland testing).

Dosage: Calcium from dairy products produces twice the drop in blood pressure as supplements do, but to get the amount necessary to prevent cancers, help avoid osteoporosis, and control hot flashes, supplementation is recommended. Recommended doses are 1,000mg to 1,200mg for men and 1,200mg to 1,600mg for women. For the best effects in osteoporosis, you should take calcium with magnesium and vitamin D. Calcium supplements should be taken in three to four doses because they are absorbed better when taken with food and in doses of 500mg or less.

The major problem with calcium is that many of the products are not very absorbable. An investigation into all calcium products revealed that of 37 over-the-counter calcium preparations, only 5 were absorbed to any significant degree. Calcium comes in several forms, including citrate, carbonate, hydroxyapatite, amino acid chelate, chloride, gluconate, lactate, pangamate, and phosphate. My recommended forms are citrate, tricalcium phosphate, and hydroxyapatite, although carbonate is more commonly used than the latter two. Calcium carbonate and phosphate should be taken with meals. Although chelated forms and coral calcium are marketed as superior to the other forms, research has not yet substantiated these claims.

Chromium

This mineral is the initial component of "glucose tolerance factor," a group of amino acids that regulate insulin-glucose transport. Deficiency of chromium is widespread in this country.

Used For: Type II diabetes; hyperglycemia caused by taking corticosteroids (see "Drug Interrelationships"); weight control; athletic performance.

Side Effects: Headaches; insomnia; irritability; can cause neurological and brain disturbances even at low dosages; can cause weight gain in women who don't exercise. At dosages greater than 1mg/day, it can cause anemia, liver problems, and renal failure.

Drug Interrelationships: Combined with niacin, it might improve glucose tolerance. Chromium may also reverse increases in blood sugar caused by the use of corticosteroids. However, because it can decrease blood sugar, it can cause hypoglycemia in diabetics taking insulin. Vitamin C can increase chromium absorption. Chromium can beneficially increase HDL cholesterol when the use of beta blockers (such as Tenormin, Inderal) lowers HDL cholesterol levels to below normal.

Disease Cautions: May worsen behavioral disorders due to alterations of chemical messengers in the brain (serotonin) when used in the picolinate form. Chromium can worsen kidney failure.

Lab Test Interference: Chromium can lower blood sugar, and reduce cholesterol and triglyceride levels in Type II diabetes; it can increase HDL concentration in patients taking beta blockers (such as atenolol, propranolol).

Dosage: Picolinate is better absorbed than the chloride or nicotinate forms. 200mcg to 300mcg three times daily is the recommended dosage.

Iron

This mineral is an essential component of hemoglobin, the primary constituent of red blood cells necessary to carry oxygen.

Used For: Iron-deficiency anemia; coughing caused by ACE inhibitors.

Side Effects: Gastrointestinal disturbances; abdominal pain.

Drug Interrelationships: Iron absorption is decreased by antacids, calcium, tetracyclines, H2 acid blockers (Tagamet, Pepcid, Zantac), and proton pump inhibitors (Prilosec, Prevacid, Aciphex). Iron levels are increased by vitamin C. Iron use decreases the absorption of vitamin E, fluoroquinolone antibiotics (such as Cipro), methyldopa, penicillamine, tetracyclines, and thyroid-replacement medications.

Food Interactions: Coffee inhibits absorption of iron, and soy reduces the absorption of iron from plant-based foods such as asparagus, broccoli, cabbage, tomatoes, and peppers.

Disease Cautions: Iron absorption is decreased in dialysis. It should not be used in patients with peptic ulcer or inflammatory bowel diseases.

Lab Test Interference: The guaiac test for detecting blood in the stools can be false positive.

Dosage: 300mg (in divided doses) daily in iron deficiency anemia. Supplementation for other causes of decreased iron is dependent on iron blood levels. It may take six months to replenish body stores of iron.

Caution: You should take iron only if blood tests reveal that you are iron deficient, not just if you feel tired, because iron intake interferes with the absorption of most other nutrients and conventional medications. If you must take iron because you have low levels, you should always take it several hours apart from all other products or medications. Iron supplementation is usually not needed and should not be used by men or post menopausal women, unless they have the above conditions and are under the supervision of a doctor.

Magnesium

This mineral is essential for proper nerve and muscle function, and is involved in more than 300 basic cellular functions. Bone contains 50 percent of the body's magnesium, which is essential for bone structure along with calcium.

Used For: Antacid; laxative; osteoporosis; angina; pre-eclampsia and eclampsia; pre-term labor; heart attack; arrhythmias caused by heart attack (intravenously); Prinzmetal angina; migraine headaches, especially pre-menstrual (used with riboflavin); cluster headaches (intravenously); PMS symptoms; pregnancy-induced leg cramps; mitral valve prolapse; hypertension (mild to moderate); kidney stones (calcium oxalate); noise-induced hearing-loss prevention; wound healing; ADHD; fibromyalgia (with malic acid); atrial fibrillation (intravenously); chronic obstructive pulmonary disease flare-up or asthma attacks (intravenously); chronic fatigue syndrome (intramuscular).

Side Effects: Gastrointestinal disturbances.

Drug Interrelationships: Boron can increase magnesium levels. Magnesium can decrease the absorption of fluoroquinolone antibiotics (such as Cipro). Magnesium levels can be decreased when using digoxin, loop and thiazide diuretics (HCTZ, Lasix), estrogens and oral contraceptives, and penicillamine.

Disease Cautions: Magnesium is contraindicated for patients with heart block. It should be used with caution in kidney failure.

Lab Test Interference: Magnesium orally can reduce serum ACE-inhibitor levels, cause a false increase in alkaline phosphatase and calcium blood levels, and intravenously can reduce levels of plasma cortisol, testosterone, and parathyroid hormone.

Dosage: Magnesium gluconate or chloride are the recommended oral forms because they have less diarrhea side effects. As a laxative, other forms can be used effectively. For hypertension, 600mg to 1,000mg of elemental magnesium per day; for diabetic control, 250mg three times daily; for fibromyalgia, 150mg to 250mg of magnesium hydroxide is used with 800mg to 1,200mg of malic acid three times a day; for angina, 200mg to 400mg three times daily; for migraines, 250mg to 400mg three times daily; for osteoporosis, 400mg to 800mg daily.

Caution: If you increase your calcium and vitamin D intakes for bone health without taking magnesium, it can intensify the risks and complications of cardiovascular disease, including hypertension.

Selenium

Epidemiological studies have shown that there are fewer cancers in regions where the soil is rich in selenium (Eastern Coastal Plain and Pacific Northwest).

Used For: AIDS patients with selenium deficiency; dandruff; cancer prevention, especially lung, colon, and prostate; prevention of heart disease and arthritis.

Side Effects: Can cause GI symptoms; fatigue; tremors; respiratory problems; nail changes; irritability. Chronic toxicity can cause hair loss; muscle tenderness; lightheadedness; garlic odor on breath; liver/kidney dysfunction.

Drug Interrelationships: Selenium can increase the tumor-killing effects of cisplatin in the presence of EDTA.

Disease Cautions: None known.

Lab Test Interference: Selenium toxicity can cause changes in the EKG test, suggesting heart attack.

Dosage: 200mcg per day for cancer prevention. Most people receive plenty of selenium in their diet so do not need supplementation. If you take a multivitamin, selenium is usually amply supplied, but caution is advised because of side effects if your *total* intake exceeds 800mcg.

Zinc

This mineral is essential for wound healing, immune function, growth and development, and protein synthesis.

Used For: Malabsorption syndromes; alcoholism; Wilson's disease; neurological recovery from head trauma; acne (used with erythromycin topically); common cold (high doses); macular degeneration (with vitamin E); Alzheimer's; eczema; benign prostatic hypertrophy; PMS; inflammatory bowel disease (Crohn's, ulcerative colitis); rheumatoid arthritis; anorexia nervosa; peptic ulcer; cold sores (topical).

Side Effects: GI disturbances; kidney inflammation and damage.

Drug Interrelationships: Zinc can decrease copper absorption, resulting in decreased immune function. Drugs that can decrease zinc levels include captopril (Capoten), penicillamine (Cuprimine), and thiazide diuretics (HydroDIURIL). Zinc levels can be increased with chlorthalidone (Hygroton) and potassium-sparing diuretics (such as spironolactone). Zinc can decrease the absorption and effectiveness of tetracyclines and fluoroquinolone antibiotics (such as Cipro).

Disease Cautions: Can decrease survival in HIV/AIDS. Zinc absorption is reduced in patients with rheumatoid arthritis. Zinc deficiency is common in malabsorption syndromes, severe or prolonged diarrhea, in cirrhosis, or after major surgery, and should be supplemented.

Food Interrelationships: Coffee may decrease zinc absorption up to 50 percent.

Dosage: For zinc deficiency, in alcoholics, or post surgery, 200mg to 300mg three times a day. For macular degeneration, acne, benign prostatic hypertrophy, or inflammatory bowel disease (Crohn's, ulcerative colitis), 45mg to 60mg per day; eczema, 30mg daily.

Caution: Studies using zinc for the common cold have been very inconsistent. Most recommend at least 15mg to 25mg of zinc gluconate or acetate (lozenges) every two hours while awake when symptoms are present, but a recent study suggests at least twice that amount. You must start taking the zinc within 24 hours of symptoms for it to be beneficial, and it should not continue after three days. Zinc lozenges taste bad.

NON-HORMONAL SUPPLEMENTS

There are more supplements produced than I could possibly mention, even in one long chapter. In every catalog and every health food store, there are literally hundreds of different substances, all being promoted to be the best cure for any number of medical conditions. Just be aware that for many of these, research is either nonexistent or has proven them ineffective. Hopefully, in the next few years, we will have more answers; but, until then, you may be wasting your money or even be allowing subtle yet harmful effects to occur to your body. However, some of these supplements have been found by research to be beneficial, or they specifically need to be mentioned because of their popularity and/or substantial promotion. These include the supplements that follow.

5-Hydroxytryptophan (5-HTP)

This essential amino acid metabolite is a precursor of both *serotonin* (an important brain neurotransmitter) and nicotinic acid.

Used For: Sleep disorders (improves the quality of sleep); fibromyalgia; anxiety; obesity (reduces carbohydrate cravings); depression; PMS; smoking cessation; ataxia (balance problems).

Side Effects: Nausea; diarrhea; anorexia; heartburn; belching; gas; headache; drowsiness; dizziness.

Drug Interrelationships: Using 5-HTP with conventional antidepressants (all types), phenothiazines, or benzodiazepines (Xanax, Valium) may cause increased side effects. Caution is advised. Should not be used in conjunction with carbidopa.

Disease Cautions: Can cause seizures in patients with Down's syndrome.

Dosage: For sleep, 100mg to 300mg 45 minutes before sleep; for depression, 300mg daily; for PMS, 600mg per day.

Caution: Do not confuse with tryptophan, which is not as effective as 5-hydroxytryptophan.

Alpha Hydroxy Acids (Malic Acid, Lactic Acid, Glycolic Acid, Tartaric Acid)

These are a group of natural fruit acids, commonly used in cosmetic products because of their skin-enhancing effects.

Used For: Light-damaged or dry skin (topical); acne (topical); fibromyalgia (oral, when used with magnesium); oral chelation (for atherosclerosis).

Side Effects: Mild GI disturbances (oral); increased sun sensitivity (topical).

Drug Interrelationships: None known.

Disease Cautions: None known.

Dosage: Oral, 800mg to 1,200mg malic acid daily with oral magnesium (fibromyalgia); malic acid, 1,200mg daily for chelation; topical, 5 percent to 12 percent concentration as lactic acid, tartaric acid, glycolic acid, or gluconolactone.

Alpha Lipoic Acid

This is a powerful antioxidant involved in carbohydrate metabolism and energy production. It has been used in Germany for more than 25 years.

Used For: Diabetic neuropathy (intravenous only) (orally, it improves nerve conduction but not symptoms); diabetes (oral and IV).

Side Effects: Skin rash; *paresthesias* (numbness, tingling).

Drug Interrelationships: None known.

Disease Cautions: Can decrease blood sugar levels in diabetics.

Dosage: 600mg three times a day.

Beta Glucans

Derived from *mucopolysaccharides* (a specific type of carbohydrate), beta glucans are primary components in cell walls of bacteria, fungi, yeasts, algae, and plants such as barley and oats. They work by preventing bacteria and viruses from attaching to binding sites; they also grab and bind harmful fats and other potentially harmful molecules in the GI tract.

Used For: Lowering cholesterol; HIV infection (intravenous); cancer (intravenous and oral); autoimmune diseases (such as lupus, rheumatoid arthritis).

Side Effects: Orally, none; intravenously, chills and fever.

Drug Interrelationships: None known.

Disease Cautions: Intravenous, can develop pustules and crusts on the palms and soles.

Dosage: For cholesterol, 7.5g twice daily; for other conditions, 500mg daily.

Bovine Cartilage: see *Glycosaminoglycans (GAGs)*

Caprylic Acid

This supplement is a fatty acid extracted from coconut or palm oil, which is known to have antifungal properties.

Used For: Yeast infections and yeast overgrowth syndrome (bloating, gas, diarrhea, fatigue, headache, depression with repeated yeast infection).

Side Effects: Mild stomach upset, headaches. Larger doses can cause yeast "die-off" symptoms (flu-like sensation).

Drug Interrelationships: None known.

Disease Cautions: Should not be used in inflammatory bowel conditions (ulcerative colitis, Crohn's disease).

Dosage: Start with 500mg one to two times per day and gradually increase to 1,000mg to 2,000mg three times a day. A three- to four-month course is necessary.

NOTE: It is thought by many practitioners that fungus is to blame for many chronic diseases, including Alzheimer's, heart disease, brain disorders, arthritis, skin rashes, allergies, obesity, asthma, intestinal disorders, and so on. However, this has never been documented by research, and there may be many other underlying causes of these diseases.

Chondroitin: see *Glycosaminoglycans (GAGs)*

Coenzyme Q10 (CoQ10)

CoQ10 was first discovered in 1957 and is used extensively in Japan, Europe, and Russia. It is derived from beets and sugar cane. It is a naturally occurring compound that is essential for cellular energy production and is an antioxidant that stabilizes cell membranes. It is found in high concentration in the heart, liver, and kidneys.

Used For: Congestive heart failure (NYHA type II); heart surgery; angina; blood pressure; heart protection from chemotherapy (Adriamycin); AIDS; diabetes; muscular dystrophy; periodontal disease; Huntington's disease (preventive delay); advanced breast cancer (20 percent of women, with other antioxidants); chronic fatigue; increased exercise tolerance; preventing migraine headaches.

Side Effects: Appetite loss; gastritis; nausea; diarrhea.

Drug Interrelationships: CoQ10 can reduce the effects of Coumadin. Some cholesterol-lowering "statins" (Lipitor, Mevacor, Zocor, Pravachol, Lescol), beta-blockers (such as atenolol, metoprolol, nadolol), and oral antidiabetic drugs (Tolinase, Micronase) can reduce blood levels of CoQ10. CoQ10 improves the benefits of L-carnitine.

Disease Cautions: CoQ10 can decrease insulin requirements in diabetics (lowers blood sugar). CoQ10 levels can increase in patients with liver or bile duct disease. CoQ10 can also lower blood pressure in patients with essential hypertension.

Lab Test Interference: Large doses can increase levels of serum aminotransferase, a liver enzyme.

Dosage: For heart failure or chemotherapy with Adriamycin, 50mg twice daily; for angina, 50mg three times a day; for hypertension, 250mg per day; for AIDS, 300mg per day; for muscular dystrophy, 50mg twice per day; for diabetes, 150mg per day; for general heart disease,

150mg to 300mg per day. For doses greater than 100mg, you should divide the doses during the day to minimize side effects.

Creatine

This supplement is widely used in professional athletics and is allowed by all athletic associations.

Used For: Enhancing exercise performance (repeated maximal bursts, not single event); congestive heart failure (increase strength, endurance); muscular dystrophies (increase strength and daily life activity); brain injury.

Side Effects: Gastrointestinal disturbances and muscle cramping.

Drug Interrelationships: None known.

Disease Cautions: Creatine should not be used in patients with kidney disease.

Dosage: For exercise performance, 20g per day for 5 days, followed by 2g to 3g per day; for heart failure, 20g per day; for muscular dystrophy, 10g per day for adults and 5g per day for children. Creatine effects are enhanced when used with a carbohydrate solution.

Caution: Water intake should be 64 ounces per day when taking creatine.

Digestive Enzymes

Enzymes are proteins that are essential for every chemical reaction that takes place in your body. Enzymes are made within our bodies, but we need to replenish them. Most of the enzymes from outside our bodies come from raw foods, but, unfortunately, most of the food we eat is processed or cooked, which destroys enzymes.

Used For: Gastroesophageal reflux disorder (GERD); gastritis, ulcers; food allergies; hiatal hernia.

Side Effects: None known.

Drug Interrelationships: Helps digest most conventional drugs and herbs.

Disease Cautions: None known.

Dosage: Take a vegetarian-based enzyme supplement containing protease, papain, amylase, lipase, bromelain, cellulase, and lactase. Take one to two tablets with each meal you eat.

Emu Oil

This oil is produced by adult emus, and is stored in a large fat pad on the animal's back. It is an essential fatty acid which can help other substances be absorbed into joint and connective tissues of the body because it penetrates skin easily. It also has local anti-inflammatory effects.

Used For: Pain, acute inflammation; cholesterol (oral); bruising (topical); insect bites; skin rejuvenation.

Side Effects: Occasional GI symptoms (oral).

Drug Interrelationships: None known.

Disease Cautions: None known.

Dosage: Oral, 7 percent Emu oil with 10 percent glycolic acid. Other combinations use aloe vera with other ingredients (such as MSM or glucosamine). Topically, apply liberally every one to two hours until relief, then as needed.

Flavonoids

These are powerful antioxidants that are found in grapes, wine, grape juice, pine bark, and green tea, as well as many other fruits and vegetables. There are many different forms and combinations of flavonoids, including bilberry, rutin, hesperidin, diosmin, quercetin, and hydroxyethylrutosides (HER).

Used For (All): Hemorrhoids; heart disease.

Hesperidin: Hot flashes.

HER: Chronic venous insufficiency, varicose veins; diabetic retinopathy; lymphedema.

Rutin, Quercetin, Bilberry: see separate summaries

Side Effects: Abdominal pain; diarrhea; gastritis; headache; dizziness; itching.

Drug Interrelationships: None known.

Disease Cautions: None known.

Dosage: Hesperidin, 150mg daily. HER, 1,000mg to 3,000mg per day. A combination of diosmin (1,350mg) and hesperidin (100mg) twice daily for four days, followed by diosmin (900mg) and hesperidin (100mg) twice daily, has been used for internal hemorrhoids.

Gamma-Oryzanol

This compound is derived from rice bran oil but is also found in wheat bran. It is a prescription drug in Japan.

Used For: High cholesterol and triglycerides; hot flashes.

Side Effects: None known.

Drug Interrelationships: None known.

Disease Cautions: None known.

Lab Test Interference: Can decrease serum TSH levels (thyroid stimulating hormone).

Dosage: 300mg daily.

Glucosamine: see *Glycosaminoglycans (GAGs)*

Glutathione (GSH)

Glutathione is one of the most widespread antioxidants in the body and is essential for numerous bodily processes, including DNA synthesis and repair, immune system function, and enzyme reactions. It is actually a tri-peptide formed from three amino acids, glutamine, cysteine, and glycine. N-acetyl cysteine (see below) is a precursor of glutathione.

Used For: Kidney damage from chemotherapy using cisplatin (intramuscular); influenza preventative; AIDS, cataracts; kidney and liver disorders; eczema.

Side Effects: None known.

Drug Interrelationships: Acetaminophen (Tylenol) and alcohol can deplete glutathione.

Disease Cautions: None known.

Dosage: 250mg daily, although oral forms may not be absorbed. Intramuscularly, 600mg on days two to five of chemotherapy.

Glycosaminoglycans (GAGs)

GAGs are components that are essential to maintaining the structure and health of arteries and other blood vessels. Most GAGs are also naturally present in the human aorta (so-called aortic GAGs). GAGs include chondroitin sulfate, glucosamine sulfate, bovine cartilage, and shark cartilage. Hyaluronic acid is a GAG used as an injection by conventional medicine for osteoarthritis of the knee.

Aortic GAGs (Mesoglycans)

Used For: Hemorrhoids; varicose veins; heart disease; stroke; coronary artery bypass; venous insufficiency; leg ulcers; lower triglycerides.

Side Effects: Mild GI symptoms.

Drug Interrelationships: None known.
Disease Cautions: None known.
Dosage: 100mg per day.

Bovine Cartilage

Used For: Anal itching; poison oak, poison ivy; acne; psoriasis; anal fissures; hemorrhoids; cancer; arthritis (subcutaneous injection).
Side Effects: Diarrhea; nausea; scrotal edema.
Drug Interrelationships: None known.
Disease Cautions: None known.
Dosage: For cancer, 3g three times per day. Topically, 5 percent cream applied two to four times per day. Rectally, 2.2g of a 2 percent suppository applied with dioctyl sodium sulfosuccinate.

Chondroitin Sulfate

Used For: Osteoarthritis (combined with NSAIDs); cataract extraction or lens implantation (with hyaluronic acid); dry eyes (ophthalmic preparation); lower risk of heart attack in patients with unstable angina or previous heart attack.
Side Effects: GI disturbances; eyelid edema; leg swelling; hair loss; palpitations; allergic reactions.
Drug Interrelationships: None known.
Disease Cautions: None known.
Dosage: 200mg to 400mg three times daily or single dose of 1,200mg. It should be used as adjunct only (commonly used with glucosamine and/or MSM). It can take two to four months before effects are noted.
Caution: A recent analysis revealed that only 5 out of 32 chondroitin products lived up to label claims. In fact, nearly half contained 10 percent or less of what the label specified, and the majority fell below the 90 percent acceptable limit set by industry standards. It was not just the cheaper brands that contained less ingredients; the same was true for exceedingly expensive ones.

Glucosamine Sulfate

Used For: Osteoarthritis of joints; spine arthritis; TMJ arthritis.
Side Effects: Mild GI disturbances; occasional drowsiness; skin reactions; headache.
Drug Interrelationships: None known.
Disease Cautions: Some glucosamine is derived from shellfish and should be used with caution in people with shellfish allergies (no cases yet substantiated). May interfere with blood sugar levels in diabetics.
Lab Test Interference: Glucosamine may increase insulin levels.
Dosage: 500mg three times a day. Unlike chondroitin, glucosamine products are closer to label claims. Most of 14 products tested contained at least 80 percent of what the label claimed, although 2 fell far short. However, 5 brands actually exceeded label claims, with the content of 1 as high as 115 percent!

Shark Cartilage

Although shark cartilage is an immune regulator, has *antiangiogenesis* ingredients (prevents new blood vessel production in cancer), and has been promoted for cancer and arthritis, no studies have supported these claims. Although claims have also been made that sharks do not get cancer, kidney, cartilage, and lymph tumors have been identified in sharks.

Used For: Pain and inflammation (topical).

Side Effects: GI symptoms; bad taste in mouth; fatigue; dizziness; decreased motor strength or sensation; can mimic signs of acute hepatitis (including jaundice, fever, abdominal pain and increased liver enzymes).

Drug Interrelationships: None known.

Disease Cautions: Can cause high calcium levels. Avoid using in parathyroid disease, and use caution if taking supplemental calcium.

Lab Test Interference: Shark cartilage can increase liver enzymes.

Dosage: No typical dose has been determined; varies from 500mg to 5,000mg a day.

HER (Hydroxyethylrutosides): see *Flavonoids*

Hesperidin: see *Flavonoids*

Huperzine-A

This substance is a chemical that is purified from Chinese club moss, an expensive and rare Chinese herb. It is known to increase brain levels of an important neurotransmitter, acetylcholine.

Used For: Alzheimer's; multi-infarct dementia; myasthenia gravis (subcutaneous injection); and senile dementia.

Side Effects: Decreased heart rate; nausea; blurred vision; sweating; decreased appetite; tremors; hyperactivity.

Drug Interrelationships: None known.

Disease Cautions: Because Huperzine-A can decrease heart rate, it should be used cautiously if you have a heart condition with slow heart rate.

Dosage: Alzheimer's, 50mcg to 200mcg twice daily; for senile dementia, 30mcg to 40mcg twice daily.

L-Arginine

This amino acid is necessary for protein synthesis and is found naturally in red meat, poultry, fish, and dairy products. It stimulates the release of several hormones, including growth hormone, *prolactin* (stimulates breast milk production) and insulin. It also increases the body's production of nitric oxide, which is a *vasodilator* (opens arteries).

Used For: Congestive heart failure; chronic angina; erectile dysfunction; migraine headache; interstitial cystitis; intermittent claudication (intravenous); nitrate intolerance; hypertension.

Side Effects: Abdominal pain; bloating; diarrhea; allergic reaction causing airway inflammation or rash.

Drug Interrelationships: Estrogens can increase the L-arginine-induced elevation of growth hormone, and progestins can decrease this response.

Lab Test Interference: Can cause elevations of kidney tests, including BUN and creatinine.

Disease Cautions: Should be used cautiously if you have asthma because of possible allergic reaction. May worsen sickle cell anemia.

Dosage: For angina, 3g to 6g three times daily; for congestive heart failure 2g to 5g three times daily; for organic erectile dysfunction, 4g to 5g per day; for interstitial cystitis, 500mg daily.

L-Carnitine

Carnitine is a vitamin-like compound that stimulates the breakdown of fats by the *mitochondria*, the parts of the cell that produce energy. Ninety-eight percent of the body's carnitine is found in heart and skeletal muscle.

Used For: Hemodialysis; HIV (intravenous, before treatment with antiretrovirals); hyperthyroidism; angina (improve exercise tolerance); congestive heart failure; heart attack, peripheral vascular disease; improving exercise performance.

Side Effects: Gastrointestinal symptoms; body odor; seizures.

Drug Interrelationships: Valproic acid (Depakene) decreases L-carnitine levels, requiring supplementation. L-carnitine improves the benefits of Coenzyme Q10.

Disease Cautions: Avoid in chronic liver disease, and with seizure disorders. Hemodialysis (kidney failure) depletes L-carnitine, so it must be supplemented.

Lab Test Interference: Can increase CD4 and CD8 counts in AIDS patients not treated with antiretrovirals, increase cholesterol, and decrease triglyceride levels when given intravenously.

Dosage: For angina or heart failure, 300mg to 500mg three times daily; after heart attacks, 2g to 6g per day.

Caution: Avoid D-carnitine and DL-carnitine, which are often found in OTC preparations and dietary supplements and are not effective.

Lecithin: see *Phosphatidylcholine*

Lycopene

Lycopene is the pigment that gives fruits and vegetables such as tomatoes their red color. It is a natural carotenoid and antioxidant, but it is absorbed only after heat processing and/or using with oil (tomato paste, ketchup, juice, pizza, etc.).

Used For: Prevention of prostate cancer; lung cancer; high blood pressure; decrease risk of heart attack; exercise-induced asthma.

Side Effects: None known.

Drug Interrelationships: None known.

Disease Cautions: None known.

Lab Test Interference: Reduces plasma PSA levels in prostate cancer.

Dosage: 5mg to 10mg, one to two times per day.

Lysine

Lysine is required for the synthesis of connective tissue and is shown to inhibit the growth of the *herpes simplex* virus.

Used For: Canker sores (*herpes simplex labialis*).

Side Effects: GI symptoms if taking more than 10g per day.

Drug Interrelationships: Lysine can increase the absorption of calcium and decrease its excretion.

Disease Cautions: Rare report of kidney failure (one case).

Dosage: 1,000mg three times daily. For recurrent canker sores, 1,000mg three times daily for six months, or 1,000mg daily for one year.

Malic Acid: see *Alpha Hydroxy Acids*

Methylsulfonylmethane (MSM)

MSM is a source of natural sulphurs for several amino acids, and it has anti-inflammatory properties. It occurs naturally in fruits, vegetables, grains, and human and cattle adrenal glands.

Used For: Osteoarthritis (in combination with other products).
Side Effects: GI disturbances, headache.
Drug Interrelationships: None known.
Disease Cautions: None known.
Dosage: 100mg to 3,000mg daily. Also used topically.

Mucopolysaccharides: see *Beta Glucans*

N-Acetylcysteine (NAC)

NAC is a free-radical scavenger and is a precursor of glutathione.

Used For: Acetaminophen (Tylenol) poisoning (intravenous); inhalation and chest injuries; acute and chronic lung conditions involving mucous production; cystic fibrosis; chronic bronchitis flare-ups; myoclonus epilepsy; unstable angina pectoris (in combination with nitroglycerin); reducing nitroglycerin tolerance; influenza; decreasing homocysteine levels; reducing dental plaque.
Side Effects: Can cause severe headaches with nitroglycerin; GI symptoms; hives; chills and fever; runny nose; asthmatic symptoms; fever blisters.
Drug Interrelationships: Nitroglycerin (see above); can decrease effectiveness of carbamazepine (Tegretol).
Disease Cautions: May cause increased symptoms in asthmatics when inhaled.
Lab Test Interference: Can interfere with blood chloride levels, blood lithium levels, urine ketones, and can elevate liver enzymes.
Dosage: Unstable angina, 600mg three times daily with nitroglycerin; for bronchitis prevention, 400mg to 600mg daily; for myoclonus epilepsy, 4g to 6g daily. For influenza, 600mg to 1,200mg daily.

NADH

NADH is made by the body and is essential for energy production. It requires nicotinamide (niacin) for its synthesis.

Used For: Parkinson's disease; chronic fatigue syndrome (CFS); Alzheimer's disease; cardiovascular disease.
Side Effects: Nausea; appetite loss.
Drug Interrelationships: None known.
Disease Cautions: None known.
Dosage: 5mg to 15mg daily.

Phosphatidylcholine (Lecithin)

This phospholipid is a major constituent of lecithin and is commonly used interchangeably with lecithin. Lecithin helps to detoxify the liver, regulate cell growth, and is part of healthy cell membranes for proper nutrient intake and toxin removal. It is both water and fat soluble, and it is found naturally in soybeans and egg yolks.

Used For: Hepatitis C (used with interferon); bipolar disorder; dermatitis and dry skin (topically).

Side Effects: GI disturbances; sweating.
Drug Interrelationships: None known.
Disease Cautions: None known.
Dosage: 15g to 25g daily.

Policosanol

This supplement is a mixture of fatty compounds derived from the outer wax of the sugar cane plant or wax of honey bees.

Used For: High cholesterol; intermittent claudication.

Side Effects: Headaches; skin redness; sleep loss; nose and gum bleeding; irritability; stomach upset.

Drug Interrelationships: Because policosanol has antiplatelet activity, it may increase bruising or bleeding if used with blood thinners.

Disease Cautions: None known.

Dosage: For cholesterol lowering, 5mg to10mg twice daily. For intermittent claudication, 10mg twice daily. Allow six to eight weeks for full effect.

Probiotics

Probiotics are colonies of beneficial microorganisms that live in the gastrointestinal tract, aiding in digestion, absorption of food, and the production of vitamins and enzymes. Unfortunately, because of many factors in our environment and aging process, beneficial bacteria are killed off, allowing overgrowth of nonbeneficial bacteria and yeast, and thus causing many gastrointestinal disturbances and other conditions. Probiotics are used to replace the killed beneficial bacteria and eradicate the harmful bacteria and yeast.

Used For: Gastroesophageal reflux disorder (GERD); ulcers; irritable bowel syndrome; inflammatory bowel disease; constipation; Candida (yeast) overgrowth; vaginal yeast infections; enhanced immunity; traveler's diarrhea; radiation sickness; allergies; rheumatoid arthritis.

Side Effects: Gas; stomach rumblings; cramping; flu-like sensation for three days to one week due to yeast die-off (avoid by decreasing dose).

Drug Interrelationships: None known.

Disease Cautions: None known.

Dosage: There are many types of beneficial bacteria used in probiotics. Look for a product that contains *L. acidophilus* and *bifidobacteria*. Other beneficial bacteria include *L salivarius*, *L. rhamnosus*, and *L. plantarum*. A good formulation will usually contain fructooligosaccharides (FOS) to promote growth. Start with ½ tablet or 1 tablet per day, then increase to the recommended dosage on the label if gas and cramping are not present.

Caution: Many probiotics have a significant die-off rate before they reach the store or your kitchen. You and the store should keep them refrigerated. Also, many of you may think that yogurt contains beneficial microorganisms that can take the place of probiotics. Yogurt products do contain beneficial microorganisms, but they are not the most important or potent. Also, many yogurt products are pasteurized after they are made, to increase shelf life, but this kills most of the good bacteria, thus destroying all the benefits. Don't rely on eating yogurt to recolonize your GI tract.

Quercetin

Also known as citrus bioflavonoid, quercetin has antioxidant and anti-inflammatory characteristics, as well as inhibitory effects on cell division in some cancers. It is abundant in green tea, onions, red wine, apples, berries, and some vegetables. In addition, it can be found in several herbs, including St. John's wort and gingko.

Used For: Cancer prevention; cancer treatment (adjunct to hyperthermia); nonbacterial prostatitis.

Side Effects: Tingling; headaches.

Drug Interrelationships: Possible interference with quinolone antibiotics (Floxin, Cipro).

Disease cautions: None known.

Dosage: 400mg to 500mg, two to three times per day.

Rutin

A citrus bioflavonoid, rutin is an antioxidant found in many natural plants (including St. John's wort, gingko, hawthorn, and eucalyptus), citrus fruits (apples), and vegetables.

Used For: Osteoarthritis (with trypsin and bromelain); glaucoma; venous insufficiency.

Side Effects: Mild gastrointestinal symptoms; headache; rash; flushing.

Drug Interrelationships: None known.

Disease Cautions: None known.

Dosage: 500mg twice daily.

S-Adenosylmethionine (SAMe)

SAMe naturally occurs in almost all bodily tissues and plays an important role in many biochemical reactions, including the manufacture of cartilage. It is a combination of an amino acid (methionine) with ATP, the energy molecule of cells.

Used For: Osteoarthritis; depression (intravenous or intramuscular); depression (oral); fibromyalgia; intrahepatic cholestasis (intravenous); AIDS-related myelopathy (intravenous); liver transplantation; chronic liver disease.

Side Effects: GI disturbances; headache; anxiety in depressed patients.

Drug Interrelationships: May cause increased side effects when used with other antidepressants or St. John's wort, but also may increase the onset of benefits of these drugs. SAMe can prevent liver dysfunction caused by drugs, including alcohol, acetaminophen, estrogens, MAO inhibitors (Nardil, Parnate), phenytoin, and steroids.

Disease Cautions: In bipolar disorders, can cause mania or hypomania.

Dosage: For depression, 400mg per day (mild depression) to 1,600mg per day (moderate to severe depression); for osteoarthritis, 400mg three times a day; for liver disease, 1,200mg to 1,600mg per day. For fibromyalgia, 800mg to 1,600mg per day. Benefits may take 30 days to occur. SAMe comes in several forms, the most bioavailable of which is the butanedisulfonate.

Shark Cartilage: see *Glycosaminoglycans (GAGs)*

St. John's Wort

Known since the early first century, St. John's wort was so named because it produces golden yellow flowers that reach peak bloom on the birthday of John the Baptist (June 24). It was used throughout the middle ages but was nearly forgotten in the late nineteenth century. It has now become one of the widest used and most popular herbs in the world.

Used For: Taken orally for mild to moderate depression; anorexia; fibromyalgia; multiple sclerosis. Applied topically for bruises, abrasions, muscle soreness, first-degree burns (such as sunburn), and wound healing.

Side Effects: Restlessness; agitation; insomnia (can take in morning); vivid dreams; GI discomfort; light sensitivity in fair-skinned individuals; intermenstrual bleeding; photodermatitis (high doses).

Drug Interrelationships: Should not be used concurrently with (at the same time as) other antidepressants, narcotics, or barbiturates because of potentiating side effects. Can reduce the levels of digoxin (heart failure), cyclosporin (organ transplant), and protease inhibitors (AIDS), and may interfere with blood levels of several other drugs, including Prozac, Prilosec, Allegra, antifungals, and chemotherapy agents. (St. John's wort interferes with a specific process in the liver that breaks down many of these pharmaceutically made drugs. There may be other drugs besides the above that are affected, but studies have not yet determined which ones, although possibilities include antiepileptics, oral contraceptives, calcium channel blockers, and macrolide antibiotics.) Can cause bleeding irregularities in women taking oral contraceptives.

Disease Cautions: Should not be used in unipolar depression or bipolar disorders; might inhibit fertility.

Dosage: 300mg three times daily, containing 0.3 percent hypericin content or 0.2mg to 1mg of total hypericin daily. If discontinuing, withdrawal symptoms can occur, so slowly decrease over at least two weeks' time.

OTHER ALTERNATIVE SUPPLEMENTS

Much like alternative methods, numerous other products are promoted by alternative practitioners and manufacturers. I have tried to discuss those that are the most commonly utilized, but there are literally thousands of other products, most of which have never been properly tested or researched, and thus I cannot make any recommendations about them at this time. Some of these, and their claims, include the following:

- Pyruvate: Greater endurance for athletes.
- IP6: Immune system enhancer, cancer preventative.
- Phosphatidylserine: Improved brain function.
- Pregnenolone: Another hormone precursor, sometimes used in place of DHEA.
- Branched chain amino acids: Lean muscle mass in athletes.
- Phenylalanine: Improved mental acuity and well-being.
- Glutamine: Preserves muscle mass, decreases addiction to chocolate.
- Taurine: Heart disease.
- Fructooligosaccharides: Helps intestinal flora.
- Noni Juice: Arthritis, varicose veins, blood pressure.

VITAMINS (ANTIOXIDANT)

Vitamins are chemical compounds necessary for growth, health, metabolism, and well-being. Some vitamins are essential parts of enzymes, the chemical molecules that facilitate the completion of chemical reactions, whereas other vitamins are essential parts of hormones. The body, however, does not manufacture vitamins; they must be supplied by outside sources—that is, food. Unfortunately, vitamins may be diluted or eliminated in the processing of food, and if you eat fast food or junk food, or otherwise have a poor diet, you can develop vitamin deficiencies, which in turn can result in a plethora of diseases and medical problems. Of the two types of vitamins, *fat-soluble* can be stored in the body's fat and used as needed (vitamins A, D, E, and K). However, too much of this type can build up and become toxic. The rest are *water-soluble* vitamins, which cannot be stored in the body and must continually be supplied through external sources.

One very important group of vitamins contains antioxidants, which are important for preventing tissue damage. Normal bodily processes involve oxidative metabolism, which produces what are called *reactive molecules* (*free radicals*). These by-products can cause extensive damage to DNA, protein, lipids, carbohydrates, and other body cells. Many free radicals are produced from the environment, such as from cigarette smoke, radon, auto exhaust, x-rays, ultraviolet light, and pesticides. In addition, cancer-causing substances (called *mutagens* and *carcinogens*) are introduced into food during cooking and storage.

Each cell of the body receives 10^{24} oxidative hits per day, but, fortunately, your body's repair enzymes are able to negate about 99 percent of those. It is the other 1 percent that is thought to cause permanent damage and induce various diseases, as well as aging. Antioxidant supplements are promoted to help nullify these harmful effects and thus prevent those diseases and slow the aging process. Four vitamins have antioxidant capabilities, vitamins E, C, A, and beta-carotene, each of which can be supplemented to help various diseased states and/or can be used as a preventive measure.

Vitamins vary greatly in quality, absorbability, and effectiveness. As with minerals, the best and most active source of vitamins is food. If you must supplement vitamins, avoid synthetically made, which are derived from either natural or synthetic sources and undergo a process of conversion. Synthetic vitamins are only 50 percent as effective as natural vitamins at best and may be harmful, especially when they're made from unhealthy sources, such as the following:

- Vitamin B_{12} is often made from activated sewage sludge and then stabilized with cyanide.
- Vitamin D is often made from irradiated oil.
- Vitamin E may be produced as a by-product in film processing.
- Calcium is often made from ground-up bones or oyster shells, or is mined from the earth.

The healthiest source of vitamins is called *co-natural*, meaning they are derived from vegetable and animal sources and do not undergo conversion or alteration. For best results, they should be taken with minerals and other nutrients.

General Recommendations for Vitamins

If you supplement your diet with vitamins, here are some recommendations to obtain the most benefits from them:

- Taking vitamins in split dosages during the day is more beneficial than taking them once per day.
- Pick a vitamin for which the label states that it has passed the 45-minute dissolution test, which indicates it will be broken down and absorbed more efficiently.
- Take vitamins with or after a meal to optimize absorption.

Vitamin A

Vitamin A can be derived from beta-carotene (see next entry), although it is commonly contained in multivitamins along with beta-carotene. Most adults have a one-year supply of vitamin A in the liver and do not require supplementation.

Used For: Vitamin A deficiency; malnourishment; acne (topical); breast cancer prevention (diet); cataract prevention (diet); lung cancer.

Side Effects: More than 15,000 IU daily can cause fatigue, malaise, abdominal discomfort and disturbances, irritability, dizziness, headache, anorexia, and psychiatric changes. Taking too much vitamin A (more than 3,000mcg daily, equivalent to 100,000 IU) can cause additional side effects too numerous to relate here, but especially can cause liver toxicity and osteoporosis.

Drug Interrelationships: If used with minocycline (Minocin), it can increase the risk of benign intracranial (brain) hypertension. Drugs that can decrease absorption of vitamin A include neomycin, cholestyramine (Questran), colestipol (Colestid), mineral oil, and orlistat (Xenical).

Disease Cautions: Vitamin A absorption is decreased in liver or pancreatic disease.

Lab Test Interference: Vitamin A may cause false elevations in bilirubin tests and in some cholesterol tests.

Beta-Carotene

Beta-carotene breaks down into vitamin A (retinol) inside the body, but it has none of the side effects of vitamin A. Therefore, it is the preferred form and has several other benefits not observed with vitamin A.

Used For: Photosensitivity in porphyria; oral leukoplakia (white spots in the mouth); exercise-induced asthma; sunscreen; prostate carcinoma prevention; breast cancer prevention (diet); macular degeneration (diet); cataracts; cervical dysplasia; slows progression of osteoarthritis.

Not Beneficial For: Heart disease prevention or treatment.

Side Effects: Can cause yellow or orange skin pigmentation in high doses and prolonged use.

Drug Interrelationships: Drugs that reduce absorption of beta-carotene include Questran, Colestid, mineral oil, Xenical (orlistat), Prevacid, Prilosec, and Aciphex.

Disease Cautions: Should not be taken if you smoke because of increased risk of lung cancer. May interfere with the benefits of angioplasty (with vitamins E and C).

Dosage: 30mg to 300mg daily. (15,000 IU to 25,000 IU).

Vitamin C (Ascorbic Acid)

This is the most commonly consumed nutrient vitamin, and it is more easily obtained in the diet, so the need for supplementation is less. Vitamin C is essential for tissue repair, immune function, and a variety of metabolic processes. It is present in fresh fruits and vegetables, especially citrus fruits.

Used For: Prevention of scurvy (vitamin C deficiency); improving iron absorption; gall bladder disease prevention, psychological stress; prevention of cancer risk (food sources); hypertension; reflex sympathetic dystrophy after wrist fractures; common cold (high doses); osteoarthritis (diet); exercise-induced asthma; photoaged facial skin (topical); stroke prevention (eating fruits, not vegetables or supplements); heart disease prevention (diet); iron deficiency anemia (see "Drug Interrelationships" below); cataract prevention (long term use); glaucoma; lowering blood lead levels; prostate and breast cancer (with vitamin K); hives; nausea of pregnancy (with vitamin K).

Side Effects: In high doses (more than 1,000mg), GI disturbances (especially diarrhea); fatigue; kidney stones; deep vein thrombosis; and thickening of the carotid artery.

Drug Interrelationships: Should not take at same time with antacids containing aluminum (take two hours before or four hours after) because absorption will be decreased. It can increase iron absorption, and so it is helpful in anemia. Drugs that can increase excretion of vitamin C, leading to lower levels, include aspirin, barbiturates, estrogen, oral contraceptives, nicotine, and tetracyclines. Large amounts of vitamin C can significantly lower B_{12} levels.

Disease Cautions: Vitamin C requirements are increased in pregnancy, lactation, stress, fever, hyperthyroidism, infection, trauma, burns, smoking, and cold exposure, and it may need to be supplemented in these conditions. Can lower blood sugar in diabetes, and can increase kidney stones. It should not be used in congenital (hereditary) anemias. Should not be used in gout (can increase uric acid levels). Vitamin C can interfere with the benefits of angioplasty (with vitamin E and beta-carotene).

Lab Test Interference: Vitamin C can interfere with the interpretation of several lab tests, including the following:

- Occult blood in stool: Used to screen for small cancers of the colon or rectum. Tests may be read falsely as normal.
- Uric Acid: Used to diagnose gout. May be falsely elevated, thus requiring unneeded medications.
- Plasma Glucose (diabetes): May be falsely elevated.
- Aspartate aminotransferase (AST, SGOT), AAT, Creatinine (liver and kidney function tests): May be falsely elevated.
- Bilirubin, LDH (liver enzymes): May be erroneously decreased, thus possibly decreasing detection of some liver diseases.

Dosage: 100mg to 1,000mg per day, depending on your condition (see introduction above) and dietary intake. Unless nutrition is very poor, most people do not need to supplement more than 500mg per day. Specific conditions (daily dose): alcoholism, cataracts, gallstones, 1,000mg to 2,000mg; glaucoma, 2,000mg; hypertension, 1,000mg; osteoarthritis, 1,000mg. Common cold, 1g to 3g daily.

Vitamin E

Vitamin E is a fat-soluble vitamin that is not easily obtained in the normal diet (at most, 60 IU daily), but that maintains body stores for four years before becoming deficient. Unlike most vitamins, it is not involved in any particular metabolic process, and it works by preventing the formation of free radicals.

Used For: Alzheimer's disease; tardive dyskinesia; Huntington's chorea; rheumatoid arthritis; sperm function and fertilization rate; kidney and eye function in type I diabetes mellitus; nitrate tolerance in angina; PMS; prevention of prostate cancer; radiation-induced fibrosis; immune function in elderly; bleeding complications in premature infants; acne; asthma; restless legs syndrome; ulcers; breast pain.

Side Effects: May have increased bleeding problems with high doses.

Drug Interrelationships: May potentiate blood thinners. It has beneficial effects with nitrates for decreasing symptoms of angina (many patients become resistant to the benefits of nitrates for reducing heart pain, and vitamin E can negate this resistance). Drugs that decrease absorption and blood levels of vitamin E include Questran, Colestid, Lopid, mineral oil, ethanol, and Xenical (orlistat). Vitamin E should be supplemented if taking these drugs.

Disease Cautions: May worsen bleeding problems in patients with vitamin K deficiency. May interfere with benefits of angioplasty (with vitamin C and beta-carotene).

Dosage: Varies from 100 IU to 3,000 IU per day, depending on the disease. Some of the more common uses with daily dosages include: male fertility (600 IU to 800 IU); Alzheimer's (400 IU to 800 IU); Huntington's chorea (3,000 IU); rheumatoid arthritis (600 IU twice daily); diabetic neuropathy (800 IU to 1,200 IU); diabetic eye disease (1,800 IU); enhancing immune function in elderly (400 IU to 800 IU); nitrate intolerance (200 IU three times daily); PMS (400 IU).

The natural form, notated as d-alpha tocopherol, is the preferred form over the synthetic form, notated as dl-tocopherol. If you do not have any of the above diseases, your intake should not exceed 1,100 IU.

Vitamins E and C in Combination

In the body, when vitamin E scavenges oxidants, it becomes a free radical itself. However, vitamin C negates this conversion, thus potentiating vitamin E's benefits. Several studies have used a combination of vitamin E with vitamin C, finding that, together, these two antioxidant vitamins are beneficial in conditions that neither vitamin alone can help as effectively.

Used For: Uveitis; pre-eclampsia; sunburn preventative; bypass surgery; colorectal cancer prevention (includes vitamin A); vascular and mixed dementia; high-risk surgical patients (lower risk of complications); slows progression of atherosclerosis.

VITAMINS (NON-ANTIOXIDANT)

Other vitamins do not have antioxidant effects but are very important for other enzymatic processes. Again, the best way to obtain these vitamins is through eating balanced meals, especially fruits and vegetables, although in some conditions, supplementation is recommended.

Folate (Folic Acid)

This is one vitamin in which the synthetic form (folic acid) is actually better absorbed than the folate found in foods. In fact, the folate in foods is almost 50 percent less available for absorption than the supplement or foods containing folic acid. Most cereals and many other food products are now fortified with folic acid, and so they are excellent sources of this important vitamin.

Used For: Pregnant women (reduces birth defects); methotrexate (chemotherapy) toxicity in treatment of rheumatoid arthritis; to decrease homocysteine levels (prevention of heart disease); methotrexate-induced GI disturbances in treatment of psoriasis; vitiligo; prevention of colon cancer; gingivitis in pregnancy; gingival hyperplasia from treatment using phenytoin; restless legs syndrome (large doses, prescription only); to decrease restenosis rate in angioplasty (with B_{12} and pyridoxine).

Side Effects: Large doses can cause altered sleep patterns; GI symptoms; irritability; confusion; impaired judgment; increased seizures; bitter taste; allergic skin reactions.

Drug Interrelationships: Zinc and vitamin B_{12} levels can be decreased by long-term use of folate. Vitamin B_{12} deficiency can therefore be masked by folate consumption, so B_{12} levels should be checked in elderly patients taking folate. Several drugs can decrease the absorption or increase excretion of folic acid, including antibiotics, carbamazepine (Tegretol), cycloserine (Seromycin), furosemide (Lasix), Glucophage, methotrexate, oral contraceptives, Mysoline, phenobarbital, aminosalicylic acid, Dilantin, Daraprim, Azulfidine, thiazide diuretics, trimethoprim, and triamterene.

Disease Cautions: Can mask pernicious anemia (caused by vitamin B_{12} deficiency); can exacerbate seizures and schizophrenia. May be deficient in inflammatory bowel diseases (Crohn's, ulcerative colitis) because of sulfasalazine use.

Dosage: 400mcg per day through supplementation or fortified foods.

Niacin and Niacinamide (Vitamin B_3)

This vitamin is essential for the metabolism of fats and is found in meats, beans, and dairy products.

Used For: *Hyperlipoproteinemia* (high cholesterol, triglycerides); heart attack (preventing a second attack); Type I diabetes (initial stages); Type II diabetes; cataract prevention; cholera; osteoarthritis.

Side Effects: Flushing; itching. Flushing can increase with concomitant use of transdermal nicotine patches, or alcohol.

Drug Interrelationships: Can increase the toxicity of carbamazepine (Tegretol) and increase the risk of myopathy (muscle inflammation and pain) from "statin" drugs (such as Lipitor, Mevacor, and so on). Questran or Colestid can decrease absorption of B_3.

Disease Cautions: Can worsen allergies; cause arrhythmias in high doses; interfere with blood sugar control in diabetes; worsen gall bladder disease; worsen ulcer disease; might precipitate gout. Should not be used with liver or kidney disease.

Lab Test Interference: Can increase blood sugar levels and can falsely increase liver enzyme tests.

Dosage: For osteoarthritis, 3g per day in divided doses (check liver enzymes after three months of use). For hyperlipidemia, 3g to 4g per day. Nonflushing products are available and preferred.

Pyridoxine (Vitamin B_6)

This vitamin is essential for the metabolism of amino acids and is important in the metabolism of carbohydrates, lipids, homocysteine, and nitrogen products.

Used For: Pregnancy-induced nausea and vomiting; PMS; heart disease (with folic acid); autism; asthma; carpal tunnel syndrome (after 3 months of use); migraines; kidney stone recurrence; ADHD; prevention of restenosis after angioplasty (with B_{12} and folic acid).

Side Effects: GI disturbances; headache; somnolence; allergic reactions; breast enlargement or soreness; light sensitivity. Long-term use of large amounts can lead to neuropathy (deterioration of peripheral nerves in the legs).

Drug Interrelationships: Interferes with metabolism of levodopa (Larodopa) for Parkinson's unless used with carbidopa. Decreases blood levels of Dilantin and phenobarbital (seizure drugs). Drugs that can lower pyridoxine levels include antibiotics, estrogens, oral contraceptives, theophylline, hydralazine, penicillamine, and INH.

Disease Cautions: None known.

Lab Test Interference: Can increase SGOT levels (liver enzyme) and decrease folic acid concentration.

Dosage: For pregnancy-induced nausea, 10mg to 25mg daily; for B_6 deficiency with oral contraceptives, 25mg to 30mg; for PMS, 50mg to 100mg daily; for asthma, 25mg to 50mg twice daily.

Riboflavin (Vitamin B_2)

This vitamin is essential for oxygen exchange in tissues and is part of most respiratory enzymes. It also increases cellular energy production.

Used For: Preventing migraine headaches; preventing cataracts.

Side Effects: In large doses, diarrhea and urinary frequency; yellow-orange discoloration of urine.

Drug Interrelationships: Probenecid (Benemid) decreases B_2 absorption. Drugs that decrease riboflavin levels include antibiotics, metoclopramide (Reglan), oral contraceptives, phenothiazines, and Probenecid (Benemid).

Disease Cautions: Riboflavin absorption is decreased in hepatitis and cirrhosis. Avoid dosages greater than 10mg if you have cataracts (increases light sensitivity).

Dosage: For migraines, 400mg per day, but it may take three months to be effective.

Thiamine (Vitamin B₁)

This vitamin is essential for metabolism of carbohydrates. It is present in many foods, including grains, nuts and meats.

Used For: Alcoholism; cirrhosis; GI diseases; diabetic neuropathy.

Side Effects: Dermatitis (rare).

Drug Interrelationships: Thiamine can increase the effects of neuromuscular blocking agents. Loop diuretics (Lasix) can deplete thiamine stores.

Disease Cautions: Thiamine is decreased in alcoholism, cirrhosis, and malabsorption syndromes and should be supplemented.

Lab Test Interference: Thiamine can cause false positive results of uric acid and urobilinogen blood levels, and can interfere with accurate determination of theophylline levels (in asthma).

Dosage: 5mg to 35mg per day in divided doses, 200mg to 300mg per day for severe deficiencies.

Vitamin B₁₂

This vitamin is essential for red blood cell production, nerve function, and cell reproduction and growth. It is also essential for the body's ability to use folate.

Used For: Pernicious anemia; deficiencies associated with pregnancy, cancers, liver or kidney disease; thyroid disease; heart disease prevention; Alzheimer's disease; asthma; hives; male infertility; bursitis (intramuscular); restless legs syndrome; prevention of restenosis after angioplasty (with pyridoxine and folic acid).

Side Effects: Diarrhea; itching.

Drug Interrelationships: Absorption of B_{12} can be decreased by aminoglycoside antibiotics, anticonvulsants, metformin (Glucophage), colchicine, Colestid, extended-release potassium preparations, and excessive alcohol intake. Stomach acid blockers (Tagamet, Zantac, Pepcid) can lead to decreased absorption during long-term use. Large amounts of vitamin C can destroy vitamin B_{12}. Nicotine, oral contraceptives, and proton pump inhibitors (Prilosec, Aciphex, Prevacid) may interfere with B_{12} absorption, but this has not been studied adequately.

Disease Cautions: Contraindicated in Lerber's disease (optic nerve atrophy). Infections, kidney failure, and folic acid or iron deficiency can impair B_{12} response. B_{12} may be deficient in Crohn's disease.

Dosage: Strict vegetarians should take 6mcg per day. Alzheimer's, 1,000mcg twice daily; asthma, 1,000mcg daily; male infertility, 1,000mcg to 2,000mcg daily; heart-disease prevention, 25mcg daily. If deficient, you can measure blood levels to monitor dosage needs, using 1mcg to 25mcg per day. There are both methylcobalamin and cyanocobalamin forms; the methyl form is more active and can be taken under the tongue.

Vitamin D

This vitamin is crucial for maintaining bone structure, and calcium is not as beneficial for building bones without vitamin D. Even in low-risk patients, 27 percent have moderate deficiencies, and 14 percent have severe deficiencies. If you live in a latitude with less sunlight, vitamin D should be screened and supplemented if too low because light activates this vitamin. It should also be screened in the elderly (especially women and during winter months), patients on anticonvulsants, those with kidney disease, and any who are homebound.

Used For: Osteopenia; osteoporosis; renal osteodystrophy; psoriasis (plaque type).

Side Effects: GI disturbances; loss of appetite; dry mouth; metallic taste; weakness; fatigue; sleepiness; headache; ringing in the ears; irritability; dizziness; muscle and bone pain.

Drug Interrelationships: Can increase the risk of cardiac arrhythmias in those taking digitalis. Drugs that can decrease vitamin D absorption include cholestyramine, Colestid, rifampin (INH), carbamazepine (Tegretol), phenytoin (Dilantin), phenobarbital, mineral oil, orlistat (Xenical), laxatives, and corticosteroids.

Disease Cautions: It is contraindicated in *hypercalcemia* (high blood calcium). Use with caution in renal disease, arteriosclerosis, heart disease, and sarcoidosis.

Dosage: (Daily): 200 IU (ages 19 to 51). 400 IU (ages 52 to 70). 600 IU (Over age 70), daily.

Vitamin K

This vitamin is essential for the production of blood coagulation (clotting) factors. It is found in many foods, including leafy green vegetables, cow's milk, meat, vegetable oils, tomatoes, and egg yolks.

Used For: Overdose of oral anticoagulants (blood thinners); bleeding problems caused by drugs or herbs; hip fractures in women; nausea of pregnancy; prostate and breast cancer (with vitamin C); liver cancer.

Side Effects: Occasional stomach irritation.

Drug Interrelationships: Antagonizes the effects of blood thinners (Coumadin, heparin, aspirin). Vitamin K levels can be decreased by cholestyramine (Questran), colestipol (Colestid), some oral antibiotics, mineral oil, and orlistat (Xenical).

Disease Cautions: Caution advised in patients with biliary fistulas or obstructive jaundice. Excessive intake can cause soft-tissue calcifications in hemodialysis patients.

Lab Test Interference: Vitamin K can also reduce urine calcium, blood erythrocytes, leukocytes, and platelets; hematocrit; and prothrombin time. Large amounts can increase serum bilirubin, urine hemoglobin, serum osteocalcin in post-menopausal women, porphyrins, urine protein, and urine urobilinogen.

Dosage: There is no typical dosage. It must be individualized and *medically supervised* because of its blood-thinning effects. For nausea of pregnancy, 5mg with 250mg vitamin C, twice daily, has been used.

Megavitamins

Megavitamins are large doses of vitamins that are primarily taken by cancer patients. It was once thought that megavitamins interfere with chemotherapy and radiation, but more recent research demonstrates that they may in fact protect normal cells from the effects of cancer treatment and increase the treatment's response rate. Furthermore, 40 percent of people who have cancer die of malnutrition rather than from their cancers, and megavitamins are thought to help prevent this poor outcome.

However, a few studies warn against using very high levels of such vitamins. For example, vitamin C has been found in higher concentrations in certain cancers (lymphoma), so it is hypothesized that further supplementation with vitamin C can interfere with chemotherapy treatment. At this time, whether or not this theory is true has not been proven. Another problem is that it is not known how high a dose is needed for the above effects. There have so far been no definitive studies done that either confirm the benefits of megavitamins nor determine the amounts necessary for those benefits.

If you have cancer, taking megavitamins will probably not be harmful and may be beneficial as long as you take well below the harmful limit. Again, however, remember that high doses of any vitamin can have potential side effects and toxicities. See the following table, "Recommended Formula for Megavitamins."

RECOMMENDED FORMULA FOR MEGAVITAMINS			
Ingredient	**Value**	**Ingredient**	**Value**
Vitamin A	Not needed	Calcium	300mg
Vitamin B_6	50mg	Chromium	200mcg
Vitamin B_{12}	800mcg	Copper	1.5mg
Thiamin (B_1)	100mg	Hesperidin	50mg
Riboflavin (B_2)	50mg	Magnesium	300mg
Niacin (B_3)	50mg	Manganese	15mg
Folic Acid (B_9)	800mcg	Molybdenum	50mcg
Vitamin C	1000mg	Potassium	90mg
Vitamin D	400 IU	Rutin	50mg
Vitamin E	400 IU	Selenium	200mcg
Vitamin K	50mcg	Vanadium	50mcg
Boron	2mg	Zinc	20mg

Multivitamins

The term *multivitamin* is a misnomer because most such products are a combination of both minerals and vitamins, and sometimes other substances. The average American woman does not reach the recommended daily allowance (RDA) for vitamin E, calcium, magnesium, iron, and zinc. Males are typically low in magnesium and zinc. It is much better to obtain these vitamins and minerals from food because you receive the extra benefits of fiber and other nutrients that are contained in food but not in multivitamins. Unfortunately, processing of the food we eat depletes much of the vitamins and minerals we need, which is why many authorities now recommend that all adults take a multivitamin. I especially recommend multivitamins in the following situations:

- Dieting, especially if less than 10 percent of calories come from fat. Supplement with A, D, and E.
- Food allergies and elimination diets.
- Lactose intolerance: Take calcium.

- Elderly: Take vitamins D, B$_6$, B$_{12}$, and calcium.
- Pregnancy: Take folic acid and iron.
- Smokers: Take vitamin C; avoid beta-carotene.
- Alcoholics: Take thiamine, B$_1$, B$_6$, B$_{12}$, C, D, and folic acid.
- Vegetarians: Take vitamins D, B$_{12}$, iron, zinc, and calcium.
- Those who rely on fast or processed food or skip meals.
- Surgery or injury **needs short-term supplementation, especially vitamins C and E and zinc.**

Treatment of disease can deplete nutrient stores, such as antibiotics altering intestinal absorption and vitamin metabolism. If supplementation is necessary, you should take a mix of minerals with vitamins because they work together synergistically. It is also better for your overall health, as well as much less expensive, to take vitamins and minerals together in one product rather than from many different sources, unless you require only specific ones. In addition, you should take multivitamins in divided doses; they are more effective when taken at different times. However, some powerful multivitamins can cause insomnia, so you may want to take the last dose in the late afternoon.

There is an incredible array of multivitamins in the marketplace and the amounts of vitamins and minerals they contain vary even more. You may think that you are receiving the amounts of vitamins necessary to prevent or reduce your medical conditions, yet you may not realize that you are actually taking minimal amounts that do not provide any benefit. To obtain high levels of vitamins through a multivitamin, you usually have to take three to six pills per day; if you are taking only one a day, you may not even be consuming the RDA (recommended daily allowance) percentage. (See Recommended Daily Allowance (RDA) and Dietary Reference Intake (DRI) of "Vitamins and Minerals").

Because every multivitamin product differs in its content and percentage of minerals and vitamins, you should always make sure that it at least contains the minerals that are essential: calcium, copper, iodine, magnesium, phosphorous, and zinc. Nonessential minerals include chromium, manganese, and molybdenum, but, unfortunately, most multivitamin products contain these anyway. Most importantly, *no* multivitamin contains enough calcium; the majority contain only 13 percent of the RDA, so you must take an additional calcium supplement.

Another problem you may encounter is with how a multivitamin is bound. Many of the binders used to manufacture multivitamins (and other vitamins as well) are not broken down efficiently in the stomach, and so you may not be absorbing all the nutrients. In general, the cheaper brands have the worse binders, although some expensive brands have the same problems. Other manufacturers promote liquid or powder vitamins, which certainly may be better absorbed than pills. However, once again, there is no quality control, so even these forms may not adequately deliver the amounts you think you are receiving. An unpleasant but good way of knowing whether your vitamins are absorbed is to inspect your stool. If they are not absorbed, you will see remnants or the entire pill still intact.

When you're looking for a good multivitamin, first make sure it does not contain any synthetics (it will say on the label whether it is synthetic or natural). The best overall daily vitamin/mineral supplement is either a "food-based" vitamin complex or a "food grown" supplement. These sources contain vitamins, minerals, enzymes, antioxidants, microproteins, complex carbohydrates, and other natural nutrients. Another alternative is to take a "superfood" combination, which contain nutrients such as chlorella, rice bran, nutritional yeast,

RECOMMENDED DAILY ALLOWANCE (RDA) AND DIETARY REFERENCE INTAKE (DRI) OF VITAMINS AND MINERALS					
Vitamin	**DRI**	**RDA**	**Mineral**	**DRI**	**RDA**
Vitamin A	3,000 IU	5,000 IU	Calcium	1,300mg	1,200mg
Vitamin B$_6$	1.7mg	2mg	Choline	550 mg	
Vitamin B$_{12}$	2.4mcg	2mcg	Chromium	35mcg	50mcg to 200mcg
Thiamin (B$_1$)	1.2mg	1.5mg	Copper	0.9mg	1.5mg to 3mg
Riboflavin (B$_2$)	1.3mg	1.8mg	Iodine	150mcg	150mcg
Niacin (B$_3$)	16mg	20mg	Iron	18mg	15mg
Folate (B$_9$)	200mcg	200mcg	Magnesium	420mg	400mg
Biotin (part of the B group)	30mcg	30mcg to 100mcg	Manganese	2.3mg	2mg to 5mg
Pantothenic Acid (part of the B group)	5mg	4mg to 7mg	Molybdenum	45mcg	75mcg to 250mcg
Vitamin C	90mg	60mg	Phosphorus	1,250mg	1,200mg
Vitamin D	600 IU	400 IU	Selenium	55mcg	70mcg
Vitamin E	22.5 IU	15 IU	Zinc	11mg	15mg
Vitamin K	120mcg	80mcg			

wheat or barley grass, powdered beets, and so on. They contain most vitamins and minerals in a natural form. However, they can be very expensive, and they may contain fillers.

If you take a multivitamin, take one that contains at least the RDA values (see Table "Recommended Daily Allowance (RDA) and Dietary Reference Intake (DRI) of Vitamins and Minerals, page 452. If you eat poorly or have one of the above-listed conditions, you might want to take up to the amounts listed in Table "Recommended Formula for Megavitamins," page 451. Note: The dietary reference intake (DRI) value is the most recent dietary recommendation of the Food and Nutrition Board of the Institute of Medicine. Both values may be on the label, so I am listing them both.

BALANCING YOUR HEALTH

This appendix gives a brief and concise guide to alternative products and whether or not they are beneficial. Certainly, it is not an in-depth analysis, but it can serve as a helpful guide. Ongoing and further research into these products will reveal both benefits and pitfalls, and most certainly the recommendations we make today will change through the years, just as conventional medical care has continually changed. In the meantime, I hope these guidelines will assist you in obtaining the products considered to be the best for your particular condition. Just remember that you usually achieve the best results for your health through a balance of methods and products, both conventional and alternative.

Reference and Referral Guide

ALTERNATIVE METHODS

Ayurvedic Medicine

Ayurvedic Foundations
Web site: www.ayur.com

The National Institute of Ayurvedic Medicine
584 Milltown Road
Brewster, NY 10509
(845) 278-8700
Fax: (845) 278-8215
Web site: www.niam.com

Energy Healing

Brugh Joy, MD
P.O. Box 1059
Lucerne Valley, CA 92356
(800) 448-9187 or (760) 248-9800
Fax: (760) 248-9899
www.brughjoy.com

Homeopathy

British Institute of Homeopathy and College of Homeopathy
580 Zion Road
Egg Harbor Township, NJ 08234-9606
(609) 927-5660
Fax: (609) 653-1289
Web site: www.britinsthom.com

The National Center for Homeopathy (NCH)
801 North Fairfax Street, Suite 306
Alexandria, VA 22314
(703) 548-7790
Fax: (703) 548-7792
Web site: www.homeopathic.org

Recommended Web sites for Homeopathy:
www.homeopathic.com
www.homeopathyhome.com

Manual Therapy

Bodywork

Alexander Technique
The American Society for the Alexander Technique
P.O. Box 60008
Florence, MA 01062
(800) 473-0620 or (413) 584-2359
Fax: (413) 584-3097
Web site: www.alexandertech.org

Feldenkrais Method
Feldenkrais Guild of North America
3611 SW Hood Ave., Suite 100
Portland, OR 97239
(800) 775-2118 or (503) 221-6612
Fax (503) 221-6616
Web site: www.feldenkrais.com

Chiropractic

American Chiropractic Association
1701 Clarendon Blvd.
Arlington, VA 22209
(800) 986-4636
Fax: (703) 243-2593
Web site: www.amerchiro.org

Massage

The American Massage Therapy Association
820 Davis Street, Suite 100
Evanston, IL 60201-4444
(847) 864-0123
Fax: (847) 864-1178
Web site: www.amtamassage.org

Osteopathic

American College of Osteopathic Family Physicians
330 East Algonquin Road, Suite 1
Arlington Heights, IL 60005
(800) 323-0794
Fax: (847) 228-9755
Web site: www.acofp.org

American Osteopathic Association
142 East Ontario Street
Chicago, IL 60611
(800) 621-1773 or (312) 202-8000
Fax: (312) 202-8200
Web site: www.aoa-net.org

Rolfing

The Rolf Institute
205 Canyon Blvd
Boulder, CO 80302
(800) 530-8875 or (303) 449-5903
Fax: (303) 449-5978
Web site: www.rolf.org

MIND-BODY TECHNIQUES

Biofeedback

Association for Applied Psychophysiology and Biofeedback
10200 W. 44th Avenue, Suite 304
Wheat Ridge, CO 80033-2840
(303) 422-8436
Fax: (303) 422-8894
Web site: www.aapb.org

Biofeedback Certification Institute of America
10200 W. 44th Avenue, Suite 310
Wheat Ridge, CO 80033-2840
(303) 420-2902
Fax: (303) 422-8894
Web site: www.bcia.org

Hypnosis

The American Society of Clinical Hypnosis
140 N. Bloomingdale Road
Bloomingdale, IL 60108-1017
(630) 980-4740
Fax: (630) 351-8490
Web site: www.asch.net

National Guild of Hypnotists
P.O. 308
Merrimack, NH 03054-0308
(603) 429-9438
Web site: www.ngh.net

Imagery

Academy for Guided Imagery, Inc.
30765 Pacific Coast Highway, #369
Malibu, CA 90265
(800) 726-2070
Web site: www.interactiveimagery.com

Brugh Joy, M.D., Inc
(See under Energy Healing)
Imagery International
1574 Coburg Road, #555
Eugene, OR 97401-4802
Web site: www.imageryinternational.org

Meditation

American Meditation Institute
60 Garner Road
Averill Park, NY 12018
(518) 674-8714
Web site: www.americanmeditation.org

Institute of Noetic Sciences
101 San Antonio Road
Petaluma, CA 94952
(707) 775-3500
Fax: (707) 781-7420
Web site: www.noetic.org

Institute of Transpersonal Psychology
744 San Antonio Road
Palo Alto, CA 94303
(650) 493-4430
Fax: (650) 493-6835
Web site: www.itp.edu

Web sites with Meditations:
www.unwind.com
www.beliefnet.com

Nambudripad Allergy Elimination Treatment (NAET)

N.A.E.T.
6714 Beach Blvd.
Buena Park, CA 90621
(714) 523-0800
Fax: (714) 523-3068
Web site: www.naet.com

Recommended Book on NAET:
Nambudripad, Devi S. *Say Goodbye to Illness*. Buena Park, CA: Delta Publishing, 1993.

Naturopathic Medicine

The American Association of Naturopathic Physicians
3201 New Mexico Avenue, NW, Suite 350
Washington, DC 20016
(866) 538-2267 or (202) 895-1392
Fax: (202) 274-1992
Web site: www.naturopathic.org

American Naturopathic Medical Association
P.O. Box 96273
Las Vegas, NV 89193
(702) 897-7053
Fax: (702) 897-7140
Web site: www.anma.com

Traditional Chinese Medicine

Acupuncture

National Certification Commission for Acupuncture and Oriental Medicine
(NCCAOM)
11 Canal Center Plaza, Suite 300
Alexandria, VA 22314
(703) 548-9004
Fax: (703) 548-9079
Web site: www.nccaom.org

Recommended Books on Acupuncture:
Bensky, Dan. *Acupuncture: A Comprehensive Text*. Seattle, WA: Eastland Press, 1981.
Kaptchuk, Ted J. *The Web That Has No Weaver*. Chicago: Contemporary Books, 1983.

Recommended Web site for Acupuncture:
www.acupuncture.com

Chinese Herbs

Balanced Healing Medical Center (BHMC)
2520 N.W. Expressway
Oklahoma City, OK 73112
(800) 640-0629 or (405) 942-1725
Fax: (405) 942-5447
Web site: www.balancedhealing.com
See listing under *Alternative and Conventional Treatments* for more information.

Health Concerns
8001 Capwell Drive
Oakland, CA 94621
Web site: www.HealthConcerns.com

Recommended Books on Chinese Herbs:
Bensky, Dan. *Chinese Herbal Medicine: Formulas and Strategies*. Seattle: Eastland Press, 1990.
Gaeddert, Andrew. *Chinese Herbs in the Western Clinic*. North Atlantic Books, 1998.

Qigong

The National Qigong (Chi Kung) Association
P.O. Box 252
Lakeland, MN 55043
(888) 815-1893
Web site: www.nqa.org

Recommended Magazine and Book on Qigong:
The Empty Vessel (magazine)
Abode of the Eternal Tao
1991 Garfield Street
Eugene, OR 97405
(800) 574-5118
Web site: www.abodetao.com

Jahnke, Roger. *The Healer Within*. San Francisco: Harper, 1997.

Recommended Videos on Qigong:
(Available at Balanced Healing Medical Center; see listing under *Alternative and Conventional Treatments*)
    Advanced Level 1 of Chi-Lel Qigong
    Body and Mind Method of Chi Lel Qigong
    Dance Like a Butterfly: Secrets of the Tai Chi Circle
    101 Miracles of Natural Healing

Yoga

Yoga Research and Education Center
(and International Association of Yoga Therapists)
P.O. Box 426
Manton, CA 96059
(530) 474-5700
Web site: www.yrec.org

Recommended Web sites for Yoga:
www.yogadirectory.com
www.yogajournal.com
www.yogasite.com

ALTERNATIVE AND CONVENTIONAL TREATMENTS (COMPLEMENTARY MEDICINE)

Balanced Healing Medical Center (BHMC)
2520 N.W. Expressway
Oklahoma City, OK 73112
(800) 640-0629 or (405) 942-1725
Fax: (405) 942-5447
Web site: www.balancedhealing.com
The Balanced Healing Medical Center provides the following:
- Most products listed in this book by mail order
- Consultation and treatment of chronic diseases and pain
- Updates regarding new research findings and further guidelines
- Current lectures and appearances by Dr. Altshuler

Herbs and Supplements

American Botanical Council
6200 Manor Road
Austin, TX 78723

(512) 926-4900
Fax: (512) 926-2345
Web site: www.herbalgram.org

Balanced Healing Medical Center
See listing under *Alternative and Conventional Treatments* for more information.

Natural Medicines Database
3120 W. March Lane
P.O. Box 8190
Stockton, CA 95208
(209) 472-2244
Fax: (209) 472-2249
Web site: www.naturaldatabase.com

Recommended Books on Herbs and Supplements:
Blumenthal, Mark (Ed.). *The Complete German Commission E Monographs* (Translation).
    Austin, TX: American Botanical Council, 1998.
Murray, Michael, and Joseph Pizzorno. *Encyclopedia of Natural Medicine*, 2nd Ed.
    Roseville, CA: Prima Publishing, 1998.

Recommended Web site for Herbs and Supplements:
www.consumerlab.com
Analyzes products for content and purity.

Infrasound Treatments

Contact Balanced Healing Medical Center (see above) for referral or purchase.

Low-Level Energy Laser (LLET)

Contact Balanced Healing Medical Center (see above) for referral or purchase.

Research

National Center for Complementary and Alternative Medicine
NCCAM Clearinghouse
P.O. Box 7923
Gaithersburg, MD 20898
(888) 644-6226
Fax: (866) 464-3616
Web site: www.nccam.nih.gov

CONVENTIONAL TREATMENT GUIDELINES FOR MAJOR DISEASES

National Guideline Clearinghouse
Web site: www.guideline.gov

Dietary Referrals

American Dietetic Association
120 South Riverside Plaza, Suite 2000
Chicago, IL 60606-6995

(800) 877-1600
Web site: www.eatright.org

Research

Recommended Periodical for Conventional Research:
Clinical Evidence (an international source of the latest research on conventional methods)
United Health Foundation
9900 Bren Road East
Minnetonka, MN 55343
Web site: www.unitedhealthfoundation.org

WOMEN'S HEALTH

Recommended Books on Women's Health:
Lee, John R. *What Your Doctor Won't Tell You About Menopause: The Breakthrough Book on Natural Progesterone*. New York: Time Warner, 1996.
Northrup, Christiane. *Women's Bodies, Women's Wisdom*. New York: Bantam Books, 1998.

Web site: www.drnorthrup.com